"This book does a good job of looking at the big picture and the interaction of different cultures that helped form our global world." — Ken Faunce, *University of Idaho*

"Students will not be overwhelmed by a rash of details and will take away a big picture about the history of the world that raises interesting questions about today." — Laura A. Smoller, *University of Arkansas at Little Rock*

"After reading the brief sections, one comes away with a better understanding of these societies than if one had waded through a conventional text." — Barbara A. Moss, *Clark Atlanta University*

"Strayer's text is characterized by a commitment to thematic focus and clarity that should be of great assistance to students as they prepare for essays and analytical questions." — Abel Alves, *Ball State University*

"The class using the Strayer chapters saw an increase of ten points, or an entire grade, when compared to classes of the last twelve years. It was remarkable. I have never been forced to give so many A grades before." — Eric Mayer, *Victor Valley College*

"Unlike most world history texts, it avoids the chronological/geographic formula and instead embraces comparison, connections, and change in a deliberately brief text: quite an achievement." — Timothy J. Coates, *College of Charleston*

"Strayer's engaging book discusses world history not as separate threads that connect and entangle at some points, but as a tapestry where complex events and issues are contextualized in a big-picture approach that emphasizes change, connection, and comparison." — Charles Didier Gondola, *Indiana University–Purdue University Indianapolis*

"An entirely new and engaging approach to the topic. Instead of the traditional chronological slog through various 'civilizations,' the author offers a unique cross-continents examination of world systems of trade and social organization." — Theresa Jordan, *Washington State University*

"The author shows a remarkable agility and flexibility in dealing with cases and examples from all over the planet." — James A. Wood, *North Carolina A&T State University*

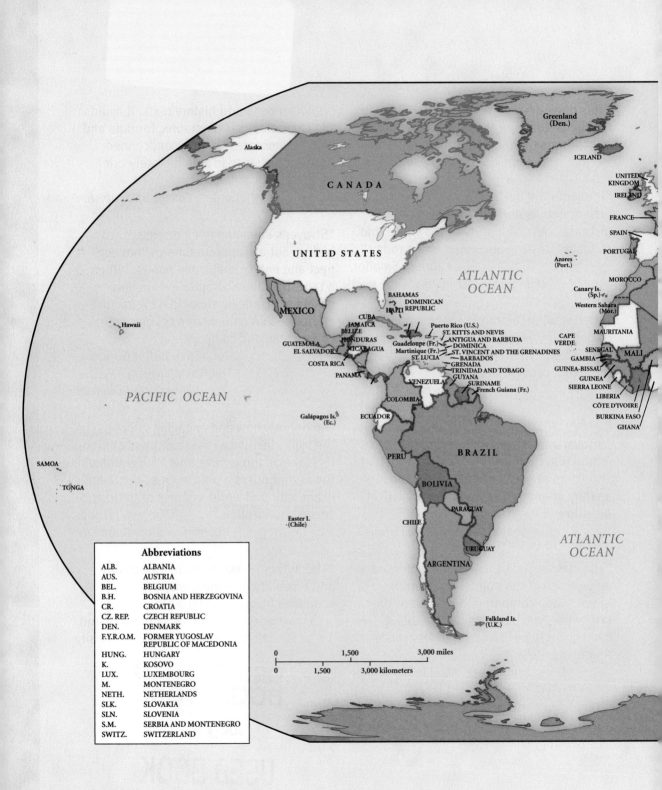

Greenland
(Den.)

Alaska

ICELAND

CANADA

UNITED
KINGDOM

IRELAND

FRANCE

SPAIN

PORTUGAL

Azores
(Port.)

ATLANTIC
OCEAN

MOROCCO

Canary Is.
(Sp.)

Western Sahara
(Mor.)

UNITED STATES

MEXICO

BAHAMAS

DOMINICAN
REPUBLIC

CUBA

JAMAICA

BELIZE

HAITI

Puerto Rico (U.S.)

ST. KITTS AND NEVIS

CAPE
VERDE

MAURITANIA

Hawaii

GUATEMALA

HONDURAS

EL SALVADOR

NICARAGUA

ANTIGUA AND BARBUDA

Guadeloupe (Fr.)

DOMINICA

MALI

SENEGAL

Martinique (Fr.)

ST. VINCENT AND THE GRENADINES

GAMBIA

ST. LUCIA

BARBADOS

GUINEA-BISSAU

COSTA RICA

GRENADA

TRINIDAD AND TOBAGO

GUINEA

PANAMA

VENEZUELA

GUYANA

SIERRA LEONE

SURINAME

LIBERIA

PACIFIC OCEAN

COLOMBIA

French Guiana (Fr.)

CÔTE D'IVOIRE

BURKINA FASO

Galápagos Is.
(Ec.)

ECUADOR

GHANA

PERU

BRAZIL

SAMOA

BOLIVIA

TONGA

PARAGUAY

Easter I.
(Chile)

CHILE

ATLANTIC
OCEAN

URUGUAY

ARGENTINA

Falkland Is.
(U.K.)

Abbreviations

ALB.	ALBANIA
AUS.	AUSTRIA
BEL.	BELGIUM
B.H.	BOSNIA AND HERZEGOVINA
CR.	CROATIA
CZ. REP.	CZECH REPUBLIC
DEN.	DENMARK
F.Y.R.O.M.	FORMER YUGOSLAV REPUBLIC OF MACEDONIA
HUNG.	HUNGARY
K.	KOSOVO
LUX.	LUXEMBOURG
M.	MONTENEGRO
NETH.	NETHERLANDS
SLK.	SLOVAKIA
SLN.	SLOVENIA
S.M.	SERBIA AND MONTENEGRO
SWITZ.	SWITZERLAND

0   1,500   3,000 miles

0   1,500   3,000 kilometers

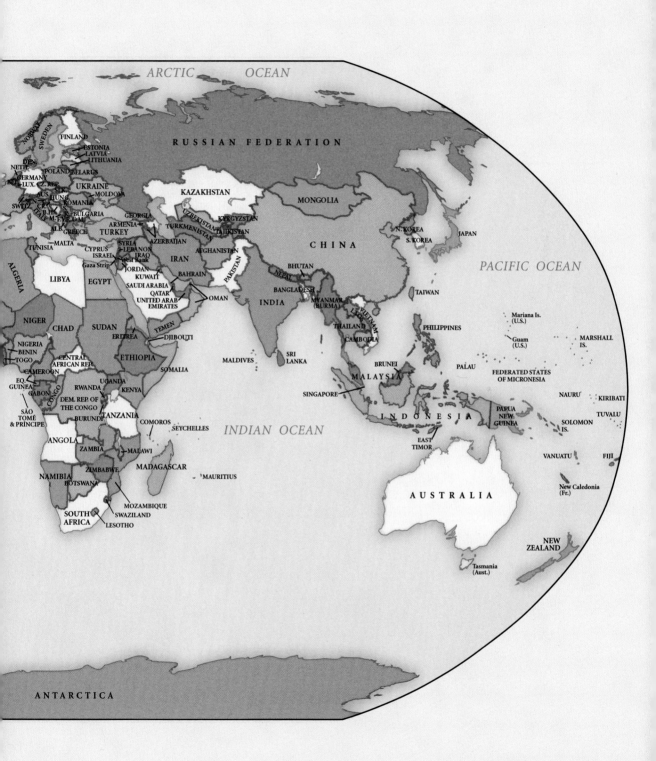

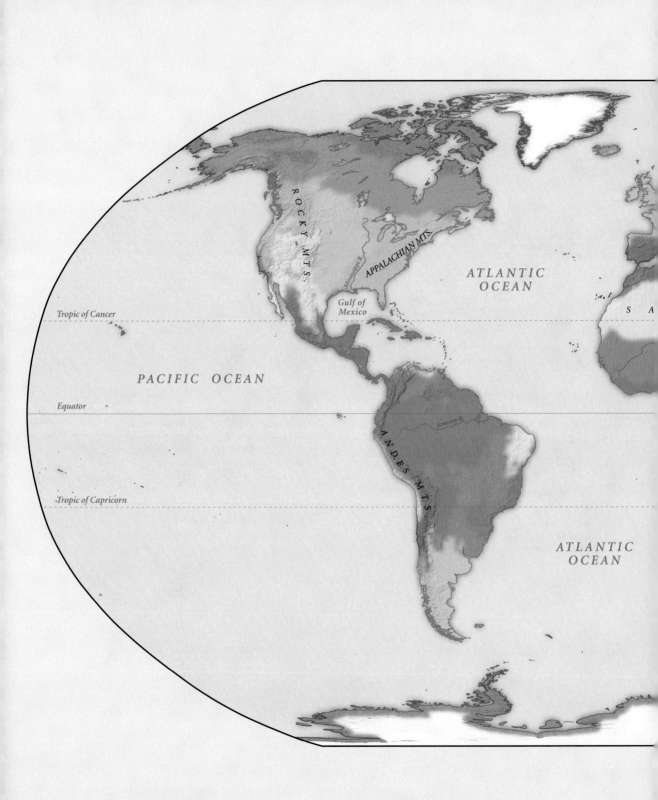

ROCKY MTS.

APPALACHIAN MTS.

Mississippi R.

ATLANTIC
OCEAN

Tropic of Cancer

Gulf of
Mexico

S   A

PACIFIC OCEAN

Equator

Amazon R.

A N D E S   M T S.

Tropic of Capricorn

ATLANTIC
OCEAN

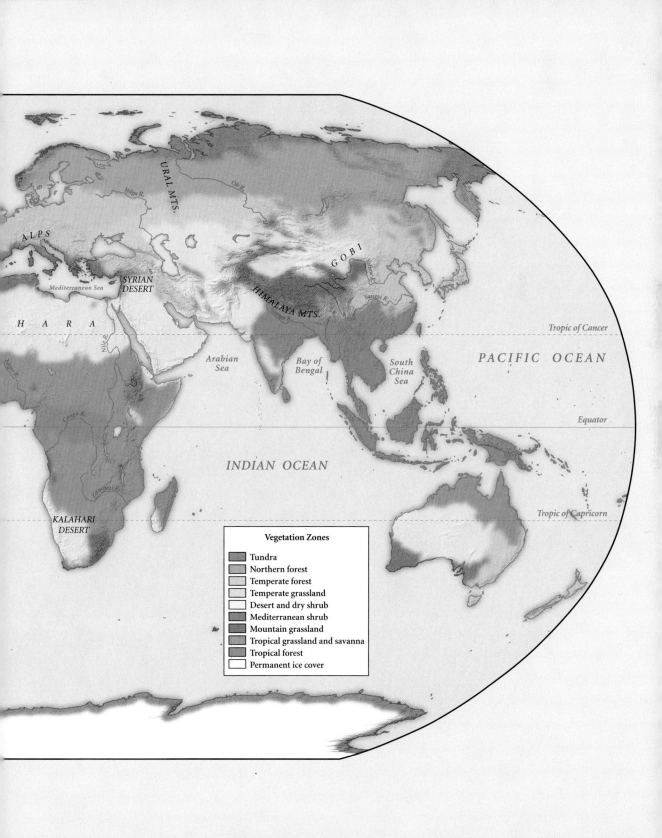

Ways of the World

A Brief Global History

VOLUME II: SINCE 1500

Ways of the World
A Brief Global History

ROBERT W. STRAYER

California State University, Monterey Bay

Bedford/St. Martin's
Boston • New York

To Alisa and her generation

For Bedford/St. Martin's
Publisher for History: Mary Dougherty
Director of Development for History: Jane Knetzger
Developmental Editor: Jim Strandberg
Senior Production Editor: Bridget Leahy
Senior Production Supervisor: Joe Ford
Executive Marketing Manager: Jenna Bookin Barry
Editorial Assistant: Lynn Sternberger
Production Assistant: Lidia MacDonald-Carr
Copyeditor: Linda McLatchie
Text and Cover Design: Joyce Weston
Cover Art: Utagawa Yoshitora, Railway timetable (detail). 1872. Arthur M. Sackler Gallery, Smithsonian Institution, Washington, D.C., Gift of Ambassador and Mrs. William Leonhart, S1998.100

Frontispiece: Indian durbar (detail). Topham/ The Image Works
Cartography: Mapping Specialists Limited
Indexer: EdIndex
Composition: Aptara®, Inc.
Printing and Binding: RR Donnelley and Sons

President: Joan E. Feinberg
Editorial Director: Denise B. Wydra
Director of Marketing: Karen R. Soeltz
Director of Editing, Design, and Production: Marcia Cohen
Assistant Director of Editing, Design, and Production: Elise S. Kaiser
Managing Editor: Elizabeth M. Schaaf

Library of Congress Control Number: 2008925891

Copyright © 2009 by Bedford/St. Martin's

Manufactured in the United States of America.

4 5 6   12 11 10 09

For information, write: Bedford/St. Martin's,
75 Arlington Street, Boston, MA 02116
(617-399-4000)

ISBN-10: 0-312-45287-X ISBN-13: 978-0-312-45287-2 (combined edition)
ISBN-10: 0-312-45288-8 ISBN-13: 978-0-312-45288-9 (Vol. 1)
ISBN-10: 0-312-45289-6 ISBN-13: 978-0-312-45289-6 (Vol. 2)
ISBN-10: 0-312-55728-0 ISBN-13: 978-0-312-55728-7 (high school edition)

Acknowledgments: Acknowledgments and copyrights can be found at the back of the book on page 765, which constitutes an extension of the copyright page.

Preface

WHEN I ENTERED COLLEGE IN 1960, there was no such thing as a world history course, either in my school or almost anywhere else in the country. When I started teaching at the college level in 1970, the study of world history was just beginning to make itself felt, and the State University of New York College at Brockport, where I taught for many years, was among the first to offer an introductory world history course. By the time I began teaching in California in 2002, world history had become an established and rapidly growing enterprise, in both secondary schools and universities, all across the country. Thus, as a teaching field, world history is a relatively new entry in the course lists of American universities, and as a subject for research and writing, it represents a new agenda within the historical profession.

This flowering of world history has coincided almost precisely with my own career in the academy. Over the course of several decades, I have been able to roam the world with history—as a student, a teacher, a scholar and writer, a traveler, and an active participant in the world history movement. My involvement in the more specialized fields of African and, later, Soviet history has likewise contributed much to the more central focus of my academic life, which is world history.

Like many others who have been attracted to this most exciting field of study, I have become something of a "specialist of the whole" rather than a specialist in one of its parts. No teacher or writer, of course, can be master of the vast array of cultures, themes, and time periods that world history encompasses. However, those of us interested in world history read widely; we look for the big picture processes and changes that have marked the human journey; we are alert to the possibilities of comparison across cultural boundaries; and we pay special attention to the multiple interactions among human communities. Students, the wider public, and professional scholars alike need the larger integrated view of the past that world history provides as well as the more focused and specialized understandings of particular countries, cultures, and peoples that most history courses offer.

On a professional level, world history has afforded me a distinctive and fulfilling career, allowing me to sample a variety of specialized fields, to interact with a remarkable community of scholars and teachers, and to engage thousands of students with the larger trajectory of the human story. More personally, my career in world history has been an immensely fruitful journey, for I have encountered times, places, and peoples that otherwise would have lain well outside my own experience. The writing of *Ways of the World* has provided an opportunity to crystallize the work of my adult life and to share it with others. Doing so has been a rare and rich privilege.

What's in a Title?

The title of a book should evoke something of its character and outlook. *Ways of the World* is intended to suggest at least three dimensions of this text.

The first is **diversity** or **variation**, for the "ways of the world," or the ways of being human in the world, have been many and constantly changing. World history, or global history as it is sometimes called, was conceived in part to counteract a Eurocentric perspective on the human past, deriving from several centuries of Western dominance on the world stage. This book seeks to embrace the experience of humankind in its vast diversity, while noticing the changing location of particular centers of innovation and wider influence.

A second meaning attached to the title *Ways of the World* involves an emphasis on major **panoramas**, **patterns**, or **pathways**, as opposed to highly detailed narratives. This reflects my own observation in the classroom, and that of many world history instructors, that students can easily feel overwhelmed by the sheer quantity of data that a course in global history can require of them. In this book, the larger patterns of world history appear in the foreground on center stage, while the plentiful details, data, and facts occupy the background, serving in supporting roles.

A third implication of the book's title lies in a certain **reflective** or **musing quality** of *Ways of the World*. It is a product of my own growing appreciation that history of any kind, and world history in particular, offers endless raw material for contemplating large questions. And so a final section in each chapter, titled "Reflections," raises questions about the nature of the historical enterprise and of the human processes it explores.

- Chapter 3, for example, about First Civilizations, ponders their ambiguous legacy—great achievements in size, complexity, innovation, and culture and equally great oppression, experienced in massive inequality, patriarchy, slavery, and war.

- Chapter 5, which deals with cultural traditions of the classical era, muses on the tensions or misunderstandings that sometimes arise between historians and the believers of various religious traditions.

- The Reflections section of Chapter 18, on the Industrial Revolution, asks whether we are presenting history as a horse race to the finish line of modernity and unduly celebrating those who arrived there first.

- Chapter 21, about the era of the world wars during the first half of the twentieth century, probes the possibility of deriving specific "lessons" from these conflicts and expresses some skepticism about the familiar notion that "history repeats itself."

Other chapters invite students to reflect on issues such as surprise or unexpectedness in the historical record and contingency or accident as modes of explanation. These Reflections sections seek to engage student readers with the larger and perhaps quasi-philosophical issues with which historians constantly grapple.

Achieving Coherence

The great virtue of world history lies in its inclusiveness, for it allows us to see the world and to see it whole, an obvious necessity given the demands of contemporary life. But that virtue is also the source of world history's greatest difficulty—telling a coherent story. How can we meaningfully present the planet's many and distinct peoples and their intersections with one another in the confines of a single book or a single term? What prevents that telling from bogging down in the endless detail of various civilizations or cultures, from losing the forest for the trees, from implying that history is just "one damned thing after another"?

Less Can Be More

Ways of the World seeks to cope with that fundamental conundrum of world history—the challenge of condensing the history of the world into a single text—in several ways. The first is relative brevity and a corresponding selectivity. This means, of course, leaving some things out or treating them more succinctly than some instructors might expect. The positive side of this brevity is that the textbook need not dominate the pedagogy of the course or overwhelm students with facts. It allows for more professorial creativity in constructing individual world history courses and in mixing and matching various reading materials. And wouldn't it be wonderful if we found students asking for "more," rather than complaining about "too much"?

Brevity also encourages a "themes and cases" rather than a "civilization-by-civilization" approach to the global past. Thus, most chapters in this book focus on a broad theme, explored on a global or transregional scale:

- classical-era empires in Chapter 4
- comparative social structures in Chapter 6
- long-distance commerce in Chapters 8 and 15
- the colonial experience in Chapter 20
- the communist experiment in Chapter 22
- twentieth-century globalization in Chapter 24

Such chapters explore a given theme in general while illustrating it with a few particular cases.

The Three Cs of World History: Change, Comparison, Connection

As a further aid to achieving coherence on a global scale, *Ways of the World* refers repeatedly to what I call the "**three Cs**" of world history. They represent some of the distinctive perspectives of world history as an academic discipline and are introduced more extensively in the prologue.

The first "C" emphasizes large-scale **changes**, both within and especially across major regions of the world. Change, of course, is a central theme in all historical study and serves to challenge "essentialist" descriptions of particular cultures or peoples. Among the macrochanges highlighted in *Ways of the World* are

- agriculture in Chapter 2
- civilization in Chapter 3
- the rise of universal religions in Chapter 5
- the changing shape of the Islamic world in Chapter 11
- industrialization in Chapter 18
- European global dominance in Chapter 19
- the rise and fall of world communism in Chapter 22

The second "C" involves frequent **comparison**. It is a technique of integration through juxtaposition, of bringing several regions or cultures into our field of vision at the same time. It encourages reflection both on the common elements of the human experience and on the many variations in that experience. Such comparisons are a prominent feature of virtually every chapter of the book. We examine the difference, for example,

- between the Agricultural Revolution in the Eastern Hemisphere and that in the Western Hemisphere (Chapter 2)
- between early Mesopotamian and Egyptian civilizations (Chapter 3)
- between the beginnings of Buddhism and the early period of Christianity (Chapter 5)
- between European and Asian empires of the early modern era (Chapter 14)
- between the Chinese and the Japanese response to European intrusion (Chapter 19)
- between Iran and Turkey within the twentieth-century Islamic world (Chapter 23)

The final "C" emphasizes **connections**, networks of communication and exchange that increasingly shaped the character of those societies that participated in them. For world historians, cross-cultural interaction becomes one of the major motors of historical change. Such connections are addressed in nearly every chapter. For example:

- Chapter 3 explores the clash of the Greeks and the Persians during the classical era.
- Chapter 8 highlights the long-distance commercial networks that linked the Afro-Eurasian world and, less extensively, the Western Hemisphere in premodern times.

- Chapter 11 focuses attention on the transregional world of Islam.
- Chapter 12 turns the spotlight on the multiple interactions of the Mongol era.
- Chapters 14 and 15 explore various facets of the transhemispheric Columbian exchange of the early modern era.
- Chapter 17 probes the linkages among the Atlantic revolutions of the late eighteenth and early nineteenth centuries.
- Chapter 24 concludes the book with an examination of globalization, highlighting its economic, feminist, religious, and environmental dimensions.

Organizing World History: Chronology, Theme, and Region

Organizing a world history textbook is, to put it mildly, a daunting task. How should we divide up the seamless stream of human experience into manageable and accessible pieces, while recognizing always that such divisions are both artificial and to some extent arbitrary? Historians, of course, debate the issue endlessly. In structuring *Ways of the World*, I have drawn on my own sense of "what works" in the classroom, on a personal penchant for organizational clarity, and on established practice in the field. The outcome has been an effort to balance three principles of organization—chronology, theme, and region—in a flexible format that can accommodate a variety of teaching approaches and organizational strategies.

The chronological principle is expressed most clearly in the overall structure of the book, which divides world history into six major periods. Each of these six parts begins with a brief **Big Picture essay** that introduces the general patterns of a particular period and raises questions about the problems historians face in dividing up the human past into meaningful chunks of time.

Part One (to 500 B.C.E.) deals in three separate chapters with beginnings—of human migration and social construction in the Paleolithic era, of agriculture, and of civilization. Each of them pursues an important theme on a global scale and illustrates that theme with regional examples treated comparatively.

Part Two, on the classical era (500 B.C.E. to 500 C.E.), likewise employs the thematic principle in exploring the major civilizations of Eurasia (Chinese, Indian, Persian, and Mediterranean), with separate chapters focusing on their empires (Chapter 4), cultural traditions (Chapter 5), and social organization (Chapter 6). This structure represents a departure from conventional practice, which usually treats the classical era on a civilization-by-civilization basis, but it allows for more effective and pointed comparison. These Eurasian chapters are followed by a single chapter (Chapter 7) that examines regionally the classical era in sub-Saharan Africa and the Americas, while asking whether their histories largely follow Eurasian patterns or depart from them.

Part Three embraces the thousand years between 500 and 1500 C.E., often known simply, and not very helpfully, as the "postclassical" era. The Big Picture essay for Part Three spotlights and seeks to explain a certain vagueness in our descriptions of this period of time, pointing out the various distinctive civilizational patterns of that millennium as well as the accelerating interactions among them. The six chapters of Part Three reflect a mix of thematic and regional principles. Chapter 8 focuses topically on commercial networks, while Chapters 9, 10, and 11 deal regionally with the Chinese, Christian, and Islamic worlds respectively. Chapter 12 treats pastoral societies as a broad theme and the Mongols as the most dramatic illustration of their impact on the larger stage of world history. Chapter 13, which bridges the two volumes of the book, presents an around-the-world tour in the fifteenth century, which serves both to conclude Volume 1 and to open Volume 2.

In considering the early modern era (1450–1750), **Part Four** treats each of its three constituent chapters thematically. Chapter 14 compares European and Asian empires; Chapter 15 lays out the major patterns of global commerce and their consequences (trade in spices, silver, furs, and slaves); and Chapter 16 focuses on cultural patterns, including the globalization of Christianity and the rise of modern science.

Part Five takes up the era of maximum European influence in the world, from 1750 to 1914. Here the Big Picture essay probes how we might avoid Eurocentrism, while describing a period of time in which Europeans were in fact increasingly central to the global story. Part Five, which charts the emergence of a distinctively modern society in Europe, devotes separate chapters to the Atlantic revolutions (Chapter 17) and the Industrial Revolution (Chapter 18). Then it turns to the growing impact of those societies on the rest of humankind—on China, the Ottoman Empire, and Japan, which are treated comparatively in Chapter 19; and on the world of formal colonies in Chapter 20.

The most recent century (1914–2008), which is treated in **Part Six**, is perhaps the most problematic for world historians, given the abundance of data and the absence of time to sort out what is fundamental and what is peripheral. The Big Picture essay that opens Part Six explores this difficulty, asking whether that century deserves the status of a separate period in the human story. Chapters 21, 22, and 23 examine respectively three major regions of the world in that century—the Western or industrial world, the communist world, and the third or developing world—while Chapter 24 explores the multiple processes of globalization, which have both linked and divided the human community in new ways.

Promoting Active Learning: Focus on Features

As all instructors know, students can often "do the assignment" or read the required chapter and yet have nearly no understanding of it when they come to class. The problem, frequently, is passive studying—a quick once-over, perhaps some highlighting of the text—but little sustained involvement with the material. A central pedagogical problem in all teaching at every level is how to encourage more active, engaged styles of learning. How can we push students to articulate in their own words the major ideas of a particular chapter or section of the text? How can we encourage them to recognize arguments, even in a textbook, and to identify and evaluate the evidence on which those arguments are based? Active learning seeks to enable students to manipulate the information of the book, using its ideas and data to answer questions, to make comparisons, to draw conclusions, to criticize assumptions, and to infer implications that are not explicitly disclosed in the book itself. This ability to use and rearrange the material of a text, not simply to recall it, lies at the heart of active college-level learning.

Ways of the World incorporates a number of features or learning aids that are designed to promote active learning, to assist students in reading the text and instructors in teaching it, and to generate more lively classroom exchanges.

- The part-opening **Big Picture essays** preview for students what follows in the subsequent chapters. In doing so, they provide a larger context for those chapters; they enable students to make comparisons with greater ease; they facilitate making connections across several chapters; and they raise questions about periodization.

- Each Big Picture essay is followed by a **Landmarks timeline**, providing a chronological overview of what follows in that particular part of the book. Each of these Landmarks is organized in a series of parallel regional timelines, allowing students to see at a glance significant developments in various regions of the world during the same time.

- A **contemporary vignette** opens each chapter with a story that links the past and the present. Chapter 1, for example, presents Gudo Mahiya, a twenty-first-century member of a gathering and hunting society in Tanzania, who rejects an opportunity to become a settled farmer or herder. Chapter 15, which describes the Atlantic slave trade, opens with a brief account of an African American woman who in 2002 visited what had been a slave port in Ghana. These vignettes seek to show the continuing resonance of the past in the lives of contemporary people.

- To encourage active learning explicitly, a series of **questions in the margins** provides students with "something to look for" as they read particular sections. Those notations also indicate what kind of question is being asked—about change, comparison, or connection, for example. Such questions relate directly to the material that follows. In Chapter 5, for example, beside a discussion of the major schools of thought in classical-era China, a marginal question asks: "Comparison: What different answers to the problem of disorder arose in classical China?" And in Chapter 17, just before a discussion of Latin American independence movements, there appears this marginal question: "Connection: How were the Spanish American revolutions shaped by the American, French, and Haitian revolutions that happened earlier?"

- To further foster active learning, the **Second Thoughts** section at the end of each chapter provides a list of particulars (people, places, events, processes, concepts) under the heading "**What's the Significance?**" inviting students to check their grasp of that chapter's material. The next part of the Second Thoughts section is a set of **Big Picture Questions**. Unlike the marginal questions, which are keyed specifically to the adjacent material, these Big Picture Questions are not directly addressed in the text. Instead, they provide opportunities for integration, comparison, analysis, and sometimes speculation. Such questions might well become the basis for engaging writing assignments, class discussions, or exam items. Finally, a limited **list of suggested readings**—books, articles, and Web sites—invites further exploration of the material in the chapter.

- **Snapshots** appear in every chapter and present succinct glimpses of particular themes, regions, or time periods, adding some trees to the forest of world history. A Snapshot in Chapter 3, for example, compares six different early writing systems, while another in Chapter 11 summarizes key achievements in Islamic science and scholarship. In Chapter 15, a Snapshot briefly summarizes the numerical dimensions of the Atlantic slave trade, and in Chapter 22, yet another Snapshot illustrates with statistical data the accomplishments, limitations, and tragedies of China under Maoist communism.

- As is always true of books published by Bedford/St. Martin's, a **rich program of maps and images** accompanies the narrative. Because history and geography are so closely related, more than 100 maps have been included in the two volumes of the book. They have been carefully chosen to orient the reader to the parts of the world described in the text. About 150 images, most of them contemporary to the times and places they illustrate, provide visual evidence of the ways people understood their worlds and their lives.

Supplements

A comprehensive collection of print and electronic resources for students and instructors accompanies this book. Developed with my collaboration, they are designed to provide a host of practical learning and teaching aids.

For Students

Print Resources

World History Matters: A Student Guide to World History Online. Based on the popular "World History Matters" Web site produced by the Center for History and New Media, this unique resource, written by Kristin Lehner (The Johns Hopkins University), Kelly Schrum (George Mason University), and T. Mills Kelly (George Mason University), combines reviews of 150 of the most useful and reliable world history Web sites, with an introduction that guides students in locating, evaluating, and correctly citing online sources. The Web sites offer opportunities for researching broad themes as well as special topics and regions and feature a range of sources, including primary documents, maps, art, photographs, statistics, and audio and video recordings. This resource is available free when packaged with the text.

Bedford Series in History and Culture.   More than 100 titles in this highly praised series combine first-rate scholarship, historical narrative, and important primary documents for undergraduate courses. Each book is brief, inexpensive, and focused on a specific topic or period. Package discounts are available.

Trade Books.   Titles published by sister companies Farrar, Straus and Giroux; Henry Holt and Company; Hill and Wang; Picador; and St. Martin's Press are available at a 50 percent discount when packaged with Bedford/St. Martin's textbooks. For more information, visit bedfordstmartins.com/tradeup.

New Media Resources

Online Study Guide at bedfordstmartins.com/strayer.   The Online Study Guide helps students synthesize the material covered in *Ways of the World*. For each chapter, it provides a multiple-choice self-test that focuses on important conceptual ideas; an identification quiz that helps students remember key people, places, and events; a flashcard activity that tests students' knowledge of key terms; and two interactive map activities intended to strengthen students' geographic skills. Instructors can monitor students' progress through an online Quiz Gradebook or receive e-mail updates.

Jules Benjamin, **A Student's Online Guide to History Reference Sources at bedfordstmartins.com/strayer.**   This Web site provides links to history-related databases, indexes, and journals, plus contact information for state, provincial, local, and professional history organizations.

The Bedford Bibliographer at bedfordstmartins.com/strayer.   *The Bedford Bibliographer*, a simple but powerful Web-based tool, assists students with the process of collecting sources and generates bibliographies in four commonly used documentation styles.

The Bedford Research Room at bedfordstmartins.com/strayer.   The Research Room, drawn from Mike Palmquist's *The Bedford Researcher*, offers a wealth of resources—including interactive tutorials, research activities, student writing samples, and links to hundreds of other places online—to support students in courses across the disciplines. The site also offers instructors a library of helpful instructional tools.

Diana Hacker's **Research and Documentation Online at bedfordstmartins .com/strayer.**   This Web site provides clear advice on how to integrate primary and secondary sources into research papers, how to cite sources correctly, and how to format in MLA, APA, *Chicago*, or CBE style.

The St. Martin's Tutorial on Avoiding Plagiarism at bedfordstmartins .com/strayer.   This online tutorial reviews the consequences of plagiarism and explains what sources to acknowledge, how to keep good notes, how to organize research, and how to integrate sources appropriately. The tutorial includes exercises to help students practice integrating sources and recognize acceptable summaries.

For Instructors

Print Resources

Instructor's Resource Manual.   This extensive manual by Eric W. Nelson (Missouri State University) and Phyllis G. Jestice (University of Southern Mississippi) offers both experienced and first-time instructors tools for presenting textbook material in exciting and engaging ways—chapter learning objectives; annotated chapter outlines; lecture strategies; tips for helping students with common misconceptions and difficult topics; a list of key terms and definitions; answer guidelines for in-text chapter questions; and suggestions for in-class activities (including using film, video, and literature), ways to start discussions, topics for debate, and analyzing primary sources. Each chapter concludes with a guide to all the chapter-specific supplements available with *Ways of the World*. A guide for first-time teaching assistants, two sample syllabi, a list of useful books for a first-time world history professor, and a list of books that form the basis of a world history reference library are also included.

New Media Resources

Instructor's Resource CD-ROM.   This disc provides instructors with ready-made and customizable PowerPoint multimedia presentations built around chapter outlines, maps, figures, and all images from the textbook, plus jpeg versions of all maps, figures, and images. The disc also contains chapter-related multiple-choice questions that can be used with the i-clicker personal response system.

Computerized Test Bank.   Written by Eric W. Nelson (Missouri State University) and Phyllis G. Jestice (University of Southern Mississippi), the test bank provides more than thirty exercises per chapter, including multiple-choice, fill-in-the-blank, short-answer, and full-length essay questions. Instructors can customize quizzes, add or edit both questions and answers, and export questions and answers to a variety of formats, including WebCT and Blackboard. The disc includes correct answers and essay outlines.

Book Companion Site at bedfordstmartins.com/strayer.   The companion Web site gathers all the electronic resources for *Ways of the World*, including the Online Study Guide and related Quiz Gradebook, at a single Web address and provides convenient links to lecture, assignment, and research materials, such as PowerPoint chapter outlines and the digital libraries at Make History.

Make History at bedfordstmartins.com/strayer.   Comprising the content of Bedford/St. Martin's five acclaimed online libraries—Map Central, the Bedford History Image Library, DocLinks, HistoryLinks, and PlaceLinks—Make History provides one-stop access to relevant digital content, including maps, images, documents, and Web links. Students and instructors alike can search this free, easy-to-use database by keyword, topic, date, or specific chapter of *Ways of the World* and download the content they find. Instructors can also create collections of content and store them online for later use or post them to the Web to share with students.

Content for Course Management Systems.   A variety of student and instructor resources developed for this textbook is ready for use in course management systems such as Blackboard, WebCT, and other platforms. This e-content includes nearly all the offerings from the book's Online Study Guide as well as the book's test bank.

Videos and Multimedia.   A wide assortment of videos and multimedia CD-ROMs on various topics in world history is available to qualified adopters.

"It Takes a Village"

In any enterprise of significance, "it takes a village," as they say. Bringing *Ways of the World* to life, it seems, has occupied the energies of several villages.

The largest of these villages consists of those many people who read the manuscript at various stages, and commented on it, sometimes at great length. I continue to be surprised at the power of this kind of collaboration. Frequently, I find that passages I had regarded as polished to a gleaming perfection benefited greatly from the collective wisdom and experience of these thoughtful reviewers. Many of the readers were commissioned by Bedford/St. Martin's and are listed here in alphabetical order, with my great thanks:

Hedrick Alixopulos, *Santa Rosa Junior College*
Abel Alves, *Ball State University*
Monty Armstrong, *Cerritos High School*
Eva Baham, *Southern University*
Cheryl Barkey, *Cabrillo College*
Eric Bobo, *Hinds Community College*
Robert W. Brown, *University of North Carolina at Pembroke*

Deborah Buffton, *University of Wisconsin–La Crosse*

Mark W. Chavalas, *University of Wisconsin–La Crosse*

Katherine Clark, *SUNY Brockport*

Timothy J. Coates, *College of Charleston*

John Hillas Cole, *Hawaii Community College*

Melinda S. Courtney, *Saddleback College*

Michael R. Davidson, *Southern Illinois University, Carbondale*

Kyle Eidahl, *Florida A&M University*

Ken Faunce, *University of Idaho*

Nancy Fitch, *California State University, Fullerton*

J. Arch Getty, *University of California, Los Angeles*

Trevor Getz, *San Francisco State University*

Charles Didier Gondola, *Indiana University–Purdue University Indianapolis*

Stephen S. Gosch, *University of Wisconsin–Eau Claire*

Howell H. Gwin Jr., *Lamar University*

John K. Hayden, *Southwestern Oklahoma State University*

Beth Hodges, *Lenoir Community College*

Bryan Jack, *Winston–Salem State University*

Michele G. Scott James, *Mira Costa College*

Theresa Jordan, *Washington State University*

Theodore Kallman, *San Joaquin Delta College*

Carol A. Keller, *San Antonio College*

John Lavalle, *Western New Mexico University*

John Mack, *Labette Community College*

Moira Maguire, *University of Arkansas at Little Rock*

Susan Maneck, *Jackson State University*

Michael Markowski, *Westminster College*

Eric Martin, *Lewis-Clark State College*

Morag Martin, *SUNY Brockport*

Eric Mayer, *Victor Valley College*

Brendan McManus, *Bemidji State University*

Eben Miller, *Southern Maine Community College*

Barbara A. Moss, *Clark Atlanta University*

Andrew Muldoon, *Metropolitan State College of Denver*

Eric Nelson, *Missouri State University*

Leonora Neville, *The Catholic University of America*

Theodore A. Nitz, *Gonzaga University*

Patricia O'Neill, *Central Oregon Community College*

Bill Palmer, *Marshall University*

Stephen Rapp, *Georgia State University*

David Rayson, *Normandale Community College*

Salvador Rivera, *SUNY Cobleskill*

Eric C. Rust, *Baylor University*

David P. Sandgren, *Concordia College*
Daniel Sarefield, *Ohio State University*
Jane Scimeca, *Brookdale Community College*
Kenneth P. Serbin, *University of San Diego*
Robert P. Sherwood, *Georgia Military College*
John M. Simpson, *Pierce College*
Laura A. Smoller, *University of Arkansas at Little Rock*
William Storey, *Millsaps College*
Mark B. Tauger, *West Virginia University*
Donna A. Vinson, *Salem State College*
Frank J. Wetta, *Ocean County College*
James A. Wood, *North Carolina Agricultural and Technical State University*
Eloy Zárate, *Pasadena City College*

Others in the village of reviewers have been friends, family, and colleagues who graciously agreed to read portions of the manuscript and offer helpful counsel: Kabir Helminski, James Horn, Elisabeth Jay, David Northrup, Lynn Parsons, Katherine Poethig, Kevin Reilly, and Julie Shackford-Bradley.

The "Bedford village" has been a second community sustaining this enterprise and the one most directly responsible for the book's appearance in print. Its unofficial chief, at least for this project, has been Jim Strandberg, the development editor assigned to this book. He has read and reread every word, perused every map, and examined every image, all with exegetical care, offering suggestions, encouragement, praise, and useful criticism. As a student and teacher of history himself, Jim has brought to this delicate task the sensitivity of a fine historian as well as the competence of an outstanding editor.

Publisher Mary Dougherty first broached the possibility of this volume and, with a manner as lovely as it is professional, has provided overall editorial leadership and a calming balm to authorial anxieties. Jane Knetzger, director of development, has overseen the project from its beginning, bore my many questions with forbearance, and, even better, provided timely answers. Company president Joan Feinberg has, to my surprise and delight, periodically kept her own experienced hand in this pot, while executive editor Beth Welch, though fully engaged in her own projects, has served as counselor from the sidelines. Photo researcher Carole Frohlich identified and acquired the many images that grace *Ways of the World* and did so with amazing efficiency and courtesy. Senior editor Louise Townsend provided initial guidance as the project got under way, and Denise Wydra, the editorial director, has offered helpful encouragement.

Operating more behind the scenes in the Bedford village, a series of highly competent and always supportive people have shepherded this book along its way. A succession of capable editorial assistants—Holly Dye, Alix Roy, and Lynn Sternberger—provided invaluable assistance in handling the manuscript, contacting reviewers, and keeping on top of the endless details that such an enterprise demands. Bridget Leahy served as project editor during the book's production and, often under considerable pressure, did so with both grace and efficiency. Copy editor Linda McLatchie polished the prose and sorted out my inconsistent usages with a seasoned and perceptive eye.

Jenna Bookin Barry and Sally Constable have overseen the marketing process, while history specialist John Hunger and a cadre of humanities specialists and sales representatives have introduced the book to the academic world. Heidi Hood and Jack Cashman supervised the development of ancillary materials to support the book, and Donna Dennison ably coordinated research for the lovely covers that mark *Ways of the World*.

Yet a further village that contributed much to *Ways of the World* involves those historians who participated with me in an earlier multi-authored world history text (*The Making of the Modern World*), published by St. Martin's Press in 1988 with a second edition in 1995: Sandria B. Freitag (India), Donald C. Holsinger (Middle East/Islamic world), James J. Horn (Latin America), Robert B. Marks (China), Joe B. Moore (Japan), Lynn H. Parsons (United States), and Robert J. Smith (Europe). Each of them is a superb scholar in his or her particular area, and all of them have an eye for the global connections and comparisons that are central to world history. Working with them was a rare privilege that taught me a great deal. I have incorporated occasional passages from this earlier work into *Ways of the World*. I am grateful to each of them.

A final and much smaller community sustained this project and its author. It is that most intimate of villages that we know as a marriage. Here I pay wholly inadequate tribute to its other member, my wife, Suzanne Sturn. She knows how I feel, and no one else needs to.

To all my fellow villagers, I offer deep thanks for perhaps the richest intellectual experience of my professional life. I am grateful beyond measure.

Robert Strayer
La Selva Beach, California

Brief Contents

Preface   *v*

Prologue: Considering World History   *xxxiii*

13. The Worlds of the Fifteenth Century   363

PART FOUR   The Early Modern World, 1450–1750   396

THE BIG PICTURE   Debating the Character of an Era   397

14. Empires and Encounters, 1450–1750   403
15. Global Commerce, 1450–1750   433
16. Religion and Science, 1450–1750   461

PART FIVE   The European Moment in World History, 1750–1914   490

THE BIG PICTURE   European Centrality and the Problem of Eurocentrism   491

17. Atlantic Revolutions and Their Echoes, 1775–1914   499
18. Revolutions of Industrialization, 1750–1914   527
19. Internal Troubles, External Threats: China, the Ottoman Empire, and Japan, 1800–1914   559
20. Colonial Encounters, 1750–1914   589

PART SIX   The Most Recent Century, 1914–2008   616

THE BIG PICTURE   The Twentieth Century: A New Period in World History?   617

21. The Collapse and Recovery of Europe, 1914–1970s   625
22. The Rise and Fall of World Communism, 1917–Present   659
23. Independence and Development in the Global South, 1914–Present   691
24. Accelerating Global Interaction, Since 1945   723

Notes   757

Index   767

Contents

Preface *v*
Maps *xxix*
Special Features *xxxi*

Prologue: Considering World History *xxxiii*
Why World History? *xxxiii*
Comparison, Connection, and Change: The Three Cs
of World History *xxxiv*

13 The Worlds of the Fifteenth Century *363*

The Shapes of Human Communities *365*
   Paleolithic Persistence • Agricultural Village Societies • Herding Peoples
Civilizations of the Fifteenth Century: Comparing China
and Europe *369*
   *Ming Dynasty China • European Comparisons: State Building and Cultural
Renewal • European Comparisons: Maritime Voyaging*
Civilizations of the Fifteenth Century: The Islamic World *378*
   *In the Islamic Heartland: The Ottoman and Safavid Empires • On the Frontiers
of Islam: The Songhay and Mughal Empires*
Civilizations of the Fifteenth Century: The Americas *382*
   The Aztec Empire • The Inca Empire
Webs of Connection *388*
A Preview of Coming Attractions: Looking Ahead to the Modern Era,
1500–2000 *390*
Reflections: What If? Chance and Contingency in World History *393*
Second Thoughts *393*
   *What's the Significance? • Big Picture Questions • Next Steps: For Further
Study*

Snapshot: **Major Developments around the World in the Fifteenth
Century** *364*
Snapshot: **Key Moments in European Maritime Voyaging** *375*
Snapshot: **World Population Growth, 1000–2000** *391*

PART FOUR   The Early Modern World, 1450–1750   396

THE BIG PICTURE   Debating the Character of an Era   397

An Early Modern Era? • A Late Agrarian Era?

Landmarks in the Early Modern Era, 1450–1750   400

14 Empires and Encounters, 1450–1750   403

European Empires in the Americas   404

The European Advantage • The Great Dying • The Columbian Exchange

Comparing Colonial Societies in the Americas   409

In the Lands of the Aztecs and the Incas • Colonies of Sugar • Settler Colonies in North America

The Steppes and Siberia: The Making of a Russian Empire   417

Experiencing the Russian Empire • Russians and Empire

Asian Empires   421

Making China an Empire • Muslims and Hindus in the Mughal Empire • Muslims, Christians, and the Ottoman Empire

Reflections: Countering Eurocentrism . . . or Reflecting It?   429

Second Thoughts   430

What's the Significance? • Big Picture Questions • Next Steps: For Further Study

Snapshot: **Ethnic Composition in Colonial Societies in Latin America**   414

Snapshot: **Demographics of the Russian Empire**   421

15 Global Commerce, 1450–1750   433

Europeans and Asian Commerce   434

A Portuguese Empire of Commerce • Spain and the Philippines • The East India Companies • Asian Commerce

Silver and Global Commerce   442

The "World Hunt": Fur in Global Commerce   445

Commerce in People: The Atlantic Slave Trade   449

The Slave Trade in Context • The Slave Trade in Practice • Comparing Consequences: The Impact of the Slave Trade in Africa

Reflections: Economic Globalization—Then and Now   457

Second Thoughts   458

What's the Significance? • Big Picture Questions • Next Steps: For Further Study

Snapshot: **Key Moments in the European Encounter with Asia**   438

Snapshot: **The Slave Trade in Numbers**   454

16 Religion and Science, 1450–1750   461

The Globalization of Christianity   *462*

  Western Christendom Fragmented: The Protestant Reformation • Christianity Outward Bound • Conversion and Adaptation in Spanish America • An Asian Comparison: China and the Jesuits

Persistence and Change in Afro-Asian Cultural Traditions   *472*

  Expansion and Renewal in the Islamic World • China: New Directions in an Old Tradition • India: Bridging the Hindu/Muslim Divide

A New Way of Thinking: The Birth of Modern Science   *477*

  The Question of Origins: Why Europe? • Science as Cultural Revolution • Science and Enlightenment • Looking Ahead: Science in the Nineteenth Century • European Science beyond the West

Reflections: Cultural Borrowing and Its Hazards   *486*

Second Thoughts   *487*

  What's the Significance? • Big Picture Questions • Next Steps: For Further Study

Snapshot: Catholic/Protestant Differences in the Sixteenth Century   *464*

Snapshot: Major Thinkers and Achievements of the Scientific Revolution   *480*

PART FIVE   The European Moment in World History, 1750–1914   *490*

THE BIG PICTURE   European Centrality and the Problem of Eurocentrism   *491*

  Eurocentric Geography and History • Countering Eurocentrism

Landmarks of the European Moment in World History, 1750–1914   *496*

17 Atlantic Revolutions and Their Echoes, 1750–1914   499

Comparing Atlantic Revolutions   *500*

  The North American Revolution, 1775–1787 • The French Revolution, 1789–1815 • The Haitian Revolution, 1791–1804 • Spanish American Revolutions, 1810–1825

Echoes of Revolution   *513*

  The Abolition of Slavery • Nations and Nationalism • Feminist Beginnings

Reflections: Revolutions Pro and Con   *523*

Second Thoughts   *524*

  What's the Significance? • Big Picture Questions • Next Steps: For Further Study

Snapshot: **Key Moments in the History of Atlantic Revolutions**   *501*

Snapshot: **Key Moments in the Growth of Nationalism**   *517*

18   Revolutions of Industrialization, 1750–1914   527

Explaining the Industrial Revolution   *528*
  Why Europe? • Why Britain?
The First Industrial Society   *534*
  The British Aristocracy • The Middle Classes • The Laboring Classes
  • Social Protest among the Laboring Classes
Variations on a Theme: Comparing Industrialization in the United States
  and Russia   *541*
  *The United States: Industrialization without Socialism • Russia: Industrialization
  and Revolution*
The Industrial Revolution and Latin America in the Nineteenth
  Century   *548*
  *After Independence in Latin America • Facing the World Economy • Becoming like
  Europe?*
Reflections: History and Horse Races   *554*
Second Thoughts   *555*
  *What's the Significance? • Big Picture Questions • Next Steps: For
  Further Study*

Snapshot: **Measuring the Industrial Revolution**   *535*

Snapshot: **The Industrial Revolution and the Global Divide**   *548*

19   Internal Troubles, External Threats: China, the Ottoman Empire, and Japan, 1800–1914   559

The External Challenge: European Industry and Empire   *561*
  New Motives, New Means • New Perceptions of the "Other"
Reversal of Fortune: China's Century of Crisis   *564*
  The Crisis Within • Western Pressures • The Failure of Conservative Modernization
The Ottoman Empire and the West in the Nineteenth Century   *571*
  *"The Sick Man of Europe" • Reform • Identity • Outcomes: Comparing China
  and the Ottoman Empire*
The Japanese Difference: The Rise of a New East Asian Power   *577*
  *The Tokugawa Background • American Intrusion and the Meiji Restoration
  • Modernization Japanese Style • Japan and the World*
Reflections: Success and Failure in History   *586*
Second Thoughts   *586*
  What's the Significance? • Big Picture Questions • Next Steps: For Further Study

Snapshot: **Chinese/British Trade at Canton, 1835–1836**   *567*

Snapshot: **Key Moments in the Rise of Japan in the Nineteenth Century and Beyond**   *582*

20 Colonial Encounters, 1750–1914   *589*

A Second Wave of European Conquests   *590*

Under European Rule   *594*

Cooperation and Rebellion • Colonial Empires with a Difference

Ways of Working: Comparing Colonial Economies   *598*

Economies of Coercion: Forced Labor and the Power of the State • Economies of Cash-Crop Agriculture: The Pull of the Market • Economies of Wage Labor: Working for Europeans • Women and the Colonial Economy: An African Case Study • Assessing Colonial Development

Believing and Belonging: Identity and Cultural Change in the Colonial Era   *607*

Education • Religion • "Race" and "Tribe"

Reflections: Who Makes History?   *613*

Second Thoughts   *614*

What's the Significance? • Big Picture Questions • Next Steps: For Further Study

Snapshot: **Long-Distance Migration in an Age of Empire, 1846–1940**   *606*

PART SIX   The Most Recent Century, 1914–2008   *616*

THE BIG PICTURE   The Twentieth Century: A New Period in World History?   *617*

Old and New in the Twentieth Century • Three Regions — One World

Landmarks of the Most Recent Century, 1914–2008   *622*

21 The Collapse and Recovery of Europe, 1914–1970s   *625*

The First World War: European Civilization in Crisis, 1914–1918   *626*

An Accident Waiting to Happen • Legacies of the Great War

Capitalism Unraveling: The Great Depression   *633*

Democracy Denied: Comparing Italy, Germany, and Japan   *636*

The Fascist Alternative in Europe • Hitler and the Nazis • Japanese Authoritarianism

A Second World War   *645*

     The Road to War in Asia • The Road to War in Europe • World War II:
     The Outcomes of Global Conflict

The Recovery of Europe   *653*

Reflections: War and Remembrance: Learning from History   *656*

Second Thoughts   *657*

     What's the Significance? • Big Picture Questions • Next Steps:
     For Further Study

Snapshot: **Comparing the Impact of the Depression**   *635*

Snapshot: **Key Moments in the History of World War II**   *650*

22   **The Rise and Fall of World Communism,**
     1917–Present   **659**

Global Communism   *660*

Comparing Revolutions as a Path to Communism   *662*

     Russia: Revolution in a Single Year • China: A Prolonged Revolutionary Struggle

Building Socialism in Two Countries   *668*

     Communist Feminism • Socialism in the Countryside • Communism and
     Industrial Development • The Search for Enemies

East versus West: A Global Divide and a Cold War   *675*

     Military Conflict and the Cold War • Nuclear Standoff and Third World Rivalry
     • The United States: Superpower of the West, 1945–1975 • The Communist World,
     1950s–1970s

Comparing Paths to the End of Communism   *681*

     China: Abandoning Communism and Maintaining the Party • The Soviet Union:
     The Collapse of Communism and Country

Reflections: To Judge or Not to Judge: The Ambiguous Legacy of
     Communism   *687*

Second Thoughts   *688*

     What's the Significance? • Big Picture Questions • Next Steps: For Further Study

Snapshot: **China under Mao, 1949–1976**   *672*

23   **Independence and Development in the Global**
     South, 1914–Present   **691**

Toward Freedom: Struggles for Independence   *692*

     The End of Empire in World History • Explaining African and Asian Independence

Comparing Freedom Struggles   *696*

     The Case of India: Ending British Rule • The Case of South Africa: Ending
     Apartheid

Experiments with Freedom   *705*

   Experiments in Political Order: Comparing African Nations and India
   • *Experiments in Economic Development: Changing Priorities, Varying Outcomes*
   • *Experiments with Culture: The Role of Islam in Turkey and Iran*

Reflections: History in the Middle of the Stream   *719*

Second Thoughts   *720*

   What's the Significance? • *Big Picture Questions* • *Next Steps: For Further Study*

Snapshot: **Key Moments in South African History**   *700*

Snapshot: **Economic Development in the Global South by the Early
Twenty-first Century**   *712*

24 Accelerating Global Interaction, Since 1945   *723*

3

Global Interaction and the Transformation of the World Economy   *724*

   Reglobalization • *Disparities and Resistance* • *Globalization and an American
Empire*

The Globalization of Liberation: Comparing Feminist Movements   *734*

   Feminism in the West • *Feminism in the Global South* • *International Feminism*

Religion and Global Modernity   *740*

   Fundamentalism on a Global Scale • *Creating Islamic Societies: Resistance and
Renewal in the World of Islam* • *Religious Alternatives to Fundamentalism*

The World's Environment and the Globalization of Environmentalism   *747*

   The Global Environment Transformed • *Green and Global*

Final Reflections: Pondering the Uses of History   *752*

Second Thoughts   *755*

   What's the Significance? • *Big Picture Questions* • *Next Steps: For Further Study*

Snapshot: **Indicators of Reglobalization**   *728*

Snapshot: **World Population Growth, 1950–2005**   *748*

Notes   *757*
Acknowledgments   *765*
Index   *767*
About the Author   *Inside back cover*

Maps

MAP 13.1   Asia in the Fifteenth Century   370

MAP 13.2   Europe in 1500   373

MAP 13.3   Africa in the Fifteenth Century   376

MAP 13.4   Empires of the Islamic World   379

MAP 13.5   The Americas in the Fifteenth Century   383

MAP 13.6   Religion and Commerce in the Afro-Eurasian World   390

MAP 14.1   European Colonial Empires in the Americas   405

MAP 14.2   The Russian Empire   418

SPOT MAP   China's Qing Dynasty Empire   422

SPOT MAP   The Mughal Empire   424

MAP 14.3   The Ottoman Empire   426

MAP 15.1   Europeans in Asia in the Early Modern Era   436

MAP 15.2   The Global Silver Trade   442

MAP 15.3   The North American Fur Trade   446

MAP 15.4   The Atlantic Slave Trade   449

MAP 16.1   Reformation Europe in the Sixteenth Century   466

SPOT MAP   The Expansion of Wahhabi Islam   474

MAP 17.1   The Expansion of the United States   502

MAP 17.2   Napoleon's European Empire   508

MAP 17.3   Latin American Independence   511

MAP 17.4   The Nations and Empires of Europe, ca. 1880   518

MAP 18.1   The Early Phase of Europe's Industrial Revolution   531

MAP 18.2   The Industrial United States in 1900   543

SPOT MAP   The 1905 Revolution in Russia   547

MAP 18.3   Latin America and the World, 1825–1935   551

MAP 19.1   China and the World in the Nineteenth Century   569

MAP 19.2   The Contraction of the Ottoman Empire   572

MAP 19.3   The Rise of Japan   585

MAP 20.1   Colonial Asia in the Early Twentieth Century   591

MAP 20.2   Conquest and Resistance in Colonial Africa   593

MAP 21.1   The World in 1914   626
MAP 21.2   Europe on the Eve of World War I   628
MAP 21.3   Europe and the Middle East after World War I   631
MAP 21.4   World War II in Asia   646
MAP 21.5   World War II in Europe   649
MAP 21.6   The Growth of European Integration   655

MAP 22.1   Russia in 1917   663
MAP 22.2   The Rise of Communism in China   667
MAP 22.3   The Global Cold War   676
MAP 22.4   The Collapse of the Soviet Empire   686

MAP 23.1   The End of European Empires   694
SPOT MAP   The Independence of British South Asia   699
MAP 23.2   South Africa after Apartheid   704
MAP 23.3   The "Worlds" of the Twentieth Century   705
MAP 23.4   Political Life in Postindependence Africa   709
SPOT MAP   Iran, Turkey, and the Middle East   715

MAP 24.1   Globalization in Action: Trade and Investment in the Early
            Twenty-first Century   726
MAP 24.2   Global Inequality: Population and Economic Development   729
MAP 24.3   Two Faces of an "American Empire"   732
MAP 24.4   The Islamic World in the Early Twenty-first Century   743
MAP 24.5   Carbon Dioxide Emissions in the Twentieth Century   750

Special Features

Landmarks

PART 4   Landmarks in the Early Modern Era, 1450–1750   400
PART 5   Landmarks of the European Moment in World History, 1750–1914   496
PART 6   Landmarks of the Most Recent Century, 1914–2008   622

Snapshots

Major Developments around the World in the Fifteenth Century   364
Key Moments in European Maritime Voyaging   375
World Population Growth, 1000–2000   391
Ethnic Composition in Colonial Societies in Latin America   414
Demographics of the Russian Empire   421
Key Moments in the European Encounter with Asia   438
The Slave Trade in Numbers   454
Catholic/Protestant Differences in the Sixteenth Century   464
Major Thinkers and Achievements of the Scientific Revolution   480
Key Moments in the History of Atlantic Revolutions   501
Key Moments in the Growth of Nationalism   517
Measuring the Industrial Revolution   535
The Industrial Revolution and the Global Divide   548
Chinese/British Trade at Canton, 1835–1836   567
Key Moments in the Rise of Japan in the Nineteenth Century and Beyond   582
Long-Distance Migration in an Age of Empire, 1846–1940   606
Comparing the Impact of the Depression   635
Key Moments in the History of World War II   650
China under Mao, 1949–1976   672
Key Moments in South African History   700
Economic Development in the Global South by the Early Twenty-first Century   712
Indicators of Reglobalization   728
World Population Growth, 1950–2005   748

Prologue
Considering World History

THE HISTORY OF THE HUMAN SPECIES HAS occupied roughly the last 250,000 to 300,000 years, a period that is conventionally divided into three major phases, based on the kind of technology that was most widely practiced. The enormously long Paleolithic age, with its gathering and hunting way of life, accounts for 95 percent or more of the time that humans have occupied the planet. People utilizing a Paleolithic technology initially settled every major landmass on the planet and constructed the first human societies. Then beginning with the first Agricultural Revolution, about 12,000 years ago, the domestication of plants and animals increasingly became the primary means of sustaining human life and societies. In giving rise to farming village societies, to pastoral communities depending on their herds of animals, and to state- and city-based civilizations, this agrarian way of life changed virtually everything and fundamentally shaped the human experience ever since. Finally around 1750, a quite sudden spurt in the rate of technological change, which we know as the Industrial Revolution, took hold. That vast increase in productivity, wealth, and human control over nature once again reshaped virtually every aspect of human life and gave rise to new kinds of societies that we call "modern."

Here then, in a single paragraph, is the history of humankind—the Paleolithic era, the age of agricultural civilizations, and, most recently and briefly, the modern industrial era. Clearly this is a world history perspective, encompassing humankind as a whole rather than focusing solely on one or another of its particular and distinctive cultures. Volume 2 of *Ways of the World* turns the spotlight on the final several centuries of the age of agriculture and then on the modern industrial era. This perspective—known variously as planetary, global, or world history—has become increasingly prominent among those who study the past. Why should this be so?

Why World History?

Not long ago—in the mid-twentieth century, for example—virtually all college-level history courses were organized in terms of particular civilizations or nations. In the United States, it was Western Civilization or some version of American History that served to introduce students to the study of the past. Since then, however, a set of profound changes has pushed the historical profession in a different direction.

The world wars of the twentieth century, revealing as they did the horrendous consequences of unchecked nationalism, persuaded some historians that a broader view of the past might contribute to notions of global citizenship. Economic and cultural globalization has highlighted both the interdependence of the world's peoples and their very unequal positions within that world. Moreover, we are aware as never before that our problems—whether they involve economic well-being, environmental deterioration, disease, or terrorism—respect no national boundaries. To many thoughtful people, a global present seemed to call for a global past. Furthermore, as colonial empires shrank and newly defined third world peoples asserted themselves on the world stage, these people also insisted that their histories be accorded equivalent treatment with those of Europe. An explosion of new knowledge about the histories of Asia, Africa, and pre-Columbian America erupted from the research of scholars around the world. All of this has generated a "world history movement," reflected in college and high school curricula, in numerous conferences and specialized studies, and in a proliferation of textbooks, of which this is one.

This world history movement has attempted to create a global understanding of the human past that highlights broad patterns cutting across particular civilizations and countries, while acknowledging in an inclusive fashion the distinctive histories of its many peoples. This is, to put it mildly, a tall order. How is it possible to encompass within a single book or course the separate stories of the world's various peoples? Surely it must be something more than just recounting the history of one civilization or culture after another. How can we distill a common history of humankind as a whole from the distinct trajectories of particular peoples? Because no world history book or course can cover everything, what criteria should we use for deciding what to include and what to leave out? Such questions have ensured no end of controversy among students, teachers, and scholars of world history, making it one of the most exciting fields of historical inquiry.

Comparison, Connection, and Change: The Three Cs of World History

Despite much debate and argument, most world historians would probably agree on three major issues or questions that define their field of study. Each of them confronts a particular problem in our understanding of the past.

The first involves constant **comparison**. Whatever else it may be, world history is a comparative discipline, seeking to identify similarities and differences in the experience of the world's peoples. In what respects did European empires in the Americas differ from the Ottoman Empire in the Middle East or the Russian Empire across northern Asia or Chinese expansion into Central Asia? Why did the Scientific and Industrial Revolutions and a modern way of life evolve first in

Western Europe rather than somewhere else? What distinguished the French, Haitian, Russian, and Chinese revolutions? How might we compare the modern transformation of capitalist, communist, and colonial societies? Did feminist movements in the developing countries resemble those of the industrial West? Describing and, if possible, explaining such similarities and differences are among the major tasks of world history.

Comparison has proven an effective tool in countering Eurocentrism, the notion that Europeans or people of European descent have long been the primary movers and shakers of the historical process. That notion arose in recent centuries when Europeans were in fact the major source of innovation in the world and did in fact exercise something close to world domination. But this temporary preeminence decisively shaped the way Europeans thought and wrote about their own histories and those of other people. In their own eyes, Europeans alone were progressive people, thanks to a cultural or racial superiority. Everyone else was stagnant, backward, savage, or barbarian. The unusual power of Europeans allowed them for a time to act on those beliefs and to impose such ways of thinking on much of the world. Comparative world history sets European achievements in a global and historical context, helping us to sort out what was distinctive about its historical development and what similarities it bore to other major regions of the world. Puncturing the pretensions of Eurocentrism has been high on the agenda of world history.

The art of comparison is a learned skill, entailing several steps. It requires, first of all, asking explicitly comparative questions and determining what particular cases will be involved. If you want to compare revolutions, for example, you would need to decide which ones you are considering—American, French, Russian, Chinese, Cuban. Defining categories of comparison is a further step. Precisely which characteristics of those revolutions will you compare—their origins, their ideologies, the social classes involved, their outcomes? Finally, how will you present your comparison? You might choose a case-by-case analysis in which you would describe, say, the American Revolution first, followed by an account of the Cuban Revolution, which makes explicit comparisons with the former. Or you might choose a thematic approach in which you would consider first the origins of both revolutions, followed by a comparison of their ideologies, and so on. You will find examples of both approaches in the chapters that follow.

A second major theme of world history involves the interactions, encounters, and **connections** among different and often distant peoples. What happened when representatives of distinct civilizations or cultures met? Focusing on cross-cultural connections represents an effort to counteract a habit of thinking about particular peoples, states, or cultures as self-contained or isolated communities. Despite the historical emergence of separate and distinct societies, none of them developed alone. Each was embedded in a network of relationships with both near and more distant peoples. The encounter with strangers, or at least with strange ideas and practices, was everywhere among the most powerful motors of change in human societies. The growing depth and significance of such cross-cultural relationships has been a distinguishing feature of the modern era, as European conquest, colonialism, commerce, and culture penetrated the entire planet. Thus world history pays attention not only to the internal developments of particular civilizations or peoples but also to the networks, webs, and cross-cultural encounters in which they were enmeshed.

Third, historians of every kind are concerned always with what changes, what persists, and why. In world history, it is the "big picture" **changes**—those that impact large segments of humankind—that are of greatest interest. What generated the amazing transformations of the "revolution of modernity" in recent centuries? What lay behind the emergence of a new balance of global power after 1500, one that featured the growing prominence of Europe on the world stage? Why did the ancient civilizations of Russia and China explode in revolution during the twentieth century? What led to the rapid collapse of Europe's global empires after World War II?

Both change and comparison provide an antidote to a persistent tendency of human thinking that historians call "essentialism." A more common term is "stereotyping." It refers to our inclination to define particular groups of people with an unchanging or essential set of characteristics. Women are nurturing; peasants are conservative; Americans are aggressive; Hindus are religious. Serious students of history soon become aware that every significant category of people contains endless divisions and conflicts and that human communities are constantly in flux. Peasants may often accept the status quo, except of course when they rebel, as they frequently have. Americans have experienced periods of official isolationism and withdrawal from the world as well as times of aggressive engagement with it. Things change.

But some things persist, even if they also change. We should not allow an emphasis on change to blind us to the continuities of human experience. A recognizably Chinese state has operated for more than 2,000 years. Slavery and patriarchy persisted as human institutions for thousands of years until they were challenged in recent centuries, and in various forms they exist still. The teachings of Buddhism, Christianity, and Islam have endured for centuries, though with endless variations and transformations.

Comparisons, connections, and changes—all of them operating on a global scale—represent three ways of bringing some coherence to the multiple and complex stories of world history. They will recur repeatedly in the pages that follow.

Ways of the World

A Brief Global History

The Worlds of the Fifteenth Century

The Shapes of Human
  Communities
  Paleolithic Persistence
  Agricultural Village Societies
  Herding Peoples
Civilizations of the Fifteenth
  Century: Comparing China
  and Europe
  Ming Dynasty China
  European Comparisons:
    State Building and Cultural
    Renewal
  European Comparisons:
    Maritime Voyaging
Civilizations of the Fifteenth
  Century: The Islamic World
  In the Islamic Heartland: The
    Ottoman and Safavid Empires
  On the Frontiers of Islam: The
    Songhay and Mughal Empires
Civilizations of the Fifteenth
  Century: The Americas
  The Aztec Empire
  The Inca Empire
Webs of Connection
A Preview of Coming
  Attractions: Looking Ahead to
  the Modern Era (1500–2000)
Reflections: What If? Chance
  and Contingency in World
  History

During 2005, Chinese authorities marked the 600th anniversary of the initial launching of their country's massive maritime expeditions in 1405. Some eighty-seven years before Columbus sailed across the Atlantic with three small ships and a crew of about ninety men, the Chinese admiral Zheng He had captained a fleet of more than 300 ships and a crew numbering some 27,000 people, which brought a Chinese naval presence into the South China Sea and the Indian Ocean as far as the East African coast. Now in 2005, China was celebrating. Public ceremonies, books, magazine articles, two television documentaries, an international symposium, a stamp in honor of Zheng He—all of this and more was part of a yearlong remembrance of these remarkable voyages.

Given China's recent engagement with the larger world, Chinese authorities sought to use Zheng He as a symbol of their country's expanding, but peaceful, role on the international stage. Until recently, however, his achievement was barely noticed in China's collective memory, and for six centuries Zheng He had been largely forgotten or ignored. Columbus, on the other hand, had long been highly visible in the West, celebrated as a cultural hero and more recently harshly criticized as an imperialist, but certainly remembered. The voyages of both of these fifteenth-century mariners were pregnant with meaning for world history. Why were they remembered so differently in the countries of their origin?

THE FIFTEENTH CENTURY, DURING WHICH BOTH ZHENG HE AND COLUMBUS undertook their momentous expeditions, proved in retrospect to mark a major turning point in the human story. At the time, of course,

The Meeting of Two Worlds: This famous sixteenth-century engraving by the Flemish artist Theodore de Bry shows Columbus landing in Hispaniola (Haiti), where the Taino people bring him presents, while the Europeans claim the island for God and queen. In light of its long-range consequences, this voyage was arguably the most important single event of the fifteenth century. (Bildarchiv Preussischer Kulturbesitz/Art Resource, NY)

Snapshot   **Major Developments around the World in the Fifteenth Century**

Region	Major Developments
Central, East, and Southeast Asia	Ming dynasty China, 1368–1644 Conquests of Timur, 1370–1406 Zheng He's maritime voyages, 1405–1433 Spread of Islam into Southeast Asia Rise of Malacca Civil war among competing warlords in Japan
South Asia/India	Timur's invasion of India, 1398 Various Muslim sultanates in northern India Rise of Hindu state of Vijayanagar in southern India Founding of Mughal Empire, 1526
Middle East	Expansion of Ottoman Empire Ottoman seizure of Constantinople, 1453 Founding of Safavid Empire in Persia, 1501 Ottoman siege of Vienna, 1529
Christendom/Europe	European Renaissance Portuguese voyages of exploration along West African coast Completion of reconquest of Spain, ending Muslim control End of the Byzantine Empire, 1453 End of Mongol rule in Russia; reign of Ivan the Great, 1462–1505
Africa	Songhay Empire in West Africa, 1464–1591 Kingdom of the Kongo in West Central Africa Expansion of Ethiopian state in East Africa Kingdom of Zimbabwe/Mwene Mutapa in southern Africa
The Americas/Western Hemisphere	Aztec Empire in Mesoamerica, 1345–1521 Inca Empire along the Andes, 1438–1533 Iroquois confederacy (New York State) "Complex" Paleolithic societies along west coast of North America
Pacific Oceania	Paleolithic persistence in Australia Chiefdoms and stratified societies on Pacific islands Yap as center of oceanic trading network with Guam and Palau

no one was aware of it. No one knew in 1405 that the huge armada under Zheng He's command would be recalled in 1433, never to sail again. And no one knew in 1492 that Columbus's minuscule fleet of three ships would utterly transform the world, bringing the people of two "old worlds" and two hemispheres permanently together, with enduring consequences for them all. The outcome of the processes set in motion by those three small ships included the Atlantic slave trade, the decimation of the native population of the Americas, the massive growth of world population, the Industrial Revolution, and the growing prominence of Europeans on the world stage. But none of these developments were even remotely foreseeable in 1492.

Thus the fifteenth century, as a hinge of major historical change, provides an occasion for a bird's-eye view of the world through a kind of global tour. This excursion around the world will serve to briefly review the human saga thus far and to establish a baseline from which the transformations of the modern era might be measured. How then might we describe the world, and the worlds, of the fifteenth century?

The Shapes of Human Communities

One way to describe the world of the fifteenth century is to identify the various types of societies that it contained. Bands of hunters and gatherers, villages of agricultural peoples, newly emerging chiefdoms or small states, nomadic/pastoral communities, established civilizations and empires—all of these social or political forms would have been apparent to a widely traveled visitor in the fifteenth century. They represented alternative ways of organizing human communities and responded to differences in the environment, in the historical development of various regions, and in the choices made by particular peoples. The balance among these distinctive kinds of societies at the end of the postclassical millennium (1500) was quite different than it had been at the beginning (500).

Paleolithic Persistence

Despite millennia of agricultural advance, substantial areas of the world still hosted gathering and hunting societies, known to scholars as Paleolithic ("old stone-age") peoples. All of Australia, much of Siberia, the arctic coastlands, and parts of Africa and the Americas fell into this category. These peoples were not simply relics of a bygone age, however. They too had changed over time, though more slowly than their agricultural counterparts, and they too interacted with their neighbors. In short, they had a history, although most history books largely ignore them after the age of agriculture arrived. Nonetheless, this most ancient way of life still had a sizable and variable presence in the world of the fifteenth century.

Consider, for example, Australia. That continent's many separate groups, some 250 of them, still practiced a gathering and hunting way of life in the fifteenth century, a pattern that continued well after Europeans arrived in the late eighteenth century.

■ Comparison

In what ways did the gathering and hunting people of Australia differ from those of the northwest coast of North America?

Over many thousands of years, these people had assimilated various material items or cultural practices from outsiders—outrigger canoes, fish hooks, complex netting techniques, artistic styles, rituals, and mythological ideas—but despite the presence of farmers in nearby New Guinea, no agricultural practices penetrated the Australian mainland. Was it because large areas of Australia were unsuited for the kind of agriculture practiced in New Guinea? Or did the peoples of Australia, enjoying an environment of sufficient resources, simply see no need to change their way of life?

Despite the absence of agriculture, Australia's peoples had mastered and manipulated their environment, in part through the practice of "firestick farming," a pattern of deliberately set fires, which they described as "cleaning up the country." These controlled burns served to clear the underbrush, thus making hunting easier and encouraging the growth of certain plant and animal species. In addition, native Australians exchanged goods among themselves over distances of hundreds of miles, created elaborate mythologies and ritual practices, and developed sophisticated traditions of sculpture and rock painting. They accomplished all of this on the basis of an economy and technology rooted in the distant Paleolithic past.

A very different kind of gathering and hunting society flourished in the fifteenth century along the northwest coast of North America among the Chinookan, Tulalip, Skagit, and other peoples. With some 300 edible animal species and an abundance of salmon and other fish, this extraordinarily bounteous environment provided the foundation for what scholars sometimes call "complex" or "affluent" gathering and hunting cultures. What distinguished the northwest coast peoples from those of Australia were permanent village settlements with large and sturdy houses, considerable economic specialization, ranked societies that sometimes included slavery, chiefdoms dominated by powerful clan leaders or "big men," and extensive storage of food.

Although these and other gathering and hunting peoples persisted still in the fifteenth century, both their numbers and the area they inhabited had contracted greatly as the Agricultural Revolution unfolded across the planet. That relentless advance of the farming frontier continued in the centuries ahead as the Russian, Chinese, and European empires encompassed the lands of the remaining Paleolithic peoples. By the early twenty-first century, what was once the only human way of life had been reduced to minuscule pockets of people whose cultures seemed doomed to a final extinction.

Agricultural Village Societies

■ Change
What kinds of changes were transforming West African agricultural village societies and those of the Iroquois as the fifteenth century dawned?

Far more numerous than hunters and gatherers were those many peoples who, though fully agricultural, had avoided incorporation into larger empires or civilizations and had not developed their own city- or state-based societies. Living usually in small village-based communities and organized in terms of kinship relations, such people predominated during the fifteenth century in much of North America, in Africa south of the equator, and in parts of the Amazon River basin and

Southeast Asia. They had created societies largely without the oppressive political authority, class inequalities, and seclusion of women that were so common in civilizations. Historians have largely relegated such societies to the periphery of world history, marginal to their overwhelming focus on large-scale civilizations. Viewed from within their own circles, though, these societies were of course at the center of things, each with its own history of migration, cultural change, social conflict, incorporation of new people, political rise and fall, and interaction with strangers.

In the forested region of what is now southern Nigeria in West Africa, for example, three quite different patterns of political development emerged in the centuries between 1000 and 1500 (see Map 13.3, p. 376). Each of them began from a base of farming village societies whose productivity was generating larger populations.

Among the Yoruba people, a series of city-states emerged, each within a walled town and ruled by an *oba*, or king (many of whom were women), who performed both religious and political functions. As in ancient Mesopotamia or classical Greece, no single state or empire encompassed all of Yorubaland. Nearby lay the kingdom of Benin, a small, highly centralized territorial state that emerged by the fifteenth century and was ruled by a warrior king named Ewuare, said to have conquered 201 towns and villages in the process of founding the new state. His administrative chiefs replaced the heads of kinship groups as major political authorities, while the ruler sponsored extensive trading missions and patronized artists who created the remarkable brass sculptures for which Benin is so famous.

East of the Niger River lay the lands of the Igbo peoples, where dense population and extensive trading networks might well have given rise to states, but the deliberate Igbo preference was to reject the kingship and state-building efforts of their neighbors, boasting on occasion that "the Igbo have no kings." Instead they relied on other institutions—title societies in which wealthy men received a series of prestigious ranks, women's associations, hereditary ritual experts serving as mediators, a balance of power among kinship groups—to maintain social cohesion beyond the level of the village. It was a "stateless society," famously described in Chinua Achebe's *Things Fall Apart,* the most widely read novel to emerge from twentieth-century Africa.

The Yoruba, Bini, and Igbo peoples did not live in isolated, self-contained societies, however. They traded actively among themselves and with more distant peoples, such as the large African kingdom of Songhay far to the north. Cotton cloth, fish, copper and iron goods, decorative objects, and more drew neighboring peoples into networks of exchange. Common artistic traditions reflected a measure of cultural unity in a politically fragmented region, and all of these peoples seem to have changed from a matrilineal to a patrilineal system of tracing their descent. Little of this registered in the larger civilizations of the Afro-Eurasian world, but to the peoples of the West African forest during the fifteenth century, these processes were central to their history and their daily lives. Soon, however, all of them would be caught up in the transatlantic slave trade and would be changed substantially in the process.

Benin Bronzes
British colonial forces in 1897 looted the palace of the king of Benin and seized more than 1,000 exquisite brass figures, most of which were associated with court ceremonies. Here is a sixteenth-century representation of the Queen Mother of Benin. (National Museum, Lagos, Nigeria/The Bridgeman Art Library)

Across the Atlantic in what is now central New York State, other agricultural village societies were also in the process of substantial change during the several centuries preceding their incorporation into European trading networks and empires. The Iroquois-speaking peoples of that region had only recently become fully agricultural, adopting maize- and bean-farming techniques that had originated long ago in Mesoamerica. As this productive agriculture took hold by 1300 or so, the population grew, the size of settlements increased, and distinct peoples emerged, such as the Onondaga, Seneca, Cayuga, Oneida, and Mohawk. Frequent warfare also erupted among them. Some scholars have speculated that as agriculture, largely seen as women's work, became the primary economic activity, "warfare replaced successful food getting as the avenue to male prestige."[1]

Whatever caused it, this increased level of conflict among Iroquois peoples triggered a remarkable political innovation—a loose alliance or confederation among five Iroquois peoples based on an agreement known as the Great Law of Peace (see Map 13.5, p. 383). It was an agreement to settle their differences peacefully through a confederation council of clan leaders, some fifty of them altogether, who had the authority to adjudicate disputes and set reparation payments. Operating by consensus, the Iroquois League of Five Nations effectively suppressed the blood feuds and tribal conflicts that had only recently been so widespread. It also coordinated their peoples' relationship with outsiders, including the Europeans, who arrived in growing numbers in the centuries after 1500.

The Iroquois League also gave expression to values of limited government, social equality, and personal freedom, concepts that some European colonists found highly attractive. One British colonial administrator declared in 1749 that the Iroquois had "such absolute Notions of Liberty that they allow no Kind of Superiority of one over another, and banish all Servitude from their Territories."[2] Such equality extended to gender relationships, for among the Iroquois, descent was matrilineal (reckoned through the woman's line), married couples lived with the wife's family, and women controlled agriculture. While men were hunters, warriors, and the primary political officeholders, women selected and could depose those leaders.

Wherever they lived in 1500, over the next several centuries independent agricultural peoples such as the Iroquois, Yoruba, and Igbo were increasingly encompassed in expanding economic networks and conquest empires based in Western Europe or in Russia. In this respect, they repeated the experience of many other village-based farming communities that had much earlier found themselves forcibly included in the powerful embrace of Egyptian, Mesopotamian, Roman, Indian, Chinese, and other civilizations.

Iroquois League

Herding Peoples

■ Significance
What role did Central Asian and West African pastoralists play in their respective regions?

Nomadic pastoral peoples impinged more directly and dramatically on civilizations than did hunting and gathering or agricultural village societies. The Mongol incursion, and the enormous empire to which it gave rise, was one in a long series of challenges from the steppes, but it was not the last. As the Mongol Empire disintegrated, a brief attempt to restore it occurred in the late fourteenth and early fifteenth centuries under the leadership of a Turkic warrior named Timur, known in the West as Tamerlane (see Map 13.1, p. 370).

With a ferocity that matched or exceeded that of his model, Chinggis Khan, Timur's army of nomads brought immense devastation yet again to Russia, Persia, and India. Timur himself died in 1405, while preparing for an invasion of China. Conflicts among his successors prevented any lasting empire, although his descendants retained control of the area between Persia and Afghanistan for the rest of the fifteenth century. That state hosted a sophisticated elite culture, particularly at its splendid capital of Samarkand, as its rulers patronized artists, poets, traders, and craftsmen. Timur's conquest proved to be the last great military success of nomadic peoples from Central Asia. In the centuries that followed, their homelands were swallowed up in the expanding Russian and Chinese empires, as the balance of power between steppe nomads of inner Eurasia and the civilizations of outer Eurasia turned decisively in favor of the latter.

In Africa, pastoral peoples stayed independent of established empires several centuries longer than the nomads of Inner Asia, for not until the late nineteenth century were they incorporated into European colonial states. The experience of the Fulbe, West Africa's largest pastoral society, provides a useful example of an African herding people with a highly significant role in the fifteenth century and beyond. From their homeland in the western fringe of the Sahara along the upper Senegal River, the Fulbe migrated gradually eastward in the centuries after 1000 C.E. (see Map 13.3, p. 376). Unlike the pastoral peoples of Inner Asia, they generally lived in small communities among agricultural peoples and paid various grazing fees and taxes for the privilege of pasturing their cattle. Relations with their farming hosts often were tense because the Fulbe resented their subordination to agricultural peoples, whose way of life they despised. That sense of cultural superiority became even more pronounced as the Fulbe, in the course of their eastward movement, slowly adopted Islam. Some of them in fact dropped out of a pastoral life and settled in towns, where they became highly respected religious leaders. In the eighteenth and nineteenth centuries, the Fulbe were at the center of a wave of religiously based uprisings, or jihads, that greatly expanded the practice of Islam and gave rise to a series of new states, ruled by the Fulbe themselves.

Civilizations of the Fifteenth Century: Comparing China and Europe

Beyond the foraging, farming, and herding societies of the fifteenth-century world were its civilizations, those city-centered and state-based societies that were far larger and more densely populated, more powerful and innovative, and much more unequal in terms of class and gender than other forms of human community. Since the First Civilizations had emerged between 3500 and 1000 B.C.E., both the geographic space they encompassed and the number of people they embraced had grown substantially. By the fifteenth century, a considerable majority of the world's population lived within one or another of these civilizations, although most of these people no doubt identified more with local communities than with a larger civilization. What might an imaginary global traveler notice about the world's major civilizations in the fifteenth century?

Ming Dynasty China

■ Description
How would you define the major achievements of Ming dynasty China?

Such a traveler might well begin his or her journey in China, heir to a long tradition of effective governance, Confucian and Daoist philosophy, a major Buddhist presence, sophisticated artistic achievements, and a highly productive economy. That civilization, however, had been greatly disrupted by a century of Mongol rule, and its population had been sharply reduced by the plague. During the Ming dynasty (1368–1644), however, China recovered (see Map 13.1). The early decades of that dynasty witnessed an effort to eliminate all signs of foreign rule, discouraging

Map 13.1 Asia in the Fifteenth Century
The fifteenth century witnessed the massive Ming dynasty voyages into the Indian Ocean as well as the last major eruption of nomadic power in Timur's empire.

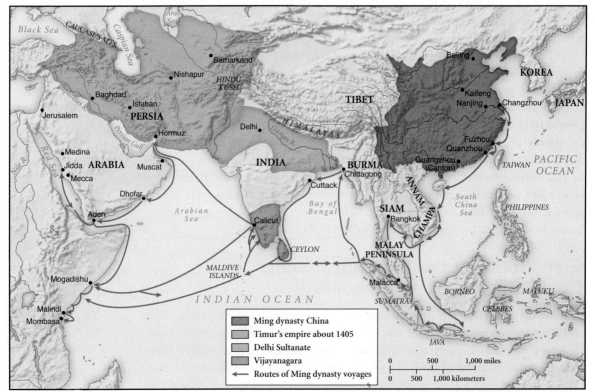

the use of Mongol names and dress, while promoting Confucian learning based on earlier models from the Han, Tang, and Song dynasties. Emperor Yongle (reigned 1402–1422) sponsored an enormous *Encyclopedia* of some 11,000 volumes. With contributions from more than 2,000 scholars, this work sought to summarize or compile all previous writing on history, geography, ethics, government, and more. Culturally speaking, China was looking to its past.

Politically, the Ming dynasty reestablished the civil service examination system that had been neglected under Mongol rule and went on to create a highly centralized government. Power was concentrated in the hands of the emperor himself, while a cadre of eunuchs (castrated men) personally loyal to the emperor exercised great authority, much to the dismay of the official bureaucrats. The state acted vigorously to repair the damage of the Mongol years by restoring millions of acres to cultivation; rebuilding canals, reservoirs, and irrigation works; and planting, according to some estimates, a billion trees in an effort to reforest China. As a result, the economy rebounded, both international and domestic trade flourished, and the population grew. During the fifteenth century, China had recovered and was perhaps the best-governed and most prosperous of the world's major civilizations.

China also undertook the largest and most impressive maritime expeditions the world had ever seen. Since the eleventh century, Chinese sailors and traders had been a major presence in the South China Sea and in Southeast Asian port cities, with much of this activity in private hands. But now, after decades of preparation, an enormous fleet, commissioned by Emperor Yongle himself, was launched in 1405, followed over the next twenty-eight years by six more such expeditions. On board more than 300 ships of the first voyage was a crew of some 27,000, including 180 physicians, hundreds of government officials, 5 astrologers, 7 high-ranking or grand eunuchs, carpenters, tailors, accountants, merchants, translators, cooks, and thousands of soldiers and sailors. Visiting many ports in Southeast Asia, Indonesia, India, Arabia, and East Africa, these fleets, captained by the Muslim eunuch Zheng He, sought to enroll distant peoples and states in the Chinese tribute system (see Map 13.1). Dozens of rulers accompanied the fleets back to China, where they presented tribute, performed the required rituals of submission, and received in return abundant gifts, titles, and trading opportunities. Chinese officials were amused by some of the exotic products to be found abroad—ostriches, zebras, and giraffes, for example. Officially described as "bringing order to the world," Zheng He's expeditions served to establish Chinese power and prestige in the Indian Ocean and to exert Chinese control over foreign trade in the

[handwritten margin note: Zheng He]

Comparing Chinese and European Ships
Among the largest vessels in Zheng He's early-fifteenth-century fleet was this "treasure ship," measuring more than 400 feet long and carrying a crew of perhaps 1,000 men. The figure at the bottom right represents one of Columbus's ships. (© Dugald Stermer)

Chinese Emperor Yongle commissioned Zheng He 1405–1433 expeditions

region. The Chinese, however, did not seek to conquer new territories, establish Chinese settlements, or spread their culture. On one of the voyages, Zheng He erected on the island of Ceylon (Sri Lanka) a tablet honoring alike the Buddha, Allah, and a Hindu deity.

The most surprising feature of these voyages was how abruptly and deliberately they were ended. After 1433, Chinese authorities simply stopped such expeditions and allowed this enormous and expensive fleet to deteriorate in port. "In less than a hundred years," wrote a recent historian of these voyages, "the greatest navy the world had ever known had ordered itself into extinction."[3] Part of the reason involved the death of the emperor Yongle, who had been the chief patron of the enterprise. Many high-ranking officials had long seen the expeditions as a waste of resources because China, they believed, was the self-sufficient "middle kingdom," requiring little from the outside world. In their eyes, the real danger to China came from the north, where nomadic barbarians constantly threatened. Finally, they viewed the voyages as the project of the court eunuchs, whom these officials despised. Even as these voices of Chinese officialdom prevailed, private Chinese merchants and craftsmen continued to settle and trade in Japan, the Philippines, Taiwan, and Southeast Asia, but they did so without the support of their government. The Chinese state quite deliberately turned its back on what was surely within its reach—a large-scale maritime empire in the Indian Ocean basin.

World View

European Comparisons: State Building and Cultural Renewal

■ **Comparison**
What political and cultural differences stand out in the histories of fifteenth-century China and Western Europe? What similarities are apparent?

At the other end of the Eurasian continent, similar processes of demographic recovery, political consolidation, cultural flowering, and overseas expansion were under way. Western Europe, having escaped Mongol conquest but devastated by the plague, began to regrow its population during the second half of the fifteenth century. As in China, the infrastructure of civilization proved a durable foundation for demographic and economic revival.

Politically, too, Europe joined China in continuing earlier patterns of state building. In China, however, this meant a unitary and centralized government that encompassed almost the whole of its civilization, while in Europe a decidedly fragmented system of many separate, independent, and highly competitive states made for a sharply divided Christendom (see Map 13.2). Many of these states—Spain, Portugal, France, England, the city-states of Italy (Milan, Venice, and Florence), various German principalities—learned to tax their citizens more efficiently, to create more effective administrative structures, and to raise standing armies. A small Russian state centered on the city of Moscow also emerged in the fifteenth century as Mongol rule faded away. Much of this state building was driven by the needs of war, a frequent occurrence in such a fragmented and competitive political environment. England and France, for example, fought intermittently for more than a century in the Hundred Years' War (1337–1453) over rival claims to territory in France. Nothing remotely similar disturbed the internal life of Ming dynasty China.

World View Political 545

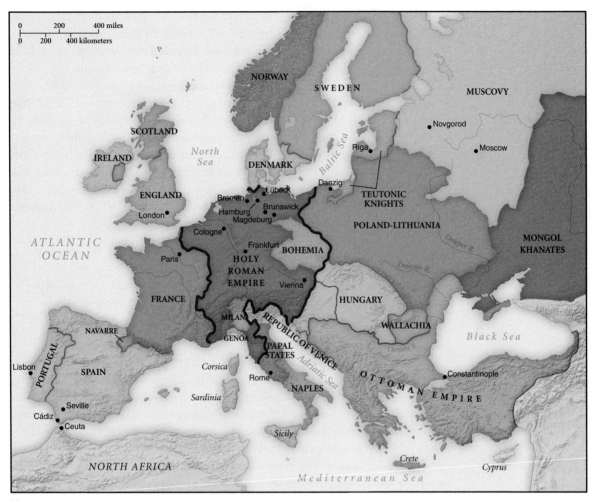

Map 13.2 Europe in 1500
By the end of the fifteenth century, Christian Europe had assumed its early modern political shape as a system of competing states threatened by an expanding Muslim Ottoman Empire.

A renewed cultural blossoming, known in European history as the Renaissance, likewise paralleled the revival of all things Confucian in Ming dynasty China. In Europe, however, that blossoming celebrated and reclaimed a classical Greek tradition that earlier had been obscured or viewed through the lens of Arabic or Latin translations. Beginning in the vibrant commercial cities of Italy between roughly 1350 and 1500, the Renaissance reflected the belief of the wealthy elite that they were living in a wholly new era, far removed from the confined religious world of feudal Europe. Educated citizens of these cities sought inspiration in the art and literature of ancient Greece and Rome—they were "returning to the sources," as they put it. Their purpose was not so much to reconcile these works with the ideas of Christianity, as the twelfth- and thirteenth-century university scholars had done, but to use them as a cultural standard to imitate and then to surpass. The elite patronized great Renaissance artists such as Leonardo da Vinci, Michelangelo, and Raphael, whose paintings and sculptures were far more naturalistic, particularly in portraying the human body, than those of their medieval counterparts.

Although religious themes remained prominent, Renaissance artists now included portraits and busts of well-known contemporary figures and scenes from ancient mythology. In the work of scholars, known as "humanists," reflections on secular topics such as grammar, history, politics, poetry, rhetoric, and ethics complemented more religious matters. For example, Niccolò Machiavelli's (1469-1527) famous work *The Prince* was a prescription for political success based on the way politics actually operated in a highly competitive Italy of rival city-states rather than on idealistic and religiously based principles. To the question of whether a prince should be feared or loved, Machiavelli replied:

> One ought to be both feared and loved, but as it is difficult for the two to go together, it is much safer to be feared than loved.... For it may be said of men in general that they are ungrateful, voluble, dissemblers, anxious to avoid danger, and covetous of gain.... Fear is maintained by dread of punishment which never fails.... In the actions of men, and especially of princes, from which there is no appeal, the end justifies the means.[4]

Heavily influenced by classical models, Renaissance figures were more interested in capturing the unique qualities of particular individuals and in describing the world as it was than in portraying or exploring eternal religious truths. In its focus on the affairs of this world, Renaissance culture reflected the urban bustle and commercial preoccupations of the Italian cities. Its secular elements challenged the otherworldliness of Christian culture, and its individualism signaled the dawning of a more capitalist economy of private entrepreneurs. A new Europe was in the making, rather more different from its own recent past than Ming dynasty China was from its pre-Mongol glory.

European Comparisons: Maritime Voyaging

■ Comparison
In what ways did European maritime voyaging in the fifteenth century differ from that of China? What accounts for these differences?

A global traveler during the fifteenth century might be surprised to find that Europeans, like the Chinese, were also launching outward-bound maritime expeditions. Initiated in 1415 by the small country of Portugal, those voyages sailed ever farther down the west coast of Africa, supported by the state and blessed by the pope (see Map 13.3). As the century ended, two expeditions marked major breakthroughs, although few suspected it at the time. In 1492, Christopher Columbus, funded by Spain, Portugal's neighbor and rival, made his way west across the Atlantic hoping to arrive in the East and, in one of history's most consequential mistakes, ran into the Americas. Five years later, in 1497, Vasco da Gama launched a voyage that took him around the tip of South Africa, along the East African coast, and, with the help of a Muslim pilot, across the Indian Ocean to Calicut in southern India.

Snapshot **Key Moments in European Maritime Voyaging**

Portuguese seize Ceuta in Morocco	1415
Prince Henry the Navigator launches Portuguese exploration of the West African coast	1420
Portuguese settle the Azores	1430s
Chinese fleets withdrawn from Indian Ocean	1433
Portuguese reach the Senegal River; beginning of Atlantic slave trade	1440s
Portuguese contact with Kongo; royal family converts to Christianity	1480s
Sugar production begins in Atlantic islands (Canaries, São Tomé)	1480s
Establishment of trading station at Elmina (in present-day Ghana)	1480s
First transatlantic voyage of Columbus	1492
John Cabot sails across North Atlantic to North America	1496
Vasco da Gama enters Indian Ocean and reaches India	1497–1498
Portuguese attacks on various Swahili cities; establishment of Fort Jesus at Mombasa; Portuguese contacts with Christian Ethiopia	1497–1520s
Magellan's voyage to Asia via the Americas; first circumnavigation of the globe	1520–1523

The differences between the Chinese and European oceangoing ventures were striking, most notably perhaps in terms of size. Columbus captained three ships and a crew of about 90, while da Gama had four ships, manned by perhaps 170 sailors. These were minuscule fleets compared to Zheng He's hundreds of ships and crew in the many thousands. "All the ships of Columbus and da Gama combined," according to a recent account, "could have been stored on a single deck of a single vessel in the fleet that set sail under Zheng He."[5]

Motivation as well as size differentiated the two ventures. Europeans were seeking the wealth of Africa and Asia—gold, spices, silk, and more. They also were in search of Christian converts and of possible Christian allies with whom to continue their long crusading struggle against threatening Muslim powers. China, by contrast, faced no equivalent power, needed no military allies in the Indian Ocean basin, and required little that these regions produced. Nor did China possess an impulse to convert foreigners to Chinese culture or religion as the Europeans surely did. Furthermore, the confident and overwhelmingly powerful Chinese fleet sought neither conquests nor colonies, while the Europeans soon tried to monopolize by force the commerce of the Indian Ocean and violently carved out huge empires in the Americas.

[handwritten margin note: World View Europe China]

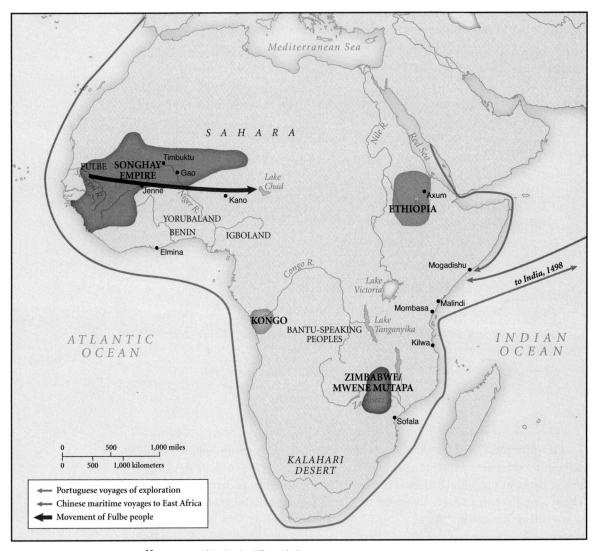

Map 13.3   Africa in the Fifteenth Century
By the 1400s, Africa was a virtual museum of political and cultural diversity, encompassing large empires, such as Songhay; smaller kingdoms, such as Kongo; city-states among the Yoruba, Hausa, and Swahili peoples; village-based societies without states at all, as among the Igbo; and nomadic pastoral peoples, such as the Fulbe. Both European and Chinese maritime expeditions touched on Africa during that century, even as Islam continued to find acceptance in the northern half of the continent.

The most striking difference in these two cases lay in the sharp contrast between China's decisive ending of its voyages and the continuing, indeed escalating, European effort, which soon brought the world's oceans and growing numbers of the world's people under its control. This is the reason that Zheng He's voyages were so long neglected in China's historical memory. They led nowhere, whereas the initial European expeditions, so much smaller and less promising, were but the initial steps on a journey to world power. But why did the Europeans continue a process that the Chinese had deliberately abandoned?

In the first place, of course, Europe had no unified political authority with the power to order an end to its maritime outreach. Its system of competing states, so unlike China's single unified empire, ensured that once begun, rivalry alone would drive the Europeans to the ends of the earth. Beyond this, much of Europe's elite had an interest in overseas expansion. Its budding merchant communities saw opportunity for profit; its competing monarchs eyed the revenue that could come from taxing overseas trade or from seizing overseas resources; the Church foresaw the possibility of widespread conversion; impoverished nobles might imagine fame and fortune abroad. In China, by contrast, support for Zheng He's voyages was very shallow in official circles, and when the emperor Yongle passed from the scene, those opposed to the voyages prevailed within the politics of the court.

Finally, the Chinese were very much aware of their own antiquity, believed strongly in the absolute superiority of their culture, and felt with good reason that, should they need something from abroad, others would bring it to them. Europeans too believed themselves unique, particularly in religious terms as the possessors of Christianity, the "one true religion." In material terms, though, they were seeking out the greater riches of the East, and they were highly conscious that Muslim power blocked easy access to these treasures and posed a military and religious threat to Europe itself. All of this propelled continuing European expansion in the centuries that followed.

Europe world view

The Waldseemüller Map of 1507
Just fifteen years after Columbus landed in the Western Hemisphere, this map, which was created by the German cartographer Martin Waldseemüller, reflected a dawning European awareness of the planet's global dimensions and location of the world's major landmasses. (Bildarchiv Preussischer Kulturbesitz/Art Resource, NY)

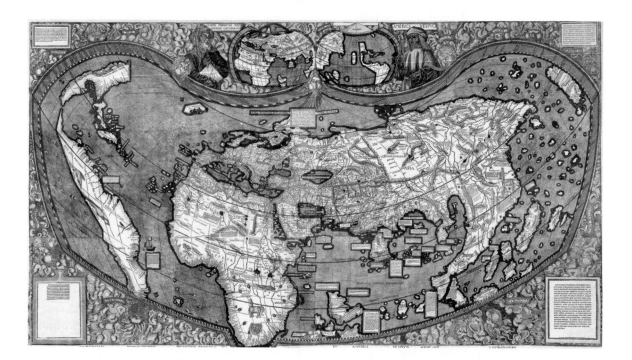

The Chinese withdrawal from the Indian Ocean actually facilitated the European entry. It cleared the way for the Portuguese to enter the region, where they faced only the eventual naval power of the Ottomans. Had Vasco da Gama encountered Zheng He's massive fleet as his four small ships sailed into Asian waters in 1498, world history may well have taken quite a different turn. As it was, however, China's abandonment of oceanic voyaging and Europe's embrace of the seas marked different responses to a common problem that both civilizations shared—growing populations and land shortage. In the centuries that followed, China's rice-based agriculture was able to expand production internally by more intensive use of the land, while the country's territorial expansion was inland toward Central Asia. By contrast, Europe's agriculture, based on wheat and livestock, expanded primarily by acquiring new lands in overseas possessions, which were gained as a consequence of a commitment to oceanic expansion.

Civilizations of the Fifteenth Century: The Islamic World

■ Comparison
What differences can you identify among the four major empires in the Islamic world of the fifteenth and sixteenth centuries?

Beyond the domains of Chinese and European civilization, our fifteenth-century global traveler would surely have been impressed with the transformations of the Islamic world. Stretching across much of Afro-Eurasia, the enormous realm of Islam experienced a set of remarkable changes during the fifteenth and early sixteenth centuries, as well as the continuation of earlier patterns. The most notable change lay in the political realm, for an Islamic civilization that had been severely fragmented since at least 900 now crystallized into four major states or empires (see Map 13.4). At the same time, a long-term process of conversion to Islam continued the cultural transformation in Afro-Eurasian societies both within and beyond these new states.

In the Islamic Heartland: The Ottoman and Safavid Empires

The most impressive and enduring of these new states was the Ottoman Empire, which lasted in one form or another from the fourteenth to the early twentieth century. It was the creation of one of the many Turkic warrior groups that had earlier migrated into Anatolia. By the mid-fifteenth century, these Ottoman Turks had already carved out a state that encompassed much of the Anatolian peninsula and had pushed deep into southeastern Europe (the Balkans), acquiring in the process a substantial Christian population. In the two centuries that followed, the Ottoman Empire extended its control to much of the Middle East, coastal North Africa, the lands surrounding the Black Sea, and even farther into Eastern Europe.

The Ottoman Empire was a state of enormous significance in the world of the fifteenth century and beyond. In its huge territory, long duration, incorporation of many diverse peoples, and economic and cultural sophistication, it was

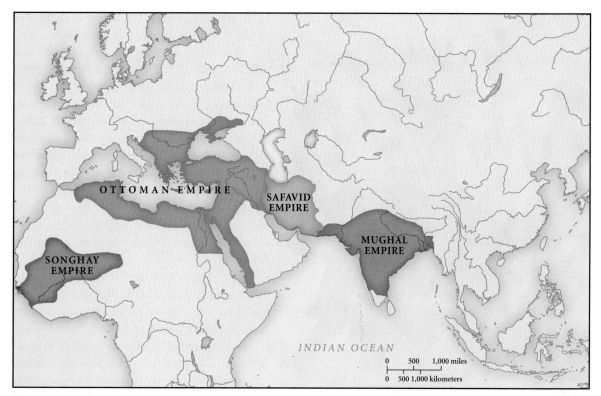

Map 13.4 Empires of the Islamic World

The most prominent political features of the vast Islamic world in the fifteenth and sixteenth centuries were four large states: the Songhay, Ottoman, Safavid, and Mughal empires.

one of the great empires of world history. In the fifteenth century, only Ming — *Ottoman* dynasty China and the Incas matched it in terms of wealth, power, and splendor. The empire represented the emergence of the Turks as the dominant people of the Islamic world, ruling now over many Arabs, who had initiated this new faith more than 800 years before. In adding "caliph" (successor to the Prophet) to their other titles, Ottoman sultans claimed the legacy of the earlier Abbasid Empire. They sought to bring a renewed unity to the Islamic world, while also serving as protector of the faith, the "strong sword of Islam."

The Ottoman Empire represented a new phase in the long encounter between Christendom and the world of Islam. In the Crusades, Europeans had taken the aggressive initiative in that encounter, but now the rise of the Ottoman Empire reversed their roles. The seizure of Constantinople in 1453 marked the final demise of Christian Byzantium and allowed Ottoman rulers to see themselves as successors to the Roman Empire. In 1529, a rapidly expanding Ottoman Empire laid siege to Vienna in the heart of Central Europe. The political and military expansion of Islam, at the expense of Christendom, seemed clearly under way. Many Europeans spoke fearfully of the "terror of the Turk."

Des obrilten Kamerling
Vnd Trüchses

Ottoman Janissaries
Originating in the fourteenth century, the Janissaries became the elite infantry force of the Ottoman Empire. Complete with uniforms, cash salaries, and marching music, they were the first standing army in the region since the days of the Roman Empire. When gunpowder technology became available, Janissary forces soon were armed with muskets, grenades, and handheld cannon. This image dates from the seventeenth century. (Austrian National Library, picture archive, Vienna: Cod. 8626, fol. 15r)

In the neighboring Persian lands to the east of the Ottoman Empire, another Islamic state was also taking shape in the late fifteenth and early sixteenth centuries—the Safavid Empire. Its leadership was also Turkic, but in this case it had emerged from a Sufi religious order founded several centuries earlier by Safi al-Din (1252–1334). The long-term significance of the Safavid Empire, which was established in the decade following 1500, was its decision to forcibly impose a Shia version of Islam as the official religion of the state. Over time, this form of Islam gained popular support and came to define the unique identity of Persian (Iranian) culture.

This Shia empire also introduced a sharp divide into the political and religious life of heartland Islam, for almost all of Persia's neighbors practiced a Sunni form of the faith. For a century (1534–1639), periodic military conflict erupted between the Ottoman and Safavid empires, reflecting both territorial rivalry and sharp religious differences. In 1514, the Ottoman sultan wrote to the Safavid ruler in the most bitter of terms:

You have denied the sanctity of divine law…you have deserted the path of salvation and the sacred commandments…you have opened to Muslims the gates of tyranny and oppression…you have raised the standard of irreligion and heresy.…[Therefore] the *ulama* and our doctors have pronounced a sentence of death against you, perjurer and blasphemer.[6]

This Sunni/Shia hostility has continued to divide the Islamic world into the twenty-first century.

On the Frontiers of Islam: The Songhay and Mughal Empires

While the Ottoman and Safavid empires brought both a new political unity and a sharp division to the heartland of Islam, two other states performed a similar role on the expanding African and Asian frontiers of the faith. In the West African savannas, the Songhay Empire rose in the second half of the fifteenth century. It was the most recent and the largest in a series of impressive states that operated at a crucial intersection of the trans-Saharan trade routes and that derived much of their revenue from taxing that commerce. Islam was a growing faith in Songhay but was limited largely to urban elites. This cultural divide within Songhay largely accounts for the religious behavior of its fifteenth-century monarch Sonni Ali (reigned 1465–1492), who gave alms and fasted during Ramadan in proper Islamic style but also enjoyed a reputation as a magician and possessed a charm thought to render his soldiers invisible to their enemies. Nonetheless, Songhay had become a major center of Islamic learning and commerce by the early sixteenth century. A North African traveler, known as Leo Africanus, remarked on the city of Timbuktu:

> Here are great numbers of [Muslim] religious teachers, judges, scholars, and other learned persons who are bountifully maintained at the king's expense. Here too are brought various manuscripts or written books from Barbary [North Africa] which are sold for more money than any other merchandise.... Here are very rich merchants and to here journey continually large numbers of negroes who purchase here cloth from Barbary and Europe.... It is a wonder to see the quality of merchandise that is daily brought here and how costly and sumptuous everything is.[7]

Sonni Ali's successor made the pilgrimage to Mecca and asked to be given the title "Caliph of the Land of the Blacks." Songhay then represented a substantial Islamic state on the African frontier of a still-expanding Muslim world.

The Mughal Empire in India bore similarities to Songhay, for both governed largely non-Muslim populations. Much as the Ottoman Empire initiated a new phase in the interaction of Islam and Christendom, so too did the Mughal Empire continue an ongoing encounter between Islamic and Hindu civilizations. Established in the early sixteenth century, the Mughal Empire was the creation of yet another Islamized Turkic group, which invaded India in 1526. Over the next century, the Mughals (a Persian term for Mongols) established unified control over most of the Indian peninsula, giving it a rare period of political unity and laying the foundation for subsequent British colonial rule. During its first several centuries, the Mughal Empire, a land of great wealth and imperial splendor, was the location of a remarkable effort to blend many Hindu groups and a variety of foreign Muslims into an effective partnership. The inclusive policies of the early Mughal emperors showed that Muslim rulers could accommodate their overwhelmingly Hindu subjects in somewhat the same fashion as Ottoman authorities provided religious autonomy for their Christian peoples. In southernmost India, however, the distinctly Hindu kingdom of Vijayanagara flourished in the fifteenth century, even as it borrowed architectural styles from the Muslim states of northern India and sometimes employed Muslim mercenaries in its military forces.

Together these four Muslim empires—Ottoman, Safavid, Songhay, and Mughal—brought to the Islamic world a greater measure of political coherence, military power, economic prosperity, and cultural brilliance than it had known since the early centuries of Islam. This new energy, sometimes called a "second flowering of Islam," impelled the continuing spread of the faith to yet new regions. The most prominent of these was oceanic Southeast Asia, which for centuries had been intimately bound up in the world of Indian Ocean commerce. By the fifteenth century, that trading network was largely in Muslim hands, and the demand for Southeast Asian spices was mounting as the Eurasian world recovered from the devastation of Mongol conquest and the plague. Growing numbers of Muslim traders, many of them from India, settled in Java and Sumatra, bringing their faith with them. Thus, unlike the Middle East and India, where Islam was established in the wake of Arab or Turkic conquest, in Southeast Asia, as in West Africa, it was introduced by traveling merchants and solidified through the activities of Sufi holy men.

The rise of Malacca, strategically located on the waterway between Sumatra and Malaya, was a sign of the times (see Map 13.1, p. 370). During the fifteenth century, it was transformed from a small fishing village to a major Muslim port city and became a springboard for the spread of Islam throughout the region. The Islam of Malacca, however, demonstrated much blending with local and Hindu/Buddhist traditions, while the city itself, like many port towns, had a reputation for "rough behavior." An Arab Muslim pilot in the 1480s commented critically:

> They have no culture at all.... You do not know whether they are Muslim or not.... They are thieves, for theft is rife among them and they do not mind.... They appear liars and deceivers in trade and labor.[8]

Nonetheless, Malacca, like Timbuktu, became a center for Islamic learning, and students from elsewhere in Southeast Asia were studying there in the fifteenth century. As the more central regions of Islam were consolidating politically, the frontier of the faith continued to move steadily outward.

Civilizations of the Fifteenth Century: The Americas

■ **Comparison**
What distinguished the Aztec and Inca empires from each other?

Across the Atlantic, centers of civilization had long flourished in Mesoamerica and in the Andes. The fifteenth century witnessed new, larger, and more politically unified expressions of those civilizations in the Aztec and Inca empires. Both were the work of previously marginal peoples who had forcibly taken over and absorbed older cultures, giving them new energy, and both were decimated in the sixteenth century at the hands of Spanish conquistadores and their diseases. To conclude this global tour of world civilizations, we will send our weary traveler to the Western Hemisphere for a brief look at these American civilizations (see Map 13.5).

The Aztec Empire

The empire known to history as the Aztec state was largely the work of the Mexica people, a seminomadic group from northern Mexico who had migrated southward and by 1325 had established themselves on a small island in Lake Texcoco. Over the next century, the Mexica developed their military capacity, served as mercenaries

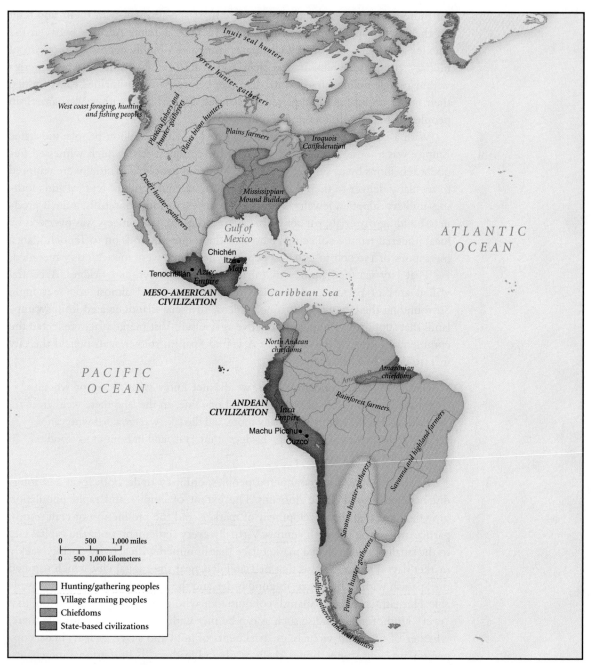

Map 13.5 The Americas in the Fifteenth Century

The Americas before Columbus represented a world almost completely separate from Afro-Eurasia. It featured similar kinds of societies, though with a different balance among them, but it completely lacked the pastoral economies that were so important in the Eastern Hemisphere.

Inuit seal hunters

Forest hunter-gatherers

West coast foraging, hunting and fishing peoples

Plateau fishers and hunter-gatherers

Plains bison hunters

Plains farmers

Iroquois Confederation

Desert hunter-gatherers

Mississippian Mound Builders

Gulf of Mexico

Chichén Itzá

Tenochtitlán · Aztec Empire

Maya

MESO-AMERICAN CIVILIZATION

Caribbean Sea

ATLANTIC OCEAN

PACIFIC OCEAN

North Andean chiefdoms

Amazonian chiefdoms

Rainforest farmers

ANDEAN CIVILIZATION

Inca Empire

Machu Picchu ·

Cuzco

Savanna and highland farmers

Savanna hunter-gatherers

Pampas hunter-gatherers

Shellfish gatherers and seal hunters

0   500   1,000 miles
0   500 1,000 kilometers

Hunting/gathering peoples
Village farming peoples
Chiefdoms
State-based civilizations

for more powerful people, negotiated elite marriage alliances with them, and built up their own capital city of Tenochtitlán. In 1428, a Triple Alliance between the Mexica and two other nearby city-states launched a highly aggressive program of military conquest, which in less than 100 years brought more of Mesoamerica within a single political framework than ever before. Aztec authorities, eager to shed their rather undistinguished past, now claimed descent from earlier Mesoamerican peoples such as the Toltecs and Teotihuacán.

With a core population recently estimated at 5 to 6 million people, the Aztec Empire was a loosely structured and unstable conquest state, which witnessed frequent rebellions by its subject peoples. Conquered peoples and cities were required to regularly deliver to their Aztec rulers impressive quantities of textiles and clothing, military supplies, jewelry and other luxuries, various foodstuffs, animal products, building materials, rubber balls, paper, and more. The process was overseen by local imperial tribute collectors, who sent the required goods on to Tenochtitlán, a metropolis of 150,000 to 200,000 people, where they were meticulously recorded.

That city featured numerous canals, dikes, causeways, and bridges. A central walled area of palaces and temples included a pyramid almost 200 feet high. Surrounding the city were "floating gardens," artificial islands created from swamplands that supported a highly productive agriculture. Vast marketplaces reflected the commercialization of the economy. A young Spanish soldier who beheld the city in 1519 described his reaction:

> Gazing on such wonderful sights, we did not know what to say, or whether what appeared before us was real, for on one side, on the land there were great cities, and in the lake ever so many more, and the lake was crowded with canoes, and in the causeway were many bridges at intervals, and in front of us stood the great city of Mexico.[9]

Beyond tribute from conquered peoples, ordinary trade, both local and long-distance, permeated Aztec domains. The extent of empire and rapid population growth stimulated the development of markets and the production of craft goods, particularly in the fifteenth century. Virtually every settlement, from the capital city to the smallest village, had a marketplace that hummed with activity during weekly market days. The largest was that of Tlatelolco, near the capital city, which stunned the Spanish with its huge size, its good order, and the immense range of goods available. Hernán Cortés, the Spanish conquistador who defeated the Aztecs, wrote that "every kind of merchandise such as can be met with in every land is for sale there, whether of food and victuals, or ornaments of gold and silver, or lead, brass, copper, tin, precious stones, bones, shells, snails and feathers."[10] Professional merchants, known as *pochteca*, were legally commoners, but their wealth, often exceeding that of the nobility, allowed them to rise in society and become "magnates of the land."

Among the "goods" that the pochteca obtained were slaves, many of whom were destined for sacrifice in the bloody rituals so central to Aztec religious life. Long a part of Mesoamerican and many other world cultures, human sacrifice

■ **Description**
How did Aztec religious thinking support the empire?

assumed an unusually prominent role in Aztec public life and thought during the fifteenth century. Tlacaelel (1398–1480), who was for more than half a century a prominent official of the Aztec Empire, is often credited with crystallizing the ideology of state that gave human sacrifice such great importance.

In the Aztecs' cyclical understanding of the world, the sun, central to all of life and identified with the their patron deity Huitzilopochtli, tended to lose its energy in a constant battle against encroaching darkness. Thus the Aztec world hovered always on the edge of catastrophe. To replenish its energy and thus postpone the descent into endless darkness, the sun required the life-giving force found in human blood. Because the gods had shed their blood ages ago in creating humankind, it was wholly proper for people to offer their own blood to nourish the gods in the present. The high calling of the Aztec state was to supply this blood, largely through its wars of expansion and from prisoners of war, who were destined for sacrifice. The victims were "those who have died for the god." The growth of the Aztec Empire therefore became the means for maintaining

Aztec Women
Within the home, Aztec women cooked, cleaned, spun and wove cloth, raised their children, and undertook ritual activities. Outside the home, they served as officials in palaces, priestesses in temples, traders in markets, teachers in schools, and members of craft workers' organizations. This domestic image comes from the sixteenth-century Florentine Codex, which was compiled by the Spanish but illustrated by Aztec artists. (Templo Mayor Library Mexico/Gianni Dagli Orti/The Art Archive)

cosmic order and avoiding utter catastrophe. This ideology also shaped the techniques of Aztec warfare, which put a premium on capturing prisoners rather than on killing the enemy. As the empire grew, priests and rulers became mutually dependent, and "human sacrifices were carried out in the service of politics."[11] Massive sacrificial rituals, together with a display of great wealth, served to impress enemies, allies, and subjects alike with the immense power of the Aztecs and their gods.

Alongside these sacrificial rituals was a philosophical and poetic tradition of great beauty, much of which mused on the fragility and brevity of human life. Here are a few lines from the fifteenth-century work of Nezahualcoyotl (1402–1472), a poet and king of the city-state of Texcoco, which was part of the Aztec Empire:

Truly do we live on Earth?
Not forever on earth; only a little while here.
Be it jade, it shatters.

Be it gold, it breaks.
Be it a quetzal feather, it tears apart.
Not forever on earth; only a little while here

Like a painting, we will be erased.
Like a flower, we will dry up here on earth.
Like plumed vestments of the precious bird,
That precious bird with an agile neck,
We will come to an end.[12]

The Inca Empire

While the Mexica were constructing an empire in Mesoamerica, a relatively small community of Quechua-speaking people, known to us as the Inca, was building the Western Hemisphere's largest imperial state along the spine of the Andes Mountains, which run almost the entire length of the west coast of South America. Much as the Aztecs drew upon the traditions of the Toltecs and Teotihuacán, the Incas incorporated the lands and cultures of earlier Andean civilizations: the Chavín, Moche, Nazca, and Chimu. The Inca Empire, however, was much larger than the Aztec state; it stretched some 2,500 miles along the Andes and contained perhaps 10 million subjects. Although the Aztec Empire controlled only part of the Mesoamerican cultural region, the Inca state encompassed practically the whole of Andean civilization during its short life in the fifteenth and early sixteenth centuries.

Both the Aztec and Inca empires represent rags-to-riches stories in which quite modest and remotely located people very quickly created by military conquest the largest states ever witnessed in their respective regions, but the empires themselves were quite different. In the Aztec realm, the Mexica rulers largely left their conquered people alone, if the required tribute was forthcoming. No elaborate administrative system arose to integrate the conquered territories or to assimilate their people to Aztec culture.

■ **Description**
In what ways did Inca authorities seek to integrate their vast domains?

The Incas, on the other hand, erected a rather more bureaucratic empire, though with many accommodations for local circumstances. At the top reigned the emperor, an absolute ruler regarded as divine, a descendant of the creator god Viracocha and the son of the sun god Inti. In theory, the state owned all land and resources, and each of the some eighty provinces in the empire had an Inca governor. At least in the central regions of the empire, subjects were grouped into hierarchical units of 10, 50, 100, 500, 1,000, 5,000, and 10,000 people, each headed by local officials, who were appointed and supervised by an Inca governor or the emperor. A separate set of "inspectors" provided the imperial center with an independent check on provincial officials. Births, deaths, marriages, and other population data were carefully recorded on *quipus*, the knotted cords that served as an accounting device. A resettlement program moved one-quarter or more of the population to new locations, in part to disperse conquered and no doubt resentful people.

Efforts at cultural integration required the leaders of conquered peoples to learn Quechua. Their sons were removed to the capital of Cuzco for instruction in Inca culture and language. Even now, millions of people from Ecuador to Chile still speak Quechua, and it is the official second language of Peru after Spanish. While the Incas required their subject peoples to acknowledge major Inca deities, these subject peoples were then largely free to carry on their own religious traditions. Human sacrifice took place on great public occasions or at times of special difficulty, but nothing remotely on the scale of the Aztec practice.

Like the Aztec Empire, the Inca state represented an especially dense and extended network of economic relationships within the "American web," but these relationships took shape in quite a different fashion. Inca demands on their conquered people were expressed, not so much in terms of tribute, but as labor service, known as *mita*, which was required periodically of every household.[13] What people produced at home usually stayed at home, but almost everyone also had to work for the state. Some labored on large state farms or on "sun farms," which supported temples and religious institutions; others herded, mined, served in the military, or toiled on state-directed construction projects. Those with particular skills were put to work manufacturing textiles, metal goods, ceramics, and stonework. The most well known of these specialists were the "chosen women," who were removed from their homes as young girls, trained in Inca ideology, and set to producing corn beer and cloth at state centers. Later they were given as wives to men of distinction or sent to serve as priestesses in various temples, where they were known as "wives of the Sun." In return for such labor services, Inca ideology, expressed in terms of family relationships, required the state to provide elaborate feasts at which large quantities of food and drink were consumed.

The Inca state played a major role in the distribution of goods as well as their production. A sixteenth-century Spanish observer wrote that "in each of the many provinces there were many storehouses filled with supplies and other needful things.... When there was no war, this stock of supplies and food was divided up among the poor and widows.... If there came a lean year, the storehouses were opened and the provinces were lent what they needed."[14] Thus the authority of the state penetrated and directed the Incas' society and economy far more than did that of the Aztecs.

If the Inca and Aztec civilizations differed sharply in their political and economic arrangements, they resembled each other more closely in their

Machu Picchu
Machu Picchu, high in the Andes Mountains, was constructed by the Incas in the 1400s on a spot long held sacred by local people. Its 200 buildings stand at some 8,000 feet above sea level, making it truly a "city in the sky." According to scholars, it was probably a royal retreat or religious center, rather than serving administrative, commercial, or military purposes. The outside world became aware of Machu Picchu only in 1911, when it was discovered by a Yale University archeologist. (Crispin Rodwell/Alamy)

gender systems. Both societies practiced what scholars call "gender parallelism," in which "women and men operate in two separate but equivalent spheres, each gender enjoying autonomy in its own sphere."[15]

In both Mesoamerican and Andean societies, such systems had emerged long before their incorporation into the Aztec and Inca empires. In the Andes, men reckoned their descent from their fathers and women from their mothers, while Mesoamericans had long viewed children as belonging equally to their mothers and fathers. Parallel religious cults for women and men likewise flourished in both societies. Inca men venerated the sun, while women worshipped the moon, with matching religious officials. In Aztec temples, both male and female priests presided over rituals dedicated to deities of both sexes. Particularly among the Incas, parallel hierarchies of male and female political officials governed the empire, while in Aztec society, women officials exercised local authority under a title that meant "female person in charge of people." Social roles were clearly defined and different for men and women, but the domestic concerns of women—childbirth, cooking, weaving, cleaning—were not regarded as inferior to the activities of men. Among the Aztec, for example, sweeping was a powerful and sacred act with symbolic significance as "an act of purification and a preventative against evil elements penetrating the center of the Aztec universe, the home."[16] In the Andes, men broke the ground, women sowed, and both took part in the harvest.

None of this meant gender equality. Men occupied the top positions in both political and religious life, and male infidelity was treated more lightly than was women's unfaithfulness. As the Inca and Aztec empires expanded, military life, limited to men, grew in prestige, perhaps skewing an earlier gender parallelism. In other ways, the new Aztec and Inca rulers adapted to the gender systems of the people they had conquered. Among the Aztecs, the tools of women's work, the broom and the weaving spindle, were ritualized as weapons; sweeping the home was believed to assist men at war; and childbirth for women was regarded as "our kind of war."[17] Inca rulers did not challenge the gender parallelism of their subjects but instead replicated it at a higher level, as the *sapay Inca* (the Inca ruler) and the *coya* (his female consort) governed jointly, claiming descent respectively from the sun and the moon.

Webs of Connection

■ Connection
In what different ways did the peoples of the fifteenth century interact with one another?

Few people in the fifteenth century lived in entirely separate and self-contained communities. Almost all were caught up, to one degree or another, in various and overlapping webs of influence, communication, and exchange. Such interactions represent, of course, one of the major concerns of world history. What kinds of webs or networks linked the various societies and civilizations of the fifteenth century?[18]

Perhaps most obvious were the webs of empire, large-scale political systems that brought together a variety of culturally different people. Christians and Muslims encountered each other directly in the Ottoman Empire, as did Hindus and Muslims in the Mughal Empire. No empire tried more diligently to integrate its diverse peoples than the fifteenth-century Incas.

Religion too linked far-flung peoples, and divided them as well. Christianity provided a common religious culture for peoples from England to Russia, although the great divide between Roman Catholicism and Eastern Orthodoxy endured, and in the sixteenth century the Protestant Reformation would shatter permanently the Christian unity of the Latin West. Although Buddhism had largely vanished from its South Asian homeland, it remained a link among China, Korea, Tibet, Japan, and parts of Southeast Asia, even as it splintered into a variety of sects and practices. More than either of these, Islam actively brought together its many peoples. In the hajj, the pilgrimage to Mecca, Africans, Arabs, Persians, Turks, Indians, and many others joined as one people as they rehearsed together the events that gave birth to their common faith. And yet the divisions and conflicts within the umma persisted, as the violent hostility between the Sunni Ottoman Empire and the Shia Safavid Empire so vividly illustrates.

Long-established patterns of trade among peoples occupying different environments and producing different goods were certainly much in evidence during the fifteenth century, as they had been for millennia. Hunting societies of Siberia funneled furs and other products of the forest into the Silk Road trading network traversing the civilizations of Eurasia. In the fifteenth century, some of the agricultural peoples in southern Nigeria were receiving horses brought overland from the drier regions to the north, where those animals flourished better. The Mississippi River in North America and the Orinoco and Amazon rivers in South America facilitated a canoe-borne commerce along those waterways. Coastal shipping in large seagoing canoes operated in the Caribbean and along the Pacific coast between Mexico and Peru. In the Pacific, the Micronesian island of Yap by the fifteenth century was the center of an oceanic trading network, which included the distant islands of Guam and Palau and used large stone disks as money. Likewise the people of Tonga, Samoa, and Fiji intermarried and exchanged a range of goods, including mats and canoes.

The great long-distance trading patterns of the Afro-Eurasian world, in operation for a thousand years or more, likewise continued in the fifteenth century, although the balance among them was changing (see Map 13.6). The Silk Road overland network, which had flourished under Mongol control in the thirteenth and fourteenth centuries, contracted in the fifteenth century as the Mongol Empire broke up and the devastation of the plague reduced demand for its products. The rise of the Ottoman Empire also blocked direct commercial contact between Europe and China, but oceanic trade from Japan, Korea, and China through the islands of Southeast Asia and across the Indian Ocean picked up considerably. Larger ships made it possible to trade in bulk goods such as grain as well as luxury products, while more sophisticated partnerships and credit mechanisms greased the wheels of commerce. A common Islamic culture over much of this vast region likewise smoothed the passage of goods among very different peoples, as it also did for the trans-Saharan trade.

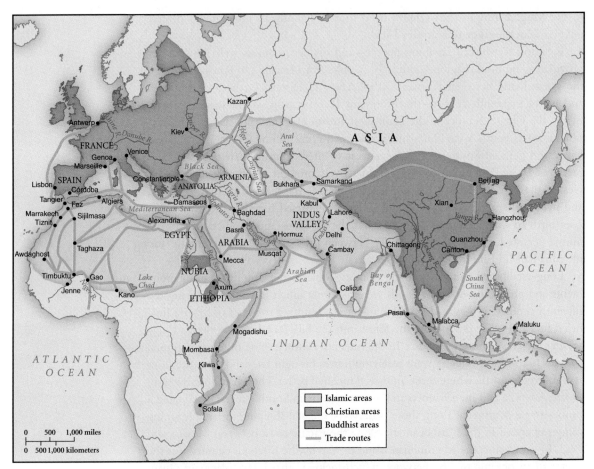

Map 13.6   Religion and Commerce in the Afro-Eurasian World

By the fifteenth century, the many distinct peoples and societies of the Eastern Hemisphere were linked to one another by ties of religion and commerce. Of course, not everyone was involved in long-distance trade, and many people in areas shown as Buddhist or Islamic on the map practiced other religions.

A Preview of Coming Attractions: Looking Ahead to the Modern Era, 1500–2000

Connections born of empire, culture, and commerce linked many of the peoples in the world of the fifteenth century, but none of them operated on a genuinely global scale. Although the densest webs of connection had been woven within the Afro-Eurasian zone of interaction, this huge region had no sustained ties with the Americas, and neither of them had meaningful contact with the peoples of Pacific Oceania. That situation was about to change as Europeans in the sixteenth century and beyond forged a set of genuinely global relationships that linked all of these regions. That enormous process and the many consequences that flowed from it marked the beginning of what historians commonly call the modern age—the more than five centuries that followed the voyages of Columbus starting in 1492.

Over those five centuries, the previously separate worlds of Afro-Eurasia, the Americas, and Pacific Oceania became inextricably linked, with enormous consequences for everyone involved. Global empires, a global economy, global cultural exchanges, global migrations, global disease, global wars, and global environmental changes have made the past 500 years a unique phase in the human journey. Those webs of communication and exchange have progressively deepened, so much so that by the end of the twentieth century few people in the world lived beyond the cultural influences, economic ties, or political relationships of a globalized world.

A second distinctive feature of the past five centuries involves the emergence of a radically new kind of human society, also called "modern," which took shape first in Europe during the nineteenth century and then in various forms elsewhere in the world. The core feature of such societies was industrialization, rooted in a sustained growth of technological innovation. The human ability to create wealth made an enormous leap forward in a very short period of time, at least by world history standards. Accompanying this economic or industrial revolution was an equally distinctive and unprecedented jump in human numbers, a phenomenon that has affected not only human beings but also many other living species and the earth itself (see the Snapshot).

Modern societies were far more urbanized and much more commercialized than ever before, as more and more people began to work for wages, to produce for the market, and to buy the requirements of daily life rather than growing or making those products for their own use. These societies gave prominence and power to holders of

Snapshot **World Population Growth, 1000–2000**[19]

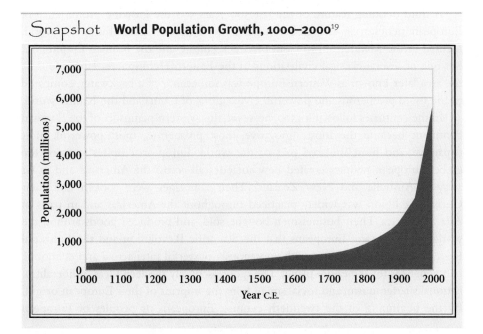

urban wealth—merchants, bankers, industrialists, educated professionals—at the expense of rural landowning elites, while simultaneously generating a substantial factory working class and diminishing the role of peasants and handicraft artisans.

Modern societies were generally governed by states that were more powerful and intrusive than earlier states and empires had been, and they offered more of their people an opportunity to play an active role in public and political life. Literacy in modern societies was far more widespread than ever before, while new national identities became increasingly prominent, competing with more local loyalties. To the mix of established religious ideas and folk traditions were now added the challenging outlook and values of modern science, with its secular emphasis on the ability of human rationality to know and manipulate the world. Modernity has usually meant a self-conscious awareness of living and thinking in new ways that deliberately departed from tradition.

This revolution of modernity, comparable in its pervasive consequences only to the Agricultural Revolution of some 10,000 years ago, introduced new divisions and new conflicts into the experience of humankind. The ancient tensions between rich and poor within particular societies were now paralleled by new economic inequalities among entire regions and civilizations and a much-altered global balance of power. The first societies to experience the modern transformation—those in Western Europe and North America—became both a threat and a source of envy to much of the rest of the world. As modern societies emerged and spread, they were enormously destructive of older patterns of human life, even as they gave rise to many new ways of living. Sorting out what was gained and what was lost during the modern transformation has been a persistent and highly controversial thread of human thought over the past several centuries.

A third defining feature of the last 500 years was the growing prominence of European peoples on the global stage. In ancient times, the European world, focused in the Mediterranean basin of Greek culture and the Roman Empire, was but one of several classical civilizations in the Eastern Hemisphere. After 500 C.E., the area later known as Western Europe was something of a backwater, compared to the more prosperous and powerful civilizations of China and the Islamic world.

In the centuries following 1500, however, this western peninsula of the Eurasian continent became the most innovative, most prosperous, most powerful, most expansive, and most imitated part of the world. European empires spanned the globe. European peoples created new societies all across the Americas and as far away as Australia and New Zealand. Their languages were spoken and their Christian religion was widely practiced throughout the Americas and in parts of Asia and Africa. Their businessmen bought, sold, and produced goods around the world. It was among Europeans that the Scientific Revolution and the Industrial Revolution first took shape, with enormously powerful intellectual and economic consequences for the entire planet. The quintessentially modern ideas of liberalism, nationalism, feminism, and socialism all bore the imprint of their European origin. By the beginning of the twentieth century, Europeans or peoples of European descent exercised unprecedented influence and control over the earth's many other peoples, a wholly novel experience in human history.

For the rest of the world, growing European dominance posed a common task. Despite their many differences, the peoples of Asia, Africa, the Middle East, the Americas, and Pacific Oceania all found themselves confronted by powerful and intrusive Europeans. The impact of this intrusion and how various peoples responded to it—resistance, submission, acceptance, imitation, adaptation—represent critically important threads in the world history of the past five centuries.

Reflections: What If? Chance and Contingency in World History

Seeking meaning in the stories they tell, historians are inclined to look for deeply rooted or underlying causes for the events they recount. And yet, is it possible that, at least on occasion, history turns less on profound and long-term causes than on coincidence, chance, or the decisions of a few that might well have gone another way?

Consider, for example, the problem of explaining the rise of Europe to a position of global power in the modern era. What if the Great Khan Ogodei had not died in 1241, requiring the forces then poised for an assault on Germany to return to Mongolia? It is surely possible that Central and Western Europe might have been overrun by Mongol armies as so many other civilizations had been, a prospect that could have drastically altered the trajectory of European history. Or what if the Chinese had decided in 1433 to continue their huge maritime expeditions, creating an empire in the Indian Ocean basin and perhaps moving on to "discover" the Americas and Europe? Such a scenario suggests a wholly different future for world history than the one that in fact occurred. Or what if the forces of the Ottoman Empire had taken the besieged city of Vienna in 1529? Might they then have incorporated even larger parts of Europe into their expanding domain, calling a halt to Europe's overseas empire-building enterprise?

None of this necessarily means that the rise of Europe was merely a fluke or an accident of history, but it does raise the issue of "contingency," the role of unforeseen or small events in the unfolding of the human story. An occasional "what if" approach to history reminds us that alternative possibilities existed in the past and that the only certainty about the future is that we will be surprised.

Second Thoughts

What's the Significance?

Paleolithic persistence	Iroquois	Ming dynasty China
Benin	Timur	Zheng He
Igbo	Fulbe	European Renaissance

To assess your mastery of the material in this chapter, see the **Online Study Guide** at bedfordstmartins.com/strayer.

Ottoman Empire	Songhay Empire	Aztec Empire
seizure of Constantinople	Timbuktu	Inca Empire
(1453)	Mughal Empire	
Safavid Empire	Malacca	

Big Picture Questions

1. Assume for the moment that the Chinese had *not* ended their maritime voyages in 1433. How might the subsequent development of world history have been different? Is there value in asking this kind of "what if" or counterfactual question? Or is it an irrelevant waste of time?

2. How does this chapter distinguish among the various kinds of societies that comprised the world of the fifteenth century? Are there other ways of categorizing the world's peoples that might work as well or better?

3. What would surprise a knowledgeable observer from 500 C.E., were he or she to make a global tour in the fifteenth century? What features of that earlier world might still be recognizable?

4. What predictions about the future might a global traveler of the fifteenth century reasonably have made? Would it depend on precisely when those predictions were made?

Next Steps: For Further Study

For Web sites and documents related to this chapter, see **Make History** at bedfordstmartins.com/strayer.

Terence N. D'Altroy, *The Incas* (2002). A history of the Inca Empire that draws on recent archeological and historical research.

Edward L. Dreyer, *Zheng He: China and the Oceans in the Early Ming Dynasty* (2006). The most recent scholarly account of the Ming dynasty voyages.

Halil Inalcik and Donald Quataert, *An Economic and Social History of the Ottoman Empire, 1300–1914* (1994). A classic study of the Ottoman Empire.

Robin Kirkpatrick, *The European Renaissance, 1400–1600* (2002). A beautifully illustrated history of Renaissance culture as well as the social and economic life of the period.

Charles Mann, *1491: New Revelations of the Americas before Columbus* (2005). A review of Western Hemisphere societies and academic debates about their pre-Columbian history.

J. R. McNeill and William H. McNeill, *The Human Web* (2003). A succinct account of the evolving webs or relationships among human societies in world history.

Michael Smith, *The Aztecs* (2003). A history of the Aztec Empire, with an emphasis on the lives of ordinary people.

"Ming Dynasty," http://www.metmuseum.org/toah/hd/ming/hd_ming.htm. A sample of Chinese art from the Ming dynasty from the collection of the Metropolitan Museum of Art.

"Renaissance Art in Italy," http://witcombe.sbc.edu/ARTHrenaissanceitaly.html. An extensive collection of painting and sculpture from the Italian Renaissance.

PART FOUR
The Early Modern World

1450–1750

Contents
Chapter 14. Empires and Encounters, 1450–1750
Chapter 15. Global Commerce, 1450–1750
Chapter 16. Religion and Science, 1450–1750

THE BIG PICTURE

Debating the Character of an Era

For the sake of clarity and the coherence of the stories they tell, historians often characterize a particular period of time in a brief phrase—the age of First Civilizations, the classical era, the age of empires, the era of revolutions, and so on. Though useful and even necessary, such capsule descriptions leave a lot out and vastly oversimplify what really happened. Historical reality is always more messy, more complicated, and more uncertain than any shorthand description can convey. Such is surely the case when we examine the three centuries spanning the years from roughly 1450 to 1750.

An Early Modern Era?

Those three centuries, which are addressed in Chapters 14 through 16, are conventionally labeled as "the early modern era." In using this term, historians are suggesting that during these three centuries we can find signs or markers of the modern era, such as those described at the end of Chapter 13: the beginnings of genuine globalization, elements of distinctly modern societies, and a growing European presence in world affairs.

The most obvious expression of globalization, of course, lay in the oceanic journeys of European explorers and the European conquest and colonial settlement of the Americas. The Atlantic slave trade linked Africa permanently to the Western Hemisphere, while the global silver trade allowed Europeans to use New World precious metals to buy their way into ancient Asian trade routes. The massive transfer of plants, animals, diseases, and people, known to scholars as the Columbian exchange, created wholly new networks of interaction across both the Atlantic and Pacific oceans, with enormous global implications. Missionaries carried Christianity far beyond Europe, allowing it to become a genuinely world religion, with a presence in the Americas, China, Japan, the Philippines, and south-central Africa. Other threads in the emerging global web were also woven as Russians marched across Siberia to the Pacific, as China expanded deep into Inner Asia, and as the Ottoman Empire encompassed much of the Middle East, North Africa, and southeastern Europe (see Chapter 14).

Scattered signs of what later generations thought of as "modernity" appeared in various places around the world. China, Japan, India, and Europe experienced the beginnings of modern population growth as the foods of the Americas—corn and potatoes, for example—provided nutrition to support larger numbers. World population more than doubled between 1400 and 1800 (from about 374 million to 968 million), even as the globalization of disease produced a demographic catastrophe in the Americas and the slave trade limited African population growth. More highly commercialized economies centered in large cities developed in various parts of Eurasia and the Americas. By the early eighteenth century, for example, Japan was one of the most urbanized societies in the world, with Edo (Tokyo) housing more than a million inhabitants and ranking as the world's largest city. In China, Southeast Asia, India, and across the Atlantic basin, more and more people found themselves, sometimes willingly and at other times involuntarily, producing for distant markets rather than for the use of their local communities.

Stronger and more cohesive states also emerged in various places, incorporating many local societies into larger units that were both able and willing to actively promote trade, manufacturing, and a common culture within their borders. France, the Dutch Republic, Russia, Morocco, the Mughal Empire, Vietnam, Burma, Siam, and Japan all represent this kind of state.[1] Their military power likewise soared as the "gunpowder revolution" kicked in around the world. Large-scale empires proliferated, and various European powers carved out new domains in the Americas. The most obviously modern cultural development took place in Europe, where the Scientific Revolution transformed, at least for members of a small educated elite, their view of the world, their approach to knowledge, and their understanding of traditional Christianity.

A Late Agrarian Era?

All of these developments give some validity to the notion of an early modern era. But this is far from the whole story, and it may be misleading if it suggests that European world domination and more fully modern societies were a "sure thing," an inevitable outgrowth of early modern developments. In fact, that future was far from clear in 1750.

Although Europeans ruled the Americas and controlled the world's sea routes, their political and military power in mainland Asia and Africa was very limited. Eighteenth-century China and Japan strictly controlled the European missionaries and merchants who operated in their societies, and African authorities frequently set the terms under which the slave trade was conducted. Islam, not Christianity, was the most rapidly spreading faith in much of Asia and Africa, and in 1750 Europe, India, and China were roughly comparable in their manufacturing output. In short, it was not obvious that Europeans would soon dominate the planet. Moreover, populations and economies had surged at various points in the past, only to fall back again in a cyclical pattern. Nothing guaranteed that the early modern surge would be any more lasting than the others.

Nor was there much to suggest that anything approaching modern industrial society was on the horizon. Animal and human muscles, wind, and water still provided almost all of the energy that powered human economies. Handicraft techniques of manufacturing had nowhere been displaced by factory-based production or steam power. Long-established elites, not middle-class upstarts, everywhere provided leadership and enjoyed the greatest privileges, while rural peasants, not urban workers, represented the primary social group in the lower classes. Kings and nobles, not parliaments and parties, governed. Male dominance was assumed to be natural almost everywhere. Modern society, with its promise of liberation from ancient inequalities and the end of poverty for most, hardly seemed around the corner.

Most of the world's peoples, in fact, continued to live in long-established ways, and their societies operated according to traditional principles. Kings ruled most of Europe, and landowning aristocrats remained at the top of the social hierarchy. Another change in ruling dynasties occurred in China, while that huge country affirmed Confucian values and a social structure that privileged landowning and officeholding elites. Most Indians practiced some form of Hinduism and owed their most fundamental loyalty to local castes, even as South Asia continued its centuries-long incorporation into the Islamic world. The realm of Islam maintained its central role in the Eastern Hemisphere as the Ottoman Empire revived the political fortunes of Islam and the religion sustained its long-term expansion into Africa and Southeast Asia.

For the majority of humankind, the three centuries between 1450 and 1750 marked less an entry into the modern era than the continuing development of older agrarian societies. It was as much a late agrarian era as an early modern age. Persistent patterns rooted in the past characterized that period, along with new departures and sprouts of modernity. Nor was change always in the direction of what we now regard as "modern." In European, Islamic, and Chinese societies alike, some people urged a return to earlier ways of living and thinking rather than embracing what was new and untried. Although Europeans were increasingly prominent on the world stage, they certainly did not hold all of the leading roles in the global drama of these three centuries.

From this mixture of what was new and what was old during the early modern era, the three chapters that follow highlight the changes. Chapter 14 turns the spotlight on the new empires of those three centuries—European, Middle Eastern, and Asian. New global patterns of long-distance trade in spices, sugar, silver, fur, and slaves represent the themes of Chapter 15. New cultural trends—both within the major religious traditions of the world and in the emergence of modern science—come together in Chapter 16. With the benefit of hindsight, we may see many of these developments as harbingers of a modern world to come, but from the viewpoint of 1700 or so, the future was open and uncertain, as it almost always is.

Landmarks in the Early Modern Era, 1450–1750

1400	1450	1500	1550

Europe

■ **1492** Columbus's first voyage to the Americas

■ **1543** Copernicus publishes heliocentric view of the universe

1400–1600 Renaissance

1400s Portuguese maritime voyages

■ **1517** Beginnings of Protestant Reformation

Africa

■ **1441** Beginnings of Atlantic slave trade

1464–1591 Songhay Empire (West Africa)

■ **1505** Portuguese attacks on Swahili cities

■ **1516** Benin begins to restrict slave trade

1506–1542 Reign of King Afonso (Kongo)

1500–1530 Christian-Muslim conflict in Ethiopia

The Americas

■ **1494** Treaty of Tordesillas divides New World between Spain and Portugal

■ **1541** Discovery of silver near Potosí

1530s First Portuguese plantations in Brazil

1532–1540 Spanish conquest of Inca Empire

■ **1519–1521** Spanish conquest of Aztec Empire

Islamic World

■ **1453** Ottoman conquest of Constantinople

1501–1722 Safavid Empire in Persia

1534–1639 Conflict between Ottoman and Safavid empires

1526–1707 Flourishing of Mughal Empire

1556–1605 Reign of Mughal emperor Akbar

1520–1566 Reign of Ottoman emperor Suleiman

■ **1529** Ottoman siege of Vienna

Asia

■ **1433** Withdrawal of Chinese fleet from Indian Ocean

■ **1498** Vasco da Gama arrives in India

■ **1550** Russian expansion across Siberia begins

■ **1582** Jesuit missionary Matteo Ricci arrives in China

■ **1565** Spanish takeover of Philippines begins

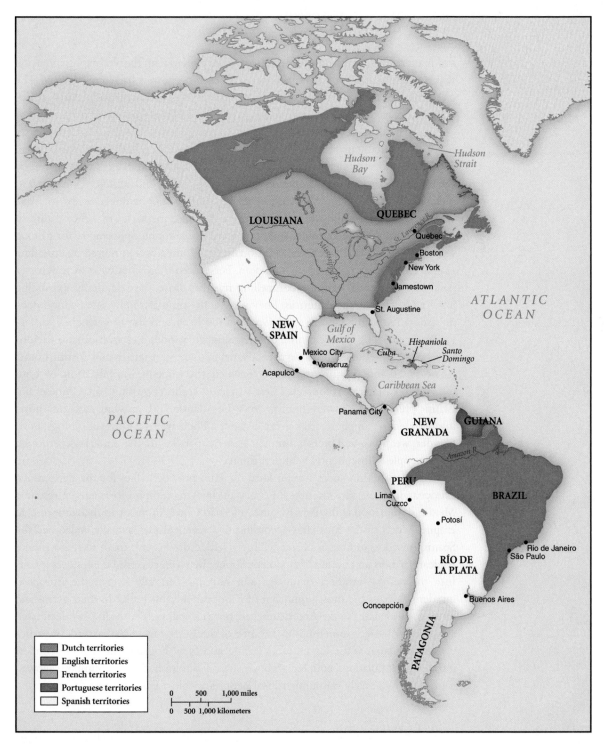

Map 14.1 European Colonial Empires in the Americas

By the beginning of the eighteenth century, European powers had laid claim to most of the Western Hemisphere. Their wars and rivalries during that century led to an expansion of Spanish and English claims, at the expense of the French.

405

and mastered, they provided a far different environment than the alternating monsoon winds of the Indian Ocean, in which Asian maritime powers had long operated. The enormously rich markets of the Indian Ocean world provided little incentive for its Chinese, Indian, or Muslim participants to venture much beyond their own waters.

Europeans, however, were powerfully motivated to do so. After 1200 or so, Europeans were increasingly aware of their marginal position in the world of Eurasian commerce and were determined to gain access to that world. Rulers were driven by the enduring rivalries of competing states. The growing and relatively independent merchant class in a rapidly commercializing Europe sought direct access to Asian wealth in order to avoid the reliance on Muslim intermediaries that they found so distasteful. Impoverished nobles and commoners alike found opportunity for gaining wealth and status in the colonies. Missionaries and others were inspired by crusading zeal to enlarge the realm of Christendom. Persecuted minorities were in search of a new start in life. All of these compelling motives drove the relentlessly expanding imperial frontier in the Americas. They were aptly summarized by one Spanish conquistador: "We came here to serve God and the King, and also to get rich."[3]

In carving out these empires, often against great odds and with great difficulty, Europeans nonetheless bore certain advantages, despite their distance from home. Their states and trading companies enabled the effective mobilization of both human and material resources. Their seafaring technology, built on Chinese and Islamic precedents, allowed them to cross the Atlantic with growing ease, transporting people and supplies across great distances. Their ironworking technology, gunpowder weapons, and horses initially had no parallel in the Americas, although many peoples subsequently acquired them.

Divisions within and between local societies provided allies for the determined European invaders. Various subject peoples of the Aztec Empire, for example, resented Mexica domination and willingly joined Hernán Cortés in the Spanish assault on that empire. Much of the Inca elite, according to a recent study, "actually welcomed the Spanish invaders as liberators and willingly settled down with them to share rule of Andean farmers and miners."[4] A violent dispute between two rival contenders for the Inca throne, the brothers Atahualpa and Huáscar, certainly helped the European invaders. Perhaps the most significant of European advantages lay in their germs and diseases, to which Native Americans had no immunities. Those diseases decimated society after society, sometimes in advance of the Europeans' actual arrival. In particular regions such as the Caribbean, Virginia, and New England, the rapid buildup of immigrant populations, coupled with the sharply diminished native numbers, allowed Europeans to actually outnumber local peoples within a few decades.

■ **Change**
What large-scale transformations did European empires generate?

The Great Dying

Whatever combination of factors explains the European acquisition of their empires in the Americas, there is no doubting their global significance. Chief among those consequences was the demographic collapse of Native American societies, a phenomenon that one prominent scholar described as "surely the great-est tragedy in the history of the human species."[5] Although precise figures remain the subject of much debate, scholars generally agree that the pre-Columbian pop-ulation of the Western Hemisphere was substantial, on the order of that of Europe, perhaps 60 million to 80 million. The greatest concentrations of people lived in the Mesoamerican and Andean zones, which were dominated by the Aztec and Inca empires. Long isolation from the Afro-Eurasian world and the lack of most domes-ticated animals meant the absence of acquired immunities to Old World diseases, such as smallpox, measles, typhus, influenza, malaria, and yellow fever.

Therefore, when they came into contact with these European and African diseases, Native American peoples died in appalling numbers, in many cases up to 90 percent of the population. The densely settled peoples of Caribbean islands virtually van-ished within fifty years of Columbus's arrival. Central Mexico, with a population estimated at some 10 million to 20 million, declined to about 1 million by 1650. A native Nahuatl account depicted the social breakdown that accompanied the small-pox pandemic: "A great many died from this plague, and many others died of hunger. They could not get up to search for food, and everyone else was too sick to care for them, so they starved to death in their beds."[6]

The situation was similar in North America. A Dutch observer in New Netherlands (later New York) reported in 1656 that "the Indians…affirm that before the arrival of the Christians, and before the small pox broke out amongst them, they were ten times as numerous as they are now, and that their population had been melted down by this disease, whereof nine-tenths of them have died."[7] To Governor Bradford of Plymouth colony (in present-day Massachusetts), such conditions represented the "good hand of God" at work, "sweeping away great multitudes of the natives…that he might make room for us."[8] Not until the late seventeenth century did native numbers begin to recuperate somewhat from this catastrophe, and even then not everywhere.

The Columbian Exchange

In sharply diminishing the population of the Americas, this "great dying" created an acute labor shortage and certainly did make room for immigrant newcomers, both colonizing Europeans and enslaved Africans. Over the several centuries of the colo-nial era and beyond, various combinations of indigenous, European, and African peoples created entirely new societies in the Americas, largely replacing the many and varied cultures that had flourished before 1492. To those colonial societies, Europeans and Africans brought not only their germs and their people but also their plants and animals. Wheat, rice, sugarcane, grapes, and many garden vegetables and fruits, as well as numerous weeds, took hold in the Americas, where they trans-formed the landscape and made possible a recognizably European diet and way of life. Even more revolutionary were their animals—horses, pigs, cattle, goats, sheep—all of which were new to the Americas and multiplied spectacularly in an environment largely free of natural predators. These domesticated animals made possible the ranching economies, the cowboy cultures, and the transformation of many Native American societies that were seen in both North and South America. Environmentally speaking, it was nothing less than revolutionary.

In the other direction, American food crops such as corn, potatoes, and cassava spread widely in the Eastern Hemisphere, where they provided the nutritional foundation for the immense population growth that became everywhere a hallmark of the modern era. In Europe, calories derived from corn and potatoes helped push human numbers from some 60 million in 1400 to 390 million in 1900. Those Amerindian crops later provided cheap and reasonably nutritious food for millions of industrial workers. Potatoes especially allowed Ireland's population to grow enormously and then condemned many of them to starvation or emigration when an airborne fungus, also from the Americas, destroyed the crop in the mid-nineteenth century. In China, corn, peanuts, and especially sweet potatoes supplemented the traditional rice and wheat to sustain China's modern population explosion. By the early twentieth century, American food plants represented about 20 percent of total Chinese food production. In Africa, corn took hold quickly and was used as a cheap food for the human cargoes of the transatlantic trade. Scholars have speculated that corn, together with peanuts and cassava, underwrote some of Africa's population growth and partially offset the population drain of the slave trade. Never before in human history had such a large-scale and consequential exchange of plants and animals operated to remake the biological environment of the planet.

Furthermore, the societies that developed within the American colonies drove the processes of globalization and reshaped the world economy of the early modern era (see Chapter 15 for a more extended treatment). The silver mines of Mexico and Peru fueled both transatlantic and transpacific commerce,

Plants and Animals of the Columbian Exchange

This eighteenth-century Peruvian painting illustrates two of the many biological species that crossed the Atlantic. Cattle from Europe flourished in the Americas, while cassava (also known as manioc), shown in the bottom of the picture, was native to South America but spread widely in Asia, and especially Africa, where its edible root provided a major source of carbohydrates. (Martinez Campañon, Trujillo del Peru, v. II, courtesy of the Biblioteca del Palacio Real/Oronoz Archives)

encouraged Spain's unsuccessful effort to dominate Europe, and enabled Europeans to buy the Chinese tea, silk, and porcelain that they valued so highly. The plantation owners of the tropical lowland regions needed workers and found them by the millions in Africa. The slave trade, which brought these workers to the colonies, and the sugar and cotton trade, which distributed the fruits of their labor abroad, created a lasting link among Africa, Europe, and the Americas, while scattering peoples of African origin throughout the Western Hemisphere.

This enormous network of communication, migration, trade, the spread of disease, and the transfer of plants and animals, all generated by European colonial empires in the Americas, has been dubbed "the Columbian exchange." It gave rise to something wholly new in world history: an interacting Atlantic world connecting four continents. Millions of years ago, the Eastern and Western hemispheres had physically drifted apart, and, ecologically speaking, they had remained largely apart. Now these two "old worlds" were joined, increasingly creating a single biological regime, a "new world" of global dimensions.

The long-term benefits of this Atlantic network were very unequally distributed. Western Europeans were clearly the dominant players in the Atlantic world, and their societies reaped the greatest rewards. Mountains of new information flooded into Europe, shaking up conventional understandings of the world and contributing to a revolutionary new way of thinking known as the Scientific Revolution. The wealth of the colonies—precious metals, natural resources, new food crops, slave labor, financial profits, colonial markets—provided one of the foundations on which Europe's Industrial Revolution was built. The colonies also provided an outlet for the rapidly growing population of European societies and represented an enormous extension of European civilization. In short, the colonial empires of the Americas greatly facilitated a changing global balance of power, which now thrust the previously marginal Western Europeans into an increasingly central and commanding role on the world stage. "[W]ithout a New World to deliver economic balance in the Old," concluded a prominent world historian, "Europe would have remained inferior, as ever, in wealth and power, to the great civilizations of Asia."[9]

Comparing Colonial Societies in the Americas

What the Europeans had discovered across the Atlantic was a second "old world," but their actions surely gave rise to a "new world" in the Americas. Their colonial empires did not simply conquer and govern established societies but rather generated wholly new societies. In at least one respect, these various colonial empires—Spanish, Portuguese, British, and French—had something in common. Each of them was viewed through the lens of the prevailing economic theory known as mercantilism. This view held that European governments served their countries' economic interests best by encouraging exports and accumulating bullion (precious metals such as silver and gold), which were believed to be the source of national prosperity. Colonies, in this scheme of things, provided closed markets for the manufactured goods of the "mother country" and, if they were lucky, supplied great quantities of bullion as well.

Beyond this shared mercantilism, though, the various colonial societies that grew up in the Americas differed sharply from one another, varying with the cultures and policies of the colonizing power. The character of the Native American cultures—the more densely populated and urbanized Mesoamerican and Andean civilizations versus the more sparsely populated rural villages of North America, for example—also shaped the new colonial societies. The kind of economy established in particular regions—settler-dominated agriculture, slave-based plantations, ranching, or mining—likewise influenced their development. Three examples indicate the differences among these new colonial societies.

In the Lands of the Aztecs and the Incas

■ Change

What was the economic foundation of colonial rule in Mexico and Peru? How did it shape the kinds of societies that arose there?

The Spanish conquest of the Aztec and Inca empires in the early sixteenth century gave Spain access to the most wealthy, urbanized, and densely populated regions of the Western Hemisphere. Within a century and well before the British had even begun their colonizing efforts in North America, the Spanish in Mexico and Peru had established nearly a dozen major cities; several impressive universities; hundreds of cathedrals, churches, and missions; an elaborate administrative bureaucracy; and a network of regulated international commerce. The economic foundation for this emerging colonial society lay in commercial agriculture, much of it on large rural estates, and in silver and gold mining. In both cases, native peoples, rather than African slaves or European workers, provided the labor, despite their much-diminished numbers. Almost everywhere it was forced labor, often directly required by colonial authorities. The loss of land to European settlers represented another incentive for wage labor, as did the growing need to repay debts to employers.

On this economic base, a distinctive social order grew up, replicating something of the Spanish class hierarchy while accommodating the racially and culturally different Indians and Africans as well as growing numbers of racially mixed people. At the top of this colonial society were the Spanish settlers, who were politically and economically dominant and seeking to become a landed aristocracy. One Spanish official commented in 1619: "The Spaniards, from the able and rich to the humble and poor, all hold themselves to be lords and will not serve [do manual labor]."[10] Politically, they increasingly saw themselves, not as colonials, but as residents of a Spanish kingdom, subject to the Spanish monarch, yet separate and distinct from Spain itself and deserving of a large measure of self-government. Therefore, they chafed under the heavy bureaucratic restrictions imposed by the Crown. "I obey but I do not enforce" was a slogan that reflected local authorities' resistance to orders from Spain.

But the Spanish minority, never more than 20 percent of the population, was itself a divided community. Descendants of the original *conquistadores* sought to protect their privileges against immigrant newcomers; Spaniards born in the Americas (creoles) resented the pretensions to superiority of those born in Spain (*peninsulares*); landowning Spaniards felt threatened by the growing wealth of commercial and mercantile groups practicing less prestigious occupations. Spanish missionaries and church authorities were often sharply critical of how these settlers treated native peoples. "By what right . . . do you keep these Indians in such a cruel and horrible servitude?" demanded a Dominican priest in 1511 to a Spanish audience in Santo Domingo that included the son of Columbus himself. "Why do you keep those who survive so oppressed and weary, not giving them enough to eat, not caring for them in their illness?"[11]

The most distinctive feature of these new colonial societies in Mexico and Peru was the emergence of a *mestizo*, or mixed-race, population, the product of unions between Spanish men and Indian women. Rooted in the sexual imbalance among Spanish immigrants (seven men to one woman in early colonial Peru, for example), the emergence of a mestizo population was facilitated by the desire of many surviving Indian women for the relative security of life in a Spanish household, where their children would not be subject to the abuse and harsh demands made on native peoples. The Spanish Crown encouraged settlers to marry into elite Indian families, and Cortés, the conqueror of Mexico, fathered children with two of Moctezuma's daughters. Over the 300 years of the colonial era, mestizo numbers grew substantially, becoming the majority of the population in Mexico sometime during the nineteenth century.

Mestizos were largely Hispanic in culture, but Spaniards looked down on them during much of the colonial era, regarding them as illegitimate, for many were not born of "proper" marriages. Despite this attitude, their growing numbers and their economic usefulness as artisans, clerks, supervisors of labor gangs, and lower-level officials in both church and state bureaucracies led to their recognition as a distinct social group. Particularly in Mexico, mestizo

Mestizos
This eighteenth-century painting by the famous Zapotec artist Miguel Cabrera shows a Spanish man, a Native American woman, and their child, who was termed a *mestizo* in Mexico. By the twentieth century, such mixed-race mestizos represented the majority of the population of Mexico, and cultural blending had become a central feature of the country's identity. (Scala/Art Resource, NY)

identity blurred the sense of sharp racial difference between Spanish and Indian peoples and became a major element in the identity of modern Mexico.

At the bottom of Mexican and Peruvian colonial societies were the indigenous peoples, known to Europeans as "Indians." Traumatized by "the great dying," they were subject to gross abuse and exploitation as the primary labor force for the mines and estates of the Spanish Empire and were required to render tribute payments to their Spanish overlords. Their empires dismantled by Spanish conquest, their religions attacked by Spanish missionaries, and their diminished numbers forcibly relocated into larger settlements, many Indians gravitated toward the world of their conquerors. Many learned Spanish; converted to Christianity; moved to cities to work for wages; ate the meat of cows, chickens, and pigs; used plows and draft animals rather than traditional digging sticks; and took their many grievances to Spanish courts.

But much that was native persisted. At the local level, Indian authorities retained a measure of autonomy, and traditional markets operated regularly. Maize, beans, and squash continued as the major elements of Indian diets in Mexico. Christian saints in many places blended easily with specialized indigenous gods, while belief in magic, folk medicine, and communion with the dead remained strong. Memories of the past also persisted, and the Tupac Amaru revolt in Peru during 1780–1781 was made in the name of the last independent Inca emperor.

Thus Spaniards, mestizos, and Indians represented the major social groups in the colonial lands of what had been the Inca and Aztec empires, while African slaves and freemen were far less numerous than elsewhere in the Americas. Despite the sharp divisions among these groups, some movement was possible. Indians who acquired an education, wealth, and some European culture might "pass" as mestizo. Likewise more fortunate mestizo families might be accepted as Spaniards over time. Colonial Spanish America was a vast laboratory of ethnic mixing and cultural change. It was dominated by Europeans to be sure, but with a rather more fluid and culturally blended society than in the racially rigid colonies of North America.

Colonies of Sugar

■ **Comparison**
How did the plantation societies of Brazil and the Caribbean differ from those of southern colonies in British North America?

A second and quite different kind of colonial society emerged in the lowland areas of Brazil, ruled by Portugal, and in the Spanish, British, French, and Dutch colonies in the Caribbean. These regions lacked the great civilizations of Mexico and Peru. Nor did they provide much mineral wealth until the Brazilian gold rush of the 1690s and the discovery of diamonds a little later. Still, Europeans found a very profitable substitute in sugar, which was much in demand in Europe, where it was used as a medicine, a spice, a sweetener, a preservative, and in sculptured forms as a decoration that indicated high status. Although commercial agriculture in the Spanish Empire served a domestic market in its towns and mining camps, these sugar-based colonies produced almost exclusively for export, while importing their food and other necessities.

Large-scale sugar production had been pioneered by Arabs, who introduced it into the Mediterranean. Europeans learned the technique and transferred it to their Atlantic island possessions and then to the Americas. For a century (1570–1670), Portuguese planters along the northeast coast of Brazil dominated the world market for sugar. Then the British, French, and Dutch turned their Caribbean territories into highly productive sugar-producing colonies, breaking the Portuguese and Brazilian monopoly.

Sugar decisively transformed Brazil and the Caribbean. Its production, which involved both growing the sugarcane and processing it into usable sugar, was very labor intensive and could most profitably occur in a large-scale, almost industrial setting. It was perhaps the first modern industry in that it produced for an international and mass market, using capital and expertise from Europe, with production facilities located in the Americas. However, its most characteristic feature—the massive use of slave labor—was an ancient practice. In the absence of a Native American population, which had been almost totally wiped out in the Caribbean or had fled inland in Brazil, European sugarcane planters turned to Africa and the Atlantic slave trade for an alternative workforce. The vast majority of the African captives transported across the Atlantic, some 80 percent or more, ended up in Brazil and the Caribbean.

Plantation Life in the Caribbean
This painting from 1823 shows the use of slave labor on a plantation in Antigua, a British-ruled island in the Caribbean. Notice the overseer with a whip supervising the tilling and planting of the field. (British Library/ HIP/Art Resource, NY)

Snapshot   **Ethnic Composition in Colonial Societies in Latin America (1825)**[12]

	Highland Spanish America	Portuguese America (Brazil)
Europeans	18.2 percent	23.4 percent
Mixed-race	28.3 percent	17.8 percent
Africans	11.9 percent	49.8 percent
Native Americans	41.7 percent	9.1 percent

Slaves worked on sugar-producing estates in horrendous conditions. The heat and fire from the cauldrons, which turned raw sugarcane into crystallized sugar, reminded many visitors of scenes from hell. These conditions, combined with disease, generated a high death rate, perhaps 5 to 10 percent per year, which required plantation owners to constantly import fresh slaves. A Jesuit observer in 1580 aptly summarized the situation: "The work is great and many die."[13]

The extensive use of African slave labor gave these plantation colonies a very different ethnic and racial makeup than that of highland Spanish America, as the Snapshot indicates. Thus, after three centuries of colonial rule, a substantial majority of Brazil's population was either partially or wholly of African descent. In the French Caribbean colony of Haiti in 1790, the corresponding figure was 93 percent.

As in Spanish America, a considerable amount of racial mixing took place in Brazil. Cross-racial unions accounted for only about 10 percent of all marriages in Brazil, but the use of concubines and informal liaisons among Indians, Africans, and Portuguese produced a substantial mixed-race population. From their ranks derived much of the urban skilled workforce and supervisors in the sugar industry. *Mulattoes*, the product of Portuguese-African unions, predominated, but as many as forty separate and named groups, each indicating a different racial mixture, emerged in colonial Brazil.

The plantation complex of the Americas, based on African slavery, extended beyond the Caribbean and Brazil to encompass the southern colonies of British North America, where tobacco, cotton, rice, and indigo were major crops, but the social outcomes of these plantation colonies were quite different than those farther south. Because European women had joined the colonial migration to North America at an early date, these colonies experienced less racial mixing and certainly demonstrated less willingness to recognize the offspring of such unions and accord them a place in society. A sharply defined racial system (with black Africans, red Native Americans, and white Europeans) evolved in North America, whereas both Portuguese and Spanish colonies acknowledged a wide variety of mixed-race groups.

Slavery too was different, being perhaps less harsh in North America than in the sugar colonies. By 1750 or so, slaves in the United States had become self-reproducing, and a century later almost all North American slaves had been born in the New World. That was never the case in Latin America, where importation of new slaves continued well into the nineteenth century. Brazilian slave owners in fact calculated the useful life of their slaves at just seven years. Nonetheless, many more slaves were voluntarily set free by their owners in Brazil than was ever the case in North America, and free blacks and mulattoes in Brazil had far greater opportunities than did their counterparts in North America. At least a few among them found positions as political leaders, scholars, musicians, writers, and artists. Some were even hired as slave catchers.

Does this mean then that racism was absent in colonial Brazil? Certainly not, but it was different than in North America. For one thing, in North America, any African ancestry, no matter how small or distant, made a person "black"; in Brazil, a person of African and non-African ancestry was considered, not black, but some other mixed-race category. Racial prejudice clearly existed in the sense that white characteristics and features were prized more highly than those of blacks, and people regarded as white had enormously greater privileges and opportunities than others. Nevertheless, color in Brazil, and in Latin America generally, was only one criterion of class status, and the perception of color changed with the educational or economic standing of individuals. A light-skinned mulatto who had acquired some wealth or education might well "pass" as a white. One curious visitor to Brazil expressed surprise upon finding a darker-skinned man serving as a local official. "Isn't the governor a mulatto?" inquired the visitor. "He was, but he isn't any more," was the reply. "How can a governor be a mulatto?"[14]

Settler Colonies in North America

A third and distinctive type of colonial society emerged in the northern British colonies of New England, New York, and Pennsylvania. Because the British were the last of the European powers to establish a colonial presence in the Americas, a full century after Spain, they found that "only the dregs were left."[15] The lands they acquired were widely regarded in Europe as the unpromising leftovers of the New World, lacking the obvious wealth and sophisticated cultures of the Spanish possessions. Until at least the eighteenth century, these British colonies remained far less prominent on the world stage than those of Spain or Portugal.

The British settlers came from a more rapidly changing society than did those from an ardently Catholic, semifeudal, authoritarian Spain. When Britain launched its colonial ventures in the seventeenth century, it had already experienced considerable conflict between Catholics and Protestants, the rise of a merchant capitalist class, the growth of a major cloth industry, the emergence of parliament as a check on the authority of kings, and the breakdown of feudalism in general.

■ Comparison
What distinguished the British settler colonies of North America from their counterparts in Latin America?

Although they brought much of their English culture with them, many of the British settlers—Puritans in Massachusetts and Quakers in Pennsylvania, for example—sought to escape aspects of an old European society rather than to re-create it, as was the case for most Spanish and Portuguese colonists. The easy availability of land, the climate and geography of North America, and the "outsider" status of many British settlers made it even more difficult to follow the Spanish or Portuguese colonial pattern of sharp class hierarchy, large rural estates, and dependent laborers.

The British settlers also were far more numerous. By 1750, they outnumbered Spanish settlers by five to one. This disparity was the most obvious distinguishing feature of the New England and middle Atlantic colonies. By the time of the American Revolution, some 90 percent or more of these colonies' populations were Europeans. Devastating diseases and a highly aggressive military policy had largely cleared the colonies of Native Americans, and their numbers did not rebound in subsequent centuries as they did in the lands of the Aztecs and the Incas. Moreover, slaves were not needed in an agricultural economy dominated by numerous small-scale independent farmers working their own land, although elite families, especially in urban areas, sometimes employed household slaves. These were almost pure settler colonies, without the racial mixing that was so prominent in Spanish and Portuguese territories.

Other differences likewise emerged. A largely Protestant England was far less interested in spreading Christianity among the remaining native peoples than were the large and well-funded missionary societies of Catholic Spain. Although religion loomed large in the North American colonies, the church and colonial state were not so intimately connected as they were in Latin America. The Protestant emphasis on reading the Bible for oneself led to a much greater mass literacy than in Latin America, where three centuries of church education still left some 95 percent of the population illiterate at independence. Furthermore, far more so than in Latin America, British settler colonies evolved traditions of local self-government. Preferring to rely on joint stock companies or wealthy individuals operating under a royal charter, Britain had nothing resembling the elaborate bureaucracy that governed Spanish colonies. For much of the seventeenth century, a prolonged power struggle between the English king and parliament meant that the British government paid little attention to the internal affairs of the colonies. Therefore, elected colonial assemblies, seeing themselves as little parliaments defending "the rights of Englishmen," vigorously contested the prerogatives of royal governors sent to administer their affairs.

The grand irony of the modern history of the Americas lay in the reversal of long-established relationships between the northern and southern continents. For thousands of years, the major centers of wealth, power, commerce, and innovation lay in Mesoamerica and the Andes. That pattern continued for much of the colonial era, as the Spanish and Portuguese colonies seemed far more prosperous and successful than their British or French counterparts. In the nineteenth and twentieth centuries, however, the balance shifted. What had once been the "dregs" of the colonial world became the United States, which was more politically stable, more democratic, more economically successful, and more internationally powerful than a divided, unstable, and economically less developed Latin America.

The Steppes and Siberia: The Making of a Russian Empire

At the same time as Western Europeans were building their empires in the Americas, the Russian Empire, which subsequently became the world's largest state, was beginning to take shape. When Columbus crossed the Atlantic, a small Russian state, centered on the city of Moscow, was emerging from two centuries of Mongol rule. That state soon conquered a number of neighboring Russian-speaking cities and incorporated them into its expanding territory. Located on the remote, cold, and heavily forested eastern fringe of Christendom, it was perhaps an unlikely candidate for constructing one of the great empires of the modern era. And yet, over the next three centuries, it did precisely that, extending Russian domination over the vast tundra, forests, and grasslands of northern Asia that lay to the south and east of Moscow. Furthermore, Russian expansion westward brought numerous Poles, Germans, Ukrainians, Belorussians, and Baltic peoples into the Russian Empire.

■ **Description**
What motivated Russian empire building?

Russian attention was drawn first to the grasslands south and east of the Russian heartland, which had long been inhabited by various nomadic pastoral peoples, who were organized in feuding tribes and clans and adjusting to the recent disappearance of the Mongol Empire. From the viewpoint of the emerging Russian state, the problem was security because these pastoral peoples, like the Mongols before them, frequently raided their agricultural Russian neighbors and sold many of them into slavery. To the east across the vast expanse of Siberia, Russian motives were quite different, for the scattered peoples of its endless forests and tundra posed no threat to Russia. Numbering only some 220,000 in the seventeenth century and speaking more than 100 languages, they were mostly hunting, gathering, and herding people, living in small-scale societies and largely without access to gunpowder weapons. What drew the Russians across Siberia was opportunity—found primarily in the "soft gold" of fur-bearing animals, whose pelts were in great demand on the world market.

Whatever motives drove it, the enormous Russian Empire, stretching to the Pacific, took shape in the three centuries between 1500 and 1800 (see Map 14.2). A growing line of wooden forts offered protection to frontier towns and trading centers as well as to mounting numbers of Russian farmers. Empire building was an extended process, involving the Russian state and its officials as well as a variety of private interests—merchants, hunters, peasant agricultural settlers, churchmen, exiles, criminals, and adventurers. For the Russian migrants to these new lands, the

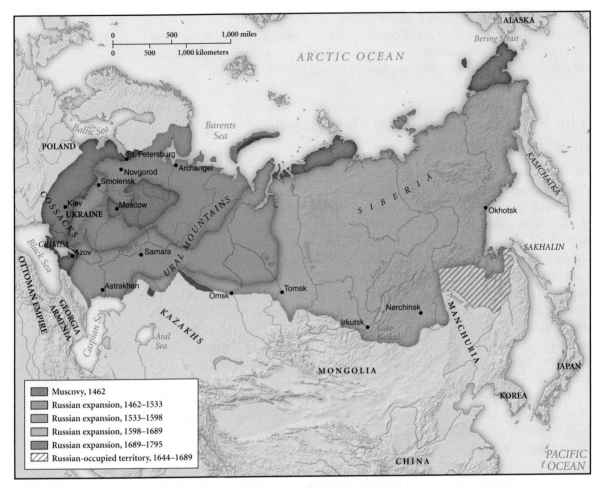

Legend:
- Muscovy, 1462
- Russian expansion, 1462–1533
- Russian expansion, 1533–1598
- Russian expansion, 1598–1689
- Russian expansion, 1689–1795
- Russian-occupied territory, 1644–1689

Map 14.2   The Russian Empire

From its beginnings as a small principality under Mongol control, Moscow became the center of a vast Russian Empire during the early modern era.

empire offered "economic and social improvements over what they had known at home—from more and better land to fewer lords and officials."[16] Political leaders and educated Russians generally defined the empire in grander terms: defending Russian frontiers; enhancing the power of the Russian state; and bringing Christianity, civilization, and enlightenment to savages. But what did that empire mean to those on its receiving end?

Experiencing the Russian Empire

■ Change

How did the Russian Empire transform the life of its conquered people and of the Russian homeland itself?

First, of course, creating an empire meant conquest, based on the precedent of Mongol domination. Although resistance was frequent, especially from nomadic peoples, in the long run Russian military might, based in modern weaponry and the organizational capacity of a powerful state, brought both the steppes and Siberia under Russian control. Everywhere Russian authorities demanded an oath of allegiance by which native peoples swore "eternal submission to the grand tsar," the monarch of the Russian Empire. They also demanded *yasak*, or tribute, paid in cash or in kind. In Siberia, this meant enormous quantities of furs, especially the extremely valuable sable, which Siberian peoples were compelled to produce. As in the Americas, devastating epidemics accompanied conquest, particularly in the more remote regions of Siberia, where local people had little immunity to small-pox or measles. Also accompanying conquest was an intermittent pressure to con-vert to Christianity. Tax breaks, exemptions from paying tribute, and the promise of land or cash provided incentives for conversion, while the destruction of many mosques and the forced resettlement of Muslims added to the pressures. Yet the Russian state did not pursue conversion with the single-minded intensity that Spanish authorities exercised in Latin America, particularly if missionary activity threatened political and social stability. The empress Catherine the Great, for exam-ple, established religious tolerance for Muslims in the late eighteenth century and created a state agency to oversee Muslim affairs.

The most profoundly transforming feature of the Russian Empire was the influx of Russian settlers, whose numbers by the end of the eighteenth century over-whelmed native peoples, thus giving their lands a distinctively Russian character. By 1720, some 700,000 Russians lived in Siberia, thus reducing the native Siberians to 30 percent of the total population, a figure that dropped to 14 percent in the nine-teenth century. The loss of hunting grounds and pasturelands to Russian agricultural settlers undermined long-standing economies and rendered local people dependent on Russian markets for grain, sugar, tea, tobacco, and alcohol. Pressures to encourage pastoralists to abandon their nomadic ways included the requirement to pay fees and to obtain permission to cross agricultural lands. Kazakh herders responded with outrage: "The grass and the water belong to Heaven, and why should we pay any fees?"[17] Intermarriage, prostitu-tion, and sexual abuse resulted in some mixed-race offspring, but these were generally absorbed as Russians rather than identified as distinctive communi-ties, as happened in Latin America.

Over the course of three centuries, both Siberia and the steppes were incorporated into the Russian state. Their native peoples were not driven into reservations or eradicated as in the

A Cossack Jail
In the vanguard of Russian expansion across Siberia were the Cossacks, bands of fiercely independent warriors consisting of peasants who had escaped serfdom as well as criminals and other adventurers. This seventeenth-century jail was part of an early Cossack settlement on the Kamchatka Peninsula at the easternmost end of Siberia. It illustrates Russian wooden architecture. (Sovfoto/Eastfoto)

Americas. Many of them, though, were Russified, adopting the Russian language and converting to Christianity, even as their traditional ways of life—hunting and herding—were much disrupted. The Russian Empire represented the final triumph of an agrarian civilization over the hunting societies of Siberia and over the pastoral peoples of the grasslands.

Russians and Empire

If the empire transformed the conquered peoples, it also fundamentally changed Russia itself. As it became a multiethnic empire, Russians diminished as a proportion of the overall population (see the Snapshot), although they remained politically dominant. Among the growing number of non-Russians in the empire, Slavic-speaking Ukrainians and Belorussians predominated, while the vast territories of Siberia and the steppes housed numerous separate peoples, but with quite small populations. The wealth of empire—rich agricultural lands, valuable furs, mineral deposits—played a major role in making Russia one of the great powers of Europe by the eighteenth century, and it has enjoyed that position ever since. This European and Christian state also became an Asian power, bumping up against China, India, Persia, and the Ottoman Empire. It was on the front lines of the encounter between Christendom and the world of Islam.

This straddling of Asia and Europe was the source of a long-standing identity problem that has troubled educated Russians for 300 years. Was Russia a backward European country, destined to follow the lead of more highly developed Western European societies? Or was it different, uniquely Slavic or even Asian, shaped by its Mongol legacy and its status as an Asian power? It is a question that Russians have not completely answered even in the twenty-first century. Either way, the very size of that empire, bordering on virtually all of the great agrarian civilizations of outer Eurasia, turned Russia, like many empires before it, into a highly militarized state, "a society organized for continuous war," according to one scholar.[18] It also reinforced the highly autocratic character of the Russian Empire because such a huge state required a powerful monarchy to hold its vast domains and highly diverse peoples together.

Clearly the Russians had created an empire, similar to those of Western Europe in terms of conquest, settlement, exploitation, religious conversion, and feelings of superiority. Like the others, the Russians recognized and distinguished among their conquered and incorporated peoples. "The All-Russian empire is unique in the world," declared an official document from 1785, "on account of its far-flung lands," which it then proceeded to enumerate one by one.[19]

Nonetheless, the Russians acquired their empire under different circumstances than did the Western Europeans. The Spanish and the British had conquered and colonized the New World, an ocean away and wholly unknown to them before 1492. They acquired those empires only after establishing themselves as distinct European states. The Russians, on the other hand, entered adjacent territories with which they had long interacted, and they did so *at the same time* that a modern

Snapshot **Demographics of the Russian Empire**[20]

Percentage of Russians in the Empire over Time

YEAR	TOTAL POPULATION (IN MILLIONS)	RUSSIANS (PERCENT OF TOTAL POPULATION)
1600	—	90
1719	15.8	71
1795	37	53
1897	125.6	44
1989 (Soviet Union)	285.7	51
2002 (Russian Federation)	145	80

Ethnic Composition of the Population in 1719 (percent)

Russians	71
Ukrainians	13
Volga/Urals peoples	6
Baltics/Scandinavians	4
Belorussians	2.4
Steppe peoples	2
Northern peoples	1
Siberians	1

Russian state was taking shape. "The British had an empire," wrote historian Geoffrey Hosking. "Russia *was* an empire."[21] Perhaps this helps explain the unique longevity of the Russian Empire. Whereas the Spanish, Portuguese, and British colonies in the Americas long ago achieved independence, the Russian Empire remained intact until the collapse of the Soviet Union in 1991. So thorough was Russian colonization that Siberia and much of the steppes remain still an integral part of the Russian state. But many internal administrative regions, which exercise a measure of autonomy, reflect the continuing presence of some 160 non-Russian peoples who were earlier incorporated into the Russian Empire.

Asian Empires

Even as Europeans were building their empires in the Americas and across Siberia, other imperial projects were likewise under way. The Chinese pushed deep into central Eurasia; Turko-Mongol invaders from Central Asia created the Mughal Empire, bringing much of Hindu South Asia within a single Muslim-ruled political system; and the Ottoman Empire brought Muslim rule to a largely Christian population in southeastern Europe and Turkish rule to largely Arab populations in North Africa and the Middle East. None of these empires had the global reach or worldwide impact of Europe's American colonies; they were regional rather than global in scope. Nor did they have the same devastating and transforming impact on their conquered peoples, for those peoples were not being exposed to new diseases. Nothing remotely approaching the catastrophic population collapse of Native American peoples occurred in these Asian empires. Moreover, the process of building these empires did not transform the imperial homeland as fundamentally as did the wealth of the Americas and to a lesser extent Siberia for European imperial powers. Nonetheless, these expanding Asian empires reflected the energies and vitality of their respective civilizations in the early modern era, and they gave rise to profoundly important cross-cultural encounters, with legacies that echoed for many centuries.

Making China an Empire

■ **Description**
What were the major features of Chinese empire building in the early modern era?

In the fifteenth century, China had declined an opportunity to construct a maritime empire in the Indian Ocean, as Zheng He's massive fleet was withdrawn and left to wither away (see Chapter 13). In the seventeenth and eighteenth centuries, however, China built another kind of empire on its northern and western frontiers that vastly enlarged the territorial size of the country and incorporated a number of non-Chinese peoples. Undertaking this enormous project of imperial expansion was China's Qing, or Manchu, dynasty (1644–1912). Strangely enough, the Qing dynasty was itself of foreign and nomadic origin, hailing from Manchuria, north of the Great Wall. Having conquered China, the Qing rulers sought to maintain their ethnic distinctiveness by forbidding intermarriage between themselves and Chinese. Nonetheless, their ruling elites also mastered the Chinese language and Confucian teachings and used Chinese bureaucratic techniques to govern the empire.

For many centuries, the Chinese had interacted with the nomadic peoples, who inhabited the dry and lightly populated regions now known as Mongolia, Xinjiang, and Tibet. Trade, tribute, and warfare ensured that these ecologically and culturally different worlds were well known to each other, quite unlike the New World "discoveries" of the Europeans. Chinese authority in the area had been intermittent and actively resisted. Then, in the early modern era, Qing dynasty China undertook an eighty-year military effort (1680–1760) that brought these huge regions solidly and permanently under Chinese control. It was largely security concerns that motivated this aggressive posture. During the late seventeenth century, the creation of a substantial state among the western Mongols, known as the Zunghars, revived Chinese memories of an earlier Mongol conquest. As in so many other

China's Qing Dynasty Empire

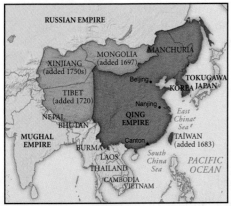

cases, Chinese expansion was viewed as a defensive necessity. The eastward movement of the Russian Empire likewise appeared potentially threatening, but this danger was resolved diplomatically, rather than militarily, in the Treaty of Nerchinsk (1689), which marked the boundary between Russia and China.

Although undertaken by the non-Chinese Manchus, the Qing dynasty campaigns against the Mongols marked the evolution of China into a Central Asian empire. The Chinese, however, have seldom thought of themselves as an imperialist power. Rather they spoke of the "unification" of the peoples of central Eurasia within a Chinese state. Nonetheless, historians have seen many similarities between Chinese expansion and other cases of early modern empire building, while noting some clear differences as well.[22]

Clearly the Qing dynasty takeover of central Eurasia was a conquest, making use of China's more powerful military technology and greater resources. Furthermore, the area was ruled separately from the rest of China through a new office called the Court of Colonial Affairs. Like other colonial powers, the Chinese made active use of local notables—Mongol aristocrats, Muslim officials, Buddhist leaders—as they attempted to govern the region as inexpensively as possible. Sometimes these native officials abused their authority, demanding extra taxes or labor service from local people and thus earning their hostility. In places, those officials imitated Chinese ways by wearing peacock feathers, decorating their hats with gold buttons, or adopting a Manchu hairstyle that was much resented by many Chinese who were forced to wear it.

More generally, however, Chinese or Qing officials did not seek to assimilate local people into Chinese culture and showed considerable respect for the Mongolian, Tibetan, and Muslim cultures of the region. People of noble rank, Buddhist monks, and those associated with monasteries were excused from the taxes and labor service required of ordinary people. Nor was the area flooded with Chinese settlers. In parts of Mongolia, for example, Qing authorities sharply restricted the entry of Chinese merchants and other immigrants in an effort to preserve the area as a source of recruitment for the Chinese military. They feared that the "soft" and civilized Chinese ways might erode the fighting spirit of the Mongols.

The long-term significance of this new Chinese imperial state was tremendous. It greatly expanded the territory of China and added a small but important minority of non-Chinese people to the empire's vast population. The borders of contemporary China are essentially those created during the Qing dynasty. Some of those peoples in the late twentieth century, particularly those in Tibet and Xinjiang, have retained their older identities and have actively sought greater autonomy or even independence from China.

Even more important, Chinese conquests, together with the expansion of the Russian Empire, utterly transformed Central Asia. For centuries, that region had been the cosmopolitan crossroads of Eurasia, hosting the Silk Road trading network, welcoming all of the major world religions, and generating an enduring encounter between the nomads of the steppes and the farmers of settled agricultural regions.

Now under Russian or Chinese rule, it became the backward and impoverished region known to nineteenth- and twentieth-century observers. Land-based commerce across Eurasia increasingly took a backseat to oceanic trade. Indebted Mongolian nobles lost their land to Chinese merchants, while nomads, no longer able to herd their animals freely, fled to urban areas, where many were reduced to begging. The incorporation of the heartland of Eurasian nomads into the Russian and Chinese empires "eliminated permanently as a major actor on the historical stage the nomadic pastoralists, who had been the strongest alternative to settled agricultural society since the second millennium B.C.E."[23] It was the end of a long era.

Muslims and Hindus in the Mughal Empire

■ Change

How did Mughal attitudes and policies toward Hindus change from the time of Akbar to that of Aurangzeb?

If the creation of a Chinese imperial state in the early modern era provoked a final clash of nomadic pastoralists and settled farmers, India's Mughal Empire hosted a different kind of encounter—a further phase in the long interaction of Islamic and Hindu cultures in South Asia. That empire was the product of Central Asian warriors, who were Muslims in religion and Turkic in culture and who claimed descent from Chinggis Khan and Timur (see Chapter 13). Their brutal conquests in the sixteenth century provided India with a rare period of relative political unity (1526–1707), as Mughal emperors exercised a fragile control over a diverse and fragmented subcontinent, which was divided into a bewildering variety of small states, principalities, tribes, castes, sects, and ethnolinguistic groups.

The central division within Mughal India was religious. The ruling dynasty and perhaps 20 percent of the population were Muslims; most of the rest practiced some form of Hinduism. Mughal India's most famous emperor, Akbar (ruled 1556–1605), clearly recognized this fundamental reality and acted deliberately to accommodate the Hindu majority. After conquering the warrior-based and Hindu Rajputs of northwestern India, Akbar married several of their princesses but did not require them to convert to Islam. He incorporated a substantial number of Hindus into the political-military elite of the empire and supported the building of Hindu temples as well as mosques, palaces, and forts.

The Mughal Empire

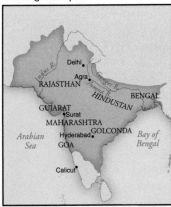

In directly religious matters, Akbar imposed a policy of toleration, deliberately restraining the more militantly Islamic ulama (religious scholars) and removing the special tax (jizya) on non-Muslims. His son Jehangir wrote proudly of his father: "He associated with the good of every race and creed and persuasion.... The professors of various faiths had room in the broad expanse of his incomparable sway."[24] Akbar went so far as to create his own state cult, a religious faith aimed at the Mughal elite. This cult drew on Islam, Hinduism, and Zoroastrianism and emphasized loyalty to the emperor himself. The overall style of the Mughal Empire was that of a blended elite culture in which both Hindus and various Muslim groups could feel comfortable. Thus Persian artists and writers were welcomed into the empire, and the Hindu epic *Ramayana* was translated into Persian, while various Persian classics appeared in Hindi and Sanskrit. In short, Akbar and his immediate successors downplayed a distinctly Islamic identity for the Mughal Empire in favor of a cosmopolitan and hybrid Indian-Persian-Turkic culture.

Such policies fostered sharp opposition among some Muslims. The philosopher Shayk Ahmad Sirhindi (1564–1624), claiming to be a "renewer" of authentic Islam in his time, strongly objected to this cultural synthesis. The worship of saints, the sacrifice of animals, and support for Hindu religious festivals all represented impure intrusions of Sufi Islam or Hinduism that needed to be rooted out. It was the duty of Muslim rulers to impose the sharia, to enforce the jizya on nonbelievers, and to remove non-Muslims from high office. This strain of Muslim thinking found a champion in the emperor Aurangzeb (1658–1707), who reversed Akbar's policy of accommodation and sought to impose Islamic supremacy. He forbade the Hindu practice of *sati*, in which a widow followed her husband to death by throwing herself on his funeral pyre. Music and dance were now banned at court, and previously tolerated vices such as gambling, drinking, prostitution, and narcotics were actively suppressed. Some Hindu temples were destroyed, and the jizya was reimposed. "Censors of public morals," posted to large cities, enforced Islamic law.

Aurangzeb's religious policies, combined with intolerable demands for taxes to support his many wars of expansion, antagonized Hindus and prompted various movements of opposition to the Mughals. "Your subjects are trampled underfoot," wrote one anonymous protester. "Every province of your empire is impoverished. . . . God is the God of all mankind, not the God of Mussalmans [Muslims] alone."[25] These opposition movements, some of them self-consciously Hindu, fatally fractured the Mughal Empire, especially after Aurangzeb's death in 1707, and opened the way for a British takeover in the second half of the eighteenth century.

Thus the Mughal Empire was the site of a highly significant encounter between two of the world's great religious traditions. It began with an experiment in multicultural empire building and ended in growing antagonism between Hindus and Muslims. In the centuries that followed, both elements of the Mughal experience would be repeated.

Muslims, Christians, and the Ottoman Empire

Like the Mughal state, the Ottoman Empire was also the creation of Turkic warrior groups, whose aggressive raiding of agricultural civilization was now legitimized in Islamic terms. Beginning around 1300 from a base area in northwestern Anatolia, these Ottoman Turks over the next three centuries swept over much of the Middle East, North Africa, and southeastern Europe to create the Islamic world's most significant empire (see Map 14.3). During those centuries, the Ottoman state was transformed from a small frontier principality to a prosperous, powerful, cosmopolitan empire, heir to both the Byzantine Empire and to leadership within the Islamic world. Its sultan combined the roles of a Turkic warrior

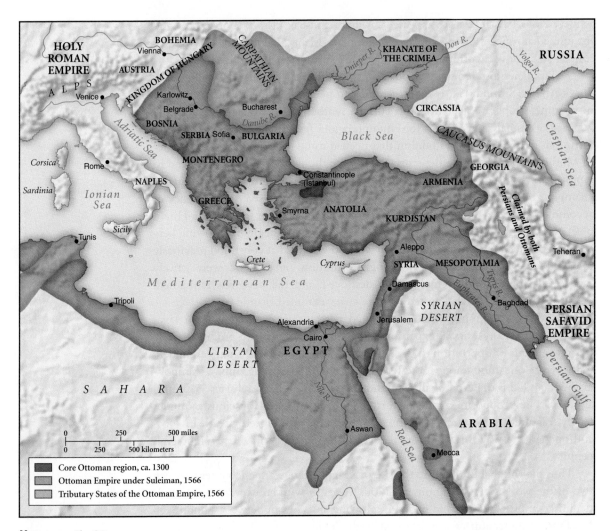

Map 14.3 The Ottoman Empire

At its high point in the mid-sixteenth century, the Ottoman Empire encompassed a vast diversity of peoples; straddled Europe, Africa, and Asia; and battled both the Austrian and Safavid empires.

prince, a Muslim caliph, and a conquering emperor, bearing the "strong sword of Islam" and serving as chief defender of the faith.

Within the Islamic world, the Ottoman Empire represented the growing prominence of Turkic people, for their empire now incorporated a large number of Arabs, among whom the religion had been born. Mecca, Medina, and Jerusalem—the holy cities of Islam—now lay in Turkic hands, while the responsibility and the prestige of protecting them belonged to the Ottoman Empire. A century-long conflict (1534–1639) between the Ottoman Empire, espousing the Sunni version of Islam, and the Persian Safavid Empire, holding fast to the Shia form of the faith, expressed a deep and enduring division within the Islamic world. Nonetheless, Persian culture, especially its poetry, painting, and traditions of imperial splendor, occupied a prominent position among the Ottoman elite.

The Ottoman Empire, like its Mughal counterpart, was the site of a highly significant cross-cultural encounter in the early modern era, adding yet another chapter to the long-running story of interaction between the Islamic world and Christendom. As the Ottoman Empire expanded across Anatolia, its largely Christian population converted in large numbers to Islam as the Byzantine state visibly weakened and large numbers of Turks settled in the region. By 1500, some 90 percent of Anatolia's inhabitants were Muslims and Turkic speakers. The climax of this Turkic assault on the Christian world of Byzantium occurred in 1453, when Constantinople fell to the invaders. Renamed Istanbul, that splendid Christian city became the capital of the Ottoman Empire. Byzantium, heir to the glory of Rome, was no more.

In the empire's southeastern European domains, known as the Balkans, the Ottoman encounter with Christian peoples unfolded quite differently than it had in Anatolia. In the Balkans, Muslims ruled over a large Christian population, but the scarcity of Turkish settlers and the willingness of the Ottoman authorities to accommodate the region's Christian churches led to far less conversion. By the early sixteenth century, only about 19 percent of the area's people were Muslims, and 81 percent were Christians.

Many of these Christians had welcomed Ottoman conquest because taxes were lighter and oppression less pronounced than under their former Christian rulers. Christian communities such as the Eastern Orthodox and Armenian churches were granted considerable autonomy in regulating their internal social, religious, educational, and charitable affairs. A substantial number of these Christians—Balkan landlords, Greek merchants, government officials, and high-ranking clergy—became part of the Ottoman elite, without converting to Islam. Jewish refugees, fleeing Christian persecution in a Spain recently "liberated" from Islamic rule, likewise found greater opportunity in the Ottoman Empire, where they became prominent in trade and banking circles. In these ways, Ottoman dealings with the Christian and Jewish populations of their empire broadly resembled Akbar's policies toward the Hindu majority of Mughal India.

In another way, however, Turkish rule bore heavily on Christians. Through a process known as the *devshirme* (the collecting or gathering), Balkan Christian communities were required to hand over a quota of young boys, who were then removed from their families, required to learn Turkish, usually converted to Islam, and trained for either civil administration or military service in elite Janissary units. Although it was a terrible blow for families who lost their children, the *devshirme* also represented a means of upward mobility within the Ottoman Empire. Nonetheless, this social gain occurred at a high price.

Even though Ottoman authorities were relatively tolerant toward Christians within their borders, the empire itself represented an enormous threat to Christendom generally. The seizure of Constantinople, the conquest of the Balkans, Ottoman naval power in the Mediterranean, and the siege of Vienna in 1529 and again in 1683 raised anew "the specter of a Muslim takeover of all of Europe."[26]

■ **Significance**
In what ways was the Ottoman Empire important for Europe in the early modern era?

One European ambassador reported fearfully in 1555 from the court of the Turkish ruler Suleiman:

> He tramples the soil of Hungary with 200,000 horses, he is at the very gates of Austria, threatens the rest of Germany, and brings in his train all the nations that extend from our borders to those of Persia.[27]

The Ottoman Siege of Vienna, 1683
In this late-seventeenth-century painting by artist Frans Geffels, the last Ottoman incursion into the Austrian Empire was pushed back with French and Polish help, marking the end of a serious Muslim threat to Christian Europe. (Historisches Museum der Stadt Wien/Gianni Dagli Orti/The Art Archive)

Indeed, the "terror of the Turk" inspired fear across much of Europe and placed Christendom on the defensive, even as Europeans were expanding aggressively across the Atlantic and into the Indian Ocean.

The Ottoman encounter with Christian Europe spawned admiration and cooperation as well as fear and trembling. The sixteenth-century French philosopher Jean Bodin praised the religious tolerance of the Ottoman sultan in contrast to Christian intolerance: "The King of the Turks who rules over a great part of Europe safeguards the rites of religion as well as any prince in this world. Yet he constrains no-one, but on the contrary permits everyone to live as his conscience

dictates."[28] The French government on occasion found it useful to ally with the Ottoman Empire against their common enemy of Habsburg Austria, while European merchants willingly violated a papal ban on selling firearms to the Turks. In the early eighteenth century, the wife of an English diplomat posted to Istanbul praised the morality of Ottoman women as well as their relative freedom: "It is easy to see they have more liberty than we do."[29] Cultural encounter involved more than conflict.

Reflections: Countering Eurocentrism... or Reflecting It?

With an emphasis on empires and cross-cultural encounter, this chapter deliberately places the more familiar narrative of European colonization in the Americas along-side the less well-known stories of Russian, Chinese, Mughal, and Ottoman empire building. The chief purpose in doing so is to counteract a Eurocentric understanding of the early modern age, in which European initiatives dominate our view of this era. It reminds us that Western Europe was not the only center of vitality and expansion and that the interaction of culturally different peoples, so characteristic of the modern age, derived from multiple sources. How often do we notice that a European Christendom creating empires across the Atlantic was also the victim of Ottoman empire building in the Balkans?

A critic of this chapter, however, might well argue that it is nonetheless a Eurocentric narrative, for it allots rather more space to the Western European empires than to the others, and it tells the European story first. What led to such an ordering of this material?

Underlying the organization of this chapter is the notion that Western European empires in the Americas were in some ways both different from and more significant than the others. They represented something wholly new in human history, an interacting Atlantic world, while the Russian, Chinese, Mughal, and Ottoman empires continued older patterns of historical development. Furthermore, the European empires had a far heavier impact on the peoples they incorporated than did the others. After all, the great tragedies of the early modern era—the population collapse of Native American societies and the Atlantic slave trade—both grew out of these European empires. Moreover, they had, arguably, a far wider impact on the world as a whole, as they extended European civilization to the vast areas of the Americas, laid the nutritional foundation for the global population explosion of modern times, and contributed to both the Scientific Revolution and the Industrial Revolution.

Counteracting Eurocentrism, while acknowledging the unique role of Europe, continues to generate controversy among both scholars and students of modern world history. It is an issue that will recur repeatedly in the chapters that follow.

Second Thoughts

What's the Significance?

"the great dying"   settler colonies   Aurangzeb
Columbian exchange   Siberia   Ottoman Empire
peninsulares   *yasak*   Constantinople, 1453
mestizo   Qing dynasty empire   *devshirme*
mulattoes   Mughal Empire
plantation complex   Akbar

Big Picture Questions

1. In comparing the European empires in the Americas with the Russian, Chinese, Mughal, and Ottoman empires, should world historians emphasize the similarities or the differences? What are the implications of each approach?
2. In what different ways was European colonial rule expressed and experienced in the Americas?
3. Why did the European empires in the Americas have such an enormously greater impact on the conquered people than did the Chinese, Mughal, and Ottoman empires?
4. In what ways did the empires of the early modern era continue patterns of earlier empires? In what ways did they depart from those patterns?

Next Steps: For Further Study

Jorge Canizares-Esguerra and Erik R. Seeman (eds), *The Atlantic in Global History* (2007). A collection of essays that treats the Atlantic basin as a single interacting region.

Alfred W. Crosby, *The Columbian Voyages, the Columbian Exchange, and Their Historians* (1987). A brief and classic account of changing understandings of Columbus and his global impact.

John Kicza, *Resilient Cultures: America's Native Peoples Confront European Colonization, 1500–1800* (2003). An account of European colonization in the Americas that casts the native peoples as active agents rather than passive victims.

Peter Perdue, *China Marches West: The Qing Conquest of Central Eurasia* (2005). Describes the process of China becoming an empire as it incorporated the non-Chinese people of Central Asia.

John F. Richards, *The Mughal Empire* (1996). A well-regarded summary by a major scholar in the field.

David R. Ringrose, *Expansion and Global Interaction, 1200–1700* (2001). A world history perspective on empire building that bridges the postclassical and early modern eras.

Willard Sutherland, *Taming the Wild Fields: Colonization and Empire on the Russian Steppe* (2004). An up-to-date account of Russian expansion in the steppes.

"1492: An Ongoing Voyage," http://www.ibiblio.org/expo/1492.exhibit/Intro.html. An interactive Web site based on an exhibit from the Library of Congress that provides a rich context for exploring the meaning of Columbus and his voyages.

Global Commerce

1450-1750

Europeans and Asian
  Commerce
  A Portuguese Empire of
    Commerce
  Spain and the Philippines
  The East India Companies
  Asian Commerce
Silver and Global Commerce
The "World Hunt": Fur in
  Global Commerce
Commerce in People: The
  Atlantic Slave Trade
  The Slave Trade in Context
  The Slave Trade in Practice
  Comparing Consequences:
    The Impact of the Slave
    Trade in Africa
Reflections: Economic
  Globalization—Then and
  Now

"I have come full circle back to my destiny: from Africa to America and back to Africa. I could hear the cries and wails of my ancestors. I weep with them and for them."[1] This is what an African American woman from Atlanta wrote in 2002 in the guest book of the Cape Coast Castle, one of the many ports of embarkation for slaves located along the coast of Ghana in West Africa. There she no doubt saw the whips and leg irons used to discipline the captured Africans as well as the windowless dungeons in which hundreds of them were crammed while waiting for the ships that would carry them across the Atlantic to the Americas. Almost certainly she also caught sight of the infamous "gate of no return," through which the captives departed to their new life as slaves.

THIS VISITOR'S EMOTIONAL ENCOUNTER WITH THE LEGACY OF THE ATLANTIC SLAVE TRADE reminds us of the enormous significance of this commerce in human beings for the early modern world and of its continuing echoes even at the beginning of the twenty-first century. The slave trade, however, was only one component of those international trading networks that shaped human interactions during the centuries between 1450 and 1750. Europeans now smashed their way into the ancient spice trade of the Indian Ocean, developing new relationships with Asian societies as a result. Silver, obtained from mines in Spanish America, enriched Western Europe, even as much of it made its way to China, where it allowed Europeans to participate more fully in the rich commerce of East Asia. Furs from North America and Siberia found a

The Atlantic Slave Trade: Among the threads of global commerce during the early modern era, none has resonated more loudly in historical memory than the Atlantic slave trade. This eighteenth-century French painting shows the sale of slaves at Goree, a major slave trading port in what is now Dakar in Senegal. A European merchant and an African authority figure negotiate the arrangement, while the shackled victims themselves wait for their fate to be decided. (Bibliothèque des Arts Décoratifs, Paris/Archives Charmet/The Bridgeman Art Library)

ready market in Europe and China, while the hunting and trapping of those fur-bearing animals transformed both natural environments and human societies. Despite their growing prominence in long-distance exchange, Europeans were far from the only active traders. Southeast Asians, Chinese, Indians, Armenians, Arabs, and Africans like-wise played major roles in the making of the world economy of the early modern era.

Thus commerce joined empire as the twin drivers of globalization during these centuries. Together they created new relationships, disrupted old patterns, brought distant peoples into contact with one another, enriched some, and impoverished or enslaved others. From the various "old worlds" of the premodern era, a single "new world" emerged—slowly, with great pain, and accompanied by growing inequali-ties. What was gained and what was lost in the transformations born of global com-merce have been the subject of great controversy ever since.

Europeans and Asian Commerce

Schoolchildren everywhere know that European empires in the Western Hemisphere grew out of an accident—Columbus's unknowing encounter with the Americas—and that new colonial societies and new commercial connections across the Atlantic were the result. In Asia, it was a very different story. The voyage (1497–1499) of the Portuguese mariner Vasco da Gama, in which Europeans sailed to India for the first time, was certainly no accident. It was the outcome of a deliberate, systematic, century-long Portuguese effort to explore a sea route to the East, by creeping slowly down the West African coast, around the tip of South Africa, up the East African coast, and finally to Calicut in southern India in 1498. There Europeans encountered an ancient and rich network of commerce that stretched from East Africa to China. They were certainly aware of the wealth of that commercial network, but largely ignorant of its workings.

■ Causation
What drove European involvement in the world of Asian commerce?

The most immediate motivation for this massive effort was the desire for trop-ical spices—cinnamon, nutmeg, mace, cloves, and, above all, pepper—which were widely used as condiments and preservatives and were sometimes regarded as aphrodisiacs. Other products of the East, such as Chinese silk, Indian cottons, rhubarb for medicinal purposes, emeralds, rubies, and sapphires, also were in great demand.

Underlying this growing interest in Asia was the more general recovery of European civilization following the disaster of the Black Death in the early four-teenth century. During the fifteenth century, Europe's population was growing again, and its national monarchies—in Spain, Portugal, England, and France—were learning how to tax their subjects more effectively and to build substantial military forces equipped with gunpowder weapons. Its cities were growing too. Some of them—in England, the Netherlands, and northern Italy, for example—were becoming centers of international commerce, giving birth to a more capitalist economy based on market exchange, private ownership, and the accumulation of capital for further investment.

For many centuries, Eastern goods had trickled into the Mediterranean through the Middle East from the network of Indian Ocean trade. From the viewpoint of an increasingly dynamic Europe, several major problems accompanied this pattern of commerce. First, of course, the source of supply for these much-desired goods lay solidly in Muslim hands. Most immediately, Muslim Egypt was the primary point of transfer into the Mediterranean basin and its European customers. The Italian commercial city of Venice largely monopolized the European trade in Eastern goods, annually sending convoys of ships to Alexandria in Egypt. Venetians resented the Muslim monopoly on Indian Ocean trade, and other European powers disliked relying on Venice as well as on Muslims. Circumventing these monopolies was yet another impetus—both religious and political—for the Portuguese to attempt a sea route to India that bypassed both Venetian and Muslim middlemen. In addition, many Europeans of the time were persuaded that a mysterious Christian monarch, known as Prester John, ruled somewhere in Asia or Africa. Joining with his mythical kingdom to continue the Crusades and combat a common Islamic enemy was likewise a goal of the Portuguese voyages.

A final problem lay in paying for Eastern goods. Few products of an economically less developed Europe were attractive in Eastern markets. Thus Europeans were required to pay cash—gold or silver—for Asian spices or textiles. This persistent trade deficit contributed much to the intense desire for precious metals that attracted early modern European explorers, traders, and conquerors. Portuguese voyages along the West African coast, for example, were seeking direct access to African goldfields. The enormously rich silver deposits of Mexico and Bolivia provided at least a temporary solution to this persistent European problem.

First the Portuguese and then the Spanish, French, Dutch, and British found their way into the ancient Asian world of Indian Ocean commerce (see Map 15.1). How they behaved in that world and what they created there differed considerably among the various European countries, but collectively they contributed much to the new regime of globalized trade.

A Portuguese Empire of Commerce

The arena of Indian Ocean commerce into which Vasco da Gama and his Portuguese successors sailed was a world away from anything they had known. It was a vast world, both in geographic extent and in the diversity of those who participated in it. East Africans, Arabs, Persians, Indians, Malays, Chinese, and others traded freely. Most of them were Muslims, though hailing from many separate communities, but Hindus, Christians, Jews, and Chinese likewise had a role in this commercial network. Had the Portuguese sought simply to participate in peaceful trading, they certainly could have done so, but it was quickly apparent that European trade goods were crude and unattractive in Asian markets and that Europeans would be unable to compete effectively. Moreover, the Portuguese soon learned that most Indian Ocean merchant ships were not heavily armed and certainly lacked the

■ **Connection**
To what extent did the Portuguese realize their own goals in the Indian Ocean?

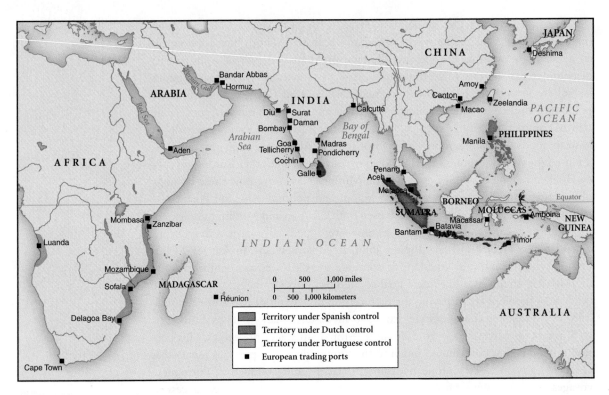

Map 15.1 Europeans in Asia in the Early Modern Era The early modern era witnessed only very limited territorial control by Europeans in Asia. Trade, rather than empire, was the chief concern of the Western newcomers, who were not, in any event, a serious military threat to major Asian states.

onboard cannons that Portuguese ships carried. Since the withdrawal of the Chinese fleet from the Indian Ocean early in the fifteenth century, no major power was in a position to dominate the sea-lanes, and the many smaller-scale merchants generally traded openly, although piracy was sometimes a problem.

Given these conditions, the Portuguese saw an opening, for their ships could outgun and outmaneuver competing naval forces, while their onboard cannons could devastate coastal fortifications. Although their overall economy lagged behind that of Asian producers, Europeans had more than caught up in the critical area of naval technology and naval warfare. This military advantage enabled the Portuguese to quickly establish fortified bases at several key locations within the Indian Ocean world—Mombasa in East Africa, Hormuz at the entrance to the Persian Gulf, Goa on the west coast of India, Malacca in Southeast Asia, and Macao on the south coast of China. With the exception of Macao, which had been obtained through bribery and negotiations with Chinese authorities, these Portuguese bases were obtained forcibly against small and weak states. In Mombasa, for example, the commander of a Portuguese fleet responded to local resistance in 1505 by burning and sacking the city, killing some 1,500 people, and seizing large quantities of cotton and silk textiles and carpets. The king of Mombasa wrote a warning to a neighboring city:

This is to inform you that a great lord has passed through the town, burning it and laying it waste. He came to the town in such strength and was of such a cruelty that he spared neither man nor woman, or old nor young—nay, not even the smallest child. . . . Nor can I ascertain nor estimate what wealth they have taken from the town.[2]

What the Portuguese created in the Indian Ocean is commonly known as a "trading post empire," for they aimed to control commerce, not large territories or populations, and to do so by force of arms rather than by economic competition. Seeking to monopolize the spice trade, the Portuguese king grandly titled himself "Lord of the Conquest, Navigation, and Commerce of Ethiopia, Arabia, Persia, and India." Portuguese authorities in the East tried to require all merchant vessels to purchase a *cartaz*, or pass, and to pay duties of 6 to 10 percent on their cargoes. They partially blocked the traditional Red Sea route to the Mediterranean and for a century or so monopolized the highly profitable route around Africa to Europe. Even so, they never succeeded in controlling much more than half of the spice trade to Europe.[3]

Failing to dominate Indian Ocean commerce as they had hoped, the Portuguese gradually assimilated themselves to its ancient patterns. They became heavily involved in carrying Asian goods to Asian ports, selling their shipping services because they were largely unable to sell their goods. Even in their major settlements, the Portuguese were outnumbered by Asian traders, and many married Asian women. Hundreds of Portuguese escaped the control of their government altogether and settled in Asian or African ports, where they learned local languages, sometimes converted to Islam, and became simply one more group in the diverse trading culture of the East.

By 1600, the Portuguese trading post empire was in steep decline. This small European country was overextended, and rising Asian states such as Japan, Burma, Mughal India, Persia, and the sultanate of Oman actively resisted Portuguese commercial control. Unwilling to accept a dominant Portuguese role in the Indian Ocean, other European countries also gradually contested Portugal's efforts to monopolize the rich spice trade to Europe.

Spain and the Philippines

Spain was the first to challenge Portugal's position. As precious and profitable spices began to arrive in Europe on Portuguese ships in the early sixteenth century, the Spanish soon realized that they were behind in the race to gain access to the riches of the East. In an effort to catch up, they established themselves on what became the Philippine Islands, named after the Spanish king Philip II. The Spanish first

The Spice Trade For thousands of years, spices were a major trade item in the Indian Ocean commercial network, as this fifteenth-century French depiction of the gathering of pepper in southern India illustrates. In the early modern era, Europeans gained direct access to this ancient network for the first time. (Bibliothèque nationale de France)

■ **Comparison**

How did the Portuguese, Spanish, Dutch, and British initiatives in Asia differ from one another?

Snapshot   **Key Moments in the European Encounter with Asia**

Vasco da Gama's arrival in India	1498
Portuguese trading post empire established	early 1500s
Spanish takeover of Philippines begins	1565
China establishes taxes payable in silver	1570s
Beginning of silver shipments from Mexico to Manila	1570s
British and Dutch East India companies begin operation in Asia	1601–1602
Missionaries expelled from Japan	early 1600s
Dutch conquest of nutmeg-producing Banda Islands	1620
French East India Company established	1664
British begin military conquest of India	1750s

encountered the region during the famous round-the-world voyage (1519–1521) of Ferdinand Magellan, a Portuguese mariner sailing on behalf of the Spanish Crown. There they found an archipelago of islands, thousands of them, occupied by culturally diverse peoples and organized in small and highly competitive chiefdoms. One of the local chiefs later told the Spanish: "There is no king and no sole authority in this land; but everyone holds his own view and opinion, and does as he prefers."[4] Some were involved in tribute trade with China, and a small number of Chinese settlers lived in the port towns. Nonetheless, the region was of little interest to the governments of China and Japan, the major powers in the area.

These conditions—proximity to China and the spice islands, small and militarily weak societies, the absence of competing claims—encouraged the Spanish to establish outright colonial rule on the islands, rather than to imitate a Portuguese-style trading post empire. Small-scale military operations, gunpowder weapons, local alliances, gifts and favors to chiefs, and the pageantry of Catholic ritual all contributed to a relatively easy and often bloodless Spanish takeover of the islands in the century or so after 1565. They remained a Spanish colonial territory until the end of the nineteenth century, when the United States assumed control following the Spanish-American War of 1898.

Accompanying Spanish rule was a major missionary effort, which turned Filipino society into the only major outpost of Christianity in Asia. That effort also opened up a new front in the long encounter of Christendom and Islam, for on the southern island of Mindanao, Islam was gaining strength and provided an ideology of resistance to Spanish encroachment for 300 years. Indeed Mindanao remains a contested part of the Philippines into the twenty-first century.

Beyond the missionary enterprise, other features of Spanish colonial practice in the Americas found expression in the Philippines. People living in scattered settlements were persuaded or forced to relocate into more concentrated Christian communities. Tribute, taxes, and unpaid labor became part of ordinary life. Large landed estates emerged, owned by Spanish settlers, Catholic religious orders, or prominent Filipinos. Women who had played a major role as ritual specialists, healers, and midwifes were now displaced by male Spanish priests, and their ceremonial instruments were deliberately defiled and disgraced. Short-lived revolts and flight to interior mountains were among the Filipino responses to colonial oppression.

Yet others fled to Manila, the new capital of the colonial Philippines. By 1600, it had become a flourishing and culturally diverse city of more than 40,000 inhabitants and was home to many Spanish settlers and officials and growing numbers of Filipino migrants. Its rising prosperity also attracted some 3,000 Japanese and more than 20,000 Chinese. Serving as traders, artisans, and sailors, the Chinese in particular became an essential element in the Spanish colony's growing economic relationship with China; however, their economic prominence and their resistance to conversion earned them Spanish hostility and clearly discriminatory treatment. Periodic Chinese revolts, followed by expulsions and massacres, were the result. On one occasion in 1603, the Spanish killed about 20,000 people, nearly the entire Chinese population of the island.

The East India Companies

Far more important than the Spanish as European competitors for the spice trade were the Dutch and English, both of whom entered Indian Ocean commerce in the early seventeenth century. Together they quickly overtook and displaced the Portuguese, often by force, even as they competed vigorously with each other as well. These rising Northern European powers were both militarily and economically stronger than the Portuguese. For example, during the sixteenth century, the Dutch had become a highly commercialized and urbanized society, and their business skills and maritime shipping operations were the envy of Europe. Around 1600, both the British and the Dutch, unlike the Portuguese, organized their Indian Ocean ventures through private trading companies, which were able to raise money and share risks among a substantial number of merchant investors. The British East India Company and the Dutch East India Company received charters from their respective governments granting them trading monopolies and the power to make war and to govern conquered peoples. Thus they established their own parallel and competing trading post empires, with the Dutch focused on the islands of Indonesia and the English on India. Somewhat later, a French company also established settlements in the Indian Ocean basin.

Operating in a region of fragmented and weak political authority, the Dutch acted to control not only the shipping but also the production of cloves, cinnamon, nutmeg, and mace. With much bloodshed, the Dutch seized control of a number of small spice-producing islands, forcing their people to sell only to the Dutch and destroying the crops of those who refused. On the Banda Islands, famous for their

■ **Change**
To what extent did the British and Dutch trading companies change the societies they encountered in Asia?

A European View of Asian Commerce
The various East India companies (British, French, and Dutch) represented the major vehicle for European commerce in Asia during the early modern era. This wall painting, dating from 1778 and titled *The East Offering Its Riches to Britannia*, hung in the main offices of the British East India Company. (© British Library Board)

nutmeg, the Dutch killed, enslaved, or left to starve virtually the entire population of some 15,000 people and then replaced them with Dutch planters, using a slave labor force to produce the nutmeg crop. For a time in the seventeenth century, the Dutch were able to monopolize the trade in nutmeg, mace, and cloves and to sell these spices in Europe and India at fourteen to seventeen times the price they paid in Indonesia.[5] While Dutch profits soared, the local economy of the Spice Islands was shattered, and their people were impoverished.

The British East India Company operated differently than its Dutch counterpart. Less well financed and less commercially sophisticated, the British were largely excluded from the rich Spice Islands by the Dutch monopoly. Thus they fell back on India, where they established three major trading settlements during the seventeenth century: Bombay, on India's west coast, and Calcutta and Madras, on the east coast. Although British naval forces soon gained control of the Arabian Sea and the Persian Gulf, largely replacing the Portuguese, on land they were no match for the powerful Mughal Empire, which ruled most of the Indian subcontinent. Therefore, the British were not in a position to practice "trade by warfare," as the Dutch did in Indonesia.[6] Rather they secured their trading bases with the permission of Mughal authorities or local rulers, with substantial payments and bribes as the price of admission to the Indian market. When some independent English traders plundered a Mughal ship in 1636, local authorities detained British East India Company officials for two months and forced them to pay a whopping fine. Although pepper and other spices remained important in British trade, British merchants came to focus much more heavily on Indian cotton textiles, which were becoming widely popular in England and its American colonies. Hundreds of villages in the interior of southern India became specialized producers for this British market.

Like the Portuguese before them, both the Dutch and English became heavily involved in trade within Asia. The profits from this "carrying trade" enabled them to purchase Asian goods without paying for them in gold or silver from Europe. Dutch and English traders also began to deal in bulk goods for a mass market—pepper, textiles, and later tea and coffee—rather than just luxury goods for an elite market. In the second half of the eighteenth century, both the Dutch and British trading post empires slowly evolved into a more conventional form of colonial domination, in which the British came to rule India and the Dutch controlled Indonesia.

Asian Commerce

Although European commerce in the Indian Ocean and the South China Sea created new linkages between East and West, historians have sometimes exaggerated their impact on Asian societies during the early modern era. Certainly the European presence was far less significant in Asia than it was in the Americas or Africa during these centuries. European political control was limited to the Philippines and a few of the Spice Islands. To the great powers of South and East Asia—Mughal India, China, and Japan—Europeans represented no real military threat and played minor roles in their large and prosperous economies. Japan provides a fascinating case study in the ability of major Asian powers to control the European intruders.

When Portuguese traders and missionaries first arrived on that island nation in the mid-sixteenth century, soon followed by Spanish, Dutch, and English traders, Japan was plagued by endemic conflict among numerous feudal lords, known as *daimyo*, each with his own cadre of *samurai* warriors. In these circumstances, the European newcomers found a hospitable welcome, for their military technology, shipbuilding skills, geographic knowledge, commercial opportunities, and even religious ideas proved useful or attractive to various elements in Japan's fractious and competitive society. The second half of the sixteenth century, for example, witnessed the growth of a substantial Christian movement, with some 300,000 converts and a Japanese-led church.

By the early seventeenth century, however, a series of remarkable military figures had unified Japan politically, under the leadership of a supreme military commander known as the *shogun*, who hailed from the Tokugawa clan. With the end of Japan's civil wars, successive shoguns came to view Europeans as a threat to the country's newly established unity rather than an opportunity. They therefore expelled Christian missionaries and violently suppressed the practice of Christianity. This policy included the execution, often under torture, of some sixty-two missionaries and thousands of Japanese converts. Shogunate authorities also forbade Japanese from traveling abroad and banned most European traders altogether, permitting only the Dutch, who appeared less interested in spreading Christianity, to trade at a single site. Thus, for two centuries (1650–1850), Japanese authorities of the Tokugawa shogunate largely closed their country off from the emerging world of European commerce, although they maintained their trading ties to China and Korea.

Despite the European naval dominance in Asian waters, Asian merchants did not disappear. Arab, Chinese, Javanese, Malay, and other traders benefited from the upsurge in seaborne commerce. Chinese merchants, for example, continued to carry most of the spice trade from Southeast Asia to China. Overland trade within Asia remained wholly in Asian hands and grew considerably. Christian merchants from Armenia were particularly active in the overland commerce linking Europe, the Middle East, and Central Asia. Tens of thousands of Indian merchants and moneylenders, mostly Hindus representing sophisticated family firms, lived through-out Central Asia, Persia, and Russia, thus connecting this vast region to markets in India. These commercial networks, equivalent in their sophistication to those of Europe, continued to operate successfully even as Europeans militarized the seaborne commerce of the Indian Ocean.

Silver and Global Commerce

■ **Significance**
What was the world historical importance of the silver trade?

Even more than the spice trade of Eurasia, it was the silver trade that gave birth to a genuinely global network of exchange (see Map 15.2). As one historian put it, silver "went round the world and made the world go round."[7] The mid-sixteenth-century discovery of enormously rich silver deposits in Bolivia, and simultaneously in Japan, suddenly provided a vastly increased supply of that precious metal. Spanish America alone produced perhaps 85 percent of the world's silver during the early modern era. Spain's sole Asian colony, the Philippines, provided a critical link in this emerging network of global commerce. Manila, the colonial capital of the Philippines, was the destination of annual Spanish shipments of silver, which were drawn from the rich mines of Bolivia, transported overland to Acapulco in Mexico, and from there shipped across the Pacific to the Philippines. This trade was the first direct and sustained link between the Americas and Asia, and it initiated a web of Pacific commerce that grew steadily over the centuries.

At the heart of that Pacific web, and of early modern global commerce gener-ally, was China's huge economy, and especially its growing demand for silver. In the

Map 15.2   The Global Silver Trade
Silver was one of the first major commodities to be exchanged on a genuinely global scale.

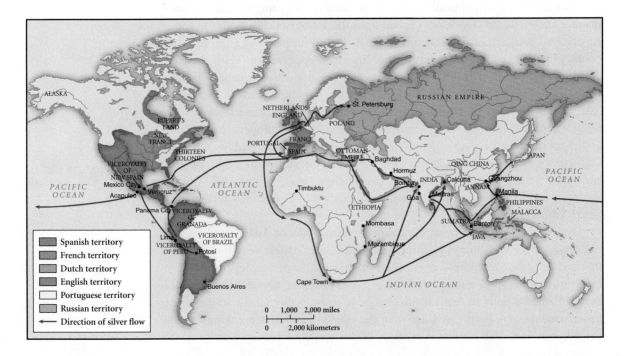

1570s, Chinese authorities consolidated a variety of tax levies into a single tax, which its huge population was now required to pay in silver. This sudden new demand for the white metal caused its value to skyrocket. It meant that foreigners with silver could now purchase far more of China's silks and porcelains than before.

This demand set silver in motion around the world, with the bulk of the world's silver supply winding up in China and much of the rest elsewhere in Asia. The routes by which this "silver drain" operated were numerous. Chinese, Portuguese, and Dutch traders flocked to Manila to sell Chinese goods in exchange for silver. European ships carried Japanese silver to China. Much of the silver shipped across the Atlantic to Spain was spent in Europe generally and then used to pay for the Asian goods that the French, British, and Dutch so greatly desired. Silver paid for some African slaves and for spices in Southeast Asia. The standard Spanish silver coin, known as a piece of eight, was used by merchants in North America, Europe, India, Russia, and West Africa as a medium of exchange. By 1600, it circulated widely in southern China. A Portuguese merchant in 1621 noted that silver "wanders throughout all the world . . . before flocking to China, where it remains as if at its natural center."[8]

In its global journeys, silver transformed much that it touched. At the world's largest silver mine in what is now Bolivia, the city of Potosí arose from a barren landscape high in the Andes, a ten-week mule trip away from Lima. "New people arrive by the hour, attracted by the smell of silver," commented a Spanish observer in the 1570s. With 160,000 people, Potosí became the largest city in the Americas and equivalent in size to London, Amsterdam, or Seville. Its wealthy European elite lived in luxury, with all the goods of Europe and Asia at their disposal. Meanwhile, the city's Native American miners worked in conditions so horrendous that some families held funeral services for men drafted to work the mines. One Spanish priest referred to Potosí as a "portrait of hell."[9]

In Spain itself, which was the initial destination for much of Latin America's silver, the precious metal vastly enriched the Crown, making Spain the envy of its European rivals during the sixteenth century. Spanish rulers could now pursue military and political ambitions in both Europe and the Americas far beyond the country's own resource base. "New World mines," concluded one scholar, "supported the Spanish empire."[10] Nonetheless, this vast infusion of wealth did not fundamentally transform the Spanish economy, because it generated more inflation of prices than

Potosí

This colonial-era painting shows the enormously rich silver mines of Potosí, then a major global source of the precious metal and the largest city in the Americas. Brutally hard work and poisonous exposure to mercury, which was used in the refining process, led to the deaths of many thousands of workers, even as the silver itself contributed to European splendor in the early modern era. (Courtesy, The Hispanic Society of America)

real economic growth. A rigid economy laced with monopolies and regulations, an aristocratic class that preferred leisure to enterprise, and a crusading insistence on religious uniformity all prevented the Spanish from using their silver windfall in a productive fashion. When the value of silver dropped in the early seventeenth century, Spain lost its earlier position as the dominant Western European power.

Japan, another major source of silver production in the sixteenth century, did better. Its military rulers, the Tokugawa shoguns, used silver-generated profits to defeat hundreds of rival feudal lords and unify the country. Unlike their Spanish counterparts, the shoguns allied with the country's vigorous merchant class to develop a market-based economy and to invest heavily in agricultural and industrial enterprises. Japanese state and local authorities alike acted vigorously to protect and renew Japan's dwindling forests, while millions of families in the eighteenth century took steps to have fewer children by practicing late marriages, contraception, abortion, and infanticide. The outcome was the dramatic slowing of Japan's population growth, the easing of an impending ecological crisis, and a flourishing, highly commercialized economy. These conditions were the foundations for Japan's remarkable nineteenth-century Industrial Revolution.

In China, silver deepened the already substantial commercialization of the country's economy. In order to obtain the silver needed to pay their taxes, more and more people had to sell something—either their labor or their products. Areas that devoted themselves to growing mulberry trees, on which silkworms fed, had to buy their rice from other regions. Thus the Chinese economy became more regionally specialized. Particularly in southern China, this surging economic growth resulted in the loss of about half the area's forest cover as more and more land was devoted to cash crops. No Japanese-style conservation program emerged to address this growing problem. An eighteenth-century Chinese poet, Wang Dayue, gave voice to the fears that this ecological transformation wrought.

> Rarer, too, their timber grew, and rarer still and rarer
> As the hills resembled heads now shaven clean of hair.
> For the first time, too, moreover, they felt an anxious mood
> That all their daily logging might not furnish them with fuel.[11]

China's role in the silver trade is a useful reminder of Asian centrality in the world economy of the early modern era. Its large and prosperous population, increasingly operating within a silver-based economy, fueled global commerce, vastly increasing the quantity of goods exchanged and the geographic range of world trade. Despite their obvious physical presence in the Americas, Africa, and Asia, economically speaking Europeans were essentially middlemen, funneling American silver to Asia and competing with one another for a place in the rich markets of Asia. The productivity of the Chinese economy was evident in Spanish America, where cheap and well-made Chinese goods easily outsold those of Spain. In 1594, the Spanish viceroy of Peru observed that "a man can clothe his wife in Chinese silks for [25 pesos], whereas he could not provide her with clothing of

Spanish silks with 200 pesos."[12] Indian cotton textiles likewise outsold European woolen or linen textiles in the seventeenth century to such an extent that French laws in 1717 prohibited the wearing of Indian cotton or Chinese silk clothing as a means of protecting French industry.

The "World Hunt": Fur in Global Commerce[13]

In the early modern era, furs joined silver, textiles, and spices as major items of global commerce. Their production had an important environmental impact as well as serious implications for the human societies that generated and consumed them. Furs, of course, had long provided warmth and conveyed status in colder regions of the world, but the integration of North America and of northern Asia (Siberia) into a larger world economy vastly increased their significance in global trade.

■ **Change**
Describe the impact of the fur trade on North American native societies.

By 1500, European population growth and agricultural expansion had sharply diminished the supply of fur-bearing animals, such as beaver, rabbits, sable, marten, and deer. Furthermore, much of the early modern era witnessed a period of cooling temperatures and harsh winters, known as the Little Ice Age, which may well have increased the demand for furs. "The weather is bitterly cold and everyone is in furs although we are almost in July," observed a surprised visitor from Venice while in London in 1604.[14] These conditions pushed prices higher. The cost of a good-quality beaver pelt, for example, quadrupled in France between 1558 and 1611. This translated into strong economic incentives for European traders to tap the immense wealth of fur-bearing animals found in North America.

Like other aspects of imperial expansion, the fur trade was a highly competitive enterprise. The French were most prominent in the St. Lawrence valley, around the Great Lakes, and later along the Mississippi River; British traders pushed into the Hudson Bay region; and the Dutch focused their attention along the Hudson River in what is now New York. They were frequently rivals for the great prize of North American furs. In the southern colonies of British North America, deerskins by the hundreds of thousands found a ready market in England's leather industry (see Map 15.3).

Only a few Europeans directly engaged in commercial trapping or hunting. They usually waited for Indians to bring the furs or skins initially to their coastal settlements and later to their fortified trading posts in the interior of North America. European merchants paid for the furs with a variety of trade goods, including guns, blankets, metal tools, rum, and brandy, amid much ceremony, haggling over prices, and ritualized gift-giving. Native Americans represented a cheap labor force in this international commercial effort, but they were not a directly coerced labor force.

Over the three centuries of the early modern era, enormous quantities of furs and deerskins found their way to Europe, where they considerably enhanced the standard of living in those cold climates. The environmental price was paid in the

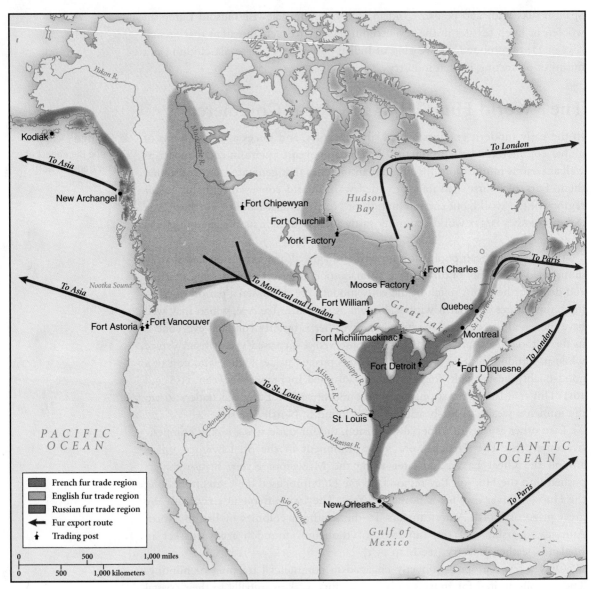

Map 15.3 The North American Fur Trade
North America, as well as Russian Siberia, funneled an apparently endless supply of furs into the circuits of global trade during the early modern era.

Americas, and it was high. A consistent demand for beaver hats led to the near extinction of that industrious animal in much of North America by the early nineteenth century. Many other fur-bearing species were seriously depleted as the trade moved inexorably westward. By the 1760s, hunters in southeastern British colonies took about 500,000 deer every year, seriously diminishing the deer population of the region.

For the Native American peoples who hunted, trapped, processed, and transported these products, the fur trade bore various benefits, particularly at the beginning. The Hurons, for example, who lived on the northern shores of Lakes Erie and Ontario in the early seventeenth century, annually exchanged some 20,000 to 30,000 pelts, mostly beaver, and in return received copper pots, metal axes, knives, cloth, firearms, and alcohol. Many of these items were of real value, which strengthened the Hurons in their relationship with neighboring peoples. These goods also enhanced the authority of Huron chiefs by providing them with gifts to distribute among their followers. At least initially, competition among Europeans ensured that Native American leaders could negotiate reasonable prices for their goods. Furthermore, their important role in the lucrative fur trade protected them for a time from the kind of extermination, enslavement, or displacement that was the fate of native peoples in Portuguese Brazil.

Nothing, however, protected them against the diseases carried by Europeans. In the 1630s and 1640s, to cite only one example of many, about half of the Hurons perished from influenza, smallpox, and other European-borne diseases. Furthermore, the fur trade generated warfare beyond anything previously known. Competition among Native American societies became more intense as the economic stakes grew higher. Catastrophic population declines owing to disease stimulated "mourning wars," designed to capture people who could be assimilated into much-diminished societies. A century of French-British rivalry for North America (1664–1763) forced Native American societies to take sides, to fight, and to die in these European imperial conflicts. Firearms, of course, made warfare far more deadly than before.

As many Native American peoples became enmeshed in commercial relationships with Europeans, they grew dependent on European trade goods. Among the Algonquians, for example, iron tools and cooking pots replaced those of stone, wood, or bone; gunpowder weapons took the place of bows and arrows; European textiles proved more attractive than traditional beaver and deerskin clothing; flint and steel were more effective for starting fires than wooden drills. A wide range of traditional crafts were thus lost, without the native peoples gaining a corresponding ability to manufacture the new items for themselves. Enthusiasm for these imported goods and continued European demands for furs and skins frequently eroded the customary restraint that characterized traditional hunting practices, resulting in the depletion of many species. One European observer wrote of the Creek Indians: "[They] wage eternal war against deer and bear . . . which is indeed carried to an unreasonable and perhaps criminal excess, since the white people have dazzled their senses with foreign superfluities."[15]

Beyond germs and guns, the most destructive of the imported goods was surely alcohol—rum and brandy, in particular. Whiskey, a locally produced grain-based alcohol, only added to the problem. With no prior experience of alcohol and little time to adjust to its easy availability, these drinks "hit Indian societies with explosive force."[16] Binge drinking, violence among young men, promiscuity, and addiction followed in many places. In 1753, Iroquois leaders complained bitterly to European authorities in Pennsylvania: "These wicked Whiskey Sellers, when they have once got the Indians in liquor, make them sell their very clothes from their backs. . . . If this practice be continued, we must be inevitably ruined."[17] In short, it was not so much the fur trade itself that decimated Native American societies, but all that accompanied it—disease, dependence, guns, alcohol, and the growing encroachment of European colonial empires.

■ Comparison
How did the North American and Siberian fur trades differ from each other? What did they have in common?

Much the same could be said about the other fur trade that was simultaneously taking shape within a rapidly expanding Russian Empire. As a new Russian state emerged from Mongol rule around the city of Moscow in the late fifteenth century, it became a major source of furs for both Western Europe and the Ottoman Empire. The profitability of that trade in furs was the chief incentive for Russia's rapid expansion during the sixteenth and seventeenth centuries across Siberia, where the "soft gold" of fur-bearing animals was abundant. With growing markets in both China and Europe, the fur trade greatly enriched the Russian state as well as many private merchants, trappers, and hunters. Here the silver trade and the fur trade intersected, as Europeans paid for Russian furs largely with American gold and silver.

The consequences for native Siberians were similar to those in North America as disease took its toll, as indigenous people became dependent on Russian goods, as the settler frontier encroached on native lands, and as many species of fur-bearing mammals were seriously depleted. In several ways, however, the Russian fur trade was unique. Whereas several European nations competed in North America and generally obtained their furs through commercial negotiations with Indian societies, no such competition accompanied Russian expansion across Siberia. Russian authorities imposed a tax or tribute, payable in furs, on every able-bodied Siberian male between eighteen and fifty years of age. To enforce the payment, they took hostages from Siberian societies, with death as a possible outcome if the required furs were not forthcoming. A further difference lay in the large-scale presence of private Russian hunters and trappers, who competed directly with their Siberian counterparts.

Fur and the Russians
This colored engraving shows a sixteenth-century Russian ambassador and his contingent arriving at the court of the Holy Roman Emperor and bearing gifts of animal pelts, the richest fruit of the expanding Russian Empire. (RIA Novosti)

Commerce in People: The Atlantic Slave Trade

Of all the commercial ties that linked the early modern world into a global network of exchange, none had more profound or enduring human consequences than the Atlantic slave trade. During the 400 years from the mid-fifteenth to the mid-nineteenth century, that trade in humankind took an estimated 11 million people from African societies, shipped them across the Atlantic in the infamous Middle Passage, and deposited them in the Americas, where they lived out their often brief lives as slaves. Countless millions more died in the process of capture and transport, before ever reaching American shores (see Map 15.4).

Beyond the multitude of individual tragedies that it spawned—capture and sale, displacement from home cultures, forced labor, beatings and brandings, broken families—the Atlantic slave trade transformed the societies of all of its participants. Within Africa itself, some societies were thoroughly disrupted; others were strengthened; many were corrupted. Elites were often enriched, while the slaves themselves, of course, were victimized beyond imagination.

In the Americas, the slave trade added a substantial African presence to the mix of European and Native American peoples. This African diaspora (the transatlantic

Map 15.4   The Atlantic Slave Trade
Stimulated by the plantation complex of the Americas, the Atlantic slave trade represented an enormous extension of the ancient practice of people owning and selling other people.

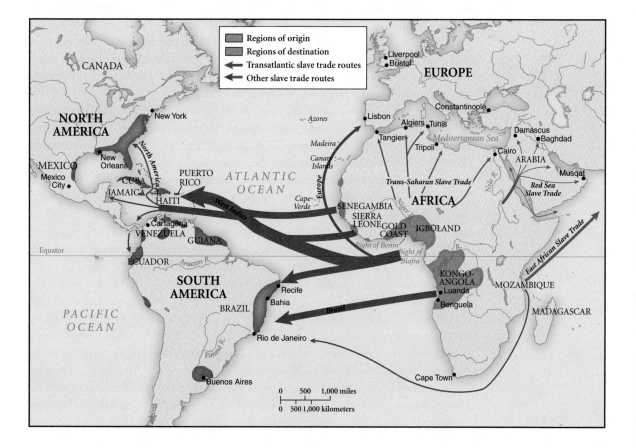

spread of African peoples) injected into these new societies issues of race that endure still in the twenty-first century. It also introduced elements of African culture, such as religious ideas, musical and artistic traditions, and cuisine, into the making of American cultures. The profits from the slave trade and the forced labor of African slaves certainly enriched European and Euro-American societies, even as the practice of slavery contributed much to the racial thinking of European peoples. Finally, slavery became a metaphor for many kinds of social oppression, quite different from plantation slavery, in the centuries that followed. Workers protested the slavery of wage labor; colonized people rejected the slavery of imperial domination; and feminists identified slavery with patriarchy.

The Slave Trade in Context

■ Comparison

What was distinctive about the Atlantic slave trade? What did it share with other patterns of slave owning and slave trading?

The Atlantic slave trade and slavery in the Americas represented the most recent large-scale expression of an almost universal human practice—the owning and exchange of human beings. With origins that go back to the earliest civilizations, slavery was widely accepted as a perfectly normal human enterprise and was closely linked to warfare and capture. Before 1500, the Mediterranean and Indian Ocean basins were the major arenas of the Old World slave trade, and southern Russia was a major source of slaves. Many African societies likewise both practiced slavery themselves and sold slaves into these international commercial networks. A trans-Saharan slave trade had long funneled African captives into Mediterranean slavery, and an East African slave trade brought Africans into the Middle East and the Indian Ocean basin. Both operated largely within the Islamic world.

Furthermore, slavery came in many forms. Although slaves were everywhere vulnerable "outsiders" to their masters' societies, in many places they could be assimilated into their owners' households, lineages, or communities. In some places, children inherited the slave status of their parents; elsewhere those children were free persons. Within the Islamic world, the preference was for female slaves by a two-to-one margin, while the later Atlantic slave trade favored males by a similar margin. Not all slaves, however, occupied degraded positions. Some in the Islamic world acquired prominent military or political status. Most slaves in the premodern world worked in their owners' households, farms, or shops, with smaller numbers laboring in large-scale agricultural or industrial enterprises.

The slavery that emerged in the Americas was distinctive in several ways. One was simply the immense size of the traffic in slaves and its centrality to the economies of colonial America. Furthermore, this New World slavery was largely based on plantation agriculture and treated slaves as a form of dehumanized property, lacking any rights in the society of their owners. Slave status throughout the Americas was inherited across generations, and there was little hope of eventual freedom for the vast majority. Nowhere else, with the possible exception of ancient Greece, was widespread slavery associated with societies affirming values of human freedom and equality. Perhaps most distinctive was the racial dimension: Atlantic slavery came to be identified wholly with Africa and with "blackness." How did this exceptional form of slavery emerge?

The origins of Atlantic slavery clearly lie in the Mediterranean world and with that now common sweetener known as sugar. Until the Crusades, Europeans knew nothing of sugar and relied on honey and fruits to sweeten their bland diets. However, as they learned from the Arabs about sugarcane and the laborious techniques for producing usable sugar, Europeans established sugar-producing plantations within the Mediterranean and later on various islands off the coast of West Africa. Sugar production was perhaps the first "modern" industry in that it required huge capital investment, substantial technology, an almost factory-like discipline among workers, and a mass market of consumers. The immense difficulty and danger of the work, the limitations attached to serf labor, and the general absence of wage workers all pointed to slavery as a source of labor for sugar plantations.

Initially, Slavic-speaking peoples from the Black Sea region furnished the bulk of the slaves for Mediterranean plantations, so much so that "Slav" became the basis for the word "slave" in many European languages. In 1453, however, when the Ottoman Turks seized Constantinople, the supply of Slavic slaves was effectively cut off. At the same time, Portuguese mariners were exploring the coast of West Africa; they were looking primarily for gold, but they also found there an alternative source of slaves available for sale. Thus, when sugar, and later tobacco and cotton, plantations took hold in the Americas, Europeans had already established links to a West African source of supply.

Largely through a process of elimination, Africa became the primary source of slave labor for the plantation economies of the Americas. Slavic peoples were no longer available; Native Americans quickly perished from European diseases; marginal Europeans were Christians and therefore supposedly exempt from slavery; and European indentured servants were expensive and temporary. Africans, on the other hand, were skilled farmers; they had some immunity to both tropical and European diseases; they were not Christians; they were, relatively speaking, close at hand; and they were readily available in substantial numbers through African-operated commercial networks.

Moreover, Africans were black. The precise relationship between slavery and European

■ **Causation**
What explains the rise of the Atlantic slave trade?

The Middle Passage
This mid-nineteenth-century painting of slaves held below deck on a Spanish slave ship illustrates the horrendous conditions of the transatlantic voyage, a journey experienced by many millions of captured Africans. (The Art Archive)

racism has long been a much-debated subject. Historian David Brion Davis has suggested the controversial view that "racial stereotypes were transmitted, along with black slavery itself, from Muslims to Christians."[18] For many centuries, Muslims had drawn on sub-Saharan Africa as one source of slaves and in the process had developed a form of racism. The fourteenth-century Tunisian scholar Ibn Khaldun wrote that black people were "submissive to slavery, because Negroes have little that is essentially human and have attributes that are quite similar to those of dumb animals."[19]

Other scholars find the origins of racism within European culture itself. For the English, argues historian Audrey Smedley, the process of conquering Ireland had generated by the sixteenth century a view of the Irish as "rude, beastly, ignorant, cruel, and unruly infidels," perceptions that were then transferred to Africans enslaved on English sugar plantations of the West Indies.[20] Whether Europeans borrowed such images of Africans from their Muslim neighbors or developed them independently, slavery and racism soon went hand in hand. "Europeans were better able to tolerate their brutal exploitation of Africans," writes a prominent world historian, "by imagining that these Africans were an inferior race, or better still, not even human."[21]

The Slave Trade in Practice

■ Connection

What roles did Europeans and Africans play in the unfolding of the Atlantic slave trade?

The European demand for slaves was clearly the chief cause of this tragic commerce, and from the point of sale on the African coast to the massive use of slave labor on American plantations, the entire enterprise was in European hands. Within Africa itself, however, a different picture emerges, for over the four centuries of the Atlantic slave trade, European demand elicited an African supply. A few early efforts by the Portuguese at slave raiding along the West African coast convinced Europeans that such efforts were unnecessary and unwise, for African societies were quite capable of defending themselves against European intrusion, and many were willing to sell their slaves peacefully. Furthermore, Europeans died like flies when they entered the interior because they lacked immunities to common tropical diseases. Thus the slave trade quickly came to operate largely with Europeans waiting on the coast, either on their ships or in fortified settlements, to purchase slaves from African merchants and political elites. Certainly Europeans tried to exploit African rivalries to obtain slaves at the lowest possible cost, and the firearms they funneled into West Africa may well have increased the warfare from which so many slaves were derived. But from the point of initial capture to sale on the coast, the entire enterprise was normally in African hands. Almost nowhere did Europeans attempt outright military conquest; instead they generally dealt as equals with local African authorities.

One English merchant in 1693 reported on his negotiations with the king of Whydah, a small kingdom on the coast of what is now Benin: "We attended his majesty with samples of our goods, and made our agreement about the prices, though not without much difficulty."[22] Those goods included both European and Indian textiles, cowrie shells (widely used as money in West Africa), European metal goods, firearms and gunpowder, tobacco and alcohol, and various decorative items such as beads. Europeans purchased some of these items—cowrie shells and Indian textiles, for example—with silver mined in the Americas. Thus the slave trade connected with commerce in silver and textiles as it became part of an emerging worldwide network of exchange. In most places most of the time, a leading scholar concluded, the slave trade took place "not unlike international trade anywhere in the world of the period."[23]

If African authorities and elite classes in many places controlled their side of the slave trade, on occasion they were almost overwhelmed by it. Many small-scale kinship-based societies, lacking the protection of a strong state, were thoroughly disrupted by raids from more powerful neighbors. Even some sizable states were destabilized. In the early sixteenth century, the kingdom of Kongo, located mostly in present-day Angola, had been badly damaged by the commerce in slaves, and the authority of its ruler had been severely undermined. In 1526, the Kongo king Afonso, himself a convert to Christianity, begged the Portuguese to halt the slave trade altogether. "We cannot calculate how great the damage is," he wrote to the king of Portugal. "[M]erchants are taking everyday our natives, sons of the land and the sons of our noblemen and vassals and our relatives."[24]

An incident along the so-called Slave Coast of West Africa during the final decades of the slave trade illustrates how even African slave traders themselves could be victimized. On this occasion in 1856, a "Yankee captain" bought some 500 slaves and then invited twenty-five "headmen or traders" aboard his ship for a drink. An American chaplain recounted what happened next as he heard the story from local people: "He [the ship's captain] was profuse in his hospitality, made them all drunk, put them in irons, sank their canoes, pocketed their money, and got under weigh. Two of the twenty five thus taken jumped overboard shortly after, and were drowned; the remainder he sold in Cuba for four hundred dollars each."[25]

Whatever the relationship between European buyers and African sellers, for the slaves themselves—who were seized in the interior, often sold several times on the harrowing journey to the coast, sometimes branded, and held in squalid slave dungeons while awaiting transportation to the New World—it was anything but a normal commercial transaction. One European engaged in the trade noted that "the negroes are so willful and loath to leave their own country, that they have often leap'd out of the canoes, boat, and ship, into the sea, and kept under water till they were drowned, to avoid being taken up and saved by our boats."[26]

Over the four centuries of the slave trade, millions of Africans underwent some such experience, but their numbers varied considerably over time. For the first 150 years (1450–1600), fewer than 4,000 slaves annually were shipped to Europe or across the Atlantic. During those years, the Portuguese were at least as much interested in African gold, spices, and textiles. Furthermore, as in Asia, they became involved in transporting African goods, including slaves, from one African port to another, thus becoming the "truck drivers" of coastal West African commerce.[27] In the seventeenth century, the pace picked up, with an average of about 10,000 slaves

Snapshot **The Slave Trade in Numbers**

The Rise and Decline of the Slave Trade[28]

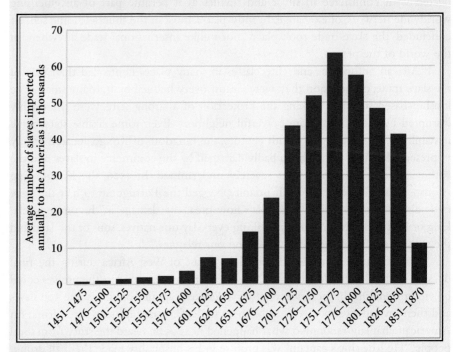

The Destination of Slaves in the Eighteenth Century[29]

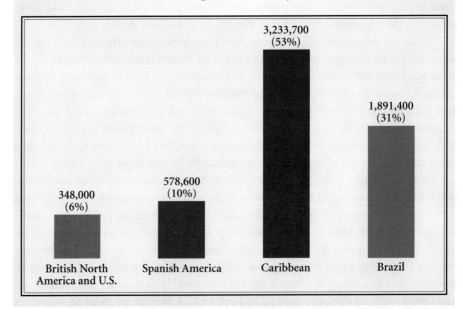

per year shipped to the Americas. By this time, the slave trade was becoming highly competitive, with the British, Dutch, and French contesting the earlier Portuguese monopoly. The eighteenth century was the high point of the slave trade as the plantation economies of the Americas boomed. By the 1750s, more than 60,000 people per year left Africa in chains, bound for the Americas and slavery.

Where did these Africans come from, and where did they go? Geographically, the slave trade drew on the societies of West Africa, from present-day Mauritania in the north to Angola in the south. Initially focused on the coastal regions, the slave trade progressively penetrated into the interior as the demand for slaves picked up. Socially, slaves were mostly drawn from various marginal groups in African societies— prisoners of war, criminals, debtors, people who had been "pawned" during times of difficulty. Thus Africans did not generally sell "their own people" into slavery. Divided into hundreds of separate, usually small-scale, and often rival communities—cities, kingdoms, microstates, clans, and villages—the various peoples of West Africa had no concept of an "African" identity. Those whom they captured and sold were normally outsiders, vulnerable people who lacked the protection of membership in an established community. When short-term economic or political advantage could be gained, such people were sold. In this respect, the Atlantic slave trade was little different from the experience of enslavement elsewhere in the world.

The destination of enslaved Africans, half a world away in the Americas, was very different. Some 80 percent wound up in Brazil or the Caribbean, where the labor demands of the plantation economy were most intense. About 5 to 6 percent found themselves in North America, with the balance in mainland Spanish America or in Europe itself (see the Snapshot). The journey across the Atlantic was horrendous almost beyond description, with the Middle Passage having an overall mortality rate of about 15 percent.

Comparing Consequences: The Impact of the Slave Trade in Africa

From the viewpoint of world history, the chief outcome of the slave trade lay in the new transregional linkages that it generated. Both commercially and demographically, Africa became a permanent part of an interacting Atlantic world. Millions of its people were now compelled to make their lives in the New World. West African economies were increasingly connected to an emerging European-centered world economy. These vast processes set in motion a chain of consequences that have transformed the lives and societies of people on both sides of the Atlantic.

■ **Change**
In what different ways did the Atlantic slave trade transform African societies?

Although the slave trade did not result in the kind of population collapse that occurred in the Americas, it certainly slowed Africa's growth at a time when Europe, China, and other regions were expanding demographically. Scholars have estimated that sub-Saharan Africa represented about 18 percent of the world's population in 1600, but only 6 percent in 1900.[30] A portion of that difference reflects the slave trade's impact on Africa's population history.

That impact derived not only from the loss of millions of people over four centuries but also from the economic stagnation and political disruption that the slave trade generated. Economically, the slave trade stimulated little positive change in Africa because those Africans who benefited most from the traffic in people were not investing in the productive capacities of African societies. Although European imports generally did not displace traditional artisan manufacturing, no technological breakthroughs in agriculture or industry increased the wealth available to these societies. Maize and manioc (cassava), introduced from the Americas, added a new source of calories to African diets, but the international demand was for Africa's people, not its agricultural products.

Within particular African societies, the impact of the slave trade differed considerably from place to place and over time. Particularly in small-scale societies that were frequently subjected to slave raiding and that had little centralized authority, insecurity was pervasive. Oral traditions in southern Ghana, for example, reported that "there was no rest in the land," that people went about in groups rather than alone, and that mothers kept their children inside when European ships appeared.[31] Some larger kingdoms such as Kongo and Oyo slowly disintegrated as access to trading opportunities and firearms enabled outlying regions to establish their independence. However, African authorities also sought to take advantage of the new commercial opportunities and to manage the slave trade in their own interests, as the contrasting experience of the neighboring kingdoms of Benin and Dahomey illustrates.[32]

The kingdom of Benin, in the forest area of present-day Nigeria, was one of the oldest and most highly developed states in the coastal hinterland of West Africa, dating perhaps to the eleventh century C.E. Its capital was a large, walled city with wide avenues, a lavish court, a wealthy elite, and a powerful monarch, or *oba*, who strictly controlled the country's trade. Benin's uniqueness lay in its relatively successful efforts to avoid a deep involvement in the slave trade and to diversify the exports with which it purchased European firearms and other goods. As early as 1516, the oba began to restrict the slave trade and soon forbade the export of male slaves altogether, a ban that lasted until the early eighteenth century. By then, the oba's authority over outlying areas had declined, and the country's major exports of pepper and cotton cloth had lost out to Asian and then European competition. In these circumstances, Benin felt compelled to resume limited participation in the slave trade. But even at the height of the trade, in the late eighteenth century, Benin exported fewer than 1,000 slaves a year.

Among the Aja-speaking peoples to the west of Benin, the situation was very different. There the slave trade had thoroughly disrupted a series of small and weak states along the coast. Some distance inland, the kingdom of Dahomey arose in the early eighteenth century, at least in part as an effort to contain the constant raiding and havoc occasioned by the coastal trade. It was a unique and highly authoritarian state in which commoners and chiefs alike were responsible directly to the king and in which the power of lineages and secret societies was considerably weakened.

For a time, Dahomey tried to limit the external slave trade, to import European craftsmen, and to develop plantation agriculture within the kingdom, but all this failed. In view of hostile relations with the neighboring kingdom of Oyo and others, Dahomey instead turned to a vigorous involvement in the slave trade, under strict royal control. The army conducted annual slave raids, and the government soon came to depend on the trade for its essential revenues. Unlike in Benin, the slave trade in Dahomey became the chief business of the state and remained so until well into the nineteenth century.

Reflections: Economic Globalization— Then and Now

The study of history reminds us of two quite contradictory truths. One is that our lives in the present bear remarkable similarities to those of people long ago. We are perhaps not as unique as we might think. The other is that our lives are very different from theirs and that things have changed substantially. This chapter about global commerce—long-distance trade in spices and textiles, silver and gold, beaver pelts and deerskins, slaves and sugar—provides both perspectives.

If we are accustomed to think about globalization as a product of the late twentieth century, early modern world history provides a corrective. Those three centuries reveal much that is familiar to people of the twenty-first century—the global circulation of goods; an international currency; production for a world market; the growing economic role of the West on the global stage; private enterprise, such as the British and Dutch East India companies, operating on a world scale; national governments eager to support their merchants in a highly competitive environment. By the eighteenth century, many Europeans dined from Chinese porcelain dishes called "china," wore Indian-made cotton textiles, and drank chocolate from Mexico, tea from China, and coffee from Yemen while sweetening these beverages with sugar from the Caribbean or Brazil. The millions who worked to produce these goods, whether slave or free, were operating in a world economy. Some industries were thoroughly international. New England rum producers, for example, depended on molasses imported from the Caribbean, while the West Indian sugar industry used African labor and European equipment to produce for a global market.

Nonetheless, early modern economic globalization was a far cry from that of the twentieth century. Most obvious perhaps were scale and speed. By 2000, immensely more goods circulated internationally and far more people produced for and depended on the world market than was the case even in 1750. Back-and-forth communications between England and India that took eighteen months in the eighteenth century could be accomplished in an hour by telegraph in the late nineteenth century and almost instantaneously via the Internet in the late twentieth century. Moreover, by 1900 globalization was firmly centered in the economies of

Europe and North America. In the early modern era, by contrast, Asia in general and China in particular remained major engines of the world economy, despite the emerging presence of Europeans around the world. By the end of the twentieth century, the booming economies of India and China suggested at least a partial return to that earlier pattern.

Early modern globalization differed in still other ways from that of the contemporary world. Economic life then was primarily preindustrial, still powered by human and animal muscles, wind, and water and lacking the enormous productive capacity that accompanied the later technological breakthrough of the steam engine and the Industrial Revolution. Finally, the dawning of a genuinely global economy in the early modern era was tied unapologetically to empire building and to slavery, both of which had been discredited by the late twentieth century. Slavery lost its legitimacy during the nineteenth century, and formal territorial empires largely disappeared in the twentieth. Most people during the early modern era would have been surprised to learn that a global economy, as it turned out, could function effectively without either of these long-standing practices.

Second Thoughts

What's the Significance?

Indian Ocean commercial network
trading post empires
Spanish Philippines

British/Dutch East India companies
Tokugawa shogunate
"silver drain"

Potosí
"soft gold"
African diaspora
Benin/Dahomey

Big Picture Questions

1. In what specific ways did trade foster change in the world of the early modern era?
2. To what extent did Europeans transform earlier patterns of commerce, and in what ways did they assimilate into those older patterns?
3. Describe and account for the differing outcomes of European expansion in the Americas (see Chapter 14), Africa, and Asia.
4. How should we distribute the moral responsibility or blame for the Atlantic slave trade? Is this a task appropriate for historians?
5. What lasting legacies of early modern globalization are evident in the early twenty-first century? Pay particular attention to the legacies of the slave trade.

Next Steps: For Further Study

Glenn J. Ames, *The Globe Encompassed: The Age of European Discovery, 1500–1700* (2007). An up-to-date survey of European expansion in the early modern era.

Andre Gunder Frank, *ReOrient: Global Economy in the Asian Age* (1998). An account of the early modern world economy that highlights the centrality of Asia.

Erik Gilbert and Jonathan Reynolds, *Trading Tastes: Commodity and Cultural Exchange to 1750* (2006). A world historical perspective on transcontinental and transoceanic commerce.

David Northrup, ed., *The Atlantic Slave Trade* (2002). A fine collection of essays about the origins, practice, impact, and abolition of Atlantic slavery.

John Richards, *The Endless Frontier* (2003). Explores the ecological consequences of early modern commerce.

John Thornton, *Africa and Africans in the Making of the Atlantic World* (1998). A well-regarded but somewhat controversial account of the slave trade, with an emphasis on African authorities as active and independent players in the process.

"Atlantic Slave Trade and Slave Life in the Americas: A Visual Record," http://hitchcock.itc.virginia .edu/Slavery/index.php. An immense collection of maps and images illustrating the slave trade and the life of slaves in the Americas.

Religion and Science

1450-1750

The Globalization of
    Christianity
    Western Christendom
    Fragmented: The Protestant
    Reformation
    Christianity Outward Bound
    Conversion and Adaptation
    in Spanish America
    An Asian Comparison: China
    and the Jesuits
Persistence and Change in
    Afro-Asian Cultural Traditions
    Expansion and Renewal in
    the Islamic World
    China: New Directions in an
    Old Tradition
    India: Bridging the
    Hindu/Muslim Divide
A New Way of Thinking: The
    Birth of Modern Science
    The Question of Origins: Why
    Europe?
    Science as Cultural Revolution
    Science and Enlightenment
    Looking Ahead: Science in
    the Nineteenth Century
    European Science beyond
    the West
Reflections: Cultural
    Borrowing and Its Hazards

"This country wasn't founded on Muslim beliefs or evolution. This country was founded on Christianity, and our students should be taught as such."[1] That was the view of one member of a rural school board in Dover, Pennsylvania, in 2004. It reflected a long-running tension between modern science and some Christian believers within the United States. The school board had mandated the teaching of "intelligent design"—the notion that life is so complex that it must have been created by some higher power—alongside evolutionary biology. A federal judge subsequently struck down the school board's policy, arguing that it violated the separation of church and state, and board members who mandated teaching intelligent design were defeated for reelection.

Few observers of the controversy paused to reflect on the historical processes of the early modern era that provide a context for this contemporary debate. It was during those three centuries that Christianity first achieved a global presence, including, of course, its transplantation to the Americas. That a religion of Middle Eastern origin should come to dominate the Western Hemisphere surely ranks high among the strange twists of world history. At the same time, the Scientific Revolution was generating among European thinkers a very different approach to the world, and it too took root in the Americas. The relationship between religion and science in the West has been long and complex, and by no means always antagonistic. But the controversy in this small Pennsylvania community in the early twenty-first century illustrates the continuing tension, at least in some places, between these alternative ways of understanding the universe. That tension has been an important

---

The Virgin of Guadalupe: According to Mexican tradition, a dark-skinned Virgin Mary appeared to an indigenous peasant named Juan Diego in 1531, an apparition reflected in this Mexican painting from 1720. Belief in the Virgin of Guadalupe represented the incorporation of Catholicism into the emerging culture and identity of Mexico. (National Palace Mexico City/Gianni Dagli Orti/The Art Archive)

thread in the cultural history of the Christian world, and much of the rest of the world as well, over the past five centuries.

ALONGSIDE NEW EMPIRES AND NEW PATTERNS OF COMMERCE, the early modern centuries also witnessed novel cultural transformations that likewise connected distant peoples. Riding the currents of European empire building and commercial expansion, Christianity was solidly established in the Americas and the Philippines; far more modestly in Siberia, China, Japan, and India; and hardly at all within the vast and growing domains of Islam. A cultural tradition largely limited to Europe now became a genuine world religion, generating a multitude of cultural encounters. While this ancient faith was spreading, a new understanding of the universe and a new approach to knowledge were taking shape among European thinkers of the Scientific Revolution, giving rise to another kind of cultural encounter—that between science and religion. In certain respects, science was a new and competing worldview, and for some it was almost a new religion. It challenged the established outlooks of many European Christians and, over the next several centuries, of other religious or cultural traditions as well. In time, science became a defining feature of global modernity, achieving a worldwide acceptance that exceeded that of Christianity or any other religious tradition.

Although Europeans were central players in the globalization of Christianity and the emergence of modern science, they did not act alone in the cultural transformations of the early modern era. Asian, African, and Native American peoples largely determined how Christianity would be accepted, rejected, or transformed as it entered new cultural environments. Science emerged within an international and not simply a European context, and it met varying receptions in different parts of the world. Islam continued a long pattern of religious expansion and renewal, even as Christianity began to compete with it as a world religion. Buddhism maintained its hold in much of East Asia, as did Hinduism in South Asia and various smaller-scale religious traditions in Africa. And Europeans themselves were certainly affected by the many "new worlds" that they now encountered. The cultural interactions of the early modern era, in short, were not a "one-way street."

The Globalization of Christianity

Despite its Middle Eastern origins, Christianity was largely limited to Europe at the beginning of the early modern era. In 1500, the world of Christendom stretched from Spain and England in the west to Russia in the east, with small and beleaguered communities of various kinds in Egypt, Ethiopia, southern India, and Central Asia. Internally, Christianity was seriously divided between the Roman Catholics of Western and Central Europe and the Eastern Orthodox of Eastern Europe and Russia. Externally, it was very much on the defensive against an expansive Islam. Muslims had ousted Christian Crusaders from their toeholds in the Holy

Land by 1300, and with the Ottoman seizure of Constantinople in 1453, they had captured the prestigious capital of Eastern Orthodoxy. The Ottoman siege of Vienna in 1529 marked a Muslim advance into the heart of Central Europe. Except in Spain, which had recently been reclaimed for Christendom after centuries of Muslim rule, the future, it must have seemed, lay with Islam rather than Christianity.

Western Christendom Fragmented: The Protestant Reformation

As if these were not troubles enough, in the early sixteenth century the Protestant Reformation shattered the unity of Roman Catholic Christianity, which for the previous 1,000 years had provided the cultural and organizational foundation of Western European civilization. The Reformation began in 1517 when a German priest, Martin Luther, publicly invited debate about various abuses within the Roman Catholic Church by posting a document, known as the Ninety-five Theses, on the door of a church in Wittenberg. In itself, this was nothing new, for many people were critical of the luxurious life of the popes, the corruption and immorality of some clergy, the Church's selling of indulgences (said to remove the penalties for sin), and other aspects of church life and practice.

What made Luther's protest potentially revolutionary, however, was its theological basis. A troubled and brooding man who was anxious about his relationship with God, Luther recently had come to a new understanding of salvation, which held that it came through faith alone. Neither the good works of the sinner nor the sacraments of the Church had any bearing on the eternal destiny of the soul, for faith was a free gift of God, graciously granted to his needy and undeserving people. To Luther, the source of these beliefs, and of religious authority in general, was not the teaching of the Church, but the Bible alone, interpreted according to the individual's conscience. All of this challenged the authority of the Church and called into question the special position of the clerical hierarchy and of the pope in particular. In sixteenth-century Europe, this was the stuff of revolution.

Contrary to Luther's original intentions, his ideas ultimately provoked a massive schism within the world of Catholic Christendom, for they came to express a variety of political, economic, and social tensions as well as religious differences. Some kings and princes, many of whom had long disputed the political authority of the pope, found in

■ **Change**
In what ways did the Protestant Reformation transform European society, culture, and politics?

The Protestant Reformation This sixteenth-century painting by the well-known German artist Lucas Cranach the Elder shows Martin Luther and his supporters using a giant quill to write their demands for religious reform on a church door. It memorializes the posting of the Ninety-five Theses in 1517, which launched the Protestant Reformation. (Dr. Henning Schleifenbaum, Siegen, Germany/Visual Connection Archive)

$Snapshot$ **Catholic/Protestant Differences in the Sixteenth Century**

	Catholic	Protestant
Religious authority	Pope and church hierarchy	The Bible, as interpreted by individual Christians
Role of the pope	Ultimate authority in faith and doctrine	Denied the authority of the pope
Ordination of clergy	Apostolic succession: direct line between original apostles and all subsequently ordained clergy	Apostolic succession denied; ordination by individual congregations or denominations
Salvation	Importance of church sacraments as channels of God's grace	By faith alone; God's grace is freely and directly granted to believers
Status of Mary	Highly prominent, ranking just below Jesus; provides constant intercession for believers	Less prominent; denied Mary's intercession on behalf of the faithful
Prayer	To God, but often through or with Mary and saints	To God alone; no role for Mary and saints
Holy Communion	Transubstantiation: bread and wine become the actual body and blood of Christ	Denied transubstantiation; bread and wine have a spiritual or symbolic significance
Role of clergy	Generally celibate; sharp distinction between priests and laypeople; mediators between God and humankind	Ministers may marry; priesthood of all believers; clergy have different functions (to preach, administer sacraments) but no distinct spiritual status

these ideas a justification for their own independence and an opportunity to gain the lands and taxes previously held by the Church. In the Protestant idea that all vocations were of equal merit, middle-class urban dwellers found a new religious legitimacy for their growing role in society, since the Roman Catholic Church was associated in their eyes with the rural and feudal world of aristocratic privilege. For common people, who were offended by the corruption and luxurious living of some bishops, abbots, and popes, the new religious ideas served to express their opposition to the entire social order, particularly in a series of German peasant revolts in the 1520s.

Although large numbers of women were attracted to Protestantism, Reformation teachings and practices did not offer them a substantially greater role in the church or society. In Protestant-dominated areas, the veneration of Mary and female saints ended, leaving the male Christ figure as the sole object of worship. Protestant opposition to celibacy and monastic life closed the convents, which had offered some women an alternative to marriage. Nor were Protestants (except the Quakers) any more willing than Catholics to offer women an official role within their churches. The importance that Protestants gave to reading the Bible for oneself stimulated education and literacy for women, but given the emphasis on women as wives and mothers subject to male supervision, they had little opportunity to use that education outside of the family.

Reformation thinking spread quickly both within and beyond Germany, thanks in large measure to the recent invention of the printing press. Luther's many pamphlets and his translation of the New Testament into German were soon widely available. "God has appointed the [printing] Press to preach, whose voice the pope is never able to stop," declared one Reformation leader.[2] As the movement spread to France, Switzerland, England, and elsewhere, however, it also splintered, amoeba-like, into a variety of competing Protestant churches—Lutheran, Calvinist, Anglican, Quaker, Anabaptist—many of which subsequently subdivided, producing a bewildering array of Protestant denominations. Each was distinctive, but none gave allegiance to Rome or the pope.

Thus to the divided societies and the fractured political system of Europe was now added the potent brew of religious difference, operating both within and between states (see Map 16.1). For more than thirty years (1562–1598), French society was torn by violence between Catholics and the Protestant minority known as Huguenots. On a single day, August 24, 1572, Catholic mobs in Paris massacred some 3,000 Huguenots, and thousands more perished in provincial towns in the weeks that followed. Finally, a war-weary monarch, Henry IV, issued the Edict of Nantes (1598), which granted a substantial measure of religious toleration to French Protestants, though with the intention that they would soon return to the Catholic Church. The culmination of European religious conflict took shape in the Thirty Years' War (1618–1648), a Catholic-Protestant struggle that began in the Holy Roman Empire but eventually engulfed most of Europe. It was a horrendously destructive war, during which, scholars estimate, between 15 and 30 percent of the German population perished from violence, famine, or disease. Finally, the Peace of Westphalia (1648) brought the conflict to an end, with some reshuffling of boundaries and an agreement that each state was sovereign, authorized to control religious affairs within its own territory. Whatever religious unity Catholic Europe had once enjoyed was now permanently broken.

The Protestant breakaway, combined with reformist tendencies within the Catholic Church itself, provoked a Catholic Counter-Reformation. In the Council of Trent (1545–1563), Catholics clarified and reaffirmed their unique doctrines and practices, such as the authority of the pope, priestly celibacy, the veneration of saints and relics, and the importance of church tradition and good works, all of which Protestants had rejected. Moreover, they set about correcting the abuses and corruption that had stimulated the Protestant movement in the first place by

Map 16.1 Reformation Europe in the Sixteenth Century

The rise of Protestantism added yet another set of religious divisions, both within and between states, to European Christendom, which was already sharply divided between the Roman Catholic Church and the Eastern Orthodox Church.

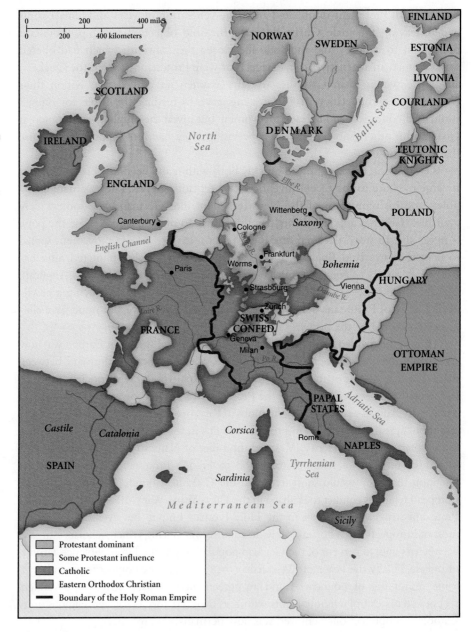

placing a new emphasis on the education of priests and their supervision by bishops. A crackdown on dissidents included the censorship of books, fines, exile, penitence, and occasionally the burning of heretics. Renewed attention was given to individual spirituality and personal piety. New religious orders, such as the Society of Jesus (Jesuits), provided a dedicated brotherhood of priests committed to the renewal of the Catholic Church and its extension abroad.

Although the Reformation was profoundly religious, it encouraged a skeptical attitude toward authority and tradition, for it had, after all, successfully challenged the immense prestige and power of the pope and the established Church. Protestant reformers fostered religious individualism as people were now encouraged to read and interpret the scriptures for themselves and to seek salvation without the mediation of the Church. For some in the centuries that followed, that skepticism and the habit of thinking independently were turned against revealed religion itself. Thus the Protestant Reformation opened some space for new directions in European intellectual life.

In short, it was a more highly fragmented but also a renewed and revitalized Christianity that established itself around the world in the several centuries after 1500.

Christianity Outward Bound

Christianity motivated European political and economic expansion and also benefited from it. The resolutely Catholic Spanish and Portuguese both viewed their movement overseas as a continuation of a long crusading tradition, which only recently had completed the liberation of their countries from Muslim control. When Vasco da Gama's small fleet landed in India in 1498, local authorities understandably asked, "What brought you hither?" The reply: they had come "in search of Christians and of spices."[3] Likewise, Columbus, upon arriving in the Americas, expressed the no doubt sincere hope that the people "might become Christians," even as he promised his Spanish patrons an abundant harvest of gold, spice, cotton, aloe wood, and slaves.[4] Neither man sensed any contradiction or hypocrisy in this blending of religious and material concerns.

■ **Connection**

How was European imperial expansion related to the spread of Christianity?

If religion drove and justified European ventures abroad, it is difficult to imagine the globalization of Christianity without the support of empire. Colonial settlers and traders, of course, brought their faith with them and sought to replicate it in their newly conquered homelands. New England Puritans, for example, planted a distinctive Protestant version of Christianity in North America, with an emphasis on education, moral purity, personal conversion, civic responsibility, and little tolerance for competing expressions of the faith. They did not show much interest in converting native peoples but sought rather to push them out of their ancestral territories. It was missionaries, mostly Catholic, who actively spread the Christian message beyond European communities. Organized in missionary orders such as the Dominicans, Franciscans, and Jesuits, Portuguese missionaries took the lead in Africa and Asia, while Spanish and French missionaries were most prominent in the Americas. Missionaries of the Russian Orthodox Church likewise accompanied the expansion of the Russian Empire across Siberia, where priests and monks ministered to Russian settlers and trappers, who often donated their first sable furs to a church or monastery.

Missionaries had their greatest success in Spanish America and in the Philippines, areas that shared two critical elements beyond their colonization by Spain. Most

Japanese Christian Martyrs
Christianity was beginning to take root in sixteenth-century Japan, but intensive persecution by Japanese authorities in the early seventeenth century largely ended that process. This monument was later erected in memory of twenty-six martyrs, Japanese and European alike, who were executed during this suppression of Christianity. (Photo Agency MH Martin Hladik, Photographer)

■ **Connection**
In what ways was European Christianity assimilated into the Native American cultures of Spanish America?

important, perhaps, was an overwhelming European presence, experienced variously as military conquest, colonial settlement, missionary activity, forced labor, social disruption, and disease. Surely it must have seemed as if the old gods had been bested and that any possible future lay with the powerful religion of the European invaders. A second common factor was the absence of a literate world religion in these two regions. Throughout the modern era, peoples solidly rooted in Confucian, Buddhist, Hindu, or Islamic traditions proved far more resistant to the Christian message than those who practiced more localized, small-scale, orally based polytheistic religions.

Conversion and Adaptation in Spanish America

Spanish America and China illustrate the difference between those societies in which Christianity became widely practiced and those that largely rejected it. Both cases, however, represent major cultural encounters of a kind that was becoming more frequent as European expansion brought the Christian faith to distant peoples with very different cultural traditions.

The decisive conquest of the Aztec and Inca empires and all that followed from it—disease, population collapse, loss of land to Europeans, forced labor, resettlement into more compact villages—created a setting in which the religion of the victors took hold in Spanish American colonies. Europeans saw their political and military success as a demonstration of the power of the Christian God. Native American peoples generally agreed, and by 1700 or earlier the vast majority had been baptized and saw themselves in some respects as Christians. After all, other conquerors such as the Aztecs and the Incas had always imposed their gods in some fashion on defeated peoples. It made sense, both practically and spiritually, to affiliate with the Europeans' God, saints, rites, and rituals. Many millions accepted baptism, contributed to the construction of village churches, attended services, and embraced images of Mary and other saints.

Earlier conquerors, however, had made no attempt to eradicate local deities and religious practices. The flexibility and inclusiveness of Mesoamerican and Andean religions had made it possible for subject people to accommodate the gods of their new rulers while maintaining their own traditions. But Europeans were different. They claimed an exclusive religious truth and sought the utter destruction of local gods and everything associated with them. Operating within a Spanish colonial regime that actively encouraged conversion, missionaries often proceeded by persuasion and patient teaching. At times, though, their frustration with the persistence of "idolatry, superstition, and error" boiled over into violent campaigns designed to uproot old religions once and for all. In 1535, the bishop of Mexico boasted that he had destroyed 500 pagan shrines and 20,000 idols. During the seventeenth and early eighteenth centuries, church authorities in the Andean region periodically launched movements of "extirpation," designed to fatally undermine native religion. They smashed religious images and ritual objects, publicly urinated on native "idols," desecrated the remains of ancestors, held religious trials and "processions of shame" aimed at humiliating offenders, and flogged "idolaters."[5]

Occasionally, overt resistance erupted. One such example was the religious revivalist movement in central Peru in the 1560s, known as Taki Onqoy ("dancing sickness"). Possessed by the spirits of local gods, or *huacas*, traveling dancers and teachers predicted that an alliance of Andean deities would soon overcome the Christian God, inflict the intruding Europeans with the same diseases that they had brought to the Americas, and restore the world of the Andes to an imagined earlier harmony. They called on native peoples to cut off all contact with the Spanish, to reject Christian worship, and to return to traditional practices. "The world has turned about," one member declared, "and this time God and the Spaniards [will be] defeated and all the Spaniards killed and their cities drowned; and the sea will rise and overwhelm them, so that there will remain no memory of them."[6]

More common than such frontal attacks on Christianity, which were quickly smashed by colonial authorities, were efforts at blending two religious traditions, reinterpreting Christian practices within an Andean framework, and incorporating local elements into an emerging Andean Christianity. Even female dancers in the Taki Onqoy movement sometimes took the names of Christian saints, seeking to appropriate for themselves the religious power of Christian figures. Within Andean Christian communities, people might offer the blood of a llama to strengthen a village church or make a cloth covering for the Virgin Mary and a shirt for an image of a huaca with the same material. Although the state cults of the Incas faded away, missionary attacks did not succeed in eliminating the influence of local huacas. Images and holy sites might be destroyed, but the souls of the huacas remained, and their representatives gained prestige. One resilient Andean resident inquired of a Jesuit missionary: "Father, are you tired of taking our idols from us? Take away that mountain if you can, since that is the God I worship."[7]

In Mexico as well, an immigrant Christianity was assimilated into patterns of local culture. Parishes were organized largely around precolonial towns or regions. Churches built on or near the sites of old temples became the focus of community identity. *Cofradias*, church-based associations of laypeople, organized community processions and festivals and made provision for a proper funeral and burial for their members. Central to an emerging Mexican Christianity were the saints who closely paralleled the functions of precolonial gods. Saints were imagined as parents of the local community and the true owners of its land, and their images were paraded through the streets on the occasion of great feasts and were collected by individual households. Although parish priests were almost always Spanish, the *fiscal*, or leader of the church staff, was a native Christian of great local prestige, who carried on the traditions and role of earlier religious specialists.

Throughout the colonial period and beyond, many Mexican Christians also took part in rituals derived from the past, with little sense that this was incompatible with Christian practice. Incantations to various gods for good fortune in hunting, farming, or healing; sacrifices of self-bleeding; offerings to the sun; divination; the use of hallucinogenic drugs—all of these rituals provided spiritual assistance in those areas of everyday life not directly addressed by Christian rites. Conversely, these practices also showed signs of Christian influence. Wax candles, normally used in Christian services, might now appear in front of a stone image of a precolonial god. The anger of a neglected saint, rather than that of a traditional god, might explain someone's illness and require offerings, celebration, or a new covering to regain his or her favor.[8] In such ways did Christianity take root in the new cultural environments of Spanish America, but it was a distinctly Andean or Mexican Christianity, not merely a copy of the Spanish version.

An Asian Comparison: China and the Jesuits

■ **Comparison**

Why were missionary efforts to spread Christianity so much less successful in China than in Spanish America?

The Chinese encounter with Christianity was very different from that of Native Americans in Spain's New World empire. The most obvious difference was the political context. The peoples of Spanish America had been defeated, their societies thoroughly disrupted, and their cultural confidence sorely shaken. China, on the other hand, encountered European Christianity between the sixteenth and eighteenth centuries during the powerful and prosperous Ming (1368–1644) and Qing (1644–1912) dynasties. Although the transition between these two dynasties occasioned several decades of internal conflict, at no point was China's political independence or cultural integrity threatened by the handful of European missionaries and traders operating in the country.

The reality of a strong, independent, confident China required a different missionary strategy, for Europeans needed the permission of Chinese authorities to operate in the country. Whereas Spanish missionaries working in a colonial setting sought primarily to convert the masses, the leading missionary order in China, the Jesuits, took deliberate aim at the official Chinese elite. Following the lead of their most famous missionary, Matteo Ricci (in China 1582–1610), many Jesuits learned Chinese, became thoroughly acquainted with classical Confucian texts, and dressed like Chinese scholars. Initially, they downplayed their mission to convert and instead emphasized their interest in exchanging ideas and learning from China's ancient culture. As highly educated men, the Jesuits carried the recent secular knowledge of Europe—science, technology, mapmaking—to an audience of curious Chinese scholars. In presenting Christian teachings, Jesuits were at pains to be respectful of Chinese culture, pointing out parallels between Confucianism and

Christianity rather than portraying it as something new and foreign. They chose to define Chinese rituals honoring the emperor or venerating ancestors as secular or civil observances rather than as religious practices that had to be abandoned. Such efforts to accommodate Chinese culture contrast sharply with the frontal attacks on Native American religions in the Spanish Empire.

The religious and cultural outcomes of the missionary enterprise likewise differed greatly in the two regions. Nothing approaching the mass conversion to Christianity of Native American peoples took place in China. During the sixteenth and seventeenth centuries, a modest number of Chinese scholars and officials—who were attracted by the personal lives of the missionaries, by their interest in Western science, and by the moral certainty that Christianity offered—did become Christians. Jesuit missionaries found favor for a time at the Chinese imperial court, where their mathematical, astronomical, technological, and mapmaking skills rendered them useful. For more than a century, they were appointed to head the Chinese Bureau of Astronomy. Among ordinary people, Christianity spread very modestly amid tales of miracles attributed to the Christian God, while missionary teachings about "eternal life" sounded to some like Daoist prescriptions for immortality. At most, though, missionary efforts over the course of some 250 years (1550–1800) resulted in 200,000 to 300,000 converts, a minuscule number in a Chinese population approaching 300 million by 1800. What explains the very limited acceptance of Christianity in early modern China?

Fundamentally, the missionaries offered little that the Chinese really needed. Confucianism for the elites and Buddhism, Daoism, and a multitude of Chinese gods and spirits at the local level adequately supplied the spiritual needs of most Chinese. Furthermore, it became increasingly clear that Christianity was an "all or nothing" faith that required converts to abandon much of traditional Chinese culture. Christian monogamy,

Jesuits in China

In this seventeenth-century Dutch engraving, two Jesuit missionaries hold a map of China. Their mapmaking skills were among the reasons that the Jesuits were initially welcomed among the educated elite of that country. (Frontispiece to *China Illustrated* by Athanasius Kircher [1601–80] 1667 [engraving], Dutch School, [17th century]/Private Collection, The Stapleton Collection/The Bridgeman Art Library)

for example, seemed to require Chinese men to put away their concubines. What would happen to these deserted women?

By the early eighteenth century, the papacy and competing missionary orders came to oppose the Jesuit policy of accommodation. The pope claimed authority over Chinese Christians and declared that sacrifices to Confucius and the veneration of ancestors were "idolatry" and thus forbidden to Christians. The pope's pronouncements represented an unacceptable challenge to the authority of the emperor and an affront to Chinese culture. In 1715, an outraged Emperor Kangxi wrote:

> I ask myself how these uncultivated Westerners dare to speak of the great precepts of China. . . . [T]heir doctrine is of the same kind as the little heresies of the Buddhist and Taoist monks. . . . These are the greatest absurdities that have ever been seen. As from now I forbid the Westerners to spread their doctrine in China; that will spare us a lot of trouble.[9]

This represented a major turning point in the relationship of Christian missionaries and Chinese society. Many were subsequently expelled, and missionaries lost favor at court.

In other ways as well, missionaries played into the hands of their Chinese opponents. Their willingness to work under the Manchurian Qing dynasty, which came to power in 1644, discredited them with those Chinese scholars who viewed the Qing as uncivilized foreigners and their rule in China as disgraceful and illegitimate. Missionaries' reputation as miracle workers further damaged their standing as men of science and rationality, for elite Chinese often regarded miracles and supernatural religion as superstitions, fit only for the uneducated masses. Some viewed the Christian ritual of Holy Communion as a kind of cannibalism. Others came to see missionaries as potentially subversive, for various Christian groups met in secret, and such religious sects had often provided the basis for peasant rebellion. Nor did it escape Chinese notice that European Christians had taken over the Philippines and that their warships were active in the Indian Ocean. Perhaps the missionaries, with their great interest in maps, were spies for these aggressive foreigners. All of this contributed to the general failure of Christianity to secure a prominent presence in China.

Persistence and Change in Afro-Asian Cultural Traditions

Although Europeans were central players in the globalization of Christianity, theirs was not the only expanding or transformed culture of the early modern era. African religious ideas and practices, for example, accompanied slaves to the Americas. Common African forms of religious revelation—divination, dream interpretation, visions, spirit possession—found a place in the Africanized versions of Christianity that emerged in the New World. Europeans frequently perceived these practices as evidence of sorcery, witchcraft, or even devil worship and tried to suppress them.

Nonetheless, syncretic (blended) religions such as Vodou in Haiti, Santeria in Cuba, and Candomble and Macumba in Brazil persisted. They derived from various West African traditions and featured drumming, ritual dancing, animal sacrifice, and spirit possession. Over time, they incorporated Christian beliefs and practices such as church attendance, the search for salvation, and the use of candles and crucifixes and often identified their various spirits or deities with Catholic saints.

Expansion and Renewal in the Islamic World

The early modern era likewise witnessed the continuation of the "long march of Islam" across the Afro-Asian world. In sub-Saharan Africa, in the eastern and western wings of India, and in Central and Southeast Asia, the expansion of the Islamic frontier, a process already almost 1,000 years in the making, extended farther still. Conversion to Islam generally did not mean a sudden abandonment of old religious practices in favor of the new. Rather it was more often a matter of "assimilating Islamic rituals, cosmologies, and literatures into . . . local religious systems."[10]

■ **Explanation**
What accounts for the continued spread of Islam in the early modern era and for the emergence of reform or renewal movements within the Islamic world?

Continued Islamization usually was not the product of conquering armies and expanding empires. It depended instead on wandering Muslim holy men, Islamic scholars, and itinerant traders, none of whom posed a threat to local rulers. In fact, such people often were useful to those rulers and their village communities. They offered literacy in Arabic, established informal schools, provided protective charms containing passages from the Quran, served as advisers to local authorities and healers to the sick, often intermarried with local people, and generally did not insist that new converts give up their older practices. What they offered, in short, was connection to the wider, prestigious, prosperous world of Islam. Islamization extended modestly even to the Americas, where enslaved African Muslims planted their faith, particularly in Brazil. There Muslims led a number of slave revolts in the early nineteenth century.

To more orthodox Muslims, this religious syncretism, which accompanied Islamization almost everywhere, became increasingly offensive, even heretical. Such sentiments played an important role in movements of religious renewal and reform that emerged throughout the vast Islamic world of the eighteenth century. Scholars and religious leaders frequently called attention to the ways in which the practice of Islam had come to deviate from the original teachings of Muhammad and the Quran. For example, in India, which was governed by the Muslim Mughal Empire, religious resistance to official policies that accommodated Hindus found concrete expression during the reign of the emperor Aurangzeb (1658–1707) (see Chapter 14). A series of religious wars in West Africa during the eighteenth and early nineteenth centuries took aim at corrupt Islamic practices and the rulers, Muslim and non-Muslim alike, who permitted them. In Southeast and Central Asia, tension grew between practitioners of localized and blended versions of Islam and those who sought to purify such practices in the name of a more authentic and universal faith.

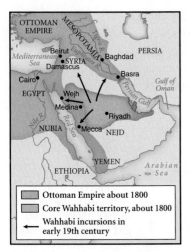

The Expansion of Wahhabi Islam

Map legend:
- Ottoman Empire about 1800
- Core Wahhabi territory, about 1800
- ← Wahhabi incursions in early 19th century

The most well known and widely visible of these Islamic renewal movements took place during the mid-eighteenth century in Arabia itself, where the religion had been born 1,000 years earlier. A young Muslim theologian, Abd al-Wahhab (1703–1792), argued that the declining fortunes of the Islamic world were the result of a gradual process of decay that had crept in over the centuries, as Muslims allowed themselves to be drawn away from the essentials of the faith. He was particularly upset by common religious practices in central Arabia that seemed to him idolatry—the widespread veneration of Sufi saints and their tombs, the adoration of natural sites, and even the respect paid to Muhammad's tomb at Mecca. All of this was a dilution of the absolute monotheism of authentic Islam.

Abd al-Wahhab began preaching among the tribes of the Arabian Desert, calling for a return to a doctrinaire Islam with an austere and puritanical lifestyle, in strict accordance with the sharia (Islamic law). When in the 1740s he joined forces with Muhammad Ibn Saud, a sympathetic local chieftain, the movement took on a political dimension and soon led to the creation of a state. Within that state, women were expected to subject themselves strictly to the traditional patronage of husbands and male relatives. Offending tombs were razed; "idols" were eliminated; books on logic were destroyed; the use of tobacco, hashish, and musical instruments was forbidden; and certain taxes not authorized by religious teaching were abolished. By the early nineteenth century, this new reformist state encompassed much of central Arabia, with Mecca itself coming under Wahhabi control in 1806. Although an Egyptian army broke the power of the Wahhabis in 1818, the movement's influence continued to spread across the Islamic world.

Together with the ongoing expansion of the religion, these movements of reform and renewal signaled the continuing cultural vitality of the "abode of Islam," even as the European presence on the world stage assumed larger dimensions. In the nineteenth and twentieth centuries, such movements persisted and became associated with resistance to the political, military, and cultural intrusion of the European West into the affairs of the Islamic world.

China: New Directions in an Old Tradition

■ **Comparison**

In what ways did Asian cultural changes in the early modern era parallel those of Europe, and in what ways were they different?

Neither China nor India experienced cultural or religious change as dramatic as that of the Reformation in Europe, nor did Confucian or Hindu cultures during the early modern era spread widely, as did Christianity and Islam. Nonetheless, neither of these traditions remained static. As in Christian Europe, challenges to established orthodoxies in China and India emerged as commercial and urban life, as well as political change, fostered new thinking.

China during the Ming and Qing dynasties continued to operate broadly within a Confucian framework, enriched now by the insights of Buddhism and Daoism to generate a system of thought called Neo-Confucianism. Chinese Ming dynasty rulers, in their aversion to the despised Mongols, embraced and actively supported this native Confucian tradition, whereas the foreign Manchu or Qing rulers did so in order to woo Chinese intellectuals to support the new dynasty. Within this context, a considerable amount of controversy, debate, and new thinking emerged during the early modern era.

During late Ming times, for example, the influential thinker Wang Yangmin (1472–1529) argued that truth and moral knowledge were innate to the human person. Thus anyone could achieve a virtuous life by introspection, without the extended education and constant striving for improvement that traditional Confucianism prescribed for an elite class of "gentlemen." Such ideas figured prominently among Confucian scholars of the sixteenth century, although critics later contended that the individualism that such thinking promoted had undermined the Ming dynasty and contributed to China's conquest by the foreign Manchus. Some Chinese Buddhists as well sought to make their religion more accessible to ordinary people, by suggesting that laypeople at home could undertake practices similar to those performed by monks in monasteries. Withdrawal from the world was not necessary for enlightenment. This kind of moral or religious individualism bore some similarity to the thinking of Martin Luther, who argued that individuals could seek salvation by "faith alone," without the assistance of a priestly hierarchy.

Another new direction in Chinese elite culture took shape in a movement known as *kaozheng*, or "research based on evidence." Intended to "seek truth from facts," kaozheng was critical of the unfounded speculation of conventional Confucian philosophy and instead emphasized the importance of verification, precision, accuracy, and rigorous analysis in all fields of inquiry. During the late Ming years, this emphasis generated works dealing with agriculture, medicine, pharmacology, botany, craft techniques, and more. In the Qing era, kaozheng was associated with a recovery and critical analysis of ancient historical documents, which sometimes led to sharp criticism of Neo-Confucian orthodoxy. It was a genuinely scientific approach to knowledge, but it was applied more to the study of the past than to the natural world of astronomy, physics, or anatomy, as in the West.

While such matters occupied the intellectual elite of China, in the cities a lively popular culture emerged among the less well educated. For city-dwellers, plays, paintings, short stories, and especially novels provided diversion and entertainment that were a step up from what could be found in teahouses and wine shops. Numerous "how-to" painting manuals allowed a larger public to participate in this favorite Chinese art form. Even though Confucian scholars disdained popular fiction, a vigorous printing industry responded to the growing demand for exciting novels. The most famous was Cao Xueqin's mid-eighteenth-century novel *The Dream of the Red Chamber*, a huge book that contained 120 chapters and some 400 characters, most of them women. It explored the social life of an eighteenth-century elite family with connections to the Chinese court.

India: Bridging the Hindu/Muslim Divide

In a largely Hindu India, ruled by the Muslim Mughal Empire, several significant cultural departures took shape in the early modern era that brought Hindus and Muslims together in new forms of religious expression. One was the flourishing of a devotional form of Hinduism known as *bhakti*. Through songs, prayers, dances, poetry, and rituals, devotees sought to achieve union with one or another of India's many deities. Appealing especially to women, the bhakti movement provided an avenue for social criticism. Its practitioners often set aside caste distinctions and disregarded the detailed rituals of the Brahmin priests in favor of direct contact with the divine. This emphasis had much in common with the mystical Sufi form of Islam and helped blur the distinction between these two traditions in India.

Among the most beloved of bhakti poets was Mirabai (1498–1547), a high-caste woman from northern India who abandoned her upper-class family and conventional Hindu practice. Upon her husband's death, tradition asserts, she declined to burn herself on his funeral pyre (a practice known as *sati*). She further offended caste restrictions by taking as her guru (religious teacher) an old untouchable shoemaker. To visit him, she apparently tied her saris together and climbed down the castle walls at night. Then she would wash his aged feet and drink the water from these ablutions. Much of her poetry deals with her yearning for union with Krishna, a Hindu deity she regarded as her husband, lover, and lord.

> What I paid was my social body, my town body, my family body, and all my inherited jewels.
> Mirabai says: The Dark One [Krishna] is my husband now.[11]

Yet another major cultural change that blended Islam and Hinduism emerged with the growth of Sikhism as a new and distinctive religious tradition in the Punjab region of northern India. Its founder, Guru Nanak (1469–1539), had been involved in the bhakti movement but came to believe that "there is no Hindu; there is no Muslim; only God." His teachings and those of subsequent gurus also set aside caste distinctions and untouchability and ended the seclusion of women, while proclaiming the "brotherhood of all mankind" as well as the essential equality

Guru Nanak
In this early-eighteenth-century manuscript painting, Guru Nanak, the founder of Sikhism, and his constant companion Mardana (with a musical instrument) encounter a robber (the man with a sword) along the road. According to the story accompanying the painting, that experience persuaded the robber to abandon his wicked ways and become a follower of the Sikh path. (© British Library Board)

of men and women. Drawing converts from Punjabi peasants and merchants, both Muslim and Hindu, the Sikhs gradually became a separate religious community. They developed their own sacred book, known as the Guru Granth (teacher book); created a central place of worship and pilgrimage in the Golden Temple of Amritsar; and pre-scribed certain dress requirements for men, including keeping hair and beards uncut, wearing a turban, and carrying a short sword. During the seventeenth century, Sikhs encountered hostility from both the Mughal Empire and some of their Hindu neigh-bors. In response, Sikhism evolved from a peaceful religious movement, blending Hindu and Muslim elements, into a militant community whose military skills were highly valued by the British when they took over India in the late eighteenth century.

A New Way of Thinking: The Birth of Modern Science

While some Europeans were actively attempting to spread the Christian faith to distant corners of the world, others were nurturing an understanding of the cos-mos very much at odds with traditional Christian teaching. These were the makers of Europe's Scientific Revolution, a vast intellectual and cultural transformation that took place between the mid-sixteenth and early eighteenth centuries. No longer would men of science rely on the external authority of divinely revealed scripture or the speculations of ancient philosophers or the received wisdom of cul-tural tradition. Instead a combination of careful observations, controlled experi-ments, and the formulation of general laws, expressed in mathematical terms, became the standard means of obtaining knowledge and understanding in every domain of life. Those who created this revolution—Copernicus from Poland, Galileo from Italy, Descartes from France, Newton from England, and many oth-ers—saw themselves as departing radically from older ways of thinking. They were the "moderns" combating the "ancients." "The old rubbish must be thrown away," wrote a seventeenth-century English scientist. "These are the days that must lay a new Foundation of a more magnificent Philosophy."[12]

The long-term significance of the Scientific Revolution can hardly be overes-timated. Within early modern Europe, it fundamentally altered ideas about the place of humankind within the cosmos and sharply challenged both the teachings and the authority of the Church. Over the past several centuries, it has substantially eroded religious belief and practice in the West. When applied to the affairs of human society, scientific ways of thinking challenged ancient social hierarchies and political systems and played a role in the revolutionary upheavals of the modern era. But science also was used to legitimize racial and gender inequalities, by defining people of color and women as inferior by nature. When married to the technolog-ical innovations of the Industrial Revolution, science fostered both the marvels of modern production and the horrors of modern means of destruction. By the twen-tieth century, science had become so widespread that it largely lost its association with European culture and became the chief symbol of global modernity.

The Question of Origins: Why Europe?

■ Comparison
Why did the Scientific Revolution occur in Europe rather than in China or the Islamic world?

Why did that breakthrough occur first in Europe and during the early modern era? The realm of Islam, after all, had generated the most advanced science in the world during the centuries between 800 and 1400. Arab scholars could boast of remarkable achievements in mathematics, astronomy, optics, and medicine, and their libraries far exceeded those of Europe.[13] And what of China? Its elite culture of Confucianism was both sophisticated and secular, less burdened by religious dogma than in the Christian or Islamic worlds; its technological accomplishments and economic growth were unmatched anywhere in the several centuries after 1000. In neither civilization, however, did these achievements lead to the kind of intellectual breakthrough that occurred in Europe.

Europe's historical development as a reinvigorated and fragmented civilization (see Chapter 10) arguably gave rise to conditions uniquely favorable to the scientific enterprise. By the twelfth and thirteenth centuries, Europeans had evolved a legal system that guaranteed a measure of independence for a variety of institutions—the Church, towns and cities, guilds, professional associations, and universities. This legal revolution was based on the idea of a "corporation," a collective group of people that was treated as a unit, a legal person, with certain rights to regulate and control its own members. Thus the Roman Catholic Church achieved some measure of autonomy from secular authorities, making Europe quite different from the Islamic world, where the separation of religious and secular law gained little traction.

Most important for the development of science in the West was the autonomy of its emerging universities. By 1215, the University of Paris was recognized as a "corporation of masters and scholars," which could admit and expel students, establish courses of instruction, and grant a "license to teach" to its faculty. Such universities—for example, in Paris, Bologna, Oxford, Cambridge, and Salamanca—became "neutral zones of intellectual autonomy" in which scholars could pursue their studies in relative freedom from the dictates of church or state authorities. Within them, the study of the natural order began to slowly separate itself from philosophy and theology and to gain a distinct identity. Their curricula featured "a basically scientific core of readings and lectures" that drew heavily on the writings of the Greek thinker Aristotle, which had only recently become available to Western Europeans. Most of the major figures in the Scientific Revolution had been trained in and were affiliated with these universities.

In the Islamic world, by contrast, science was patronized by a variety of local authorities, but it occurred largely outside the formal system of higher education. Within colleges known as madrassas, Quranic studies and religious law held the central place, whereas philosophy and natural science were viewed with great suspicion. To religious scholars, the Quran held all wisdom, and scientific thinking might well challenge it. An earlier openness to free inquiry and religious toleration was increasingly replaced by a disdain for scientific and philosophical inquiry, for it seemed to lead only to uncertainty and confusion. "May God protect us from useless knowledge" was a saying that reflected this outlook. Nor did Chinese authorities permit independent institutions of higher learning in which scholars could conduct their studies in relative freedom. Instead Chinese education focused on preparing for a rigidly defined set of civil service examinations and emphasized the humanistic and moral texts of classical Confucianism. "The pursuit of scientific subjects," one recent historian concluded, "was thereby relegated to the margins of Chinese society."[14]

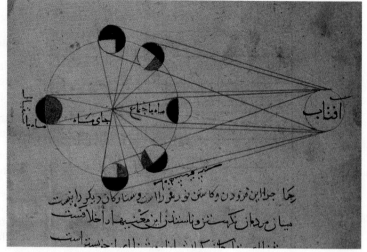

Muslim Astronomy and the Scientific Revolution
This diagram of the eclipses of the moon by the eleventh-century Muslim mathematician and astronomer al-Biruni is a reminder of Muslim scientific achievements, some of which stimulated European scientific thinking. (Roland and Sabrina Michaud/Rapho/Eyedea)

Beyond its distinctive institutional development, Western Europe was in a position to draw extensively upon the knowledge of other cultures, especially that of the Islamic world. Arab medical texts, astronomical research, and translations of Greek classics played a major role in the birth of European natural philosophy (as science was then called) between 1000 and 1500. In constructing his proofs for a sun-centered solar system, Copernicus in the sixteenth century almost certainly drew upon astronomical work and mathematical formulations undertaken 200 to 300 years earlier in the Islamic world, particularly at the famous Muslim observatory of Maragha in present-day Iran.

In the sixteenth through the eighteenth centuries, Europeans found themselves at the center of a massive new exchange of information as they became aware of lands, peoples, plants, animals, societies, and religions from around the world. This tidal wave of new knowledge, uniquely available to Europeans, clearly shook up older ways of thinking and opened the way to new conceptions of the world. The sixteenth-century Italian doctor, mathematician, and writer Girolamo Cardano (1501–1576) clearly expressed this sense of wonderment: "The most unusual [circumstance of my life] is that I was born in this century in which the whole world became known; whereas the ancients were familiar with but a little more than a third part of it." He worried, however, that amid this explosion of knowledge, "certainties will be exchanged for uncertainties."[15] It was precisely those uncertainties—skepticism about established views—that provided such a fertile cultural ground for the emergence of modern science.

Science as Cultural Revolution

Before the Scientific Revolution, educated Europeans held a view of the world that derived from Aristotle, perhaps the greatest of the ancient Greek philosophers, and from Ptolemy, a Greco-Egyptian mathematician and astronomer who lived in

■ Change
What was revolutionary about the Scientific Revolution?

Snapshot   **Major Thinkers and Achievements of the Scientific Revolution**

Thinker/Scientist	Achievements
Nicolaus Copernicus (Polish; 1473–1543)	Posited that sun is at the center of solar system, earth rotates on its axis, and earth and planets revolve around the sun
Andreas Vesalius (Flemish; 1514–1564)	"Father of anatomy"; made detailed drawings of human body based on dissection
Francis Bacon (English; 1561–1626)	Emphasized observation and experimentation as the key to modern science
Galileo Galilei (Italian; 1564–1642)	Developed an improved telescope; discovered sunspots, mountains on the moon, and Jupiter's moons; performed experimental work on the velocity of falling objects
Johannes Kepler (German; 1571–1630)	Posited that planets follow elliptical, not circular, orbits; described laws of planetary motion
William Harvey (English; 1578–1657)	Described the circulation of the blood and the function of the heart
René Descartes (French; 1596–1650)	Emphasized the importance of mathematics and logical deduction in understanding the physical world; invented analytical geometry
Isaac Newton (English; 1642–1727)	Synthesized earlier findings around the concept of universal gravitation; invented calculus; formulated concept of inertia and laws of motion

Alexandria during the second century C.E. To medieval European thinkers, the earth was stationary and at the center of the universe, and around it revolved the sun, moon, and stars embedded in ten spheres of transparent crystal. This understanding coincided well with the religious purpose of the Catholic Church because the attention of the entire universe was centered on the earth, where the drama of salvation took place, and on its human inhabitants. It was a universe of divine purpose, with angels guiding the hierarchically arranged spheres along their way while God watched over the whole from his realm beyond the spheres. The Scientific Revolution was revolutionary because it fundamentally challenged this understanding of the universe.

The initial breakthrough came from the Polish mathematician and astronomer Nicolaus Copernicus, whose famous book *On the Revolutions of the Heavenly Spheres* was published in the year of his death, 1543. Its essential argument was that "at the middle of all things lies the sun" and that the earth, like the other planets, revolved around it. Thus the earth was no longer unique or at the center of God's attention.

Other European scientists built on Copernicus's central insight, and some even argued that other inhabited worlds and other kinds of humans existed. Less speculatively, in the early seventeenth century Johannes Kepler, a German mathematician, showed that the planets followed elliptical orbits, undermining the ancient belief that they moved in perfect circles. The Italian Galileo Galilei developed an improved telescope, with which he observed sunspots, or blemishes, moving across the face of the sun. This called into question the traditional notion that no change or imperfection marred the heavenly bodies. His discovery of the moons of Jupiter and many new stars suggested a cosmos far larger than the bounded or finite universe of traditional astronomy. Some thinkers began to discuss the notion of an infinite universe in which humankind occupied a mere speck of dust in an unimaginable vastness. The French mathematician and philosopher Blaise Pascal (1623–1662) perhaps spoke for many when he wrote: "The eternal silence of infinite space frightens me."[16]

The culmination of the Scientific Revolution came in the work of Sir Isaac Newton, the Englishman who formulated the modern laws of motion and mechanics, which were scarcely modified until the twentieth century. Central to Newton's thinking was the concept of universal gravitation. "All bodies whatsoever," Newton declared, "are endowed with a principle of mutual gravitation."[17] Here was the grand unifying idea of early modern science. The radical implication of this view was that the heavens and the earth, long regarded as separate and distinct spheres, were not so different after all, for the motion of a cannonball on earth or the falling of an apple from a tree obeyed the same natural laws that governed the orbiting planets.

By the time Newton died, the view of the physical universe held by educated Europeans had substantially changed. It was no longer propelled by angels and spirits but functioned on its own according to timeless principles that could be described mathematically. In Kepler's view, "the machine of the universe is not similar to a divine animated being but similar to a clock."[18] Furthermore, it was a machine that regulated itself, requiring neither God nor angels to account for its normal operation. Knowledge of that universe could be obtained through human reason alone—by observation, deduction, and experimentation—without the aid of ancient authorities or divine revelation. The French philosopher René Descartes resolved "to seek no other knowledge than that which I might find within myself, or perhaps in the book of nature."[19]

Like the physical universe, the human body also lost some of its mystery. The careful dissections of cadavers and animals enabled doctors and scientists to describe the human body with much greater accuracy and to understand the circulation of the blood throughout the body. The heart was no longer the mysterious center of the body's heat and the seat of its passions; instead it was just another machine, a complex muscle that functioned as a pump.

Much of this thinking developed in the face of strenuous opposition from the Catholic Church, for both its teachings and its authority were under attack. The

Italian philosopher Giordano Bruno, proclaiming an infinite universe and many worlds, was burned at the stake in 1600. Galileo too was compelled by the Church to publicly renounce his belief that the earth moved around an orbit and rotated on its axis.

But not all was conflict between the Church and an emerging science. None of the early scientists rejected Christianity. Galileo himself proclaimed the compatibility of science and faith when he wrote that "God is no less excellently revealed in Nature's actions than in the sacred statements of the Bible."[20] Newton was a serious biblical scholar and saw no necessary contradiction between his ideas and belief in God. "This most beautiful system of the sun, planets, and comets," he declared, "could only proceed from the counsel and dominion of an intelligent Being."[21] The Church gradually accommodated as well as resisted the new ideas, admitting that science was competent in its limited sphere but insisting that religion held the key to ultimate questions concerning human salvation and the larger purpose of the universe.

Science and Enlightenment

■ **Change**

In what ways did the Enlightenment challenge older patterns of European thinking?

Initially limited to a small handful of scholars, the ideas of the Scientific Revolution spread to a wider European public during the eighteenth century. That process was aided by novel techniques of printing and book-making, by a popular press, and by a host of scientific societies. Moreover, the new approach to knowledge—rooted in human reason, skeptical of authority, expressed in natural laws—was now applied to human affairs, not just to the physical universe. The Scottish professor Adam Smith (1723–1790), for example, formulated laws that accounted for the operation of the economy and which, if followed, would generate inevitably favorable results for society. Growing numbers of people believed that the long-term outcome of scientific development would be "enlightenment," a term that has come to define the eighteenth century in European history. If human reason could discover the laws that governed the universe, surely it could uncover ways in which humankind might govern itself more effectively.

"What is Enlightenment?" asked the prominent German intellectual Immanuel Kant (1724–1804). "It is man's emergence from his self-imposed . . . inability to use one's own understanding without another's guidance. . . . Dare to know! 'Have the courage to use your own understanding' is therefore the motto of the enlightenment."[22] Although they often disagreed sharply with one another, Enlightenment thinkers shared this belief in the power of knowledge to transform human society. They also shared a satirical, critical style, a commitment to open-mindedness and inquiry, and in various degrees a hostility to established political and religious authority.

Many took aim at arbitrary governments, the "divine right of kings," and the aristocratic privileges of European society. The English philosopher John Locke (1632–1704) offered principles for constructing a constitutional government, a contract between rulers and ruled that was created by human ingenuity rather than divinely prescribed. Any number of writers, including many women, advocated education for women as a means of raising their status in society.

Much of Enlightenment thinking was directed against the superstition, ignorance, and corruption of established religion. In his *Treatise on Toleration*, the French writer Voltaire (1694–1778) reflected the outlook of the Scientific Revolution as he commented sarcastically on religious intolerance.

> This little globe, nothing more than a point, rolls in space like so many other globes; we are lost in its immensity. Man, some five feet tall, is surely a very small part of the universe. One of these imperceptible beings says to some of his neighbors in Arabia or Africa: "Listen to me, for the God of all these worlds has enlightened me; there are nine hundred million little ants like us on the earth, but only my anthill is beloved of God; He will hold all others in horror through all eternity; only mine will be blessed, the others will be eternally wretched."[23]

Voltaire's own faith, like many others among the "enlightened," was deism. Deists believed in a rather abstract and remote Deity, sometimes compared to a clockmaker, who had created the world, but not in a personal God who intervened in history or tampered with natural law. Others became *pantheists,* who believed that God and nature were identical. Among the most radical were the several Dutchmen who wrote the *Treatise of Three Imposters*, which claimed that Moses, Jesus, and Muhammad were fraudulent imposters who based their teachings on "the ignorance of Peoples [and] resolved to keep them in it."[24]

Though solidly rooted in Europe, Enlightenment thought was influenced by the growing global awareness of its major thinkers. Voltaire, for example, idealized China as an empire governed by an elite of secular scholars selected for their talent, which stood in sharp contrast to continental Europe, where aristocratic birth and military prowess were far more important. Throughout much of the eighteenth century, a fad for things Chinese—furniture styles, decorative arts, dishes, lacquerware, wallpaper—shaped the tastes of European elites.

The central theme of the Enlightenment—and what made it potentially revolutionary—was the idea of progress. Human society was not fixed by tradition or divine command but could be changed, and improved, by human action guided by reason. This view was a sharp departure from much of premodern social thinking, and it inspired those who later made the American, French, Haitian, and Latin American revolutions (see Chapter 17). No one expressed this soaring confidence in the "real improvement of humanity" more effectively than the French thinker the Marquis de Condorcet (1743–1794). The future, in his view,

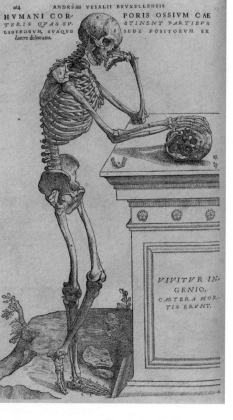

Uncovering the Human Skeleton
This drawing by the sixteenth-century Flemish anatomist Andreas Vesalius suggests a rational and philosophical approach to the human predicament, even as it presents the human skeleton with scientific precision. (Courtesy, National Library of Medicine)

promised the end of slavery, racism, gender inequality, supernatural religion, political tyranny, and contagious disease. "The day will come when the sun will shine only on free men, born knowing no other master but their reason," he declared. "The perfectibility of humanity is indefinite."[25] Born of the Scientific Revolution, that was the faith of the Enlightenment. For some, it was virtually a new religion.

The age of the Enlightenment also witnessed a reaction against too much reliance on human reason. Jean-Jacques Rousseau (1712–1778) minimized the importance of book learning for the education of children and prescribed instead an immersion in nature, which taught self-reliance and generosity rather than the greed and envy fostered by "civilization." The Romantic movement in art and literature appealed to emotion, intuition, passion, and imagination rather than cold reason and scientific learning. Religious awakenings—complete with fiery sermons, public repentance, and intense personal experience of sin and redemption—shook Protestant Europe and North America. Science and the Enlightenment surely challenged religion, and for some they eroded religious belief and practice. Just as surely, though, religion persisted, adapted, and revived for many others.

Looking Ahead: Science in the Nineteenth Century

■ Change
How did nineteenth-century developments in the sciences challenge the faith of the Enlightenment?

The perspectives of the Enlightenment were challenged not only by romanticism and religious "enthusiasm" but also by the continued development of science itself. This remarkable phenomenon justifies a brief look ahead at several scientific developments in the nineteenth century.

Modern science was a cumulative and self-critical enterprise, which in the nineteenth century and after was applied to new domains of human inquiry in ways that undermined some of the assumptions of the Enlightenment. In the realm of biology, for example, Charles Darwin (1809–1882) laid out a complex argument that all of life was in flux, that over millions of years new species of plants and animals were continuously emerging and becoming extinct. Human beings were not excluded from this vast process, for they too were the work of evolution operating through natural selection. Darwin's famous books *The Origin of Species* (1859) and *The Descent of Man* (1871) were as shattering to traditional religious views as Copernicus's ideas about a sun-centered universe had been several centuries earlier.

At the same time, Karl Marx (1818–1883) articulated a view of human history that likewise emphasized change and struggle. Conflicting social classes—slave owners and slaves, nobles and peasants, capitalists and workers—successively drove the process of historical transformation. Although he was describing the evolution of human civilization, Marx saw himself as a scientist. He based his theories on extensive historical research; like Newton and Darwin, he sought to formulate general laws that would explain events in a rational way. Nor did he believe in heavenly intervention, chance, or the divinely endowed powers of kings. The coming of socialism, in this view, was not simply a good idea; it was inscribed in the laws of historical development.

Like the intellectuals of the Enlightenment, Darwin and Marx believed strongly in progress, but in their thinking, conflict and struggle rather than reason and education were the motors of progress. The image of the tranquil, rational, and autonomous individual created by the Enlightenment was fading. Individuals of all species were now viewed as caught in vast systems of biological, economic, and social conflict.

The work of the Viennese doctor Sigmund Freud (1856–1939) applied scientific techniques to the operation of the human mind and emotions and in doing so cast further doubt on Enlightenment conceptions of human rationality. At the core of each person, Freud argued, lay primal impulses toward sexuality and aggression, which were only barely held in check by the thin veneer of social conscience derived from civilization. Our neuroses arose from the ceaseless struggle between our irrational drives and the claims of conscience. This too was a far cry from the Enlightenment conception of the human condition.

European Science beyond the West

In the long run, the achievements of the Scientific Revolution spread globally, becoming the most widely sought-after product of European culture and far more desired than Christianity, democracy, socialism, or Western literature. In the early modern era, however, the level of interest in European scientific thinking within major Asian societies was both modest and selective.

■ **Connection**
In what ways was European science received in the major civilizations of Asia in the early modern era?

In China, for example, Qing dynasty emperors and scholars were most interested in European astronomy and mathematics, derived largely from Jesuit missionaries, because those disciplines proved useful in predicting eclipses, reforming the calendar, and making accurate maps of the empire. European medicine, however, held little interest for Chinese physicians before the nineteenth century. But the reputation of the Jesuits suffered when it became apparent in the 1760s that for two centuries the missionaries had withheld information about Copernican views of a sun-centered solar system because those ideas had been condemned by the Church. Nonetheless, European science had a substantial impact on a number of Chinese scholars as it interacted with the data-based kaozheng movement, described by one participant as "an ant-like accumulation of facts."[26] European mathematics was of particular interest to kaozheng researchers who were exploring the history of Chinese mathematics. To encourage their skeptical colleagues that the barbarian Europeans had something to offer in this field, some Chinese scholars argued that European mathematics had in fact grown out of much earlier Chinese ideas and could therefore be adopted with comfort.[27] In such ways, early modern Chinese thinkers selectively assimilated Western science very much on their own terms.[28]

Although Japanese authorities largely closed their country off from the West in the early seventeenth century (see Chapter 15), one window remained open. Alone among Europeans, the Dutch were permitted to trade in Japan at a single location near Nagasaki, but not until 1720 did the Japanese lift the ban on importing Western books. Then a number of European texts in medicine, astronomy, geography, mathematics, and other disciplines were translated and studied by a small group of Japanese scholars. They were especially impressed with Western anatomical studies, for in Japan dissection was work fit only for outcasts. Returning from an autopsy conducted by Dutch physicians, several Japanese observers reflected on their experience: "We remarked to each other how amazing the autopsy had been, and how inexcusable it had been for us to be ignorant of the anatomical structure of the human body."[29] Nonetheless, this small center of "Dutch learning," as it was called, remained isolated amid a pervasive Confucian-based culture. Not until the mid-nineteenth century, when Japan was forcibly opened to Western penetration, would European science assume a prominent place in Japanese culture.

Like China and Japan, the Ottoman Empire in the sixteenth and seventeenth centuries was an independent, powerful, successful society whose intellectual elites saw no need for a wholesale embrace of things European. Ottoman scholars were conscious of the rich tradition of Muslim astronomy and chose not to translate the works of major European scientists such as Copernicus, Kepler, or Newton, although they were broadly aware of European scientific achievements by 1650. Insofar as they were interested in these developments, it was for their practical usefulness in making maps and calendars rather than for their larger philosophical implications. In any event, the notion of a sun-centered solar system did not cause the kind of upset that it did in Europe.[30]

More broadly, theoretical science of any kind—Muslim or European—faced an uphill struggle in the face of a conservative Islamic educational system. In 1580, for example, a highly sophisticated astronomical observatory was dismantled under pressure from conservative religious scholars and teachers, who interpreted an outbreak of the plague as God's displeasure with those who were seeking to penetrate his secrets. As in Japan, the systematic embrace of Western science would have to await the nineteenth century, when the Ottoman Empire was under far more intense European pressure and reform seemed more necessary.

Reflections: Cultural Borrowing and Its Hazards

Ideas are important in human history. They shape the mental or cultural worlds that people everywhere inhabit, and they often influence behavior as well. Many of the ideas developed or introduced during the early modern era have had enormous and continuing significance in the centuries that followed. The Western Hemisphere was solidly incorporated into Christendom. A Wahhabi version of Islam remains the official faith of Saudi Arabia into the twenty-first century and has influenced many contemporary Islamic revival movements. Modern science and the associated notions of progress have become for many people something approaching a new religion.

Accompanying the development of these ideas has been a great deal of cultural borrowing. Filipinos, Siberians, and many Native American peoples borrowed Christianity from Europeans. Numerous Asian and African peoples borrowed Islam from the Arabs. Northern Indian Sikhs drew upon both Hindu and Muslim teachings. Europeans borrowed scientific ideas from the Islamic world.

In virtually every case, though, that borrowing was selective rather than wholesale, even when it took place under conditions of foreign domination or colonial rule. Many peoples who appropriated Christianity or Islam certainly did not accept the rigid exclusivity and ardent monotheism of those faiths. Elite Chinese were far more interested in European astronomy and mathematics than in Western medicine, while Japanese scholars became fascinated with the anatomical work of the Dutch. Neither, however, adopted Christianity in a widespread manner.

Borrowing was frequently the occasion for serious conflict. Some objected to much borrowing at all, particularly when it occurred under conditions of foreign domination or foreign threat. Thus members of the Taki Onqoy movement in Peru sought to wipe out Spanish influence and control, while Chinese and Japanese authorities clamped down firmly on European missionaries, even as they maintained some interest in European technological and scientific skills. Another kind of conflict derived from the efforts to control the terms of cultural borrowing. For example, European missionaries and Muslim reformers alike sought to root out "idolatry" among native converts.

To ease the tensions of cultural borrowing, efforts to "domesticate" foreign ideas and practices proliferated. Thus the Jesuits in China tried to point out similarities between Christianity and Confucianism, and Native American converts identified Christian saints with their own gods and spirits. By the late seventeenth century, some local churches in central Mexico had come to associate Catholicism less with the Spanish than with ancient pre-Aztec communities and beliefs that were now restored to their rightful position.

The pace of global cultural borrowing and its associated tensions stepped up even more as Europe's modern transformation unfolded in the nineteenth century and as its imperial reach extended and deepened around the world.

Second Thoughts

What's the Significance?

Protestant Reformation
Catholic Counter-Reformation
Taki Onqoy
Jesuits in China
Wahhabi Islam

Wang Yangmin
kaozheng
Mirabai
Sikhism
Copernicus

Newton
the European Enlightenment
Voltaire
Condorcet and the idea of
   progress

To assess your mastery of the material in this chapter, see the **Online Study Guide** at bedfordstmartins.com/strayer.

Big Picture Questions

1. Why did Christianity take hold in some places more than in others?
2. In what ways was the missionary message of Christianity shaped by the cultures of Asian and American peoples?
3. Compare the processes by which Christianity and Islam became world religions.
4. In what ways did the spread of Christianity, Islam, and modern science give rise to culturally based conflicts?
5. Based on Chapters 13 through 16, how does the history of Islam in the early modern era challenge a Eurocentric understanding of those centuries?

Next Steps: For Further Study

For Web sites and documents related to this chapter, see **Make History** at bedfordstmartins.com/strayer.

Natana J. Delong-Bas, *Wahhabi Islam: From Revival and Reform to Global Jihad* (2004). A careful study of the origins of Wahhabi Islam and its subsequent development.

Patricia B. Ebrey et al., *East Asia: A Cultural, Social, and Political History* (2005). A broad survey by major scholars in the field.

Geoffrey C. Gunn, *First Globalization: The Eurasian Exchange, 1500–1800* (2003). Explores the two-way exchange of ideas between Europe and Asia in the early modern era.

Toby E. Huff, *The Rise of Early Modern Science* (2003). A fascinating and controversial explanation as to why modern science arose in the West rather than in China or the Islamic world.

Steven Shapin, *The Scientific Revolution* (1996). A brief, accessible, and scholarly account of the emergence of modern science.

Paul R. Spickard and Kevin M. Cragg, *A Global History of Christians* (1994). A broad-brush account of the global spread of Christianity and its various expressions in different cultures.

Internet Modern History Sourcebook, "The Scientific Revolution," http://www.fordham.edu/halsall/mod/modsbook09.html. A collection of primary-source documents dealing with the breakthrough to modern science in Europe.

PART FIVE

The European Moment in World History

1750–1914

Contents

Chapter 17. Atlantic Revolutions and Their Echoes, 1750–1914
Chapter 18. Revolutions of Industrialization, 1750–1914
Chapter 19. Internal Troubles, External Threats: China, the Ottoman
Empire, and Japan, 1800–1914
Chapter 20. Colonial Encounters, 1750–1914

European Centrality and the Problem of Eurocentrism

During the century and a half between 1750 and 1914, sometimes referred to as the "long nineteenth century," two new and related phenomena held center stage in the global history of humankind and represent the major themes of the four chapters that follow. The first of these, explored in Chapters 17 and 18, was the creation of a new kind of human society, commonly called "modern," which was the outgrowth of the Scientific, French, and Industrial revolutions, all of which took shape in Western Europe. Those societies generated many of the ideas that have guided human behavior over the past several centuries—notions of progress, constitutional government, political democracy, socialism, nationalism, feminism, and opposition to slavery.

The second theme of this long nineteenth century, which is addressed in Chapters 19 and 20, was the growing ability of these modern societies to exercise enormous power and influence over the rest of humankind. In some places, this occurred within growing European empires, such as those that governed India, Southeast Asia, and Africa. Elsewhere, it took place through less formal means—economic penetration, military intervention, diplomatic pressure, missionary activity—in states that remained officially independent, such as China, Japan, the Ottoman Empire, and various countries in Latin America.

Together, these two phenomena thrust Western Europe, and to a lesser extent North America, into a new and far more prominent role in world history than ever before, for it was in those European societies that modern ways of living emerged most fully. Those societies, and their North American offspring, also came to exercise a wholly unprecedented role in world affairs, as they achieved, collectively, something approaching global dominance by the early twentieth century.

Eurocentric Geography and History

That unprecedented power included the ability to rewrite geography and history in ways that centered the human story on Europe and to impose those views on other people. Thus maps placed Europe at the center of the world, while dividing Asia in half. Europe was granted continental status, even though it was more accurately only the western peninsula of Asia, much as India was its southern peninsula. Other regions of the world, such as the Far East or the Near (Middle) East, were defined in terms of their distance from Europe. The entire world came to measure

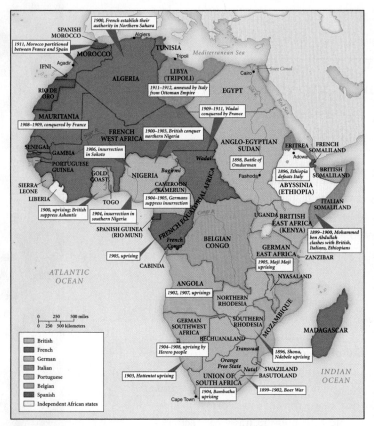

Conquest and Resistance in Colonial Africa (p. 593)

longitude from a line, known as the prime meridian, that passes through the Royal Astronomical Observatory in Greenwich, England.

History textbooks as well often reflected a Europe-centered outlook, sometimes blatantly. In 1874, the American author William O. Swinton wrote *An Outline of the World's History*, a book intended for use in high school and college classes, in which he flatly declared that "the race to which we belong, the Aryan, has always played the leading part in the great drama of the world's progress."[1] Other peoples and civilizations, by contrast, were long believed to be static and unchanging, thus largely lacking any real history. Most Europeans assumed that these "backward" peoples and regions were either headed in the European direction or doomed to extinction. Until the mid-twentieth century, such ideas went largely unchallenged in the Western world. Their implication was that history was a race toward the finish line of modernity. That Europeans arrived there first seemed to suggest something unique, special, or superior about them or their culture, while everyone else struggled to overcome their inadequacy and catch up.

As the discipline of world history took shape in the decades after World War II, scholars and teachers actively sought to counteract such a Eurocentric understanding of the past, but they faced a special problem in dealing with recent centuries. How can we avoid an inappropriate Eurocentrism when dealing with a phase of world history in which Europeans were in fact central? The long nineteenth century, after all, was "the European moment," a time when Europeans were clearly the most powerful, most innovative, most prosperous, most expansive, and most widely imitated people on the planet.

Countering Eurocentrism

At least five answers to this dilemma are reflected in the chapters that follow. You may want to look for examples of them as you read. The first is simply to remind ourselves how recent and perhaps how brief the European moment in world history has been. Other peoples too had times of "cultural flowering" that granted them a period of primacy or influence—for example, the Greeks (500 B.C.E.–200 C.E.), Indians of South Asia (200–600 C.E.), Arabs (600–1000), Chinese (1000–1500), Mongols (1200–1350), Incas and Aztecs (fifteenth century)—but all of these were limited to particular regions of Afro-Eurasia or the Americas.[2] Even though the European moment operated on a genuinely global scale, Western peoples have enjoyed their worldwide primacy for at most two centuries. Some scholars have suggested that the events of the late twentieth and early twenty-first centuries—the end of colonial empires,

Railroads (p. 534)

the rise of India and especially China, and the assertion of Islam—mark the end, or at least the erosion, of the age of Europe.

Second, we need to remember that the rise of Europe occurred within an international context. It was the withdrawal of the Chinese naval fleet that allowed Europeans to dominate the Indian Ocean in the sixteenth century, while Native Americans' lack of immunity to European diseases and their own divisions and conflicts greatly assisted the European takeover. Europe's Scientific Revolution drew upon earlier Islamic science and was stimulated by the massive amounts of new information pouring in from around the world. The Industrial Revolution, which is explored in Chapter 18, likewise benefited from New World resources and markets and from the stimulus of superior Asian textile and pottery production. Chapters 19 and 20 make clear that European control of other regions everywhere enlisted the cooperation of local elites. None of this diminishes the remarkable—indeed revolutionary—transformations of the European moment in world history. Rather it suggests that they did not derive wholly from some special European genius or long-term advantage but emerged from a unique intersection of European historical development with that of other peoples, regions, and cultures.

A third reminder is that the rise of Europe to a position of global dominance was not an easy or automatic process. Frequently it occurred in the face of ferocious resistance and rebellion, which often required Europeans to modify their policies and practices. The so-called Indian mutiny in mid-nineteenth-century South Asia, a massive uprising against British colonial rule, did not end British control, but it substantially transformed the character of the colonial experience. In

Africa, fear of offending Muslim sensibilities persuaded the British to keep European missionaries and mission schools out of northern Nigeria during the colonial era. Even when Europeans exercised political power, they could not do so precisely as they pleased. Empire, formal and informal alike, was always in some ways a negotiated arrangement.

Fourth, peoples the world over made active use of Europeans and European ideas for their own purposes, seeking to gain advantage over local rivals or to benefit themselves in light of new conditions. In Southeast Asia, for example, a number of highland minority groups, long oppressed by the dominant lowland Vietnamese, viewed the French invaders as liberators and assisted in their takeover of Vietnam. Hindus in India used the railroads, which had been introduced by the British, to go on pilgrimages to holy sites more easily, while the printing press made possible the more widespread distribution of their sacred texts. During the Haitian Revolution, which is explored in Chapter 17, enslaved Africans made use of radical French ideas about "the rights of man" in ways that most Europeans never intended. The leaders of a massive Chinese peasant upheaval in the mid-nineteenth century adopted a unique form of Christianity to legitimate their revolutionary assault on an ancient social order. Recognizing that Asian and African peoples remained active agents, pursuing their own interests even in oppressive conditions, is another way of countering residual Eurocentrism.

What was borrowed from Europe was always adapted to local circumstances. Thus Japanese or Russian industrial development did not wholly follow the pattern of England's Industrial Revolution. The Christianity that took root in the Americas or later in Africa evolved in culturally distinctive ways. Ideas of nationalism, born in Europe, were used to oppose European imperialism throughout Asia and Africa. Chinese socialism in the twentieth century departed in many ways from the vision of Karl Marx. The most interesting stories of modern world history are not simply those of European triumph or the imposition of Western ideas and practices, but of encounters, though highly unequal, among culturally different peoples. It was from these encounters, not just from the intentions and actions of Europeans, that the dramatic global changes of the modern era arose.

A fifth and final antidote to Eurocentrism in an age of European centrality lies in the recognition that although Europeans gained an unprecedented prominence on the world stage, they were not the only game in town, nor were they the sole preoccupation of Asian, African, and Middle Eastern peoples. While China confronted Western aggression in the nineteenth century, it was also absorbing a huge population increase and experiencing massive peasant rebellions that grew out of distinctly Chinese conditions. The long relationship of Muslim and Hindu cultures in India continued to evolve under British colonial rule as it had for centuries under other political systems. West African societies in the nineteenth century experienced a wave of religious wars that created new states and extended and transformed the practice of Islam, and that faith continued its centuries-long spread on the continent even under European colonial rule. A further wave of wars and state formation in southern Africa transformed the political and ethnic landscape, even as European penetration picked up speed.

None of this diminishes the significance of the European moment in world history, but it sets that moment in a larger context of continuing patterns of historical development and of interaction and exchange with other peoples.

Landmarks of the European Moment in World History, 1750–1914

1750	1775	1800	1825	
Europe	**1780s** Beginnings of British Industrial Revolution	**1799–1814** Reign of Napoleon	**1848** Publication of Karl Marx's *Communist Manifesto*	
		1789–1799 French Revolution		
	1780s Beginnings of antislavery movement			
North America	**1775–1783** American Revolution **1787** U.S. Constitutional Convention	**1803** Louisiana Purchase	**1845–1848** Mexican-American War	
			1848 Women's Rights Convention, Seneca Fall, New York	
			1849 California gold rush	
Latin America	**1783–1830** Life of Simón Bolívar			
	1791–1803 Haitian Revolution	**1810–1825** Latin American wars of independence		
		1810 Hidalgo-Morelos rebellion in Mexico		
Africa		**1798** Napoleon's invasion of Egypt **1815–1840** Rise of Zulu kingdom in South Africa		
		1804–1817 Fulbe wars and establishment of Sokoto caliphate in West Africa		
		1805–1848 Reign of Muhammad Ali in Egypt **1830** French invasion of Algeria		
East Asia		**1793** Chinese rejection of British request for open trade	**1830s** Famines and rebellions in Japan	
			1838–1842 First Opium War	
South, Southwest, and Southeast Asia			**1839–1876** Tanzimat reforms in Ottoman Empire	

1740s–1818 Wahhabi movement of Islamic renewal in Arabia

1750s Beginnings of British takeover in India

1850	1875	1900	1925

1861 Emancipation of serfs in Russia

1870–1871 Unification of Italy and Germany

1905 Revolution in Russia

1914 Outbreak of World War I

1861–1865 U.S. Civil War

1867 Dominion of Canada established

1890 Massacre at Wounded Knee

1898–1902 Spanish-American War (US acquires the Philippines)

1850s Beginning of railroad building in Cuba, Chile, and Brazil

1869 First school for girls in Mexico

1886–1888 Cuba and Brazil abolish slavery

1904–1914 Construction of Panama Canal

1910–1920 Mexican Revolution

1850s High point of East African slave trade

1875–1900 Colonial conquest of Africa

1882–1898 Samori Toure's resistance to French aggression in West Africa

1904–1905 Maji Maji rebellion in German East Africa (Tanzania)

1899–1902 Boer War in South Africa

1853 Arrival in Japan of Commodore Perry

1850–1864 Taiping Uprising in China

1868 Meiji restoration in Japan

1899–1901 Boxer Rebellion in China

1910 Japan annexes Korea

1911 Chinese Revolution

1904–1905 Russo-Japanese War

1857–1858 Indian mutiny/rebellion

1883 Ilbert Bill/White Mutiny in India

1876 Ottoman constitution established

1885 Indian National Congress established

1908 Young Turk takeover in Ottoman Empire

1858–1893 French conquest of Indochina

1869 Opening of Suez Canal

CHAPTER SEVENTEEN

Atlantic Revolutions and Their Echoes

1750-1914

Comparing Atlantic
    Revolutions
    The North American
        Revolution, 1775–1787
    The French Revolution,
        1789–1815
    The Haitian Revolution,
        1791–1804
    Spanish American
        Revolutions, 1810–1825
Echoes of Revolution
    The Abolition of Slavery
    Nations and Nationalism
    Feminist Beginnings
Reflections: Revolutions Pro
    and Con

On July 14, 1989, France celebrated the bicentennial of its famous revolution with a huge parade in Paris. At the head of that parade, strangely enough, were a number of Chinese students, pushing empty bicycles. Just a few weeks earlier, those students had been part of massive demonstrations in Beijing's Tiananmen Square, demanding from their communist government the kind of democratic political rights that the French Revolution had inspired two centuries before. In the process, they had created a thirty-foot-tall papier-mâché Goddess of Democracy, which resembled the Statue of Liberty, a French gift to the United States. Chinese authorities had violently crushed those demonstrations, and now a few students who had escaped to France were paying tribute to the ideals that the French Revolution had unleashed. Their empty bicycles symbolized thousands of their colleagues who had been killed or jailed during the Chinese struggle for democracy. Thus the reverberations of the French Revolution of 1789 still echoed two centuries later and half a world away.

ESSENTIAL AS IT WAS TO THE HISTORY OF EUROPE, the French Revolution holds an even larger significance as the centerpiece of a more extensive revolutionary process that unfolded all around the Atlantic world in the century or so following 1775. The upheaval in France was, of course, preceded by the American Revolution, which gave birth to the United States. It was followed by the Haitian Revolution, the first successful slave revolt in history, and by the Latin American revolutions, in

---

The Three Estates of Old-Regime France: This satirical eighteenth-century illustration represents the three estates of prerevolutionary French society as women, with the peasant woman carrying a nun and an aristocratic lady on her back. Such social tensions contributed much to the making of the French Revolution. (Réunion des Musées Nationaux/Art Resource, NY)

which Spanish and Portuguese colonial rule was ended and the modern states of Latin America emerged. Further revolutionary outbreaks shook various European societies in 1830, 1848, and 1870. These upheavals also had an impact well beyond the Atlantic world. The armies of revolutionary France, for example, invaded Egypt, Poland, and Russia, carrying seeds of change. The ideals that animated these Atlantic revolutions inspired efforts in many countries to abolish slavery, to extend the right to vote, and to secure greater equality for women. Nationalism, perhaps the most potent ideology of the modern era, was nurtured in the Atlantic revolutions and shaped much of nineteenth- and twentieth-century world history. And the principles of equality that were articulated in these revolutions later found expression in socialist and communist movements.

Comparing Atlantic Revolutions

■ Causation

In what ways did the ideas of the Enlightenment contribute to the Atlantic revolutions?

Writing to a friend in 1772, before any of the Atlantic revolutions had occurred, the French intellectual Voltaire asked, "My dear philosopher, doesn't this appear to you to be the century of revolutions?"[1] He was certainly on target: in the century that followed, revolutionary outbreaks punctuated the histories of three continents, with influences and echoes even farther afield. Nor were these various revolutions— in North America, France, Haiti, and Latin America—entirely separate and distinct events, for they clearly influenced one another. The American revolutionary leader Thomas Jefferson was the U.S. ambassador to France on the eve of the French Revolution, and while there he provided advice and encouragement to French reformers and revolutionaries. Simón Bolívar, a leading figure in Spanish American struggles for independence, twice visited Haiti, where he received military aid from the first black government in the Americas.

Beyond such direct connections, the various Atlantic revolutionaries shared a set of common ideas. The Atlantic basin had become a world of intellectual and cultural exchange as well as one of commercial and biological intercourse. The ideas that animated the Atlantic revolutions derived from the European Enlightenment and were shared across the ocean in newspapers, books, and pamphlets. At the heart of these ideas was the radical notion that human political and social arrangements could be engineered, and improved, by human action. Thus conventional and long-established ways of living and thinking—the divine right of kings, state control of trade, aristocratic privilege, the authority of a single church— were no longer sacrosanct and came under repeated attack. New ideas of liberty, equality, free trade, religious tolerance, republicanism, and human rationality were in the air. Politically, the core notion was "popular sovereignty," which meant that the authority to govern derived from the people rather than from God or from established tradition. As the Englishman John Locke (1632–1704) had argued, the "social contract" between ruler and ruled should last only as long as it served the people well. In short, it was both possible and desirable to start over in the construction of human communities.

$\mathcal{S}$napshot **Key Moments in the History of Atlantic Revolutions**

American Declaration of Independence	1776
British recognition of American independence	1783
U.S. Constitutional Convention	1787
Tupac Amaru revolt in Peru	1780s
Outbreak of French Revolution	1789
Haitian Revolution	1791–1804
French Terror, execution of Louis XVI	1793–1794
Napoleon's rise to power	1799
High point of Napoleon's empire	1810–1811
Hidalgo-Morales rebellion in Mexico	1810–1813
Wars of Spanish American independence	1810–1825
Final defeat of Napoleon	1815
Independence of Brazil from Portugal	1822

Such ideas generated endless controversy. Were liberty and equality compatible? What kind of government—unitary and centralized or federal and decentralized—best ensured freedom? And how far should liberty be extended? Except in Haiti, the chief beneficiaries of these revolutions were propertied white men of the "middling classes." Although women, slaves, Native Americans, and men without property did not gain much from these revolutions, the ideas that accompanied these upheavals gave them ammunition for the future. Because their overall thrust was to extend political rights further than ever before, these Atlantic movements have often been referred to as "democratic revolutions."

Beneath a common political vocabulary and a broadly democratic character, the Atlantic revolutions differed substantially from one another. They were triggered by different circumstances, expressed quite different social and political tensions, and varied considerably in their outcomes. Liberty, noted Simón Bolívar, "is a succulent morsel, but one difficult to digest."[2] "Digesting liberty" occurred in quite distinct ways in the various sites of the Atlantic revolutions.

The North American Revolution, 1775–1787

Every schoolchild in the United States learns early that the American Revolution was a struggle for independence from oppressive British rule. That struggle was launched with the Declaration of Independence in 1776, resulted in an unlikely military victory by 1781, and generated a federal constitution in 1787, joining thirteen

■ Change
What was revolutionary about the American Revolution, and what was not?

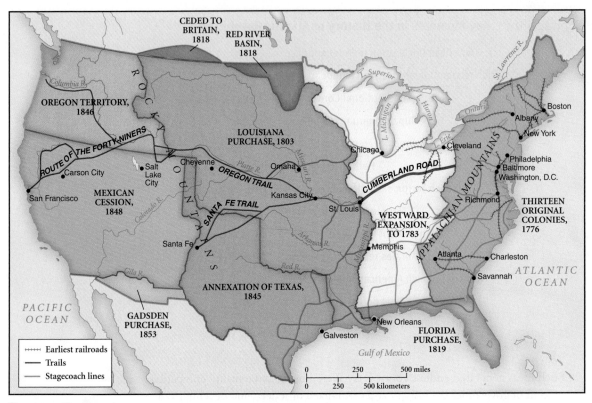

Map 17.1 The Expansion of the United States

The union of the thirteen British colonies in North America provided the foundation for the westward and transcontinental expansion of the United States during the nineteenth century, a process that turned the country into a global power by the early twentieth century.

formerly separate colonies into a new nation (see Map 17.1). It was the first in a series of upheavals that rocked the Atlantic world and beyond in the century that followed. But was it a genuine revolution? What, precisely, did it change?

In its break with Britain, the American Revolution marked a decisive political change, but in other ways it was, strangely enough, a conservative movement, because it originated in an effort to preserve the existing liberties of the colonies rather than to create new ones. For much of the seventeenth and eighteenth centuries, the British colonies in North America enjoyed a considerable degree of local autonomy as the British government was embroiled in its own internal conflicts and various European wars. Furthermore, Britain's West Indian colonies seemed more profitable and of greater significance than those of North America. In these circumstances, local elected assemblies in North America, dominated by the wealthier property-owning settlers, achieved something close to self-government. Colonists came to regard such autonomy as a birthright and part of their English heritage. Thus, until the mid-eighteenth century, almost no one in the colonies thought of breaking away from England because participation in the British Empire provided many advantages—protection in war, access to British markets, and confirmation of their continuing identity as "Englishmen"—and few drawbacks.

Within these colonies, English settlers had developed societies described by a leading historian as "the most radical in the contemporary Western world." Certainly class distinctions were real and visible, and a small class of wealthy "gentlemen"—the Adamses, Washingtons, Jeffersons, and Hancocks—wore powdered wigs, imitated the latest European styles, were prominent in political life, and were generally deferred to by ordinary people. But the ready availability of land following the elimination of Native Americans, the scarcity of people, and the absence of both a titled nobility and a single established church meant that social life was far more open than in Europe. No legal distinctions differentiated clergy, aristocracy, and commoners, as they did in France. All free people, which of course excluded black slaves, enjoyed the same status before the law. These conditions made for less poverty, more economic opportunity, fewer social differences, and easier relationships among the classes than in Europe. The famous economist Adam Smith observed that British colonists were "republican in their manners ... and their government" well before their independence from England.[3]

Thus the American Revolution did not grow out of social tensions within the colonies, but from a quite sudden and unexpected effort by the British government to tighten its control over the colonies and to extract more revenue from them. As Britain's global struggle with France drained its treasury and ran up its national debt, British authorities, beginning in the 1760s, looked to America to make good these losses. Abandoning its neglectful oversight of the colonies, Britain began to act like a genuine imperial power, imposing a variety of new taxes and tariffs on the colonies without their consent, for they were not represented in the British parliament. By challenging their economic interests, their established traditions of local autonomy, and their identity as true Englishmen, such measures infuriated many of the colonists. Armed with the ideas of the Enlightenment—popular sovereignty, natural rights, the consent of the governed—they went to war, and by 1781 they had prevailed, with considerable aid from the French.

What was revolutionary about the American experience was not so much the revolution itself but the kind of society that had already emerged within the colonies. Independence from Britain was not accompanied by any wholesale social transformation. Rather the revolution accelerated the established democratic tendencies of the colonial societies. Political authority remained largely in the hands of existing elites who had led the revolution, although property requirements for voting were lowered and more white men of modest means, such as small farmers and urban artisans, were elected to state legislatures.

This widening of political participation gradually eroded the power of traditional gentlemen, but no women or people of color shared in these gains. Land was not seized from its owners, except in the case of pro-British loyalists who had fled the country. Although slavery was gradually abolished in the northern states, where it counted for little, it remained firmly entrenched in the southern states, where it counted for much. Chief Justice John Marshall later gave voice to this conservative understanding of the American Revolution: "All contracts and rights, respecting property, remained unchanged by the Revolution."[4] In the century that followed independence, the United States did become the world's most democratic country, but it was less the direct product of the revolution and more the gradual working out in a reformist fashion of earlier practices and the principles of equality announced in the Declaration of Independence.

Nonetheless, many American patriots felt passionately that they were creating "a new order for the ages." James Madison in the *Federalist Papers* made the point clearly: "We pursued a new and more noble course . . . and accomplished a revolution that has no parallel in the annals of human society." Supporters abroad agreed. On the eve of the French Revolution, a Paris newspaper proclaimed that the United States was "the hope and model of the human race."[5] In both cases, they were referring primarily to the political ideas and practices of the new country. The American Revolution, after all, initiated the political dismantling of Europe's New World empires. The "right to revolution," proclaimed in the Declaration of Independence and made effective only in a great struggle, inspired revolutionaries and nationalists from Simón Bolívar in nineteenth-century Latin America to Ho Chi Minh in twentieth-century Vietnam. Moreover, the new U.S. Constitution— with its Bill of Rights, checks and balances, separation of church and state, and federalism—was one of the first sustained efforts to put the political ideas of the Enlightenment into practice. That document, and the ideas that it embraced, echoed repeatedly in the political upheavals of the century that followed.

The French Revolution, 1789–1815

■ **Comparison**
How did the French Revolution differ from the American Revolution?

Act Two in the drama of the Atlantic revolutions took place in France, beginning in 1789, although it was closely connected to Act One in North America. Thousands of French soldiers had provided assistance to the American colonists and now returned home full of republican enthusiasm. Thomas Jefferson, the U.S. ambassador in Paris, reported that France "has been awakened by our revolution."[6] More immediately, the French government, which had generously aided the Americans in an effort to undermine its British rivals, was teetering on the brink of bankruptcy and had long sought reforms that would modernize the tax system and make it more equitable. In a desperate effort to raise taxes against the opposition of the privileged classes, the French king, Louis XVI, had called into session an ancient parliamentary body, the Estates General. It consisted of representatives of the three "estates," or legal orders, of prerevolutionary France: the clergy, the nobility, and the commoners. The first two estates comprised about 2 percent of the population, and the Third Estate included everyone else. When that body convened in 1789, representatives of the Third Estate soon organized themselves as the National Assembly, with the sole authority to make laws for the country. A few weeks later they drew up the Declaration of the Rights of Man and Citizen, which forthrightly declared that "men are born and remain free and equal in rights." These actions, unprecedented and illegal in the *ancien régime* (the Old Regime), launched the

French Revolution and radicalized many of the participants in the National Assembly.

That revolution was quite different from its North American predecessor. Whereas the American Revolution expressed the tensions of a colonial relationship with a distant imperial power, the French insurrection was driven by sharp conflicts within French society. Members of the titled nobility—privileged, prestigious, and wealthy—resented and resisted the monarchy's efforts to subject them to new taxes. Educated middle-class groups, such as doctors, lawyers, lower-level officials, and merchants, were growing in numbers and sometimes in wealth and were offended by the remaining privileges of the aristocracy, from which they were excluded. Ordinary urban residents, many of whose incomes had declined for a generation, were particularly hard-hit in the late 1780s by the rapidly rising price of bread and widespread unemployment. Peasants in the countryside, though largely free of serfdom, were subject to a variety of hated dues imposed by their landlords, taxes from the state, obligations to the Church, and the requirement to work without pay on public roads. As Enlightenment ideas penetrated French society, more and more people, mostly in the Third Estate but including some priests and nobles, found a language with which to articulate these grievances. The famous French writer Jean-Jacques Rousseau had told them that it was "manifestly contrary to the law of nature ... that a handful of people should gorge themselves with superfluities while the hungry multitude goes in want of necessities."[7]

These social conflicts gave the French Revolution, especially during its first five years, a much more violent, far-reaching, and radical character than its American counterpart. It was a profound social upheaval, more comparable to the revolutions of Russia and China in the twentieth century than to the earlier American Revolution. Initial efforts to establish a constitutional monarchy gave way to more radical measures, as internal resistance and foreign opposition produced a fear that the revolution might be overturned. In the process, urban crowds organized insurrections. Some peasants attacked the castles of their lords, burning the documents that recorded their dues and payments. The National Assembly decreed the end of all legal privileges and abolished what remained of feudalism in France. Even slavery was abolished, albeit briefly. Church lands were sold to raise revenue, and priests were put under government authority.

In early 1793, King Louis XVI and his queen, Marie Antoinette, were executed, an act of regicide that shocked traditionalists all across Europe and marked a new stage in revolutionary violence. What followed was the Terror of 1793–1794. Under the leadership of Maximilien Robespierre and his Committee of Public Safety, tens of thousands deemed enemies of the revolution lost their lives on the guillotine. Shortly thereafter, Robespierre himself was arrested and guillotined, accused of leading France into tyranny and dictatorship. "The revolution," remarked one of its victims, "was devouring its own children."

Accompanying attacks on the old order were efforts to create a wholly new society, symbolized by a new calendar with the Year 1 in 1792, marking a fresh start for

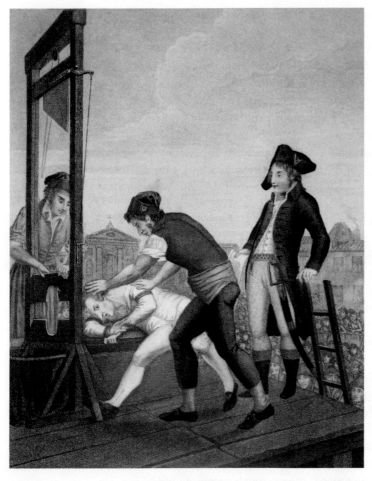

The Execution of Robespierre
The beheading of the radical leader Robespierre, who had himself brought thousands of others to the guillotine, marked a decisive turning point in the unfolding of the French Revolution and the end of its most violent phase. (Musée de la Revolution Française, Vizille, France/ Bridgeman Art Library)

France. Unlike the Americans, who sought to restore or build upon earlier freedoms, French revolutionaries perceived themselves to be starting from scratch and looked to the future. For the first time in its history, the country became a republic and briefly passed universal male suffrage, although it was never implemented. The old administrative system was rationalized into eighty-three territorial departments, each with a new name. As revolutionary France prepared for war against its threatened and threatening neighbors, it created the world's largest army, with some 800,000 men, and all adult males were required to serve. Led by officers from the middle and even lower classes, this was an army of citizens representing the nation.

The impact of the revolution was felt in many ways. Streets got new names; monuments to the royal family were destroyed; titles vanished; people referred to one another as "citizen so-and-so." Real politics in the public sphere emerged for the first time as many people joined political clubs, took part in marches and demonstrations, served on local committees, and ran for public office. Common people, who had identified primarily with their local community, now began to think of themselves as belonging to a nation. The state replaced the Catholic Church as the place for registering births, marriages, and deaths, and revolutionary festivals substituted for church holidays.

More radical revolutionary leaders deliberately sought to convey a sense of new beginnings. A Festival of Unity held in 1793 to mark the first anniversary of the end of monarchy burned the crowns and scepters of the royal family in a huge bonfire while releasing a cloud of 3,000 white doves. The Cathedral of Notre Dame was temporarily turned into the Temple of Reason, while a "Hymn to Liberty" combined traditional church music with the explicit message of the Enlightenment:

> Oh Liberty, sacred Liberty
> Goddess of an enlightened people
> Rule today within these walls.
> Through you this temple is purified.

Liberty! Before you reason chases out deception,
Error flees, fanaticism is beaten down.
Our gospel is nature
And our cult is virtue.
To love one's country and one's brothers,
To serve the Sovereign People—
These are the sacred tenets
And pledge of a Republican.[8]

The French Revolution differed from the American Revolution also in the way its influence spread. At least until the United States became a world power at the end of the nineteenth century, what inspired others was primarily the example of its revolution and its constitution. French influence, by contrast, spread through conquest, largely under the leadership of Napoleon Bonaparte (ruled 1799–1814). A highly successful general who seized power in 1799, Napoleon is often credited with taming the revolution in the face of growing disenchantment with its more radical features and with the social conflicts it generated. He preserved many of its more moderate elements, such as civil equality, a secular law code, religious freedom, and promotion by merit, while reconciling with the Catholic Church and suppressing the revolution's more democratic elements in a military dictatorship. In short, Napoleon kept the revolution's emphasis on social equality but dispensed with liberty.

Like many of the revolution's ardent supporters, Napoleon was intent on spreading its benefits far and wide. In a series of brilliant military campaigns, his forces subdued most of Europe, thus creating the continent's largest empire since the days of the Romans (see Map 17.2). Within that empire, Napoleon imposed such revolutionary practices as ending feudalism, proclaiming equality of rights, insisting on religious toleration, codifying the laws, and rationalizing government administration. In many places, these reforms were welcomed, and seeds of further change were planted. But French domination was also resented and resisted, stimulating national consciousness throughout Europe. That too was a seed that bore fruit in the century that followed. More immediately, national resistance, particularly from Russia and Britain, brought down Napoleon and his amazing empire by 1815 and marked an end to the era of the French Revolution, though not to the potency of its ideas.

The Haitian Revolution, 1791–1804

Nowhere did the example of the French Revolution echo more loudly than in the French Caribbean colony of Saint Domingue, later renamed Haiti (see Map 17.3, p. 511). Widely regarded as the richest colony in the world, Saint Domingue boasted 8,000 plantations, which in the late eighteenth century produced some 40 percent of the world's sugar and perhaps half of its coffee. Slaves, about 500,000 of them, made up the vast majority of its population. Whites numbered about 40,000, sharply divided between very well-to-do plantation owners, merchants, and lawyers and those known as *petits blancs*, or poor whites. A third social group consisted of some 30,000 *gens de*

■ **Comparison**
What was distinctive about the Haitian Revolution, both in world history generally and in the history of Atlantic revolutions?

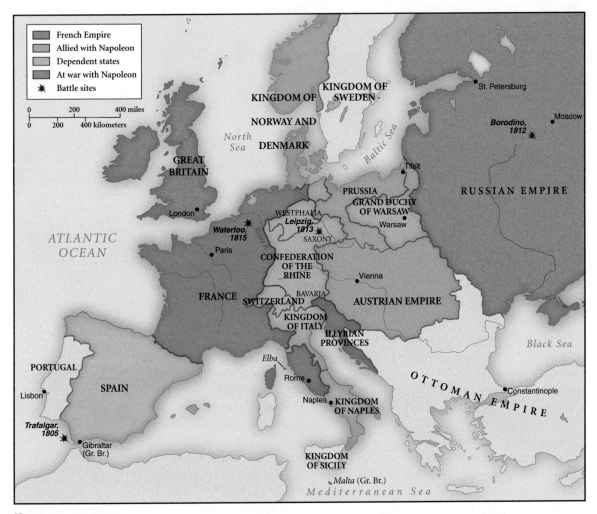

Map 17.2 Napoleon's European Empire

The French Revolution spawned a French empire, under Napoleon's leadership, that encompassed most of Europe and served to spread the principles of the revolution.

couleur libres, or free people of color, many of them of mixed-race background. Saint Domingue was a colonial society very different from the New England colonies or even the southern colonies of British North America. Given its enormous inequalities and its rampant exploitation, this Caribbean colony was primed for explosion.

In such a volatile setting, the ideas and example of the French Revolution lit several fuses and set in motion a spiral of violence that engulfed the colony for more than a decade. The principles of the revolution, however, meant different things to different people. To the *grands blancs*—the rich white landowners—it suggested greater autonomy for the colony and fewer economic restrictions on trade, but they resented the demands of the *petits blancs*, who sought equality of citizenship for all whites. Both white groups were adamantly opposed to the insistence of free people of color that the "rights of man" meant equal treatment for all free people regardless of race. To the slaves, the promise of the French Revolution's ideas was a personal freedom that threatened the entire slave labor system. In a massive slave revolt beginning in 1791, triggered by rumors that the French king had already declared an end to slavery, they burned 1,000 plantations and killed hundreds of whites as well as mixed-race people.

Soon warring factions of slaves, whites, and free people of color battled one another. Spanish and British forces, seeking to enlarge their own empires at the expense of the French, only added to the turmoil. Amid the confusion, brutality, and massacres of the 1790s, power gravitated toward the slaves, now led by the astute Toussaint Louverture, himself a former slave. He and his successor overcame internal resistance, outmaneuvered the foreign powers, and even defeated an attempt by Napoleon to reestablish French control.

When the dust settled in the early years of the nineteenth century, it was clear that something remarkable and unprecedented had taken place, a revolution unique in the Atlantic world and in world history. Socially, the last had become first. In the only completely successful slave revolt in world history, "the lowest order of the society—slaves—became equal, free, and independent citizens."9 Politically, they had thrown off French colonial rule, becoming the second independent republic in the Americas and the first non-European state to

PL. VII.

Wraak door het leger der zwarten genomen van de wreedheden, hun door de Franschen aangedaan.

The Haitian Revolution
This early-nineteenth-century engraving, entitled *Revenge Taken by the Black Army*, illustrates both the violence and the racial dimension of the upheaval in Haiti. (Schomburg Center, NY/Art Resource, NY)

emerge from Western colonialism. They renamed their country Haiti, a term meaning "mountainous" or "rugged" in the language of the original Taino people. It was a symbolic break with Europe and represented some connection with the long-deceased native inhabitants of the land. Some, in fact, referred to themselves as "Incas." At the formal declaration of Haiti's independence on January 1, 1804, Jean-Jacques Dessalines, the new country's first head of state, declared: "I have given the French cannibals blood for blood; I have avenged America."10 In defining all Haitians as "black," Haiti directly confronted an emerging racism, even as they declared all citizens legally equal regardless of race, color, or class. Economically, the country's plantation system, oriented wholly toward the export of sugar and coffee, had been largely destroyed. As whites fled or were killed, both private and state lands were redistributed among former slaves and free blacks, and Haiti became a nation of small-scale farmers producing mostly for their own needs, with a much smaller export sector.

The destructiveness of the Haitian Revolution; its bitter internal divisions of race, color, and class; and continuing external opposition contributed much to Haiti's abiding poverty as well as to its authoritarian and unstable politics. In the early nineteenth century, however, it was a source of enormous hope and of great fear. Within weeks of the Haitian slave uprising in 1791, Jamaican slaves had composed songs in its honor, and it was not long before slave owners in the Caribbean and North America observed a new "insolence" in their slaves. Certainly its example inspired other slave rebellions, gave a boost to the dawning abolitionist movement, and has been a source of pride for people of African descent ever since.

To whites throughout the hemisphere, the cautionary phrase "remember Haiti" reflected a sense of horror at what had occurred there and a determination not to allow political change to reproduce that fearful outcome again. Particularly in Latin America, it injected a deep caution and social conservatism in the elites that led their countries to independence in the early nineteenth century. Ironically, though, the Haitian Revolution also led to a temporary expansion of slavery elsewhere. Cuban plantations and their slave workers considerably increased their production of sugar as that of Haiti declined. Moreover, Napoleon's defeat in Haiti persuaded him to sell to the United States the French territories known as the Louisiana Purchase, from which a number of "slave states" were carved out. In such contradictory ways did the echoes of the Haitian Revolution reverberate in the Atlantic world.

Spanish American Revolutions, 1810–1825

■ **Connection**
How were the Spanish American revolutions shaped by the American, French, and Haitian revolutions that happened earlier?

The final act in a half century of Atlantic revolutionary upheaval took place in the Spanish and Portuguese colonies of mainland Latin America (see Map 17.3). Their revolutions were shaped by preceding events in North America, France, and Haiti as well as by their own distinctive societies and historical experience. As in British North America, native-born elites in the Spanish colonies (known as *creoles*) were offended and insulted by the Spanish monarchy's efforts during the eighteenth century to exercise greater power over its colonies and to subject them to heavier taxes and tariffs. Creole intellectuals also had become familiar with ideas of popular sovereignty, republican government, and personal liberty derived from the European Enlightenment. Why did these conditions, similar to those in North America, lead initially only to scattered and uncoordinated protests rather than to outrage, declarations of independence, war, and unity, as had occurred in the British colonies? Why, in short, did Spanish American struggles for independence occur decades later than those of British North America?

The settlers in the Spanish colonies had little tradition of local self-government such as had developed in North America. Their society was far more authoritarian and divided by class, and their culture was informed by the strict Catholicism of the Counter-Reformation. In addition, whites throughout Latin America were vastly outnumbered by Native Americans, people of African ancestry, or those of mixed race.

All of these factors help explain the delayed movement for independence, despite the example of North America and similar provocations.

Despite their growing disenchantment with Spanish rule, creole elites did not so much generate a revolution as have one thrust upon them by events in Europe. In 1808, Napoleon invaded Spain and Portugal, deposing the Spanish king Ferdinand VII and forcing the Portuguese royal family into exile in Brazil. With legitimate royal authority now in disarray, Latin Americans were forced to take action. The outcome, ultimately, was independence for the various states of Latin America, established almost everywhere by 1826. But the way in which it occurred and the kind of societies it generated differed greatly from the experience of both North America and Haiti.

The process lasted more than twice as long as it did in North America, partly because Latin American societies were so conflicted and divided by class, race, and region. In North America, violence was directed almost entirely

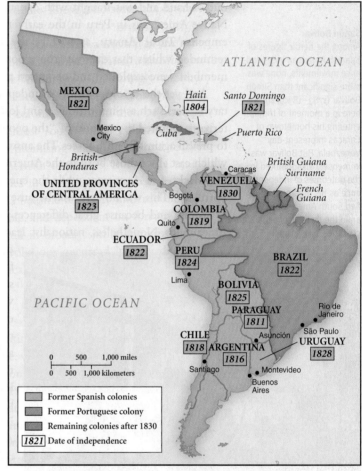

Map 17.3 Latin American Independence
With the exception of Haiti, Latin American revolutions brought independence to new states but offered little social change or political opportunity for the vast majority of people.

against the British and seldom spilled over into domestic disputes, except for some bloody skirmishes with loyalists. Even then, little lasting hostility occurred, and some loyalists were able to reenter U.S. society after independence was achieved. In Mexico, by contrast, the move toward independence began in 1810 in a peasant insurrection, driven by hunger for land and by high food prices and led successively by two priests, Miguel Hidalgo and José Morelos. Alarmed by the social radicalism of the Hidalgo-Morelos rebellion, creole landowners, with the support of the Church, raised an army and crushed the insurgency. Later that alliance of clergy and creole elites brought Mexico to a more socially controlled independence in 1821. Violent conflict among Latin Americans, along lines of race, class, and ideology, accompanied the struggle against Spain in many places.

The entire independence movement in Latin America took place under the shadow of a great fear—the dread of social rebellion from below—that had little counterpart in North America. The great violence of the French and Haitian revolutions was a lesson to Latin American elites that political change could easily get

Map 17.4 The Nations and Empires of Europe, ca. 1880

By the end of the nineteenth century, the national principle had substantially reshaped the map of Europe, especially in the unification of Germany and Italy. However, several major empires (Russian, Austro-Hungarian, and Ottoman) remained, each with numerous subject peoples who likewise sought national independence.

Governments throughout the Western world claimed now to act on behalf of their nations and deliberately sought to instill national loyalties in their citizens through schools, public rituals, the mass media, and military service. Russian authorities, for example, imposed the use of the Russian language, even in parts of the country where it was not widely spoken. They succeeded, how-

ever, only in producing a greater awareness of Ukrainian, Polish, and Finnish nationalism.

As it became more prominent in the nineteenth century, nationalism took on a variety of political ideologies. Some supporters of liberal democracy and representative government, as in France or the United States, saw nationalism, with its emphasis on "the people," as an aid to their aspirations toward wider involvement in political life. Often called "civic nationalism," such a view identified the nation with a particular territory and maintained that people of various cultural backgrounds could assimilate into the dominant culture, as in the process of "becoming American." Other versions of nationalism, in Germany for example, sometimes defined the nation in racial terms, which excluded those who did not share a common ancestry, such as Jews. In the hands of conservatives, nationalism could be used to combat socialism and feminism, for those movements only divided the nation along class or gender lines. Thus nationalism generated endless controversy because it provided no clear answer to the question of who belonged to the nation or who should speak for it.

Nor was nationalism limited to the Euro-American world in the nineteenth century. An "Egypt for the Egyptians" movement arose in the 1870s as British and

Nationalism in Poland
In the eighteenth century, Poland had been divided among Prussia, Austria, and Russia and disappeared as a separate and independent state. Polish nationalism found expression in the nineteenth century in a series of revolts, among which was a massive uprising in 1863, directed against Poland's Russian occupiers. This famous painting by Polish artist Jan Matejko shows a crowd of Polish prisoners awaiting transportation to imprisonment in Siberia, while Russian military officers supervise a blacksmith, who fastens fetters on a woman representing Poland. (Courtesy, Czartoryski Museum, Cracow)

French intervention in Egyptian affairs deepened. When Japan likewise confronted European aggression in the second half of the nineteenth century, its long sense of itself as a distinct culture was readily transformed into an assertive modern nationalism. Small groups of Western-educated men in British-ruled India began to think of their enormously diverse country as a single nation. The Indian National Congress, established in 1885, gave expression to this idea. The notion of the Ottoman Empire as a Turkish national state rather than a Muslim or dynastic empire took hold among a few people. By the end of the nineteenth century, some Chinese intellectuals began to think in terms of a Chinese nation beset both by a foreign ruling dynasty and by predatory Europeans. Along the West African coast, the idea of an "African nation" stirred among a handful of freed slaves and missionary-educated men. Although Egyptian and Japanese nationalism gained broad support, elsewhere in Asia and Africa such movements would have to wait until the twentieth century, when they exploded with enormous power on the stage of world history.

Feminist Beginnings

■ Significance
What were the achievements and limitations of nineteenth-century feminism?

A third echo of the Atlantic revolutions lay in the emergence of a feminist movement. Although scattered voices had earlier challenged patriarchy, never before had an organized and substantial group of women called into question this most fundamental and accepted feature of all preindustrial civilizations—the subordination of women to men. Then, in the century following the French Revolution, such a challenge took shape, especially in Europe and North America. In the twentieth century, feminist thinking transformed "the way in which women and men work, play, think, dress, worship, vote, reproduce, make love and make war."[19] How did this extraordinary process get launched in the nineteenth century?

Thinkers of the European Enlightenment had challenged many ancient traditions, including on occasion that of women's intrinsic inferiority. The French writer Condorcet, for example, called for "the complete destruction of those prejudices that have established an inequality of rights between the sexes." The French Revolution then raised the possibility of re-creating human societies on new foundations. Many women participated in these events, and a few insisted, unsuccessfully, that the revolutionary ideals of liberty and equality must include women. In her *Declaration of the Rights of Woman*, the French feminist Olympe de Gouges wrote in 1791: "Woman, wake up; the tocsin [warning bell] of reason is being heard throughout the whole universe; discover your rights."[20]

Within the growing middle classes of industrializing societies, more women found both educational opportunities and some freedom from household drudgery. Such women increasingly took part in temperance movements, charities, abolitionism, and missionary work, as well as socialist and pacifist organizations. Some of their working-class sisters became active trade unionists. On both sides of the Atlantic, small numbers of these women began to develop a feminist consciousness that viewed women as individuals with rights equal to those of men.[21] Others, particularly in France, based their claims less on abstract notions of equality and more on the distinctive role of women as mothers. "It is above all this holy function of motherhood . . . ," wrote one advocate of "maternal feminism," "which requires that women watch over the futures of their children and gives women the right to intervene not only in all acts of civil life, but also in all acts of political life."[22] The first organized expression of this new feminism took place at a women's rights conference in Seneca Falls, New York, in 1848. At that meeting, Elizabeth Cady Stanton drafted a statement that began by paraphrasing the Declaration of Independence: "We hold these truths to be self-evident, that all men and women are created equal."

From the beginning, feminism was a transatlantic movement in which European and American women attended the same conferences, corresponded regularly, and read one another's work. Access to schools, universities, and the professions were among their major concerns as growing numbers of women sought these previously unavailable opportunities. The more radical among them refused to take their husbands' surname or wore trousers under their skirts. Elizabeth Cady Stanton published a Women's Bible, eliminating the parts she found offensive. As heirs to the French Revolution, feminists ardently believed in progress and insisted that it must now include a radical transformation of the position of women.

By the 1870s, feminist movements in the West were focusing primarily on the issue of suffrage and were gaining a growing constituency. Now many ordinary middle-class housewives and working-class mothers joined their better-educated sisters in the movement. By 1914, some 100,000 women took part in French feminist organizations, while the National American Woman Suffrage Association claimed 2 million members. Most operated through peaceful protest and persuasion, but the British Women's Social and Political Union organized a campaign of violence that included blowing up railroad stations, slashing works of art, and smashing department store windows. One British activist, Emily Davison, threw herself in front of the king's horse during a race in Britain in 1913 and was trampled to death. By the beginning of the twentieth century in the most highly industrialized countries of the West, the women's movement had become a mass movement.

That movement had some effect. By 1900, upper- and middle-class women had gained entrance to universities, though in small numbers, and women's literacy rates were growing steadily. In the United States, a number of states passed legislation allowing women to manage and control their own property and wages, separate from their husbands. Divorce laws were liberalized in some places. Professions such as medicine opened to a few, and teaching beckoned to many more. In Britain, Florence Nightingale professionalized nursing and attracted thousands of women into it, while Jane Addams in the United States virtually invented social work, which also became a female-dominated profession. Progress was slower in the political domain. In 1893, New Zealand became the first country to give the vote to all adult women; Finland followed in 1906. Elsewhere widespread voting rights for women in national elections were not achieved until after World War I and in France not until 1945.

Women's Suffrage
What began as a few isolated voices of feminist protest in the early nineteenth century had become by the end of the century a mass movement in the United States and Western Europe. Here, in a photograph of an American suffrage parade in 1912, is an illustration of that movement in action. (The Granger Collection, New York)

Beyond these concrete accomplishments, the movement prompted an unprecedented discussion about the role of women in modern society. In Henrik Ibsen's play *A Doll's House* (1879), the heroine Nora, finding herself in a loveless and oppressive marriage, leaves both her husband and her children. European audiences were riveted, and many were outraged. Writers, doctors, and journalists addressed previously taboo sexual topics, including homosexuality and birth control. Socialists too found themselves divided about women's issues. Did the women's movement distract from the class solidarity that Marxism proclaimed, or did it provide added energy to the workers' cause? Feminists themselves disagreed about the proper basis for women's rights. Some took their stand on the modern idea of human equality: "whatever is right for a man is right for a woman." Others argued that women's traditional role as mothers, the guardians of family life and social virtue, provided the stronger case for women's rights.

Not surprisingly, feminism provoked bitter opposition. Some academic and medical experts argued that the strains of education and life in the world outside the home would cause serious reproductive damage and as a consequence depopulate the nation. Thus feminists were viewed as selfish, willing to sacrifice the family or even the nation while pursuing their individual goals. Some saw suffragists, like Jews and socialists, as "a foreign body in our national life." Never before in any society had such a passionate and public debate about the position of women erupted. It was a novel feature of Western historical experience in the aftermath of the Atlantic revolutions.

Like nationalism, a concern with women's rights spread beyond Western Europe and the United States, though less widely. An overtly feminist newspaper was established in Brazil in 1852, and an independent school for girls was founded in Mexico in 1869. A handful of Japanese women and men, including the empress Haruko, raised issues about marriage, family planning, and especially education as the country began its modernizing process after 1868, but the state soon cracked down firmly, forbidding women from joining political parties or even attending political meetings. In Russia, the most radical feminist activists operated within socialist or anarchist circles, targeting the oppressive tsarist regime. Within the Islamic world and in China, some modernists came to feel that education and a higher status for women strengthened the nation in its struggles for development and independence and therefore deserved support. Huda Sharawi, founder of the first feminist organization in Egypt, returned to Cairo in 1923 from an international conference in Italy and threw her veil into the sea. Many upper-class Egyptian women soon followed her example.

Nowhere did nineteenth-century feminism have really revolutionary consequences. But as an outgrowth of the French and Industrial revolutions, it raised issues that echoed repeatedly and more loudly in the century that followed.

⼿ Reflections: Revolutions Pro and Con

Not long before he died in 1976, the Chinese revolutionary and communist leader Zhou Enlai was asked what he thought about the French Revolution. His famous reply—"It's too early to say"—highlights the endless controversies that revolutions everywhere have spawned. Long after the dust had settled from these Atlantic upheavals, their legacies have continued to provoke controversy. Were these revolutions necessary? Did they really promote the freedoms that they advertised? Did their benefits outweigh their costs in blood and treasure?

To the people who made these revolutions, benefited from them, or subsequently supported them, they represented an opening to new worlds of human possibility, while sweeping away old worlds of oppression, exploitation, and privilege. Modern revolutionaries acted on the basis of Enlightenment ideas—that the structure of human societies was not forever ordained by God or tradition and that it was both possible and necessary to reconstruct those societies. They also saw themselves as correcting ancient and enduring injustices. To those who complained about the violence of revolutions, supporters pointed to the violence that maintained the status quo and the unwillingness of privileged classes to accommodate changes that threatened those privileges. It was persistent injustice that made revolution necessary and perhaps inevitable.

To their victims, critics, and opponents, revolutions appeared quite different. Conservatives generally viewed human societies, not as machines whose parts could be easily rearranged, but as organisms that evolved slowly. Efforts at radical and sudden change only invited disaster, as the unrestrained violence of the French Revolution at its height demonstrated. The brutality and bitterness of the Haitian Revolution arguably contributed much to the unhappy future of that country. Furthermore, critics charged that revolutions were largely unnecessary, since societies were in fact changing. France was becoming a modern society and feudalism was largely gone well before the revolution exploded. Slavery was ended peacefully in many places, and democratic reform proceeded gradually throughout the nineteenth century. Was this not a preferable alternative to that of revolutionary upheaval?

Historians too struggle with the passions of revolution—both pro and con—as they seek to understand the origins and consequences of these momentous events. Were revolutions the product of misery, injustice, and oppression? Or did they reflect the growing weakness of established authorities, the arrival of new ideas, or the presence of small groups of radical activists able to fan the little fires of ordinary discontent into revolutionary conflagrations? The outcomes of revolutions have been as contentious as their beginnings. Did the American Revolution enable the growth of the United States as an economic and political "great power"? Did the Haitian Revolution stimulate the later end of slavery elsewhere in the Atlantic world? Did the French Revolution and the threat of subsequent revolutions encourage the democratic reforms that followed in the nineteenth century? Such questions have been central to an understanding of eighteenth-century revolutions as well as to those that followed in Russia, China, and elsewhere in the twentieth century.

Second Thoughts

To assess your mastery of the material in this chapter, see the **Online Study Guide** at bedfordstmartins.com/strayer.

What's the Significance?

North American Revolution
French Revolution
Declaration of the Rights of
     Man and Citizen
Napoleon Bonaparte

Haitian Revolution
Latin American
     revolutions
abolitionist movement
nationalism

*Declaration of the Rights of
     Woman*
maternal feminism
Elizabeth Cady Stanton

Big Picture Questions

1. Make a chart comparing the North American, French, Haitian, and Spanish American revolutions. What categories of comparison would be most appropriate to include?
2. Do revolutions originate in oppression and injustice, in the weakening of political authorities, in new ideas, or in the activities of small groups of determined activists?
3. "The influence of revolutions endured long after they ended." To what extent does this chapter support or undermine this idea?

4. In what ways did the Atlantic revolutions and their echoes give a new and distinctive shape to the emerging societies of nineteenth-century Europe and the Americas?

Next Steps: For Further Study

Benedict Anderson, *Imagined Communities: Reflections on the Origins and Spread of Nationalism* (1991). A now-classic though controversial examination of the process by which national identities were created.

Bonnie S. Anderson, *Joyous Greetings: The First International Women's Movement, 1830–1860* (2000). Describes the beginnings of transatlantic feminism.

Laurent Dubois and John Garrigus, *Slave Revolution in the Caribbean, 1789–1804* (2006). A brief and up-to-date summary of the Haitian Revolution, combined with a number of documents.

Susan Dunn, *Sister Revolutions* (1999). A stimulating comparative study of the American and French revolutions.

Eric Hobsbawm, *The Age of Revolution, 1789–1848* (1999). A highly respected survey by a well-known British historian.

Lynn Hunt, ed., *The French Revolution and Human Rights* (1996). A collection of documents, with a fine introduction by a prominent scholar.

"Liberty, Equality, Fraternity: Exploring the French Revolution," http://chnm.gmu.edu/revolution/browse/images/#. A collection of cartoons, paintings, and artifacts illustrating the French Revolution.

For Web sites and documents related to this chapter, see **Make History** at bedfordstmartins.com/strayer.

half between 1750 and 1900. It drew upon the Scientific Revolution and accompanied the unfolding legacy of the French Revolution to utterly transform European society and to propel Europe into a position of global dominance. Not since the breakthrough of the Agricultural Revolution some 12,000 years ago had human ways of life been so fundamentally altered. But the Industrial Revolution, unlike its agricultural predecessor, began independently in only one place, Western Europe and more specifically Great Britain. From there, it spread far more rapidly than agriculture, though very unevenly, to achieve a worldwide presence in less than 250 years. Far more than Europe's Christian religion, its democratic political values, or its capitalist economic framework, the techniques of its Industrial Revolution have been intensely sought after virtually everywhere.

In any long-term reckoning, the history of industrialization is very much an unfinished story. It is hard to know whether we are at the beginning of a movement leading to worldwide industrialization, stuck in the middle of a world permanently divided into rich and poor countries, or approaching the end of an environmentally unsustainable industrial era. Whatever the future holds, this chapter focuses on the early stages of an immense transformation in the global condition of humankind.

Explaining the Industrial Revolution

At the heart of the Industrial Revolution lay a great acceleration in the rate of technological innovation, leading to an enormously increased output of goods and services. Particularly significant were new sources of energy—coal-fired steam engines early on and petroleum-fueled engines later. In Britain, where that revolution began, industrial output increased some fiftyfold between 1750 and 1900. It was a wholly unprecedented and previously unimaginable jump in the capacity of human societies to produce wealth. Lying behind it was not simply this or that invention—the spinning jenny, power loom, steam engine, or cotton gin—but a "culture of innovation," a widespread and almost obsessive belief that things could be endlessly improved. Until 1750 or even 1800, however, Europeans held no across-the-board technological advantage over China, India, or the Islamic world. These major Eurasian civilizations existed then in a state of rough technological equilibrium.

Early signs of the technological creativity that spawned the Industrial Revolution appeared in eighteenth-century Britain, where a variety of innovations transformed cotton textile production. It was only in the nineteenth century, though, that Europeans in general and the British in particular more clearly forged ahead. The great breakthrough was the steam engine, which provided an inanimate and almost limitless source of power beyond that of wind, water, or muscle and could be used to drive any number of machines as well as locomotives and oceangoing ships. Soon the Industrial Revolution spread beyond the textile industry to iron and steel production, railroads and steamships, food processing, construction, chemicals, electricity, the telegraph and telephone, rubber, pottery, printing, and much more. Agriculture too was affected as mechanical reapers, chemical fertilizers, pesticides, and refrigeration transformed this most ancient of industries. Technical innovation occurred in more modest ways as well. Patents for horseshoes in the United States, for example, grew from fewer than five per year before 1840 to thirty to forty per year by the end of the century. Furthermore, industrialization spread beyond Britain to continental Western Europe and then in the second half of the century to the United States, Russia, and Japan.

In the twentieth century, the Industrial Revolution became global when a number of Asian and Latin American countries developed substantial industrial sectors. Oil, natural gas, and nuclear reactions became widely available sources of energy, and new industries emerged in automobiles, airplanes, consumer durable goods, electronics, computers, and on and on. It was a cumulative process that, despite periodic ups and downs, accelerated over time. More than anything else, this continuous emergence of new techniques of production and the economic growth that they made possible mark the past 250 years as a distinct phase of human history.

Why Europe?

The Industrial Revolution has long been a source of great controversy among scholars. Why did it occur first in Europe? Within Europe, why did it occur first in Great Britain? And why did it take place in the late eighteenth and nineteenth centuries? Earlier explanations that sought the answer in some unique and deeply rooted feature of European society, history, or culture have been challenged by world historians because such views seemed to suggest that Europe alone was destined to lead the way to modern economic life. This approach not only was Eurocentric and deterministic but also flew in the face of much recent research in at least three ways.

■ Causation
In what respects did the roots of the Industrial Revolution lie within Europe? In what ways did that transformation have global roots?

First, other areas of the world had experienced times of great technological and scientific flourishing. Between 750 and 1100 C.E., the Islamic world generated major advances in shipbuilding, the use of tides and falling water to generate power, papermaking, textile production, chemical technologies, water mills, clocks, and much more.[2] India had long been the world center of cotton textile production, the first place to turn sugarcane juice into crystallized sugar, and the source of many agricultural innovations and mathematical inventions. To the Arabs of the ninth century C.E., India was a "place of marvels."[3] More than either of these, China was clearly the world leader in technological innovation between 700 and 1400 C.E., prompting various scholars to suggest that China was on the edge of an industrial revolution by 1200 or so. For reasons much debated among historians, all of these flowerings of technological creativity had slowed down considerably or stagnated by the early modern era, when the pace of technological change in Europe began to pick up. But their earlier achievements certainly suggest that Europe was not alone in its capacity for technological innovation.

Nor did Europe enjoy any overall economic advantage as late as 1750. Over the past twenty years or so, historians have carefully examined the economic conditions of various Eurasian societies in the eighteenth century and found them surprisingly alike. Economic indicators such as life expectancies, patterns of consumption and nutrition, wage levels, general living standards, widespread free markets, and prosperous merchant communities suggest broadly similar conditions across the major civilizations of Europe and Asia.[4] Thus Europe had no obvious economic lead, even on the eve of the Industrial Revolution. Rather, according to one leading scholar, "there existed something of a global economic parity between the most advanced regions in the world economy."[5]

A final reason for doubting any unique European capacity for industrial development lies in the relatively rapid spread of industrial techniques to many parts of the world over the past 250 years (a fairly short time by world history standards). Although the process has been highly uneven, industrialization has taken root, to one degree or another, in Japan, China, India, Brazil, Mexico, Indonesia, South Africa, Saudi Arabia, Thailand, South Korea, and elsewhere. Such a pattern weakens any suggestion that European culture or society was exceptionally compatible with industrial development.

Thus contemporary historians are inclined to see the Industrial Revolution erupting rather quickly and quite unexpectedly between 1750 and 1850 (see Map 18.1). Two intersecting factors help to explain why this process occurred in Europe rather than elsewhere. One lies in certain patterns of Europe's internal development that favored innovation. Its many small and highly competitive states, taking shape in the twelfth or thirteenth centuries, arguably provided an "insurance against economic and technological stagnation," which the larger Chinese, Ottoman, or Mughal empires perhaps lacked.[6] If so, then Western Europe's failure to re-create the earlier unity of the Roman Empire may have acted as a stimulus to innovation.

Furthermore, the relative newness of these European states and their monarchs' desperate need for revenue in the absence of an effective tax-collecting bureaucracy pushed European royals into an unusual alliance with their merchant classes. Small groups of merchant capitalists might be granted special privileges, monopolies, or even tax-collecting responsibilities in exchange for much-needed loans or payments to the state. It was therefore in the interest of governments to actively encourage commerce and innovation. Thus states granted charters and monopolies to private trading companies, and governments founded scientific societies and offered prizes to promote innovation. In this way, European merchants and other innovators from the fifteenth century onward gained an unusual degree of freedom from state control and in some places a higher social status than their counterparts in more established civilizations. In Venice and Holland, merchants actually controlled the state. In short, by the eighteenth century major Western European societies were highly commercialized and governed by states generally supportive of private commerce. Such internally competitive economies, coupled with a highly competitive system of rival states, fostered innovation in the new civilization taking shape in Western Europe.

Europe's societies, of course, were not alone in developing market-based economies by the eighteenth century. Japan, India, and especially China were likewise

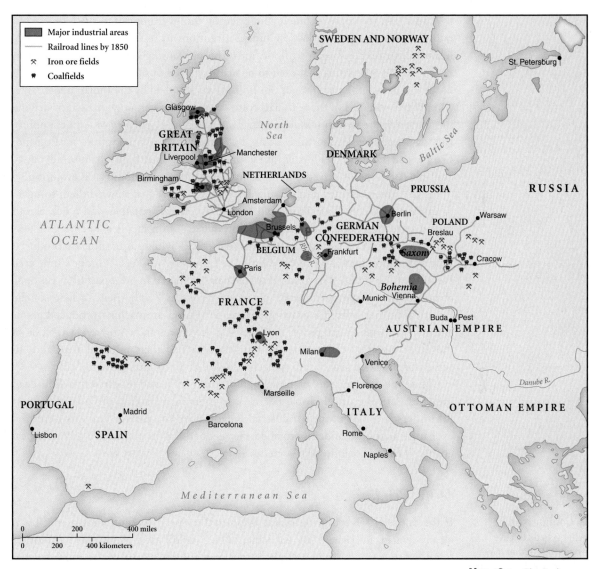

Map 18.1 The Early Phase of Europe's Industrial Revolution
From its beginning in Great Britain, industrialization spread by 1850 across northwestern Europe to include parts of France, Germany, Belgium, Bohemia, and Italy.

highly commercialized. However, in the several centuries after 1500, Western Europe alone "found itself at the hub of the largest and most varied network of exchange in history."[7] Widespread contact with culturally different peoples was yet another factor that historically has generated extensive change and innovation. This new global network, largely the creation of Europeans themselves, greatly energized European commerce and brought Europeans into direct contact with peoples around the world.

For example, Asia, home to the world's richest and most sophisticated societies, was the initial destination of European voyages of exploration. The German philosopher Gottfried Wilhelm Leibniz (1646–1716) encouraged Jesuit missionaries in China "not to worry so much about getting things European to the Chinese but rather about getting remarkable Chinese inventions to us."[8] Inexpensive and well-made Indian textiles began to flood into Europe, causing one English observer to note: "Almost everything that used to be made of wool or silk, relating either to dress of the women or the furniture of our houses, was supplied by the Indian trade."[9] The competitive stimulus of these Indian cotton textiles was certainly one factor driving innovation in the British textile industry. Likewise, the popularity of Chinese porcelain and Japanese lacquerware prompted imitation and innovation in England, France, and Holland.[10] Thus competition from desirable, high-quality, and newly available Asian goods played a role in stimulating Europe's Industrial Revolution.

In the Americas, Europeans found a windfall of silver that allowed them to operate in Asian markets. They also found timber, fish, maize, potatoes, and much else to sustain a growing population. Later, slave-produced cotton supplied an emerging textile industry with its key raw material at low prices, while sugar, similarly produced with slave labor, furnished cheap calories to European workers. "Europe's Industrial Revolution," concluded historian Peter Stearns, "stemmed in great part from Europe's ability to draw disproportionately on world resources."[11] The new societies of the Americas further offered a growing market for European machine-produced goods and generated substantial profits for European merchants and entrepreneurs. None of the other empires of the early modern era enriched their imperial heartlands so greatly or provided such a spur to technological and economic growth.

Thus the intersection of new, highly commercialized, competitive European societies with the novel global network of their own making provides a context for understanding Europe's Industrial Revolution. Commerce and cross-cultural exchange, acting in tandem, provided the seedbed for the impressive technological changes of the first industrial societies.

Why Britain?

■ **Comparison**
What was distinctive about Britain that may help to explain its status as the breakthrough point of the Industrial Revolution?

If the Industrial Revolution was a Western European phenomenon generally, it clearly began in Britain in particular. The world's first Industrial Revolution unfolded spontaneously in a country that concentrated some of the more general features of European society. It was both unplanned and unexpected.

Britain was the most highly commercialized of Europe's larger countries. Its landlords had long ago "enclosed" much agricultural land, pushing out the small farmers and producing for the market. A series of agricultural innovations—crop rotation, selective breeding of animals, lighter plows, higher-yielding seeds—increased agricultural output, kept food prices low, and freed up labor from the countryside. The guilds, which earlier had protected Britain's urban artisans, had largely disappeared by the eighteenth century, allowing employers to run their manufacturing enterprises as they saw fit. Coupled with a rapidly growing population, these processes ensured a ready supply of industrial workers who had few alternatives available to them. Furthermore, British aristocrats, unlike their counterparts in

Europe, had long been interested in commerce, and some took part in new mining and manufacturing enterprises. British commerce, moreover, extended around the world, its large merchant fleet protected by the Royal Navy. The wealth of empire and global commerce, however, were not themselves sufficient for spawning the Industrial Revolution, especially when we consider that Spain, the earliest beneficiary of American wealth, remained one of the more slowly industrializing European countries into the twentieth century.

British political life encouraged commercialization and economic innovation. Its policy of religious toleration, formally established in 1688, welcomed people with technical skills regardless of their faith, whereas France's persecution of its Protestant minority had chased out some of its most skilled workers. The British government favored men of business with tariffs to keep out cheap Indian textiles, with laws that made it easy to form companies and to forbid workers' unions, with roads and canals that helped create a unified internal market, and with patent laws that served to protect the interests of inventors. Checks on royal authority—trial by jury and the growing authority of parliament, for example—provided a freer arena for private enterprise than elsewhere in Europe.

Europe's Scientific Revolution also took a distinctive form in Great Britain in ways that fostered technological innovation.[12] Whereas science on the continent was largely based on logic, deduction, and mathematical reasoning, in Britain it was much more concerned with observation and experiment, precise measurements, mechanical devices, and practical commercial applications. Discoveries about atmospheric pressure and vacuums, for example, played an important role in the invention and improvement of the steam engine. Even though most inventors were artisans or craftsmen rather than scientists, in eighteenth-century Britain they were in close contact with scientists, makers of scientific instruments, and entrepreneurs, whereas in continental Europe these groups were largely separate. The British Royal Society, an association of natural philosophers (scientists) established in 1660, saw its role as one of promoting "useful knowledge." To this end, it established "mechanics' libraries," published broadsheets and pamphlets on recent scientific advances, and held frequent public lectures and demonstrations. The integration of science and technology became widespread and permanent after 1850, but for a century before, it was largely a British phenomenon.

Finally, several accidents of geography and history contributed something to Britain's Industrial Revolution. The country had a ready supply of coal and iron ore, often located close to each other and within easy reach of major industrial centers. Although Britain took part in the wars against Napoleon, the country's island location protected it from the kind of invasions that so many continental European states experienced during the era of the French Revolution. Moreover, Britain's relatively fluid society allowed for adjustments in the face of social changes without widespread revolution. By the time the dust settled from the immense disturbance of the French Revolution, Britain was well on its way to becoming the world's first industrial society.

Railroads
The popularity of railroads, long a symbol of the Industrial Revolution, is illustrated in this early-nineteenth-century water-color, which shows a minia-ture train offered as a paid amusement for enthusiasts in London's Euston Square. (Science Museum, London, UK/The Bridgeman Art Library)

The First Industrial Society

Wherever it took hold, the Industrial Revolution generated, within a century or less, an economic miracle, at least in comparison with earlier technologies. The British textile industry, which used 52 million pounds of cotton in 1800, consumed 588 million pounds in 1850. Britain's output of coal soared from 5.23 million tons in 1750 to 68.4 million tons a century later.[13] Railroads crisscrossed Britain and much of Europe like a giant spider web (see Map 18.1, p. 531). Most of this dramatic increase in production occurred in mining, manufacturing, and services. Thus agriculture, for millennia the overwhelmingly dominant eco-nomic sector in every civilization, shrank in relative importance. In Britain, for exam-ple, agriculture generated only 8 percent of national income in 1891 and employed fewer than 8 percent of working Britons in 1914. Accompanying this vast economic change was an epic transformation of social life. "In two centuries," wrote one promi-nent historian, "daily life changed more than it had in the 7,000 years before."[14] Nowhere were the revolutionary dimensions of industrialization more apparent than in Great Britain, the world's first industrial society.

The social transformation of the Industrial Revolution both destroyed and cre-ated. Referring to the impact of the Industrial Revolution on British society, histo-rian Eric Hobsbawm said: "[I]n its initial stages it destroyed their old ways of living and left them free to discover or make for themselves new ones, if they could and knew how. But it rarely told them how to set about it."[15] For many people, it was an enormously painful, even traumatic process, full of social conflict, insecurity, and false starts as well as new opportunities, an eventually higher standard of living, and greater participation in public life. Scholars, politicians, journalists, and ordinary people have endlessly debated the gains and losses associated with the Industrial Revolution. Amid the controversy, however, one thing is clear: not everyone was affected in the same way.

The British Aristocracy

■ **Change**
How did the Industrial Revolution transform British society?

Individual landowning aristocrats, long the dominant class in Britain, suffered little in material terms from the Industrial Revolution. In the mid-nineteenth century, a few thousand families still owned more than half of the cultivated land in Britain,

Snapshot **Measuring the Industrial Revolution**[16]

Railroads are one useful measure of industrial development. This graph illustrates both Britain's head start and the beginning catch-up efforts of other countries.

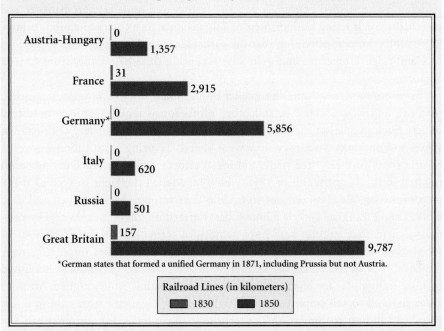

Austria-Hungary — 0 — 1,357
France — 31 — 2,915
Germany* — 0 — 5,856
Italy — 0 — 620
Russia — 0 — 501
Great Britain — 157 — 9,787

*German states that formed a unified Germany in 1871, including Prussia but not Austria.

Railroad Lines (in kilometers)
1830   1850

most of it leased to tenant farmers, who in turn employed agricultural wage labor-ers to work it. Rapidly growing population and urbanization sustained a demand for food products grown on that land. For most of the nineteenth century, landowners continued to dominate the British parliament.

As a class, however, the British aristocracy, like large landowners in every indus-trial society, declined. As urban wealth became more important, landed aristocrats had to make way for the up-and-coming businessmen, manufacturers, and bankers who had been newly enriched by the Industrial Revolution. The aristocracy's declining political clout was demonstrated in the 1840s when high tariffs on for-eign agricultural imports, designed to protect the interests of British landlords, were finally abolished. By the end of the century, landownership had largely ceased to be the basis of great wealth, and businessmen, rather than aristocrats, led the major political parties. Even so, the titled nobility of dukes, earls, viscounts, and barons retained great social prestige and considerable personal wealth. Many among them found an outlet for their energies and opportunities for status and enrichment in the vast domains of the British Empire, where they went as colonial administrators or settlers. Famously described as a "system of outdoor relief for the aristocracy," the empire provided a cushion for a declining class.

The Middle Classes

■ Change
How did Britain's middle classes change during the nineteenth century?

Those who benefited most conspicuously from industrialization were members of that amorphous group known as the "middle classes." At its upper levels, the middle class contained extremely wealthy factory and mine owners, bankers, and merchants. Such rising businessmen readily assimilated into aristocratic life, buying country houses, obtaining seats in parliament, sending their sons to Oxford or Cambridge University, and gratefully accepting titles of nobility from Queen Victoria.

Far more numerous were the smaller businessmen, doctors, lawyers, engineers, teachers, journalists, scientists, and other professionals required in any industrial society. Such people set the tone for a distinctly middle-class society with its own values and outlooks. Politically they were liberals, favoring constitutional government, private property, free trade, and social reform within limits. Their agitation resulted in the Reform Bill of 1832, which broadened the right to vote to many men of the middle class, but not to middle-class women. Ideas of thrift and hard work, a rigid morality, and cleanliness characterized middle-class culture. The central value of that culture was "respectability," a term that combined notions of social status and virtuous behavior. Nowhere were these values more effectively displayed than in the Scotsman Samuel Smiles's famous book *Self-Help*, published in 1859. Individuals are responsible for their own destiny, Smiles argued. An hour a day devoted to self-improvement "would make an ignorant man wise in a few years." According to Smiles, this enterprising spirit was what distinguished the prosperous middle class from Britain's poor. The misery of the poorer classes was "voluntary and self-imposed—the results of idleness, thriftlessness, intemperance, and misconduct."[17]

Women in such middle-class families were increasingly cast as homemakers, wives, and mothers, charged with creating an emotional haven for their men and a refuge from a heartless and cutthroat capitalist world. They were also the moral center of family life and the educators of "respectability" as well as the managers of consumption in a setting in which "shopping," a new concept in eighteenth-century Britain, became a central activity. An "ideology of domesticity" defined the home and charitable activities as the proper sphere for women, while paid employment and public life beckoned to men.

The Industrial Middle Class
This late-nineteenth-century painting shows a prosperous French middle-class family, attended by a servant. (Chateau de Versailles/SuperStock, Inc.)

The English poet Alfred, Lord Tennyson, aptly expressed this understanding in his poem "The Princess":

Man for the field and woman for the hearth:
Man for the sword and for the needle she:
Man with the head and woman with the heart:
Man to command and woman to obey.
All else confusion.

Middle-class women played a very different role from women in the peasant farm or the artisan's shop, where wives, though clearly subordinate, worked productively alongside their husbands. By the late nineteenth century, however, some middle-class women began to enter the teaching, clerical, and nursing professions.

As Britain's industrial economy matured, it also gave rise to a sizable "lower middle class," which included people employed in the growing service sector as clerks, salespeople, bank tellers, hotel staff, secretaries, telephone operators, police officers, and the like. By the end of the nineteenth century, this growing class represented about 20 percent of Britain's population and provided new employment opportunities for women as well as men. In just twenty years (1881–1901), the number of female secretaries in Britain rose from 7,000 to 90,000. Almost all were single and expected to return to the home after marriage. For both men and women, such employment represented a claim on membership in the larger middle class and a means of distinguishing themselves clearly from a "working class" tainted by manual labor.

The Laboring Classes

The overwhelming majority of Britain's nineteenth-century population—some 70 percent or more—were, of course, neither aristocrats nor members of the middle classes. They were manual workers in the mines, ports, factories, construction sites, workshops, and farms of an industrializing Britain. Although their conditions varied considerably and changed over time, the laboring classes were the people who suffered most and benefited least from the epic transformations of the Industrial Revolution. Their efforts to accommodate, resist, protest, and change those conditions contributed much to the texture of the first industrial society.

The lives of the laboring classes were shaped primarily by the new working conditions of the industrial era. Chief among those conditions was the rapid urbanization of British society. Liverpool's population alone grew from 77,000 to 400,000 in the first half of the nineteenth century. By 1851, a majority of Britain's population lived in towns and cities, an enormous change from the overwhelmingly rural life of almost all previous civilizations. By the end of the century, London was the world's largest city, with more than 6 million inhabitants.

These cities were vastly overcrowded and smoky, with wholly inadequate sanitation, periodic epidemics, endless row houses and warehouses, few public services or open spaces, and inadequate water supplies. This was the environment in which

DEATH'S DISPENSARY.
OPEN TO THE POOR, GRATIS, BY PERMISSION OF THE PARISH.

The Urban Poor of Industrial Britain
This 1866 political cartoon shows an impoverished urban family forced to draw its drinking water from a polluted public well, while a figure of Death operates the pump. (The Granger Collection, New York)

most urban workers lived in the first half of the nineteenth century. Nor was there much personal contact between the rich and the poor of industrial cities. Benjamin Disraeli's novel *Sybil*, published in 1845, described these two ends of the social spectrum as "two nations between whom there is no intercourse and no sympathy; who are ignorant of each other's habits, thoughts and feelings, as if they were dwellers in different zones or inhabitants of different planets."

The industrial factories to which growing numbers of desperate people looked for employment offered a work environment far different from the artisan's shop or the tenant's farm. Long hours, low wages, and child labor were nothing new for the poor, but the routine and monotony of work, dictated by the factory whistle and the needs of machines, imposed novel and highly unwelcome conditions of labor. Also objectionable were the direct and constant supervision and the rules and fines aimed at enforcing work discipline. The ups and downs of a capitalist economy made industrial work insecure as well as onerous. Unlike their middle-class sisters, many girls and young women of the laboring classes worked in mills or as domestic servants in order to supplement meager family incomes, but after marriage they too usually left outside paid employment because a man who could not support his wife was widely considered a failure. Within the home, however, many working-class women continued to earn money by taking in boarders, doing laundry, or sewing clothes.

Social Protest among the Laboring Classes

For workers of the laboring classes, industrial life "was a stony desert, which they had to make habitable by their own efforts."[18] Such efforts took many forms. By 1815, about 1 million workers, mostly artisans, had created a variety of "friendly societies." With dues contributed by members, these working-class self-help groups provided insurance against sickness, a decent funeral, and an opportunity for social life in an otherwise bleak environment. Other skilled artisans, who had been displaced by machine-produced goods and forbidden to organize in legal unions, sometimes wrecked the offending machinery and burned the mills that had taken their jobs. The class consciousness of working people was such that one police informer reported that "most every creature of the lower order both in town and country are on their side."[19]

Others acted within the political arena by joining movements aimed at obtaining the vote for working-class men, a goal that was gradually achieved in the second half of the nineteenth century. When trade unions were legalized in 1824, growing numbers of factory workers joined these associations in their efforts to achieve better wages and working conditions. Initially their strikes, attempts at nationwide organization, and the threat of violence made them fearful indeed to the upper classes. One British newspaper in 1834 described unions as "the most dangerous institutions that were ever permitted to take root, under shelter of law, in any country,"[20] although they later became rather more "respectable" organizations.

Socialist ideas of various kinds gradually spread within the working class, challenging the assumptions of a capitalist society. Robert Owen (1771–1858), a wealthy British cotton textile manufacturer, urged the creation of small industrial communities, cooperatively run by the workers themselves. He established one such community, with a ten-hour workday, spacious housing, decent wages, and education for children, at his mill in New Lanark in Scotland.

Of more lasting significance was the socialism of Karl Marx (1818–1883). German by birth, Marx spent much of his life in England, where he witnessed the brutal conditions of Britain's Industrial Revolution and wrote voluminously about history and economics. To Marx, the story line of the human past and the motor of historical change had always been "class struggle," the bitter conflict of "oppressor and oppressed." In his own time, that struggle took the form of sharpening hostility between the *bourgeoisie*, who owned industrial capital, and the *proletariat*, his term for the industrial working class. For Marx, class struggle was the central dynamic of industrial capitalist societies.

■ **Change**
How did Karl Marx understand the Industrial Revolution? In what ways did his ideas have an impact in the industrializing world of the nineteenth century?

As a phase of human history, capitalism bore great promise, for it had unleashed, as Marx put it in the *Communist Manifesto*, "more massive and more colossal productive forces than have all preceding generations together," which meant, of course, that the end of poverty was in sight. And yet, according to Marx, capitalist societies could never deliver on that promise because private property, competition, and class hostility prevented those societies from distributing the abundance of industrial economies to the workers whose labor had created that abundance. Capitalism therefore was fatally flawed, doomed to inevitable collapse amid a working-class revolution as society polarized into rich and poor. After that revolution, Marx looked forward to a communist future in which the great productive potential of industrial technology would be placed in service to the entire community, thus ending forever the ancient conflict between rich and poor.

In the later decades of the nineteenth century, such ideas echoed among more radical trade unionists and some middle-class intellectuals in Britain, and even more so in a rapidly industrializing Germany and elsewhere, but the British working-class movement by then was not overtly revolutionary. When a working-class political party, the Labour Party, was established in the 1890s, it advocated a

reformist program and a peaceful democratic transition to socialism, largely rejecting the class struggle and revolutionary emphasis of Marxism.

A major factor producing a moderate working-class movement lay in the improv-
ing material conditions during the second half of the nineteenth century. Marx had
expected industrial capitalist societies to polarize into a small wealthy class and a huge
and increasingly impoverished proletariat. However, standing between "the captains
of industry" and the workers was a sizable middle and lower-middle class, constitut-
ing perhaps 30 percent of the population, most of whom were not really wealthy but
were immensely proud that they were not manual laborers. Marx had not foreseen
the development of this intermediate social group, nor had he imagined that workers could better their standard of living within a capitalist framework. But they did.
Wages rose under pressure from unions; cheap imported food improved working-class
diets; infant mortality rates fell; and shops and chain stores catering to working-class
families multiplied. As English male workers gradually obtained the right to vote,
politicians had an incentive to legislate in their favor, by abolishing child labor, regulating factory conditions, and even, in 1911, inaugurating a system of relief for the
unemployed. Sanitary reform considerably cleaned up the "filth and stink" of early-
nineteenth-century cities, and urban parks made a modest appearance. Contrary to
Marx's expectations, capitalist societies demonstrated some capacity for reform.

Socialist Protest
Socialism, a response to the injustices and inequalities of industrial capitalism, spread throughout Europe in the nineteenth and early twenti-eth centuries. Here a group of French socialists in 1908 are demonstrating in mem-ory of an earlier uprising, the Paris commune of 1871. (Demonstration at Père-Lachaise for the commemoration of the Paris Commune, by Socialist party, French Section of the International Workingmen's Association, group of La Villette, 1st May 1908 [coloured photo], Gondry, [19th–early 20th century]/ Private Collection/The Bridgeman Art Library)

Manifestation du Père Lachaise
Parti Socialiste, Section Française de l'Internationale Ouvrière
Groupe de la Villette

Nonetheless, as the twentieth century dawned, industrial Britain could hardly be described as a stable or contented society. Immense inequalities still separated the classes. Some 40 percent of the working class continued to live in conditions then described as "poverty." A mounting wave of strikes from 1910 to 1913 testified to the intensity of class conflict. The Labour Party was becoming a major force in parliament. Some socialists and some feminists were becoming radicalized. "Wisps of violence hung in the English air," wrote Eric Hobsbawm, "symptoms of a crisis in economy and society, which the [country's] self-confident opulence…could not quite conceal."[21] The world's first industrial society remained a dissatisfied and conflicted society.

It was also a society in economic decline relative to industrial newcomers such as Germany and the United States. Britain paid a price for its early lead, for its businessmen became committed to machinery that became obsolete as the century progressed. Latecomers invested in more modern equipment and in various ways had surpassed the British by the early twentieth century.

Variations on a Theme: Comparing Industrialization in the United States and Russia

Not for long was the Industrial Revolution confined to Britain. It soon spread to continental Western Europe, and by the end of the nineteenth century, it was well under way in the United States, Russia, and Japan. The globalization of industrialization had begun. Everywhere it took hold, industrialization bore a range of outcomes broadly similar to those in Britain. New technologies and sources of energy generated vast increases in production and spawned an unprecedented urbanization as well. Class structures changed as aristocrats, artisans, and peasants declined as classes, while the middle classes and a factory working class grew in numbers and social prominence. Middle-class women generally withdrew from paid labor altogether, and their working-class counterparts sought to do so after marriage. Working women usually received lower wages than their male counterparts, had difficulty joining unions, and were subject to charges that they were taking jobs from men. Working-class frustration and anger gave rise to trade unions and socialist movements, injecting a new element of social conflict into industrial societies.

Nevertheless, different histories, cultures, and societies ensured that the Industrial Revolution unfolded variously in the diverse countries in which it became established. Differences in the pace and timing of industrialization, the size and shape of major industries, the role of the state, the political expression of social conflict, and many other factors have made this process rich in comparative possibilities. French industrialization, for example, occurred more slowly and perhaps less disruptively than did that of Britain. Germany focused initially on heavy industry—iron, steel, and coal—rather than on the textile industry with which Britain had begun. Moreover, German industrialization was far more highly concentrated in huge companies called cartels, and it generated a rather more militant and Marxist-oriented labor movement than in Britain.

Nowhere were the variations in the industrializing process more apparent than in those two vast countries that lay on the periphery of Europe. To the west across the Atlantic Ocean was the United States, a young, vigorous, democratic, expanding country, populated largely by people of European descent, along with a substantial number of slaves of African origin. To the east was Russia, with its Eastern Orthodox Christianity, an autocratic tsar, a huge population of serfs, and an empire stretching across all of northern Asia. In the early nineteenth century, the French observer Alexis de Tocqueville famously commented on these two emerging giants.

> The Anglo-American relies upon personal interest to accomplish his ends and gives free scope to the unguided strength and common sense of the people; the Russian centers all the authority of society in a single arm.... Their starting-point is different and their courses are not the same; yet each of them seems marked out by the will of Heaven to sway the destinies of half the globe.

By the early twentieth century, his prediction seemed to be coming true. Industrialization had turned the United States into a major global power and in Russia had spawned an enormous revolutionary upheaval that made that country the first outpost of global communism.

The United States: Industrialization without Socialism

■ Comparison
What were the differences between industrialization in the United States and that in Russia?

American industrialization began in the textile industry of New England during the 1820s but grew explosively in the half century following the Civil War (1861–1865) (see Map 18.2). The country's huge size, the ready availability of natural resources, its growing domestic market, and its relative political stability combined to make the United States the world's leading industrial power by 1914. At that time, it produced 36 percent of the world's manufactured goods, compared to 16 percent for Germany, 14 percent for Great Britain, and 6 percent for France. Furthermore, U.S. industrialization was closely linked to that of Europe. About one-third of the capital investment that financed its remarkable growth came from British, French, and German capitalists. Like many former colonies in the twentieth century, the United States initially relied on foreign capital for its development, although its overall economic strength was sufficient to avoid the dependency and underdevelopment that more recent emerging nations have so frequently experienced.

As in other second-wave industrializing countries, the U.S. government played an important role, though less directly than in Germany or Japan. Tax breaks, huge grants of public land to the railroad companies, laws enabling the easy formation of corporations, and the absence of much overt regulation of industry all fostered the rise of very large business enterprises. The U.S. Steel Corporation, for example, by 1901 had an annual budget three times the size of the federal government. In this

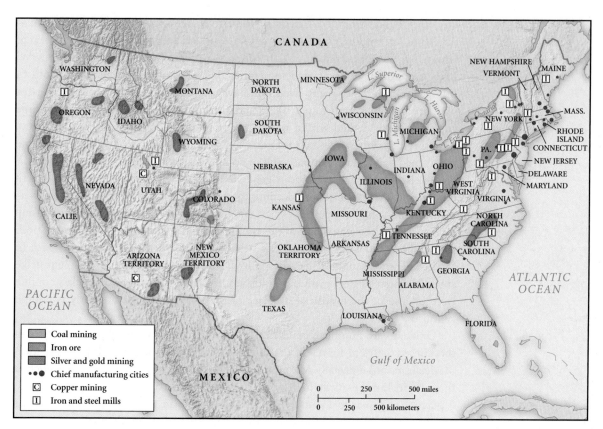

Map 18.2 The Industrial United States in 1900
By the early twentieth century, manufacturing industries were largely in the Northeast and Midwest, whereas mining operations were more widely scattered across the country.

respect, the United States followed the pattern of Germany but differed from that of France and Britain, where family businesses still predominated.

The United States also pioneered techniques of mass production, using interchangeable parts, the assembly line, and "scientific management" to produce for a mass market. The nation's advertising agencies, Sears Roebuck's and Montgomery Ward's mail-order catalogs, and urban department stores generated a middle-class "culture of consumption." When the industrialist Henry Ford in the early twentieth century began producing the Model T at a price that many ordinary people could afford, he famously declared: "I am going to democratize the automobile." More so than in Europe, with its aristocratic traditions, self-made American industrialists of fabulous wealth such as Henry Ford, Andrew Carnegie, and John D. Rockefeller became cultural heroes, widely admired as models of what anyone could achieve with daring and hard work in a land of endless opportunity.

Nevertheless, well before the first Model T rolled off the assembly line, serious social divisions of a kind common to European industrial societies mounted. Preindustrial America had prided itself on its lack of European-style slums, but by the 1850s, and even more so by the 1890s, a growing gap had opened between the poor and the working class on the one hand and the middle class and the rich on

■ **Explanation**
Why did Marxist socialism not take root in the United States?

the other hand. Around Carnegie's Homestead steel plant near Pittsburgh stood thousands of workers' shacks. Employees worked every day of the year except Christmas and the Fourth of July, often for twelve hours a day. In crowded Manhattan, often the first (and sometimes the last) stopping point for millions of European immigrants, many lived in the infamous "dumbbell" tenements: five- or six-story buildings with four families and two toilets on each floor. In every large city, these slums existed within walking distance of the mansions of the well-to-do. To some, the contrast was a disgrace to the economic system that produced it, while others held that it was a natural result of competition and "the survival of the fittest."

As elsewhere, such conditions generated much labor protest, the formation of unions, and strikes, sometimes leading to violence. In 1877, when the eastern railroads announced a 10 percent wage cut for their workers, strikers disrupted rail service across the eastern half of the country, smashed equipment, and rioted. Both state militias and federal troops were called out to put down the movement. In 1892, the entire National Guard of Pennsylvania was sent to suppress a violent strike at the Homestead steel plant near Pittsburgh. Class consciousness and class conflict were intense in the industrial America of the late nineteenth and early twentieth centuries.

Unlike many European countries, however, no major political party emerged in the United States to represent the interests of the working class. Nor did the ideas of socialism, and especially Marxism, appeal to American workers nearly as much as they did in Europe. At its high point, the Socialist Party of America garnered just 6 percent of the vote for its presidential candidate in the 1912 election, whereas socialists at the time held more seats in Germany's parliament than any other party. Even in the depths of the Great Depression of the 1930s, no major socialist movement emerged to champion American workers. How might we explain this distinctive feature of American industrial development?

One answer lies in the relative conservatism of major American union organizations, especially the American Federation of Labor. Its focus on skilled workers excluded the more radical unskilled laborers, and its refusal to align with any party limited its influence in the political arena. Furthermore, the immense religious, ethnic, and racial divisions of American society contrasted sharply with the more homogeneous populations of many European countries. Catholics and Protestants; English, Irish, Germans, Slavs, Jews, and Italians; whites and blacks—such differences undermined the class solidarity of American workers, making it far more difficult to sustain class-oriented political parties and a socialist labor movement. Moreover, the country's remarkable economic growth generated on average a higher standard of living for American workers than their European counterparts experienced. Land was cheaper, and home ownership was more available. Workers with property generally found socialism less attractive than those without. By 1910, a particularly large group of white-collar workers in sales, services, and offices outnumbered factory laborers. Their middle-class aspirations further diluted impulses toward radicalism.

The seamy side of American industrialization did not go unchallenged, however. "Populists," whose ideas echoed most loudly among small farmers in the U.S. South, West, and Midwest, systematically denounced banks, industrialists, monopolies, the existing money system, and both major political parties, which they saw as being controlled by the corporate interests of the eastern part of the country. But populism, after reaching a high point in the mid-1890s, found scant support in the growing industrial areas, even among the workers at whom some of its rhetoric was aimed. More successful, especially after 1900, were the Progressives, who sought to remedy the ills of industrialization through reforms such as wages-and-hours legislation, better sanitation standards, antitrust laws, and greater governmental intervention in the economy. Conservatives sometimes accused Progressives of being socialists and radicals, but nothing could have been further from the minds of men such as Presidents Theodore Roosevelt and Woodrow Wilson, both of whom championed their ideas. Socialism came to be defined as fundamentally "un-American" in a country that so valued individualism and so feared "big government." It was a distinctive feature of the American response to industrialization.

Russia: Industrialization and Revolution

As a setting for the Industrial Revolution, it would be hard to imagine two more different environments than the United States and Russia. If the United States was the Western world's most exuberant democracy in the nineteenth century, Russia remained the sole outpost of absolute monarchy, in which the state exercised far greater control over individuals and society than anywhere in the Western world. At the beginning of the twentieth century, Russia still had no national parliament, no legal political parties, and no nationwide elections. The tsar, answerable to God alone, ruled unchecked. Furthermore, Russian society was dominated by a titled nobility of various ranks, whose upper levels included great landowners, who furnished the state with military officers and leading government officials. Until 1861, most Russians were peasant serfs, bound to the estates of their masters, subject to sale, greatly exploited, and largely at the mercy of their owners. In Russia at least, serfdom approximated slavery. A vast cultural gulf separated these two classes. Many nobles were highly Westernized, some speaking French better than Russian, whereas their serfs were steeped in a backwoods Orthodox Christianity that incorporated pre-Christian spirits, spells, curses, and magic.

Russian Serfdom
This nineteenth-century cartoon by the French artist Gustave Doré shows Russian noblemen gambling with tied bundles of stiff serfs. Serfdom was not finally abolished in Russia until 1861. (The Granger Collection, New York)

A further difference between Russia and the United States lay in the source of social and economic change. In the United States, such change bubbled up from society as free farmers, workers, and businessmen sought new opportunities and operated in a political system that gave them varying degrees of expression. In autocratic Russia, change was far more often initiated by the state itself, in its continuing efforts to catch up with the more powerful and innovative states of Europe. This kind of "transformation from above" found an early expression in the reign of Peter the Great (reigned 1689–1725). His massive efforts included vast administrative changes, the enlargement and modernization of Russian military forces, a new educational system for the sons of noblemen, and dozens of manufacturing enterprises. Russian nobles were instructed to dress in European styles and to shave their sacred and much-revered beards. The newly created capital city of St. Petersburg was to be Russia's "window on the West." One of Peter's successors, Catherine the Great (reigned 1762–1796), followed up with further efforts to Europeanize Russian cultural and intellectual life, viewing herself as heir to the European Enlightenment.

Such state-directed change continued in the nineteenth century with the freeing of the serfs in 1861, an action stimulated by military defeat at the hands of British and French forces in the Crimean War (1854–1856). To many thoughtful Russians, serfdom seemed incompatible with modern civilization and held back the country's overall development, as did its economic and industrial backwardness. Thus, beginning in the 1860s, Russia began a program of industrial development, which was more heavily directed by the state than was the case in Western Europe or the United States.

By the 1890s, Russia's Industrial Revolution was launched and growing rapidly. It focused particularly on railroads and heavy industry and was fueled by a substantial amount of foreign investment. By 1900, Russia ranked fourth in the world in steel production and had major industries in coal, textiles, and oil. Its industrial enterprises, still modest in comparison to those of Europe, were concentrated in a few major cities—Moscow, St. Petersburg, and Kiev, for example—and took place in factories far larger than in most of Western Europe.

All of this contributed to the explosive social outcomes of Russian industrialization. A growing middle class of businessmen and professionals increasingly took shape. As modern and educated people, many in the middle class objected strongly to the deep conservatism of tsarist Russia and sought a greater role in political life, but they were also dependent on the state for contracts and jobs and for suppressing the growing radicalism of the workers, which they greatly feared. Although factory workers constituted only about 5 percent of Russia's total population, they quickly developed an unusually radical class consciousness, based on harsh conditions and the absence of any legal outlet for their grievances. Until 1897, a thirteen-hour working day was common. Ruthless discipline and overt disrespect from supervisors created resentment, while life in large and unsanitary barracks added to workers' sense of injustice. In the absence of legal unions or political parties, these grievances often erupted in the form of large-scale strikes.

■ Change
What factors contributed to the making of a revolutionary situation in Russia by the beginning of the twentieth century?

In these conditions, a small but growing number of educated Russians found in Marxist socialism a way of understanding the changes they witnessed daily and hope for the future in a revolutionary upheaval of workers. In 1898, they created an illegal Russian Social-Democratic Labor Party and quickly became involved in workers' education, union organizing, and, eventually, revolutionary action. By the early twentieth century, the strains of rapid change and the state's continued intransigence had reached the bursting point, and in 1905, following its defeat in a naval war with Japan, Russia erupted in spontaneous insurrection. Workers in Moscow and St. Petersburg went on strike and created their own representative councils, called soviets. Peasant uprisings, student demonstrations, revolts of non-Russian nationalities, and mutinies in the military all contributed to the upheaval. Recently formed political parties, representing intellectuals of various persuasions, came out into the open.

The 1905 Revolution in Russia

The 1905 revolution, though brutally suppressed, forced the tsar's regime to make more substantial reforms than it had ever contemplated. It granted a constitution, legalized both trade unions and political parties, and permitted the election of a national assembly, called the Duma. Censorship was eased, and plans were under way for universal primary education. Industrial development likewise continued at a rapid rate, so that by 1914 Russia stood fifth in the world in terms of overall output. But in the first half of that year, some 1,250,000 workers, representing about 40 percent of the entire industrial workforce, went out on strike.

Thus the tsar's limited political reforms, which had been granted with great reluctance and were often reversed in practice, failed to tame working-class radicalism or to bring social stability to Russia. In 1906–1907, when a newly elected and radically inclined Duma refused to cooperate with the tsar's new political system, Tsar Nicholas II twice dissolved that elected body and finally changed the electoral laws to favor the landed nobility. Consequently, in Russian political life, the people generally, and even the middle class, had only a limited voice. The representatives of even the privileged classes had become so alienated by the government's intransigence that many felt revolution was inevitable. Various revolutionary groups, many of them socialist, published pamphlets and newspapers, organized trade unions, and spread their messages among workers and peasants. Particularly in the cities, these revolutionary parties had an impact. They provided a language through which workers could express their grievances; they created links among workers from different factories; and they furnished leaders who were able to act when the revolutionary moment arrived.

World War I provided that moment. The enormous hardships of that war, coupled with the immense social tensions of industrialization within a still autocratic political system, sparked the Russian Revolution of 1917. That massive upheaval quickly brought to power the most radical of the socialist groups operating in the country—the Bolsheviks, led by the charismatic Vladimir Ulyanov, better known as Lenin. Only in Russia was industrialization associated with violent social revolution, and this was the most distinctive feature of Russia's modern historical development. And only in Russia was a socialist political party, inspired by the teachings of Karl Marx, able to seize power, thus launching the modern world's first socialist society, with enormous implications for the twentieth century.

The Industrial Revolution and Latin America in the Nineteenth Century

Beyond the world of Europe and North America, only Japan underwent a major industrial transformation during the nineteenth century, part of that country's overall response to the threat of European aggression. (See Chapter 19 for a more detailed examination of Japan in the nineteenth century.) Elsewhere—in colonial India, Egypt, the Ottoman Empire, China, and Latin America—very modest experiments in modern industry were undertaken, but nowhere did they drive the kind of major social transformation that had taken place in Britain, Europe, North America, and Japan. However, even in societies that did not experience their own Industrial Revolution, the profound impact of European and North American industrialization was hard to avoid. Such was the case in Latin America during the nineteenth century.

Snapshot   **The Industrial Revolution and the Global Divide**[22]

During the nineteenth century, the Industrial Revolution generated an enormous and unprecedented economic division in the world, as measured by the share of manufacturing output. What patterns can you see in this table?

SHARE OF TOTAL WORLD MANUFACTURING OUTPUT (PERCENT)

	1750	1800	1860	1880	1900
Europe as a Whole	**23.2**	**28.1**	**53.2**	**61.3**	**62.0**
UNITED KINGDOM	1.9	4.3	19.9	22.9	18.5
FRANCE	4.0	4.2	7.9	7.8	6.8
GERMANY	2.9	3.5	4.9	8.5	13.2
RUSSIA	5.0	5.6	7.0	7.6	8.8
United States	**0.1**	**0.8**	**7.2**	**14.7**	**23.6**
Japan	**3.8**	**3.5**	**2.6**	**2.4**	**2.4**
The Rest of the World	**73.0**	**67.7**	**36.6**	**20.9**	**11.0**
CHINA	32.8	33.3	19.7	12.5	6.2
SOUTH ASIA (INDIA/PAKISTAN)	24.5	19.7	8.6	2.8	1.7

After Independence in Latin America

The struggle for independence in Latin America had lasted far longer and proved far more destructive than in North America. Decimated populations, diminished herds of livestock, flooded or closed silver mines, abandoned farms, shrinking international trade and investment capital, and empty national treasuries were some of the conditions under which Latin American countries greeted independence. Furthermore, the four major administrative units (vice-royalties) of Spanish America ultimately dissolved into eighteen separate countries, and regional revolts wracked Brazil in the early decades of its independent life. A number of international wars in the postindependence century likewise shook these new nations. Mexico lost huge territories to the United States (1846–1848); an alliance of Argentina, Brazil, and Uruguay went to war with Paraguay (1864–1870) in a conflict that devastated Paraguay's small population; Peru and Bolivia briefly united and then broke apart in a bitter conflict (1836–1839).

Within these new countries, political life was turbulent and unstable. Conservatives favored centralized authority and sought to maintain the social status quo of the colonial era in alliance with the Catholic Church, which at independence owned perhaps half of all productive land. Their often bitter opponents were liberals, who attacked the Church in the name of Enlightenment values, sought at least modest social reforms, and preferred federalism. In many countries, conflicts between these factions, often violent, enabled military strongmen known as *caudillos* to achieve power as defenders of order and property, although they too succeeded one another with great frequency. One of them, Antonio López de Santa Anna of Mexico, was president of his country at least nine separate times between 1833 and 1855. Constitutions too replaced one another with bewildering speed. Bolivia had ten constitutions during the nineteenth century, while Ecuador and Peru each had eight.

Social life did not change fundamentally in the aftermath of independence. Slavery, it is true, was abolished in most of Latin America by midcentury, although it persisted in both Brazil and Cuba until the late 1880s. Most of the legal distinctions among various racial categories also disappeared, and all free people were considered, at least officially, equal citizens. Nevertheless, productive economic resources such as businesses, ranches, and plantations remained overwhelmingly in the hands of creole whites, who were culturally oriented toward Europe. The military provided an avenue of mobility for a few skilled and ambitious mestizo men, some of whom subsequently became *caudillos*. Other mixed-race people found a place in a small middle class as teachers, shopkeepers, or artisans. The vast majority—blacks, Indians, and many mixed-race people—remained impoverished, working small subsistence farms or laboring in the mines or on the *haciendas* (plantations) of the well-to-do. Only rarely did the poor and dispossessed actively rebel against their social betters. One such case was the Caste War of Yucatán (1847–1901), a prolonged struggle of the Maya people of Mexico, aimed at cleansing their land of European and mestizo intruders.

Facing the World Economy

■ Connection
In what ways and with
what impact was Latin
America linked to the
global economy of the
nineteenth century?

During the second half of the century, a measure of political consolidation took hold in Latin America, and countries such as Mexico, Peru, and Argentina entered periods of greater stability. At the same time, Latin America as a whole became more closely integrated into a world economy driven by the industrialization of Western Europe and North America. The new technology of the steamship cut the sailing time between Britain and Argentina almost in half, while the underwater telegraph instantly brought the latest news and fashions of Europe to Latin America.

The most significant economic outcome of this growing integration was a rapid growth of Latin American exports to the industrializing countries, which now needed the food products, raw materials, and markets of these new nations. Latin American landowners, businessmen, and governments proved eager to supply those needs, and in the sixty years or so after 1850, an export boom increased the value of Latin American goods sold abroad by a factor of ten.

Mexico continued to produce large amounts of silver, supplying more than half the world's new supply until 1860. Now added to the list of raw materials flowing out of Latin America were copper from Chile, a metal that the growing electrical industry required; tin from Bolivia, which met the mounting demand for tin cans; and nitrates from Chile and guano (bird droppings) from Peru, both of which were used for fertilizer. Wild rubber from the Amazon rain forest was in great demand for bicycle and automobile tires, as was sisal from Mexico, used to make binder twine for the proliferating mechanical harvesters of North America. Bananas from Central America, beef from Argentina, cacao from Ecuador, coffee from Brazil and Guatemala, and sugar from Cuba also found eager markets in the rapidly growing and increasingly prosperous world of industrializing countries. In return for these primary products, Latin Americans imported the textiles, machinery, tools, weapons, and luxury goods of Europe and the United States (see Map 18.3).

Accompanying this burgeoning commerce was large-scale investment of European capital in Latin America, $10 billion alone between 1870 and 1919. Most of this capital came from Great Britain, which invested more in Argentina in the late nineteenth century than in its colony of India, although France, Germany, Italy, and the United States also contributed to this substantial financial transfer. By 1910, U.S. business interests controlled 40 percent of Mexican property and produced half of its oil. Much of this capital was used to build railroads, largely to funnel Latin American exports to the coast, where they were shipped to overseas markets. Mexico had only 390 miles of railroad in 1876; it had 15,000 miles in 1910. By 1915, Argentina, with 22,000 miles of railroad, had more track per person than the United States.

■ Comparison
Did Latin America follow or
diverge from the historical
path of Europe during the
nineteenth century?

Becoming like Europe?

To the economic elites of Latin America, who were intent on making their countries resemble Europe or the United States, all of this was progress. In some respects,

U.S. Interventions

Puerto Rico, 1898–on
Panama, 1903
Cuba, 1898–1902, 1905–09, 1917–21
Haiti, 1915–34
Mexico, 1914, 1916–17
Nicaragua, 1909, 1912–25, 1927–32
Dominican Republic, 1916–24

MEXICO
$1329

CUBA
$471

$11 $16 $44

$99 $42
$19 $12
$61 $28

VENEZUELA
$161

COLOMBIA
$77

ECUADOR
$41

PERU
$197

BOLIVIA
$59

BRAZIL
$1913

PARAGUAY
$27

ARGENTINA
$4001

CHILE
$668

$475

Legend:
- Bananas
- Cacao
- Cattle
- Coffee
- Copper and tin
- Cotton
- Guano
- Henequen
- Nitrate
- Oil
- Rubber
- Sheep
- Silver
- Sugar
- Tobacco
- Wheat
- Yerba mate

$161   Foreign investment (in millions of U.S. dollars around 1914)
← European immigration
← U.S. intervention

Map 18.3 Latin America and the World, 1825–1935
During the nineteenth and early twentieth centuries, Latin American countries interacted with the industrializing world via investment, trade, immigration, and military intervention from the United States.

they were surely right. Economies were growing and producing more than ever before. The population also was burgeoning; it increased from about 30 million in 1850 to more than 77 million in 1912 as public health measures (such as safe drinking water, inoculations, sewers, and campaigns to eliminate mosquitoes that carried yellow fever) brought down death rates.

Urbanization also proceeded rapidly. By the early twentieth century, wrote one scholar, "Latin American cities lost their colonial cobblestones, white-plastered walls, and red-tiled roofs. They became modern metropolises, comparable to urban giants anywhere. Streetcars swayed, telephones jangled, and silent movies flickered from Montevideo and Santiago to Mexico City and Havana."[23] Buenos Aires, Argentina's metropolitan center, boasted 750,000 people in 1900 and billed itself the "Paris of South America." There the educated elite, just like the English, drank tea in the afternoon, while discussing European literature, philosophy, and fashion, usually in French.

To become more like Europe, Latin America sought to attract more Europeans. Because civilization, progress, and modernity apparently derived from Europe, many Latin American countries actively sought to increase their European populations by deliberately recruiting impoverished people with the promise, mostly unfulfilled, of a new and prosperous life in the New World. Argentina received the largest wave of European immigrants (some 2.5 million between 1870 and 1915), mostly from Spain and Italy. Brazil and Uruguay likewise attracted substantial numbers of European newcomers.

Only a quite modest segment of Latin American society saw any great benefits from the export boom and all that followed from it. Upper-class landowners certainly gained as exports flourished and their property values soared. Middle-class urban dwellers—merchants, office workers, lawyers, and other professionals—also grew in numbers and prosperity as their skills proved valuable in a modernizing society. As a percentage of the total population, however, these were narrow elites. In Mexico in the mid-1890s, for example, the landowning upper class made up no more than 1 percent and the middle classes perhaps 8 percent of the population. Everyone else was lower-class, and most of them were impoverished.[24]

A new but quite small segment of this vast lower class emerged among urban workers who labored in the railroads, ports, mines, and a few factories. They organized themselves initially in a variety of mutual aid societies, but by the end of the nineteenth century, they were creating unions and engaging in strikes. To authoritarian governments interested in stability and progress, such activity was highly provocative and threatening, and they acted harshly to crush or repress unions and strikes. In 1906, the Mexican dictator Porfirio Díaz invited the Arizona Rangers to suppress a strike at Cananea near the U.S. border, an action that resulted in dozens of deaths. The following year in the Chilean city of Iquique, more than 1,000 men, women, and children were slaughtered by police when nitrate miners protested their wages and working conditions.

The vast majority of the lower class lived in rural areas, where they suffered the most and benefited the least from the export boom. Government attacks on communal landholding and peasant indebtedness to wealthy landowners combined to push many farmers off their land or into remote and poor areas where they could barely make a living. Many wound up as dependent laborers or peons on the haciendas of the wealthy, where their wages were often too meager to support a family. Thus women and children, who had earlier remained at home to tend the family plot, were required to join their menfolk as field laborers. Many immigrant Italian farmworkers in Argentina and Brazil were unable to acquire their own farms, as they had expected, and so drifted into the growing cities or returned to Italy.

Although local protests and violence were frequent, only in Mexico did these vast inequalities erupt into a nationwide revolution. There, in the early twentieth century, middle-class reformers joined with workers and peasants to overthrow the long dictatorship of Porfirio Díaz (1876–1911). What followed was a decade of bloody conflict (1910–1920) that cost Mexico some 1 million lives, or roughly 10 percent of the population. Huge peasant armies under charismatic leaders such as Pancho Villa and Emiliano Zapata helped oust Díaz. Intent on seizing land and redistributing it to the peasants, they then went on to attack many of Mexico's large haciendas. But unlike the later Russian and Chinese revolutions, in which the most

radical elements seized state power, Villa and Zapata proved unable to do so, in part because they were hobbled by factionalism and focused on local or regional issues. Despite this limitation and its own internal conflicts, the Mexican Revolution transformed the country. When the dust settled, Mexico had a new constitution (1917) that proclaimed universal suffrage; provided for the redistribution of land; stripped the Catholic Church of any role in public education and forbade it to own land; announced unheard-of rights for workers, such as a minimum wage and an eight-hour workday; and placed restrictions on foreign ownership of property. Much of Mexico's history in the twentieth century involved working out the implications of these nationalist and reformist changes. The revolution's direct influence, however, was largely limited to Mexico itself, without the wider international impact of the Russian and Chinese upheavals.

Perhaps the most significant outcome of the export boom lay in what did *not*

The Mexican Revolution
Women were active participants in the Mexican Revolution. They prepared food, nursed the wounded, washed clothes, and at times served as soldiers on the battlefield, as illustrated in this cover image from a French magazine in 1913. (© Archivo Iconografico, S.A./Corbis)

happen, for nowhere in Latin America did it jump-start a thorough Industrial Revolution, despite a few factories that processed foods or manufactured textiles, clothing, and building materials. The reasons are many. A social structure that relegated some 90 percent of its population to an impoverished lower class generated only a very small market for manufactured goods. Moreover, economically powerful groups such as landowners and cattlemen benefited greatly from exporting agricultural products and had little incentive to invest in manufacturing. Domestic manufacturing enterprises could only have competed with cheaper and higher-quality foreign goods if they had been protected for a time by high tariffs. But Latin American political leaders had thoroughly embraced the popular European doctrine of prosperity through free trade, and many governments depended on taxing imports to fill their treasuries.

Instead of its own Industrial Revolution, Latin Americans developed a form of economic growth that was largely financed by capital from abroad and dependent on European and North American prosperity and decisions. Brazil experienced this kind of dependence when its booming rubber industry suddenly collapsed in 1910–1911, after seeds from the wild rubber tree had been illegally exported to Britain and were used to start competing and cheaper rubber plantations in Malaysia.

Later critics saw this "dependent development" as a new form of colonialism, expressed in the power exercised by foreign investors. The influence of the U.S.-owned United Fruit Company in Central America was a case in point. Allied with large landowners and compliant politicians, the company pressured the governments of these "banana republics" to maintain conditions favorable to U.S. business. This indirect or behind-the-scenes imperialism was supplemented by repeated U.S. military intervention in support of American corporate interests in Cuba, Haiti, the Dominican Republic, Nicaragua, and Mexico. The United States also controlled the Panama Canal and acquired Puerto Rico as a territory in the aftermath of the Spanish-American War (see Map 18.3, p. 551).

Thus, despite its domination by people of European descent and its close ties to the industrializing countries of the Atlantic world, Latin America's historical trajectory in the nineteenth century diverged considerably from that of Europe and North America.

Reflections: History and Horse Races

Historians and students of history seem endlessly fascinated by "firsts"—the first breakthrough to agriculture, the first civilization, the first domestication of horses, the first use of gunpowder, the first printing press, and so on. Each of these firsts presents a problem of explanation: why did it occur in some particular time and place rather than somewhere else or at some other time? Such questions have assumed historical significance both because "first achievements" represent something new in the human journey and because many of them conveyed unusual power, wealth, status, or influence on their creators.

Nonetheless, the focus on firsts can be misleading as well. Sometimes those who accomplished something first have seen themselves as generally superior to those who embraced that innovation later. Historians too can sometimes adopt a winners-and-losers mentality, inviting a view of history as a horse race toward some finish line of accomplishment. Most first achievements in history, however, were not the result of intentional efforts but rather were the unexpected outcome of converging circumstances.

The Industrial Revolution is a case in point. Understanding the European beginnings of this immense breakthrough is certainly justified by its pervasive global consequences and its global spread over the past several centuries. In terms of our ability to dominate the natural environment and to extract wealth from it, the Industrial Revolution marks a decisive turning point in human history. But Europeans' attempts to explain their Industrial Revolution have at times stated or implied their own superiority. In the nineteenth century, many Europeans saw their technological mastery as a sure sign of their cultural and racial superiority as they came to use "machines as the measure of men."[25] In attempting to answer the "why Europe?" question, historians too have sometimes sought the answer in some distinct or even superior feature of European civilization.

In emphasizing the unexpectedness of the first Industrial Revolution, and the global context within which it occurred, world historians have attempted to avoid a "history as horse race" syndrome. Clearly the first industrial breakthrough in Britain was not a self-conscious effort to win a race; it was the surprising outcome of countless decisions by many people to further their own interests. Subsequently, however, other societies and their governments quite deliberately tried to catch up, seeking the wealth and power that the Industrial Revolution promised.

The rapid spread of industrialization across the planet, though highly uneven, promises to diminish the importance of the "why Europe?" issue. Just as no one views agriculture as a Middle Eastern phenomenon, even though it occurred first in that region, it seems likely that industrialization will be seen increasingly as a global process rather than one uniquely associated with Europe. If industrial society proves to be a sustainable future for humankind—and this is presently an open question—historians of the future will probably be more interested in the pattern of its global spread and in efforts to cope with its social and environmental consequences than with its origins in Western Europe.

Second Thoughts

What's the Significance?

steam engine	Karl Marx	Russian Revolution of 1905
Indian cotton textiles	proletariat	*caudillo*
British Royal Society	Labour Party	Latin American export boom
middle-class values	socialism in the United States	Mexican Revolution
lower middle class	Progressives	dependent development

To assess your mastery of the material in this chapter, see the **Online Study Guide** at bedfordstmartins.com/strayer.

Big Picture Questions

1. What was revolutionary about the Industrial Revolution?
2. What was common to the process of industrialization everywhere, and in what ways did it vary from place to place?
3. What did humankind gain from the Industrial Revolution, and what did it lose?
4. In what ways might the Industrial Revolution be understood as a global rather than simply a European phenomenon?

Next Steps: For Further Study

For Web sites and documents related to this chapter, see **Make History** at bedfordstmartins.com/strayer.

John Charles Chasteen, *Born in Blood and Fire* (2006). A lively and well-written account of Latin America's turbulent history since the sixteenth century.

David S. Landes, *The Wealth and Poverty of Nations* (1998). An argument that culture largely shapes the possibilities for industrialization and economic growth.

Robert B. Marks, *The Origins of the Modern World* (2007). An effective summary of new thinking about the origins of European industrialization.

Peter Stearns, *The Industrial Revolution in World History* (1998). A global and comparative perspective on the Industrial Revolution.

Peter Waldron, *The End of Imperial Russia, 1855–1917* (1997). A brief account of Russian history during its early industrialization.

Bridging World History, Units 18 and 19, http://www.learner.org/channel/courses/worldhistory. An innovative world history Web site that provides pictures, video, and text dealing with "Rethinking the Rise of the West" and "Global Industrialization."

CHAPTER NINETEEN

Internal Troubles, External Threats

China, the Ottoman Empire, and Japan

1800-1914

The External Challenge:
European Industry and
Empire
New Motives, New Means
New Perceptions of the
"Other"
Reversal of Fortune: China's
Century of Crisis
The Crisis Within
Western Pressures
The Failure of Conservative
Modernization
The Ottoman Empire and the
West in the Nineteenth
Century
"The Sick Man of Europe"
Reform
Identity
Outcomes: Comparing China
and the Ottoman Empire
The Japanese Difference:
The Rise of a New East
Asian Power
The Tokugawa Background
American Intrusion and the
Meiji Restoration
Modernization Japanese Style
Japan and the World
Reflections: Success and
Failure in History

In the early twenty-first century, the issue of Japanese history textbooks became a serious matter in the relationship between Japan and its Chinese and Korean neighbors. From a Chinese point of view, those textbooks had minimized or whitewashed Japanese atrocities committed against China during World War II. In particular, many Chinese were outraged at the treatment of the so-called Rape of Nanjing, which witnessed the killing of perhaps 200,000 people, most of them civilians, and the rape of countless women. "Nanjing city was soaked with bloodshed and piles of bodies were everywhere," declared one survivor of those events. "Japanese rightist groups distort history and attempt to cover the truth of Nanjing Massacre. This makes me extremely angry."[1] For Koreans, the issue was the Japanese use of Korean "comfort women," sexual slaves forced to service Japanese troops. Japan, they argued, had not sufficiently acknowledged this outrage in their history textbooks, nor had the Japanese government adequately apologized for it.

To an observer from, say, the fifteenth century or even the eighteenth century, all of this—Japanese aggression during World War II, its enormous economic success after the war, and the continuing fear and resentment of Japan reflected in the textbook controversy—would have seemed strange indeed. For many centuries, after all, Japan had lived in the shadow of its giant Chinese neighbor, borrowing many elements of Chinese culture. Certainly it was never a threat to China. Beginning in the mid-nineteenth century, however, a remarkable reversal of roles occurred in East Asia when both China and Japan experienced a series of internal crises and, at the same time, had to confront

---

Carving Up the Pie of China: In this French cartoon from the late 1890s, the Great Powers of the day (from left to right: Great Britain's Queen Victoria, Germany's Kaiser Wilhelm, Russia's Tsar Nicholas II, a female figure representing France, and the Meiji emperor of Japan) participate in dividing China, while a Chinese figure behind them tries helplessly to stop the partition of his country. (Gianni Dagli Orti/The Art Archive)

the novel reality of an industrialized, newly powerful, intrusive Europe. It was their very different responses to these internal crises and external challenges that led to their changed relationship in the century or more that followed and to the continuing suspicions and tensions that still characterize their relationship.

CHINA AND JAPAN WERE NOT ALONE IN FACING AN EXPANSIVE EUROPE. During the nineteenth century, and in some places earlier, most of the peoples of Asia, the Middle East, and Africa, as well as those living in the newly independent states of Latin America, were required to deal with European or American imperialism of one kind or another. Whatever their other differences, this was a common thread that gave these diverse peoples something of a shared history.

But—and this can hardly be emphasized too strongly—dealing with Europe was not the only item on their agendas. Islamic revival and the rise and fall of their own states occupied many African peoples; population growth and peasant rebellion wracked China; the great empires of the Islamic world shrank or disappeared; Hindus and Muslims persisted in their sometimes competitive and sometimes cooperative relationship in India; and rivalry among competing elites troubled Latin American societies. Encounters with an expansive Europe were conditioned everywhere by particular local circumstances. Those encounters provided a mirror in which the peoples of Asia and Africa viewed themselves, as they alternately celebrated, criticized, and sought to transform their own cultures.

This chapter examines the experience of societies that confronted these crises while retaining their formal independence, with China, the Ottoman Empire, and Japan as primary examples. The following chapter turns the spotlight on the colonial experience of those societies that fell under the official control of one or another of the European powers. In both cases, they were dealing with a new thrust of European expansion, one that drew its energy from the Industrial Revolution.

Four dimensions of European imperialism confronted these societies. First, they faced the immense military might and political ambitions of rival European states. Second, they became enmeshed in networks of trade, investment, and sometimes migration that radiated out from an industrializing and capitalist Europe to generate a new world economy. Third, they were touched by various aspects of traditional European culture, as some among them learned the French, English, or German language; converted to Christianity; or studied European literature and philosophy. Finally, Asians and Africans engaged with the culture of modernity— its scientific rationalism; its technological achievements; its belief in a better future; and its ideas of nationalism, socialism, feminism, and individualism. In that epic encounter, they sometimes resisted, at other times accommodated, and almost always adapted what came from the West. They were active participants in the global drama of nineteenth-century world history, not simply its passive victims or beneficiaries.

The External Challenge: European Industry and Empire

More than any other period, the nineteenth century was Europe's age of global expansion. During that century, Europe became the center of the world economy, with ties of trade and investment in every corner of the globe. Between 1812 and 1914, millions of Europeans migrated to new homes outside Europe. Missionaries and explorers penetrated the distant interiors of Asia and Africa. European states incorporated India, Africa, Southeast Asia, and the islands of the Pacific into their overseas colonial empires and seriously diminished the sovereignty and independence of the once proud domains of China, the Ottoman Empire, and Persia. Many newly independent states in Latin America became economically dependent on Europe and the United States (see Chapter 18). How can we explain such dramatic changes in the scope, character, and intensity of European expansion?

New Motives, New Means

Behind much of Europe's nineteenth-century expansion lay the massive fact of the Industrial Revolution. That process gave rise to new economic needs, many of which found solutions abroad. The enormous productivity of industrial technology and Europe's growing affluence now created the need for extensive raw materials and agricultural products. The demand for a wide variety of products—wheat from the American Midwest and southern Russia, meat from Argentina, bananas from Central America, rubber from Brazil, cocoa and palm oil from West Africa, tea from Ceylon, gold and diamonds from South Africa—radically changed patterns of economic and social life in the countries of their origin.

■ **Change**
In what ways did the Industrial Revolution shape the character of nineteenth-century European imperialism?

Furthermore, Europe needed to sell its own products. One of the peculiarities of industrial capitalism was that it periodically produced more manufactured goods than its own people could afford to buy. By 1840, for example, Britain was exporting 60 percent of its cotton-cloth production, annually sending 200 million yards to Europe, 300 million yards to Latin America, and 145 million yards to India. This last figure is particularly significant because for centuries Europe had offered little that Asian societies were willing to buy. Part of European and American fascination with China during the nineteenth and twentieth centuries lay in the enormous potential market represented by its huge population.

Much the same could be said for capital, for European investors often found it more profitable to invest their money abroad than at home. Between 1910 and 1913, Britain was sending about half of its savings abroad as foreign investment. In 1914, it had about 3.7 billion pounds sterling invested abroad, about equally divided between Europe, North America, and Australia on the one hand and Asia, Africa, and Latin America on the other hand.

Wealthy Europeans also saw social benefits to foreign markets, which served to keep Europe's factories humming and its workers employed. The English imperialist Cecil Rhodes confided his fears to a friend:

> Yesterday I attended a meeting of the unemployed in London and having listened to the wild speeches which were nothing more than a scream for bread, I returned home convinced more than ever of the importance of imperialism.... In order to save the 40 million inhabitants of the United Kingdom from a murderous civil war, the colonial politicians must open up new areas to absorb the excess population and create new markets for the products of the mines and factories.... The British Empire is a matter of bread and butter. If you wish to avoid civil war, then you must become an imperialist.[2]

Thus imperialism promised to solve the class conflicts of an industrializing society while avoiding revolution or the serious redistribution of wealth.

But what made imperialism so broadly popular in Europe, especially in the last quarter of the nineteenth century, was the growth of mass nationalism. By 1871, the unification of Italy and Germany made Europe's always competitive political system even more so, and much of this rivalry spilled over into the struggle for colonies or economic concessions in Asia and Africa. Colonies and spheres of influence abroad became a symbol of national "Great Power" status, and their acquisition was a matter of urgency, even if they possessed little immediate economic value. After 1875, it seemed to matter, even to ordinary people, whether some remote corner of Africa or some obscure Pacific island was in British, French, or German hands. Imperialism, in short, appealed on economic and social grounds to the wealthy or ambitious, seemed politically and strategically necessary in the game of international power politics, and was emotionally satisfying to almost everyone. It was a potent mix.

If the industrial era made overseas expansion more desirable or even urgent, it also provided new means for achieving those goals. Steam-driven ships, moving through the new Suez Canal, allowed Europeans to reach distant Asian and African ports more quickly and predictably and to penetrate the interior rivers as well. The underwater telegraph made possible almost instant communication with far-flung outposts of empire. The discovery of quinine to prevent malaria greatly reduced European death

The Gatling Gun
The Gatling gun, which was designed by the American Richard Gatling during the Civil War and named after him, was one of the earliest machine guns. By the late nineteenth century, this weapon gave European powers and the United States an enormous military advantage. (Courtesy, Royal Artillery Historical Trust)

rates in the tropics. Breech-loading rifles and machine guns vastly widened the military gap between Europeans and everyone else.

New Perceptions of the "Other"

Industrialization also occasioned a marked change in the way Europeans perceived themselves and others. In earlier centuries, Europeans had defined others largely in religious terms. "They" were heathen; "we" were Christian. Even as they held on to their sense of religious superiority, Europeans nonetheless adopted many of the ideas and techniques of more advanced societies. They held many aspects of Chinese and Indian civilization in high regard; they freely mixed and mingled with Asian and African elites and often married their women; some even saw the more technologically simple peoples of Africa and America as "noble savages."

■ **Change**
What contributed to changing European views of Asians and Africans in the nineteenth century?

With the advent of the industrial age, however, Europeans developed a secular arrogance that fused with or in some cases replaced their notions of religious superiority. They had, after all, unlocked the secrets of nature, created a society of unprecedented wealth, and used both to produce unsurpassed military power. These became the criteria by which Europeans judged both themselves and the rest of the world.

By such standards, it is not surprising that their opinions of other cultures dropped sharply. The Chinese, who had been highly praised in the eighteenth century, were reduced in the nineteenth century to the image of "John Chinaman," weak, cunning, obstinately conservative, and, in large numbers, a distinct threat, the "yellow peril" of late-nineteenth-century European fears. African societies, which had been regarded even in the slave-trade era as nations and their leaders as kings, were demoted in nineteenth-century European eyes to the status of tribes led by chiefs as a means of emphasizing their "primitive" qualities.

Increasingly, Europeans viewed the culture and achievements of Asian and African peoples through the prism of a new kind of racism, expressed now in terms of modern science. Although physical differences had often been a basis of fear or dislike, in the nineteenth century Europeans increasingly used the prestige and apparatus of science to support their racial preferences and prejudices. Phrenologists, craniologists, and sometimes physicians used allegedly scientific methods and numerous instruments to classify the size and shape of human skulls and concluded, not surprisingly, that those of whites were larger and therefore more advanced. Nineteenth-century biologists, who classified the varieties of plants and animals, applied these notions of rank to varieties of human beings as well. The result was a hierarchy of races, with the whites, naturally, on top and the less developed "child races" beneath them. Race, in this view, determined human intelligence, moral development, and destiny. "Race is everything," declared the British anatomist Robert Knox in 1850; "civilization depends on it."[3] Furthermore, as the germ theory of disease took hold in nineteenth-century Europe, it was accompanied by fears that contact with "inferior" peoples threatened the health and even the biological future of more advanced or "superior" peoples.

PROGRESSIVE DEVELOPMENT OF MAN.—(2) EVOLUTION ILLUSTRATED WITH THE SIX CORRESPONDING LIVING FORMS.

European Racial Images
This nineteenth-century chart, depicting the "Progressive Development of Man" from apes to modern Europeans, reflected the racial categories that were so prominent at the time. It also highlights the influence of Darwin's evolutionary ideas as they were applied to varieties of human beings. (The Granger Collection, New York)

These ideas influenced how Europeans viewed their own global expansion. Almost everyone saw it as inevitable, a natural outgrowth of a superior civilization. For many, though, this viewpoint was tempered with a genuine, if condescending, sense of responsibility to the "weaker races" that Europe was fated to dominate. "Superior races have a right, because they have a duty," declared the French politician Jules Ferry in 1883. "They have the duty to civilize the inferior races."[4] That "civilizing mission," as Europeans regarded it, included bringing Christianity to the heathen, good government to disordered lands, work discipline and production for the market to "lazy natives," a measure of education to the ignorant and illiterate, clothing to the naked, and health care to the sick, while suppressing "native customs" that ran counter to Western ways of living. All of this was defined as "progress" and "civilization."

Another, harsher side to the ideology of imperialism derived from an effort to apply, or perhaps misapply, the evolutionary thinking of Charles Darwin to an understanding of human history. The key concept of this "social Darwinism," though not necessarily shared by Darwin himself, was "the survival of the fittest," suggesting that European dominance inevitably involved the displacement or destruction of backward peoples or "unfit" races. Referring to native peoples of Australia, a European bishop declared:

> Everyone who knows a little about aboriginal races is aware that those races which are of a low type mentally and who are at the same time weak in constitution rapidly die out when their country comes to be occupied by a different race much more rigorous, robust and pushing than themselves.[5]

Such views made imperialism, war, and aggression seem both natural and progressive, for they served to weed out the weaker peoples of the world, allowing the stronger to flourish. These were some of the ideas with which industrializing and increasingly powerful Europeans confronted the peoples of Asia and Africa in the nineteenth century. Among those confrontations, none was more important than Europe's encounter with China.

Reversal of Fortune: China's Century of Crisis

In 1793 in a famous letter to King George III, the Chinese emperor Qianlong sharply rebuffed British requests for a less restricted trading relationship with his country. "Our Celestial Empire possesses all things in great abundance," he declared.

"There was therefore no need to import the manufactures of outside barbarians." Qianlong's snub simply continued the pattern of the previous several centuries, during which Chinese authorities had strictly controlled and limited the activities of European missionaries and merchants. By 1912, little more than a century later, China's long-established imperial state had collapsed, and the country had been transformed from a central presence in the Afro-Eurasian world to a weak and dependent participant in a European-dominated world system. It was a stunning reversal of fortune for a country that in Chinese eyes was the civilized center of the entire world—in their terms, the Middle Kingdom.

The Crisis Within

In many ways, China was the victim of its own earlier success. Its robust economy and American food crops had enabled massive population growth, from about 100 million people in 1685 to some 430 million in 1853. Unlike Europe, though, where a similar population spurt took place, no Industrial Revolution accompanied this vast increase in the number of people, nor was agricultural production able to keep up. The result was growing pressure on the land, smaller farms for China's huge peasant population, and, in all too many cases, unemployment, impoverishment, misery, and starvation.

■ **Causation**
What accounts for the massive peasant rebellions of nineteenth-century China?

Furthermore, China's famed centralized and bureaucratic state did not enlarge itself to keep pace with the growing population. In 1400, the lowest administrative unit, a county, encompassed perhaps 50,000 people and was governed by a magistrate and a small staff. By 1800, that magistrate was responsible for 200,000 people, with no increase in his staff. Thus the state was increasingly unable to effectively perform its many functions, such as tax collection, flood control, social welfare, and public security. Gradually the central state lost power to provincial officials and local gentry. Among such officials, corruption was endemic, and harsh treatment of peasants was common. According to an official report issued in 1852, "[D]ay and night soldiers are sent out to harass taxpayers. Sometimes corporal punishments are imposed upon tax delinquents; some of them are so badly beaten to exact the last penny that blood and flesh fly in all directions."[6]

This combination of circumstances, traditionally associated with a declining dynasty, gave rise to growing numbers of bandit gangs roaming the countryside and, even more dangerous, to outright peasant rebellion. Beginning in the late eighteenth century, such rebellions drew upon a variety of peasant grievances and found leadership in charismatic figures proclaiming a millenarian religious message. Increasingly they also expressed opposition to the Qing dynasty on account of its foreign Manchurian origins. "We wait only for the northern region to be returned to a Han emperor," declared one rebel group in the early nineteenth century.[7]

The culmination of China's internal crisis lay in the Taiping Uprising, which set much of the country aflame between 1850 and 1864. This was a different kind of peasant upheaval. Its leaders rejected Confucianism, Daoism, and Buddhism alike, finding their ideology in a unique form of Christianity. Its leading figure, Hong

Xiuquan (1814–1864), proclaimed himself the younger brother of Jesus, sent to cleanse the world of demons and to establish a "heavenly kingdom of great peace." Nor were these leaders content to restore an idealized Chinese society; instead they insisted on genuinely revolutionary change. They called for the abolition of private property; a radical redistribution of land; the equality of men and women; the end of foot binding, prostitution, and opium smoking; and the organization of society into sexually segregated military camps of men and women. Hong fiercely denounced the Qing dynasty as foreigners who had "poisoned China" and "defiled the emperor's throne." His cousin, Hong Rengan, developed plans for transforming China into an industrial nation, complete with railroads, health insurance for all, newspapers, and widespread public education.

With a rapidly swelling number of followers, Taiping forces swept out of southern China and established their capital in Nanjing in 1853. For a time, the days of the Qing dynasty appeared to be over. But divisions and indecisiveness within the Taiping leadership and their inability to link up with other rebel groups also operating in China provided an opening for Qing dynasty loyalists to rally and by 1864 to crush this most unusual of peasant rebellions. Western military support for pro-Qing forces likewise contributed to their victory. It was not the imperial military forces of the central government that defeated the rebels, however. Instead provincial gentry landowners, fearing the radicalism of the Taiping program, mobilized their own armies, which in the end destroyed the revolutionary rebels.

Thus the Qing dynasty was saved, but it was also weakened as the provincial gentry consolidated their power at the expense of the central state. The intense conservatism of both imperial authorities and their gentry supporters postponed any resolution of China's peasant problem, delayed any real change for China's women, and deferred any vigorous efforts at modernization until the communists came to power in the mid-twentieth century. More immediately, the devastation and destruction occasioned by this massive civil war seriously disrupted and weakened China's economy. Vast expanses of the Yangzi River valley became virtual wastelands, and travelers reported walking for days in previously densely populated regions without seeing a living person. Estimates of the number of lives lost range from 20 million to 30 million. In human terms, it was the most costly conflict in the world of the nineteenth century, and it took China more than a decade to recover from that devastation. China's internal crisis in general and the Taiping Uprising in particular also provided a highly unfavorable setting for the country's encounter with a Europe newly invigorated by the Industrial Revolution.

Western Pressures

■ **Connection**

What was the impact of Western pressures on China during the nineteenth century?

Nowhere was the shifting balance of global power in the nineteenth century more evident than in China's changing relationship with Europe, a transformation that registered most dramatically in the famous Opium Wars. Derived from Arab traders in the eighth century or earlier, opium had long been used on a small scale as a

Snapshot   **Chinese/British Trade at Canton, 1835–1836**[8]

What do these figures suggest about the role of opium in British trade with China?
Calculate opium exports as a percentage of British exports to China, Britain's trade deficit
without opium, and its trade surplus with opium. What did this pattern mean for China?

	Item	Value (in Spanish dollars)
British Exports to Canton	Opium	17,904,248
	Cotton	8,357,394
	All other items (sandlewood, lead, iron, tin, cotton yarn and piece goods, tin plates, watches, clocks)	6,164,981
	Total	32,426,623
British Imports from Canton	Tea (black and green)	13,412,243
	Raw silk	3,764,115
	Vermilion	705,000
	All other goods (sugar products, camphor, silver, gold, copper, musk)	5,971,541
	Total	23,852,899

drinkable medicine, regarded as a magical cure for dysentery and described by one
poet as "fit for Buddha."[9] It did not become a serious problem until the late eighteenth century, when the British began to use opium, grown and processed in
India, to cover their persistent trade imbalance with China. By the 1830s, British,
American, and other Western merchants had found an enormous, growing, and
very profitable market for this highly addictive drug. From 1,000 chests (each
weighing roughly 150 pounds) in 1773, China's opium imports exploded to more
than 23,000 chests in 1832.

By then, Chinese authorities recognized a mounting problem on many levels.
Because opium importation was illegal, it had to be smuggled into China, thus flout-
ing Chinese law. Bribed to turn a blind eye to the illegal trade, many officials were
corrupted. Furthermore, a massive outflow of silver to pay for the opium reversed
China's centuries-long ability to attract much of the world's silver supply, and this
imbalance caused serious economic problems. Finally, China found itself with many
millions of addicts—men and women, court officials, students preparing for exams,
soldiers going into combat, and common laborers seeking to overcome the pain and
drudgery of their work. Following an extended debate at court in 1836—whether

Addiction to Opium
Throughout the nineteenth century, opium imports created a massive addiction problem in China, as this photograph of an opium den from around 1900 suggests. Not until the early twentieth century did the British prove willing to curtail the opium trade from their Indian colony. (Hulton-Deutsch Collection/Corbis)

to legalize the drug or to crack down on its use—the emperor decided on suppression. An upright official, Commissioner Lin Zexu, led the campaign against opium use as a kind of "drug czar." His measures included seizing and destroying, without compensation, more than 3 million pounds of opium from Western traders and expelling them from the country.

The British, offended by this violation of property rights and emboldened by their new military power, determined to teach the Chinese a lesson about the virtues of free trade and the "proper" way to conduct relations among countries—and so began the first Opium War in 1839. The Treaty of Nanjing, which ended the conflict in 1842, largely on British terms, imposed numerous restrictions on Chinese sovereignty. Besides agreeing to pay a $21 million indemnity to the British and ceding the island of Hong Kong, the treaty required China to open five ports to trade, fixed the tariff on imported goods at a low 5 percent, and granted foreigners the right to live in China under their own laws. Its provisions reflected the changed balance of global power that had emerged with Britain's Industrial Revolution. To the Chinese, that agreement represented the first of the "unequal treaties" that seriously eroded China's independence by the end of the century.

But it was not the last of these treaties. Britain's victory in a second Opium War (1856–1858) was accompanied by the brutal vandalizing of the emperor's exquisite Summer Palace outside Beijing, resulted in the opening of yet more treaty ports to foreign traders, allowed foreigners to travel and buy land in China, opened the country to Christian missionaries, and permitted Western powers to patrol some of China's interior waterways. Following military defeats at the hands of the French (1885) and Japanese (1895), China lost control of Vietnam, Korea, and Taiwan. By the end of the century, the Western nations plus Japan and Russia all had carved out spheres of influence within China, granting them special privileges to establish military bases, extract raw materials, and build railroads. Many Chinese believed that their country was being "carved up like a melon" (see Map 19.1).

Coupled with its internal crisis, China's encounter with European imperialism had reduced the proud Middle Kingdom to dependency on the Western powers as it became part of a European-based "informal empire." China was no longer the center of civilization to which barbarians paid homage and tribute, but just one nation in a world of nation-states, and a beleaguered one at that. The Qing dynasty remained in power, but in a weakened condition, which served

directed against I
many held respon

The Qing dy
extensive reform
ination system ar
little too late." In
millennia collaps
was the end of a
the country's futu

The Otton
in the Nin

Like China, the I
little need to lear
with an expandir
though, Islamic c
Its most promine
of the Balkans a
sixteenth and sev
abrupt than that
Empire nor Chir
as the changing
"defensive moder
independence; an
values, even as c
modernity.

"The Sick M

In 1750, the Otto
Islamic world. Fr
Arab world, from
Mecca, governed
Christians in the
to the Prophet M
mary representati
end, of the ninet
with Europe fron
Powers of the We
Muslim world, th
was unable to pre
Asia—from fallin

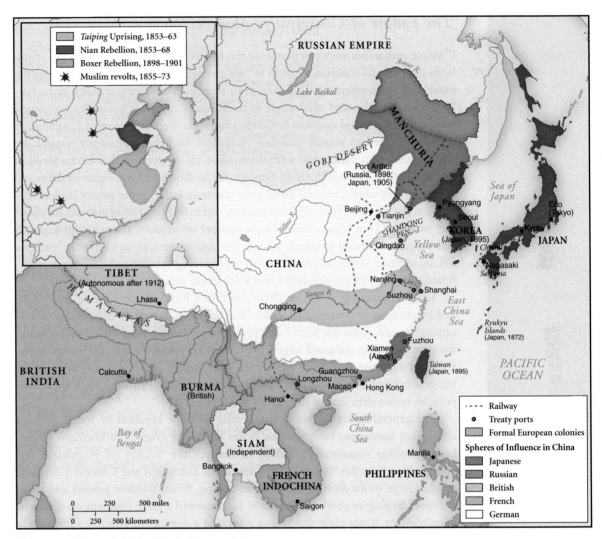

Map 19.1   China and the World in the Nineteenth Century
As China was reeling from massive internal upheavals during the nineteenth century, it also faced external assaults from Russia, Japan, and various European powers. By the end of the century, large parts of China were divided into spheres of influence, each affiliated with one of the major industrial powers of the day.

European interests well. Thus imperialism had enfeebled the Chinese state at precisely the time when China required a strong government to manage its entry into the modern world. Restrictions imposed by the unequal treaties also inhibited China's industrialization, as foreign goods and foreign investment flooded the country largely unrestricted. Chinese businessmen mostly served foreign interests rather than developing as an independent capitalist class able to lead the country's economic modernization.

■ Connection
Why was China unable
respond effectively to
mounting pressures fr
the West in the
nineteenth century?

Ottoman reforms began in the late eighteenth century when Sultan Selim III attempted to set up new military and administrative structures alongside traditional institutions as a means of enhancing and centralizing state power. Selim sent ambassadors to the courts of Europe, studied their administrative methods, imported European advisers, and established technical schools to train future officials. More far-reaching measures, known as *Tanzimat* ("reorganization"), emerged in the several decades after 1839 as the Ottoman leadership sought to provide the economic, social, and legal underpinnings for a strong and newly recentralized state. Factories producing cloth, paper, and armaments; modern mining operations; reclamation and resettlement of agricultural land; telegraphs, steamships, railroads, and a modern postal service; Western-style law codes and courts; new elementary and secondary schools—all of these new departures began a long process of modernization and Westernization in the Ottoman Empire.

Even more revolutionary, at least in principle, were changes in the legal status of the empire's diverse communities. In an effort to integrate non-Muslim subjects more effectively into the state, the principle of equality of all citizens before the law was accepted. An imperial proclamation of 1839 declared:

> Every distinction or designation tending to make any class whatever of the subjects of my Empire inferior to another class, on account of their religion, language or race shall be forever effaced.... No subject of my Empire shall be hindered in the exercise of the religion that he professes.... All the subjects of my Empire, without distinction of nationality, shall be admissible to public employment.

The Ottoman Empire and the West
The intense interaction of the Ottoman Empire and the world of European powers is illustrated in this nineteenth-century Austrian painting, which depicts an elaborate gathering of Ottoman officials with members of the Austrian royal family around 1850. (Miramare Palace Trieste/Alfredo Dagli Orti/The Art Archive)

This declaration represented a dramatic change that challenged the fundamentally Islamic character of the state. Mixed tribunals with representatives from various religious groups were established to hear cases involving non-Muslims. More Christians were appointed to high office. A mounting tide of secular legislation and secular schools, drawing heavily on European models, now competed with traditional Islamic institutions.

Identity

The reform process raised profound and highly contested questions about political and cultural identity. What was the Ottoman Empire, and who were its people? Even the modest innovations of Selim III stirred the hostility of powerful factions among both the ulama (religious scholars) and the Janissaries, who saw them in conflict with Islam. Opposition to his measures was so strong that Selim was forced from power in 1807. Subsequent sultans, however, crushed this conservative opposition while bringing the ulama more thoroughly under state control than elsewhere in the Islamic world.

■ Comparison

In what different ways did various groups define the Ottoman Empire during the nineteenth century?

Outside the Ottoman Empire, movements of Islamic renewal (see Chapter 16) began to express opposition to European encroachment while providing a prescription for rebuilding threatened societies. In Sumatra (present-day Indonesia), an Islamic renewal movement that sought to correct immorality and to impose the veil on women and Arab dress on men became a war of resistance to Dutch penetration in the early nineteenth century. Prominent Muslim leaders in the Caucasus regions of Chechnya and Dagestan organized jihads against Russian intrusion and simultaneously sought to purify the practice of Islam by eliminating local religious traditions. The French invasion of Algeria in 1830 provoked a Muslim-based resistance movement, which was also an effort to create an Islamic state.

Such political expressions of Islamic renewal had little impact in the Ottoman Empire of the mid-nineteenth century, when the Tanzimat reforms were being implemented. To those who supported these reforms, the Ottoman Empire was a secular state whose people were loyal to the dynasty that ruled it, rather than a primarily Muslim state based on religious principles. This was the outlook of a new class spawned by the reform process itself—lower-level officials, military officers, writers, poets, and journalists, many of whom had a modern Western-style education. Dubbed the "Young Ottomans," they were active during the middle decades of the nineteenth century, when they urged the extension of Westernizing reforms to the political system. Rejecting the despotism of Ottoman rulers, they favored a constitutional regime like that of Great Britain. Only such a political system could mobilize the energies of the country to overcome backwardness and preserve the state against European aggression. Known as Islamic modernism, such ideas found expression in many parts of the Muslim world in the second half of the century. Muslim societies, they argued, needed to embrace Western technical and scientific knowledge, while rejecting its materialism. Moreover, they believed it was possible to find in Islam itself the basis for freedom, progress, rationality, and patriotism. It was not necessary to choose between Western-style modernity and Islam. The growing influence of the Young Ottomans was reflected in the adoption of a short-lived constitution for the empire in 1876, which limited the authority of the sultan and established a representative government.

No sooner had Sultan Abd al-Hamid II (ruled 1876–1909) accepted the constitution than he suspended it and purged his government of the more radical reformers, using the occasion of a Russian invasion to act decisively. For the next three decades, he ruled as a reactionary autocrat, suppressing liberal and nationalist sentiments among his diverse and restive subjects, though continuing many of the educational, economic, and technical reforms of the earlier era. He sought to bolster his authority by reactivating the old claim that the Ottoman rulers were caliphs, speaking for the entire Islamic world. This claim was yet another answer to the question of identity. The Ottoman Empire would be a despotic state with a pan-Islamic identity. Thus Abd al-Hamid II restored the ulama to a position of prestige, if not real power, and reintroduced the distinction between Muslim and non-Muslim subjects.

Opposition to this revived despotism soon surfaced among both military and civilian elites known as the Young Turks. Largely abandoning any reference to Islam, they advocated a militantly secular public life. Furthermore, some among them began to think about the Ottoman regime neither as a dynastic state nor as a pan-Islamic empire, but as a Turkish national state. This was a revolutionary notion, drawn from the growing nationalism of the empire's subject peoples and ultimately from Europe. It went against the grain of Islamic thinking, which focused loyalty on a community of faith, not of ethnicity. It also challenged the longtime Ottoman practice of incorporating a variety of cultural groups into a common political system. Moreover, at the time few people were aware of a distinctly Turkish ethnic identity. By the beginning of the twentieth century, however, a number of writers and intellectuals began to articulate the notion of a "Turkish nation" and to define its unique character. To the writer Ziya Gokalp, Turkish nationality was based fundamentally on language and was expressed in folk stories and popular songs.

A military coup in 1908 allowed the Young Turks to exercise real power. They pushed for a radical secularization of schools, courts, and law codes; permitted elections and competing parties; established a single Law of Family Rights for all regardless of religion; and encouraged Turkish as the official language of the empire. They also opened up modern schools for women, allowed them to wear Western clothing, restricted polygamy, and permitted women to obtain divorces in some situations. But the nationalist conception of Ottoman identity antagonized non-Turkic peoples and helped stimulate Arab and other nationalisms in response. For some, a secular nationality was becoming the most important public loyalty, with Islam relegated to private life. Such nationalist sentiments contributed to the complete disintegration of the Ottoman Empire following World War I, but the secularizing and Westernizing principles of the Young Turks informed the policies of the Turkish republic that replaced it.

Outcomes: Comparing China and the Ottoman Empire

By the beginning of the twentieth century, both China and the Ottoman Empire, recently centers of proud and vibrant civilizations, had experienced the consequences of a rapidly shifting balance of global power. Now they were "semicolonies" within the "informal empires" of Europe, although they retained sufficient independence for their governments to launch catch-up efforts of defensive modernization. But neither was able to create the industrial economies or strong states required to fend off European intrusion and restore their former status in the world. Despite their diminished power, both China and the Ottoman Empire gave rise to new nationalist conceptions of society, which were initially small and limited in appeal but of great significance for the future.

In the early twentieth century, that future witnessed the end of both the Chinese and Ottoman empires. In China, the collapse of the imperial system in 1911 was followed by a vast revolutionary upheaval that by 1949 led to a Communist regime within largely the same territorial space as the old empire. By contrast, the collapse of the Ottoman Empire following World War I led to the creation of a new but much smaller nation-state in the Turkish heartland of the old empire, having lost its vast Arab and European provinces.

China's twentieth-century revolutionaries rejected traditional Confucian culture far more thoroughly than the secularizing leaders of modern Turkey rejected Islam. Almost everywhere in the Islamic world, traditional religion retained its hold on the private loyalties of most people and later in the twentieth century became a basis for social renewal in many places. Islamic civilization, unlike its Chinese counterpart, had many independent centers and was never so closely associated with a single state. Furthermore, it was embedded in a deeply religious tradition that was personally meaningful to millions of adherents, in contrast to the more elitist and secular outlook of Confucianism. All of this perhaps facilitated the survival and renewal of Islamic civilization in the twentieth century in a way that was not possible for traditional Chinese civilization.

The Japanese Difference: The Rise of a New East Asian Power

Like China and the Ottoman Empire, the island country of Japan confronted the aggressive power of the West during the nineteenth century, most notably in the form of U.S. Commodore Matthew Perry's "black ships," which steamed into Tokyo Bay in 1853 and forcefully demanded that this reclusive nation open up to more "normal" relations with the world. However, the outcome of that encounter differed sharply from the others. In the second half of the nineteenth century, Japan undertook a radical transformation of its society—a "revolution from above," according to some historians—turning it into a powerful, modern, united, industrialized nation. It was an achievement that neither China nor the Ottoman Empire was able to duplicate. Far from succumbing to Western domination, Japan joined the club of imperialist countries by creating its own East Asian empire, largely at the expense of China. In building a society that was both modern and distinctly Japanese, Japan demonstrated that modernity was not a uniquely European phenomenon. This "Japanese miracle," as some have called it, was both promising and ominous for the rest of Asia. How had it occurred?

The Tokugawa Background

■ Comparison
How did Japan's historical development differ from that of China and the Ottoman Empire during the nineteenth century?

For 250 years prior to Perry's arrival, Japan had been governed by a shogun (a military ruler) from the Tokugawa family who acted in the name of a revered but powerless emperor, who lived in Kyoto, 300 miles away from the seat of power in Edo (Tokyo). The chief task of this Tokugawa shogunate was to prevent the return of civil war among some 260 rival feudal lords, known as daimyo, each of whom had a cadre of armed retainers, the famed samurai warriors of Japanese tradition.

Based on their own military power and political skills, successive shoguns gave Japan more than two centuries of internal peace (1600–1850). To control the restive daimyo, they strictly regulated internal travel and communication and required the daimyo to spend alternate years in the capital of Edo, leaving their families behind as hostages during their absence. Nonetheless, the daimyo, especially the more powerful ones, retained substantial autonomy in their own domains and behaved in some ways like independent states with separate military forces, law codes, tax systems, and currencies. With no national army, no uniform currency, and little central authority at the local level, Tokugawa Japan was "pacified...but not really unified."[11] To further stabilize the country, the Tokugawa regime issued highly detailed rules governing the occupation, residence, dress, hairstyles, and behavior of the four hierarchically ranked status groups into which Japanese society was divided—samurai at the top, then peasants, artisans, and, at the bottom, merchants.

■ Change
In what ways was Japan changing during the Tokugawa era?

Much was changing within Japan during these 250 years of peace in ways that belied the control and orderliness of Tokugawa regulations. For one thing, the samurai, in the absence of wars to fight, evolved into a salaried bureaucratic or administrative class amounting to 5 to 6 percent of the total population, but they were still fiercely devoted to their daimyo lords and to their warrior code of loyalty, honor, and self-sacrifice.

More generally, centuries of peace contributed to a remarkable burst of economic growth, commercialization, and urban development. Entrepreneurial peasants, using fertilizers and other agricultural innovations, grew more rice than ever before and engaged in a variety of rural manufacturing enterprises as well. By 1750, Japan had become perhaps the world's most urbanized country, with about 10 percent of its population living in sizable towns or cities. Edo, with a million residents, was the world's largest city. Well-functioning markets linked urban and rural areas, marking Japan as an emerging capitalist economy. The influence of Confucianism encouraged education and generated a remarkably literate population, with about

40 percent of men and 15 percent of women able to read and write. Although no one was aware of it at the time, these changes during the Tokugawa era provided a solid foundation for Japan's remarkable industrial growth in the late nineteenth century.

These changes also undermined the shogunate's efforts to freeze Japanese society in the interests of stability. Some samurai found the lowly but profitable path of commerce too much to resist. "No more shall we have to live by the sword," declared one of them in 1616 while renouncing his samurai status. "I have seen that great profit can be made honorably. I shall brew *sake* and soy sauce, and we shall prosper."[12] Many merchants, though hailing from the lowest-ranking status group, prospered in the new commercial environment and supported a vibrant urban culture, while not a few daimyo found it necessary, if humiliating, to seek loans from these social inferiors. Thus merchants had money, but little status, whereas samurai enjoyed high status but were often indebted to inferior merchants. Both resented their position.

Despite prohibitions to the contrary, many peasants moved to the cities, becoming artisans or merchants and imitating the ways of their social betters. A decree of 1788 noted that peasants "have become accustomed to luxury and forgetful of their status." They wore inappropriate clothing, used umbrellas rather than straw hats in the rain, and even left the villages for the city. "Henceforth," declared the shogun, "all luxuries should be avoided by the peasants. They are to live simply and devote themselves to farming."[13] This decree, like many others before it, was widely ignored.

More than social change undermined the Tokugawa regime. Corruption was widespread, to the disgust of many. The shogunate's failure to deal successfully with a severe famine in the 1830s eroded confidence in its effectiveness. At the same time, a mounting wave of local peasant uprisings and urban riots expressed the many grievances of the poor. The most striking of these outbursts left the city of Osaka in flames in 1837. Its leader, Oshio Heihachiro, no doubt spoke for many ordinary people when he wrote:

> We must first punish the officials who torment the people so cruelly; then we must execute the haughty and rich Osaka merchants. Then we must distribute the gold, silver, and copper stored in their cellars, and bands of rice hidden in their storehouses.[14]

From the 1830s on, one scholar concluded, "there was a growing feeling that the *shogunate* was losing control."[15]

American Intrusion and the Meiji Restoration

It was foreign intervention that brought matters to a head. Since the expulsion of European missionaries and the harsh suppression of Christianity in the early seventeenth century (see Chapter 15), Japan had deliberately limited its contact with the West to a single port, where only the Dutch were allowed to trade. By the early nineteenth century, however, various European countries and the United States

The "Opening" of Japan
This nineteenth-century Japanese woodblock print depicts Commodore Perry's meeting with a Japanese official in 1853. It was this encounter that launched Japan on a series of dramatic changes that resulted in the country's modernization and its emergence as one of the world's major industrialized powers by the early twentieth century. (Bettmann/Corbis)

were knocking at the door. All were turned away, and even shipwrecked sailors or whalers were expelled, jailed, or executed. As it happened, it was the United States that forced the issue, sending Commodore Perry in 1853 to demand humane treatment for castaways, the right of American vessels to refuel and buy provisions, and the opening of ports for trade. Authorized to use force if necessary, Perry presented his reluctant hosts, among other gifts, with a white flag for surrender should hostilities follow.

In the end, conflict was avoided. Aware of what had happened to China in resisting European demands, Japan agreed to a series of unequal treaties with various Western powers. That humiliating capitulation to the demands of the "foreign devils" further eroded support for the shogunate, triggered a brief civil war, and by 1868 led to a political takeover by a group of young samurai from southern Japan. This decisive turning point in Japan's history was known as the Meiji restoration, for the country's new rulers claimed that they were restoring to power the young emperor, then a fifteen-year-old boy whose throne name was Meiji, or Enlightened Rule. Having eliminated the shogunate, these patriotic young men soon made their goals clear—to save Japan from foreign domination, not by futile resistance, but by a thorough transformation of Japanese society, drawing upon all that the modern West had to offer. "Knowledge shall be sought throughout the world," they declared, "so as to strengthen the foundations of imperial rule."

Japan now had a government committed to a decisive break with the past, and it had acquired that government without massive violence or destruction. By contrast, the defeat of the Taiping Uprising had deprived China of any such opportunity for a fresh start, while saddling it with enormous devastation and massive loss of life. Furthermore, Japan was of less interest to Western powers than either China, with its huge potential market and reputation for riches, or the Ottoman Empire, with its strategic location at the crossroads of Asia and Europe. The American Civil War and its aftermath likewise deflected U.S. ambitions in the Pacific for a time, further reducing the Western pressure on Japan.

■ **Change**
Does Japan's nineteenth-century transformation deserve to be considered revolutionary?

Modernization Japanese Style

These circumstances gave Japan some breathing space, and its new rulers moved quickly to take advantage of that unique window of opportunity by directing a cascading wave of dramatic changes that rolled over the country in the last three decades of the nineteenth century. Those reforms, which were revolutionary in their cumulative effect, transformed Japan far more thoroughly than even the most radical of the Ottoman efforts, let alone the modest self-strengthening policies of the Chinese.

The first task was genuine national unity, which required an attack on the power and privileges of both the daimyo and the samurai. By 1871, the new regime had abolished the daimyo domains with their considerable autonomy, replacing them with a system of prefectures, whose appointed governors were responsible to the central government. That government now collected the nation's taxes and raised a national army based on conscription from all social classes.

Thus the samurai lost their ancient role as the country's warrior class and with it their cherished right to carry swords. The old Confucian-based social order was largely dismantled as class restrictions on occupation, residence, marriage, and clothing were abolished, and almost all Japanese became legally equal as common-ers. Limitations on travel and trade likewise fell as a nationwide economy came to parallel the centralized state. Although there was some opposition to these mea-sures, including a brief rebellion of resentful samurai in 1877, it was on the whole a remarkably peaceful process in which a segment of the old ruling class abolished its own privileges. Many, but not all, of these displaced elites found a "soft landing" in the army, bureaucracy, or business enterprises of the new regime, thus easing a painful transition.

Accompanying these social and political changes was a widespread and eager fascination with almost everything Western. Knowledge about the West—its science and technology; its various political and constitutional arrangements; its legal and educational systems; its dances, clothing, and hairstyles—was enthusiastically sought out by official missions to the West, by hundreds of students sent to study abroad, and by many ordinary Japanese at home. Western writers were translated into Japanese; for example, Samuel Smiles's *Self-Help*, which focused on "achieving suc-cess and rising in the world," sold a million copies. "Civilization and Enlightenment" was the slogan of the time, and both were to be found in the West. The most prominent popularizer of Western knowledge, Fukuzawa Yukichi, summed up the chief lesson of his studies in the mid-1870s—Japan was backward and needed to learn from the West. "If we compare the knowledge of the Japanese and Westerners, in letters, in technique, in commerce, or in industry, from the largest to the smallest matter, there is not one thing in which we excel....In Japan's pres-ent condition there is nothing in which we may take pride vis-à-vis the West."[16]

After this initial wave of uncritical enthusiasm for everything Western receded, Japan proceeded to borrow more selectively and to combine foreign and Japanese elements in distinctive ways. For example, the constitution of 1889, drawing heav-ily on German experience, introduced an elected parliament, political parties, and democratic ideals, but that constitution was presented as a gift from a sacred emperor descended from the Sun Goddess. The parliament could advise, but ulti-mate power, and particularly control of the military, lay theoretically with the

Snapshot   **Key Moments in the Rise of Japan in the Nineteenth Century and Beyond**

Famines, urban and rural rebellions	1830s
Commodore Perry arrives in Japan	1853
Meiji restoration	1868
Government-run enterprises in railroad construction, manufacturing, and mining	1870s
Western dress prescribed for court and official ceremonies	1872
Samurai rebellion crushed	1877
Government sells state industries to private investors	1880s
Ito Hirobumi travels to Europe to study political systems	1882
Peak of peasant protest against high taxes and prices	1883–1884
Women banned from political parties and meetings	1887
Japan's modern constitution announced	1889
Sino-Japanese War	1894–1895
Japan's labor movement crushed	by 1901
Anglo-Japanese alliance marks Japan's acceptance as Great Power	1902
Russo-Japanese War	1904–1905
Universal primary education	1905
Japanese annexation of Korea	1910
Meiji emperor dies	1912

emperor and in practice with an oligarchy of prominent reformers acting in his name. Likewise, a modern educational system, which achieved universal primary schooling by the early twentieth century, was also laced with Confucian-based moral instruction and exhortations of loyalty to the emperor. Neither Western-style feminism nor Christianity made much headway in Meiji Japan, but Shinto, an ancient religious tradition featuring ancestors and nature spirits, was elevated to the status of an official state cult. Japan's earlier experience in borrowing massively but selectively from Chinese culture perhaps served it better in these new circumstances than either the Chinese disdain for foreign cultures or the reluctance of many Muslims to see much of value in the infidel West.

At the core of Japan's effort at defensive modernization lay its state-guided industrialization program. The government took over and modernized Tokugawa and daimyo enterprises, such as iron foundries, munitions plants, and dockyards. It

Japan's Modernization
In Japan, as in Europe, railroads quickly became a popular symbol of the country's modernization, as this woodblock print from the 1870s illustrates. (Visual Arts Library [London]/Alamy)

established model factories to produce cement, chemicals, glass, sugar, and silk and cotton goods. It also opened mines, built railroads, and established postal, telegraph, and banking systems. Subsequently many of these state enterprises were sold off to private investors. By the early twentieth century, Japan's industrialization was well under way. Its major cities enjoyed mass-circulation newspapers, movie theaters, and electric lights. All of this was accomplished through its own resources and without the massive foreign debt that so afflicted Egypt and the Ottoman Empire. Although the country was still overwhelmingly agrarian, Japan's factories were now producing not only textiles for export but also munitions for the military and industrial goods for private industry. No other country outside of Europe and North America had been able to launch its own Industrial Revolution in the nineteenth century. It was a distinctive feature of Japan's modern transformation.

Less distinctive, however, were the social results of that process. Taxed heavily to pay for Japan's ambitious modernization program, many peasant families slid into poverty. Their sometimes violent protests peaked in 1883–1884 with attacks on government offices and moneylenders' homes that were aimed at destroying records of debt. Despite substantial private relief efforts, the Japanese countryside witnessed infanticide, the sale of daughters, and starvation.

As elsewhere during the early stages of industrial growth, urban workers were treated harshly. The majority of Japan's textile workers were young women from poor families in the countryside. Their pay was at or below subsistence, and a combination of bad food, overwork, terrible working conditions, and jail-like dormitories left many cast-off employees in their twenties without mates but with terminal diseases such as tuberculosis and dependent for survival on degrading occupations such as prostitution. Resistance to these conditions was reflected in a high turnover rate, strikes, and efforts to organize unions. A series of repressive laws allowed the government and employers to treat unions and strikes as criminal activities. These laws were used so effectively that the budding labor movement had been crushed by the end of 1901. But the authorities also began to draw upon familiar themes of service to state and emperor and new ideas of the enterprise as a family, which would emerge after World War I as a primary means of eliciting worker loyalty to the firm.

Japan and the World

■ Connection
How did Japan's relationship to the larger world change during its modernization process?

Japan's modern transformation soon registered internationally. By the early twentieth century, its economic growth, openness to trade, and embrace of "civilization and enlightenment" from the West persuaded the Western powers to revise the unequal treaties in Japan's favor. This had long been a primary goal of the Meiji regime, and the Anglo-Japanese Treaty of 1902 now acknowledged Japan as an equal player among the Great Powers of the world.

Not only did Japan escape from its semicolonial entanglements with the West, but it also launched its own empire-building enterprise, even as European powers and the United States were carving up much of Asia and Africa into colonies or spheres of influence. It was what industrializing Great Powers did in the late nineteenth century, and Japan followed suit. Successful wars against China (1894–1895) and Russia (1904–1905) established Japan as a formidable military competitor in East Asia and the first Asian state to defeat a major European power. Through those victories, Japan also gained colonial control of Taiwan and Korea and a territorial foothold in Manchuria.

Japan's entry onto the broader global stage was felt in many places (see Map 19.3). It added yet one more imperialist power to those already burdening a beleaguered China. Defeat at the hands of Japanese upstarts shocked Russia and triggered the 1905 revolution in that country. To Europeans and Americans, Japan was now an economic, political, and military competitor in Asia.

In the world of subject peoples, the rise of Japan and its defeat of Russia generated widespread admiration among those who saw Japan as a model for their own modern development and perhaps as an ally in the struggle against imperialism. Some Poles, Finns, and Jews viewed the Russian defeat in 1905 as an opening for their own liberation from the Russian Empire and were grateful to Japan for the opportunity. Despite Japan's aggression against their country, many Chinese reformers and nationalists found in the Japanese experience valuable lessons for themselves. Thousands flocked to Japan to study its achievements. Newspapers throughout the Islamic world celebrated Japan's victory over Russia as an "awakening of the East," which might herald Muslims' own liberation. Some Turkish women gave their children Japanese names. Indonesian Muslims from Aceh wrote to the Meiji emperor asking for help in their struggle against the Dutch, and Muslim poets wrote odes in his honor. The Egyptian nationalist Mustafa Kamil spoke for many when he

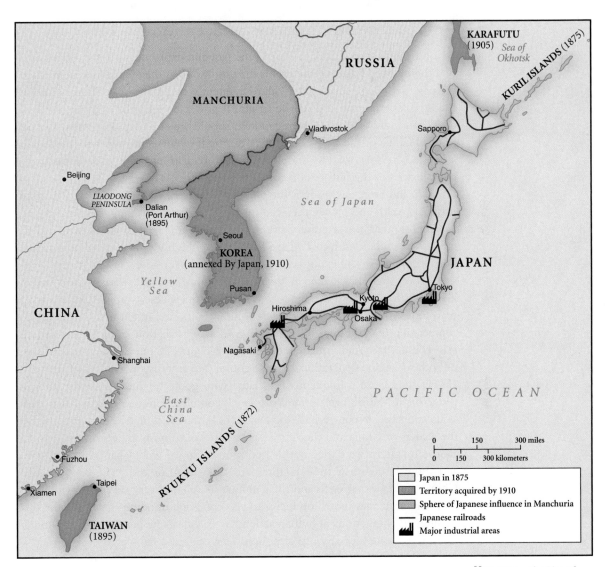

Map 19.3 The Rise of Japan

As Japan modernized after the Meiji restoration, it launched an empire-building program that provided a foundation for further expansion in the 1930s and during World War II.

declared: "We are amazed by Japan because it is the first Eastern government to utilize Western civilization to resist the shield of European imperialism in Asia."[17]

Those who directly experienced Japanese imperialism in Taiwan or Korea no doubt had a less positive view, for its colonial policies matched or exceeded the brutality of European practices. In the twentieth century, China and much of Southeast Asia suffered bitterly under Japanese imperial aggression. Nonetheless, both the idea of Japan as a liberator of Asia from the European yoke and the reality of Japan as an imperial power in its own right derived from the country's remarkable modern transformation and its unique response to the provocation of Western intrusion.

⊔̄⊤ Reflections: Success and Failure in History

Beyond describing what happened in the past and explaining why, historians often find themselves evaluating the events they study. When they make judgments about the past, notions of success and failure frequently come into play. Should Europe's Industrial Revolution and its rise to global power be regarded as a success? If so, does that imply that others were failures? Should we consider Japan more success-ful than China or the Ottoman Empire during the nineteenth century? Three con-siderations suggest that we should be very careful in applying these ideas to the complexities of the historical record.

First, and most obviously, is the question of criteria. If the measure of success is national wealth and power, then the Industrial Revolution surely counts as a great accomplishment. But if preservation of the environment, spiritual growth, and the face-to-face relationships of village life are more highly valued, then industrializa-tion, according to some, might be more reasonably considered as a disaster.

Second, there is the issue of "success for whom?" British artisans who lost their livelihood to industrial machines as well as those Japanese women textile workers who suffered through the early stages of industrialization might be forgiven for not appreciating the "success" of their countries' transformation, even if their middle-class counterparts and subsequent generations benefited. In cases such as this, issues of both social and generational justice complicate any easy assessment of the past.

Finally, success is frequently associated with good judgment and wise choices, yet actors in the historical drama are never completely free in making their deci-sions, and none, of course, have the benefit of hindsight, which historians enjoy. Did the leaders of China and the Ottoman Empire fail to push industrial development more strongly, or were they not in a position to do so? Were Japanese leaders wiser and more astute than their counterparts elsewhere, or did their knowledge of China's earlier experience and their unique national history simply provide them with circumstances more conducive to success? Such questions regarding the pos-sibilities and limitations of human action have no clear-cut answers, but they might caution us about any easy use of notions of success and failure.

Second Thoughts

What's the Significance?

To assess your mastery of the material in this chapter, see the **Online Study Guide** at bedfordstmartins.com/strayer.

social Darwinism	China, 1911	informal empire
Taiping Uprising	"the sick man of Europe"	Tokugawa Japan
Opium Wars	Tanzimat reforms	Meiji restoration
unequal treaties	Young Ottomans	Russo-Japanese War,
self-strengthening movement	Sultan Abd al-Hamid II	1904–1905
Boxer Rebellion	Young Turks	

Big Picture Questions

1. How did European expansion in the nineteenth century differ from that of the early modern era (see Chapters 14–16)?

2. What differences can you identify in how China, the Ottoman Empire, and Japan experienced Western imperialism and confronted it? How might you account for those differences?

3. "The response of each society to European imperialism grew out of its larger historical development and its internal problems." What evidence might support this statement?

4. What kind of debates, controversies, and conflicts were generated by European intrusion within each of the societies examined in this chapter?

Next Steps: For Further Study

William Bowman et al., *Imperialism in the Modern World* (2007). A collection of short readings illustrating the various forms and faces of European expansion over the past several centuries.

Carter V. Finley, *The Turks in World History* (2004). Places the role of Turkish-speaking peoples in general and the Ottoman Empire in particular in a global context.

Maurice Jansen, *The Making of Modern Japan* (2000). A well-regarded account of Japan since 1600 by a leading scholar.

Jonathan Spence, *The Search for Modern China* (1999). Probably the best single-volume account of Chinese history from about 1600 through the twentieth century.

E. Patricia Tsurumi, *Factory Girls: Women in the Thread Mills of Meiji Japan* (1990). Examines the lives of women in Japan's nineteenth-century textile factories.

Arthur Waley, *The Opium War through Chinese Eyes* (1968). An older classic that views the Opium War from various Chinese points of view.

Justin Jesty, "Japanese History from 1868 to the Present," http://ceas.uchicago.edu/outreach/1868%20to%20Present.pdf. A guide to modern Japanese history, with many links to pictures, documents, and further information.

For Web sites and documents related to this chapter, see **Make History** at bedfordstmartins.com/strayer.

CHAPTER TWENTY

Colonial Encounters

1750-1914

A Second Wave of European
Conquests
Under European Rule
Cooperation and Rebellion
Colonial Empires with a
Difference
Ways of Working: Comparing
Colonial Economies
Economies of Coercion:
Forced Labor and the Power
of the State
Economies of Cash-Crop
Agriculture: The Pull of the
Market
Economies of Wage Labor:
Working for Europeans
Women and the Colonial
Economy: An African Case
Study
Assessing Colonial
Development
Believing and Belonging:
Identity and Cultural
Change in the Colonial Era
Education
Religion
"Race" and "Tribe"
Reflections: Who Makes
History?

In mid-1967, I was on summer break from a teaching assignment with the Peace Corps in Ethiopia and was traveling with some friends in neighboring Kenya, just four years after that country had gained its independence from British colonial rule. The bus we were riding on broke down, and I found myself hitchhiking across Kenya, heading for Uganda. Soon I was picked up by a friendly Englishman, one of Kenya's many European settlers who had stayed on after independence. At one point, he pulled off the road to show me a lovely view of Kenya's famous Rift Valley, and we were approached by a group of boys selling baskets and other tourist items. They spoke to us in perfect English, but my British companion replied to them in Swahili. He later explained that Europeans generally did not speak English with the "natives."

Several years later, while conducting research for my Ph.D. dissertation about British missionaries in Kenya in the early twentieth century, I came across a letter from one of them in which he argued against the teaching of English to Africans. Among his reasons were "the danger in which such a course would place our white women and girls" and "the danger of organizing against the government and Europeans."[1] Perhaps such fears—grounded in the intense colonial concern to maintain distance and distinction between whites and blacks, for both sexual and political reasons—were the origin of my helpful driver's reluctance to speak his own language with Kenyans. Maintaining racial boundaries was a central feature of many nineteenth- and early-twentieth-century colonial societies and, in the case of my new British acquaintance, one that persisted even after the colonial era had ended.

The Imperial Durbar of 1903: To mark the coronation of British monarch Edward VII and his installation as the Emperor of India, colonial authorities in India mounted an elaborate assembly, or *durbar*. The durbar was intended to showcase the splendor of the British Empire, and its pageantry included sporting events; a state ball; a huge display of Indian arts, crafts, and jewels; and an enormous parade in which a long line of British officials and Indian princes passed by on bejeweled elephants. (Topham/The Image Works)

FOR MANY MILLIONS OF AFRICANS AND ASIANS, colonial rule—by the British, French, Germans, Italians, Belgians, Portuguese, Russians, or Americans—was the major new element in their historical experience during the nineteenth century. Between roughly 1750 and 1950, much of the Afro-Asian-Pacific world was enveloped within this new wave of European empire building. The encounter with European power in these colonized societies was more immediate, and often more intense, than in those regions that were buffered by their own independent governments, such as Latin America, China, and the Ottoman Empire. Of course, no single colonial experience characterized these two centuries across this vast region. Much depended on the cultures and prior history of various colonized people. Policies of the colonial powers sometimes differed sharply and changed over time. Men and women experienced the colonial era differently, as did traditional elites, Western-educated classes, urban artisans, peasant farmers, and migrant laborers. Furthermore, the varied actions and reactions of such people, despite their oppression and exploitation, shaped the colonial experience, perhaps as much as the policies, practices, and intentions of their temporary European rulers. All of them—colonizers and colonized alike—were caught up in the flood of change that accompanied the Industrial Revolution and a new burst of European imperialism.

A Second Wave of European Conquests

■ Comparison

In what different ways did the colonial takeover of Asia and Africa occur?

If the sixteenth- and seventeenth-century takeover of the Americas represented the first phase of European colonial conquests, the century and a half between 1750 and 1900 was a second and quite distinct round of that larger process. Now it was focused in Asia and Africa rather than in the Western Hemisphere. It featured a number of new players—Germany, Italy, Belgium, the United States, Japan—who were not at all involved in the earlier phase, while the Spanish and Portuguese now had only minor roles. In mainland Asia and Africa, nineteenth-century European conquests nowhere had the devastating demographic consequences that had so sharply reduced the Native American populations. Furthermore, this second wave of European colonial conquests, at least by the mid-nineteenth century, was conditioned by Europe's Industrial Revolution. In both their formal colonies and their "informal empires" (Latin America, China, the Ottoman Empire, and for a time Japan), European motives and activities were shaped by the military capacity and economic power that the Industrial Revolution conveyed. In general, Europeans preferred informal control, for it was cheaper and less likely to provoke wars. But where rivalry with other European states made it impossible or where local governments were unable or unwilling to cooperate, Europeans proved more than willing to undertake the expense and risk of conquest and outright colonial rule.

The construction of these second-wave European empires in the Afro-Asian world, like empires everywhere, involved military force or the threat of using it. Initially, the European military advantage lay in organization, drill and practice, and command structure. Increasingly in the nineteenth century, the Europeans also

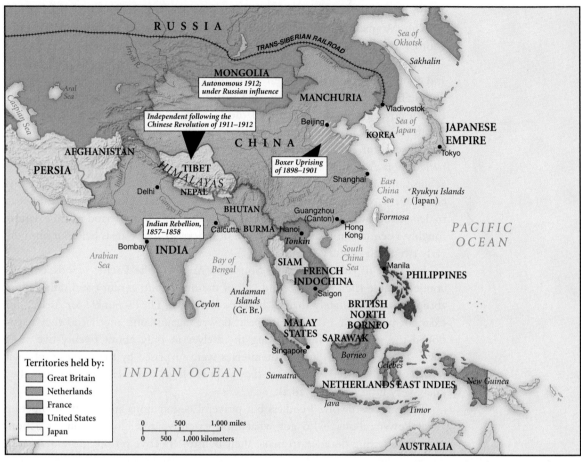

RUSSIA

TRANS-SIBERIAN RAILROAD

Sea of Okhotsk

Sakhalin

MONGOLIA
Autonomous 1912; under Russian influence

MANCHURIA

Vladivostok

Independent following the Chinese Revolution of 1911–1912

Beijing

Sea of Japan

KOREA

JAPANESE EMPIRE

Tokyo

Aral Sea

AFGHANISTAN

C H I N A

Boxer Uprising of 1898–1901

PERSIA

TIBET

HIMALAYAS

Delhi   NEPAL

Shanghai

East China Sea

Ryukyu Islands (Japan)

Caspian Sea

BHUTAN

Ganges R.

Yangzi R.

Guangzhou (Canton)

Formosa

PACIFIC OCEAN

Indian Rebellion, 1857–1858

Calcutta   BURMA   Hanoi

Hong Kong

Bombay   INDIA

Tonkin

South China Sea

Arabian Sea

Bay of Bengal

SIAM

FRENCH INDOCHINA

Manila

PHILIPPINES

Ceylon

Andaman Islands (Gr. Br.)

Saigon

BRITISH NORTH BORNEO

MALAY STATES

SARAWAK

Borneo

Singapore

INDIAN OCEAN

Sumatra

Celebes

New Guinea

NETHERLANDS EAST INDIES

Java

Timor

Territories held by:
- Great Britain
- Netherlands
- France
- United States
- Japan

0   500   1,000 miles
0   500   1,000 kilometers

AUSTRALIA

Map 20.1 Colonial Asia in the Early Twentieth Century
By the early 1900s, several of the great population centers of Asia had come under the colonial control of Britain, the Netherlands, France, the United States, or Japan.

possessed overwhelming advantages in firepower, deriving from the recently invented repeating rifles and machine guns. A much-quoted jingle by the English writer Hilaire Belloc summed up the situation:

Whatever happens we have got
The Maxim gun [an automatic machine gun] and they have not.

Nonetheless, Europeans had to fight, often long and hard, to create their new empires, as countless wars of conquest attest. In the end, though, they prevailed almost everywhere, largely against adversaries who did not have Maxim guns or in some cases any guns at all. Thus were African and Asian peoples of all kinds incorporated within one or another of the European empires. Gathering and hunting bands in Australia, agricultural village societies on Pacific islands and in Africa, pastoralists of the Sahara and Central Asia, residents of states large and small, and virtually everyone in the large and complex civilizations of India and Southeast Asia—all of them alike lost the political sovereignty and freedom of action they had previously exercised. For some, such as Hindus governed by the Muslim Mughal Empire, it was an exchange of one set of foreign rulers for another. But now all were subjects of a European colonial state.

The passage to colonial status occurred in various ways. For the peoples of India and Indonesia, colonial conquest grew out of earlier interaction with European trading firms. Particularly in India, the British East India Company, rather than the British government directly, played the leading role in the colonial takeover of South Asia. The fragmentation of the Mughal Empire and the absence of any overall sense of cultural or political unity both invited and facilitated European penetration. A similar situation of many small and rival states assisted the Dutch acquisition of Indonesia. However, neither the British nor the Dutch had a clear-cut plan for conquest. Rather it evolved slowly as local authorities and European traders made and unmade a variety of alliances over a long period of time, lasting roughly a century in India (1750–1850). In Indonesia, a few areas held out until the early twentieth century (see Map 20.1).

For most of Africa, mainland Southeast Asia, and the Pacific islands, colonial conquest came later, in the second half of the nineteenth century, and rather more abruptly and deliberately than in India or Indonesia. The "scramble for Africa," for example, pitted half a dozen European powers against one another as they partitioned the entire continent among themselves in only about twenty-five years (1875–1900). European leaders themselves were surprised by the intensity of their rivalries and the speed with which they acquired huge territories, about which they knew very little (see Map 20.2).

That process involved endless but peaceful negotiations among the competing Great Powers about "who got what" and extensive and bloody military action, sometimes lasting decades, to make their control effective on the ground. Among the most difficult to subdue were those decentralized societies without a formal state structure. In such cases, Europeans confronted no central authority with which they could negotiate or that they might decisively defeat. It was a matter of village-by-village conquest against extended resistance. As late as 1925, one British official commented on the process as it operated in central Nigeria: "I shall of course go on walloping them until they surrender. It's a rather piteous sight watching a village being knocked to pieces and I wish there was some other way, but unfortunately there isn't."[2]

The South Pacific territories of Australia and New Zealand, both of which were taken over by the British during the nineteenth century, were more similar to the earlier colonization of North America than to contemporary patterns of Asian and African conquest. In both places, conquest was accompanied by massive European settlement and diseases that reduced native numbers by 75 percent or more by 1900. Like Canada and the United States, these became settler colonies, "neo-European" societies in the Pacific. Aboriginal Australians constituted only about 2.4 percent of their country's population in the early twenty-first century, and the indigenous Maori were a minority of about 15 percent in New Zealand. With the exception

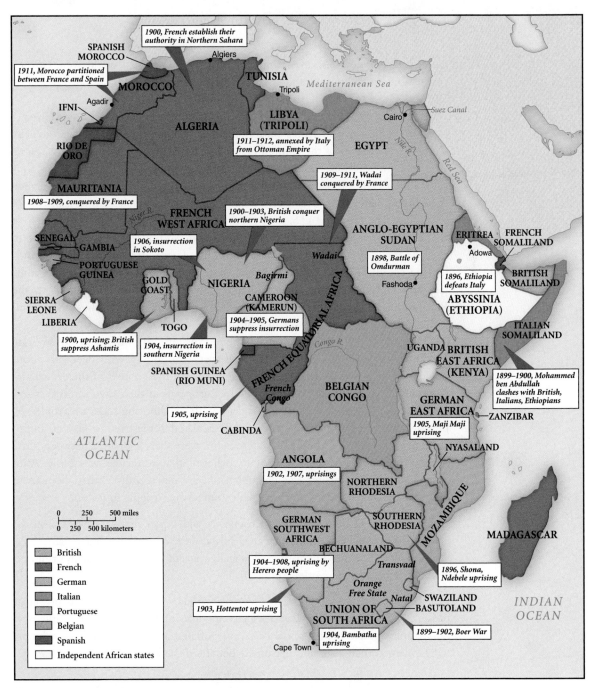

Map 20.2 Conquest and Resistance in Colonial Africa

By the early twentieth century, the map of Africa reflected the outcome of the "scramble for Africa," a conquest that was heavily resisted in many places. The boundaries established during that process still provide the political framework for Africa's independent states.

The following labels appear on the map:

- 1900, French establish their authority in Northern Sahara
- 1911, Morocco partitioned between France and Spain
- 1908–1909, conquered by France
- 1906, insurrection in Sokoto
- 1900, uprising; British suppress Ashantis
- 1904, insurrection in southern Nigeria
- 1900–1903, British conquer northern Nigeria
- 1911–1912, annexed by Italy from Ottoman Empire
- 1909–1911, Wadai conquered by France
- 1904–1905, Germans suppress insurrection
- 1898, Battle of Omdurman
- 1896, Ethiopia defeats Italy
- 1899–1900, Mohammed ben Abdullah clashes with British, Italians, Ethiopians
- 1905, uprising
- 1905, Maji Maji uprising
- 1902, 1907, uprisings
- 1904–1908, uprising by Herero people
- 1903, Hottentot uprising
- 1904, Bambatha uprising
- 1896, Shona, Ndebele uprising
- 1899–1902, Boer War

Map legend:
- British
- French
- German
- Italian
- Portuguese
- Belgian
- Spanish
- Independent African states

Scale: 0 – 250 – 500 miles / 0 – 250 – 500 kilometers

of Hawaii, nowhere else in the nineteenth-century colonial world were existing populations so decimated and overwhelmed as they were in Australia and New Zealand.

Elsewhere other variations on the theme of imperial conquest unfolded. Japan's takeover of Taiwan and Korea bore marked similarities to European actions. The westward expansion of the United States and the Russian penetration of Central Asia brought additional millions under European control as these two states continued their earlier territorial growth. Filipinos acquired new colonial rulers when the United States took over from Spain following the Spanish-American War of 1898. Some 13,000 freed U.S. slaves, seeking greater freedom than was possible at home, migrated to West Africa, where they became, ironically, a colonizing elite in the land they named Liberia. Ethiopia and Siam (Thailand) were notable for avoiding the colonization to which their neighbors succumbed. Those countries' military and diplomatic skills, their willingness to make modest concessions to the Europeans, and the rivalries of the imperialists all contributed to these exceptions to the rule of colonial takeover in East Africa and Southeast Asia.

These broad patterns of colonial conquest dissolved into thousands of separate encounters as Asian and African societies were confronted with decisions about how to respond to encroaching European power in the context of their local circumstances. Many initially sought to enlist Europeans in their own internal struggles for power or in their external rivalries with neighboring states or peoples. As pressures mounted and European demands escalated, some tried to play off imperial powers against one another. Many societies were sharply divided between those who wanted to fight and those who believed that resistance was futile. After extended resistance against French aggression, the nineteenth-century Vietnamese emperor Tu Duc argued with those who wanted the struggle to go on.

> Do you really wish to confront such a power with a pack of [our] cowardly soldiers? It would be like mounting an elephant's head or caressing a tiger's tail. . . . With what you presently have, do you really expect to dissolve the enemy's rifles into air or chase his battleships into hell?[3]

Others negotiated, attempting to preserve as much independence and power as possible. The rulers of the East African kingdom of Buganda, for example, saw opportunity in the British presence and negotiated an arrangement that substantially enlarged their state and personally benefited the kingdom's elite class.

Under European Rule

In many places and for many people, incorporation into European colonial empires was a traumatic experience. Especially for small-scale societies, the loss of life, homes, cattle, crops, and land could be devastating. In 1902, a British soldier in East Africa described what happened in a single village: "Every soul was either shot or bayoneted. . . . We burned all the huts and razed the banana plantations to the ground."[4]

For the Vietnamese elite, schooled for centuries in Chinese-style Confucian thinking, conquest meant that the natural harmonies of life had been badly disrupted; it was a time when "water flowed uphill." Nguyen Khuyen (1835–1909), a senior Vietnamese official, retired to his ancestral village to farm and write poetry after the French conquest. There he expressed his anguish at the passing of the world he had known.

> Fine wine but no good friends,
> So I buy none though I have the money.
> A poem comes to mind, but I choose not to write it down.
> If it were written, to whom would I give it?
> The spare bed hangs upon the wall in cold indifference.
> I pluck the lute, but it just doesn't sound right.[5]

Many others also withdrew into private life, feigning illness when asked to serve in public office under the French.

Cooperation and Rebellion

Although violence was a prominent feature of colonial life both during conquest and after, various groups and many individuals willingly cooperated with colonial authorities to their own advantage. Many men found employment, status, and security in European-led armed forces. The shortage and expense of European administrators and the difficulties of communicating across cultural boundaries made it necessary for colonial rulers to rely heavily on a range of local intermediaries. Thus Indian princes, Muslim emirs, and African chiefs, often from elite or ruling families, found it possible to retain much of their earlier status and privileges while gaining considerable wealth by exercising authority, both legally and otherwise, at the local level. For example, in French West Africa, an area eight times the size of France itself and with a population of about 15 million in the late 1930s, the colonial state consisted of just 385 French administrators and more than 50,000 African chiefs. Thus colonial rule rested upon and reinforced the most conservative segments of Asian and African societies.

■ **Explanation**
Why might subject people choose to cooperate with the colonial regime? What might prompt them to rebel or resist?

Both colonial governments and private missionary organizations had an interest in promoting a measure of European education. From this process arose a small Western-educated class, whose members served the colonial state, European businesses, and Christian missions as teachers, clerks, translators, and lower-level administrators. A few received higher education abroad and returned home as lawyers, doctors, engineers, or journalists. As colonial governments and business enterprises became more sophisticated, Europeans increasingly depended on the Western-educated class at the expense of the more traditional elites.

If colonial rule enlisted the willing cooperation of some, it provoked the bitter opposition of many others. Thus periodic rebellions, both large and small, punctuated the history of colonial regimes everywhere. The most famous among them was

THE DEVILFISH IN EGYPTIAN WATERS.

An Egyptian View of British Imperialism
In this late-nineteenth-century Egyptian cartoon, the British Empire is portrayed as an octopus whose tentacles are already attached to many countries, while one tentacle is about to grasp still another one, Egypt. (The Granger Collection, New York)

the Indian Rebellion of 1857–1858, which was triggered by the introduction into the colony's military forces of a new cartridge smeared with animal fat from cows and pigs. The first animal was sacred to Hindus and the second deeply offensive to Muslims, and both groups viewed the innovation as a plot to render them defiled and to convert them to Christianity. Behind this incident were many groups of people with a whole series of grievances generated by the British colonial presence: local rulers who had lost power; landlords deprived of their estates or their rent; peasants overtaxed and exploited by urban moneylenders and landlords alike; unemployed weavers displaced by machine-manufactured textiles; and religious leaders threatened by missionary activities. A mutiny among Indian troops in Bengal triggered the rebellion, which soon spread to other regions of the colony and other social groups. Soon much of India was aflame. Rebel leaders presented their movement as an effort to revitalize the defunct Mughal Empire and thereby attracted many with strong resentments against the British. Although it was crushed in 1858, the rebellion greatly widened the racial divide in colonial India and eroded British tolerance for those they viewed as "nigger natives" who had betrayed their trust. It made the British more conservative and cautious about deliberately trying to change Indian society for fear of provoking another rebellion. Moreover, it convinced the British government to assume direct control over India, ending the era of British East India Company rule in the subcontinent.

Colonial Empires with a Difference

■ **Comparison**

What was distinctive about European colonial empires of the nineteenth century?

At one level, European colonial empires were but the latest in a very long line of imperial creations, all of which had enlisted cooperation and experienced resistance from their subject peoples, but the nineteenth-century European version of empire differed from the others in several remarkable ways. One was the prominence of race in distinguishing rulers and ruled, as the high tide of "scientific racism" in Europe coincided with the acquisition of Asian and African colonies (see Chapter 19). In East Africa, for example, white men were referred to as "bwana" (Swahili for "master"), whereas Europeans regularly called African men "boy." Education for colonial subjects was both limited and skewed toward practical subjects rather than scientific and literary studies, which were widely regarded as inappropriate for the "primitive mind" of "natives." Particularly affected by European racism were those whose Western education and aspirations most clearly threatened the racial divide. Europeans were exceedingly reluctant to allow even the most highly educated Asians and Africans to enter the higher ranks of the colonial civil service. A proposal in 1883 to allow Indian judges to hear cases involving whites provoked outrage and massive demonstrations among European inhabitants of India.

In those colonies that had a large European settler population, the pattern of racial separation was much more pronounced than in places such as Nigeria, which had few permanently settled whites. The most extreme case was South Africa, where a large European population and the widespread use of African labor in mines and industries brought blacks and whites into closer and more prolonged contact than elsewhere. The racial fears that were aroused resulted in extraordinary efforts to establish race as a legal, not just a customary, feature of South African society. This racial system provided for separate "homelands," educational systems, residential areas, public facilities, and much more. In what was eventually known as apartheid, South African whites attempted the impossible task of creating an industrializing economy based on cheap African labor, while limiting African social and political integration in every conceivable fashion.

A further distinctive feature of nineteenth-century European empires lay in the extent to which colonial states were able to penetrate the societies they governed. Centralized tax-collecting bureaucracies, new means of communication and transportation, imposed changes in landholding patterns, integration of colonial economies into a global network of exchange, public health and sanitation measures, and the activities of missionaries all touched the daily lives of many people far more deeply than in most earlier empires. Not only were Europeans foreign rulers, but they also bore the seeds of a very different way of life, which grew out of their own modern transformation.

Nineteenth-century European colonizers were extraordinary as well in their penchant for counting and classifying their subject people. With the assistance of anthropologists and missionaries, colonial governments collected a vast amount of information, sought to organize it "scientifically," and used it to manage the unfamiliar, complex, varied, and fluctuating societies that they governed. In India, the British found in classical texts and Brahmin ideology an idealized description of the caste system, based on the notion of four ranked and unchanging varnas, which made it possible to bring order out of the immense complexity and variety of caste as it actually operated. Thus the British invented or appropriated a Brahmin version of "traditional India" that they favored and sought to preserve, while scorning as "non-Indian" the new elite educated in European schools and enthusiastic about Western ways of life. This view of India reflected the great influence of Brahmins on British thinking and clearly served the interests of this Indian upper class.

Likewise within African colonies, Europeans identified, and sometimes invented, distinct tribes, each with its own clearly defined territory, language, customs, and chief. The notion of a "tribal Africa" expressed the Western view that African societies were primitive or backward, representing an earlier stage of human development. It was also a convenient idea, for it reduced the enormous complexity and fluidity of African societies to a more manageable state and thus made colonial administration easier.

Finally, European colonial policies contradicted their own core values and their practices at home to an unusual degree. While nineteenth-century Britain and France were becoming more democratic, their colonies were essentially dictatorships, offering perhaps order and stability, but certainly not democratic government, because few colonial subjects were participating citizens. Empire of course was wholly at odds with European notions of national independence, and ranked racial classifications went against the grain of both Christian and Enlightenment ideas of human equality. Furthermore, many Europeans were distinctly reluctant to encourage within their colonies the kind of modernization—urban growth, industrialization, individual values, religious skepticism—that was sweeping their own societies. They feared that this kind of social change, often vilified as "detribalization," would encourage unrest, challenging colonial rule. As a model for social development, they much preferred "traditional" rural society, with its established authorities and social hierarchies, though shorn of abuses such as slavery and sati (widow-burning). Such contradictions between what Europeans preached at home and what they practiced in the colonies became increasingly apparent to many Asians and Africans and played a major role in undermining the foundations of colonial rule in the twentieth century.

Ways of Working: Comparing Colonial Economies

Colonial rule affected the lives of its subject people in many ways, but the most pronounced change was in their ways of working. The colonial state—with its power to tax, to seize land for European enterprises, to compel labor, and to build railroads, ports, and roads—played an important role in these transformations. Even more powerful was the growing integration of Asian and African societies into a world economy that increasingly demanded their gold, diamonds, copper, tin, rubber, coffee, cotton, sugar, cocoa, and many other products. But the economic transformations born of these twin pressures were far from uniform. Various groups—migrant workers and cash-crop farmers, plantation laborers and domestic servants, urban elites and day laborers, men and women—experienced the colonial era differently as their daily working lives underwent profound changes.

To various degrees, old ways of working were eroded almost everywhere in the colonial world. Subsistence farming, in which peasant families produced largely for their own needs, diminished as growing numbers directed at least some of their energies to working for wages or selling what they produced for a cash income.

That money was both necessary to pay their taxes and school fees and useful for buying the various products—such as machine-produced textiles, bicycles, and kerosene—that the industrial economies of Europe sent their way. As in Europe, artisans suffered greatly when cheaper machine-manufactured merchandise displaced their own handmade goods. A flood of inexpensive textiles from Britain's new factories ruined the livelihood of tens of thousands of India's handloom weavers. Iron smelting largely disappeared in Africa, and occupations such as blacksmithing and tanning lost ground. Furthermore, Asian and African merchants, who had earlier handled the trade between their countries and the wider world, were squeezed out by well-financed European commercial firms.

Economies of Coercion: Forced Labor and the Power of the State

Many of the new ways of working that emerged during the colonial era derived directly from the demands of the colonial state. The most obvious was required and unpaid labor on public projects, such as building railroads, constructing government buildings, and transporting goods. In French Africa, all "natives" were legally obligated for "statute labor" of ten to twelve days a year, a practice that lasted through 1946. It was much resented. A resident of British West Africa, interviewed in 1996, bitterly recalled this feature of colonial life: "They [British officials] were rude, and they made us work for them a lot. They came to the village and just rounded us up and made us go off and clear the road or carry loads on our heads."[6]

■ **Connection**
How did the power of colonial states transform the economic lives of colonial subjects?

The most infamous cruelties of forced labor occurred during the early twentieth century in the Congo Free State, then governed personally by Leopold II of Belgium. Private companies in the Congo, operating under the authority of the state, forced villagers to collect rubber, which was much in demand for bicycle and automobile tires, with a reign of terror and abuse that cost millions of lives. One refugee from these horrors described the process.

> We were always in the forest to find the rubber vines, to go without food, and our women had to give up cultivating the fields and gardens. Then we starved.... We begged the white man to leave us alone, saying we could get no more rubber, but the white men and their soldiers said "Go. You are only beasts yourselves...." When we failed and our rubber was short, the soldiers came to our towns and killed us. Many were shot, some had their ears cut off; others were tied up with ropes round their necks and taken away.[7]

Eventually such outrages were widely publicized in Europe, where they created a scandal, forcing the Belgian government to take control of the Congo in 1908 and ending Leopold's reign of terror.

A variation on the theme of forced labor took shape in the so-called cultivation system of the Netherlands East Indies (Indonesia) during the nineteenth century.

Colonial Violence in the Congo
These young boys with severed hands were among the victims of a brutal regime of forced labor undertaken in the Congo during the late nineteenth and early twentieth centuries. Such mutilation was punishment for their villages' inability to supply the required amount of wild rubber. (Courtesy, Anti-Slavery Organization, London)

Peasants were required to cultivate 20 percent or more of their land in cash crops such as sugar or coffee to meet their tax obligation to the state. Sold to government contractors at fixed and low prices, those crops, when resold on the world market, proved highly profitable for Dutch traders and shippers as well as for the Dutch state and its citizens. According to one scholar, the cultivation system "performed a miracle for the Dutch economy," enabling it to avoid taxing its own people and providing capital for its Industrial Revolution.[8] It also enriched and strengthened the position of those "traditional authorities" who enforced the system, often by using lashings and various tortures, on behalf of the Dutch. For the peasants of Java, however, it meant a double burden of obligations to the colonial state as well as to local lords. Many became indebted to moneylenders when they could not meet those obligations. Those demands, coupled with the loss of land and labor now excluded from food production, contributed to a wave of famines during the mid-nineteenth century in which hundreds of thousands perished.

The forced cultivation of cash crops was widely and successfully resisted in many places. In German East Africa, for example, colonial authorities in the late nineteenth century imposed the cultivation of cotton, which seriously interfered with production of local food crops. Here is how one man remembered the experience:

> The cultivation of cotton was done by turns. Every village was allotted days on which to cultivate. . . . After arriving you all suffered very greatly. Your back and your buttocks were whipped and there was no rising up once you stooped to dig. . . . And yet he [the German] wanted us to pay him tax. Were we not human beings?[9]

Such conditions prompted a massive rebellion in 1905 and persuaded the Germans to end the forced growing of cotton. In Mozambique, where the Portuguese likewise brutally enforced cotton cultivation, a combination of peasant sabotage, the planting of unauthorized crops, and the smuggling of cotton across the border to more profitable markets ensured that Portugal never achieved its goal of becoming self-sufficient in cotton production. In such ways did the actions of the colonized alter or frustrate the plans of the colonizers.

Economies of Cash-Crop Agriculture: The Pull of the Market

Many Asian and African peoples had produced quite willingly for an international market long before they were enclosed within colonial societies. They offered for trade items such as peanuts and palm oil in West Africa, cotton in Egypt, spices in Indonesia, and pepper and textiles in India. In some places, colonial rule created conditions that facilitated and increased cash-crop production to the advantage of local farmers. British authorities in Burma, for example, acted to encourage rice production among small farmers by ending an earlier prohibition on rice exports, providing irrigation and transportation facilities, and enacting land tenure laws that facilitated private ownership of small farms. Under these conditions, the population of the Irrawaddy Delta boomed, migrants from Upper Burma and India poured into the region, and rice exports soared. Local small farmers benefited considerably because they were now able to own their own land, build substantial houses, and buy imported goods. For several decades in the late nineteenth century, standards of living improved sharply. It was a very different situation from that of peasants forced to grow crops that seriously interfered with their food production.

Profitable cash-crop farming also developed in the southern Gold Coast (present-day Ghana), a British territory in West Africa. Unlike Burma, it was African farmers themselves who took the initiative to develop export agriculture. Planting cacao trees in huge quantities, they became the world's leading supplier of cocoa, used to make chocolate, by 1911. Cacao was an attractive crop because, unlike cotton, it was compatible with the continued production of foods and did not require so much labor time. In the early twentieth century, it brought a new prosperity to many local farmers. "A hybrid society was taking shape," wrote one scholar, "partly peasant, in that most members farmed their own land with family labor . . . and partly capitalist, in that a minority employed wage laborers, produced chiefly for the market, and reinvested profits."[10]

That success brought new problems in its wake. A shortage of labor fostered the employment of former slaves as dependent and exploited workers and also generated tensions between the sexes when some men married women for their labor power but refused to support them adequately. Moreover, the labor shortage brought a huge influx of migrants from the drier interior parts of West Africa, generating ethnic and class tensions. Furthermore, many colonies came to specialize in one or two cash crops, creating an unhealthy dependence when world market prices dropped. Thus African and Asian farmers were increasingly subject to the uncertain rhythms of the international marketplace as well as to those of the seasons and the weather.

Economies of Wage Labor: Working for Europeans

Yet another new way of working in colonial societies involved wage labor in some European enterprise. Driven by the need for money, by the loss of land adequate to support their families, or sometimes by the orders of colonial authorities, millions of

■ **Change**
How did cash-crop agriculture transform the lives of colonized peoples?

■ **Change**
What kinds of wage labor were available in the colonies? Why might people take part in it? How did doing so change their lives?

colonial subjects across Asia and Africa sought employment in European-owned plantations, mines, construction projects, and homes. All across Southeast Asia in the later nineteenth and early twentieth centuries, huge plantations sprouted, which were financed from Europe and which grew sugarcane, rubber, tea, tobacco, sisal (used for making rope), and more. Impoverished workers by the hundreds of thousands came from great distances—India, China, Java—finding their way to these plantations, where they were subject to strict control, often housed in barracks, and paid poorly, with women receiving 50 to 75 percent of a man's wage. Disease was common, and death rates were twice or more that of the colony as a whole. In southern Vietnam in 1927 alone, one in twenty plantation workers died. British colonial authorities in India facilitated the migration of millions of Indians to work sites elsewhere in the British Empire—Trinidad, Fiji, Malaysia, Ceylon, South Africa, Kenya, and Uganda, for example—with some laboring as indentured workers and others as independent merchants.

In Africa more than in Asia, people migrated to European farms or plantations because they had lost their own land. In the settler colonies of Africa—Algeria, Kenya, Southern Rhodesia (Zimbabwe), and South Africa, for example—permanent European communities, with the help of colonial governments, obtained huge tracts of land, much of which had previously been home to African societies. A 1913 law in South Africa legally defined 88 percent of the land as belonging to whites, who were then about 20 percent of the population. Much of highland Kenya, an

Economic Change in the Colonial World
These workers on a Ceylon tea plantation in the early twentieth century are moving sacks of tea into a drying house in preparation for export. The Lipton label on the bags is a reminder of the role of large-scale foreign investment in the economic transformations of the colonial era. (Hulton-Deutsch Collection/Corbis)

enormously rich agricultural region that was home to the Gikuyu and Kamba peoples, was taken over by some 4,000 white farmers. Some Africans stayed on the land as squatters, working for the new landowners as the price of remaining on what had been their own land. Others were displaced to "native reserves," limited areas that could not support their growing populations, thus forcing many to work for wages on European farms.

Mines were another source of wage labor for many. In the British-ruled Malay States (Malaysia), tin mining accelerated greatly in the late nineteenth century, and by 1895 that colony produced some 55 percent of the world's tin. Operated initially by Chinese and later by European entrepreneurs, these mines drew many millions of impoverished Chinese workers on strictly controlled three-year contracts. Appalling living conditions, disease, and accidents generated extraordinarily high death rates. The gold and diamond mines of South Africa likewise set in motion a huge pattern of labor migration that encompassed all of Africa south of the Belgian Congo. With skilled and highly paid work reserved for white miners, Africans were relegated largely to unskilled labor at a fraction of white wages. Furthermore, they were recruited on short-term contracts, lived in all-male prisonlike barracks that were often surrounded by barbed wire, and were forced to return home periodically to prevent them from establishing a permanent family life near the mines.

The rapidly swelling cities of the colonial world—Lagos, Nairobi, Cairo, Calcutta, Rangoon, Batavia, Singapore, Saigon—required no coercion to attract would-be wage earners, particularly from the late nineteenth century on. Racially segregated, often unsanitary, and greatly overcrowded, these cities nonetheless were seen as meccas of opportunity for people all across the social spectrum. Traditional elites, absentee landlords, and wealthy Chinese businessmen occupied the top rungs of Southeast Asian cities. Western-educated people everywhere found opportunities as teachers, doctors, and professional specialists, but more often as clerks in European business offices and government bureaucracies. Skilled workers on the railways or in the ports represented a working-class elite, while a few labored in the factories that processed agricultural goods or manufactured basic products such as beer, cigarettes, cement, and furniture. Far more numerous were the construction workers, rickshaw drivers, food sellers, domestic servants, prostitutes, and others who made up the urban poor of colonial cities. In 1955, a British investigating commission described life in Nairobi, the capital of Kenya, one of Britain's richest colonies.

> The wages of the majority of African workers are too low to enable them to obtain accommodation which is adequate to any standard. The high cost of housing relative to wages is in itself a cause of overcrowding, because housing is shared to lighten the cost. This, with the high cost of food in towns, makes family life impossible for the majority.[11]

Thus, after more than half a century of colonial rule, British authorities themselves acknowledged that normal family life in the colony's major urban center proved out of reach for the vast majority. It was quite an admission.

Women and the Colonial Economy: An African Case Study

■ **Change**
How were the lives of African women altered by colonial economies?

If economic life in European empires varied greatly from place to place, even within the same colony, it also offered a different combination of opportunities and hardships to women than it did to men, as the experience of colonial Africa shows.[12] In precolonial times, African women were almost everywhere active farmers, with responsibility for planting, weeding, and harvesting in addition to food preparation and child care. Men cleared the land, built houses, herded the cattle, and in some cases assisted with field work. Within this division of labor, women were expected to feed their own families and were usually allocated their own fields for that purpose. Many also were involved in local trading activity. Though clearly subordinate to men, African women nevertheless had a measure of economic autonomy.

As the demands of the colonial economy grew, women's lives diverged more and more from those of men. In colonies where cash-crop agriculture was dominant, men often withdrew from subsistence production in favor of more lucrative export crops. Among the Ewe people of southern Ghana, men almost completely dominated the highly profitable cacao farming, whereas women assumed near total responsibility for domestic food production. In neighboring Ivory Coast, women had traditionally grown cotton for their families' clothing; but when that crop acquired a cash value, men insisted that cotton grown for export be produced on their own personal fields. Thus men acted to control the most profitable aspects of cash-crop agriculture and in doing so greatly increased the subsistence workload of women. One study from Cameroon estimated that women's working hours increased from forty-six per week in precolonial times to more than seventy by 1934.

Further increasing women's workload and differentiating their lives from those of men was labor migration. As more and more men sought employment in the cities, on settler farms, or in the mines, their wives were left to manage the domestic economy almost alone. In many cases, women also had to supply food to men in the cities to compensate for very low urban wages. They often took over such traditionally male tasks as breaking the ground for planting, milking the cows, and supervising the herds, in addition to their normal responsibilities. In South Africa, where the demands of the European economy were particularly heavy, some 40 to 50 percent of able-bodied adult men were absent from the rural areas, and women headed 60 percent of households. In

Women in Colonial Africa
The movement of many African men into wage labor thrust even more of the domestic responsibilities onto women. Here in a photograph from colonial Kenya in 1936 a woman carries on the ancient craft of making clay pots. (Elspeth Huxley/ Huxley Collection/Images of Empire, British Empire & Commonwealth Museum)

Botswana, which supplied much male labor to South Africa, married couples by the 1930s rarely lived together for more than two months at a time. In such situations, the lives and cultures of men and women increasingly diverged, with one focused on the cities and working for wages and the other on village life and subsistence agriculture.

Women coped with these difficult circumstances in a number of ways. Many sought closer relations with their families of birth rather than with their absent husbands' families, as would otherwise have been expected. Among the Luo of Kenya, women introduced laborsaving crops, adopted new farm implements, and earned some money as traders. In the cities, they established a variety of self-help associations, including those for prostitutes and for brewers of beer.

The colonial economy sometimes provided a measure of opportunity for enterprising women, particularly in small-scale trade and marketing. In some parts of West Africa, women came to dominate this sector of the economy by selling foodstuffs, cloth, and inexpensive imported goods, while men or foreign firms controlled the more profitable wholesale and import-export trade. Such opportunities sometimes gave women considerable economic autonomy. By the 1930s, for example, Nupe women in northern Nigeria had gained sufficient wealth as itinerant traders that they were contributing more to the family income than their husbands and frequently lent money to them. Among some Igbo groups in southern Nigeria, men were responsible for growing the prestigious yams, but women's crops—especially cassava—came to have a cash value during the colonial era, and women were entitled to keep the profits from selling it. "What is man? I have my own money" expressed the growing economic independence of such women.[13]

At the other end of the social scale, women of impoverished rural families, by necessity, often became virtually independent heads of household in the absence of their husbands. Others took advantage of new opportunities in mission schools, towns, and mines to flee the restrictions of rural patriarchy. Such challenges to patriarchal values elicited various responses from men, including increased accusations of witchcraft against women and fears of impotence. Among the Shona in Southern Rhodesia, and no doubt elsewhere, senior African men repeatedly petitioned the colonial authorities for laws and regulations that would criminalize adultery and restrict women's ability to leave their rural villages.[14] The control of women's sexuality and mobility was a common interest of European and African men.

Assessing Colonial Development

Beyond the many and varied changes that transformed the working lives of millions in the colonial world lies the difficult and highly controversial question of the overall economic impact of colonial rule on Asian and African societies. Defenders, both then and now, praise it for jump-starting modern growth, but numerous critics cite a record of exploitation and highlight the limitations and unevenness of that growth. Amid the continuing debates, three things seem reasonably clear. First,

■ Change
Did colonial rule bring "progress" in its wake?

colonial rule served, for better or worse, to further the integration of Asian and African economies into a global network of exchange, now centered in Europe. In many places, that process was well under way before conquest imposed foreign rule, and elsewhere it occurred without formal colonial control. Nonetheless, it is apparent that within the colonial world far more land and labor were devoted to production for the global market at the end of the colonial era than at its beginning.

Second, Europeans could hardly avoid conveying to the colonies some elements of their own modernizing process. It was in their interests to do so, and many felt duty bound to "improve" the societies they briefly governed. Modern administrative and bureaucratic structures facilitated colonial control; communication and transportation infrastructure (railroads, motorways, ports, telegraphs, postal services) moved products to the world market; schools trained the army of intermediaries on which colonial rule depended; and modest health care provisions fulfilled some of the "civilizing mission" to which many Europeans felt committed. These elements of modernization made an appearance, however inadequately, during the colonial era.

Third, nowhere in the colonial world did a breakthrough to modern industrial society of Japanese dimensions occur. When India became independent after two centuries of colonial rule by the world's first industrial society, it was still one of the poorest of the world's developing countries. The British may not have created Indian poverty, but neither did they overcome it to any substantial degree. Scholars continue to debate the reasons for that failure: was it the result of deliberate British policies, or was it due to the conditions of Indian society? The nationalist movements that surged across Asia and Africa in the twentieth century had their own answer. To their many millions of participants, colonial rule, whatever its earlier promise, had become an economic dead end, whereas independence represented a grand opening to new and more hopeful possibilities. Paraphrasing a famous teaching of Jesus, Kwame Nkrumah, the first prime minister of an independent Ghana, declared, "Seek ye first the political kingdom, and all these other things [schools, factories, hospitals, for example] will be added unto you."

Snapshot   Long-Distance Migration in an Age of Empire, 1846–1940[15]

The age of empire was also an age of global migration. Beyond the long-distance migration shown here, shorter migrations within particular regions or colonies set millions more into motion.

Origins	Destination	Numbers
Europe	Americas	55–58 million
India, southern China	Southeast Asia, Indian Ocean rim, South Pacific	48–52 million
Northeast Asia, Russia	Manchuria, Siberia, Central Asia, Japan	46–51 million

Believing and Belonging: Identity and Cultural Change in the Colonial Era

The experience of colonial rule—its racism, its exposure to European culture, its social and economic upheavals—contributed much to cultural change within Asian and African societies. Coping with these enormous disruptions induced many colonized peoples to alter the ways they thought about themselves and their communities. Cultural identities, of course, are never static, but the transformations of the colonial era catalyzed substantial and quite rapid changes in what people believed and in how they defined the societies to which they belonged. Those transformed identities continued to echo long after European rule had ended.

Education

For an important minority, it was the acquisition of Western education, obtained through missionary or government schools, that generated a new identity. To previously illiterate people, the knowledge of reading and writing of any kind often suggested an almost magical power. Within the colonial setting, it could mean an escape from some of the most onerous obligations of living under European control, such as forced labor. More positively, it meant access to better-paying positions in government bureaucracies, mission organizations, or business firms and to the exciting imported goods that their salaries could buy. Moreover, education often provided social mobility and elite status within their own communities and an opportunity to achieve, or at least approach, equality with whites in racially defined societies. An African man from colonial Kenya described an encounter he had as a boy in 1938 with a relative who was a teacher in a mission school.

> Aged about 25, he seems to me like a young god with his smart clothes and shoes, his watch, and a beautiful bicycle. I worshipped in particular his bicycle that day and decided that I must somehow get myself one. As he talked with us, it seemed to me that the secret of his riches came from his education, his knowledge of reading and writing, and that it was essential for me to obtain this power.[16]

Many such people ardently embraced European culture, dressing in European clothes, speaking French or English, building European-style houses, getting married in long white dresses, and otherwise emulating European ways. Some of the early Western-educated Bengalis from northeastern India boasted about dreaming in English and deliberately ate beef, to the consternation of their elders. In a well-known poem entitled "A Prayer for Peace," Léopold Senghor, a highly educated West African writer and political leader, enumerated the many crimes of colonialism and yet confessed, "I have a great weakness for France." Asian and African colonial societies now had a new cultural divide: between the small number who had mastered to varying degrees the ways of their rulers and the vast majority who had

■ **Change**
What impact did Western education have on colonial societies?

The Educated Elite
Throughout the Afro-Asian world of the nineteenth century, the European presence generated a small group of people who enthusiastically embraced the culture and lifestyle of Europe. Here King Chulalongkorn of Siam poses with the crown prince and other young students, all of them garbed impeccably in European clothing. (Hulton-Deutsch Collection/Corbis)

not. Literate Christians in the East African kingdom of Buganda referred with contempt to their "pagan" neighbors as "they who do not read."

Many among the Western-educated elite saw themselves as a modernizing vanguard who were leading the regeneration of their societies, in association with colonial authorities. For them, at least initially, the colonial enterprise was full of promise for a better future. The Vietnamese teacher and nationalist Nguyen Thai Hoc, while awaiting execution in 1930 by the French for his revolutionary activities, wrote about his earlier hopes: "At the beginning, I had thought to cooperate with the French in Indochina in order to serve my compatriots, my country, and my people, particularly in the areas of cultural and economic development."[17] Senghor too wrote wistfully about an earlier time when "we could have lived in harmony [with Europeans]."

In nineteenth-century India, Western-educated people organized a variety of reform societies, which sought a renewed Indian culture that was free of idolatry, child marriages, caste, and discrimination against women, while drawing inspiration from the classic texts of Hinduism. For them, European education was an instrument of progress and liberation from the stranglehold of tradition. Ram Mohan Roy (1772–1833), perhaps the foremost of these Indian reformers, sought from the colonial regime "European gentlemen of talent and education to instruct the natives of India in mathematics, natural philosophy, chemistry, anatomy and other useful sciences which the natives of Europe have carried to a degree of perfection that has raised them above the inhabitant of other parts of the world."[18]

Such fond hopes for the renewal of Asian and African societies through colonial rule would be bitterly disappointed. Europeans generally declined to treat their Asian and African subjects—even those with a Western education—as equal partners in the enterprise of renewal. The frequent denigration of their cultures as primitive, backward, uncivilized, or savage certainly rankled, particularly among the well-educated. "My people of Africa," wrote the West African intellectual James Aggrey in the 1920s, "we were created in the image of God, but men have made us think that we are chickens, and we still think we are; but we are eagles. Stretch forth your wings and fly."[19]

Religion

Religion too provided the basis for new or transformed identities during the colonial era. Most dramatic were those places where widespread conversion to Christianity took place, such as New Zealand, the Pacific islands, and especially non-Muslim Africa. Some 10,000 missionaries had descended on Africa by 1910; by the 1960s, about 50 million Africans, roughly half of the non-Muslim population, claimed a Christian identity. The attractions of the new faith were many. As in the Americas centuries earlier, military defeat shook confidence in the old gods and local practices, fostering openness to new sources of supernatural power that could operate in the wider world now impinging on their societies. Furthermore, Christianity was widely associated with modern education, and, especially in Africa, mission schools were the primary providers of Western education. The young, the poor, and many women—all of them oppressed groups in many African societies— found new opportunities and greater freedom in some association with missions. Moreover, the spread of the Christian message was less the work of

■ Change
What were the attractions of Christianity within some colonial societies?

The Missionary Factor
Among the major change agents of the colonial era were the thousands of Christian missionaries who brought not only a new religion but also elements of European medicine, education, gender roles, and culture. Here is an assembly at a mission school for girls in New Guinea in the early twentieth century. (Rue des Archives/The Granger Collection, New York)

European missionaries than of those many thousands of African teachers, catechists, and pastors who brought the new faith to remote villages as well as the local communities that begged for a teacher and supplied the labor and materials to build a small church or school.

■ **Change**
How and why did Hinduism emerge as a distinct religious tradition during the colonial era in India?

As elsewhere, Christianity in Africa soon became Africanized. Within mission-based churches, many converts continued using protective charms and medicines and consulting local medicine men, all of which caused their missionary mentors to speak frequently of "backsliding." Other converts continued to believe in their old gods and spirits but now deemed them evil and sought their destruction. Furthermore, thousands of separatist movements established a wide array of independent churches, which were thoroughly Christian but under African rather than missionary control and which in many cases incorporated African cultural practices and modes of worship. It was a twentieth-century "African Reformation."

In India, where Christianity made only very modest inroads, leading intellectuals and reformers began to define their region's endlessly varied beliefs, practices, sects, rituals, and schools of philosophy as a more distinct, unified, and separate religion that we now know as Hinduism. It was in part an effort to provide for India a religion wholly equivalent to Christianity, "an accessible tradition and a feeling of historical worth when faced with the humiliation of colonial rule."[20] To Swami Vivekananda (1863–1902), one of nineteenth-century India's most influential religious figures, a revived Hinduism, shorn of its distortions, offered a means of uplifting the country's village communities, which were the heart of Indian civilization. Moreover, it could offer spiritual support to a Western world mired in materialism and militarism, a message that he took to the First World Parliament of Religions held in 1893 in Chicago. Here was India speaking back to Europe.

Hinduism in the West
The cultural interactions of the colonial era brought Asian traditions such as Hinduism to the attention of small groups in Europe and the United States. The visit of India's Swami Vivekananda to the First World Parliament of Religions in Chicago in 1893 was part of that process, illustrated here by a famous poster that circulated at that event. (Courtesy, Goes Lithographics, Chicago, after photo by Frank Parlato Jr. Image provided by www.vivekananda.net)

> Let the foreigners come and flood the land with their armies, never mind. Up, India and conquer the world with your spirituality. . . . The whole of the Western world is a volcano which may burst tomorrow, go to pieces tomorrow. . . . Now is the time to work so that India's spiritual ideas may penetrate deep into the West.[21]

This new notion of Hinduism provided a cultural foundation for emerging ideas of India as a nation, but it also contributed to a clearer sense of Muslims as a distinct community in India. Before the British takeover, little sense of commonality united the many diverse communities who practiced Islam—urban and rural dwellers; nomads and farmers; artisans, merchants, and state officials. But the British had created separate inheritance laws for all Muslims and all Hindus; in their census taking, they counted the numbers of people within these now sharply distinguished groups; and they allotted seats in local councils according to these artificial categories. As some anti-British patriots began to cast India in Hindu terms, the idea of Muslims as a separate community, which was perhaps threatened by the much larger number of Hindus, began to make sense to some who practiced Islam. In the early twentieth century, a young Hindu Bengali schoolboy noticed that "our Muslim school-fellows were beginning to air the fact of their being Muslims rather more consciously than before and with a touch of assertiveness."[22] Here were the beginnings of what became in the twentieth century a profound religious and political division within the South Asian peninsula.

"Race" and "Tribe"

In Africa as well, intellectuals and ordinary people alike forged new ways of belonging as they confronted the upheavals of colonial life. Central to these new identities were notions of race and ethnicity. By the end of the nineteenth century, a number of African thinkers, familiar with Western culture, began to define the idea of an "African identity." Previously, few if any people on the continent had regarded themselves as Africans. Rather they were members of particular local communities, usually defined by language; some were also Muslims; and still others inhabited some state or empire. Now, however, influenced by the common experience of colonial oppression and by a highly derogatory European racism, well-educated Africans began to think in broader terms, similar to Indian reformers who were developing the notion of Hinduism. It was an effort to revive the cultural self-confidence of their people by articulating a larger, common, and respected "African tradition," equivalent to that of Western culture.

■ **Change**
In what way were "race" and "tribe" new identities in colonial Africa?

This effort took many shapes. One line of argument held that African culture and history in fact possessed the very characteristics that Europeans exalted. Knowing that Europeans valued large empires and complex political systems, African intellectuals pointed with pride to the ancient kingdoms of Ethiopia, Mali, Songhay, and others. C. A. Diop, a French-educated scholar from Senegal, insisted that Egyptian civilization was in fact the work of black Africans. Turning European assumptions on their head, Diop argued that Western civilization owed much to Egyptian influence and was therefore derived from Africa. Black people, in short, had a history of achievement fully comparable to that of Europe and therefore deserved just as much respect and admiration.

An alternative approach to defining an African identity lay in praising the differences between African and European cultures. The most influential proponent of such views was Edward Blyden (1832–1912), a West African born in the West Indies and educated in the United States, who later became a prominent scholar and political official in Liberia. Blyden accepted the assumption that the world's various races were different but argued that each had its own distinctive contribution to make to world civilization. The uniqueness of African culture, Blyden wrote, lay in its communal, cooperative, and egalitarian societies, which contrasted sharply with Europe's highly individualistic, competitive, and class-ridden societies; in its harmonious relationship with nature as opposed to Europe's efforts to dominate and exploit the natural order; and particularly in its profound religious sensibility, which Europeans had lost in centuries of attention to material gain. Like Vivekananda in India, Blyden argued that Africa had a global mission "to be the spiritual conservatory of the world."[23]

In the twentieth century, such ideas resonated with a broader public. Hundreds of thousands of Africans took part in World War I, during which they encountered other Africans as well as Europeans. Some were able to travel widely. Contact with American black leaders such as Booker T. Washington, W. E. B. DuBois, and Marcus Garvey and with West Indian intellectuals further stimulated among a few a sense of belonging to an even larger pan-African world. Such notions underlay the growing nationalist movements that contested colonial rule as the twentieth century unfolded.

For the vast majority, however, the most important new sense of belonging that evolved from the colonial experience was not the notion of "Africa"; rather, it was the idea of "tribe" or, in the language of contemporary scholars, that of ethnic identity. African peoples, of course, had long recognized differences among themselves based on language, kinship, clan, village, or state, but these were seldom sharp or clearly defined. Boundaries fluctuated and were hazy; local communities often incorporated a variety of culturally different peoples. The idea of an Africa sharply divided into separate and distinct "tribes" was in fact a European notion that facilitated colonial administration and reflected Europeans' belief in African primitiveness. When the British, for example, began to govern the peoples living along the northern side of Lake Tanganyika, in present-day Tanzania, they found a series of communities that were similar to one another in language and customs but that governed themselves separately and certainly had not regarded themselves as a tribe. It was British attempts to rule them as a single people, first through a "paramount chief" and later through a council of chiefs and elders, that resulted in their being called, collectively, the Nyakyusa. A tribe had been born. By requiring people to identify their tribe on applications for jobs, schools, and identity cards, colonial governments spread the idea of tribe widely within their colonies.

New ethnic identities were not simply imposed by Europeans; Africans increasingly found ethnic or tribal labels useful. This was especially true in rapidly growing urban areas. Surrounded by a bewildering variety of people and in a setting where competition for jobs, housing, and education was very intense, migrants to the city found it helpful to categorize themselves and others in larger ethnic terms. Thus, in many colonial cities, people who spoke similar languages, shared a common culture, or came from the same general part of the country began to think of themselves as a single people—a new tribe. They organized a rich variety of ethnic or tribal associations to provide mutual assistance while in the cities and to send money back home to build schools or clinics. Migrant workers, far from home and concerned to protect their rights to land and to their wives and families, found a sense of security in being part of a recognized tribe, with its chiefs, courts, and established authority.

The Igbo people of southeastern Nigeria represent a case in point. Prior to the twentieth century, they were organized in a series of independently governed village groups. Although they spoke related languages, they had no unifying political system and no myth of common ancestry. Occupying a region of unusually dense population, many of these people eagerly seized on Western education and moved in large numbers to the cities and towns of colonial Nigeria. There they gradually discovered what they had in common and how they differed from the other peoples of Nigeria. By the 1940s, they were organizing on a national level and calling on Igbos everywhere to "sink all differences" in order to achieve "tribal unity, cooperation, and progress of all the Igbos." Fifty years earlier, however, no one had regarded himself or herself as an Igbo. One historian summed up the process of creating African ethnic identities in this way: "Europeans believed Africans belonged to tribes; Africans built tribes to belong to."[24]

⊢⊣ Reflections: Who Makes History?

Winners may write history, but they do not make history, at least not alone. Dominant groups everywhere—slave owners, upper classes, men generally, and certainly colonial rulers—have found their actions constrained and their choices limited by the sheer presence of subordinated people and the ability of those people to act. Europeans who sought to make their countries self-sufficient in cotton by requiring colonized Africans to grow it generally found themselves unable to achieve that goal. Missionaries who tried to impose their own understanding of Christianity in the colonies found their converts often unwilling to accept missionary authority or the cultural framework in which the new religion was presented. In the twentieth century, colonial rulers all across Asia and Africa found that their most highly educated subjects became the leaders of those movements seeking to end colonial rule. Clearly this was not what they had intended.

In recent decades, historians have been at pains to uncover the ways in which subordinated people—slaves, workers, peasants, women, the colonized—have been able to act in their own interests, even within the most oppressive conditions. This kind of "history from below" found expression in a famous book about American slavery that was subtitled "The World the Slaves Made." Historians of women's lives have sought to depict women not only as victims of patriarchy but also as historical actors in their own right. Likewise, colonized people in any number of ways actively shaped the history of the colonial era. On occasion, they resisted and rebelled; in various times and places, they embraced, rejected, and transformed a transplanted Christianity; many eagerly sought Western education but later turned it against the colonizers; women both suffered from and creatively coped with the difficulties of colonial life; and everywhere people created new ways of belonging. None of this diminishes the hardships, the enormous inequalities of power, or the exploitation and oppression of the colonial experience. Rather it suggests that history is often made through the struggle of unequal groups and that the outcome corresponds to no one's intentions.

Perhaps we might let Karl Marx have the last word on this endlessly fascinating topic: "Men make their own history," he wrote, "but they do not make it as they please nor under conditions of their own choosing." In the colonial experience of the nineteenth and early twentieth centuries, both the colonizers and the colonized "made history," but neither was able to do so as they pleased.

Second Thoughts

What's the Significance?

To assess your mastery of the material in this chapter, see the **Online Study Guide** at bedfordstmartins.com/strayer.

scramble for Africa	cash-crop agriculture	colonial racism
Indian Rebellion, 1857–1858	Western-educated elite	Edward Blyden
Congo Free State/Leopold II	Africanization of Christianity	colonial tribalism
cultivation system	Swami Vivekananda	

Big Picture Questions

1. Why were Asian and African societies incorporated into European colonial empires later than those of the Americas? How would you compare their colonial experiences?

2. In what ways did colonial rule rest upon violence and coercion, and in what ways did it elicit voluntary cooperation or generate benefits for some people?

3. In what respects were colonized people more than victims of colonial conquest and rule? To what extent could they act in their own interests within the colonial situation?

4. Was colonial rule a transforming, even a revolutionary, experience, or did it serve to freeze or preserve existing social and economic patterns? What evidence can you find to support both sides of this argument?

Next Steps: For Further Study

For Web sites and documents related to this chapter, see **Make History** at bedfordstmartins.com/strayer.

A. Adu Boahen, *African Perspectives on Colonialism* (1987). A prominent African scholar examines the colonial experience.

Alice Conklin and Ian Fletcher, *European Imperialism, 1830–1930* (1999). A collection of both classical reflections on empire and examples of modern scholarship.

Scott B. Cook, *Colonial Encounters in the Age of High Imperialism* (1996). Seven case studies of the late-nineteenth-century colonial experience.

Adam Hochschild, *King Leopold's Ghost* (1999). A journalist's evocative account of the horrors of early colonial rule in the Congo.

Douglas Peers, *India under Colonial Rule* (2006). A concise and up-to-date exploration of colonial India.

Bonnie Smith, ed., *Imperialism* (2000). A fine collection of documents, pictures, and commentary on nineteenth- and twentieth-century empires.

Margaret Strobel, *Gender, Sex, and Empire* (1994). A brief account of recent historical thinking about colonial life and gender.

"History of Imperialism," http://members.aol.com/TeacherNet/World.html. A Web site with dozens of links to documents, essays, maps, cartoons, and pictures dealing with modern empires.

PART SIX

The Most Recent Century

1914–2008

Contents

Chapter 21. The Collapse and Recovery of Europe, 1914–1970s
Chapter 22. The Rise and Fall of World Communism, 1917–Present
Chapter 23. Independence and Development in the Global South, 1914–Present
Chapter 24. Accelerating Global Interaction since 1945

The Twentieth Century: A New Period in World History?

Dividing up time into coherent segments—periods, eras, ages—is the way historians mark major changes in the lives of individuals, local communities, social groups, nations, and civilizations and also in the larger story of humankind as a whole. Because all such divisions are artificial, imposed by scholars on a continuously flowing stream of events, they are endlessly controversial and never more so than in the case of the twentieth century.

Does this most recent 100-year period represent a separate phase of world history? Granting it that status has become conventional in many world history textbooks, including this one, but there are reasons to wonder whether future generations will view it in the same way. One problem, of course, lies in its brevity—less than 100 years, compared to the many centuries or millennia that comprise earlier periods. Furthermore, an immense overload of information about these decades makes it difficult to distinguish "the forest from the trees." We cannot be sure what will prove of lasting significance and what will later seem of only passing importance. Furthermore, because we are so close to the events we study and obviously ignorant of the future, we cannot know if or when this most recent period of world history will end. Or, as some have argued, has it ended already, perhaps with the collapse of the Soviet Union in 1991 or with the attacks of September 11, 2001? If so, are we now in yet another phase of historical development?

We are more certain about the beginning of the twentieth century than its end. For most historians, it was the outbreak of World War I in 1914 that marked the start of a new era. That terrible conflict, after all, represented a fratricidal civil war within Western civilization; it triggered the Russian Revolution and the beginning of world communism; it stimulated many in the colonial world to work for their own independence; and the way it ended set the stage for an even more terrible struggle in World War II.

Old and New in the Twentieth Century

Like most historical periods, the twentieth century both carried on from the past and developed distinctive characteristics. Whether that combination of the old and new merits the designation of a separate era in world history will likely be debated for a long time to come. For our purposes, it will be enough to highlight both the continuities with the past and the sharp changes of this most recent century.

Consider, for example, the world wars that played such an important role in the first half of the century. They grew out of Europeans' persistent inability to embody their civilization within a single state or empire, as China had long done. They also represent a further stage of European rivalries around the globe that had been going on for four centuries. Nonetheless, the world wars of the twentieth century were also new in the extent to which whole populations were mobilized to fight them and in the enormity of the destruction that they caused. During World War II, for example, Hitler's attempted extermination of the Jews in the Holocaust and the United States' dropping of atomic bombs on Japanese cities marked something new in the history of human conflict.

The communist phenomenon provides another illustration of the blending of old and new. The Russian (1917) and Chinese (1949) revolutions, both of which were enormous social upheavals, brought to power regimes committed to remaking their societies from top to bottom along socialist lines. They were the first large-scale attempts in modern world history to undertake such a gigantic task, and in doing so they broke sharply with the capitalist democratic model of the West. They also created a new and global division of humankind, expressed most dramatically in the cold war between the communist East and the capitalist West. On the other hand, the communist experience also drew much from the past. The great revolutions of the twentieth century derived from long-standing conflicts in Russian and Chinese society, particularly between impoverished and exploited peasants and dominant landlord classes. The ideology of those communist governments came from the thinking of the nineteenth-century German intellectual Karl Marx. Their intention, like that of their capitalist enemies, was modernization and industrialization. They simply claimed to do it better—more rapidly and more justly.

Another distinguishing feature of the twentieth century lay in the disintegration of its great empires—the Austro-Hungarian, Ottoman, Russian, British, French, Japanese, Soviet, and more—and in their wake the emergence of dozens of new nation-states. At one level, this is simply the latest turn of the wheel in the endless rise and fall of empires, dating back to the ancient Assyrians. But something new occurred this time, for the very idea of empire was rendered illegitimate in the twentieth century, much as slavery lost its international acceptance in the nineteenth century. The superpowers of the second half of the twentieth century—the Soviet Union and the United States—both claimed an anticolonial ideology, even as both of them constructed their own "empires" of a different kind. By the beginning of the twenty-first century, a world of more than 200 nation-states had come to pass, each claiming sovereignty and legal equality with all the others. This represented a distinctly new global ordering of peoples.

The less visible underlying processes of the twentieth century, just like the more dramatic wars, revolutions, and political upheavals, also had roots in the past as well as new expressions in the new century. Perhaps the most fundamental process was explosive population growth, as human numbers more than quadrupled since 1900, leaving the planet with about 6.7 billion people by 2008. This was an absolutely

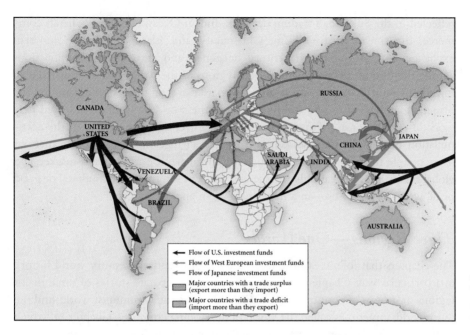

Globalization in Action:
Trade and Investment in the
Early Twenty-first Century
(p. 726)

unprecedented rate of growth that conditioned practically every other feature of the century's history. Still, this new element of twentieth-century world history built upon earlier achievements, most notably the increased food supply deriving from the global spread of American crops such as corn and potatoes. Improvements in medicine and sanitation, which grew out of the earlier Scientific and Industrial revolutions, likewise drove down death rates and thus spurred population growth.

While global population increased fourfold in the twentieth century, industrial output grew fortyfold. This unprecedented economic growth, despite large variations over time and place, was associated with a cascading rate of scientific and technological innovation as well as with the extension of industrial production to many regions of the world. This too was a wholly novel feature of twentieth-century world history and, combined with population growth, resulted in an extraordinary and mounting human impact on the environment. Historian J. R. McNeill wrote that "this is the first time in human history that we have altered ecosystems with such intensity, on such a scale, and with such speed. . . . The human race, without intending anything of the sort, has undertaken a gigantic uncontrolled experiment on the earth."[1] From a longer-term perspective, of course, these developments represent a continued unfolding of the Scientific and Industrial revolutions. Both began in Europe, but in the twentieth century they largely lost their unique association with the West as they took hold in many cultures. Furthermore, the human impact on the earth itself and other living creatures has a history dating back to the extinction of some large mammals at the hands of Paleolithic hunters.

Much the same might be said about that other grand process of twentieth-century world history—globalization. It too has a genealogy reaching deep into the past, reflected in the Silk Road trading network; Indian Ocean and trans-Saharan commerce; the spread of Buddhism, Christianity, and Islam; and the Columbian exchange. But the twentieth century deepened and extended the connections among the distinct peoples, nations, and regions of the world in ways unparalleled in earlier centuries. A few strokes on a keyboard can send money racing around the planet; radio, television, and the Internet link the world in an unprecedented network of communication; the warming of the lower atmosphere due to the accumulation of greenhouse gases portends radical changes for the whole planet; far more people than ever before produce for and depend on the world market; and global inequalities increasingly surface as sources of international conflict. For good or ill, we live—all of us—in a new phase of an ancient process.

Three Regions—One World

The chapters that follow explore these themes of twentieth-century world history in a particular way. Chapters 21, 22, and 23 tell the separate stories of three major regions or groups of countries—the Western world; the communist world; and the third world, sometimes called the world of developing countries. Chapter 21, which focuses on the Western world of capitalist countries, highlights the dramatic changes that occurred at the center of the global network. The European heartland of the world system collapsed in war and economic depression during the first half of the century but recovered in the second half as leadership of the Western world passed to the United States.

Accompanying those changes internal to the West was the profound challenge of world communism. Chapter 22 addresses four features of the communist phenomenon: the revolutionary origins of communism, especially in Russia and China; the efforts of those two communist giants to build new and socialist societies; the global conflict of the cold war, which arose from the expansion of communism; and the amazing abandonment of communism as the century ended.

Chapter 23 turns the historical spotlight on the colonial world of Asia and Africa. Two major themes serve to structure the twentieth-century history of this vast region. The first focuses attention on the struggles for independence, the end of colonial empires, and the emergence of dozens of new nations. The second describes the increasingly important role on the global stage that these new states have played in the second half of the century. The assertion of African, Asian, and Middle Eastern peoples, joined by those of Latin America, made the world of 2000 a very different place from that of a century earlier.

These twentieth-century histories of the Western world, the communist world, and the third world not only paralleled one another but also frequently intersected and overlapped, as Chapters 21, 22, and 23 repeatedly indicate. All of them, however, were also part of an even larger story, known everywhere now as globalization. The post–World War II acceleration of this much older process is the grand theme of Chapter 24, which examines four dimensions of recent globalization—economic relationships, feminism, religious fundamentalism, and environmentalism.

Perhaps there is enough that is new about the twentieth century to treat it, tentatively, as a distinct era in human history, but only what happens next will determine how this most recent century will be understood by later generations. Will it be regarded as the beginning of the end of the modern age, as human demands upon the earth prove unsustainable? Or will it be seen as the midpoint of an ongoing process that extends a full modernity to the entire planet? Like all of our ancestors, every one of them, we too live in a fog when contemplating our futures and see more clearly only in retrospect. In this strange way, the future shapes the telling of the past, even as the past shapes the living of the future.

Landmarks of the Most Recent Century, 1914–2008

1910	1920	1930	1940	1950	

The Western/Developed World

■ **1919** Treaty of Versailles, ending World War I

1914–1918 World War I

■ **1929** Stock market crash and beginning of Great Depression

■ **1933** Hitler's rise to power in Germany

■ **1937** Japan invades China, beginning World War II in Asia

■ **1945** Bombing of Hiroshima/Nagasaki (first use of nuclear weapons in combat)

1957 ■ European Economic Community established

1939–1945 World War II/Holocaust in Europe

The Communist World

■ **1921** Founding of Chinese Communist Party

■ **1917** Russian Revolution

1929–1953 Stalin in power in USSR

1934–1935 Long March in China

1945–1950 Expansion of communism in Eastern Europe

■ **1949** Communist triumph in Chinese Revolution

1950–1953 Korean War

The Third World/Developing World

1923–1938 Turkey's secular modernization/Kemal Atatürk

■ **1919** May Fourth movement in China

■ **1928** Muslim Brotherhood established in Egypt

■ **1947** Independence of India/Pakistan

■ **1949** Independence of Indonesia

1959 ■ Cuban Revolution

The Whole World (Markers of Globalization)

1919–1946 League of Nations

■ **1945** Founding of United Nations

■ **1945** World Bank/International Monetary Fund established

1946–1991 Cold war

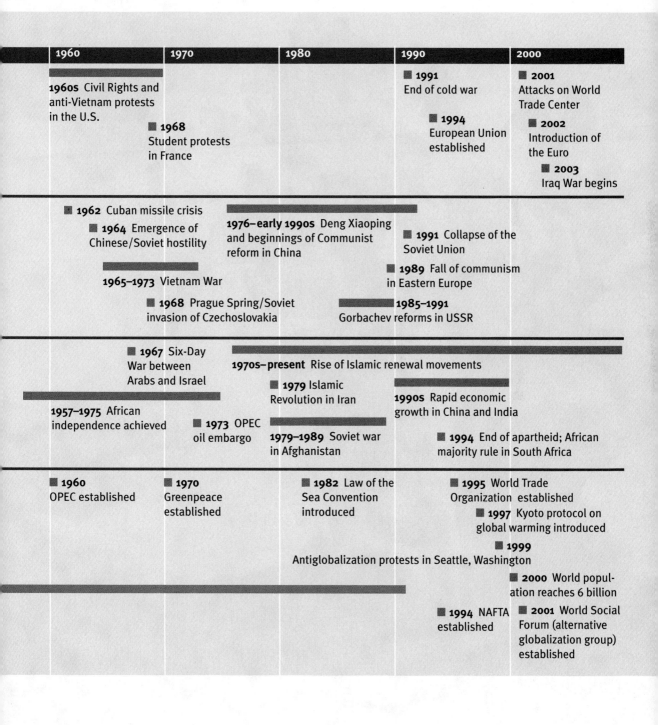

1960	1970	1980	1990	2000

1960s Civil Rights and anti-Vietnam protests in the U.S.

1968 Student protests in France

1991 End of cold war

1994 European Union established

2001 Attacks on World Trade Center

2002 Introduction of the Euro

2003 Iraq War begins

1962 Cuban missile crisis

1964 Emergence of Chinese/Soviet hostility

1976–early 1990s Deng Xiaoping and beginnings of Communist reform in China

1991 Collapse of the Soviet Union

1965–1973 Vietnam War

1989 Fall of communism in Eastern Europe

1968 Prague Spring/Soviet invasion of Czechoslovakia

1985–1991 Gorbachev reforms in USSR

1967 Six-Day War between Arabs and Israel

1970s–present Rise of Islamic renewal movements

1979 Islamic Revolution in Iran

1957–1975 African independence achieved

1990s Rapid economic growth in China and India

1973 OPEC oil embargo

1979–1989 Soviet war in Afghanistan

1994 End of apartheid; African majority rule in South Africa

1960 OPEC established

1970 Greenpeace established

1982 Law of the Sea Convention introduced

1995 World Trade Organization established

1997 Kyoto protocol on global warming introduced

1999 Antiglobalization protests in Seattle, Washington

2000 World population reaches 6 billion

1994 NAFTA established

2001 World Social Forum (alternative globalization group) established

CHAPTER TWENTY-ONE

The Collapse and Recovery of Europe

1914–1970s

The First World War:
  European Civilization in
  Crisis, 1914–1918
  An Accident Waiting to
  Happen
  Legacies of the Great War
Capitalism Unraveling: The
  Great Depression
Democracy Denied:
  Comparing Italy, Germany,
  and Japan
  The Fascist Alternative in
  Europe
  Hitler and the Nazis
  Japanese Authoritarianism
A Second World War
  The Road to War in Asia
  The Road to War in Europe
  World War II: The Outcomes
  of Global Conflict
The Recovery of Europe
Reflections: War and
  Remembrance: Learning
  from History

In November 2005, at the age of 109, Alfred Anderson died in a nursing home in Scotland. He was one of a rapidly dwindling group of men who had served in World War I. He was also, apparently, the last survivor of the famous Christmas truce of 1914, when British and German soldiers, enemies on the battlefield of that war, briefly mingled, exchanged gifts, and played football in the "no-man's land" that lay between their entrenchments in Belgium. "I was told," he said several years before his death, "that I was fighting a war that would end all wars, but that wasn't the case." He was especially dismayed when in 2003 his own unit, the famous Black Watch regiment, was ordered into Iraq along with other British forces.[1] Despite his disappointment at the many conflicts that followed World War I, Anderson's own lifetime had witnessed the fulfillment of the promise of the Christmas truce. By the time he died, the major European nations had put aside their centuries-long hostilities, and war between Britain and Germany, which had erupted twice in the twentieth century, seemed unthinkable. What happened to Europe, and to the larger civilization of which it was a part, during the life of this one man is the focus of this chapter.

THE "GREAT WAR," WHICH CAME TO BE CALLED THE FIRST WORLD WAR (1914–1918), effectively launched the twentieth century, considered as a new phase of world history. That bitter conflict—essentially a European civil war with a global reach—was followed by the economic meltdown of the Great Depression, by the rise of Nazi Germany and the horror of

---

Over the Top: Among the most famous paintings to emerge from World War I, this work depicts the absurdity, futility, and despair that accompanied trench warfare during that conflict. More specifically, it reflects the experience of an eighty-man British unit that was sent "over the top" in late 1917; sixty-eight of them perished in the first few minutes of the battle. Three months later, John Nash, one of the twelve survivors, painted this haunting picture from his memory of that horrendous experience. (Imperial War Museum, London, UK/The Bridgeman Art Library)

the Holocaust, and by an even bloodier and more destructive World War II. During those three decades, Western Europe, for more than a century the dominant and dominating center of the modern "world system," largely self-destructed, in a process with profound and long-term implications far beyond Europe itself. By 1945, an outside observer might well have thought that Western civilization, which for several centuries was in the ascendancy on the global stage, had damaged itself beyond repair.

In the second half of the century, however, that civilization proved quite resilient. Its Western European heartland recovered remarkably from the devastation of war, rebuilt its industrial economy, and set aside its war-prone nationalist passions in a loose European Union. But as Europe revived after 1945, it lost both its overseas colonial possessions and its position as the political, economic, and military core of Western civilization. That role now passed across the Atlantic to the United States. This was a major change in the historical development of the West. The offspring now overshadowed its parent.

Map 21.1   The World in 1914
A map of the world in 1914 shows an unprecedented situation in which one people—Europeans or those of European descent—exercised enormous control and influence over virtually the entire planet.

The First World War: European Civilization in Crisis, 1914–1918

Since 1500, Europe had assumed an increasingly prominent position on the global stage, driven by its growing military capacity and the marvels of its Scientific and Industrial revolutions. By 1900, Europeans, or people with a European ancestry, largely controlled the world's other peoples through their formal empires, their informal influence, or the weight of their numbers (see Map 21.1). That unique

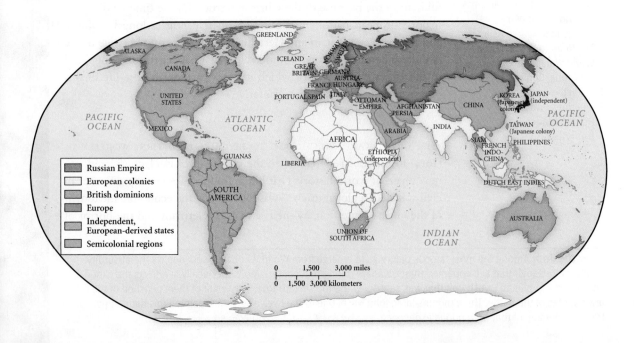

situation provided the foundation for Europeans' pride, self-confidence, and sense of superiority. Few could have imagined that this "proud tower" of European dominance would lie shattered less than half a century later. The starting point in that unraveling was the First World War.

An Accident Waiting to Happen

Europe's modern transformation and its global ascendancy were certainly not accompanied by a growing unity or stability among its own peoples—quite the opposite. The most obvious division was among its competing states, a long-standing feature of European political life. Those historical rivalries further sharpened as both Italy and Germany joined their fragmented territories into two major new powers around 1870. German unification had occurred in the context of a short war with France (the Franco-Prussian War of 1870–1871), which embittered relations between these two large countries for the next half century. More generally, the arrival on the international scene of a powerful and rapidly industrializing Germany, seeking its "place in the sun" as Kaiser Wilhelm put it, was a disruptive new element in European political life, especially for the more established powers, such as Britain, France, and Russia. Since the defeat of Napoleon in 1815, a fragile and fluctuating balance of power had generally maintained the peace among Europe's major countries. By the early twentieth century, that balance of power was expressed in two rival alliances, the Triple Alliance of Germany, Austria, and Italy and the Triple Entente of Russia, France, and Britain. It was those commitments, undertaken in the interests of national security, that transformed a minor incident in the Balkans into a conflagration that consumed all of Europe.

That incident occurred on June 28, 1914, when a Serbian nationalist assassinated the heir to the Austrian throne, Archduke Franz Ferdinand. To the rulers of Austria, the surging nationalism of Serbian Slavs was a mortal threat to the cohesion of their fragile multinational empire, which included other Slavic peoples as well, and they determined to crush it. But behind Austria lay its far more powerful ally, Germany; and behind tiny Serbia lay Russia, with its self-proclaimed mission of protecting other Slavic peoples; and allied to Russia were the French and the British. Thus a system of alliances intended to keep the peace created obligations that drew the Great Powers of Europe into a general war by early August 1914 (see Map 21.2).

The outbreak of that war was an accident, in that none of the major states planned or predicted the archduke's assassination or deliberately sought a prolonged conflict, but the system of rigid alliances made Europe prone to that kind of accident. Moreover, behind those alliances lay other factors that contributed to the eruption of war and shaped its character. One of them was a mounting popular nationalism (see Chapter 17). Slavic nationalism and Austrian opposition to it certainly lay at the heart of the war's beginning. More important, the rulers of the major countries of Europe saw the world as an arena of conflict and competition

■ **Explanation**
What aspects of Europe's nineteenth-century history contributed to the First World War?

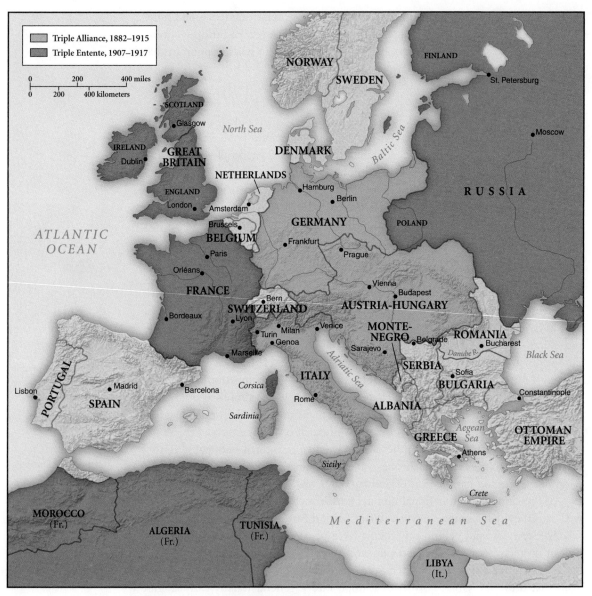

Map 21.2 Europe on the Eve of World War I
Despite many elements of common culture, Europe in 1914 was a powder keg, with its major states armed to the teeth and divided into two rival alliances. In the early stages of the war, Italy changed sides to join the French, British, and Russians.

among rival nation-states. The Great Powers of Europe competed intensely for colonies, spheres of influence, and superiority in armaments. Schools, mass media, and military service had convinced millions of ordinary Europeans that their national identities were profoundly and personally meaningful. The public pressure of these competing nationalisms allowed statesmen little room for compromise and ensured widespread popular support, at least initially, for the decision to go to war. Men rushed to recruiting offices, fearing that the war might end before they could enlist. Celebratory parades sent them off to the front. For conservative governments, the prospect of war was a welcome occasion for national unity in the face of the mounting class- and gender-based conflicts of European society.

Also contributing to the war was an industrialized militarism. Europe's armed rivalries had long ensured that military men enjoyed great social prestige, and most heads of state wore uniforms in public. All of the Great Powers had substantial standing armies and, except for Britain, relied on conscription (compulsory military service) to staff them. One expression of the quickening rivalry among these states was a mounting arms race in naval warships, particularly between Germany and Britain. Furthermore, each of the major states had developed elaborate "war plans" spelling out in great detail the movement of men and materials that should occur immediately upon the outbreak of war. Such plans created a hair-trigger mentality, since each country had an incentive to strike first so that its particular strategy could be implemented on schedule and without interruption or surprise. The rapid industrialization of warfare had generated an array of novel weapons, including submarines, tanks, airplanes, poison gas, machines guns, and barbed wire. This new military technology contributed to the staggering casualties of the war, including some 10 million deaths; perhaps twice that number wounded, crippled, or disfigured; and countless women for whom there would be no husbands or children.

Europe's imperial reach around the world likewise shaped the scope and conduct of the war. It funneled colonial troops and laborers by the hundreds of thousands into the war effort, with men from Africa, India, China, Southeast Asia, Australia, New Zealand, Canada, and South Africa taking part in the conflict. Battles raged in Africa and the South Pacific as British and French forces sought to seize German colonies abroad. Japan, allied with Britain, took various German possessions in China and the Pacific and made heavy demands on China itself. The Ottoman Empire, which entered the conflict on the side of Germany, became the site of intense military actions and witnessed an Arab revolt against Ottoman control. Finally, the United States, after initially seeking to avoid involvement in European quarrels, joined the war in 1917 when German submarines threatened American shipping. Some 2 million Americans took part in the first U.S. military action on European soil and helped turn the tide in favor of the British and French. Thus the war, though centered in Europe, had global dimensions and certainly merited its familiar title as a "world war."

Legacies of the Great War

The Great War was a conflict that shattered almost every expectation. Most Europeans believed in the late summer of 1914 that "the boys will be home by Christmas," but instead the war ground relentlessly on for more than four years

■ Change
In what ways did World War I mark new departures in the history of the twentieth century?

THESE WOMEN ARE DOING THEIR BIT

LEARN TO MAKE MUNITIONS

Women and the Great War
World War I temporarily brought a halt to the women's suffrage movement as well as to women's activities on behalf of international peace. Most women on both sides actively supported their countries' war efforts, as suggested by this British wartime poster, inviting women to work in the munitions industry. (Eileen Tweedy/The Art Archive)

before ending in a German defeat in November 1918. At the beginning, most military experts expected a war of movement and attack, but it soon bogged down on the western front into a war of attrition, in which "trench warfare" resulted in enormous casualties while gaining or losing only a few yards of muddy, blood-soaked ground. Extended battles lasting months—such as those at Verdun and the Somme—generated casualties of a million or more each, as the destructive potential of industrialized warfare made itself tragically felt. Moreover, everywhere it became a "total war," requiring the mobilization of each country's entire population. Thus the authority of governments expanded greatly. The German state, for example, assumed such control over the economy that its policies became known as "war socialism." Vast propaganda campaigns sought to arouse citizens by depicting a cruel and inhuman enemy who killed innocent children and violated women. In factories, women replaced the men who had left for the battlefront, while labor unions agreed to suspend strikes and accept sacrifices for the common good.

No less surprising were the outcomes of the war. In the European cockpit of that conflict, the unprecedented casualties, particularly among elite and well-educated groups, and the physical destruction, especially in France, led to a widespread disillusionment among intellectuals with their own civilization. The war seemed to mock the Enlightenment values of progress, tolerance, and rationality. Who could believe any longer that the West was superior or that its vaunted science and technology were unquestionably good things? In the most famous novel to emerge from the war, the German veteran Erich Remarque's *All Quiet on the Western Front*, one soldier expressed what many no doubt felt: "It must all be lies and of no account when the culture of a thousand years could not prevent this stream of blood being poured out."

Furthermore, from the collapse of the German, Russian, and Austrian empires emerged a new map of Central Europe with an independent Poland, Czechoslovakia, Yugoslavia, and other nations (see Map 21.3). Such new states were based on the principle of "national self-determination," a concept championed by the U.S. president Woodrow Wilson, but each of them also contained dissatisfied ethnic minorities, who claimed the same principle. In Russia, the strains of war triggered a vast revolutionary upheaval that brought the radical Bolsheviks to power in 1917 and took Russia out of the war. Thus was launched world communism, which was to play such a prominent role in the history of the twentieth century (see Chapter 22).

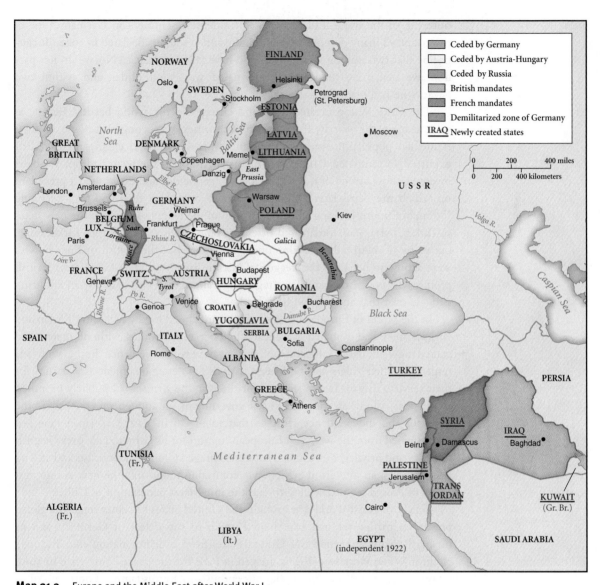

Map 21.3   Europe and the Middle East after World War I

The Great War brought into existence a number of new states that were carved out of the old German, Austro-Hungarian, Russian, and Ottoman empires. Turkey and the new states in Europe were independent, but those in the Middle East—Syria, Palestine, Iraq, and Transjordan—were administered by Britain or France as mandates of the League of Nations.

The Treaty of Versailles, which formally concluded the war in 1919, proved in retrospect to have established conditions that generated a second world war only twenty years later. In that treaty, Germany lost its colonial empire and 15 percent of its European territory, was required to pay heavy reparations to the winners, had its military forces severely restricted, and had to accept sole responsibility for the outbreak of the war. All of this created immense resentment in Germany. One of the country's many demobilized and disillusioned soldiers declared in 1922:"It cannot be that two million Germans should have fallen in vain....No, we do not pardon, we demand—vengeance."[2] His name was Adolf Hitler, and within two decades he had begun to exact that vengeance.

The Great War generated profound changes in the world beyond Europe as well. During the war itself, Ottoman authorities, suspecting that some of their Armenian population were collaborating with the Russian enemy, massacred or deported an estimated 1 million Armenians. Although the term had not yet been invented, those atrocities merit the label of "genocide" and established a precedent on which the Nazis later built. The war also brought a final end to a declining Ottoman Empire, creating the modern map of the Middle East, with the new states of Turkey, Syria, Iraq, Jordan, and Palestine. Thus Arabs emerged from Turkish rule, but many of them fell for a time under the control of the British or French, who were acting on behalf of the League of Nations (see Map 21.3). Conflicting British promises to both Arabs and Jews regarding Palestine set the stage for an enduring struggle over that ancient and holy land.

In the world of European colonies, the war echoed loudly. Millions of Asian and African men had watched Europeans butcher one another without mercy, had gained new military skills and political awareness, and returned home with less respect for their rulers and with expectations for better treatment as a reward for their service. To gain Indian support for the war, the British had publicly promised to put that colony on the road to self-government, an announcement that set the stage for the independence struggle that followed. In East Asia, Japan emerged strengthened from the war, with European support for its claim to take over German territory and privileges in China. That news enraged Chinese nationalists and among a few sparked an interest in Soviet-style communism, for only the new communist rulers of Russia seemed willing to end the imperialist penetration of China.

Finally, the First World War brought the United States to center stage as a global power. Its manpower had contributed much to the defeat of Germany, and its financial resources turned the United States from a debtor nation into Europe's creditor. When Woodrow Wilson arrived in Paris for the peace conference in 1919, he was greeted with an almost religious enthusiasm, for his famous Fourteen Points seemed to herald a new kind of international life, one based on moral principles rather than secret deals and imperialist machinations. Particularly appealing to many was his idea for the League of Nations, a new international peacekeeping organization based on the principle of "collective security" and intended to avoid any repetition of the horrors of the war just ended. Wilson's idealistic vision largely failed, however. Germany was treated more harshly than he had wished. And in his own country, the U.S. Senate refused to join the league, on which he had pinned his hopes for a lasting peace. Its opponents feared that Americans would be forced to bow to "the will of other nations." That refusal seriously weakened the League of Nations as a vehicle for a new international order.

Capitalism Unraveling: The Great Depression

The aftermath of war brought substantial social and cultural changes to the European and American victors in that conflict. Integrating millions of returning veterans into ordinary civilian life was no easy task, for they had experienced horrors almost beyond imagination. Governments sought to accommodate them—for example, with housing programs called "homes for heroes" and with an emphasis on traditional family values. French authorities proclaimed Mother's Day as a new holiday designed to encourage childbearing and thus replace the millions lost in the war.

Nonetheless, the war had loosened the hold of tradition in many ways. Enormous casualties promoted social mobility, allowing commoners to move into positions previously dominated by aristocrats. Women increasingly gained the right to vote. Young middle-class women, sometimes known as "flappers," began to flout convention by appearing at nightclubs, smoking, dancing, drinking hard liquor, cutting their hair short, wearing more revealing clothing, and generally expressing a more open sexuality. A new consumerism encouraged those who could to acquire cars, washing machines, vacuum cleaners, electric irons, gas ovens, and other newly available products. Radio and the movies now became vehicles of popular culture, transmitting American jazz to Europe and turning Hollywood stars into international celebrities.

Far and away the most influential change of the postwar decades lay in the Great Depression. If World War I represented the political collapse of Europe, this catastrophic downturn suggested that its economic system was likewise failing. During the nineteenth century, European industrial capitalism had spurred the most substantial economic growth in world history and had raised the living standards of millions, but to many people it was a troubling system. Its very success generated an individualistic materialism that seemed to conflict with older values of community and spiritual life. To socialists and many others, its immense social inequalities were unacceptable. Furthermore, its evident instability—with cycles of boom and bust, expansion and recession—generated profound anxiety and threatened the livelihood of both industrial workers and those who had gained a modest toehold in the middle class.

■ **Connection**
In what ways was the Great Depression a global phenomenon?

Never had the instabilities of capitalism been so evident or so devastating as during the decade that followed the outbreak of the Great Depression in 1929. All across the Euro-American heartland of the capitalist world, this vaunted economic system seemed to unravel. For the rich, it meant contracting stock prices that wiped out paper fortunes almost overnight. On the day that the American stock market initially crashed (October 24, 1929), eleven Wall Street financiers committed suicide, some by jumping out of skyscrapers. Banks closed, and many people lost their life's savings. Investment dried up, world trade dropped by 62 percent within a few years, and businesses contracted when they were unable to sell their products. For ordinary people, the worst feature of the Great Depression was the loss of work. Unemployment soared everywhere, and in both Germany and the United States it

The Great Depression
This photograph of an impoverished American mother of three children, which was taken in 1936, came to symbolize the agonies of the Depression and the apparent breakdown of capitalism in the United States. (Library of Congress)

reached 30 percent or more by 1932 (see the Snapshot on p. 635). Vacant factories, soup kitchens, bread lines, shantytowns, and beggars came to symbolize the human reality of this economic disaster.

Explaining its onset, its spread from America to Europe and beyond, and its continuation for a decade has been a complicated task for historians. Part of the story lies in the United States' booming economy during the 1920s. In a country physically untouched by the war, wartime demand had greatly stimulated agricultural and industrial capacity. By the end of the 1920s, its farms and factories were producing more goods than could be sold because a highly unequal distribution of income meant that many people could not afford to buy the products that American factories were churning out. Nor were major European countries able to purchase those goods. Germany and Austria had to make huge reparation payments and were able to do so only with extensive U.S. loans. Britain and France, which were much indebted to the United States, depended on those reparations to repay their loans. Furthermore, Europeans generally had recovered enough to begin producing some of their own goods, and their expanding production further reduced the demand for American products. Meanwhile, a speculative stock market frenzy had driven up stock prices to an unsustainable level. When that bubble burst in late 1929, this intricately connected and fragile economic network across the Atlantic collapsed like a house of cards.

Much as Europe's worldwide empires had globalized the war, so too its economic linkages globalized the Great Depression. Countries or colonies tied to exporting one or two products were especially hard-hit. Chile, which was dependent on copper mining, found the value of its exports cut by 80 percent. In an effort to maintain the price of coffee, Brazil destroyed enough of its coffee crop to have supplied the world for a year. Colonial Southeast Asia, the world's major rubber-producing region, saw the demand for its primary export drop dramatically as automobile sales in Europe and the United States were cut in half. In Britain's West African colony of the Gold Coast (present-day Ghana), farmers who had staked their economic lives on producing cocoa for the world market were badly hurt by the collapse of commodity prices. Depending on a single crop or product rendered these societies extraordinarily vulnerable to changes in the world market.

The Great Depression sharply challenged the governments of capitalist countries, which generally had believed that the economy would regulate itself through the market. The market's apparent failure to self-correct led many people to look twice at the Soviet Union, a communist state whose more equal distribution of income and state-controlled economy had generated an impressive growth with no unemployment in the 1930s, even as the capitalist world was reeling. No Western country opted for the dictatorial and draconian socialism of the USSR, but in Britain, France, and Scandinavia, the Depression energized a "democratic socialism" that sought greater regulation of the economy and a more equal distribution of wealth through peaceful means and electoral politics.

The United States' response to the Great Depression came in the form of President Franklin Roosevelt's New Deal (1933–1942), a complex tangle of reforms intended to restore pre-Depression prosperity and to prevent future calamities. These measures reflected the thinking of John Maynard Keynes, a prominent British economist who argued that government actions and spending programs could moderate the recessions and depressions to which capitalist economies were prone. Although this represented a departure from standard economic thinking, none of it was really "socialist," even if some of the New Deal's opponents labeled it as such.

Nonetheless, Roosevelt's efforts permanently altered the relationship among government, the private economy, and individual citizens. Through immediate programs of public spending (for dams, highways, bridges, and parks), the New Deal sought to "prime the pump" of the economy and thus reduce unemployment. The

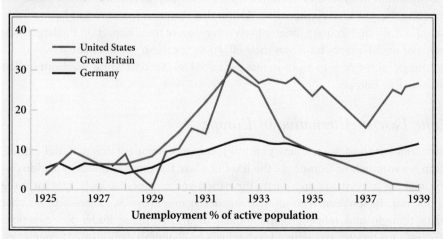

Snapshot   **Comparing the Impact of the Depression**[3]

As industrial production dropped during the Depression, unemployment soared. Yet the larger Western capitalist countries differed considerably in the duration and extent of this unemployment. Note especially the differences between Germany and the United States. How might you account for this difference?

New Deal's longer-term reforms, such as the Social Security system, the minimum wage, and various relief and welfare programs, attempted to build an economic floor below which the poor, the unemployed, and the elderly could not fall. By supporting the organization of labor unions, the New Deal strengthened their hand against business. Through farm subsidies, it created a permanent agribusiness that made possible continued production without the risk of falling prices. Finally, the vast array of government agencies that were created during the New Deal instituted a new degree of federal regulation and supervision of the economy.

Ultimately, none of the New Deal's programs worked very well to end the Great Depression. Not until the massive government spending required by World War II kicked in did that economic disaster abate in the United States. The most successful efforts to cope with the Depression came from unlikely places—Nazi Germany and an increasingly militaristic Japan.

Democracy Denied: Comparing Italy, Germany, and Japan

Despite the victory of the democratic powers in World War I—Britain, France, and the United States—their democratic political ideals and cultural values of liberalism and individual freedom came under sharp attack in the aftermath of that bloody conflict. One challenge derived from communism, which was initiated in the Russian Revolution of 1917 and expressed most fully in the cold war during the second half of the twentieth century (see Chapter 22). In the 1920s and 1930s, however, the more immediate challenge to the victors in the Great War came from highly authoritarian, intensely nationalistic, territorially aggressive, and ferociously anti-communist regimes, particularly those that took shape in Italy, Germany, and Japan. The common features of these three countries drew them together by 1936–1937 in a political alliance directed against the Soviet Union and international communism. In 1940, they solidified their relationship in a formal military alliance, creating the so-called Axis powers. Within this alliance, Germany and Japan clearly stand out, though in quite different ways, in terms of their impact on the larger patterns of world history, for it was their efforts to "establish and maintain a new order of things," as the Axis Pact put it, that generated the Second World War both in East Asia and in Europe.

The Fascist Alternative in Europe

■ **Change**
In what ways did fascism challenge the ideas and practices of European liberalism and democracy?

Between 1919 and 1945, a new political ideology, known as fascism, found expression across much of Europe. At the level of ideas, fascism was intensely nationalistic, seeking to revitalize and purify the nation and to mobilize its people for some grand task. Its spokesmen condoned violence against enemies, exalted action rather than thought and reflection, and looked to a charismatic leader for direction. Fascists also bitterly condemned individualism, liberalism, feminism, parliamentary democracy, and communism, all of which, they argued, divided and weakened the nation. In their determination to overthrow existing regimes, they were revolutionary; in their celebration of traditional values and their opposition to much of modern life, however, they were conservative or reactionary.

Such ideas appealed to dissatisfied or unfulfilled people in all social classes. In the devastation that followed the First World War, the numbers of such people grew substantially. Some among the middle and upper classes feared the advance of socialism and communism; small-scale merchants, artisans, and farmers felt threatened with the loss of their independence to either big business or socialist revolution; demobilized soldiers had few prospects and nursed many resentments; intellectuals were appalled by the materialism and artificiality of modern life. Such people had lost faith in the capacity of liberal democracy and capitalism to create a good society and to protect their interests. Some among them proved a receptive audience for the message of fascism.

Small fascist movements appeared in many Western European countries, including France, Great Britain, and the Netherlands, but they had little political impact. More substantial movements took shape in Austria, Hungary, and Romania. In Spain, the rise of a fascist movement led to a bitter civil war (1936–1939) and a dictatorial regime that lasted into the 1970s. But in Italy and especially in Germany, such movements achieved prolonged power in major states, with devastating consequences for Europe and the world.

The fascist alternative took shape first in Italy. That nation had become a unified state only in 1870 and had yet to develop a thoroughly modern and democratic culture. Conservative landlords controlled most of the rural areas both economically and politically. In the north, however, a significant industrial society arose in the late nineteenth century, and with it came considerable tension between a factory working class and a substantial middle class. The First World War introduced still other social disruptions in the form of resentful veterans, who lacked both employment and popular respect, and patriots who believed that Italy had not gained the territory it deserved from the Treaty of Versailles. During the economic crisis following the war, trade unions, peasant movements, and various communist and socialist parties threatened the established social order with a wave of strikes and land seizures.

Into this setting stepped a charismatic orator and a former journalist with a socialist background, Benito Mussolini (1883–1945). With the help of a private army of disillusioned veterans and jobless men known as the Black Shirts, Mussolini swept to power in 1922, promising an alternative to both communism and ineffective democratic rule. Considerable violence accompanied Mussolini's rise to power as bands of Black Shirts destroyed the offices of socialist newspapers, attacked striking workers, and forced socialists to drink castor oil. Fearful of communism, big business threw its support to Mussolini, who promised order in the streets, an end to bickering party-based politics, and the maintenance of the traditional social order. That Mussolini's government allegedly made the trains run on time became

The Faces of European Fascism
Benito Mussolini (left) and Adolf Hitler came to symbolize fascism in Europe in the several decades between the two world wars. In this photograph from September 1937, they are reviewing German troops in Munich during Mussolini's visit to Germany, a trip that deepened the growing relationship between their two countries. (Luce/Keystone/Getty Images)

■ Comparison
What was distinctive about the German expression of fascism? What was the basis of popular support for the Nazis?

evidence that these promises might be fulfilled. The symbol of this movement was the *fasces*, a bundle of birch rods bound together around an axe, which represented power and strength in unity and derived from ancient Rome. Thus fascism was born.

Mussolini promised his mass following a generous social program, but once he attained power, he concentrated instead on building state power. Democracy in Italy was suspended, and opponents were imprisoned, deported, or sometimes executed. Independent labor unions and peasant groups were disbanded, as were all political parties except the Fascist Party. In economic life, a "corporate state" took shape, at least in theory, in which workers, employers, and various professional groups were organized into corporations that were supposed to settle their disagreements and determine economic policy under the supervision of the state.

Culturally, fascists invoked various aspects of traditional Italian life. Mussolini, though personally an atheist, embraced the Catholic culture of Italy in a series of agreements with the Church (the Lateran Accords of 1929) that made the Vatican a sovereign state and Catholicism Italy's national religion. In fascist propaganda, women were portrayed in highly traditional terms as domestic creatures, particularly as mothers creating new citizens for the fascist state, with no hint of equality or liberation. Nationalists were delighted when Italy invaded Ethiopia in 1935, avenging the embarrassing defeat that Italians suffered at the hands of Ethiopians in 1896. In the eyes of Mussolini and fascist believers, all of this was the beginning of a "new Roman Empire" that would revitalize Italian society and give it a global mission.

Hitler and the Nazis

Far more important in the long run was the German expression of European fascism, which took shape as the Nazi Party under the leadership of Adolf Hitler (1889–1945). In many respects, it was similar to its Italian counterpart. Both espoused an extreme nationalism, openly advocated the use of violence as a political tool, generated a single-party dictatorship, were led by charismatic figures, despised parliamentary democracy, hated communism, and viewed war as a positive and ennobling experience.[4] The circumstances that gave rise to the Nazi movement were likewise broadly similar to those of Italian fascism, although the Nazis did not achieve national power until 1933. As World War I ended, the German imperial state, itself less than a half century old, collapsed, and democratic politicians of a new government—known as the Weimar Republic—were left to negotiate the peace settlement. Traditional elites were either disgraced or had withdrawn from public life because their regime had lost the war. However, these defeated leaders never explicitly took responsibility for the defeat; instead they attacked the democratic politicians who had the unfortunate task of signing the peace settlement and enforcing it. In this atmosphere, there arose a myth that Germany had not really lost the war but that civilians, especially socialists, communists, and Jews, had betrayed the nation, "stabbing it in the back."

As in postwar Italy, liberal or democratic political leaders during the 1920s faced the active or silent animosity of much of the German population. Vigilante groups of veterans (the Freikorps) assassinated hundreds of liberal politicians, journalists, and supporters of the Weimar regime, and they received only mild punishments from conservative judges, who also detested the republic. These small groups of discontented veterans, hostile to democracy, gradually drew support from the middle classes as well as from conservative landowners because of the ruinous inflation of 1923 and then the Great Depression. The German economy largely ground to a halt in the early 1930s amid massive unemployment among workers and the middle class alike. Everyone demanded decisive governmental action. Many industrial workers turned to socialists and communists for answers; others looked to fascism. Large numbers of middle-class people deserted moderate political parties in favor of conservative and radical right-wing movements.

This was the context in which Adolf Hitler's National Socialist, or Nazi, Party gained growing public support. Founded shortly after the end of World War I, the Nazi Party under Hitler's leadership proclaimed a message of intense German nationalism cast in terms of racial superiority, bitter hatred for Jews as an alien presence, passionate opposition to communism, a determination to rescue Germany from the humiliating requirements of the Treaty of Versailles, and a willingness to decisively tackle the country's economic problems. Throughout the 1920s, the Nazis were a minor presence in German politics, gaining only 2.6 percent of the vote in the national elections of 1928. Just four years later, however, in the wake of the Depression's terrible impact and the Weimar government's inability to respond effectively, the Nazis attracted 37 percent of the vote. In 1933, Hitler was legally installed as the chancellor of the German government. Thus did the Weimar Republic, a democratic regime that never gained broad support, give way to the Third Reich.

Once in power, Hitler quickly suppressed all other political parties, abolished labor unions, arrested thousands of opponents, controlled the press and radio, and in general assumed police power over society far more thoroughly than Italian fascists were able to achieve. German workers, for example, never rose up to challenge the Nazi regime, whereas Italian workers engaged in mass strikes in early 1943 against the fascist state.[5]

By the late 1930s, Hitler apparently had the support of a considerable majority of the population, in large measure because his policies successfully brought Germany out of the Depression. The government invested heavily in projects such as superhighways, bridges, canals, and public buildings and, after 1935, in rebuilding and rearming the country's diminished military forces. These policies drove down the number of unemployed Germans from 6.2 million in 1932 to fewer than 500,000 in 1937. Two years later Germany had a labor shortage. Erna Kranz, a teenager in the 1930s, later remembered the early years of Nazi rule as "a glimmer of hope … not just for the unemployed but for everybody because we all knew that we were downtrodden. … It was a good time … there was order and discipline."[6] Millions agreed with her.

For many countries still suffering from the Depression throughout the 1930s, Hitler seemed to have found the secret for recovery: economic planning, controlled wages and prices, government investment, and enforced peace between capital and labor. This was a radical departure from the principles of capitalism. Still, neither Hitler nor Mussolini chose to dispossess the capitalists so long as they cooperated by producing goods that the regime required.

Other factors as well contributed to Nazi popularity. Like Italian fascists, Hitler masterfully invoked rural and traditional values that many Germans feared losing in their increasingly urban and materialistic culture. Far more so than in Italy, he used Jews as a symbol of the urban, capitalist, and foreign influences that were corrupting "true" German culture. The Nazis reflected and reinforced a current of anti-Semitism that had deep roots in Germany and most of Europe. More than elsewhere, though, the Nazis projected their distaste for modern life and for recent German history onto the Jews. In his book *Mein Kampf* (*My Struggle*), Hitler outlined his case against the Jews and his call for the racial purification of Germany in vitriolic terms.

Nazi Hatred of the Jews
This picture served as the cover of a highly anti-Semitic book of photographs entitled *The Eternal Jew*, published by the Nazis in 1937. It effectively summed up many of the themes of the Nazi case against the Jews, showing them as ugly and subhuman, as the instigators of communism (the hammer and sickle on a map of Russia), as greedy capitalists (coins in one hand), and as seeking to dominate the world (the whip). (akg-images)

> The black-haired Jewish youth, with Satanic joy on his face, lurks in wait for hours for the innocent girls he plans to defile with his blood, and steal the young girl from her people. With every means at hand, he seeks to undermine the racial foundations of the people they would subjugate. … [But] a people which is racially pure and is conscious of its blood will never be able to be subjugated by the Jews. The Jew in this world will forever only be the masters of a bastardized people.

This insistence on a racial revolution was a central feature of the Nazi program and differed from the racial attitudes in Italy, where Jews were a tiny minority of the population and deeply assimilated into Italian culture. Early on Mussolini had ridiculed Nazi racism, but as Germany and Italy drew closer together, Italy too began a program of overt anti-Semitism, though nothing approaching the extremes that characterized Nazi Germany.

Soon after coming to power, Hitler implemented policies that increasingly restricted Jewish life, such as exclusion from universities, professional organizations, and civil employment. In 1935, the Nuremberg Laws forbade sexual relations or marriage between Jews and other Germans and forced Jews to identify themselves in public by wearing the Star of David. Ostracism escalated to terror on the night of November 9, 1938, known as *Kristallnacht*, when Nazis smashed and looted Jewish shops. Such actions made clear the Nazis' determination to rid Germany of its Jewish population, thus putting into effect the most radical element of Hitler's program, although it was not yet apparent that this "racial revolution" would mean the mass killing of Europe's Jews. That horrendous development emerged only in the context of World War II.

Meanwhile, in schools and in massive torchlight ceremonies, the Nazis celebrated the superiority of the German race, its folk culture, and its ancient heroes. Although Hitler relied on modern technology to create his war machine, in his public speeches he was the mystical leader, the Führer, whose deeds were beyond the rational understanding of his people. Intuition and force rather than reason and compromise should rule Germany. "The stronger must dominate," he declared, "and must not blend with the weaker orders and sacrifice their powers." Hitler's own power rested ultimately on the willingness of most Germans to surrender their right to question and analyze; instead they followed a mesmerizing orator, a leader who, they believed, would direct them to national greatness and personal fulfillment.

If World War I and the Great Depression brought about the political and economic collapse of Europe, the Nazi phenomenon represented a moral collapse within the West, deriving from a highly selective incorporation of earlier strands of European culture. On the one hand, the Nazis actively rejected some of the values—rationalism, tolerance, democracy, human equality—that for many people had defined the core of Western civilization since the Enlightenment. On the other hand, they claimed the legacy of modern science, particularly in their concern to classify and rank various human groups. Thus they drew heavily on the "scientific racism" of the nineteenth century and its expression in phrenology, which linked the size and shape of the skull to human behavior and personality. Moreover, in their effort to purify German society, the Nazis reflected the Enlightenment confidence in the perfectibility of humankind and in the social engineering necessary to achieve it.

Japanese Authoritarianism

In various ways, the modern history of Japan paralleled that of Italy and Germany. All three were newcomers to great power status, with Japan joining the club of

■ Comparison
How did Japan's experience during the 1920s and 1930s resemble that of Germany, and how did it differ?

industrializing and empire-building states only in the late nineteenth century as its sole Asian member (see Chapter 19). Like Italy and Germany, Japan had a rather limited experience with democratic politics, for its elected parliament was constrained by a very small electorate (only 1.5 million men in 1917) and by the exalted position of a semidivine emperor and his small coterie of elite advisers. During the 1930s, Japan too moved toward authoritarian government and a denial of democracy at home, even as it launched an aggressive program of territorial expansion in East Asia.

Despite these broad similarities, Japan's history in the first half of the twentieth century was clearly distinctive. In sharp contrast to Italy and Germany, Japan's participation in World War I was minimal, and its economy grew considerably as other industrialized countries were engaged in the European war. At the peace conference ending that war, Japan was seated as an equal participant, allied with the winning side of democratic countries such as Britain, France, and the United States.

During the 1920s, Japan seemed to be moving toward a more democratic politics and Western cultural values. Universal male suffrage was achieved in 1925; cabinets led by leaders of the major parties, rather than bureaucrats or imperial favorites, governed the country; and a two-party system began to emerge. Supporters of these developments generally embraced the dignity of the individual, free expression of ideas, and greater gender equality. Education expanded; an urban consumer society developed; middle-class women entered new professions; young women known as *moga* (modern girls) sported short hair and short skirts, while dancing with *mobo* (modern boys) at jazz clubs and cabarets. To such people, the Japanese were becoming world citizens and their country was becoming "a province of the world" as they participated increasingly in a cosmopolitan and international culture.

In this environment, the accumulated tensions of Japan's modernizing and industrializing processes found expression. "Rice riots" in 1918 brought more than a million people into the streets of urban Japan to protest the rising price of that essential staple. Union membership tripled in the 1920s as some factory workers began to think in terms of entitlements and workers' rights rather than the benevolence of their employers. In rural areas, tenant unions multiplied, and disputes with landowners increased amid demands for a reduction in rents. A mounting women's movement advocated a variety of feminist issues, including suffrage and the end of legalized prostitution. "All the sleeping women are now awake and moving," declared Yosano Akiko, a well-known poet, feminist, and social critic. Within the political arena, a number of "proletarian parties"—the Labor-Farmer Party, the Socialist People's Party, and a small Japan Communist Party—promised in various ways to "bring about the political, economic and social emancipation of the proletarian class."[7]

To many people in established elite circles—bureaucrats, landowners, industrialists, military officials—all of this was alarming, even appalling, and suggested echoes of the Russian Revolution of 1917. A number of political activists were arrested, and a few were killed. A Peace Preservation Law, enacted in 1925, promised long prison sentences or even the death penalty to anyone who organized against the existing imperial system of government or private property.

As in Germany, however, it was the impact of the Great Depression that paved the way for harsher and more authoritarian action. That worldwide economic catastrophe hit Japan hard. Shrinking world demand for silk impoverished millions of rural dwellers who raised silkworms. Japan's exports fell by half between 1929 and 1931, leaving a million or more urban workers unemployed. Many young workers returned to their rural villages only to find food scarce, families forced to sell their daughters to urban brothels, and neighbors unable to offer the customary money for the funerals of their friends. In these desperate circumstances, many began to doubt the ability of parliamentary democracy and capitalism to address Japan's "national emergency." Politicians and business leaders alike were widely regarded as privileged, self-centered, and heedless of the larger interests of the nation.

Such conditions energized a growing movement in Japanese political life known as Radical Nationalism or the Revolutionary Right. It was expressed in dozens of small groups and was especially appealing to younger army officers. The movement's many separate organizations shared an extreme nationalism, hostility to parliamentary democracy, a commitment to elite leadership focused around an exalted emperor, and dedication to foreign expansion. The manifesto of one of those organizations, the Cherry Blossom Society, expressed these sentiments clearly in 1930.

> As we observe recent social trends, top leaders engage in immoral conduct, political parties are corrupt, capitalists and aristocrats have no understanding of the masses, farming villages are devastated, unemployment and depression are serious.... The rulers neglect the long term interests of the nation, strive to win only the pleasure of foreign powers and possess no enthusiasm for external expansion.... The people are with us in craving the appearance of a vigorous and clean government that is truly based upon the masses, and is genuinely centered around the Emperor.[8]

Members of such organizations managed to assassinate a number of public officials and prominent individuals, in the hope of provoking a return to direct rule by the emperor, and in 1936 a group of junior officers attempted a military takeover of the government, which was quickly suppressed. In sharp contrast to developments in Italy and Germany, however, no right-wing party gained wide popular support, nor was any such party able to seize power in Japan. Although individuals and small groups sometimes espoused ideas similar to those of European fascists, no major fascist party emerged. Nor did Japan produce any charismatic leader on the order of Mussolini or Hitler. People arrested for political crimes were neither criminalized nor exterminated, as in Germany, but instead were subjected to a process of "resocialization" that brought the vast majority of them to renounce their "errors" and return to the "Japanese way." Japan's established institutions of government were sufficiently strong, and traditional notions of the nation as a family headed by the emperor were sufficiently intact, to prevent the development of a widespread fascist movement able to take control of the country.[9]

In the 1930s, though, Japanese public life clearly changed in ways that reflected the growth of right-wing nationalist thinking. Parties and the parliament continued to operate, and elections were held, but major cabinet positions now went to prominent bureaucratic or military figures rather than to party leaders. The military in particular came to exercise a more dominant role in Japanese political life, although military men had to negotiate with business and bureaucratic elites as well as party leaders. Censorship limited the possibilities of free expression, and a single news agency was granted the right to distribute all national and most international news to the country's newspapers and radio stations. An Industrial Patriotic Federation replaced independent trade unions with factory-based "discussion councils" to resolve local disputes between workers and managers.

Established authorities also adopted many of the ideological themes of the Radical Right. In 1937, the Ministry of Education issued a new textbook, *The Cardinal Principles of Our National Polity*, for use in all Japanese schools. That document proclaimed the Japanese to be "intrinsically quite different from the so-called citizens of Occidental [Western] countries." Those nations were "conglomerations of separate individuals" with "no deep foundation between ruler and citizen to unite them." In Japan, by contrast, an emperor of divine origin related to his subjects as a father to his children. It was a natural, not a contractual, relationship, expressed most fully in the "sacrifice of the life of a subject for the Emperor." In addition to studying this text, students were now required to engage in more physical training, in which Japanese martial arts replaced baseball in the physical education curriculum.

The erosion of democracy and the rise of the military in Japanese political life reflected long-standing Japanese respect for the military values of its ancient samurai warrior class as well as the relatively independent position of the military in Japan's Meiji constitution. The state's success in quickly bringing the country out of the Depression likewise fostered popular support. As in Nazi Germany, state-financed credit, large-scale spending on armaments, and public works projects enabled Japan to emerge from the Depression more rapidly and more fully than major Western countries. "By the end of 1937," noted one Japanese laborer, "everybody in the country was working."[10] By the mid-1930s, the government increasingly assumed a supervisory or managerial role in economic affairs that included subsidies to strategic industries; profit ceilings on major corporations; caps on wages, prices, and rents; and a measure of central planning. Private property, however, was retained, and the huge industrial enterprises called *zaibatsu* continued to dominate the economic landscape.

Although Japan during the 1930s shared some common features with fascist Italy and Nazi Germany, it remained, at least internally, a less repressive and more pluralistic society than either of those European states. Japanese intellectuals and writers had to contend with government censorship, but they retained some influence in the country. Generals and admirals exercised great political authority as the role of an elected parliament declined, but they did not govern alone. Political prisoners were few and were not subjected to execution or deportation as in European fascist states. Japanese conceptions of their racial purity and uniqueness were directed largely against foreigners rather than an internal minority. Nevertheless, like Germany and Italy, Japan developed extensive imperial ambitions. Those projects of conquest and empire building collided with the interests of established world powers such as the United States and Britain, launching a second, and even more terrible, global war.

A Second World War

World War II, even more than the Great War, was a genuinely global conflict with independent origins in both Asia and Europe. Their common feature lay in dissatisfied states in both continents that sought to fundamentally alter the international arrangements that had emerged from World War I. Many Japanese, like their counterparts in Italy and Germany, felt stymied by Britain and the United States as they sought empires that they regarded as essential for their national greatness and economic well-being.

The Road to War in Asia

World War II began in Asia before it occurred in Europe. In the late 1920s and the 1930s, Japanese imperial ambitions mounted as the military became more prominent and powerful in Japan's political life and as an earlier cultural cosmopolitanism gave way to more nationalist sentiments. An initial problem was the rise of Chinese nationalism, which seemed to threaten Japan's sphere of influence in Manchuria, which had been acquired after the Russo-Japanese War of 1904–1905. Acting independently of civilian authorities in Tokyo, units of the Japanese military seized control of Manchuria in 1931 and established a puppet state called Manchukuo. This action infuriated Western powers, prompting Japan to withdraw from the League of Nations, to break politically with its Western allies, and in 1936 to align more closely with Germany and Italy. By that time, relations with an increasingly nationalist China had deteriorated further, leading to a full-scale attack on heartland China in 1937 and escalating a bitter conflict that would last another eight years. World War II in Asia had begun (see Map 21.4).

As the war with China unfolded, the view of the world held by Japanese authorities and many ordinary people hardened. Increasingly, they felt isolated, surrounded, and threatened. A series of international agreements in the early 1920s that had granted Japan a less robust naval force than Britain or the United States as well as anti-Japanese immigration policies in the United States convinced some Japanese that European racism prevented the West from acknowledging Japan as an equal power. Furthermore, Japan was quite dependent on foreign and especially American sources of strategic goods. By the late 1930s, some 73 percent of Japan's scrap iron, 60 percent of its imported machine tools, 80 percent of its oil, and about half of its

■ **Comparison**

In what ways were the origins of World War II in Asia and in Europe similar to each other? How were they different?

Map 21.4 World War II in Asia
Japanese aggression temporarily dislodged the British, French, Dutch, and Americans from their colonial possessions in Asia, while inflicting vast devastation on China.

copper came from the United States, which was becoming increasingly hostile to Japanese ambitions in Asia. Western imperialist powers—the British, French, and Dutch—controlled resource-rich colonies in Southeast Asia. Finally, the Soviet Union, which was proclaiming an alien communist ideology, loomed large in northern Asia. To growing numbers of Japanese, their national survival was at stake.

Thus in 1940–1941, Japan extended its military operations to the French, British, Dutch, and American colonies of Indochina, Malaya, Burma, Indonesia, and the Philippines in an effort to acquire those resources that would free it from dependence on the West. In carving out this Pacific empire, the Japanese presented themselves as liberators and modernizers, creating an "Asia for Asians" and freeing their continent from European dominance. Experience soon showed that Japan's concern was far more for Asia's resources than for its liberation and that Japanese rule exceeded in brutality even that of the Europeans.

A decisive step in the development of World War II in Asia lay in the Japanese attack on the United States at Pearl Harbor in Hawaii in December 1941. Japanese authorities undertook that attack with reluctance and only after negotiations to end American hostility to Japan's empire-building enterprise proved fruitless and an American oil embargo was imposed on Japan in July 1941. American opinion in the 1930s increasingly saw Japan as aggressive, oppressive, and a threat to U.S. economic interests in Asia. In the face of this hostility, Japan's leaders felt that the alternatives for their country boiled down to either an acceptance of American terms, which they feared would reduce Japan to a second- or third-rank power, or a war with an uncertain outcome. Given those choices, the decision for war was made more with foreboding than with enthusiasm. A leading Japanese admiral made the case for war in this way in late 1941: "The government has decided that if there were no war the fate of the nation is sealed. Even if there is a war, the country may be ruined. Nevertheless a nation that does not fight in this plight has lost its spirit and is doomed."[11]

As a consequence of the attack on Pearl Harbor, the United States entered the war in the Pacific, beginning a long and bloody struggle that ended only with the use of atomic bombs against Hiroshima and Nagasaki in 1945. The Pearl Harbor action also joined the Asian theater of the war and the ongoing conflict in Europe into a single global struggle that pitted Germany, Italy, and Japan (the Axis powers) against the United States, Britain, and the Soviet Union (the Allies).

The Road to War in Europe

If Japan was the dissatisfied power in Asia, Nazi Germany occupied that role in Europe even more sharply. As a consequence of its defeat in World War I and the harsh terms of the Treaty of Versailles, many Germans harbored deep resentments about their country's position in the international arena. Taking advantage of those resentments, the Nazis pledged to rectify the treaty's perceived injustices. Thus, to most historians, the origins of World War II in Europe lie squarely in German aggression, although with many twists and turns and encouraged by the initial

that set a new standard for human depravity and has haunted the world's conscience ever since. Millions more whom the Nazis deemed inferior, undesirable, or dangerous—Russians, Poles, and other Slavs; Gypsies, or the Roma; mentally or physically handicapped people; homosexuals; communists; and Jehovah's Witnesses—likewise perished in Germany's efforts at racial purification.

On an even larger scale than World War I, this second global conflict rearranged the architecture of world politics. As the war ended, Europe was impoverished, its industrial infrastructure was shattered, many of its great cities were in ruins, and millions of its people were homeless or displaced. Within a few years, this much-weakened Europe was effectively divided, with its western half operating under an American umbrella and the eastern half subject to Soviet control. It was clear that Europe's dominance in world affairs was finished.

Over the next two decades, Europe's greatly diminished role in the world registered internationally when its Asian and African colonies achieved independence. Not only had the war weakened both the will and the ability of European powers to hold onto their colonies, but it had also emboldened nationalist and anticolonial movements everywhere (see Chapter 23). Japanese victories in Southeast Asia had certainly damaged European prestige, for British, Dutch, and American military forces fell to Japanese conquerors, sometimes in a matter of weeks. Japanese authorities staged long and brutal marches of Western prisoners of war, partly to drive home to local people that the era of Western domination was over. Furthermore, tens of thousands of Africans had fought for the British or the French, had seen white people die, had enjoyed the company of white women, and had returned home with very different ideas about white superiority and the permanence of colonial rule. Colonial subjects everywhere were very much aware that U.S. president Franklin Roosevelt and British prime minister Winston Churchill had solemnly declared in 1941 that "we respect the right of all peoples to choose the form of government under which they will live." Many asked whether those principles should not apply to people in the colonial world as well as to Europeans.

A further outcome of World War II lay in the consolidation and extension of the communist world. The Soviet victory over the Nazis, though bought at an unimaginable cost in blood and treasure, gave immense credibility to the communist regime and to its leader, Joseph Stalin. In the decades that followed, Soviet authorities nurtured a virtual cult of the war: memorials were everywhere; wedding parties made pilgrimages to them, and brides left their bouquets behind; May 9, Victory Day, saw elaborately orchestrated celebrations; veterans were honored and granted modest privileges. Furthermore, communist parties, largely dominated by the Soviet Union and supported by its armed forces, took power all across Eastern Europe, pushing the communist frontier deep into the European heartland. Even more important was a communist takeover in China in 1949. The Second World War allowed the Chinese Communist Party to gain support and credibility by leading the struggle against Japan. By 1950, the communist world seemed to many in the West very much on the offensive (see Chapter 22).

The horrors of two world wars within a single generation prompted a renewed interest in international efforts to maintain the peace in a world of competing and sovereign states. The chief outcome was the United Nations (UN), established in 1945 as a successor to the moribund League of Nations. As a political body dependent on agreement among its most powerful members, the UN proved more effective as a forum for international opinion than as a means of resolving the major conflicts of the postwar world, particularly the Soviet/American hostility during the cold war decades. Further evidence for a growing internationalism lay in the creation in late 1945 of the World Bank and International Monetary Fund, whose purpose was to regulate the global economy, prevent another depression, and stimulate economic growth, especially in the poorer nations.

What these initiatives shared was the dominant presence of the United States. Unlike the aftermath of World War I, when an isolationist United States substantially withdrew from world affairs, the half century following the end of World War II witnessed the emergence of the United States as a global superpower. This was one of the major outcomes of the Second World War and a chief reason for the remarkable recovery of a badly damaged and discredited Western civilization.

The Recovery of Europe

The tragedies that afflicted Europe in the first half of the twentieth century—fratricidal war, economic collapse, the Holocaust—were wholly self-inflicted, and yet despite the sorry and desperate state of heartland Europe in 1945, that civilization had not permanently collapsed. In the twentieth century's second half, Europeans rebuilt their industrial economies and revived their democratic political systems, while the United States, a European offshoot, assumed a dominant and often dominating role both within Western civilization and in the world at large.

Three factors help to explain this astonishing recovery. One is the apparent resiliency of an industrial society, once it has been established. The knowledge, skills, and habits of mind that made industrial societies work remained intact, even if the physical infrastructure had been largely destroyed. Thus even the most terribly damaged countries—Germany, the Soviet Union, and Japan—had substantially recovered, both economically and demographically, within a quarter of a century. A second factor lay in the ability of the major Western European countries to integrate their recovering economies. After centuries of military conflict climaxed by the horrors of the two world wars, the major Western European powers were at last willing to put aside some of their prickly nationalism in return for prolonged peace and a general prosperity.

Perhaps most important, Europe had long ago spawned an overseas extension of its own civilization in what became the United States. In the twentieth century, that country served as a reservoir of military manpower, economic resources, and political leadership for the West as a whole. By 1945, the center of gravity within Western civilization had shifted decisively, relocated now across the Atlantic. With

■ **Change**
How was Europe able to recover from the devastation of war?

Europe diminished, divided, and on the defensive against the Communist threat, leadership of the Western world passed, almost by default, to the United States. It was the only major country physically untouched by the war. Its economy had demonstrated enormous productivity during that struggle and by 1945 was generating fully 50 percent of total world production. Its overall military strength was unmatched, and it was in sole possession of the atomic bomb, the most powerful weapon ever constructed. Thus the United States became the new heartland of the West as well as a global superpower. In 1941, the publisher Henry Luce had proclaimed the twentieth century as "the American century." As the Second World War ended, that prediction seemed to be coming true.

An early indication of the United States' intention to exercise global leadership took shape in its efforts to rebuild and reshape shattered European economies. Known as the Marshall Plan, that effort funneled into Europe some $12 billion, at the time a very large amount, together with numerous advisers and technicians. It was motivated by some combination of genuine humanitarian concern, a desire to prevent a new depression by creating overseas customers for American industrial goods, and an interest in undermining the growing appeal of European communist parties. This economic recovery plan was successful beyond anyone's expectations. Between 1948 and the early 1970s, Western European economies grew rapidly, generating a widespread prosperity and improving living standards; at the same time, Western Europe became both a major customer for American goods and a major competitor in global markets.

The Marshall Plan also required its European recipients to cooperate with one another. After decades of conflict and destruction almost beyond description, many Europeans were eager to do so. That process began in 1951 when Italy, France, West Germany, Belgium, the Netherlands, and Luxembourg created the European Coal and Steel Community to jointly manage the production of these critical items. In 1957, these six countries deepened their level of cooperation by establishing the European Economic Community (EEC), more widely known as the Common Market, whose members reduced their tariffs and developed common trade policies. Over the next half century, the EEC expanded its membership to include almost all of Europe, including many former communist states. In 1994, the EEC was renamed the European Union, and in 2002 twelve of its members adopted a common currency, the euro (see Map 21.6). All of this sustained Europe's remarkable economic recovery and expressed a larger European identity, although it certainly did not erase deeply rooted national loyalties. Nor did it lead, as some had hoped, to a political union, a United States of Europe.

Beyond economic assistance, the American commitment to Europe soon came to include political and military security against the distant possibility of renewed German aggression and the more immediate communist threat from the Soviet Union. Without that security, economic recovery was unlikely to continue. Thus was born the military and political alliance known as the North Atlantic Treaty Organization (NATO) in 1949. It committed the United States and its nuclear arsenal to the defense of Europe against the Soviet Union, and it firmly anchored West Germany within the Western alliance. Thus, as Western Europe revived economically,

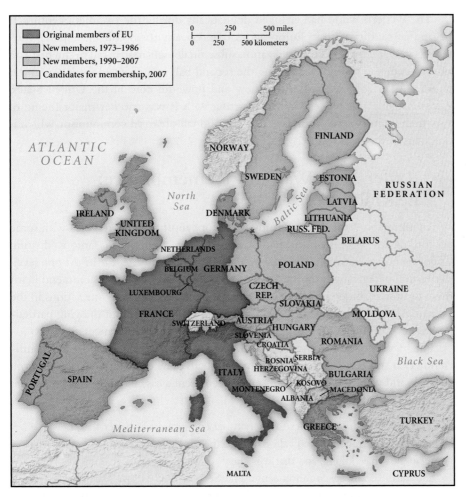

Map 21.6 The Growth of European Integration Gradually during the second half of the twentieth century, Europeans put aside their bitter rivalries and entered into various forms of economic cooperation with one another, although these efforts fell short of complete political union. This map illustrates the growth of what is now called the European Union (EU). Notice the eastward expansion of the EU following the collapse of communism in Eastern Europe and the Soviet Union.

Map legend:
- Original members of EU
- New members, 1973–1986
- New members, 1990–2007
- Candidates for membership, 2007

it did so under the umbrella of U.S. political and military leadership, which Europeans generally welcomed. It was perhaps an imperial relationship, but to historian John Gaddis, it was "an empire by invitation" rather than by imposition.[13]

A parallel process in Japan, which was under American occupation between 1945 and 1952, likewise revived that country's devastated but already industrialized economy. In the two decades following the occupation, Japan's economy grew at the remarkable rate of 10 percent a year, and the nation became an economic giant on the world stage. This "economic miracle" received a substantial boost from some $2 billion in American aid during the occupation and even more from U.S. military purchases in Japan during the Korean War (1950–1953). Furthermore, the democratic constitution imposed on Japan by American occupation authorities required that "land, sea, and air forces, as well as other war potential, will never be maintained." This meant that Japan, even more so than Europe, depended on the United States for its military security. Because it spent only about 1 percent of its gross national product on defense, more was available for productive investment.

The Western world had changed dramatically during the twentieth century. It began that century with its European heartland clearly the dominant imperial center of a global network. That civilization substantially self-destructed in the first half of the century, but it revived during the second half in a changed form—without its Afro-Asian colonies and with a new and powerful core in the United States. Accompanying this process and intersecting with it was another major theme of twentieth-century world history—the rise and fall of world communism, which is the focus of the next chapter.

Reflections: War and Remembrance: Learning from History

When asked about the value of studying history, most students respond with some version of the Spanish-born philosopher George Santayana's famous dictum: "Those who cannot remember the past are condemned to repeat it." At one level, this notion of learning from the "lessons of history" has much to recommend it, for there is, after all, little else except the past on which we can base our actions in the present. And yet historians in general are notably cautious about drawing particular lessons from the past and applying them to present circumstances.

For one thing, the historical record, like the Bible or any sacred text, is sufficiently rich and complex to allow many people to draw quite different lessons from it. The world wars of the twentieth century represent a case in point, as writer Adam Gopnik has pointed out:

> The First World War teaches that territorial compromise is better than full-scale war, that an "honor-bound" allegiance of the great powers to small nations is a recipe for mass killing, and that it is crazy to let the blind mechanism of armies and alliances trump common sense. The Second teaches that searching for an accommodation with tyranny by selling out small nations only encourages the tyrant, that refusing to fight now leads to a worse fight later on.... The First teaches us never to rush into a fight, the Second never to back down from a bully.[14]

Did the lessons of the First World War lead Americans to ignore the rise of fascism until the country was directly threatened by Japanese attack? Did the lessons of World War II contribute to unnecessary wars in Vietnam and more recently in Iraq? There are no easy answers to such questions, for the lessons of history are many, varied, and changing.

Behind any such lesson is the common assumption that history repeats itself. This too is a notion to which historians bring considerable skepticism. They are generally more impressed with the complexity and particularity of major events such as wars rather than with their common features. Here is a further basis for caution in easily drawing lessons from the past.

But the wars of the past century perhaps share one broad similarity: all of them led to unexpected consequences. Few people expected the duration and carnage of

World War I. The Holocaust was literally unimaginable when Hitler took power in 1933 or even at the outbreak of the Second World War in 1939. Who would have expected an American defeat at the hands of the Vietnamese? And the invasion of Iraq in 2003 has generated a long list of surprises for the United States, including the absence of weapons of mass destruction and a prolonged insurgency. History repeats itself most certainly only in its unexpectedness.

Second Thoughts

What's the Significance?

World War I	fascism	total war
Treaty of Versailles	Mussolini	Holocaust
Woodrow Wilson/Fourteen	Nazi Germany/Hitler	Marshall Plan
Points	Revolutionary Right (Japan)	European Economic
Great Depression	World War II in Asia	Community
New Deal	World War II in Europe	NATO

To assess your mastery of the material in this chapter, see the **Online Study Guide** at bedfordstmartins.com/strayer.

Big Picture Questions

1. What explains the disasters that befell Europe in the first half of the twentieth century?
2. In what ways were the world wars a motor for change in the history of the twentieth century?
3. To what extent were the two world wars distinct and different conflicts, and in what ways were they related to each other? In particular, how did the First World War and its aftermath lay the foundations for World War II?
4. In what ways did Europe's internal conflicts between 1914 and 1945 have global implications?

Next Steps: For Further Study

Michael Burleigh, *The Third Reich: A New History* (2001). A fresh and thorough look at the Nazi era in Germany's history.

John Keegan, *The Second World War* (2005). A comprehensive account by a well-known scholar.

Bernd Martin, *Japan and Germany in the Modern World* (1995). A comparative study of these two countries' modern history and the relationship between them.

Mark Mazower, *Dark Continent* (2000). A history of Europe in the twentieth century that views the era as a struggle among liberal democracy, fascism, and communism.

Michael S. Nieberg, *Fighting the Great War: A Global History* (2006). Explores the origins and conduct of World War I.

Dietman Rothermund, *The Global Impact of the Great Depression, 1929–1939* (1996). Examines the origins of the Depression in America and Europe and its impact in Asia, Africa, and Latin America.

First World War.com, http://www.firstworldwar.com. A Web site rich with articles, documents, photos, diaries, and more that illustrate the history of World War I.

"Nazi Rule," http://www.ushmm.org/outreach/nrule.htm. A great Web site, sponsored by the U.S. Holocaust Memorial Museum, for exploring various aspects of the Nazi experience.

For Web sites, images, and documents related to this chapter, see **Make History** at bedfordstmartins.com/strayer.

ЛЕНИН –
ЖИЛ,
ЛЕНИН –
ЖИВ,
ЛЕНИН –
БУДЕТ ЖИТ

ВЛ. МАЯКОВСКИЙ.

The Rise and Fall of World Communism

1917–PRESENT

Global Communism

Comparing Revolutions as a
Path to Communism
  Russia: Revolution in a Single
  Year
  China: A Prolonged
  Revolutionary Struggle

Building Socialism in Two
Countries
  Communist Feminism
  Socialism in the Countryside
  Communism and Industrial
  Development
  The Search for Enemies

East versus West: A Global
Divide and a Cold War
  Military Conflict and the Cold War
  Nuclear Standoff and Third
  World Rivalry
  The United States: Superpower
  of the West, 1945–1975
  The Communist World,
  1950s–1970s

Comparing Paths to the End
of Communism
  China: Abandoning
  Communism and
  Maintaining the Party
  The Soviet Union: The Collapse
  of Communism and Country

Reflections: The Ambiguous
Legacy of Communism

"I was living in Germany on the day the wall came down and well remember talking to my German neighbour. With tears streaming down his face he kept saying in English and German: 'I never thought I would live to see this.'

"For anyone who didn't experience the Wall, it will be hard to imagine what an overwhelming feeling of relief, of joy, of unreality filled one that this monster was dead, and people had conquered it."[1]

Both of these eyewitness comments referred to that remarkable day, November 9, 1989, when the infamous Berlin Wall in Germany was breached. Built in 1961 to prevent the residents of communist East Berlin from escaping to the West, that concrete barrier had become a potent symbol of communist tyranny. Its fall, amid the overthrow of communist governments all across Eastern Europe, was part of a larger process that marked the collapse or the abandonment of communism as the twentieth century entered its final decade. In the midst of that euphoria, it was hard to remember that earlier in the century communism had been greeted with enthusiasm by many people—in Russia, China, Cuba, Vietnam, and elsewhere—as a promise of liberation from inequality, oppression, exploitation, and backwardness.

IT WOULD BE HARD TO OVERESTIMATE THE SIGNIFICANCE OF COMMU-NISM IN THE WORLD OF THE TWENTIETH CENTURY. Communist regimes came to power almost everywhere in the tumultuous wake of war, rev-olution, or both. Once established, those regimes set about a thorough and revolutionary transformation of their societies—"building social-ism," as they so often put it. Internationally, world communism posed a

Lenin: Vladimir Ulyanov, better known as Lenin, was the Bolshevik leader of the Russian Revolution. He became the iconic symbol of world communism and in his own country was the focus of a semireligious cult. This widely distributed Soviet propaganda poster reads "Lenin lived; Lenin lives; Lenin will live." (David King Collection)

profound military and political/ideological threat to the Western world of capitalism and democracy, particularly during the decades of the cold war (1946–1991). That struggle divided continents, countries, and cities into communist and non-communist halves. It also prompted a global rivalry between the United States and the Soviet Union (USSR) for influence in the third world. Most hauntingly, it spawned an arms race in horrendously destructive nuclear weapons that sent schoolchildren scrambling under their desks during air raid drills, while sober scientists speculated about the possible extinction of human life, and perhaps all life, in the event of a major war.

Then, to the amazement of everyone, it was over, more with a whimper than with a bang. The last two decades of the twentieth century witnessed the collapse of communist regimes or the abandonment of communist principles practically everywhere. The great global struggle of capitalism and communism, embodied in the United States and the Soviet Union, was resolved in favor of the former far more quickly and much more peacefully than anyone had imagined possible.

Global Communism

■ **Description**
When and where did communism exercise influence during the twentieth century?

Modern communism found its political and philosophical roots in nineteenth-century European socialism, inspired by the teachings of Karl Marx (see Chapter 18). Although most European socialists came to believe that they could achieve their goals peacefully and through the democratic process, those who defined themselves as communists in the twentieth century disdained such reformism and advocated uncompromising revolution as the only possible route to a socialist future. Russia was the first country to experience such a revolution. Other movements that later identified or allied with the Soviet Union, as the Russian Empire was renamed after its 1917 revolution, likewise defined themselves as communist. In Marxist theory, that term also referred to a final stage of historical development when social equality and collective living would be most fully developed, wholly without private property. Socialism was an intermediate stage along the way to that final goal.

At communism's high point in the 1970s, almost one-third of the world's population lived in societies governed by communist regimes. By far the most significant were the Soviet Union, the world's largest country in size, and China, the world's largest country in population. This chapter focuses primarily on a comparison of these two large-scale experiments in communism and their global impact.

Beyond the Soviet Union and China, communism also came to Eastern Europe in the wake of World War II and the extension of the Soviet military presence there. In Asia, following Japan's defeat in that war, its Korean colony was partitioned, with the northern half coming under Soviet and therefore communist control. In Vietnam, a much more locally based communist movement, under the leadership of Ho Chi Minh, embodied both a socialist vision and Vietnamese nationalism as it battled Japanese, French, and later American invaders and established communist control first in the northern half of the country and after 1975 throughout the whole country. The victory of the Vietnamese communists spilled over into neighboring Laos and Cambodia, where communist parties took power in the mid-1970s. In Latin America, Fidel Castro led a revolutionary nationalist movement against a repressive and American-backed government in Cuba. On coming to power in 1959, he moved toward communism and an alliance with the Soviet Union. Finally, a shaky communist regime took power in Afghanistan in 1979, propped up briefly only by massive Soviet military support. None of these countries had achieved the kind of advanced industrial capitalism that Karl Marx had viewed as a prerequisite for revolution and socialism. In one of history's strange twists, the great revolutions of the twentieth century took place instead in largely agrarian societies.

In addition to those countries where communist governments exercised state power, communist parties took root in still other places, where they exercised various degrees of influence. In the aftermath of World War II, such parties played important political roles in Greece, France, and Italy. In the 1950s, a small communist party in the United States became the focus of an intense wave of fear and political repression known as McCarthyism. Revolutionary communist movements threatened established governments in the Philippines, Malaya, Indonesia, Bolivia, Peru, and elsewhere, sometimes provoking brutal crackdowns by those governments. A number of African states in the 1970s proclaimed themselves Marxist for a time and aligned with the Soviet Union in international affairs. All of this was likewise part of global communism.

These differing expressions of communism were linked to one another in various ways. They shared a common ideology derived from European Marxism, although it was substantially modified in many places. That ideology minimized the claims of national loyalty and looked forward to an international revolutionary movement of the lower classes and a worldwide socialist federation. The Russian Revolution of 1917 served as an inspiration and an example to aspiring revolutionaries elsewhere, and the new Soviet Communist Party and government provided them aid and advice. Through an organization called Comintern (Communist International), Soviet authorities also sought to control their policies and actions.

During the cold war decades, the Warsaw Pact brought the Soviet Union and Eastern European communist states together in a military alliance designed to counter the threat from the Western capitalist countries of the NATO alliance. A parallel organization called the Council on Mutual Economic Assistance tied Eastern European economies tightly to the economy of the Soviet Union. A Treaty of Friendship between the Soviet Union and China in 1950 joined the two communist giants in an alliance that caused many in the West to view communism as a unified international movement aimed at their destruction. Nevertheless, rivalry, outright hostility, and on occasion military conflict marked the communist world as much or more than solidarity and cooperation. Eastern European resentment of their Soviet overlords was expressed in periodic rebellions, even as the Soviet Union and China came close to war in the late 1960s.

Although the globalization of communism found expression primarily in the second half of the twentieth century, that process began with two quite distinct and different revolutionary upheavals—one in Russia and the other in China—in the first half of that century.

Comparing Revolutions as a Path to Communism

■ **Comparison**
Identify the major differences between the Russian and Chinese revolutions.

Communist movements of the twentieth century quite self-consciously drew on the mystique of the earlier French Revolution, which suggested that new and better worlds could be constructed by human actions. Communist revolutions, like their French predecessor, ousted old ruling classes and dispossessed landed aristocracies. They too involved vast peasant upheavals in the countryside and an educated leadership with roots in the cities. All three revolutions—French, Russian, and Chinese—found their vision of the good society in a modernizing future, not in some nostalgic vision of the past. Communists also worried lest their revolutions end up in a military dictatorship like that of Napoleon following the French Revolution.

But the communist revolutions were distinctive as well. They were made by highly organized parties guided by a Marxist ideology, were committed to an industrial future, pursued economic as well as political equality, and sought the abolition of private property. In doing so, they mobilized, celebrated, and claimed to act on behalf of society's lower classes—exploited urban workers and impoverished rural peasants. The middle classes, who were the chief beneficiaries of the French Revolution, numbered among the many victims of the communist upheavals. The Russian and Chinese revolutions shared these features, but in other respects they differed sharply from each other.

Russia: Revolution in a Single Year

In Russia, the communists came to power on the back of a revolutionary upheaval that took place within a single year, 1917. The immense pressures of World War I, which was going very badly for the Russians, represented the catalyst for that revolution as the accumulated tensions of Russian society exploded (see Chapter 18). Much exploited and suffering from wartime shortages, workers, including many women, took to the streets to express their outrage at the incompetence and privileges of their social betters. Activists from various parties, many of them socialist, recruited members, organized demonstrations, published newspapers, and plotted revolution. By February 1917, Tsar Nicholas II had lost almost all support and was forced to abdicate the throne, thus ending the Romanov dynasty, which had ruled Russia for more than three centuries.

That historic event opened the door to a massive social upheaval. Ordinary soldiers, seeking an end to a terrible war and despising their upper-class officers, deserted in substantial numbers. In major industrial centers such as St. Petersburg and Moscow, new trade unions arose to defend workers' interests, and some workers

Map 22.1 Russia in 1917
During the First World War, the world's largest state, bridging both Europe and Asia, exploded in revolution in 1917. The Russian Revolution brought to power the twentieth century's first communist government and launched an international communist movement that eventually incorporated about one-third of the world's people.

seized control of their factories. Grassroots organizations of workers and soldiers, known as "soviets," emerged to speak for ordinary people. Peasants, many of whom had been serfs only a generation or two ago, seized landlords' estates, burned their manor houses, and redistributed the land among themselves. Non-Russian nationalists in Ukraine, Poland, Muslim Central Asia, and the Baltic region demanded greater autonomy or even independence (see Map 22.1).

This was social revolution, and it quickly demonstrated the inadequacy of the Provisional Government, which had come to power after the tsar abdicated. Consisting of middle-class politicians and some socialist leaders, that government was divided and ineffectual, unable or unwilling to meet the demands of Russia's revolutionary masses. Nor was it willing to take Russia out of the war, as many were now demanding. Impatience and outrage against the Provisional Government provided an opening for more radical groups. The most effective were the Bolsheviks, a small socialist party with a determined and charismatic leader, Vladimir Ulyanov, more commonly known as Lenin. He had long believed that Russia, despite its industrial backwardness, was nonetheless ready for a socialist revolution that would, he expected, spark further revolutions in the more developed countries of Europe. Thus backward Russia would be a catalyst for a more general socialist breakthrough.

■ **Change**
Why were the Bolsheviks able to ride the Russian Revolution to power?

It was a striking revision of Marxist thinking to accommodate the conditions of a largely agrarian Russian society.

In the desperate circumstances of 1917, his party's message—an end to the war, land for the peasants, workers' control of factories, self-determination for non-Russian nationalities—resonated with an increasingly rebellious public mood, particularly in the major cities. Lenin and the Bolsheviks also called for the dissolution of the Provisional Government and a transfer of state power to the new soviets. On the basis of this program, the Bolsheviks—claiming to act on behalf of the highly popular soviets, in which they had a major presence—seized power in late October during an overnight coup in the capital city of St. Petersburg. Members of the discredited Provisional Government fled or were arrested, even as the Bolsheviks also seized power elsewhere in the country.

Taking or claiming power was one thing; holding onto it was another. A three-year civil war followed in which the Bolsheviks, now officially calling their party "communist," battled an assortment of enemies—tsarist officials, landlords, disaffected socialists, and regional nationalist forces, as well as troops from the United States, Britain, France, and Japan, all of which were eager to crush the fledgling communist regime. Remarkably, the Bolsheviks held on and by 1921 had staggered to victory over their divided and uncoordinated opponents. One thing that helped the Bolsheviks was their signing of a separate peace treaty with Germany, thus taking Russia out of World War I, but at a great, though temporary, cost in terms of Russian territory.

During the civil war (1918–1921), the Bolsheviks had harshly regimented the economy, seized grain from angry peasants, suppressed nationalist rebellions, and perpetrated bloody atrocities, as did their enemies as well. But they also had integrated many lower-class men into the Red Army, as Bolshevik military forces were known, and into new local governments, providing them an avenue of social mobility not previously available. By battling foreign troops from the United States, Britain, France, and Japan, the Bolsheviks claimed to be defending Russia from imperialists and protecting the downtrodden masses from their exploiters. The civil war exaggerated even further the Bolsheviks' authoritarian tendencies and their inclination to use force. Shortly after that war ended, they renamed their country the Union of Soviet Socialist Republics and set about its transformation.

For the next twenty-five years, the Soviet Union remained a communist island in a capitalist sea. The next major extension of communist control occurred in Eastern Europe in the aftermath of World War II, but it took place quite differently than in Russia. The war had ended with Soviet military forces occupying much of Eastern Europe. Furthermore, Stalin, the USSR's longtime leader, had determined that Soviet security required "friendly" governments in the region so as to permanently end the threat of invasion from the West. When the Marshall Plan seemed to suggest American plans to incorporate Eastern Europe into a Western economic network, Stalin acted to install fully communist governments, loyal to himself, in Poland, East Germany, Czechoslovakia, Hungary, Romania, and Bulgaria. Backed by the pressure and presence of the Soviet army, communism was largely imposed on Eastern Europe from outside rather than growing out of a domestic revolution, as had happened in Russia itself.

Local communist parties had some domestic support, deriving from their role in the resistance against the Nazis and their policies of land reform. In Hungary and Poland, for example, communist pressures led to the redistribution of much land to poor or landless peasants, and in free elections in Czechoslovakia in 1946, communists received 38 percent of the vote. Furthermore, in Yugoslavia, a genuinely popular communist movement had played a leading role in the struggle against Nazi occupation and came to power on its own with little Soviet help. Its leader, Josef Broz, known as Tito, openly defied Soviet efforts to control it, claiming that "our goal is that everyone should be master in his own house."[2]

China: A Prolonged Revolutionary Struggle

Communism triumphed in the ancient land of China in 1949, about thirty years after the Russian Revolution, likewise on the heels of war and domestic revolution. But that revolution, which was a struggle of decades rather than a single year, was far different from its earlier Russian counterpart. The Chinese imperial system had collapsed in 1911, under the pressure of foreign imperialism, its own inadequacies, and mounting internal opposition (see Chapter 19). Unlike Russia, where intellectuals had been discussing socialism for half a century or more before the revolution, the ideas of Karl Marx were barely known in China in the early twentieth century. Not until 1921 was a small Chinese Communist Party (CCP) founded, aiming its efforts initially at organizing the country's minuscule urban working class.

Over the next twenty-eight years, that small party, with an initial membership of only sixty people, grew enormously, transformed its strategy, found a charismatic leader in Mao Zedong, engaged in an epic struggle with its opponents, fought the Japanese heroically, and in 1949 emerged victorious as the rulers of China. The victory was all the more surprising because the CCP faced a far more formidable foe than the weak Provisional Government over which the Bolsheviks had triumphed in Russia. That opponent was

■ **Change**
What was the appeal of communism in China before 1949?

Mao Zedong and the Long March
An early member of China's then minuscule Communist Party, Mao rose to a position of dominant leadership during the Long March of 1934–1935, when beleaguered communists from southeastern China trekked to a new base area in the north. This photograph shows Mao on his horse during that epic journey of some 6,000 miles. (Collection J.A. Fox/Magnum Photos)

the *Guomindang*, or Nationalist Party, which governed China after 1928. Led by a military officer, Chiang Kai-shek, that party promoted a measure of modern development (railroads, light industry, banking, airline services) in the decade that followed. However, the impact of these achievements was limited largely to the cities, leaving the rural areas, where most people lived, still impoverished. The Guomindang's base of support was also narrow, deriving from urban elites, rural landlords, and Western powers.

Chased out of China's cities in a wave of Guomindang-inspired anticommunist terror in 1927, the CCP groped its way toward a new revolutionary strategy, quite at odds with both classical Marxism and Russian practice. Whereas the Bolsheviks had found their primary audience among workers in Russia's major cities, Chinese communists increasingly looked to the country's peasant villages for support. Thus European Marxism was adapted once again, this time to fit the situation in a mostly peasant China. Still, it was no easy sell. Chinese peasants did not rise up spontaneously against their landlords, as Russian peasants had. However, years of guerrilla warfare, experiments with land reform in areas under communist control, efforts to empower women, and the creation of a communist military force to protect liberated areas from Guomindang attack and landlord reprisals—all of this slowly gained for the CCP a growing measure of respect and support among China's peasants. In the process, Chinese communists discovered an effective leader in Mao Zedong, the son of a prosperous Chinese peasant family and a professional revolutionary since the early 1920s.

It was Japan's brutal invasion of China that gave the CCP a decisive opening, for that attack destroyed Guomindang control over much of the country and forced it to retreat to the interior, where it became even more dependent on conservative landlords. The CCP, by contrast, grew from just 40,000 members in 1937 to more than 1.2 million in 1945, while the communist-led People's Liberation Army mushroomed to 900,000 men, supported by an additional 2 million militia troops (see Map 22.2). Much of this growing support derived from the vigor with which the CCP waged war against the Japanese invaders. Using guerrilla warfare techniques learned in the struggle against the Guomindang, communist forces established themselves behind enemy lines and, despite periodic setbacks, offered a measure of security to many Chinese faced with Japanese atrocities. The Guomindang, by contrast, sometimes seemed to be more interested in eliminating the communists than in actively fighting the Japanese. Furthermore, in the areas it controlled, the CCP reduced rents, taxes, and interest payments for peasants; taught literacy to adults; and mobilized women for the struggle. As the war drew to a close, more radical action followed. Teams of activists, called cadres, encouraged poor peasants to "speak bitterness" in public meetings, to "struggle" with landlords, and to "settle accounts" with them.

Thus the CCP frontally addressed both of China's major problems—foreign imperialism and peasant exploitation. It expressed Chinese nationalism as well as a demand for radical social change. It gained a reputation for honesty that contrasted

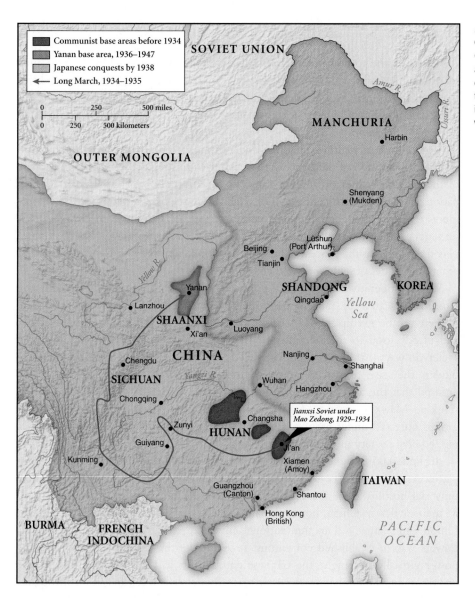

Map 22.2 The Rise of Communism in China
Communism arose in China at the same time as the country was engaged in a terrible war with Japan and in the context of a civil war with Guomindang forces.

sharply with the massive corruption of Guomindang officials. It put down deep roots among the peasantry in a way that the Bolsheviks never did. And whereas the Bolsheviks gained support by urging Russian withdrawal from the highly unpopular First World War, the CCP won support by aggressively pursuing the struggle against Japanese invaders during World War II. In 1949, four years after the war's end, the Chinese communists swept to victory over the Guomindang, many of whose followers fled to Taiwan. Mao Zedong announced triumphantly in Beijing's Tiananmen Square that "the Chinese people have stood up."

Building Socialism in Two Countries

Once they came to power, the communist parties of the Soviet Union and China set about the construction of socialist societies. In the Soviet Union, this massive undertaking occurred under the leadership of Joseph Stalin in the 1920s and 1930s. The corresponding Chinese effort took place during the 1950s and 1960s with Mao Zedong at the helm.

To communist regimes, building socialism meant first of all the modernization and industrialization of their backward societies. In this respect, they embraced many of the material values of Western capitalist societies and were similar to the new nations of the twentieth century, all of which were seeking development. The communists, however, sought a distinctly socialist modernity. This involved a frontal attack on long-standing inequalities of class and gender, an effort to prevent the making of new inequalities as the process of modern development unfolded, and the promotion of cultural values of selflessness and collectivism that could support a socialist society.

Those imperatives generated a political system thoroughly dominated by the Communist Party. Top-ranking party members enjoyed various privileges but were expected to be exemplars of socialism in the making by being disciplined, selfless, and utterly loyal to their country's Marxist ideology. The party itself penetrated society in ways that Western scholars called "totalitarian," for other parties were forbidden, the state controlled almost the entire economy, and political authorities ensured that the arts, education, and the media conformed to approved ways of thinking. Mass organizations for women, workers, students, and various professional groups operated under party control, with none of the independence that characterized civil society in the West.

In undertaking these tasks, the Soviet Union and China started from different places. As the first successful communist revolution, the Bolsheviks faced almost universal hostility from the capitalist Great Powers and international intervention in their civil war. China, however, had a secure northern border with the Soviet Union and confronted an international environment in which one of the Great Powers was an established communist state. Unlike the Bolsheviks, who came to power virtually overnight, the Chinese communists had substantial administrative and governing experience; by the early 1940s, they already ruled an area with 100 million inhabitants. Finally, whereas the Bolsheviks had little presence among the peasantry and lacked experience in the countryside, the Chinese communists came to power as the champions of the rural masses, who constituted some 80 percent of China's population.

In economic terms, China faced even more daunting prospects than did the Soviet Union. Its population was far greater, its industrial base far smaller, and the availability of new agricultural land far more limited than in the Soviet Union. China's literacy and modern education as well as its transportation network were likewise much less developed. Even more than the Soviets, Chinese communists had to build a modern society from the ground up.

Communist Feminism

Among the earliest and most revolutionary actions of these new communist regimes were efforts at liberating and mobilizing their women. Communist countries in fact pioneered forms of "women's liberation" that only later were adopted in the West. This communist feminism was largely state-directed, with the initiative coming from the top rather than bubbling up from grassroots movements as in the West. In the Soviet Union, where a small women's movement had taken shape in pre–World War I Russia, the new communist government almost immediately issued a series of laws and decrees regarding women. They declared full legal and political equality for women; marriage became a civil procedure among freely consenting adults; divorce was legalized and made easier, as was abortion; illegitimacy was abolished; women no longer had to take their husbands' surnames; pregnancy leave for employed women was mandated; and women were actively mobilized as workers in the country's drive to industrialization.

In 1919, the party set up a special organization called Zhenotdel (Women's Department), whose radical leaders, all women, pushed a decidedly feminist agenda in the 1920s. They organized numerous conferences for women, trained women to run day-care centers and medical clinics, published newspapers and magazines aimed at a female audience, provided literacy and prenatal classes, and encouraged Muslim women to take off their veils. Much of this encountered opposition from male communist officials and from ordinary people as well, and Stalin abolished Zhenotdel in 1930. While it lasted, though, it was a remarkable experiment in women's liberation by means of state action, animated by an almost utopian sense of new possibilities set loose by the revolution.

Similar policies took shape in communist China. The Marriage Law of 1950 was a direct attack on patriarchal and Confucian traditions. It decreed free choice in marriage, relatively easy divorce, the end of concubinage and child marriage, permission for widows to remarry, and equal property rights for women. A short but intense campaign by the CCP in the early 1950s sought to implement these changes, often against strenuous opposition. The party also launched a Women's Federation, a mass organization that enrolled millions of women. Its leadership, however, was far less radical than that of the Bolshevik feminists who led Zhenotdel in the

■ **Change**
What changes did communist regimes bring to the lives of women?

Mobilizing Women for Communism
As the Soviet Union mobilized for rapid economic development in the 1930s, women entered the workforce in great numbers. Here two young women are mastering the skills of driving a tractor on one of the large collective farms that replaced the country's private agriculture. (Sovfoto/Eastfoto)

1920s. In China, there was little talk of "free love" or the "withering away of the family," as there had been in the USSR. Nevertheless, like their Soviet counterparts, Chinese women became much more actively involved in production outside the home. By 1978, 50 percent of agricultural workers and 38 percent of nonagricultural laborers were female. "Women can do anything" became a famous party slogan in the 1960s.

Still, women's liberation communist style had definite limits. Fearing that the women's question would detract from his emphasis on industrial production, Stalin declared it "solved" in 1930. Little direct discussion of women's issues was permitted in the several decades that followed. In neither the Soviet Union nor China did the Communist Party undertake a direct attack on male domination within the family. Thus the double burden of housework and child care plus paid employment continued to afflict most women. Moreover, women appeared only very rarely in the top political leadership of either country.

Socialism in the Countryside

■ Comparison
How did the collectivization of agriculture differ between the USSR and China?

In their effort to build socialism, both the Soviet Union and China first expropriated landlords' estates and redistributed that land on a much more equitable basis to the peasantry. Such actions were not socialist, for peasants initially received their land as private property, but they were thoroughly revolutionary. In Russia, the peasants had spontaneously redistributed the land among themselves, and the victorious Bolsheviks merely ratified their actions. In China after 1949, it was a more prolonged and difficult process. Hastily trained land reform teams were dispatched to the newly liberated areas, where they mobilized the poorer peasants in thousands of separate villages to confront and humiliate the landlords or the more wealthy peasants and seized their land, animals, tools, houses, and money for redistribution to the poorer members of the village. In the villages, the land reform teams encountered the age-old deference that peasants traditionally had rendered to their social superiors. One young woman activist described the confrontational meetings intended to break this ancient pattern.

> "Speak bitterness meetings," as they were called, would help [the peasants] to understand how things really had been in the old days, to realize that their lives were not blindly ordained by fate, that poor peasants had a community of interests, having suffered similar disasters and misery in the past—and that far from owing anything to the feudal landlords, it was the feudal landlords who owed them a debt of suffering beyond all reckoning.[3]

It was, as Mao Zedong put it, "not a dinner party." Approximately 1 million to 2 million landlords were killed in the process, which was largely over by 1952.

A second and more distinctly socialist stage of rural reform sought to end private property in land by collectivizing agriculture. In China, despite brief resistance from richer peasants, collectivization during the 1950s was a generally peaceful process, owing much to the close relationship between the Communist Party and the peasantry, which had been established during three decades of struggle. This contrasted markedly with the experience of the Soviet Union from 1928 to 1933, when peasants were forced into collective farms and violence was extensive. Russian peasants slaughtered and consumed hundreds of thousands of animals rather than surrender them to the collectives. Stalin singled out the richer peasants, known as *kulaks*, for exclusion from the new collective farms. Some were killed, and many others were deported to remote areas of the country. With little support or experience in the countryside, Soviet communists, who came mostly from the cities, were viewed as intrusive outsiders in Russian peasant villages. A terrible famine ensued, with some 5 million deaths from starvation or malnutrition.

China pushed the collectivization process further than the Soviet Union did, particularly in huge "people's communes" during the Great Leap Forward in the late 1950s. It was an effort to mobilize China's enormous population for rapid development and at the same time to move toward a more fully communist society with an even greater degree of social equality and collective living. Administrative chaos, disruption of marketing networks, and bad weather combined to produce a massive famine that killed an amazing 20 million people or more between 1959 and 1962, dwarfing even the earlier Soviet famine.

Communism and Industrial Development

Both the Soviet Union and China defined industrialization as a fundamental task of their regimes. That process was necessary to end humiliating backwardness and poverty, to provide the economic basis for socialism, and to create the military strength that would enable their revolutions to survive in a hostile world. Though strongly anticapitalist, communists everywhere were ardent modernizers.

■ **Change**
What were the achievements of communist efforts at industrialization? What problems did these achievements generate?

When the Chinese communists began their active industrialization efforts in the early 1950s, they largely followed the model pioneered by the Soviet Union in the late 1920s and the 1930s. That model involved state ownership of property, centralized planning embodied in successive five-year plans, priority to heavy industry, massive mobilization of the nation's human and material resources, and intrusive Communist Party control of the entire process. Both countries experienced major—indeed unprecedented—economic growth. The Soviet Union constructed the foundations of an industrial society in the 1930s that proved itself in the victory over Nazi Germany in World War II and which by the 1960s and 1970s generated substantially improved standards of living. China too quickly expanded its output (see the Snapshot). In addition, both countries achieved massive improvements in their literacy rates and educational opportunities, allowing far greater social mobility for millions of people than ever before. In both countries, industrialization fostered a similar set of social outcomes: rapid urbanization, exploitation of the countryside to provide for modern industry in the cities, and the growth of a privileged bureaucratic and technological elite intent on pursuing their own careers and passing on their new status to their children.

Snapshot **China under Mao, 1949–1976**

The following table reveals some of the achievements, limitations, and tragedies of China's communist experience during the era of Mao Zedong.[4]

Steel production	from 1.3 million to 23 million tons
Coal production	from 66 million to 448 million tons
Electric power generation	from 7 million to 133 billion kilowatt-hours
Fertilizer production	from 0.2 million to 28 million tons
Cement production	from 3 million to 49 million tons
Industrial workers	from 3 million to 50 million
Scientists and technicians	from 50,000 to 5 million
"Barefoot doctors" posted to countryside	1 million
Annual growth rate of industrial output	11 percent
Annual growth rate of agricultural output	2.3 percent
Total population	from 542 million to 1 billion
Average population growth rate per year	2 percent
Per capita consumption of rural dwellers	from 62 to 124 yuan annually
Per capita consumption of urban dwellers	from 148 to 324 yuan
Overall life expectancy	from 35 to 65 years
Counterrevolutionaries killed (1949–1952)	between 1 million and 3 million
People labeled "rightists" in 1957	550,000
Deaths from famine during Great Leap Forward	20 million or more
Deaths during Cultural Revolution	500,000
Officials sent down to rural labor camps during Cultural Revolution	3 million or more
Urban youth sent down to countryside (1967–1976)	17 million

Perhaps the chief difference in the industrial histories of the Soviet Union and China lies in the leadership's response to these social outcomes. In the Soviet Union under Stalin and his successors, they were largely accepted. Industrialization was centered in large urban areas, which pulled from the countryside its most ambitious and talented people. A highly privileged group of state and party leaders emerged in the Stalin era and largely remained the unchallenged ruling class of the country until the 1980s. Even in the 1930s, the outlines of a conservative society, which had discarded much of its revolutionary legacy, were apparent. Stalin himself endorsed Russian patriotism, traditional family values, individual competition, and substantial differences in wages to stimulate production, even as an earlier commitment to egalitarianism was substantially abandoned. Increasingly the invocation of revolutionary values was devoid of real content, and by the 1970s the perception of official hypocrisy was widespread.

The unique feature of Chinese history under Mao Zedong's leadership was a recurrent effort to combat these perhaps inevitable tendencies of any industrializing process and to revive and preserve the revolutionary spirit, which had animated the Communist Party during its long struggle for power. By the mid-1950s, Mao and some of his followers had become persuaded that the Soviet model of industrialization was leading China away from socialism and toward new forms of inequality, toward individualistic and careerist values, and toward an urban bias that privileged the cities at the expense of the countryside. The Great Leap Forward of 1958–1960 marked Mao's first response to these distortions of Chinese socialism. It promoted small-scale industrialization in the rural areas rather than focusing wholly on large enterprises in the cities; it tried to foster widespread and practical technological education for all rather than relying on a small elite of highly trained technical experts; and it envisaged an immediate transition to full communism in the "people's communes" rather than waiting for industrial development to provide the material basis for that transition. The disruptions and resentments occasioned by this Great Leap Forward, coupled with a series of droughts, floods, and typhoons, threw China into a severe crisis, including a massive famine that brought death and malnutrition to some 20 million people between 1959 and 1962.

In the mid-1960s, Mao launched yet another campaign—the Great Proletarian Cultural Revolution—to combat the capitalist tendencies that he believed had penetrated even the highest ranks of the Communist Party itself. The Cultural Revolution also involved new policies to bring health care and education to the countryside and to reinvigorate earlier efforts at rural industrialization under local rather than central control. In these ways, Mao struggled, though without great success, to overcome the inequalities associated with China's modern development and to create a model of socialist modernity quite distinct from that of the Soviet Union.

Substituting Manpower for Machinery
Lacking sophisticated equipment, Chinese communist leaders pursued a labor-intensive form of development, mobilizing the country's huge population in constructing the economic infrastructure for its industrial development. Here thousands of workers using ancient techniques participate in the building of a modern dam during China's Great Leap Forward in 1958. (Henry Cartier-Bresson/Magnum Photos)

The Search for Enemies

■ Explanation
Why did communist
regimes generate terror
and violence on such a
massive scale?

Despite their totalitarian tendencies, the communist societies of the Soviet Union and China were laced with conflict. Under both Stalin and Mao, those conflicts erupted in a search for enemies that disfigured both societies. An elastic concept of "enemy" came to include not only surviving remnants from the old prerevolutionary elites but also, and more surprisingly, high-ranking members and longtime supporters of the Communist Party who allegedly had been corrupted by bourgeois ideas. Refracted through the lens of Marxist thinking, these people became class enemies who had betrayed the revolution and were engaged in a vast conspiracy, often linked to foreign imperialists, to subvert the socialist enterprise and restore capitalism. In the rhetoric of the leadership, the class struggle continued and in fact intensified as the triumph of socialism drew closer.

In the Soviet Union, that process culminated in the Terror, or the Great Purges, of the late 1930s, which enveloped tens of thousands of prominent communists, including virtually all of Lenin's top associates, and millions of more ordinary people. Based on suspicious associations in the past, denunciations by colleagues, connections to foreign countries, or simply bad luck, such people were arrested, usually in the dead of night, and then tried and sentenced either to death or to long years in harsh and remote labor camps known as the gulag. Many of the accused were linked, almost always falsely, to the Nazis, who were then a real and growing external threat to the Soviet Union. A series of show trials publicized the threat that these "enemies of the people" allegedly posed to the country and its revolution. Close to 1 million people were executed between 1936 and 1941. Perhaps an additional 4 million or 5 million were sent to the gulag, where they were forced to work in horrendous conditions and died in appalling numbers. Victimizers too were numerous: the Terror consumed the energies of a huge corps of officials, investigators, interrogators, informers, guards, and executioners, many of whom themselves were arrested, exiled, or executed in the course of the purges.

In the Soviet Union, the search for enemies occurred under the clear control of the state. In China, however, it became a much more public process, escaping the control of the leadership, particularly during the Cultural Revolution of 1966–1969. Mao had become convinced that many within the Communist Party had been seduced by capitalist values of self-seeking and materialism and were no longer animated by the idealistic revolutionary vision of earlier times. Therefore, he called for rebellion, against the Communist Party itself. Millions of young people responded, and, organized as Red Guards, they set out to rid China of those who were "taking the capitalist road." Following gigantic and ecstatic rallies in Beijing, they fanned out across the country and attacked local party and government officials, teachers, intellectuals, factory managers, and others they defined as enemies. Rival revolutionary groups soon began fighting with one another, violence erupted throughout the country, and civil war threatened China. Mao found himself forced to call in the military to restore order and Communist Party control. Both the Soviet Terror and the Chinese Cultural

Revolution badly discredited the very idea of socialism and contributed to the ultimate collapse of the communist experiment at the end of the century.

East versus West: A Global Divide and a Cold War

Not only did communist regimes bring revolutionary changes to the societies they governed, but they also launched a global conflict that restructured international life and touched the lives of almost everyone, particularly in the twentieth century's second half. That rift began soon after the Russian Revolution when the new communist government became the source of fear and loathing to many in the Western capitalist world. The common threat of Nazi Germany temporarily made unlikely allies of the Soviet Union, Britain, and the United States, but a few years after World War II ended, that division erupted again in what became known as the cold war. Underlying that conflict were the geopolitical and ideological realities of the postwar world. The Soviet Union and the United States were now the major political/military powers, replacing the shattered and diminished states of Western Europe, but they represented sharply opposed views of history, society, politics, and international relations. Conflict, in retrospect, seemed almost inevitable.

Military Conflict and the Cold War

The initial arena of the cold war was Europe, where Soviet insistence on security and control in Eastern Europe clashed with American and British desires for open and democratic societies with ties to the capitalist world economy. What resulted were rival military alliances (NATO and the Warsaw Pact), a largely voluntary American sphere of influence in Western Europe, and an imposed Soviet sphere in Eastern Europe. The heavily fortified border between Eastern and Western Europe came to be known as the Iron Curtain. Thus Europe was bitterly divided; tensions flared across this dividing line, particularly in Berlin; but no shooting war occurred between the two sides (see Map 22.3).

■ **Connection**
In what different ways was the cold war expressed?

By contrast, the extension of communism into Asia—China, Korea, and Vietnam—globalized the cold war and led to its most destructive and prolonged "hot wars." A North Korean invasion of South Korea in 1950 led to both Chinese and American involvement in a bitter three-year war (1950–1953), which ended in an essential standoff that left the Korean peninsula divided still in the early twenty-first century. Likewise in Vietnam, military efforts by South Vietnamese communists and the already communist North Vietnamese government to unify their country prompted massive American intervention in the 1960s, peaking at some 550,000 U.S. troops. To American authorities, a communist victory opened the door to further communist expansion in Asia and beyond. Armed and supported by the Soviets and Chinese and willing to endure enormous losses, the Vietnamese communists bested the Americans, who were hobbled by growing protest at home. The Vietnamese united their country under communist control by 1975.

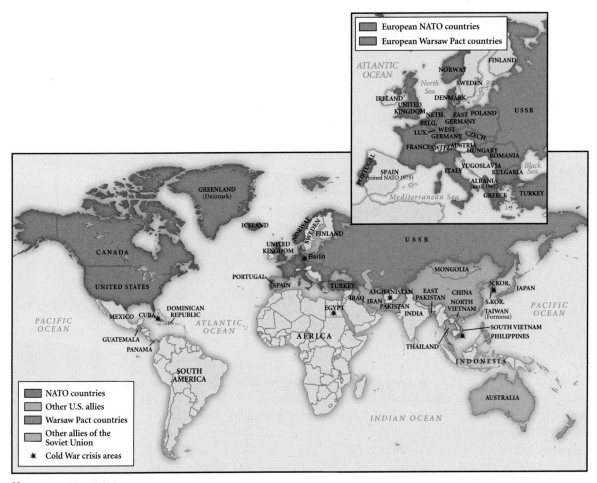

Map 22.3   The Global Cold War

The cold war sharply divided the world as a whole as well the continent of Europe; the countries of Korea, Vietnam, and Germany; and the city of Berlin. In many places, it also sparked crises that brought the nuclear-armed superpowers of the United States and the USSR to the brink of war, although in every case they managed to avoid direct military conflict between themselves.

A third major military conflict of the cold war era occurred in Afghanistan, where a Marxist party had taken power in 1978. Soviet leaders were delighted at this extension of communism on their southern border, but radical land reforms and efforts to liberate Afghan women soon alienated much of this conservative Muslim country and led to a mounting opposition movement. Fearing the overthrow of a new communist state and its replacement by Islamic radicals, Soviet forces intervened militarily and were soon bogged down in a war they could not win. For a full decade (1979–1989), that war was a "bleeding wound," sustained in part by U.S. aid to Afghan guerrillas. Under widespread international pressure, Soviet forces finally withdrew in 1989, and the Afghan communist regime soon collapsed. In Vietnam and Afghanistan, both superpowers painfully experienced the limits of their power.

The most haunting battle of the cold war era was the one that never happened. The setting was Cuba. When the revolutionary Fidel Castro came to power in 1959, his nationalization of American assets provoked great U.S. hostility and efforts to overthrow his regime. Such pressure only pushed this revolutionary nationalist closer to the Soviet Union, and gradually he began to think of himself and his revolution as Marxist. Soviet authorities were elated. "You Americans must realize what Cuba means to us old Bolsheviks," declared one high-ranking Soviet official. "We have been waiting all our lives for a country to go communist without the Red Army. It has happened in Cuba, and it makes us feel like boys again."[5] Fearing the loss of their newfound Caribbean ally to American aggression, the Soviet leader Nikita Khrushchev, who had risen to power after Stalin's death in 1953, secretly deployed nuclear-tipped Soviet missiles to Cuba, believing that this would deter further U.S. action against Castro. When the missiles were discovered in October 1962, the world held its breath for thirteen days as American forces blockaded the island and prepared for an invasion. A nuclear exchange between the superpowers seemed imminent, but that catastrophe was averted by a compromise between Khrushchev and U.S. president John F. Kennedy. Under the terms of that compromise, the Soviets removed their missiles from Cuba in return for an American promise not to invade the island.

Nuclear Standoff and Third World Rivalry

The Cuban missile crisis gave concrete expression to the most novel and dangerous dimension of the cold war—the arms race in nuclear weapons. An American monopoly on those weapons when World War II ended prompted the Soviet Union to redouble its efforts to acquire them, and in 1949 it succeeded. Over the next forty years, the world moved from a mere handful of nuclear weapons to a global arsenal of close to 60,000 warheads. Delivery systems included bomber aircraft and missiles that could rapidly propel numerous warheads across whole continents and oceans with accuracies measured in hundreds of feet. During those decades, the world's many peoples lived in the shadow of weapons whose destructive power is scarcely within the bounds of human imagination. A single bomb in a single instant could obliterate any major city in the world. The detonation of even a small fraction of the weapons then in the arsenals of the Soviet Union and the United States could reduce the target countries to radioactive rubble and social chaos. Responsible scientists seriously discussed the possible extinction of the human species under such conditions.

Awareness of this possibility is surely the primary reason that no shooting war of any kind occurred between the two

The Hydrogen Bomb
During the 1950s and early 1960s, tests in the atmosphere of ever larger and more sophisticated hydrogen bombs made images of enormous fireballs and mushroom-shaped clouds the universal symbol of these weapons, which were immensely more powerful than the atomic bombs dropped on Japan. The American test pictured here took place in 1957. (Image courtesy The Nuclear Weapon Archive)

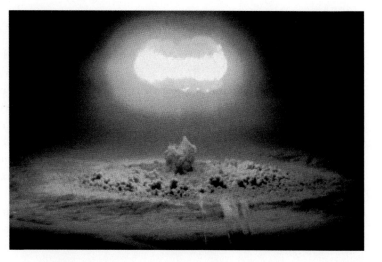

superpowers. During the two world wars, the participants had been greatly surprised by the destructiveness of modern weapons. During the cold war, however, the leaders of the two superpowers knew beyond any doubt that a nuclear war would produce only losers and utter catastrophe. Already in 1949, Stalin had observed that "atomic weapons can hardly be used without spelling the end of the world."[6] Furthermore, the deployment of reconnaissance satellites made it possible to know with some clarity the extent of the other side's arsenals. Particularly after the frightening Cuban missile crisis of 1962, both sides carefully avoided further nuclear provocation, even while continuing the buildup of their respective arsenals. Moreover, because they feared that a conventional war would escalate to the nuclear level, they implicitly agreed to sidestep any direct military confrontation at all.

Still, opportunities for conflict abounded as the U.S.-Soviet rivalry spanned the globe. Using military and economic aid, educational opportunities, political pressure, and covert action, both sides courted third world countries just emerging from colonial rule. Cold war fears of communist penetration prompted U.S. intervention, sometimes openly and often secretly, in Iran, the Philippines, Guatemala, El Salvador, Chile, the Congo, and elsewhere, and in the process the United States frequently supported anti-communist but corrupt and authoritarian regimes. However, neither superpower was able to completely dominate its supposed third-world allies, many of whom resisted the role of pawns in superpower rivalries. Some countries, such as India, took a posture of nonalignment in the cold war, while others tried to play off the superpowers against each other. Indonesia received large amounts of Soviet and Eastern European aid, but that did not prevent it from destroying the Indonesian Communist Party in 1965, butchering half a million suspected communists in the process. When the Americans refused to assist Egypt in building the Aswan Dam in the mid-1950s, that country developed a close relationship with the Soviet Union. Later, in 1972, Egypt expelled 21,000 Soviet advisers and aligned more clearly with the United States.

The United States: Superpower of the West, 1945–1975

■ Connection
In what ways did the United States play a global role after World War II?

World War II and the cold war provided the context for the emergence of the United States as a global superpower, playing a role that has often been compared to that of Great Britain in the nineteenth century. Much of that effort was driven by the perceived demands of the cold war, during which the United States spearheaded the Western effort to contain a worldwide communist movement that seemed to be on the move. A series of global alliances and military bases sought to create a barrier against further communist expansion and to provide launching points for military action should it become necessary. By 1970, one writer observed, "the United States had more than 1,000,000 soldiers in 30 countries, was a member of four regional defense alliances and an active participant in a fifth, had mutual defense treaties with 42 nations, was a member of 53 international organizations, and was furnishing military or economic aid to nearly 100 nations across the face of the globe."[7]

The need for quick and often secret decision making gave rise in the United States to a strong or "imperial" presidency and a "national security state," in which defense and intelligence agencies acquired great power within the government and were often unaccountable to Congress. With power so focused in the executive branch, critics charged that democracy itself was undermined. Fear of internal subversion produced an intense anticommunism in the 1950s and in general narrowed the range of political debate in the country as both parties competed to appear "tough on communism." All of this served to strengthen the influence of what U.S. president Dwight Eisenhower (1953–1961) called the "military-industrial complex," a coalition of the armed services, military research laboratories, and private defense industries that both stimulated and benefited from increased military spending and cold war tensions.

Sustaining this immense military effort was a flourishing U.S. economy and an increasingly middle-class society. Private spending for houses, automobiles, and durable goods as well as public spending for schools, superhighways, and cold war armaments spurred this remarkable growth. The United States, of course, was the only major industrial society to escape the physical devastation of war on its own soil. As World War II ended, the United States was the world's largest creditor, controlled two-thirds of the world's gold, and accounted for half of its manufacturing and shipping. "The whole world is hungry for American goods," wrote one American economist in 1945. "Everyone would like to have the opportunity of riding in American automobiles, of drinking American fruit juices, and of possessing electric refrigerators and other conveniences of life."[8] Americans were a "people of plenty," ready and willing "to show to other countries the path that may lead them to plenty like our own."[9] Beyond their goods, Americans sent their capital abroad in growing amounts—from $19 billion in 1950 to $81 billion in 1965. Huge American firms such as General Motors, Ford, Mobil, Sears, General Electric, and Westinghouse established factories, offices, and subsidiaries in many countries and sold their goods locally. The U.S. dollar replaced the British pound as the most trusted international currency.

Accompanying the United States' political and economic penetration of the world was its popular culture. In musical terms, first jazz, then rock-and-roll, and most recently rap have found receptive audiences abroad, particularly among the young. Blacks in South Africa took up American "Negro spirituals." In the Soviet Union, American rock-and-roll became the music of dissent and a way of challenging the values of communist culture. Muslim immigrants to France as well as young Japanese have developed local traditions of rap. By the 1990s, American movies took about 70 percent of the market in Europe, and some 20,000 McDonald's restaurants in 100 countries served 30 million customers every day. Various American brand names—Kleenex, Coca-Cola, Jeep, Spam, Nike, Kodak—became common points of reference around the world. English became a global language, while American slang terms—"groovy," "crazy," "cool"—were integrated into many of the world's languages.

The Communist World, 1950s–1970s

■ **Description**
Describe the strengths and weaknesses of the communist world by the 1970s.

On the communist side, the cold war was accompanied by considerable turmoil both within and among the various communist states. Joseph Stalin, Soviet dictator and acknowledged leader of the communist world in general, died in 1953 as that global conflict was mounting. His successor, Nikita Khrushchev, stunned his country and communists everywhere with a lengthy speech delivered to a party congress in 1956 in which he presented a devastating but incomplete account of Stalin's crimes, particularly those against party members. "Everywhere and in everything, he [Stalin] saw 'enemies,' 'two-facers,' and 'spies,'" declared Khrushchev. "Possessing unlimited power, he indulged in great willfulness and choked a person morally and physically."[10] These revelations shocked many of the party faithful, for Stalin had been viewed as the "genius of all time." Now he was presented as a criminal.

In the Soviet Union, the superpower of the communist world, the cold war justified a continuing emphasis on military and defense industries after World War II and gave rise to a Soviet version of the military-industrial complex. Sometimes called a "metal-eater's alliance," this complex joined the armed forces with certain heavy industries to press for a weapons buildup that benefited both. Soviet citizens, even more than Americans, were subject to incessant government propaganda that glorified the Soviet system and vilified that of their American opponents.

As the communist world expanded, so too did divisions and conflicts among its various countries. Many in the West had initially viewed world communism as a monolithic force whose disciplined members meekly followed Soviet dictates in cold war solidarity against the West. And Marxists everywhere contended that revolutionary socialism would erode national loyalties as the "workers of the world" united in common opposition to global capitalism. Nonetheless, the communist world experienced far more bitter and divisive conflict than did the Western alliance, which was composed of supposedly warlike, greedy, and highly competitive nations.

Czechoslovakia, 1968
In August 1968, Soviet forces invaded Czechoslovakia, where a popular reform movement proclaiming "socialism with a human face" threatened to erode established communist control. The Soviet troops that crushed this so-called Prague Spring were greeted by thousands of peaceful street demonstrators begging them to go home. (Bettmann/Corbis)

In Eastern Europe, Yugoslav leaders early on had rejected Soviet domination of their internal affairs and charted their own independent road to socialism. Fearing that reform movements might lead to contagious defections from the communist bloc, Soviet forces actually invaded their supposed allies in Hungary (1956–1957) and Czechoslovakia (1968) to crush such groups. In the early 1980s, Poland was seriously threatened with a similar action. The brutal suppression of these reform movements gave credibility to Western perceptions of the cold war as a struggle between tyranny and freedom and badly tarnished the image of Soviet communism as a reasonable alternative to capitalism.

Even more startling, the two communist giants, the Soviet Union and China, found themselves sharply opposed, owing to territorial disputes, ideological differences, and rivalry for communist leadership. The Chinese bitterly criticized Khrushchev for backing down in the Cuban missile crisis, while to the Soviet leadership, Mao was insanely indifferent to the possible consequences of a nuclear war. In 1960, the Soviet Union backed away from an earlier promise to provide China with the prototype of an atomic bomb and abruptly withdrew all Soviet advisers and technicians, who had been assisting Chinese development. By the late 1960s, China on its own had developed a modest nuclear capability, and the two countries were at the brink of war, with the Soviet Union hinting at a possible nuclear strike on Chinese military targets. Their enmity certainly benefited the United States, which in the 1970s was able to pursue a "triangular diplomacy," easing tensions and simultaneously signing arms control agreements with the USSR and opening a formal relationship with China. Beyond this central conflict, a communist China in fact went to war against a communist Vietnam in 1979, while Vietnam invaded a communist Cambodia in the late 1970s. Nationalism proved more powerful than communist solidarity, even in the face of cold war hostilities with the West.

Despite its many internal conflicts, world communism remained a powerful global presence during the 1970s, reaching the greatest extent of its worldwide expansion. China was emerging from the chaos of the Cultural Revolution. The Soviet Union had achieved its long-sought goal of matching U.S. military might; in response, the Americans launched a major buildup of their own military forces in the early 1980s. Despite American hostility, Cuba remained a communist outpost in the Western Hemisphere, with impressive achievements in education and health care for its people. Communism triumphed in Vietnam, dealing a major setback to the United States. A number of African countries affirmed their commitment to Marxism. Few people anywhere expected that within two decades most of the twentieth century's experiment with communism would be gone.

Comparing Paths to the End of Communism

More rapidly than its beginning, and far more peacefully, the communist era came to an end during the last two decades of the twentieth century. It was a drama in three acts. Act One began in China during the late 1970s, following the death of its towering revolutionary leader Mao Zedong in 1976. Over the next several decades, the CCP gradually abandoned almost everything that had been associated with Maoist socialism, even as the party retained its political control of the country. Act Two took place in Eastern Europe in the "miracle year" of 1989, when popular movements toppled despised communist governments one after another all across the region. The final and climactic act in this "end of communism" drama occurred in 1991 in the Soviet Union, where the entire "play" had opened seventy-four years

■ Change
What explains the rapid end of the communist era?

earlier. There the reformist leader Mikhail Gorbachev had come to power in 1985 intending to revive and save Soviet socialism from its accumulated dysfunctions. Those efforts, however, only exacerbated the country's many difficulties and led to its political disintegration on Christmas Day of 1991. The curtain had fallen on the communist era and on the cold war as well.

Behind these separate stories lay two general failures of the communist experiment, measured both by their own standards and by those of the larger world. The first was economic. Despite their early successes, communist economies by the late 1970s showed no signs of catching up to the more advanced capitalist countries. The highly regimented Soviet economy in particular was largely stagnant; its citizens were forced to stand in long lines for consumer goods and complained endlessly about their poor quality and declining availability. This was enormously embarrassing, for it had been the proud boast of communist leaders everywhere that they had found a better route to modern prosperity than their capitalist rivals. Furthermore, these comparisons were increasingly well known, thanks to the global information revolution. They had security implications as well, for economic growth, even more than military capacity, was the measure of state power as the twentieth century approached its end.

The second failure was moral. The horrors of Stalin's Terror and the gulag, of Mao's Cultural Revolution, of something approaching genocide in communist Cambodia — all of this wore away at communist claims to moral superiority over capitalism. Moreover, this erosion occurred as global political culture more widely embraced democracy and human rights as the universal legacy of humankind, rather than the exclusive possession of the capitalist West. In both economic and moral terms, the communist path to the modern world was increasingly seen as a road to nowhere.

Communist leaders were not ignorant of these problems, and particularly in China and the Soviet Union, they moved aggressively to address them. But their approach to doing so varied greatly, as did the outcomes of those efforts. Thus, much as the Russian and Chinese revolutions differed and their approaches to building socialism diverged, so too did these communist giants chart distinct paths during the final years of the communist era.

China: Abandoning Communism and Maintaining the Party

As the dust settled from the political shakeout following Mao's death in 1976, Deng Xiaoping emerged as China's "paramount leader," committed to ending the periodic upheavals of the Maoist era while fostering political stability and economic growth. Soon previously banned plays, operas, films, and translations of Western classics reappeared, and a "literature of the wounded" exposed the sufferings of the Cultural Revolution. Some 100,000 political prisoners, many of them high-ranking communists, were released and restored to important positions. A party evaluation of Mao severely criticized his mistakes during the Great Leap Forward and the Cultural Revolution, while praising his role as a revolutionary leader.

Even more dramatic were Deng's economic reforms. In the rural areas, these reforms included a rapid dismantling of the country's system of collectivized farming and a return to something close to small-scale private agriculture. Impoverished Chinese peasants eagerly embraced these new opportunities and pushed them even further than the government had intended. Industrial reform proceeded more gradually. Managers of state enterprises were given greater authority and encouraged to act like private owners, making many of their own decisions and seeking profits. China opened itself to the world economy and welcomed foreign investment in special enterprise zones along the coast, where foreign capitalists received tax breaks and other inducements. Local governments and private entrepreneurs joined forces in thousands of flourishing "township and village enterprises" that produced food, clothing, building materials, and much more.

The outcome of these reforms was stunning economic growth, the most rapid and sustained in world history, and a new prosperity for millions. Better diets, lower mortality rates, declining poverty, massive urban construction, and surging exports accompanied China's rejoining of the world economy, contributed to a much-improved material life for many of its citizens, and prompted much commentary about China as the economic giant of the twenty-first century. On the other hand, the country's burgeoning economy also generated massive corruption among Chinese officials, sharp inequalities between the coast and the interior, a huge problem of urban overcrowding, terrible pollution in major cities, and periodic inflation as the state loosened its controls over the economy. Urban vices such as street crime, prostitution, gambling, drug addiction, and a criminal underworld, which had been largely eliminated after 1949, surfaced again in China's booming cities. Nonetheless, something remarkable had occurred in China: an essentially capitalist economy had been restored, and by none other than the Communist Party itself. Mao's worst fears had been realized, as China "took the capitalist road."

Although the party was willing to largely abandon communist economic policies, it was adamantly unwilling to relinquish its political monopoly or to promote democracy at the national level. "Talk about democracy in the abstract," Deng Xiaoping declared, "will inevitably lead to the unchecked spread of ultra-democracy and anarchism, to the complete disruption of political stability, and to the total failure of our modernization program.... China will once again be plunged into chaos, division, retrogression, and darkness."[11] Such attitudes associated democracy with the chaos and uncontrolled mass action of the Cultural Revolution. Thus, when a

After Communism in China Although the Communist Party still governed China in the early twenty-first century, communist values of selflessness, community, and simplicity had been substantially replaced for many by Western-style consumerism. Here a group of young people in Shanghai are eating at a Kentucky Fried Chicken restaurant, drinking Pepsi, wearing clothing common to modern youth everywhere, and using their ubiquitous cell phones. (Mike Kemp/Corbis)

democracy movement, spearheaded by university and secondary school students, surfaced in the late 1980s, Deng ordered the brutal crushing of its brazen demonstration in Beijing's Tiananmen Square before the television cameras of the world.

China entered the new millennium as a rapidly growing economic power with an essentially capitalist economy presided over by an intact and powerful Communist Party. Culturally, some combination of nationalism, consumerism, and a renewed respect for ancient traditions had replaced the collectivist and socialist values of the Maoist era. It was a strange and troubled hybrid.

The Soviet Union: The Collapse of Communism and Country

■ **Comparison**

How did the end of communism in the Soviet Union differ from communism's demise in China?

By the mid-1980s, the reformist wing of the Soviet Communist Party, long squelched by an aging conservative establishment, had won the top position in the party as Mikhail Gorbachev assumed the role of general secretary. Like Deng Xiaoping in China, Gorbachev was committed to aggressively tackling the country's many problems—economic stagnation, a flourishing black market, public apathy, and cynicism about the party. His economic program, launched in 1987 and known as *perestroika* ("restructuring"), paralleled aspects of the Chinese approach by freeing state enterprises from the heavy hand of government regulation, permitting small-scale private businesses called cooperatives, offering opportunities for private farming, and cautiously welcoming foreign investment in joint enterprises.

Heavy resistance to these modest efforts from entrenched party and state bureaucracies persuaded Gorbachev to seek allies outside of official circles. The vehicle was *glasnost* ("openness"), a policy of permitting a much wider range of cultural and intellectual freedoms in Soviet life. He hoped that glasnost would overcome the pervasive, long-standing distrust between society and the state and would energize Soviet society for the tasks of economic reform. "We need *glasnost*," Gorbachev declared, "like we need the air."[12]

In the late 1980s, glasnost hit the Soviet Union like a bomb. Newspapers and TV exposed social pathologies that previously had been presented solely as the product of capitalism. Stories about social problems such as crime, prostitution, child abuse, suicide, corruption, and homelessness flooded the public media. Viewers learned that the abortion rate in the USSR was the highest in the world, and they discovered something of the degrading process of obtaining one. Films broke the ban on nudity and explicit sex. TV reporters climbed the wall of a secluded villa to film the luxurious homes of the party elite. Soviet history was also reexamined as revelations of Stalin's crimes poured out of the media. Mass graves were uncovered, and a former executioner described on camera precisely how he had shot people. The Bible and the Quran became more widely available, atheistic propaganda largely ceased, and thousands of churches and mosques were returned to believers and opened for worship. Plays, poems, films, and novels that had long been buried "in the drawer" were now released to a public that virtually devoured them. "Like an excited boy reads a note from his girl," wrote one poet, "that's how we read the papers today."[13]

Beyond glasnost lay democratization and a new parliament with real powers, chosen in competitive elections. When those elections occurred in 1989, dozens of leading communists were rejected at the polls. And when the new parliament met and actually debated controversial issues, its televised sessions were broadcast to a transfixed audience of 100 million or more. In foreign affairs, Gorbachev moved to end the cold war by making unilateral cuts in Soviet military forces, engaging in arms control negotiations with the United States, and, most important, refusing to intervene as communist governments in Eastern Europe were overthrown. Thus the Soviet reform program was far more broadly based than that of China, for it embraced dramatic cultural and political changes, which Chinese authorities refused to consider.

Despite his good intentions, almost nothing worked out as Gorbachev had anticipated. Far from strengthening socialism and reviving a stagnant Soviet Union, the reforms led to its further weakening and collapse. In a dramatic contrast with China's booming economy, that of the Soviet Union spun into a sharp decline as its planned economy was dismantled before a functioning market-based system could emerge. Inflation mounted; consumer goods were in short supply, and ration coupons reappeared; many feared the loss of their jobs. Unlike Chinese peasants, few Soviet farmers were willing to risk the jump into private farming, and few foreign investors found the Soviet Union a tempting place to do business.

Furthermore, the new freedoms provoked demands that went far beyond what Gorbachev had intended. A democracy movement of unofficial groups and parties now sprang to life, many of them seeking a full multiparty democracy and a capitalist economy. They were joined by independent labor unions, which actually went on strike, something unheard of in the "worker's state." Most corrosively, a multitude of nationalist movements used the new freedoms to insist on greater autonomy, or even independence, from the Soviet Union. In the Baltic republics of Latvia, Lithuania, and Estonia, nationalists organized a human chain some 370 miles long, sending the word "freedom" along the line of a million people. Even in Russia, growing numbers came to feel that they too might be better off without the Soviet Union. In the face of these mounting demands, Gorbachev resolutely refused to use force to crush the protesters, another sharp contrast with the Chinese experience.

Events in Eastern Europe now intersected with those in the Soviet Union. Gorbachev's reforms had lit a fuse in these Soviet satellites, where communism had been imposed and maintained from outside. If the USSR could practice glasnost and hold competitive elections, why not Eastern Europe as well? This was the background for the "miracle year" of 1989. Massive demonstrations, last-minute efforts at reforms, the breaching of the Berlin Wall, the surfacing of new political groups—all of this and more quickly overwhelmed the highly unpopular communist regimes of Poland, Hungary, East Germany, Bulgaria, Czechoslovakia, and Romania, which were quickly swept away. This success then emboldened nationalists and democrats in the Soviet Union. If communism had been overthrown in Eastern Europe, perhaps it was possible to do so in the USSR as well. Soviet conservatives and patriots, however, were outraged. To them, Gorbachev had stood idly by while the political gains of World War II, for which the Soviet Union had paid in rivers of blood, vanished before their eyes. It was nothing less than treason.

Gorbachev's perceived betrayal was just one of the grievances that motivated a short-lived conservative attempt to restore the old order in August 1991. Leading state, party, and military officials placed Gorbachev under house arrest, occupied Moscow with tanks and troops, and prepared for mass arrests, but popular resistance ensured that this effort collapsed within three days. Ironically, this failed coup energized those who sought an end to both communism and the Soviet Union, and by the end of the year, the Soviet Union and its communist regime had passed into history. From the wreckage of the Soviet Union emerged fifteen new and independent states, following the internal political divisions of the USSR (see Map 22.4). Within Russia itself, the Communist Party was actually banned for a time in the place of its origin. Once again, nationalism had trumped socialism.

The Soviet collapse represented a unique phenomenon in the world of the late twentieth century. Simultaneously, the world's largest state and its last territorial empire vanished; the first Communist Party disintegrated; a powerful command

Map 22.4 The Collapse of the Soviet Empire
Soviet control over its Eastern European dependencies vanished as those countries threw off their communist governments in 1989. Then, in 1991, the Soviet Union itself disintegrated into fifteen separate states, none of them governed by communist parties.

economy broke down; an official socialist ideology was repudiated; and a forty-five-year global struggle between the East and the West ended. In Europe, Germany was reunited, and a number of former communist states joined NATO and the European Union, ending the division of that continent. At least for the moment, capitalism and democracy seemed to triumph over socialism and authoritarian governments. In many places, the end of communism allowed simmering ethnic tensions to explode into open conflict. Beyond the disintegration of the Soviet Union, both Yugoslavia and Czechoslovakia fragmented, the former amid terrible violence and the latter peacefully. Chechens in Russia, Abkhazians in Georgia, Russians in the Baltic states and Ukraine, Tibetans in China—all of these "minorities" found themselves in opposition to the states in which they lived.

As the twenty-first century dawned, the communist world had shrunk considerably from its high point just three decades earlier. In the Soviet Union and Eastern Europe, communism had disappeared entirely as the governing authority and dominant ideology, although communist parties continued to play a role in some countries. China had largely abandoned its communist economic policies as a market economy took shape. Like China, Vietnam and Laos remained officially communist, even while they pursued Chinese-style reforms, though more cautiously. Even Cuba, which was beset by economic crisis in the 1990s after massive Soviet subsidies ended, allowed small businesses, private food markets, and tourism to grow, while harshly repressing opposition political groups. An impoverished North Korea remained the most unreformed and Stalinist of the remaining communist countries.

International tensions born of communism remained only in East Asia and the Caribbean. North Korea's threat to develop nuclear weapons posed a serious international issue. Continuing tension between China and Taiwan as well as between the United States and Cuba were hangovers from the cold war era. But either as a primary source of international conflict or as a compelling path to modernity and social justice, communism was effectively dead. The communist era in world history had ended.

Reflections: To Judge or Not to Judge: The Ambiguous Legacy of Communism

Should historians or students of history make moral judgments about the people and events they study? On the one hand, some would argue, scholars do well to act as detached and objective observers of the human experience, at least as much as possible. The task is to describe what happened and to explain why things turned out as they did. Whether we approve or condemn the outcomes of the historical process is, in this view, beside the point. On the other hand, all of us, scholars and students alike, stand somewhere. We are members of particular cultures; we have values and outlooks on the world that inevitably affect the way we write or think about the past. Perhaps it is better to recognize and acknowledge these limitations than to pretend some unattainable objectivity that places us above it all. Furthermore, making judgments is a way of connecting with the past, of affirming our continuing relationship with those who have gone before us. It shows that we care.

The question of making judgments arises strongly in any examination of the communist phenomenon. In a United States without a strong socialist tradition, sometimes saying anything positive about communism or even noting its appeal to millions of people has brought charges of whitewashing its crimes. Within the communist world, even modest criticism was usually regarded as counterrevolutionary and was largely forbidden and harshly punished. Certainly few observers were neutral in their assessment of the communist experiment.

Were the Russian and Chinese revolutions a blow for human freedom and a cry for justice on the part of oppressed people, or did they simply replace one tyranny with another? Was Stalinism a successful effort to industrialize a backward country or a ferocious assault on its moral and social fabric? Do Chinese reforms that were initiated in the late twentieth century represent a return to sensible policies of modernization, a continued denial of basic democratic rights, or an opening to capitalist inequalities, corruption, and acquisitiveness? Passionate debate continues on all of these questions.

Communism, like many human projects, has been an ambiguous enterprise. On the one hand, communism brought hope to millions by addressing the manifest injustices of the past; by providing new opportunities for women, workers, and peasants; by promoting rapid industrial development; and by ending Western domination. On the other hand, communism was responsible for mountains of crimes—millions killed and wrongly imprisoned; massive famines partly caused by radical policies; human rights violated on an enormous scale; lives uprooted and distorted by efforts to achieve the impossible.

Studying communism challenges our inclination to want definitive answers and clear moral judgments. Can we hold contradictory elements in some kind of tension? Can we affirm our own values while acknowledging the ambiguities of life, both past and present? Doing so is arguably among the essential tasks of growing up and achieving intellectual maturity. That is the gift, both painful and enormously enriching, that the study of history offers to us all.

Second Thoughts

What's the Significance?

To assess your mastery of the material in this chapter, see the **Online Study Guide** at bedfordstmartins.com/strayer.

Russian Revolution	Zhenotdel	Nikita Khrushchev
Bolsheviks/Lenin	collectivization	Mikhail Gorbachev
Guomindang	Cultural Revolution	Deng Xiaoping
Chinese Revolution	Stalin	perestroika/glasnost
Mao Zedong	Great Purges/Terror	
building socialism	Cuban missile crisis	

Big Picture Questions

1. What was the appeal of communism, in terms of both its promise and its achievements? To what extent did it fulfill that promise?
2. Why did the communist experiment, which was committed to equality and a humane socialism, generate such oppressive, brutal, and totalitarian regimes?
3. What is distinctive about twentieth-century communist industrialization and modernization compared to the same processes in the West a century earlier?
4. What was the global significance of the cold war?
5. "The end of communism was as revolutionary as its beginning." Do you agree with this statement?
6. In what different ways did the Soviet Union and China experience communism during the twentieth century?

Next Steps: For Further Study

Archie Brown, *The Gorbachev Factor* (1996). A careful examination of Gorbachev's role in the collapse of the Soviet Union.

Jung Chang, *Wild Swans* (2004). A compelling view of twentieth-century Chinese history through the eyes of three generations of women in a single family.

Timothy Check, *Mao Zedong and China's Revolutions* (2002). A collection of documents about the Chinese Revolution and a fine introduction to the life of Mao.

John L. Gaddis, *The Cold War: A New History* (2005). An overview by one of the most highly regarded historians of the cold war.

Peter Kenez, *A History of the Soviet Union from the Beginning to the End* (1999). A thoughtful overview of the entire Soviet experience.

Maurice Meisner, *Mao's China and After* (1999). A provocative history of Mao's China and what followed.

Robert Strayer, *The Communist Experiment: Revolution, Socialism, and Global Conflict in the Twentieth Century* (2007). A comparative study of Soviet and Chinese communism.

"Mao Zedong Reference Archive," http://www.marxists.org/reference/archive/mao. A Web site offering the translated writings of Mao, including poetry and some images.

"Soviet Archives Exhibit," http://www.ibiblio.org/expo/soviet.exhibit/entrance.html. A rich Web site from the Library of Congress, focusing on the operation of the Soviet system and relations with the United States.

For Web sites and documents related to this chapter, see **Make History** at bedfordstmartins.com/strayer.

CHAPTER TWENTY-THREE

Independence and Development in the Global South

1914- PRESENT

Toward Freedom: Struggles for Independence
  The End of Empire in World History
  Explaining African and Asian Independence
Comparing Freedom Struggles
  The Case of India: Ending British Rule
  The Case of South Africa: Ending Apartheid
Experiments with Freedom
  Experiments in Political Order: Comparing African Nations and India
  Experiments in Economic Development: Changing Priorities, Varying Outcomes
  Experiments with Culture: The Role of Islam in Turkey and Iran
Reflections: History in the Middle of the Stream

"During my lifetime I have dedicated myself to this struggle of the African people. I have fought against white domination, and I have fought against black domination. I have cherished the ideal of a democratic and free society in which all persons live together in harmony and with equal opportunity. It is an ideal which I hope to live for and to achieve. But, if need be, it is an ideal for which I am prepared to die."[1]

Nelson Mandela, South Africa's nationalist leader, first uttered these words in 1964 at his trial for treason, sabotage, and conspiracy to overthrow the apartheid government of his country. Convicted of those charges, he spent the next twenty-seven years in prison, sometimes working at hard labor in a stone quarry. Often the floor was his bed, and a bucket was his toilet. For many years, he was allowed one visitor a year for thirty minutes and permitted to write and receive one letter every six months. When he was finally released from prison in 1990 under growing domestic and international pressure, he concluded his first speech as a free person with the words originally spoken at his trial. Four years later in 1994, South Africa held its first election in which blacks and whites alike were able to vote. The outcome of that election made Mandela the country's first black African president, and it linked South Africa to dozens of other countries all across Africa and Asia that had thrown off European rule or the control of white settlers during the second half of the twentieth century.

THAT PROCESS—VARIOUSLY CALLED THE STRUGGLE FOR INDEPENDENCE OR DECOLONIZATION—was immensely significant. It marked a dramatic

Nelson Mandela: In April 1994, the long struggle against apartheid and white domination in South Africa came to an end in the country's first democratic and nonracial election. The symbol of that triumph was Nelson Mandela, long a political prisoner, head of the African National Congress, and the country's first black African president. He is shown here voting in that historic election. (Peter Turnley/Corbis)

change in the world's political architecture, as nation-states triumphed over the empires that had structured much of African and Asian life in the nineteenth and early twentieth centuries. It mobilized millions of people, thrusting them into political activity and sometimes into violence and warfare. Decolonization signaled the declining legitimacy of both empire and race as credible bases for political or social life. It promised not only national freedom but also personal dignity, abundance, and opportunity.

What followed in the decades after independence was equally significant. Political, economic, and cultural experiments proliferated across these newly independent nations, which during the cold war were labeled as the third world and now are often referred to as developing countries or the Global South. Their peoples, who represented the vast majority of the world's population, faced enormous challenges: the legacies of empire; their own deep divisions of language, ethnicity, religion, and class; their rapidly growing numbers; the competing demands of the capitalist West and the communist East; the difficult tasks of simultaneously building modern economies, stable politics, and coherent nations; and all of this in a world still shaped by the powerful economies of the wealthy, already industrialized nations. The emergence of the developing countries onto the world stage as independent and assertive actors has been a distinguishing feature of world history in this most recent century.

Toward Freedom: Struggles for Independence

In 1900, European colonial empires in Africa and Asia appeared as permanent features of the world's political landscape. Well before the end of the twentieth century, they were gone. The first major breakthroughs occurred in Asia and the Middle East in the late 1940s, when India, Pakistan, Burma, Indonesia, Iraq, Jordan, and Israel achieved independence. The period from the mid-1950s through the mid-1970s was the age of African independence as colony after colony, more than fifty in total, emerged into what was then seen as the bright light of freedom (see Map 23.1, p. 694).

The End of Empire in World History

■ Comparison
What was distinctive about the end of Europe's African and Asian empires compared to other cases of imperial disintegration?

At one level, this vast process was but the latest case of imperial dissolution, a fate that had overtaken earlier empires, including the Assyrian, Roman, Arab, and Mongol empires. But never before had the end of empire been so associated with the mobilization of the masses around a nationalist ideology; nor had these earlier cases generated a plethora of nation-states, each claiming an equal place in a world of nation-states. More comparable perhaps was that first decolonization, in which the European colonies in the Americas threw off British, French, Spanish, or Portuguese rule during the late eighteenth and early nineteenth centuries (see Chapter 17). Like their twentieth-century counterparts, these new nations claimed an international status equivalent to that of their former rulers. In the Americas, however, many of the colonized people were themselves of European origin, sharing much of their culture with their colonial rulers. In that respect, the African and Asian struggles of the twentieth century were very different, for they not only asserted political independence but also affirmed the vitality of their cultures, which had been submerged and denigrated during the colonial era.

The twentieth century witnessed the demise of many empires. The Austrian and Ottoman empires collapsed following World War I, giving rise to a number of new states in Europe and the Middle East. The Russian Empire also unraveled, although it was soon reassembled, under the auspices of the Soviet Union. World War II ended the German and Japanese empires. African and Asian movements for independence shared with these other "end of empire" stories the ideal of national self-determination. This novel idea—that humankind was naturally divided into distinct peoples or nations, each of which deserved an independent state of its own—was loudly proclaimed by the winning side of both world wars. The belief in national self-determination gained a global following in the twentieth century and rendered empire illegitimate in the eyes of growing numbers of people.

Empires without territory, such as the powerful influence that the United States exercised in Latin America and elsewhere, likewise came under attack from highly nationalist governments. An intrusive U.S. presence was certainly one factor stimulating the Mexican Revolution, which began in 1910. One of the outcomes of that upheaval was the nationalization in 1937 of Mexico's oil industry, much of which was owned by American and British investors. Similar actions accompanied Cuba's revolution of 1959–1960 and also occurred in other places throughout Latin America and elsewhere. National self-determination likewise lay behind the disintegration of the Soviet Union in 1991, when the last of the major territorial empires of the twentieth century came to an inglorious end with the birth of fifteen new states. Although the winning of political independence for Europe's African and Asian colonies was perhaps the most spectacular challenge to empire in the twentieth century, that achievement was part of a larger pattern in modern world history (see Map 23.1).

Explaining African and Asian Independence

As the twentieth century closed, the end of European empires seemed an almost "natural" phenomenon, for colonial rule had lost any credibility as a form of political order. What could be more natural than for people to seek to rule themselves? Yet at the beginning of the century, few observers were predicting the collapse of these empires, and the idea that "the only legitimate government is self-government" was not nearly so widespread as it subsequently became. This situation has presented historians with a problem of explanation—how to account for the fall of European colonial empires and the emergence of dozens of new nation-states.

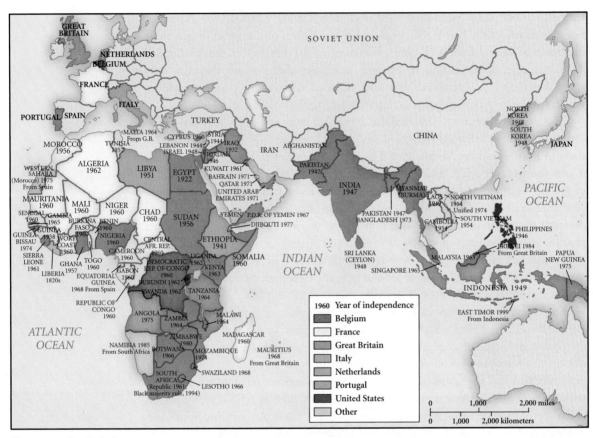

Map 23.1   The End of European Empires
In the second half of the twentieth century, under pressure from nationalist movements, Europe's Asian and African empires dissolved into dozens of new independent states.

■ Change
What international circumstances and social changes contributed to the end of colonial empires?

One approach to explaining the end of colonial empires focuses attention on fundamental contradictions in the entire colonial enterprise that arguably rendered its demise more or less inevitable. The rhetoric of both Christianity and material progress sat awkwardly with the realities of colonial racism, exploitation, and poverty. The increasingly democratic values of European states ran counter to the essential dictatorship of colonial rule. The ideal of national self-determination was profoundly at odds with the possession of colonies that were denied any opportunity to express their own national character. The enormously powerful force of nationalism, having earlier driven the process of European empire building, now played a major role in its disintegration. Colonial rule, in this argument, dug its own grave.

But why did this "fatal flaw" of European colonial rule lead to independence in the post–World War II era rather than earlier or later? In explaining the timing of the end of empire, historians frequently use the notion of "conjuncture," the coming together of several separate developments at a particular time. At the international level, the world wars had weakened Europe, while discrediting any sense of European moral superiority. Both the United States and the Soviet Union, the new global superpowers, generally opposed the older European colonial empires.

Meanwhile, the United Nations provided a prestigious platform from which to conduct anticolonial agitation. All of this contributed to the global illegitimacy of empire, a moral transformation that was enormously encouraging to Africans and Asians seeking political independence.

At the same time, social and economic circumstances within the colonies themselves generated the human raw material for anticolonial movements. By the early twentieth century in Asia and the mid-twentieth century in Africa, a second or third generation of Western-educated elites, largely male, had arisen throughout the colonial world. These young men were thoroughly familiar with European culture, were deeply aware of the gap between its values and its practices, no longer viewed colonial rule as a vehicle for their peoples' progress as their fathers had, and increasingly insisted on independence now. Moreover, growing numbers of ordinary people also were receptive to this message. Veterans of the world wars; young people with some education but no jobs commensurate with their expectations; a small class of urban workers who were increasingly aware of their exploitation; small-scale traders resentful of European privileges; rural dwellers who had lost land or suffered from forced labor; impoverished and insecure newcomers to the cities—all of these groups had reason to believe that independence held great promise.

A third approach to explaining the end of colonial empires puts the spotlight squarely on particular groups or individuals whose deliberate actions brought down the colonial system. Here the emphasis is on the "agency"—the deliberate initiatives—of historical actors rather than on impersonal contradictions or conjunctures. But which set of actors were most important in this end-of-empire drama?

Particularly in places such as West Africa or India, where independence occurred peacefully and through a negotiated settlement, the actions of colonial rulers have received considerable attention from historians. As the twentieth century wore on, these rulers were increasingly on the defensive and were actively planning for a new political relationship with their Asian and African colonies. With the colonies integrated into a global economic network and with local elites now modernized and committed to maintaining those links, outright colonial rule seemed less necessary to many Europeans. It was now possible to imagine retaining profitable economic interests in Asia and Africa without the expense and bother of formal colonial government. Deliberate planning for decolonization included gradual political reforms; investments in railroads, ports, and telegraph lines; the holding of elections; and the writing of constitutions. To some observers, it seemed as if independence was granted by colonial rulers rather than gained or seized by nationalist movements.

But these reforms and, ultimately, independence itself occurred only under considerable pressure from mounting nationalist movements. Creating such movements was no easy task. Political leaders, drawn from the ranks of the educated few, organized political parties, recruited members, plotted strategy, developed an ideology, and negotiated with one another and with the colonial state. The most prominent among them became the "fathers" of their new countries as independence

■ **Description**
What obstacles confronted the leaders of movements for independence?

dawned—Mahatma Gandhi and Jawaharlal Nehru in India, Sukarno in Indonesia, Ho Chi Minh in Vietnam, Kwame Nkrumah in Ghana, and Nelson Mandela in South Africa. In places where colonial rule was particularly intransigent—settler-dominated colonies and Portuguese territories, for example—leaders also directed military operations and administered liberated areas.

Agency within nationalist movements was not limited to leaders and the educated few. Millions of ordinary people decided to join Gandhi's nonviolent campaigns; tens of thousands of freedom fighters waged guerrilla warfare in Algeria, Kenya, Mozambique, and Zimbabwe; workers went on strike; market women in West Africa joined political parties, as did students, farmers, and the unemployed. In short, the struggle for independence did not happen automatically. It was deliberately made by the conscious personal choices of innumerable individuals across Asia and Africa.

In some places, that struggle produced independence within a few years, four in the case of the Belgian Congo. Elsewhere it was measured in decades. But everywhere it was a contested process. Those efforts were rarely if ever cohesive movements of uniformly oppressed people. More often they were fragile alliances of conflicting groups and parties representing different classes, ethnic groups, religions, or regions. Beneath the common goal of independence, they struggled with one another over questions of leadership, power, strategy, ideology, and the distribution of material benefits, even as they fought and negotiated with their colonial rulers. The very notion of "national self-government" posed obvious but often contentious questions: What group of people constituted the "nation" that deserved to rule itself? And who should speak for it?

Comparing Freedom Struggles

Two of the most extended freedom struggles—in India and South Africa—illustrate both the variations and the complexity of this process, which was so central to twentieth-century world history. India was among the first colonies to achieve independence and provided both a model and an inspiration to others, whereas South Africa, though not formally a colony, was among the last to throw off political domination by whites.

The Case of India: Ending British Rule

■ Change
How did India's nationalist movement change over time?

Surrounded by the Himalayas and the Indian Ocean, the South Asian peninsula, commonly known as India, enjoyed a certain geographic unity. But before the twentieth century few of its people thought of themselves as "Indians." Cultural identities were primarily local and infinitely varied, rooted in differences of family, caste, village, language, region, tribe, and religious practice. Various efforts in earlier centuries—during the Mauryan, Gupta, and Mughal empires, for example—had briefly brought large areas of the subcontinent within a single political system, but always these were imperial overlays, constructed on top of enormously diverse Indian societies.

So too was British colonial rule, but the British differed from earlier invaders in ways that promoted a growing sense of Indian identity. Unlike previous foreign rulers, the British never assimilated into Indian society because their acute sense of racial and cultural distinctiveness kept them apart. This served to intensify Indians' awareness of their collective difference from their alien rulers. Furthermore, British railroads, telegraph lines, postal services, administrative networks, newspapers, and schools as well as the English language bound India's many regions and peoples together more firmly than ever before and facilitated communication among its educated elite. Early-nineteenth-century cultural nationalists, seeking to renew and reform Hinduism, registered this sense of India as a cultural unit.

The most important political expression of an all-Indian identity took shape in the Indian National Congress (INC), which was established in 1885. This was an association of English-educated Indians—lawyers, journalists, teachers, business-men—drawn overwhelmingly from regionally prominent high-caste Hindu families. Its founding represented the beginning of a new kind of political protest, quite different from the rebellions, banditry, and refusal to pay taxes that had periodically erupted in the rural areas of colonial India. The INC was largely an urban phenomenon and quite moderate in its demands. Initially, its well-educated members did not seek to overthrow British rule; rather they hoped to gain greater inclusion within the political, military, and business life of British India. From such positions of influence, they argued, they could better protect the interests of India than could their foreign-born rulers. The British mocked their claim to speak for ordinary Indians, referring to them as "babus," a derogatory term that implied a semiliterate "native" with only a thin veneer of modern education.

Even in the first two decades of the twentieth century, the INC remained largely an elite organization; as such, it had difficulty gaining a mass following among India's vast peasant population. That began to change in the aftermath of World War I. To attract Indian support for the war effort, the British in 1917 had promised "the gradual development of self-governing institutions," a commitment that energized nationalist politicians to demand more rapid political change. Furthermore, British attacks on the Islamic Ottoman Empire antagonized India's Muslims. The end of the war was followed by a massive influenza epidemic, which cost the lives of millions of Indians. Finally, a series of repressive actions, including the killing of some 400 people who had defied a ban on public meetings to celebrate a

Mahatma Gandhi
The most widely recognized and admired figure in the global struggle against colonial rule was India's Mahatma Gandhi. In this famous photograph, he is sitting cross-legged on the floor, clothed in a traditional Indian garment called a *dhoti*, while nearby stands a spinning wheel, symbolizing the independent and nonindustrial India that Gandhi sought. (Margaret Bourke-White/Time Life Pictures/Getty Images)

Hindu festival in the city of Amritsar, antagonized many. This was the context in which Mohandas Gandhi (1869–1948) arrived on the Indian political scene and soon transformed it.

■ Change
What was the role of Gandhi in India's struggle for independence?

Gandhi was born in the province of Gujarat in western India to a pious Hindu family of the Vaisya, or business, caste. He was married at the age of thirteen, had only a mediocre record as a student, and eagerly embraced an opportunity to study law in England when he was eighteen. He returned as a shy and not very successful lawyer, and in 1893 he accepted a job with an Indian firm in South Africa, where a substantial number of Indians had migrated as indentured laborers during the nineteenth century. While in South Africa, Gandhi personally experienced overt racism for the first time and as a result soon became involved in organizing Indians, mostly Muslims, to protest that country's policies of racial segregation. He also developed a concept of India that included Hindus and Muslims alike and pioneered strategies of resistance that he would later apply in India itself. His emerging political philosophy, known as *satyagraha* ("truth force"), was an active and confrontational, though nonviolent, approach to political action. As Gandhi argued,

> Non-violence means conscious suffering. It does not mean meek submission to the will of the evil-doer, but it means the pitting of one's whole soul against the will of the tyrant.... [I]t is possible for a single individual to defy the whole might of an unjust empire to save his honour, his religion, his soul.[2]

Returning to India in 1914, Gandhi quickly rose within the leadership ranks of the INC. During the 1920s and 1930s, he applied his approach in periodic mass campaigns that drew support from an extraordinarily wide spectrum of Indians—peasants and the urban poor, intellectuals and artisans, capitalists and socialists, Hindus and Muslims. The British responded with periodic repression as well as concessions that allowed a greater Indian role in political life. Gandhi's conduct and actions—his simple and unpretentious lifestyle, his support of Muslims, his frequent reference to Hindu religious themes—appealed widely in India and transformed the INC into a mass organization. To many ordinary people, Gandhi possessed magical powers and produced miraculous events. He was the Mahatma, the Great Soul.

His was a radicalism of a different kind. He did not call for social revolution but sought the moral transformation of individuals. He worked to raise the status of India's untouchables (the lowest and most ritually polluting groups within the caste hierarchy), although he launched no attack on caste in general and accepted support from capitalists and socialists alike. His critique of India's situation went far beyond colonial rule. "India is being ground down," he argued, "not under the English heel, but under that of modern civilization"—its competitiveness, its materialism, its warlike tendencies, its abandonment of religion.[3] Almost alone among nationalist leaders in India or elsewhere, Gandhi opposed a modern industrial future for his country, seeking instead a society of harmonious self-sufficient villages drawing on ancient Indian principles of duty and morality.

Gandhi and the INC or Congress Party leadership had to contend with a wide range of movements, parties, and approaches, whose very diversity tore at the national unity that they so ardently sought. Whereas Gandhi rejected modern industrialization, his own chief lieutenant, Jawaharlal Nehru, thoroughly embraced science, technology, and industry as essential to India's future. Nor did everyone accept Gandhi's nonviolence or his inclusive definition of India. A militant Hindu organization preached hatred of Muslims and viewed India as an essentially Hindu nation. To some in the Congress Party, movements to improve the position of women or untouchables seemed a distraction from the chief task of gaining independence from Britain. Whether to participate in British-sponsored legislative bodies without complete independence also became a divisive issue. Furthermore, a number of smaller parties advocated on behalf of particular regions or castes. India's nationalist movement, in short, was beset by division and controversy.

By far the most serious threat to a unified movement derived from the growing divide between the country's Hindu and Muslim populations. As early as 1906, the formation of an All-India Muslim League contradicted the Congress Party's claim to speak for all Indians. As the British allowed more elected Indian representatives on local councils, the League demanded separate electorates, with a fixed number of seats on local councils for Muslims. As a distinct minority within India, some Muslims feared that their voice could be swamped by a numerically dominant Hindu population, despite Gandhi's inclusive philosophy. Some Hindu politicians confirmed those fears when they cast the nationalist struggle in Hindu religious terms, hailing their country, for example, as a goddess, *Bande Mataram* (Mother India). When elections in 1937 gave the Congress Party control of many provincial governments, some of those governments began to enforce the teaching of Hindi in schools and to protect cows from slaughter, both of which antagonized Muslims.

As the movement for independence gained ground, the Muslim League and its leader, Muhammad Ali Jinnah, increasingly argued that those parts of India that had a Muslim majority should have a separate political status. They called it Pakistan, the land of the pure. In this view, India was not a single nation, as Gandhi had long argued. Jinnah put his case succinctly:

> The Muslims and Hindus belong to two different religious philosophies, social customs, and literatures. They neither intermarry nor interdine [eat] together and, indeed, they belong to two different civilizations.[4]

With great reluctance and amid mounting violence, Gandhi and the Congress Party finally agreed to partition as the British declared their intention to leave India after World War II.

Thus colonial India became independent in 1947 as two countries—a Muslim Pakistan, itself divided into two wings 1,000 miles apart, and a secular but mostly Hindu India. Dividing

■ **Description**
What conflicts and differences divided India's nationalist movement?

The Independence of British South Asia

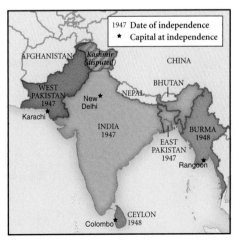

colonial India in this fashion was horrendously painful. A million people or more died in the communal violence that accompanied partition, and some 12 million refugees moved from one country to the other to join their religious compatriots. Gandhi himself, desperately trying to stem the mounting tide of violence in India's villages, refused to attend the independence celebrations. He was assassinated in 1948 by a Hindu extremist. The great triumph of independence, secured from the powerful British Empire, was shadowed by an equally great tragedy in the violence of partition.

■ **Comparison**
Why was African majority rule in South Africa delayed until 1994, whereas the overthrow of European colonialism had occurred much earlier in the rest of Africa and Asia?

The Case of South Africa: Ending Apartheid

The setting for South Africa's freedom struggle was very different from the situation in India. In the twentieth century, that struggle was not waged against an occupying European colonial power, for South Africa had in fact been independent of Great Britain since 1910. That independence, however, had been granted to a government wholly controlled by a white settler minority, which represented less than

$\mathcal{S}$napshot   **Key Moments in South African History**

Earliest humans in South Africa	by 50,000 years ago
Arrival of iron-using, Bantu-speaking agricultural peoples	by 500 C.E.
First Dutch settlement	1652
Shaka and creation of a Zulu state	early 19th century
British takeover of South Africa	1806
Great Trek: Afrikaner migration to the interior to escape more liberal British rule	1830s
European conquest of interior African societies	mid- to late 19th century
Gold and diamond mining begins	late 19th century
Great Britain defeats Afrikaners in Boer War	1899–1902
South Africa independent under white minority government	1910
African National Congress established	1912
National Party comes to power; apartheid formally established	1948
Sharpville massacre	1960
ANC launches armed struggle	1961
Black Consciousness movement; urban insurrection	1970s
Nelson Mandela released from prison	1990
ANC comes to power following first all-race elections	1994

20 percent of the total population; the country's black African majority had no political rights whatever within the central state. Black South Africans' struggle therefore was against this internal opponent rather than against a distant colonial authority, as in India. Economically, the most prominent whites were of British descent; they or their forebears had come to South Africa during the nineteenth century, when Great Britain was the ruling colonial power. But the politically dominant section of the white community, known as Boers or Afrikaners, was descended from the early Dutch settlers, who had arrived in the mid-seventeenth century. The term "Afrikaner" reflected their image of themselves as "white Africans," permanent residents of the continent rather than colonial intruders. They had unsuccessfully sought independence from a British-ruled South Africa in a bitter struggle (the Boer War, 1899–1902), and a sense of difference and antagonism lingered. Despite a certain hostility between white South Africans of British and Afrikaner background, both felt that their way of life and standard of living were jeopardized by any move toward black African majority rule. The intransigence of this sizable and threatened settler community helps explain why African rule was delayed until 1994, while India, lacking any such community, had achieved independence almost a half century earlier.

Unlike a predominantly agrarian India, South Africa by the early twentieth century had developed a mature industrial economy, based initially in gold and diamond mining, but by midcentury including secondary industries such as steel, chemicals, automobile manufacturing, rubber processing, and heavy engineering. Particularly since the 1960s, the economy benefited from extensive foreign investment and loans. Almost all black Africans were involved in this complex modern economy, working in urban industries or mines, providing labor for white-owned farms, or receiving payments from relatives who did. The extreme dependence of most Africans on the white-controlled economy rendered individuals highly vulnerable to repressive action, but collectively the threat to withdraw their essential labor also gave them a powerful weapon.

A third unique feature of the South African situation was the overwhelming prominence of race, expressed most clearly in the policy of apartheid, which attempted to separate blacks from whites in every conceivable way while retaining their labor power in the white-controlled economy. An enormous apparatus of repression enforced that system. Rigid "pass laws" monitored and tried to control the movement of Africans into the cities, where they were subjected to extreme forms of social segregation. In the rural areas, a series of impoverished and overcrowded "native reserves," or Bantustans, served as ethnic homelands that kept Africans divided along tribal lines. Even though racism was present in colonial India, nothing of this magnitude developed there.

As in India, various forms of opposition—such as resistance to conquest, rural rebellions, urban strikes, and independent churches—arose to contest the manifest injustices of South African life. There too an elite-led political party provided an organizational umbrella for many of the South African resistance

■ Change
How did South Africa's struggle against white domination change over time?

efforts in the twentieth century. Established in 1912, the African National Congress (ANC), like its Indian predecessor, was led by educated, professional, and middle-class Africans who sought, not to overthrow the existing order, but to be accepted as "civilized men" within that society. They appealed to the liberal, humane, and Christian values that white society claimed. For four decades, its leaders pursued peaceful and moderate protest—petitions, multiracial conferences, delegations appealing to the authorities—even as racially based segregationist policies were implemented one after another. By 1948, when the Afrikaner-led National Party came to power on a platform of apartheid, it was clear that such "constitutional" protest had produced nothing.

During the 1950s, a new and younger generation of the ANC leadership, which now included Nelson Mandela, broadened its base of support and launched nonviolent civil disobedience—boycotts, strikes, demonstrations, and the burning of the hated passes that all Africans were required to carry. All of these actions were similar to and inspired by the tactics that Gandhi had used in India twenty to thirty years earlier. The government of South Africa responded with tremendous repression, including the shooting of sixty-nine unarmed demonstrators at Sharpville in 1960, the banning of the ANC, and the imprisonment of its leadership. This was the context in which Mandela was arrested and sentenced to his long prison term.

Independence in Kenya, East Africa
Almost everywhere in the colonial world, the struggle for independence climaxed in a formal and joyful ceremony in which power was transferred from the colonial authority to the leader of the new nation. Here a jubilant Jomo Kenyatta takes the oath of office in 1964 as Kenya's first president, while a dour and bewigged British official looks on. (Bettmann/Corbis)

At this point, the freedom struggle in South Africa took a different direction than it had in India. Its major political parties were now illegal. Underground nationalist leaders turned to armed struggle, authorizing selected acts of sabotage and assassination, while preparing for guerrilla warfare in camps outside the country. Active opposition within South Africa was now primarily expressed by student groups that were part of the Black Consciousness movement, an effort to foster pride, unity, and political awareness among the country's African majority. Such young people were at the center of an explosion of protest in 1976 in a sprawling, segregated, impoverished black neighborhood called Soweto, outside Johannesburg, in which hundreds were killed. The initial trigger for the uprising was the government's decision to enforce education for Africans in the hated language of the white Afrikaners rather than English. However, the momentum of the Soweto rebellion persisted, and by the mid-1980s, spreading urban violence and the radicalization of urban young people had forced the government to declare a state of emergency. Furthermore, South Africa's black labor movement, legalized only in 1979, became increasingly active and political. In June 1986, to commemorate the tenth anniversary of the Soweto uprising, the Congress of South African Trade Unions orchestrated a general strike involving some 2 million workers.

Beyond this growing internal pressure, South Africa faced mounting international demands to end apartheid as well. A variety of responses to apartheid—exclusion from most international sporting events, including the Olympics; the refusal of many artists and entertainers to perform in South Africa; economic boycotts; the withdrawal of private investment funds—isolated South Africa from a Western world in which its white rulers claimed membership. This was another feature of the South African freedom movement that had no parallel in India.

The combination of these internal and external pressures persuaded many white South Africans by the late 1980s that discussion with African nationalist leaders was the only alternative to a massive, bloody, and futile struggle to preserve white privileges. The outcome was the abandonment of key apartheid policies, the release of Nelson Mandela from prison, the legalization of the ANC, and a prolonged process of negotiations that in 1994 resulted in national elections, which brought the ANC to power. To the surprise of almost everyone, the long nightmare of South African apartheid came to an end without a racial bloodbath (see Map 23.2).

As in India, the South African nationalist movement that finally won freedom was divided and conflicted. Unlike India, though, these divisions did not occur along religious lines. Rather it was race, ethnicity, and ideology that generated dissension and sometimes violence. Whereas the ANC generally favored a broad alliance of everyone opposed to apartheid (black Africans, Indians, "coloreds" or mixed-race people, and sympathetic whites), a smaller group known as the Pan Africanist Congress rejected cooperation with other racial groups and limited its membership to black Africans. During the urban uprisings of the 1970s and 1980s, young people supporting the Black Consciousness movements and those following Mandela and the ANC waged war against each other in the townships of South African cities. Perhaps most threatening to the unity of the nationalist struggle were the separatist tendencies of the Zulu-based Inkatha Freedom Party. Its leader, Gatsha Buthelezi, had cooperated with the apartheid state and even received funding from it. As negotiations for a transition to African rule unfolded in the early 1990s, considerable violence between Inkatha followers, mostly Zulu migrant workers, and ANC supporters broke out in a number of cities. None of this, however, approached the massive killing of Hindus and Muslims that accompanied the partition of India. South Africa, unlike India, acquired its political freedom as an intact and unified state.

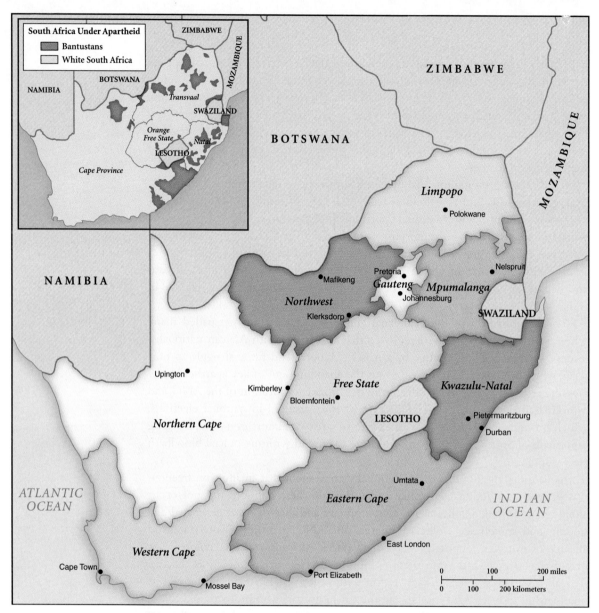

Map 23.2 South Africa after Apartheid
Under apartheid, all black Africans were officially designated as residents of small, scattered, impoverished Bantustans, shown on the inset map. Many black Africans, of course, actually lived in white South Africa, where they worked. The main map shows the new internal organization of the country as it emerged after 1994, with the Bantustans abolished and the country divided into nine provinces.

Experiments with Freedom

Africa's first modern nationalist hero, Kwame Nkrumah of Ghana, paraphrased a biblical quotation when he urged his followers, "Seek ye first the political kingdom and all these other things will be added unto you." However, would winning the political kingdom of independence or freedom from European rule really produce "all these other things"—opportunity for political participation, industrial growth and economic development, reasonably unified nations, and a better life for all? That was the central question confronting the new nations emerging from colonial rule. They were joined in that quest by already independent but nonindustrialized countries and regions such as China, Thailand, Ethiopia, Iran, Turkey, and Central and South America. Together they formed the bloc of nations known variously as the third world, the developing countries, or the Global South (see Map 23.3). In the second half of the twentieth century, these countries represented perhaps 75 percent of the world's population. They accounted for almost all of the fourfold increase in human numbers that the world experienced during the twentieth century. That immense surge in global population, at one level a great triumph for the human species, also underlay many of the difficulties these nations faced as they conducted their various experiments with freedom.

Almost everywhere, the moment of independence generated something close to euphoria. Having emerged from the long night of colonial rule, free peoples

Map 23.3   The "Worlds" of the Twentieth Century During the cold war, the term "third world" referred to those countries not solidly in either the Western or the Communist bloc of nations. Gradually it came to designate developing countries, those less wealthy and less industrialized societies seeking to catch up to the more developed countries of Europe, North America, and Japan. China, Vietnam, and Cuba, although governed by communist regimes, have been widely regarded as part of the developing world as well.

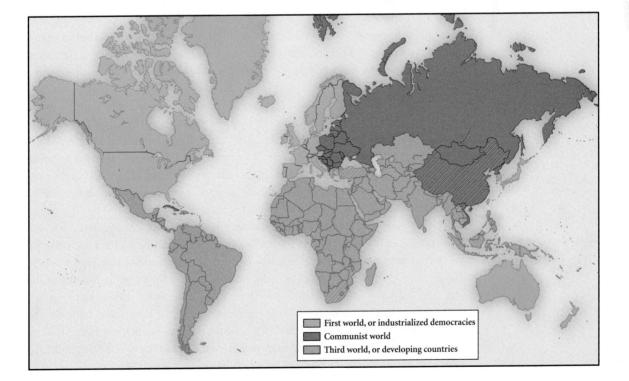

First world, or industrialized democracies
Communist world
Third world, or developing countries

were undertaking what Indian prime minister Nehru called a "tryst with destiny." The developing countries would be laboratories for new approaches to building states, nations, and modern economies. In the decades that followed, experiments with freedom multiplied, but the early optimism was soon tempered by the difficulties and disappointments of those tasks.

Experiments in Political Order: Comparing African Nations and India

All across the developing world, efforts to create political order had to contend with a set of common conditions. Populations were exploding. Expectations for independence ran very high, often exceeding the available resources. Most developing countries were culturally diverse, with little loyalty to the central state. Nonetheless, public employment mushroomed as the state assumed greater responsibility for economic development. In conditions of widespread poverty and weak private economies, groups and individuals sought to capture the state, or parts of it, both for the salaries and status it offered and for the opportunities for private enrichment that political office provided.

This was the formidable setting in which developing countries had to hammer out their political systems. The range of that effort was immense: Communist Party control in China, Vietnam, and Cuba; multiparty democracy in India and South Africa; one-party democracy in Tanzania and Senegal; military regimes for a time in much of Latin America and Africa; personal dictatorships in Uganda and the Philippines. In many places, one kind of political system followed another in kaleidoscopic succession. The political evolution of postindependence Africa illustrates the complexity and the difficulty of creating a stable political order in developing countries.

Although colonial rule had been highly authoritarian and bureaucratic with little interest in African participation, during the 1950s the British, the French, and the Belgians attempted, rather belatedly, to transplant democratic institutions to their colonies. They established legislatures, permitted elections, allowed political parties to operate, and in general anticipated the development of constitutional, parliamentary, multiparty democracies similar to their own. It was with such institutions that most African states greeted independence.

By the early 1970s, however, few such regimes were left among the new states of Africa. Many of the apparently popular political parties that had led the struggle for independence lost mass support and were swept away by military coups. When the army took power in Ghana in 1966, no one lifted a finger to defend the party that had led the country to independence only nine years earlier. Other states evolved into one-party systems, sometimes highly authoritarian and bureaucratic and sometimes more open and democratic. Still others degenerated into personal tyrannies or dictatorships. Freedom from colonial rule certainly did not automatically generate the internal political freedoms associated with democracy.

The contrast between Africa's political evolution and that of India has been particularly striking. In India, Western-style democracy, including regular elections, multiple parties, civil liberties, and peaceful changes in government, has been practiced almost continuously since independence. The struggle for independence in India had been a far more prolonged affair, thus providing time for an Indian political leadership to sort itself out. Furthermore, the British began to hand over power in a gradual way well before complete independence was granted in 1947. Thus a far larger number of Indians had useful administrative or technical skills than was the case in Africa. In sharp contrast to most African countries, the nationalist movement in India was embodied in a single national party (the Congress Party), which encompassed a wide variety of other parties and interest groups. Its leadership was genuinely committed to democratic practice. Even the tragic and painful partition of colonial India into two countries eliminated a major source of internal discord as independent India was born. Moreover, Indian statehood could be built on cultural and political traditions that were far more deeply rooted than in most African states.

■ Comparison
Why was Africa's experience with political democracy so different from that of India?

Explaining the initial rejection of democracy in Africa has been a major concern of politicians and scholars alike. Some have argued, on the basis of paternalistic or even racist assumptions, that Africans were not ready for democracy or that they lacked some crucial ingredient for democratic politics—an educated electorate, a middle class, or perhaps a thoroughly capitalist economy. Others suggested that Africa's traditional culture, based on communal rather than individualistic values and concerned to achieve consensus rather than majority rule, was not compatible with the competitiveness of party politics.

■ Change
What accounts for the ups and downs of political democracy in postcolonial Africa?

Furthermore, some argued, Western-style democracy was simply inadequate for the tasks of development confronting the new states. Creating national unity was certainly more difficult when competing political parties identified primarily with particular ethnic or "tribal" groups, as was frequently the case in Africa. Similarly, the immense problems that inevitably accompany the early stages of economic development may be compounded by the heavy demands of a political system based on universal suffrage. Certainly Europe did not begin its modernizing process with such a system. Why, many Africans asked, should they be expected to do so?

Beyond these general considerations, more immediate conditions likewise undermined the popular support of many postindependence governments in Africa and discredited their initial democracies. One was widespread economic disappointment. By almost any measure, African economic performance since independence has been the poorest in the developing world. This has translated into students denied the white-collar careers they expected, urban migrants with little opportunity for work, farmers paid low prices for their cash crops, consumers resentful about shortages and inflation, and millions of impoverished and malnourished peasants pushed to the brink of starvation. These were people for whom independence was unable to fulfill even the most minimal of expectations, let alone the grandiose visions of a better life that so many had embraced in the early 1960s. Since modern governments everywhere staked their popularity on economic performance, it is little wonder that many Africans became disaffected and withdrew their support from governments they had enthusiastically endorsed only a few years earlier.

Nevertheless, economic disappointment did not affect everyone to the same extent, and for some, independence offered great opportunities for acquiring status, position, and wealth. Unlike the situation in Latin America and parts of Asia, those who benefited most from independence were not large landowners, for most African societies simply did not have an established class whose wealth was based in landed estates. Rather they were members of the relatively well-educated elite who had found high-paying jobs in the growing bureaucracies of the newly independent states. The privileges of this dominant class were widely resented. Government ministers in many countries earned the title "Mr. Ten Percent," a reference to the bribes or "gifts" they received from private contractors working for the state. This kind of resentment broke out in Zaire between 1964 and 1968 in the form of a widespread peasant rebellion calling for a "second independence" against the "new whites" of the elite class.

Frequently, however, the resentments born of inequality and of competition for jobs, housing, educational opportunities, development projects, and political position found expression in ethnic conflict, as Africa's immense cultural diversity became intensely politicized. In many places, a judicious balancing of appointments and budgetary allocations among major ethnic groups contained conflict within a peaceful political process. Elsewhere it led to violence. An ethnically based civil war in Nigeria during the late 1960s cost the lives of millions, while in the mid-1990s ethnic hatred led Rwanda into the realm of genocide.

Thus economic disappointment, class resentments, and ethnic conflict eroded support for the transplanted democracies of the early independence era. The most common alternative involved government by soldiers, a familiar pattern in Latin America as well. By the early 1980s, the military had intervened in at least thirty of Africa's forty-six independent states and actively governed more than half of them (see Map 23.4). Usually, the military took power in a crisis, after the civilian government had lost most of its popular support. The soldiers often claimed that the nation was in grave danger, that corrupt civilian politicians had led the country to the brink of chaos, and that only the military had the discipline and strength to put things right. And so they swept aside the old political parties and constitutions and vowed to begin anew, while promising to return power to civilians and restore democracy at some point in the future.

Since the early 1980s, a remarkable resurgence of Western-style democracy has brought popular movements, multiparty elections, and new constitutions to a number of African states, including Ghana, Kenya, Mali, Senegal, and Zambia (see Map 23.4). It was part of a late-twentieth-century democratic revival of global dimensions that included Southern and Eastern Europe, most of Latin America, and parts of Asia and the Middle East. How can we explain this rather sudden, though still fragile, resumption of democracy in Africa? Perhaps the most important internal

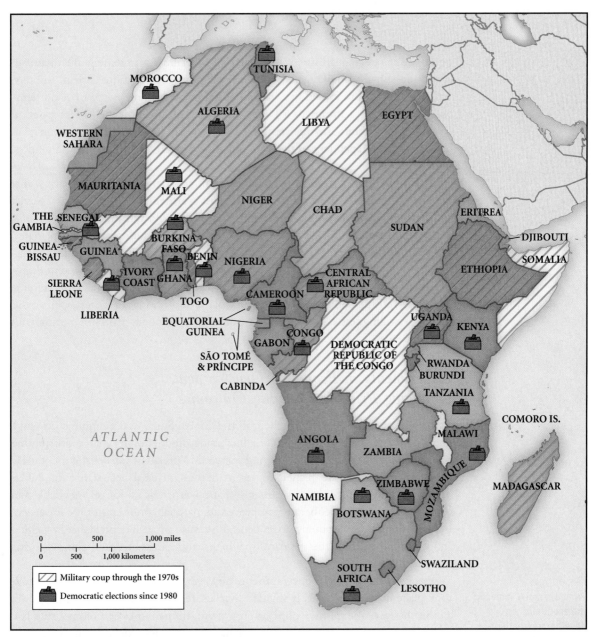

Map 23.4 Political Life in Postindependence Africa

The several decades after independence witnessed a wave of military regimes in Africa. However, since 1980 or so, a number of African countries have held reasonably free, multiparty elections, indicating a growing, but uncertain, interest in democratic practice.

factor was the evident failure of authoritarian governments to remedy the disastrous economic situation. Disaffected students, religious organizations, urban workers, and women's groups joined in a variety of grassroots movements to demand democratic change as a means to a better life. This pressure from below for political change reflected the growing strength of civil society in many African countries as organizations independent of the state provided a social foundation for the renewal of democracy.

Such movements found encouragement in the demands for democracy that accompanied the South African struggle against apartheid and the collapse of Soviet and Eastern European communism. The end of the cold war reduced the willingness of the major industrial powers to underwrite their authoritarian client states. For many Africans, democracy increasingly was viewed as a universal political principle to which they could also aspire rather than an alien and imposed system deriving from the West. None of this provided an immediate solution for the economic difficulties, ethnic conflicts, and endemic corruption of African societies, but it did suggest a willingness to continue the political experiments that had begun with independence.

Experiments in Economic Development: Changing Priorities, Varying Outcomes

At the top of the agenda everywhere in the Global South was economic development, a process that meant growth or increasing production as well as distributing the fruits of that growth to raise living standards. This quest for development, now operating all across the planet, represented the universal acceptance of beliefs unheard of not many centuries earlier—that poverty was no longer inevitable and that it was possible to deliberately improve the material conditions of life for everyone. Economic development was a central promise of all independence struggles, and it was increasingly the standard by which people measured and granted legitimacy to their governments.

■ **Change**
What obstacles impeded the economic development of third-world countries?

Achieving economic development, however, proved immensely difficult. It took place in societies sharply divided by class, religion, ethnic group, and gender and in the face of explosive population growth. In many places, colonial rule had provided only the most slender foundations for modern development to these newly independent nations, which had low rates of literacy, few people with managerial experience, a weak private economy, and transportation systems oriented to export rather than national integration. Furthermore, the entire effort occurred in a world split by rival superpowers and economically dominated by the powerful capitalist economies of the West. Despite their political independence, most developing countries had little leverage in negotiations with the wealthy nations of the Global North and their immense transnational corporations. It was hardly an auspicious environment in which to seek a fundamental economic transformation.

Beyond these structural difficulties, it was hard for leaders of developing countries to know what strategies to pursue. The academic field of "development economics" was new; its experts disagreed and often changed their minds; and conflicting political pressures, both internal and international, only added to the confusion. All of this resulted in considerable controversy, changing policies, and much experimentation.

One fundamental issue lay in the role of the state. All across the developing world and particularly in newly independent nations, most people expected that state authorities would take major responsibility for spurring the economic development of their countries. After all, the private economy was weakly developed; few entrepreneurs had substantial funds to invest; the example of rapid Soviet industrialization under state direction was hopeful; and state control held the promise of protecting vulnerable economies from the ravages of international capitalism. Some state-directed economies had real successes. China launched a major industrialization effort and massive land reform under the leadership of the Communist Party. A communist Cuba, even while remaining dependent on its sugar production, wiped out illiteracy and provided basic health care to its entire population, raising life expectancy to seventy-six years by 1992, equivalent to that of the United States. Elsewhere as well—in Turkey, India, South Korea, and much of Africa—the state provided tariffs, licenses, loans, subsidies, and overall planning, while most productive property was owned privately.

Yet in the last several decades of the twentieth century, an earlier consensus in favor of state direction largely collapsed, replaced by a growing dependence on the market to generate economic development. This was most apparent in the abandonment of much communist planning in China and the return to private farming (see Chapter 22). India and many Latin American and African states privatized their state-run industries and substantially reduced the role of the state in economic affairs. In part, this sharp change in economic policies reflected the failure, mismanagement, and corruption of many state-run enterprises, but it also was influenced by the collapse in the Soviet Union of the world's first state-dominated economy. Western pressures, exercised through international organizations such as the World Bank, likewise pushed developing countries in a capitalist direction. In China and India, the new approach generated rapid economic growth, but also growing inequalities and social conflict. As the new millennium dawned, a number of Latin American countries—Venezuela, Brazil, and Bolivia, for example—once again asserted a more prominent role for the state in their quests for economic development and social justice.

Other issues as well inspired debate. In many places, an early emphasis on city-based industrial development, stirred by visions of a rapid transition to modernity, led to a neglect or exploitation of rural areas and agriculture. This "urban bias" subsequently came in for much criticism and some adjustment in spending priorities. A growing recognition of the role of women in agriculture led to charges of "male bias" in development planning and to mounting efforts to assist women farmers

■ **Change**
In what ways did thinking about the role of the state in the economic life of developing countries change? Why did it change?

Snapshot   **Economic Development in the Global South by the Early Twenty-first Century**[5]

This table samples the economic performance of fourteen developing countries and five major regions of the Global South by the early twenty-first century. Similar data for the United States, Japan, and Russia are included for comparative purposes. Which indicators of development do you find most revealing? What aspects

Regions and Sample Countries	Average Annual Population Growth Rate, 2000–2004 (%)	Gross National Income per Capita, 2003–2004 (U.S. $)	Per Capita Purchasing Power 2004 (U.S. $)	Adult Literacy (%)
Russia	−0.5	3,410	9,620	99
East Asia	0.9	1,280	5,070	85
China	0.7	1,290	5,530	91
Philippines	2	1,170	4,890	93
Latin America	1.4	3,600	7,660	88
Mexico	1.4	6,770	9,590	90
Brazil	1.2	3,090	8,020	88
Guatemala	2.6	2,130	4,140	69
Middle East and North Africa	1.8	2,000	5,760	74
Egypt	1.8	1,310	4,120	80
Turkey	1.5	3,750	7,680	88
Iran	1.2	2,300	7,550	77
Saudi Arabia	2.8	10,430	14,010	79
South Asia	1.7	590	2,830	64
India	1.5	620	3,100	61
Indonesia	1.3	1,140	3,460	88
Subsaharan Africa	2.2	600	1,850	61
Nigeria	2.4	390	930	67
Congo	3	120	680	65
Tanzania	2	330	660	69
High-income countries	0.7	32,040	30,970	91
U.S.A.	1	41,000	39,710	99
Japan	0.2	37,180	30,040	99

of development does each of them measure? Based on these data, which countries or regions would you consider the most and the least successful? Does your judgment about "success" vary depending on which measure you use?

Life Expectancy in Years		Infant Mortality (Deaths under Age 5 per 1,000)		CO$_2$ Emission per Capita (Metric Tons)
MALE	FEMALE	1990	2003	
60	72	21	21	9.9
68	71	59	41	2.1
69	73	49	37	2.2
68	72	63	36	1
68	74	53	33	2.7
71	77	46	28	4.3
65	73	60	35	1.8
63	69	82	47	0.9
67	70	80	56	4.2
68	71	104	39	2.2
66	71	78	39	3.3
68	71	72	39	4.9
72	75	44	26	18.1
62	64	130	86	0.9
63	64	123	87	1.1
65	69	91	41	1.3
45	46	187	171	0.7
44	45	235	198	0.3
45	46	205	205	0.1
42	43	163	165	0.1
75	81	11	7	12.4
75	80	11	8	19.8
78	85	6	5	9.3

Microloans
Bangladesh's Grameen Bank pioneered an innovative approach to economic development by offering modest loans to poor people, enabling them to start small businesses. Here a group of women who received such loans meet in early 2004 to make an installment payment to an officer of the bank. (Rafiqur Rahman/Reuters/Corbis)

directly. Women also were central to many governments' increased interest in curtailing population growth. Women's access to birth control, education, and employment, it turned out, provided powerful incentives to limit family size. Another debate pitted the advocates of capital- and technology-driven projects (dams and factories, for example) against those who favored investment in "human capital," such as education, technical training, health care, and nutrition. The benefits and drawbacks of foreign aid, investment, and trade have likewise been contentious issues. Should developing countries seek to shield themselves from the influences of international capitalism, or are they better off vigorously engaging with the global economy?

Economic development was never simply a matter of technical expertise or deciding among competing theories. Every decision was political, involving winners and losers in terms of power, advantage, and wealth. Where to locate schools, roads, factories and clinics, for example, provoked endless controversies, some of them expressed in terms of regional or ethnic rivalries. It was an experimental process, and the stakes were high.

The results of those experiments have varied considerably, as the Snapshot indicates. East Asian countries in general have had the strongest record of economic growth. South Korea, Taiwan, Singapore, and Hong Kong were dubbed "newly industrialized countries," and China boasted the most rapid economic growth in the world by the end of the twentieth century, replacing Japan as the world's second-largest economy. In the 1990s, Asia's other giant, India, opened itself more fully to the world market and launched rapid economic growth with a powerful high-tech sector and an expanding middle class. Oil-producing countries reaped a bonanza when they were able to demand much higher prices for that essential commodity in the 1970s and after. Several Latin American states (Chile and Brazil, for example) entered the world market vigorously and successfully with growing industrial sectors. Limited principally to Europe, North America, and Japan in the nineteenth century, industrialization had become a global phenomenon in the twentieth century.

Elsewhere, the story was very different. In most of Africa, much of the Arab world, and parts of Asia—regions representing about one-third of the world's population—there was little sign of catching up and frequent examples of declining standards of living since the end of the 1960s. Between 1980 and 2000, the average income in forty-three of Africa's poorest countries dropped by 25 percent, pushing living standards for many below what they had been at independence.

Scholars and politicians alike argue about the reasons for such sharp variations. Variables such as geography and natural resources, differing colonial experiences, variations in regional cultures, the degree of political stability and social equality, state economic policies, population growth rates, and varying forms of involvement with the world economy have been invoked to explain the widely diverging trajectories among developing countries.

Experiments with Culture: The Role of Islam in Turkey and Iran

The quest for economic development represented the embrace of an emerging global culture of modernity—with its scientific outlook, its technological achievements, and its focus on material values. It also exposed developing countries to the changing culture of the West, including feminism, rock and rap, sexual permissiveness, consumerism, and democracy. But the peoples of the Global South also had inherited cultural patterns from the more distant past—Hindu, Confucian, Islamic, Aztec, or one of many African cultures, for example. A common issue all across the developing world involved the uneasy relationship between these older traditions and the more recent outlooks associated with modernity and the West. This tension provided the raw material for a series of cultural experiments in the twentieth century, and nowhere were they more consequential than in the Islamic world. No single answer emerged to the question of how Islam and modernity should relate to each other, but the experience of Turkey and Iran illustrate two quite different approaches to this fundamental issue.

In the aftermath of World War I, modern Turkey emerged from the ashes of the Ottoman Empire as a republic, led by a determined general, Mustafa Kemal Atatürk (1881–1938). During the 1920s and 1930s, he presided over a dramatic national cultural revolution, continuing in a more radical and single-minded fashion the modernizing reforms of the Ottoman Empire in the nineteenth century. Seeking far more than national independence, he wanted to create a thoroughly modern and Western Turkish society and viewed many traditional Islamic institutions, beliefs, and practices as obstacles to that goal. Within a few years, the caliphate had been officially ended, Sufi orders disbanded, religious courts abolished, and the sharia replaced by Swiss legal codes. Public education was completely secularized, and the Latin alphabet replaced the Arabic script for writing the Turkish language. Religious leaders (the ulama) were brought more firmly under state control. In 1932, the government even ordered that the call to prayer should be made in Turkish rather than Arabic, although this reform was later

■ Comparison

In what ways did cultural revolutions in Turkey and Iran reflect different understandings of the role of Islam in modern societies?

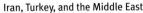
Iran, Turkey, and the Middle East

Westernization in Turkey
Mustafa Kemal Atatürk, the founder of modern Turkey, often appeared in public in elegant European dress, symbolizing for his people a sharp break with traditional Islamic ways of living. Here he is dancing with his adopted daughter at her high-society wedding in 1929. (Hulton Archive/Getty Images)

abandoned. Almost everything that had made Islam an official part of Ottoman public life was dismantled. In Atatürk's view, Islam should become a modernized personal religion, available to the individual citizens of a secular Turkish state.

The most visible symbols of Atatürk's revolutionary program occurred in the realm of dress. Turkish men were ordered to abandon the traditional headdress known as the *fez* and to wear brimmed hats. According to Atatürk,

> A civilized, international dress is worthy and appropriate for our nation, and we will wear it. Boots or shoes on our feet, trousers on our legs, shirt and tie, jacket and waist-coat—and of course, to complete these, a cover with a brim on our heads.[6]

Although women were not forbidden to wear the veil, many elite women abandoned it and set the tone for feminine fashion in Turkey. In other ways as well, women gained new legal rights. Polygamy was abolished, as was a husband's right to repudiate his wife or wives. Under the European-style legal codes, women achieved equal rights to divorce, child custody, inheritance, and education. By the mid-1930s, they had been granted the right to vote in national elections, a full decade before French women gained that right.

These reforms represented the most ambitious attempts at cultural transformation in the Middle East. Like Japan in the late nineteenth century, it was a "revolution from above" led by military and civilian officials unburdened by close ties to traditional landholding groups. State-organized enterprises were set up with centralized economic planning on the Soviet model, though without the redistribution of wealth and social revolution that was part of the Soviet experience. Landlords kept their lands, and most property was owned privately. In fact, there was considerable continuity with earlier patterns of Turkish life. Despite the imitation of Western European parliamentary politics, the Turkish government remained authoritarian. Despite the attacks on Islamic symbols, Turkish society at the local level remained firmly attached to Islamic traditions. Turkey underwent a cultural revolution in public life, but not a social or economic revolution.

After Atatürk's death in 1938, some of his more radical decrees were moderated, and a multiparty parliamentary system was allowed to develop. By the end of the twentieth century, a variety of other movements and parties emerged, some calling for the restoration of Islam to a more prominent role in society and the state. In early

2008, for example, the Turkish parliament voted to end the earlier prohibition of women wearing headscarves in universities. Nevertheless, the essential secularism of the Turkish state remained an enduring legacy of the Atatürk revolution. He and his successors had provided a distinctive answer to the question of what it meant to be modern in an Islamic setting. It entailed fully embracing modern culture and Western ways in public life and relegating Islam to the sphere of private life. Clearly, large numbers of Turkish and other Muslims did not find that solution satisfactory.

A very different answer emerged in Iran in the final quarter of the twentieth century. By that time all across the Islamic world, disappointments abounded with the social and economic results of political independence and secular development, while hostility to continuing Western cultural, military, and political intrusion grew apace. These conditions gave rise to numerous movements of Islamic revival or renewal that cast the religion as a guide to public as well as private life. If Western models of a good society had failed, it seemed reasonable to many people to turn their attention to distinctly Islamic solutions.

Iran became the epicenter of Islamic revival in the 1970s as opposition mounted to the modernizing, secularizing, American-supported government of the shah, Muhammad Reza Pahlavi (reigned 1941–1979). Some resented his close relationship with the Americans and the British as well as the heavy-handed brutality of his secret police. His land reform program had alienated landowners and upset traditional village life. Small merchants, shopkeepers, and artisans were threatened by modern stores, large government agencies, and imported foreign goods. Rural migrants to the rapidly growing cities, especially Tehran, lived an insecure life and were forced to cope with inflation, unemployment, and falling standards of living. Furthermore, the shah had provoked the Shia religious establishment by attempting to redistribute religious lands; by initiating reforms that offered women greater rights and a literacy program that threatened to replace religious schools; and by permitting the growth of Western political, economic, and cultural influences in the country. His decision to replace the Islamic calendar with one derived from Persian imperial history further alienated his subjects, as did the building of a Hyatt Hotel, which served foreign wines and liquors, near a religious sanctuary in the city of Meshed.

In a politically repressive Iran, opposition to the shah's regime came to focus on the mosque. Unlike their counterparts in Turkey, the Shia ulama in Iran had maintained their independence from the state and had often criticized both the shah's government and Western intervention in Iranian affairs. Thus the Shia leaders increasingly became the voice of opposition. One elderly cleric in particular, the Ayatollah Ruholla Khomeini, organized opposition from exile in Paris and became the center of a growing movement demanding the shah's removal. In the late 1970s, his taped messages, which were distributed through a network of local religious leaders, triggered massive urban demonstrations that paralyzed the government and strikes that shut down oil production. As the nation revolted and slipped into anarchy, the shah abdicated, and in early 1979 he and his family fled the country. The Ayatollah Khomeini returned to Iran to a hero's welcome and appointed his own government.

Khomeini believed that the purpose of government was to apply the law of Allah. Thus the sharia became the law of the land, and religious leaders themselves assumed the reins of government. Widespread purges ousted secular officials, who were replaced by Islamic activists. Actions of the parliament had to be approved by a clerical Council of Guardians. Culturally, the new regime sought the moral purification of the country under state control. Discos and bars were closed, and alcoholic drinks were forbidden. Boys and girls could no longer attend school together, and the curriculum was revised to emphasize Islamic studies and the Arabic language. An Islamic dress law required women to wear a veil and loose-fitting clothing to conceal their figures. In the early years, revolutionary guards patrolled the streets, while Islamic societies were established in many organizations; both groups served to enforce proper behavior. Khomeini made clear his posture toward much of Western culture.

[J]ust what is the social life we are talking about? Is it those hotbeds of immorality called theatres, cinemas, dancing, and music? Is it the promiscuous presence in the streets of lusting young men and women with arms, chests, and thighs bared? Is it the ludicrous wearing of a hat like the Europeans or the imitation of their habit of wine drinking? . . . Let these shameful practices come to an end, so that the dawn of a new life may break![7]

Women and the Iranian Revolution
One of the goals of Iran's Islamic Revolution was to enforce a more modest and traditional dress code for the country's women. In this photo from 2004, a woman clad in a burka and talking on her cell phone walks past a poster of the Ayatollah Khomeini, who led that revolution in 1979. (AP Images)

In other respects, however, the new regime was less than revolutionary. Despite some efforts to respond to the demands of the poor for social justice, no class upheaval or radical redistribution of wealth followed; private property was maintained, and a new privileged elite emerged. Nor did an Islamic revolution mean the abandonment of economic modernity. The country's oil revenues continued to fund its development, and by the early twenty-first century, Iran was actively pursuing nuclear power and perhaps nuclear weapons, much to the consternation of the West. Like Turkey earlier in the century, Iran had experienced a cultural revolution without major social or economic change. But it was a cultural revolution that moved in precisely the opposite direction from that of Turkey—toward, rather than away from, the Islamization of public life.

Reflections: History in the Middle of the Stream

Historians are usually more at ease telling stories that have clear endings, such as those that describe ancient Egyptian civilization, Chinese maritime voyages, the collapse of the Aztec Empire, or the French Revolution. There is a finality to these stories and a distance from them, making it easier for historians to assume the posture of detached observer, even if their understandings of those events change over time. Finality, distance, and detachment are harder to come by when historians are narrating the history of the past century, for many of its processes are clearly not over. The United States' role as a global superpower and its war in Iraq, the fate of democracy in Latin America and Africa, the rise of China and India as economic giants, the position of Islam in Turkey and Iran—all of these are unfinished stories, their outcomes unknown and unknowable. In dealing with such matters, historians write from the middle of the stream, often uncomfortably, rather than from the banks, where they might feel more at ease.

In part, that discomfort arises from questions about the future that such issues inevitably raise. Can the spread of nuclear weapons be halted? Will democracy flourish globally? Are Islamic and Christian civilizations headed for a global clash? Can African countries replicate the economic growth experience of India and China? Historians in particular are uneasy about responding to such questions because they are so aware of the unexpectedness and surprising quality of the historical process. Yet those questions about the future are legitimate and important, for as the nineteenth-century Danish philosopher Søren Kierkegaard remarked: "Life can only be understood backward, but it is lived forward." History, after all, is the only guide we have to the possible shape of that future. So, like everyone before us, we stumble on, both individually and collectively, largely in the dark, using analogies from the past as we make our way ahead.

These vast uncertainties about the future provide a useful reminder that although we know the outcomes of earlier human stories—the Asian and African struggles for independence, for example—those who lived that history did not. Such awareness can perhaps engender in us a measure of humility, a kind of sympathy, and a sense of common humanity with those whose lives we study. However we may differ from our ancestors across time and place, we share with them an immense ignorance about what will happen next.

Second Thoughts

What's the Significance?

To assess your mastery of the material in this chapter, see the **Online Study Guide** at bedfordstmartins.com/strayer.

decolonization	Muhammad Ali Jinnah	democracy in Africa
Indian National Congress	African National Congress	economic development
Mahatma Gandhi	Nelson Mandela	Kemal Atatürk
satyagraha	Black Consciousness	Ayatollah Khomeini
Muslim League	Soweto	

Big Picture Questions

1. In what ways did the colonial experience and the struggle for independence shape the agenda of developing countries in the second half of the twentieth century?
2. To what extent did the experience of the former colonies and developing countries in the twentieth century parallel that of the earlier "new nations" in the Americas in the eighteenth and nineteenth centuries?
3. How would you compare the historical experience of India and China in the twentieth century?
4. From the viewpoint of the early twenty-first century, to what extent had the goals of nationalist or independence movements been achieved?

Next Steps: For Further Study

For Web sites and documents related to this chapter, see **Make History** at bedfordstmartins.com/strayer.

Chinua Achebe, *Anthills of the Savannah* (1989). A brilliant fictional account of postindependence Nigeria by that country's foremost novelist.

Fredrick Cooper, *Africa since 1940* (2002). A readable overview of the coming of independence and efforts at development by a leading historian of Africa.

Ramachandra Guha, *India after Gandhi: The History of the World's Largest Democracy* (2007). A thoughtful account of India's first six decades of independence.

John Isbister, *Promises Not Kept* (2006). A thoughtful consideration of the obstacles to and struggles for development in the Global South.

Nelson Mandela, *Long Walk to Freedom: The Autobiography of Nelson Mandela* (1995). Mandela's account of his own amazing life as nationalist leader and South African statesman.

W. David McIntyre, *British Decolonization, 1946–1997* (1998). A global history of the demise of the British Empire.

Complete site on Mahatma Gandhi, http://www.mkgandhi.org. A wealth of resources for exploring the life of Gandhi.

CHAPTER TWENTY-FOUR

Accelerating Global Interaction

SINCE 1945

Global Interaction and the
Transformation of the World
Economy
Reglobalization
Disparities and Resistance
Globalization and an
American Empire
The Globalization of
Liberation: Comparing
Feminist Movements
Feminism in the West
Feminism in the Global
South
International Feminism
Religion and Global
Modernity
Fundamentalism on a Global
Scale
Creating Islamic Societies:
Resistance and Renewal in
the World of Islam
Religious Alternatives to
Fundamentalism
The World's Environment and
the Globalization of
Environmentalism
The Global Environment
Transformed
Green and Global
Final Reflections: Pondering
the Uses of History

"I think every Barbie doll is more harmful than an American missile," declared Iranian toy seller Masoumeh Rahimi in early 2002. To Rahimi, Barbie's revealing clothing, her shapely appearance, and her close association with Ken, her longtime unmarried companion, were "foreign to Iran's culture." Thus she warmly welcomed the arrival of Sara and Dara, two Iranian Muslim dolls meant to counteract the negative influence of Barbie and Ken, who had long dominated Iran's toy market. Sara and her brother Dara depicted eight-year-old twins. Sara came complete with a headscarf to cover her hair in modest Muslim fashion and a full-length white chador enveloping her from head to toe. They were described as helping each other solve problems, while looking to their loving parents for guidance, hardly the message that Barbie and Ken conveyed.[1]

The widespread availability of Barbie in Muslim Iran provides one small example of the power of global commerce in the world of the early twenty-first century. The creation of Sara and Dara illustrates resistance to the cultural values associated with this American product. Still, Sara and Barbie had something in common: both were manufactured in China. This triangular relationship of the United States, Iran, and China neatly symbolized the growing integration of world economies and cultures as well as the divergences and conflicts that this process generated. Those linked but contrasting patterns are the twin themes of this final chapter.

DURING THE TWENTIETH CENTURY, AN INCREASINGLY DENSE WEB OF POLITICAL RELATIONSHIPS, economic transactions, and cultural influences cut across the world's many peoples, countries, and regions, binding them

---

One World: This NASA photograph, showing both the earth and the moon, reveals none of the national, ethnic, religious, or linguistic boundaries that have long divided humankind. Such pictures have both reflected and helped create a new planetary consciousness among growing numbers of people. (Image created by Reto Stockli, Nazmi El Saleous, and Marit Jentoft-Nilsen, NASA GSFC)

more tightly, but also more contentiously, together. By the 1990s, this process of accelerating engagement among distant peoples was widely known as globalization.

Although the term was relatively new, the process was not. From the viewpoint of world history, the genealogy of globalization reaches far into the past. The Arab, Mongol, Russian, Chinese, and Ottoman empires; the Silk Road, Indian Ocean, and trans-Saharan trade routes; the spread of Buddhism, Christianity, and especially Islam—all of these connections had long linked the societies of the Eastern Hemisphere, bringing new rulers, religions, products, diseases, and technologies to many of its peoples. Later, in the centuries after 1500, European maritime voyages and colonizing efforts launched the Columbian exchange, incorporating the Western Hemisphere and inner Africa firmly and permanently into a genuinely global network of communication, exchange, and often exploitation. During the nineteenth century, as the Industrial Revolution took hold and Western nations began a new round of empire building in Asia and Africa, that global network tightened further, and its role as generator of social and cultural change only increased.

These were the foundations on which twentieth-century globalization was built. A number of prominent developments of the past century—the world wars, the Great Depression, communism, the cold war, the end of empire—which were explored in the last three chapters, operated on a global scale. But global interaction, while continuing earlier patterns, vastly accelerated its pace after World War II. Those contacts and interactions among geographically and culturally distant peoples gave rise to a world more densely connected and converging than ever before, but also to a world deeply divided, unequal, conflicted, and violent. To illustrate this accelerating globalization, this chapter examines four major processes: the transformation of the world economy, the emergence of a global feminism, the confrontation of world religions with modernity, and the growing awareness of humankind's enormous impact on the environment.

Global Interaction and the Transformation of the World Economy

■ Change
What factors contributed to economic globalization during the twentieth century?

When most people speak of globalization, they are referring to the immense growth in international economic transactions that took place in the second half of the twentieth century and that continues into the twenty-first. Many have come to see this process as almost natural, certainly inevitable, and practically unstoppable. Yet the first half of the twentieth century, particularly the decades between the two world wars, witnessed a deep contraction of global economic linkages as the aftermath of World War I and then the Great Depression wreaked havoc on the world economy. International trade, investment, and labor migration dropped sharply as major states turned inward, favoring high tariffs and economic autonomy in the face of a global economic collapse.

The aftermath of World War II was very different. The capitalist victors in that conflict, led by the United States, were determined to avoid any return to such

Depression-era conditions. At a conference in Bretton Woods, New Hampshire, in 1944, they forged a set of agreements and institutions (the World Bank and the International Monetary Fund) that laid the foundation for postwar globalization. This "Bretton Woods system" negotiated the rules for commercial and financial dealings among the major capitalist countries, while promoting relatively free trade, stable currency values linked to the U.S. dollar, and high levels of capital investment.

Technology also contributed to the acceleration of economic globalization. Containerized shipping, huge oil tankers, and air express services dramatically lowered transportation costs, while fiber optic cables and later the Internet provided the communication infrastructure for global economic interaction. Population growth, especially when tied to growing economies and modernizing societies, further fueled globalization as dozens of new nations, eager for modern development, entered the world economy.

What kind of economic globalization was taking shape? In the 1970s and after, major capitalist countries such as the United States and Great Britain abandoned many earlier political controls on economic activity as their leaders and businesspeople increasingly viewed the entire world as a single market. Known as neoliberalism, this approach to the world economy favored the reduction of tariffs, the free global movement of capital, a mobile and temporary workforce, the privatization of many state-run enterprises, the curtailing of government efforts to regulate the economy, and both tax and spending cuts. Powerful international lending agencies such as the World Bank and the International Monetary Fund imposed such free-market and pro-business conditions on many poor countries if they were to qualify for much-needed loans. The collapse of the state-controlled economies of the communist world only furthered such unrestricted global capitalism. In this view, the market, operating both globally and within nations, was the most effective means of generating the holy grail of economic growth. By the end of the twentieth century, as economic historian Jeffrey Frieden put it, "capitalism was global and the globe was capitalist."[2]

A World Economy
Indian-based call centers that serve North American or European companies and customers have become a common experience of globalization for many. Here employees in one such call center in Patna, a major city in northeastern India, undergo voice training in order to communicate more effectively with their English-speaking callers. (Indiapicture/Alamy)

Reglobalization

These were the foundations for a dramatic quickening of global economic transactions after World War II, a "reglobalization" of the world economy following the contractions of the 1930s. This immensely significant process was expressed in the accelerating circulation of goods, capital, and people.

■ **Connection**
In what ways has economic globalization linked the world's peoples more closely together?

World trade, for example, skyrocketed from a value of some $57 billion in 1947 to well over $7 trillion in 2001. Department stores and supermarkets around the world stocked their shelves with goods from every part of the globe. Twinings of London marketed its 120 blends of tea in more than 100 countries, and the Australian-based Kiwi shoe polish was sold in 180 countries. In 2005, about 70 percent of WalMart products reportedly included components from China. By then, Toyota had displaced Ford as the second-largest car seller in the United States and was edging up on the number one spot.

Money as well as goods achieved an amazing global mobility in three ways. The first was *foreign direct investment*, whereby a firm in, say, the United States opens a factory in China or Mexico (see Map 24.1). Such investment exploded after 1960 as companies in the rich countries sought to take advantage of cheap labor, tax breaks, and looser environmental regulations in the developing countries. A second form of money in motion has been the short-term movement of capital, in which investors annually spent trillions of dollars purchasing foreign currencies or stocks likely to increase in value and often sold them quickly thereafter, with unsettling consequences. A third form of capital movement involved the personal funds of individuals. By the end of the twentieth century, international credit cards had

Map 24.1 Globalization in Action: Trade and Investment in the Early Twenty-first Century
World trade has surged in the last half century, but the balance of trade among countries has made some nations net exporters and others net importers. Investment by transnational corporations around the world has been another major expression of globalization. Note that the United States and Europe are both major givers and receivers of foreign investment.

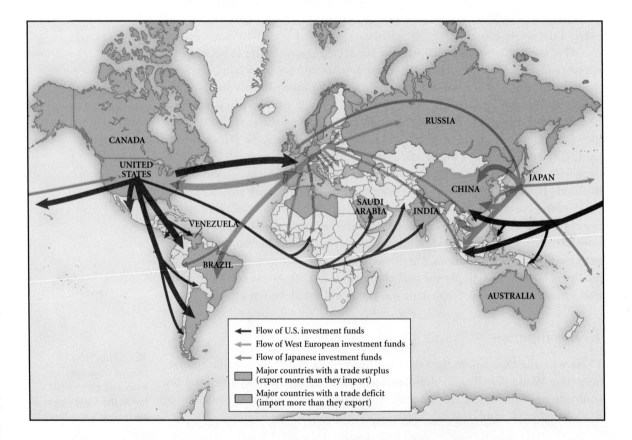

taken hold almost everywhere, allowing for easy transfer of money across national borders. In 2003, MasterCard was accepted at some 32 million businesses in 210 countries or territories.

Central to the acceleration of economic globalization have been huge global businesses known as transnational corporations (TNCs), which produce goods or deliver services simultaneously in many countries. For example, Mattel Corporation produced Barbie, that quintessentially American doll, in factories located in Indonesia, Malaysia, and China, using molds from the United States, plastic and hair from Taiwan and Japan, and cotton cloth from China. From distribution centers in Hong Kong, more than a billion Barbies were sold in 150 countries by 1999. Burgeoning in number since the 1960s, those TNCs, such as Royal Dutch Shell, Sony, and General Motors, often were of such an enormous size and economic clout that they dwarfed many countries. By 2000, 51 of the world's 100 largest economic units were in fact TNCs, not countries. In the permissive economic circumstances of recent decades, such firms have been able to move their facilities quickly from place to place in search of the lowest labor costs or the least restrictive environmental regulations. Nike, for example, during one five-year period closed twenty factories and opened thirty-five others, often thousands of miles apart.

More than ever workers too were on the move in a rapidly globalizing world economy. Examples included South Asians and West Indians seeking work and a better life in Great Britain; Algerians and West Africans in France; Yugoslavs in Germany and Switzerland; Mexicans, Cubans, and Haitians in the United States. By 2003, some 4 million Filipino domestic workers were employed in 130 countries. Young women by the hundreds of thousands from poor countries have been recruited as sex workers in wealthy nations, sometimes in conditions approaching slavery. Many highly educated professionals—doctors, nurses, engineers, computer specialists—left their homes in the Global South in a "brain drain" that clearly benefited the Global North. These flows of migrating laborers often represented a major source of income to their home countries. They also provided an inexpensive source of labor for their adopted countries, even as their presence generated mounting political and cultural tensions. Beyond those seeking work, millions of others sought refuge in the West from political oppression or civil war at home, and hundreds of millions of short-term international travelers and tourists joined the swelling ranks of people in motion.

Disparities and Resistance

What was the impact of these tightening economic links for nations and peoples around the world? That question has prompted enormous debate and controversy. Amid the swirl of contending opinion, one thing seemed reasonably clear: economic globalization accompanied, and arguably helped generate, the most remarkable spurt of economic growth in world history. On a global level, total world output grew from a value of $7.1 trillion in 1950 to $55.9 trillion in 2003 and on a per

■ **Connection**
What new or sharper divisions has economic globalization generated?

Snapshot   **Indicators of Reglobalization**[3]

Telephone lines	from 150 million in 1965 to 1.5 billion in 2000
Mobile telephones	from 0 in 1978 to more than 1 billion in 2004
Internet users	from 0 in 1985 to 934 million in 2004
International air travelers	from 25 million in 1950 to 400 million in 1996
Export processing zones	from 0 in 1957 to 3,000 in 2002
Daily foreign exchange turnover	from $15 billion in 1973 to $1.9 trillion in 2004
International bank loans	from $9 billion in 1972 to $1.465 trillion in 2000
World stock of foreign direct investment	from $66 billion in 1960 to $7.1 trillion in 2002
Value of international trade	from $629 billion in 1960 to $7.43 trillion in 2001
Number of transnational companies	from 7,000 in the late 1960s to 65,000 in 2001

capita basis from $2,835 to $8,753.[4] This represents an immense, rapid, and unprecedented creation of wealth with a demonstrable impact on human welfare. Life expectancies grew almost everywhere, infant mortality declined, and literacy increased. The UN Human Development Report in 1997 concluded that "in the past 50 years, poverty has fallen more than in the previous 500."[5]

Far more problematic has been the distribution of this new wealth. Since Europe's Industrial Revolution took hold in the early nineteenth century, a wholly new division appeared within the human community—between the rich industrialized countries, primarily in Europe and North America, and everyone else. In 1820, the ratio between the income of the top and bottom 20 percent of the world's population was three to one. By 1991, it was eighty-six to one.[6] The accelerated economic globalization of the twentieth century did not create this global rift, but it arguably has worsened the gap and certainly has not greatly diminished it. Even that well-known capitalist financier and investor George Soros, a billionaire many times over, acknowledged this reality in 2000: "The global capitalist system has produced a very uneven playing field. The gap between the rich and the poor is getting wider."[7] That gap has been evident, often tragically, in great disparities in incomes, medical care, availability of clean drinking water, educational and employment opportunities, access to the Internet, and dozens of other ways. It has shaped the life chances of practically everyone (see Map 24.2).

These disparities were the foundations for a new kind of global conflict. As the East/West division of capitalism and communism faded, differences between the rich nations of the Global North and the developing countries of the Global South assumed greater prominence in world affairs. Highly contentious issues have

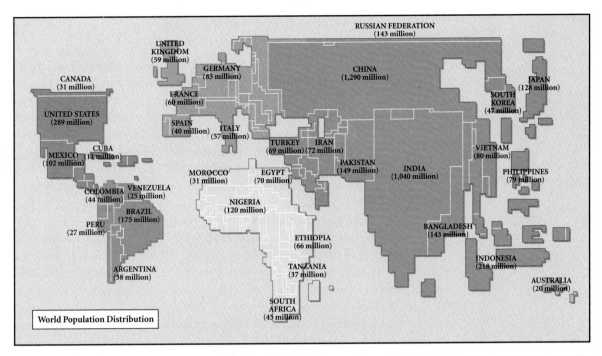

World Population Distribution

RUSSIAN FEDERATION (143 million)
UNITED KINGDOM (59 million)
GERMANY (83 million)
CHINA (1,290 million)
JAPAN (128 million)
CANADA (31 million)
FRANCE (60 million)
SOUTH KOREA (47 million)
UNITED STATES (289 million)
SPAIN (40 million)
ITALY (57 million)
TURKEY (69 million)
IRAN (72 million)
VIETNAM (80 million)
MEXICO (102 million)
CUBA (11 million)
PAKISTAN (149 million)
INDIA (1,040 million)
PHILIPPINES (79 million)
MOROCCO (31 million)
EGYPT (70 million)
VENEZUELA (25 million)
COLOMBIA (44 million)
NIGERIA (120 million)
BRAZIL (175 million)
PERU (27 million)
BANGLADESH (143 million)
ETHIOPIA (66 million)
INDONESIA (218 million)
TANZANIA (37 million)
ARGENTINA (38 million)
AUSTRALIA (20 million)
SOUTH AFRICA (45 million)

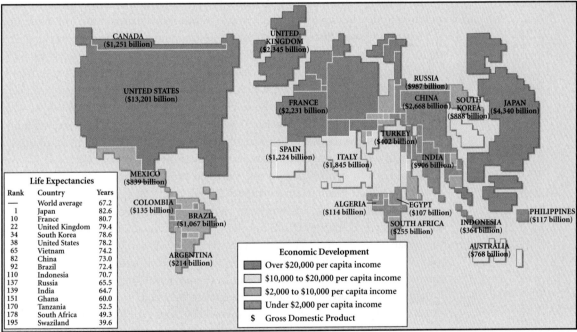

CANADA ($1,251 billion)
UNITED KINGDOM ($2,345 billion)
RUSSIA ($987 billion)
UNITED STATES ($13,201 billion)
FRANCE ($2,231 billion)
CHINA ($2,668 billion)
SOUTH KOREA ($888 billion)
JAPAN ($4,340 billion)
SPAIN ($1,224 billion)
ITALY ($1,845 billion)
TURKEY ($402 billion)
INDIA ($906 billion)
MEXICO ($839 billion)
COLOMBIA ($135 billion)
ALGERIA ($114 billion)
EGYPT ($107 billion)
PHILIPPINES ($117 billion)
BRAZIL ($1,067 billion)
SOUTH AFRICA ($255 billion)
INDONESIA ($364 billion)
AUSTRALIA ($768 billion)
ARGENTINA ($214 billion)

Life Expectancies

Rank	Country	Years
—	World average	67.2
1	Japan	82.6
10	France	80.7
22	United Kingdom	79.4
34	South Korea	78.6
38	United States	78.2
65	Vietnam	74.2
82	China	73.0
92	Brazil	72.4
110	Indonesia	70.7
137	Russia	65.5
139	India	64.7
151	Ghana	60.0
170	Tanzania	52.5
178	South Africa	49.3
195	Swaziland	39.6

Economic Development

- Over $20,000 per capita income
- $10,000 to $20,000 per capita income
- $2,000 to $10,000 per capita income
- Under $2,000 per capita income
- $ Gross Domestic Product

Map 24.2 Global Inequality: Population and Economic Development

These two maps illustrate in graphic form the global inequalities of the early twenty-first century. The first shows the relative size of the world's population by region and country; the second shows the size of the economy measured by total gross domestic product and per capita income. Illustrating yet another indication of the global economic divide are figures for overall life expectancy, an indicator that has narrowed more sharply than have others.

included the rules for world trade, availability of and terms for foreign aid, representation in international economic organizations, the mounting problem of indebtedness, and environmental and labor standards. Such matters surfaced repeatedly in international negotiations during the last half of the twentieth century and into the twenty-first. In the 1970s, for example, a large group of developing countries joined together to demand a new international economic order that was more favorable to the poor countries. Not much success attended this effort. More recently, developing countries have contested protectionist restrictions on their agricultural exports imposed by the rich countries, which were eager to protect their own politically powerful farmers.

Beyond active resistance by the rich nations, a further obstacle to reforming the world economy in favor of the poor lay in growing disparities among the developing countries themselves (see Chapter 23). The oil-rich economies of the Middle East had little in common with the banana-producing countries of Central America. The rapidly industrializing states of China, India, and South Korea had quite different economic agendas than impoverished African countries. These disparities made common action difficult to achieve.

Economic globalization has generated inequalities not only at the global level and among developing countries, but also within individual nations, rich and poor alike. In the United States, for example, a shifting global division of labor required the American economy to shed millions of manufacturing jobs. With recent U.S. factory wages perhaps thirty times those of China, many companies moved their manufacturing operations offshore to Asia or Latin America. This left many relatively unskilled American workers in the lurch, forcing them to work in the low-wage service sector, even as other Americans were growing prosperous in emerging high-tech industries. Even some highly skilled work, such as computer programming, was outsourced to lower-wage sites in India, Ireland, Russia, and elsewhere.

Globalization divided Mexico as well. The northern part of the country, with close business and manufacturing ties to the United States, grew much more prosperous than the south, which was largely a rural agricultural area and had a far more slowly growing economy. Beginning in 1994, southern resentment boiled over in the Chiapas rebellion, which featured a strong antiglobalization platform. Its leader, Subcomandante Marcos, referred to globalization as a "process to eliminate that multitude of people who are not useful to the powerful."[8] China's rapid economic growth likewise fostered mounting inequality between its rural households and those in its burgeoning cities, where income by 2000 was three times that of the countryside. Economic globalization may have brought people together as never before, but it also divided them sharply.

The hardships and grievances of those left behind or threatened by the march toward economic integration have fueled a growing popular movement aimed at criticizing and counteracting globalization. Known variously as an antiglobalization, alternative globalization, or global justice movement, it emerged in the 1990s as an international coalition of political activists, concerned scholars and students, trade unions, women's and religious organizations, environmental groups, and others, hailing from rich and poor countries alike. Thus opposition to neo-liberal globalization was itself global in scope. That opposition, though reflecting a variety of viewpoints, largely agreed that free-trade, market-driven corporate globalization lowered labor standards, fostered ecological degradation, prevented poor countries from protecting themselves against financial speculators, ignored local cultures, disregarded human rights, and enhanced global inequality, while favoring the interests of large corporations and the rich countries.

This movement appeared dramatically on the world's radar screen in late 1999 in Seattle at a meeting of the World Trade Organization (WTO). An international body representing 149 nations and charged with negotiating the rules for global commerce and promoting free trade, the WTO had become a major target of globalization critics. "The central idea of the WTO," argued one of them, "is that *free trade*—actually the values and interests of global corporations—should supersede all other values."[9] Tens of thousands of protesters—academics, activists, farmers, labor union leaders from all over the world—descended on Seattle in what became a violent, chaotic, and much-publicized protest. At the city's harbor, protest organizers created a Seattle Tea Party around the slogan "No globalization without representation," echoing the Boston Tea Party of 1773. Subsequent meetings of the WTO and other high-level international economic gatherings were likewise greeted with large-scale protest and a heavy police presence. In 2001, alternative globalization activists created the World Social Forum, an annual gathering to coordinate strategy, exchange ideas, and share experiences, under the slogan "Another world is possible." It was an effort to demonstrate that neo-liberal globalization was not inevitable and that the processes of a globalized economy could and should be regulated and subjected to public accountability.

Globalization and an American Empire

For many people, opposition to this kind of globalization also expressed resistance to mounting American power and influence in the world. An "American Empire," some have argued, is the face of globalization (see Map 24.3), but scholars, commentators, and politicians have disagreed as to how best to describe the United States' role in the postwar world. Certainly it has not been a colonial territorial empire such as that of the British or the French in the nineteenth century. Americans generally, seeking to distinguish themselves from Europeans, have vigorously denied that they were an empire at all.

In some ways, the U.S. global presence might be seen as an "informal empire," similar to the ones that Europeans exercised in China and the Middle East during the nineteenth century. In both cases, economic penetration, political pressure, and periodic military action sought to create societies and governments compatible with the values and interests of the dominant power, but without directly governing large populations for long periods of time. In its economic dimension,

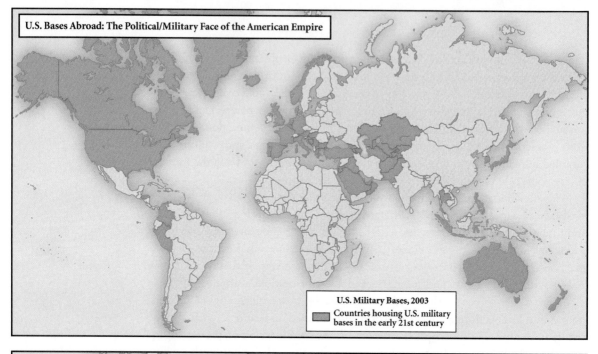

U.S. Bases Abroad: The Political/Military Face of the American Empire

U.S. Military Bases, 2003
Countries housing U.S. military bases in the early 21st century

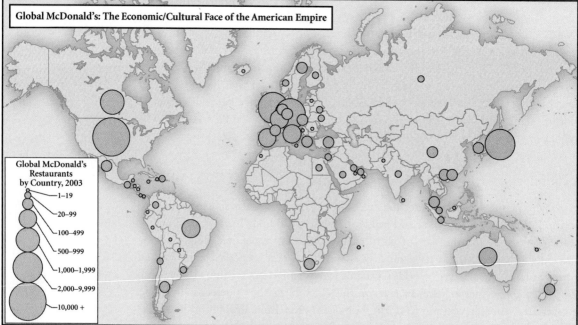

Global McDonald's: The Economic/Cultural Face of the American Empire

Global McDonald's Restaurants by Country, 2003
1–19
20–99
100–499
500–999
1,000–1,999
2,000–9,999
10,000 +

Map 24.3 Two Faces of an "American Empire"
Those who argue that the United States constructed an empire in the second half of the twentieth century point both to its political/military alliances around the world and to U.S. economic and cultural penetration of many countries. The distribution of U.S. military bases and of McDonald's restaurants indicates something of the scope of America's global presence in the early twenty-first century.

American dominance has been termed an "empire of production," which uses its immense wealth to entice or intimidate potential collaborators.[10] Some scholars have emphasized the United States' frequent use of force around the world, while others have focused attention on the "soft power" of its cultural attractiveness, its political and cultural freedoms, the economic benefits of cooperation, and the general willingness of many to follow the American lead voluntarily.

With the collapse of the Soviet Union and the end of the cold war by the early 1990s, U.S. military dominance was now unchecked by any equivalent power. When the United States was attacked by Islamic militants on September 11, 2001, that power was unleashed first against Afghanistan (2001), which had sheltered the al-Qaeda instigators of that attack, and then against Iraq (2003), where Saddam Hussein allegedly had been developing weapons of mass destruction. In the absence of the Soviet Union, the United States could act unilaterally without fear of triggering a conflict with another major power. Although the Afghan and Iraqi regimes were quickly defeated, establishing a lasting peace and rebuilding badly damaged Muslim countries proved a difficult task. Thus, within a decade of the Soviet collapse, the United States found itself in yet another global struggle, an effort to contain or eliminate Islamic terrorism.

In the final quarter of the twentieth century, as its relative military strength peaked, the United States faced growing international economic competition. The recovery of Europe and Japan and the emergent industrialization of South Korea, Taiwan, China, and India substantially reduced the United States' share of overall world production from about 50 percent in 1945 to 20 percent in the 1980s. Accompanying this relative decline was a sharp reversal of the country's trade balance as U.S. imports greatly exceeded its exports. Once the world's leading creditor, the United States now became its leading debtor. Lee Iacocca, president of Chrysler Corporation, registered the dismay that many Americans felt at this turn in their fortunes: "We send Japan low-value soybeans, wheat, corn, coal, and cotton. They send us high-value autos, motorcycles, TV sets, and oil well casings. It's 1776 and we're a colony again."[11]

However it might be defined, the exercise of American power, like that of many empires, was resisted abroad and contested at home. In Vietnam, Cuba, Iraq, and elsewhere, armed struggle against U.S. intervention was both costly and painful. During the cold war, the governments of India, Egypt, and Ethiopia sought to diminish American influence in their affairs by turning to the Soviet Union or playing off the two superpowers against each other. Even France, resenting U.S. domination, withdrew from the military structure of NATO in 1967 and expelled all foreign-controlled troops from the country. Many intellectuals, fearing the erosion of their own cultures in the face of well-financed American media around the world, have decried American "cultural imperialism." By the early twenty-first century, the United States' international policies—such as its refusal to accept the jurisdiction of the International Criminal Court; its refusal to ratify the Kyoto protocol on global warming; its doctrine of preemptive war, which was exercised in Iraq; and its apparent use of torture—had generated widespread opposition.

Within the United States as well, the global exercise of American power generated controversy. The Vietnam War, for example, divided the United States more sharply than at any time since the Civil War. It split families and friendships, churches and political parties. It alienated the United States from many of its traditional allies. The war in Vietnam provided a platform for a growing number of critics, both at home and abroad, who had come to resent American cultural and economic dominance in the post-1945 world. It stimulated a new sense of activism among students in the nation's colleges and universities. Finally, the Vietnam War gave rise to charges that the cold war had undermined American democracy by promoting an overly powerful, "imperial" presidency, by creating a culture of secrecy and an obsession with national security, and by limiting political debate in the country. Not a few came to see America itself as an imperialist power. A similar set of issues, protests, and controversies followed the American invasion of Iraq in the early twenty-first century.

The Globalization of Liberation: Comparing Feminist Movements

More than goods, money, and people traversed the planet during the twentieth century. So too did ideas, and none was more powerful than the ideology of liberation. Communism promised workers and peasants liberation from capitalist oppression. Nationalism offered subject peoples liberation from imperialism. Advocates of democracy sought liberation from authoritarian governments.

The 1960s in particular witnessed an unusual convergence of protest movements around the world, suggesting the emergence of a global culture of liberation. Within the United States, the civil rights demands of African Americans and Hispanic Americans; the youthful counterculture of music, sex, and drugs; and the prolonged and highly divisive protests against the war in Vietnam gave the 1960s a distinctive place in the country's recent history. Across the Atlantic, swelling protests against unresponsive bureaucracy, consumerism, and middle-class values likewise erupted, most notably in France in 1968. There a student-led movement protesting conditions in universities attracted the support of many middle-class people, who were horrified at the brutality of the police, and stimulated an enormous strike among some 9 million workers. France seemed on the edge of another revolution. Related but smaller-scale movements took place in Germany, Italy, and elsewhere.

The communist world too was rocked by protest. In 1968, the new Communist Party leadership in Czechoslovakia, led by Alexander Dubcek, initiated a sweeping series of reforms aimed at creating "socialism with a human face." Censorship ended, generating an explosion of free expression in what had been a highly repressive regime; unofficial political clubs emerged publicly; victims of earlier repression were rehabilitated; secret ballots for party elections were put in place. To the conservative leaders of the Soviet Union, this "Prague Spring" seemed to challenge communist rule itself, and they sent troops and tanks to crush it. Across the world in communist

China, another kind of protest was taking shape in that country's Cultural Revolution (see Chapter 22).

In the developing countries, a substantial number of political leaders, activists, scholars, and students developed the notion of a "third world." Their countries, many of which had recently broken free from colonial rule, would offer an alternative to both a decrepit Western capitalism and a repressive bureaucratic Soviet communism. They claimed to pioneer new forms of economic development, of grassroots democracy, and of cultural renewal. By the late 1960s, the icon of this third world-ideology was Che Guevara, the Argentine-born revolutionary who had embraced the Cuban Revolution and subsequently attempted to replicate its experience of liberation through guerrilla warfare in parts of Africa and Latin America. Various aspects of his life story—his fervent anti-imperialism, which was cast as a global struggle; his self-sacrificing lifestyle; his death in 1967 at the hands of the Bolivian military—made him a heroic figure to third-world revolutionaries as well as to Western radicals, who were disgusted with the complacency and materialism of their own societies.

No expression of the global culture of liberation held a more profound potential for change than feminism, for it represented a rethinking of the most fundamental and personal of all human relationships—that between women and men. Feminism had begun in the West in the nineteenth century with a primary focus on suffrage and in several countries had achieved the status of a mass movement by the outbreak of World War I (see Chapter 17). The twentieth century witnessed the globalization of feminism as organized efforts to address the concerns of women took shape across the world. Communist governments—in the Soviet Union, China, and Cuba, for example—mounted vigorous efforts to gain the support of women and to bring them into the workforce by attacking major elements of older patriarchies (see Chapter 22). But feminism took hold in many cultural and political settings, where women confronted different issues, adopted different strategies, and experienced a range of outcomes.

Che Guevara
In life, Che was an uncompromising but failed revolutionary, while in death he became an inspiration to third-world liberation movements and a symbol of radicalism to many in the West. His image appeared widely on T-shirts and posters, and in Cuba itself a government-sponsored cult featured schoolchildren chanting each morning "We will be like Che." This billboard image of Che was erected in Havana in 1988. (Tim Page/Corbis)

Feminism in the West

In the West, organized feminism had lost momentum by the end of the 1920s, when most countries had achieved universal suffrage. When it revived in the 1960s in both Western Europe and the United States, it did so with a quite different agenda. In France, for example, the writer and philosopher Simone de Beauvoir in 1949 had

■ Comparison
What distinguished feminism in the industrialized countries from that of the Global South?

published *The Second Sex*, a book arguing that women had historically been defined as "other," or deviant from the "normal" male sex. The book soon became a central statement of a reviving women's movement. French feminists dramatized their concerns publicly in the early 1970s when some of them attempted to lay a wreath at the tomb of the unknown soldier in Paris, declaring, "Someone is even more unknown than the soldier: his wife." They staged a counter–Mother's Day parade under the slogan "Celebrated one day; exploited all year." To highlight their demand to control their own bodies, some 343 women signed a published manifesto stating that they had undergone an abortion, which was then illegal in France.

Across the Atlantic, millions of American women responded to Betty Friedan's book *The Feminine Mystique* (1963), which disclosed the identity crisis of educated women who were unfulfilled by marriage and motherhood. Some adherents of this second-wave feminism took up the equal rights agenda of their nineteenth-century predecessors, but with an emphasis now on employment and education rather than voting rights.

A more radical expression of American feminism took shape from the experience of women who had worked in other kinds of radical politics, such as the civil rights movement. Widely known as "women's liberation," this approach took broader aim at patriarchy as a system of domination, similar to those of race and class. One manifesto from 1969 declared:

> We are exploited as sex objects, breeders, domestic servants, and cheap labor. We are considered inferior beings, whose only purpose is to enhance men's lives.... Because we live so intimately with our oppressors, we have been kept from seeing our personal suffering as a political condition.[12]

Thus liberation for women meant becoming aware of their own oppression, a process that took place in thousands of consciousness-raising groups across the country. Many such women preferred direct action rather than the political lobbying favored by equal rights feminists. They challenged the Miss America contest of 1968 by tossing stink bombs in the hall, crowning a live sheep as their Miss America, and disposing of girdles, bras, high-heeled shoes, tweezers, and other "instruments of oppression" in a Freedom Trashcan. They also brought into open discussion issues involving sexuality, insisting that free love, lesbianism, and celibacy should be accorded the same respect as heterosexual marriage.

Yet another strand of Western feminism emerged from women of color. For many of them, the concerns of white, usually middle-class, feminists were hardly relevant to their oppression. Black women had always worked outside the home and so felt little need to be liberated from the chains of homemaking. Whereas white women might find the family oppressive, African American women viewed it as a secure base from which to resist racism. Solidarity with black men, rather than separation from them, was essential in confronting a racist America. Viewing mainstream feminism as "a family quarrel between White women and White men," many women of African descent in the United States and Britain established their own organizations, with a focus on racism and poverty.[13]

Feminism in the Global South

As women mobilized outside of the Western world during the twentieth century, they faced very different situations than did white women in the United States and Europe. For much of Asia, Africa, and Latin America, the predominant issues—colonialism, racism, the struggle for independence, poverty, development, political oppression, and sometimes revolution—were not directly related to gender. Women were affected by and engaged with all of these efforts and were welcomed by nationalist and communist leaders, mostly men, who needed their support. Once independence or the revolution was achieved, however, the women who had joined those movements often were relegated to marginal positions.

The different conditions within developing countries sometimes generated sharp criticism of Western feminism. To many African feminists in the 1970s and beyond, the concerns of their American or European sisters were too individualistic, too focused on sexuality, and insufficiently concerned with issues of motherhood, marriage, and poverty to be of much use. Furthermore, they resented Western feminists' insistent interest in cultural matters such as female circumcision and polygamy, which sometimes echoed the concerns of colonial-era missionaries and administrators. Western feminism could easily be seen as a new form of cultural imperialism. Moreover, many African governments and many African men defined feminism of any kind as "un-African" and associated with a hated colonialism.

Women's movements in the Global South took shape around a wide range of issues, not all of which were explicitly gender based. In the East African country of Kenya, a major form of mobilization was the women's group movement. Some 27,000 small associations of women, which were an outgrowth of traditional self-help groups, had a combined membership of more than a million by the late 1980s. They provided support for one another during times of need, such as weddings, births, and funerals; they took on community projects, such as building water cisterns, schools, and dispensaries; in one province, they focused on providing permanent iron roofing for their homes. Some became revolving loan societies or bought land or businesses. One woman testified to the sense of empowerment she derived from membership in her group.

> I am a free woman. I bought this piece of land through my group. I can lie on it, work on it, keep goats or cows. What more do I want? My husband cannot sell it. It is mine.[14]

Elsewhere, other issues and approaches predominated. In the North African Islamic kingdom of Morocco, a more centrally directed and nationally focused feminist movement targeted the country's Family Law Code, which still defined women as minors. In 2004, a long campaign by Morocco's feminist movement, often with the help of supportive men and a liberal king, resulted in a new Family Law Code, which recognized women as equals to their husbands and allowed them to initiate divorce and to claim child custody, all of which had previously been denied.

Mothers of Missing Children
This group of Brazilian mothers in Rio de Janeiro gathered every week during the mid-1990s to bring pressure on the government to find their missing children, generally believed to have been seized by criminal gangs engaged in child prostitution and illegal adoption. Often seeking loved ones who probably were executed by government or paramilitary death squads, such "mothers of the disappeared" have been active in many Latin American countries.
(AP Images/Diego Guidice)

In Chile, a women's movement emerged as part of a national struggle against the military dictatorship of General Augusto Pinochet, who ruled the country from 1973 to 1990. Because they were largely regarded as "invisible" in the public sphere, women were able to organize extensively, despite the repression of the Pinochet regime. From this explosion of organizing activity emerged a women's movement that crossed class lines and party affiliations. Human rights activists, most of them women, called attention to the widespread use of torture and to the "disappearance" of thousands of opponents of the regime, while demanding the restoration of democracy. Poor urban women by the tens of thousands organized soup kitchens, craft workshops, and shopping collectives, all aimed at the economic survival of their families. Smaller numbers of middle-class women brought more distinctly feminist perspectives to the movement and argued pointedly for "democracy in the country and in the home." This diverse women's movement was an important part of the larger national protest that returned Chile to democratic government in 1990.

In South Korea as in Chile, women's mobilization contributed to a "mass people's movement" that brought a return to democracy by the late 1980s, after a long period of highly authoritarian rule. The women's movement in South Korea drew heavily on the experience of young female workers in the country's export industries. In those factories, they were poorly paid, were subjected to exhausting working conditions and frequent sexual harassment, and lived in crowded company dormitories, often called "chicken coops." Such women spearheaded a democratic trade union movement during the 1970s, and in the process many of them developed both a feminist and a class consciousness.

International Feminism

Perhaps the most impressive achievement of feminism in the twentieth century was its ability to project the "woman question" as a global issue and to gain international recognition for the view that "women's rights are human rights."[15] Like slavery and empire before it, patriarchy lost at least some of its legitimacy during this most recent century, although clearly it has not been vanquished.

Feminism registered as a global issue when the United Nations, under pressure from women activists, declared 1975 as International Women's Year and the next ten years as the Decade for Women. The United Nations also sponsored a series of World Conferences on Women over the next twenty years. By 2006, 183 nations had ratified a UN Convention to Eliminate Discrimination against Women, which committed them to promote women's legal equality, to end discrimination, to actively encourage women's development, and to protect women's human rights. Clearly this international attention to women's issues was encouraging to feminists operating in their own countries and in many places stimulated both research and action.

This growing international spotlight on women's issues also revealed sharp divisions within global feminism. One issue was determining who had the right to speak on behalf of women at international gatherings—the official delegates of male-dominated governments or the often more radical unofficial participants representing various nongovernmental organizations. North/South conflicts also surfaced at these international conferences. In preparing for the Mexico City gathering in 1975, the United States attempted to limit the agenda to matters of political and civil rights for women, whereas delegates from third-world and communist countries wanted to include issues of economic justice, decolonization, and disarmament. Feminists from the South resented the dominance and contested the ideas of their Northern sisters. One African group highlighted the differences.

> While patriarchal views and structures oppress women all over the world, women are also members of classes and countries that dominate others and enjoy privileges in terms of access to resources. Hence, contrary to the best intentions of "sisterhood," not all women share identical interests.[16]

Nor did all third-world groups have identical views. Some Muslim delegates at the Beijing Conference in 1995 opposed a call for equal inheritance for women, because Islamic law required that sons receive twice the amount that daughters inherit. In contast, Africans, especially in non-Muslim countries, were aware of how many children had been orphaned by AIDS and felt that girls' chances for survival depended on equal inheritance.

Beyond such divisions within international feminism lay a global backlash among those who felt that its radical agenda had undermined family life, the proper relationship of men and women, and civilization generally. To Phyllis Schlafly, a prominent American opponent of the Equal Rights Amendment, feminism was a "disease" that brought in its wake "fear, sickness, pain, anger, hatred, danger, violence, and all manner of ugliness."[17] In the Islamic world, Western-style feminism, with its claims of gender equality and open sexuality, was highly offensive to many and fueled movements of religious revivalism that invited or compelled women to wear the veil and sometimes lead a highly restricted life. The Vatican, some Catholic and Muslim countries, and at times the U.S. government took strong exception to aspects of global feminism, particularly its emphasis on reproductive rights, including access to abortion and birth control. Thus feminism was global as the twenty-first century dawned, but it was very diverse and much contested.

Religion and Global Modernity

Beyond liberation and feminism, a further dimension of cultural globalization took shape in the challenge that modernity presented to the world's religions. To the most "advanced" thinkers of the past several hundred years—Enlightenment writers in the eighteenth century, Karl Marx in the nineteenth, socialist intellectuals and secular-minded people in the twentieth—supernatural religion was headed for extinction in the face of modernity, science, communism, or globalization. In some places—Britain, France, the Netherlands, and the Soviet Union, for example—religious belief and practice had declined sharply. Moreover, the spread of a scientific culture around the world persuaded small minorities everywhere, often among the most highly educated, that the only realities worth considering were those that could be measured with the techniques of science. To such people, all else was superstition, born of ignorance. Nevertheless, the far more prominent trends of the last century have been those that involved the further spread of major world religions, their resurgence in new forms, their opposition to elements of a secular and global modernity, and their political role as a source of community identity and conflict. Contrary to earlier expectations, religion has played an unexpectedly powerful role in this most recent century.

Buddhism, Christianity, and Islam had long functioned as transregional cultures, spreading far beyond their places of origin. That process continued in the twentieth century. Buddhist ideas and practices such as meditation found a warm reception in the West, as did yoga, originally a mind-body practice of Indian origin. Christianity of various kinds spread widely in non-Muslim Africa and South Korea and less extensively in parts of India. By the end of the century, it was growing even in China, where perhaps 7 percent of China's population—some 82 million people—claimed allegiance to the faith. No longer a primarily European or North American religion, Christianity by the early twenty-first century found some 62 percent of its adherents in Asia, Africa, and Latin America. Moreover, millions of migrants from the Islamic world planted their religion solidly in Europe and North America. In the United States, for example, a substantial number of African Americans and smaller numbers of European Americans engaged in Islamic practice. More than ever before, religious pluralism characterized the world's societies, confronting people with the need to make choices in a domain of life previously regarded as given and fixed.

Fundamentalism on a Global Scale

■ Change
In what respect did the various religious fundamentalisms of the twentieth century express hostility to global modernity?

Religious vitality in the twentieth century was expressed not only in the spread of particular traditions to new areas but also in the vigorous response of those traditions to the modernizing and globalizing world in which they found themselves. One such response has been widely called "fundamentalism," a militant piety—defensive, assertive, and exclusive—that took shape to some extent in every major religious tradition. Many features of the modern world, after all, appeared threatening to established religion. The scientific and secular focus of global modernity directly challenged the core beliefs of supernatural religion. Furthermore, the social upheavals connected with capitalism, industrialization, and globalization thoroughly upset customary class, family, and gender relationships that had long been sanctified by religious tradition. Nation-states, often associated with particular religions, were likewise undermined by the operation of a global economy and challenged by the spread of alien cultures. In much of the world, these disruptions came at the hands of foreigners, usually Westerners, in the form of military defeat, colonial rule, economic dependency, and cultural intrusion.

To such threats, fundamentalism represented a religious response, characterized by one scholar as "embattled forms of spirituality…experienced as a cosmic war between the forces of good and evil."[18] Although fundamentalisms everywhere have looked to the past for ideals and models, their rejection of modernity was selective, not wholesale. What they sought was an alternative modernity, infused with particular religious values. Most, in fact, made active use of modern technology to communicate their message and certainly sought the potential prosperity associated with modern life. Extensive educational and propaganda efforts, political mobilization of their followers, social welfare programs, and sometimes violence ("terrorism" to their opponents) were among the means that fundamentalists employed.

The term "fundamentalism" derived from the United States, where religious conservatives in the early twentieth century were outraged by critical and "scientific" approaches to the Bible, by Darwinian evolution, and by liberal versions of Christianity that accommodated these heresies. They called for a return to the fundamentals of the faith, which included the inerrancy of the scriptures, the virgin birth and physical resurrection of Jesus, and a belief in miracles. After World War II, American Protestant fundamentalism came to oppose political liberalism and "big government," the sexual revolution of the 1960s, homosexuality and abortion rights, and secular humanism generally. Many fundamentalists saw the United States on the edge of an abyss. For one major spokesman, Francis Schaeffer (1912–1984), the West was about to enter

> an electronic dark age, in which the new pagan hordes, with all the power of technology at their command, are on the verge of obliterating the last strongholds of civilized humanity. A vision of darkness lies before us. As we leave the shores of Christian Western man behind, only a dark and turbulent sea of despair stretches endlessly ahead…unless we fight.[19]

And fight they did. At first, fundamentalists sought to separate themselves from the secular world in their own churches and schools, but from the 1970s on, they entered the political arena as the "religious right," determined to return America to a "godly path." "We have enough votes to run this country," declared Pat Robertson, a major fundamentalist evangelist and broadcaster, who ran for president in 1988. Conservative fundamentalist Christians, no longer willing to restrict their activities to personal conversion, had emerged as a significant force in American political life by the end of the century.

In the very different setting of independent India, another fundamentalist movement—known as *Hindutva*, or Hindu nationalism—took shape during the 1980s. Like American fundamentalism, it represented a politicization of religion within a democratic context. To its advocates, India was, and always had been, an essentially Hindu country, even though it had been overwhelmed in recent centuries by Muslim invaders, then by the Christian British, and most recently by the secular state of the postindependence decades. The leaders of modern India, they argued, and particularly its first prime minister, Jawaharlal Nehru, were "the self-proclaimed secularists who…seek to remake India in the Western image," while repudiating its basically Hindu religious character. The Hindutva movement took political shape in an increasingly popular party called the Bharatiya Janata Party (BJP), with much of its support coming from urban middle-class or upper-caste people who resented the state's efforts to cater to the interests of Muslims, Sikhs, and the lower castes. Muslims in particular were defined as outsiders, potentially more loyal to a Muslim Pakistan than to India. The BJP became a major political force in India during the 1980s and 1990s, winning a number of elections at both the state and national levels and promoting a distinctly Hindu identity in education, culture, and religion.

Creating Islamic Societies: Resistance and Renewal in the World of Islam

■ Change
From what sources did Islamic renewal movements derive?

The most prominent of the fundamentalisms that emerged in the late twentieth century was surely that of Islam, which was permanently etched in Americans' memory in the image of Osama bin Laden and the destruction of the World Trade Center on September 11, 2001. However, this violent event was only one expression of a much larger phenomenon—an effort among growing numbers of Muslims to create a new religious/political order centered on the teachings of Islam.

Emerging strongly in the last quarter of the century, this Islamic activism gained strength from the enormous disappointments that had accumulated in the Muslim world by the 1970s. Political independence had given rise to major states—Egypt, Iran, Algeria, and others—that pursued essentially Western and secular policies of nationalism, socialism, and economic development, often with only lip service to an Islamic identity. These policies were not very successful, however. A number of endemic problems—vastly overcrowded cities with few services, widespread unemployment, pervasive corruption, slow economic growth, a mounting gap between the rich and poor—flew in the face of the great expectations that had accompanied the struggle against European domination. Despite independence from a century or more of humiliating Western imperialism, foreign intrusion still persisted. Israel, widely regarded as an outpost of the West, had been reestablished as a Jewish state in the very center of the Islamic world in 1948. In 1967, Israel inflicted a devastating defeat on Arab forces in the Six-Day War and seized various Arab territories, including the holy city of Jerusalem. Furthermore, broader signs of

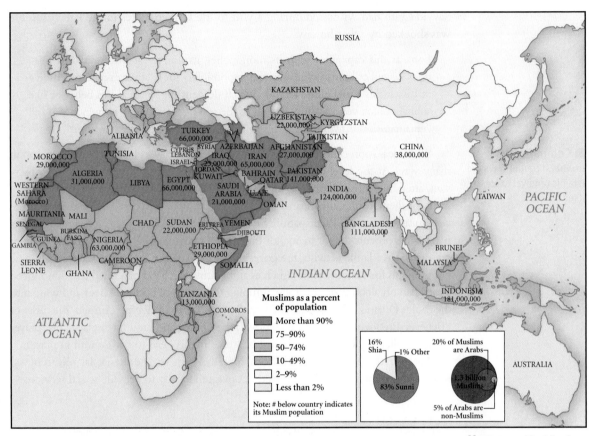

Map 24.4 The Islamic World in the Early Twenty-first Century

An Islamic world of well over a billion people incorporated much of the Afro-Asian landmass but was divided among many nations and along linguistic and ethnic lines as well. The long-term split between the majority Sunnis and the minority Shias also sharpened in the new millennium.

Western cultural penetration—secular schools, alcohol, Barbie dolls, European and American movies, scantily clad women—appeared frequently in the Muslim world.

This was the context in which the idea of an Islamic alternative to Western models of modernity began to take hold. The intellectual and political foundations of this Islamic renewal had been established earlier in the century. Its leading figures, such as the Indian Mawlana Mawdudi and the Egyptian Sayyid Qutb, insisted that the Quran and the sharia (Islamic law) provided a guide for all of life—political, economic, and spiritual—and a blueprint for a distinctly Islamic modernity not dependent on Western ideas. It was the departure from Islamic principles, they argued, that had led the Islamic world into decline and subordination to the West, and only a return to the "straight path of Islam" would ensure a revival of Muslim societies. That effort to return to Islamic principles was labeled "jihad," an ancient and evocative religious term that refers to "struggle" or "striving" to please God. In its twentieth-century political expression, jihad included the defense of an authentic Islam against Western aggression and vigorous efforts to achieve the Islamization of social and political life within Muslim countries. It was a posture that would enable Muslims to resist the seductive but poisonous culture of the West, which

Sayyid Qutb had witnessed during a visit to the United States in the late 1940s. He was shocked by what he saw.

> Look at this capitalism with its monopolies, its usury…at this individual freedom, devoid of human sympathy and responsibility for relatives except under force of law; at this materialistic attitude which deadens the spirit; at this behavior like animals which you call "free mixing of the sexes"; at this vulgarity which you call "emancipation of women"; at this evil and fanatical racial discrimination.[20]

■ Comparison
In what different ways did Islamic renewal express itself?

Such ideas soon echoed widely all across the Islamic world and found expression in many ways. At the level of personal life, many people became more religiously observant, attending mosque, praying regularly, and fasting. Substantial numbers of women, many of them young, urban, and well educated, adopted modest Islamic dress and the veil quite voluntarily. Participation in Sufi mystical practices increased. Furthermore, many governments sought to anchor themselves in Islamic rhetoric and practice. Under pressure from Islamic activists, the government of Sudan in the 1980s adopted Quranic punishments for various crimes (such as amputating the hand of a thief) and announced a total ban on alcohol, dramatically dumping thousands of bottles of beer and wine into the Nile. During the 1970s, President Anwar Sadat of Egypt claimed the title of "Believer-President," referred frequently to the Quran, and proudly displayed his "prayer mark," a callus on his forehead caused by touching his head to the ground in prayer.

All over the Muslim world, from North Africa to Indonesia, Islamic renewal movements spawned organizations that operated legally to provide social services—

Hamas in Action

The Palestinian militant organization Hamas, founded in 1987 as an offshoot of Egypt's Muslim Brotherhood, illustrates two dimensions of Islamic radicalism. On the one hand, Hamas repeatedly sent suicide bombers to target Israeli civilians and sought the elimination of the Israeli state. A group of would-be suicide bombers are shown here in white robes during the funeral of colleagues killed by Israeli security forces in late 2003. On the other hand, Hamas ran a network of social services, providing schools, clinics, orphanages, summer camps, soup kitchens, and libraries for Palestinians. The classroom pictured here was part of a school founded by Hamas. (Andrea Comas/Reuters/Corbis; Abid Katib/Getty Images)

schools, clinics, youth centers, legal-aid centers, financial institutions, publishing houses—that the state offered inadequately or not at all. Islamic activists took leadership roles in unions and professional organizations of teachers, journalists, engineers, doctors, and lawyers. Such people embraced modern science and technology but sought to embed these elements of modernity within a distinctly Islamic culture. Some served in official government positions or entered political life where it was possible to do so. The Algerian Islamic Salvation Front was poised to win elections in 1992, when a frightened military government intervened to cancel the elections, an action that plunged the country into a decade of bitter civil war. In Turkey, Egypt, Jordan, Iraq, Palestine, and Lebanon, Islamic parties made impressive electoral showings in the 1990s and the early twenty-first century.

Another face of Islamic renewal, however, sought the violent overthrow of what they saw as compromised regimes in the Muslim world. One such group, the Egyptian Islamic Jihad, assassinated President Sadat in 1981, following Sadat's brutal crackdown on both Islamic and secular opposition groups. One of the leaders of Islamic Jihad explained:

> We have to establish the Rule of God's Religion in our own country first, and to make the Word of God supreme.... There is no doubt that the first battlefield for jihad is the extermination of these infidel leaders and to replace them by a complete Islamic Order.[21]

Two years earlier in Mecca, members of another radical Islamic group sought the overthrow of the Saudi government. They despised its alliance with Western powers, the corrupt and un-Islamic lifestyle of its leaders, and the disruptive consequences of its oil-fueled modernization program. They even invaded the Grand Mosque, Islam's most sacred shrine. In Iran (1979) and Afghanistan (1996), Islamic movements succeeded in coming to power and began to implement a radical program of Islamization based on the sharia (see Chapter 23 for Iran).

Islamic revolutionaries also took aim at hostile foreign powers. Hamas in Palestine and Hezbollah in Lebanon, supported by the Islamic regime in Iran, targeted Israel with popular uprisings, suicide bombings, and rocket attacks in response to the Israeli occupation of Arab lands. For some, Israel's very existence was illegitimate. The Soviet invasion of Afghanistan in 1979 prompted widespread opposition aimed at liberating the country from atheistic communism and creating an Islamic state. Sympathetic Arabs from the Middle East flocked to the aid of their Afghan compatriots.

Among them was the young Osama bin Laden, a wealthy Saudi Arab, who created an organization, al-Qaeda (meaning "the base" in Arabic), to funnel fighters and funds to the Afghan resistance. At the time, bin Laden and the Americans were on the same side, both opposing Soviet expansion into Afghanistan, but they soon parted ways. Returning to his home in Saudi Arabia, bin Laden became disillusioned and radicalized when the government of his country allowed the stationing of "infidel" U.S. troops in Islam's holy land during and after the first American war against Iraq in 1991. By the mid-1990s, he had found a safe haven in Taliban-ruled Afghanistan, from which he and other leaders of al-Qaeda planned their now infamous attack on the World Trade Center and other targets. Although they had no standing as Muslim clerics, in 1998 they issued a *fatwa*, or religious edict, declaring war on America.

> [F]or over seven years the United States has been occupying the lands of Islam in the holiest of places, the Arabian Peninsula, plundering its riches, dictating to its rulers, humiliating its people, terrorizing its neighbors, and turning its bases in the Peninsula into a spearhead through which to fight the neighboring Muslim peoples.... [T]he ruling to kill the Americans and their allies—civilians and military—is an individual duty for every Muslim who can do it in any country in which it is possible to do it, in order to liberate the al-Aqsa Mosque in Jerusalem and the holy mosque (in Mecca) from their grip, and in order for their armies to move out of all the lands of Islam, defeated and unable to threaten any Muslim.[22]

Elsewhere as well—in East Africa, Indonesia, Great Britain, Spain, Saudi Arabia, and Yemen—al-Qaeda or groups associated with it launched scattered attacks on Western interests. At the international level, the great enemy was not Christianity itself or even Western civilization, but irreligious Western-style modernity, U.S. imperialism, and an American-led economic globalization so aptly symbolized by the World Trade Center. Ironically, al-Qaeda itself was a modern and global organization, many of whose members were highly educated professionals from a variety of countries. Despite their focus on the West, the struggles undertaken by politicized Islamic activists were as much within the Islamic world as they were with the external enemy. If Islamic fundamentalism represented a clash of cultures or civilizations, that collision took place among different conceptions of Islam at least as sharply as with the outlook and practices of the modern West.

Religious Alternatives to Fundamentalism

Militant revolutionary fundamentalism has certainly not been the only religious response to modernity and globalization within the Islamic world. Many who shared a concern to embed Islamic values more centrally in their societies have acted peacefully and within established political structures. Considerable debate among them has raised questions about the proper role of the state, the difference between the eternal law of God (sharia) and the human interpretations of it, the rights of women, the possibility of democracy, and many other issues. Some Muslim intellectuals and political leaders have called for a dialogue between civilizations; others have argued that traditions can change in the face of modern realities without losing their distinctive Islamic character. In 1996, Anwar Ibrahim, a major political and intellectual figure in Malaysia, insisted that

> [Southeast Asian Muslims] would rather strive to improve the welfare of the women and children in their midst than spend their days elaborately defining the nature and institutions of the ideal Islamic state. They do not believe it

makes one less of a Muslim to promote economic growth, to master the information revolution, and to demand justice for women.[23]

Within other religious traditions as well, believers found various ways of responding to global modernity. More liberal or mainstream Christian groups spoke to the ethical issues arising from economic globalization. Many Christian organizations, for example, were active in agitating for debt relief for poor countries. Pope John Paul II was openly concerned about "the growing distance between rich and poor, unfair competition which puts the poor nations in a situation of ever-increasing inferiority." "Liberation theology," particularly in Latin America, sought a Christian basis for action in the areas of social justice, poverty, and human rights, while viewing Jesus as liberator as well as savior. In Asia, a growing movement known as "socially engaged Buddhism" addressed the needs of the poor through social reform, educational programs, health services, and peacemaking action during times of conflict and war. The Dalai Lama has famously advocated a peaceful resolution of Tibet's relationship with China. Growing interest in communication and exchange among the world's religions was expressed at a World Peace Summit in 2000, when more than 1,000 religious and spiritual leaders met to explore how they might more effectively confront the world's many conflicts. In short, religious responses to global modernity were articulated in many voices.

The World's Environment and the Globalization of Environmentalism

Even as world religions, fundamentalist and otherwise, challenged global modernity on cultural or spiritual grounds, burgeoning environmental movements in the 1960s and after did so with an eye to the human impact on the earth and its many living creatures, including ourselves. Among the distinctive features of the twentieth century, none has been more pronounced than humankind's growing ability to alter the natural order and the mounting awareness of this phenomenon. When the wars, revolutions, and empires of this most recent century have faded from memory, environmental transformation and environmental consciousness may well seem to future generations the decisive feature of that century.

The Global Environment Transformed

Underlying the environmental changes of the twentieth century were three other factors that vastly magnified the human impact on earth's ecological systems far beyond anything previously known.[24] One was the explosion of human numbers, an unprecedented quadrupling of the world's population in a single century. Another lay in the amazing new ability of humankind to tap the energy potential of fossil fuels—coal in the nineteenth century and oil in the twentieth. Hydroelectricity, natural gas, and nuclear power added to the energy resources

■ Change
How can we explain the dramatic increase in the human impact on the environment in the twentieth century?

Snapshot **World Population Growth, 1950–2005**[25]

The great bulk of the world's population growth in the second half of the twentieth century occurred in the developing countries of Asia, Africa, the Middle East, and Latin America.

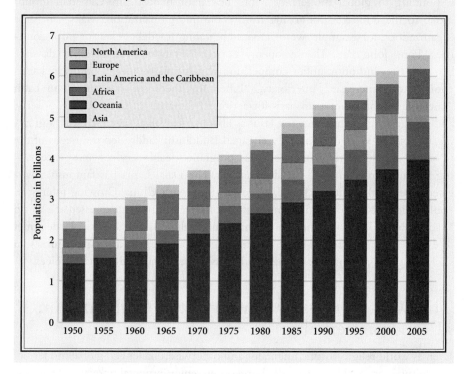

available to our species. These new sources of energy made possible a third contribution to environmental transformation—phenomenal economic growth—as modern science and technology immensely increased the production of goods and services. None of this occurred evenly across the planet. An average North American in the 1990s, for example, used 50 to 100 times more energy than an average Bangladeshi. But almost everywhere—in capitalist, communist, and developing countries alike—the idea of economic growth as something possible and desirable took hold as a part of global culture.

These three factors were the foundations for the immense environmental transformations of the twentieth century. Human activity had always altered the natural order, usually on a local basis, but now the scale of those disruptions assumed global proportions. The growing numbers of the poor and the growing consumption of the rich led to the doubling of cropland and a corresponding contraction of the world's forests and grasslands. With diminished habitats, numerous species of plants and animals either disappeared or were threatened with extinction. The human remaking of the environment also greatly increased the population of cattle, pigs, chickens, rats, and dandelions.

The global spread of modern industry, which was heavily dependent on fossil fuels, created a pall of air pollution in many major cities. By the 1970s, traffic police in Tokyo frequently wore face masks. In Mexico City, officials estimated in 2002 that air pollution killed 35,000 people every year. Industrial pollution in the Soviet Union rendered about half of the country's rivers severely polluted by the late 1980s, while fully 20 percent of its population lived in regions defined as "ecological disasters." The release of chemicals known as chlorofluorocarbons thinned the ozone layer, which protects the earth from excessive ultraviolet radiation.

The most critical and intractable environmental transformation was global warming. By the end of the twentieth century, a worldwide scientific consensus had emerged that the vastly increased burning of fossil fuels, which emit heat-trapping greenhouse gases, as well as the loss of trees that would otherwise remove carbon dioxide from the air, had begun to warm the atmosphere significantly. Although considerable disagreement existed about the rate and likely consequences of this process, concern about melting glaciers and polar ice caps, rising sea levels, thawing permafrost, extreme hurricanes, further species extinctions, and other ecological threats punctuated global discussion of this issue. It was clearly a global phenomenon, and it prompted a global awareness of the problem (see Map 24.5).

Green and Global

Environmentalism began in the nineteenth century as Romantic poets such as William Blake and William Wordsworth denounced the industrial era's "dark satanic mills," which threatened the "green and pleasant land" of an earlier England. The "scientific management" of nature, both in industrializing countries and in European colonies, represented another element of emerging environmental awareness among a few. So did the "wilderness idea," which aimed to preserve untouched areas from human disruption.[26] None of these strands of environmentalism attracted a mass following or provoked a global response. Not until the second half of the twentieth century, and then quite rapidly, did environmentalism achieve a worldwide dimension, although it was expressed in many quite different ways.

This second-wave environmentalism began in the West with the publication in 1962 of Rachel Carson's *Silent Spring*, an exposure of the chemical contamination of the environment that threatened both human health and the survival of many other species. She wrote of a "strange stillness" in a world where the songs of birds might no longer be heard. The book touched a nerve, generating an enormous response and effectively launching the environmental movement in the United States. Here, as virtually everywhere else, the impetus for action came from the grass roots and citizen protest. By the early 1990s, some 14 million Americans, one in seven adults, had joined one of the many environmental organizations—national or local—that aimed much of their effort at lobbying political parties and businesses. In Europe, the Club of Rome, a global think tank, issued a report in 1972 called *Limits to Growth*, which warned of resource exhaustion and the collapse of industrial society in the face of

■ Comparison
What differences emerged between environmentalism in the Global North and that in the Global South?

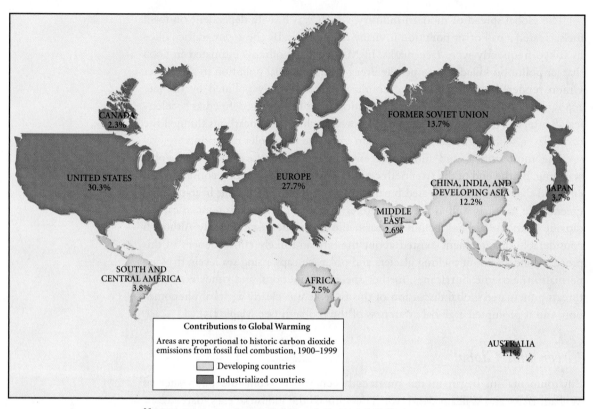

Map 24.5   Carbon Dioxide Emissions in the Twentieth Century
The source of carbon dioxide emissions, the chief human contribution to global warming, was distributed quite unevenly across the planet. Although the industrialized countries have been largely responsible for those emissions during the twentieth century, India and China in particular have assumed a much greater role in this process as their industrialization boomed in the early twenty-first century. The historically unequal distribution of those emissions has prompted much controversy between the countries of the Global North and the Global South about who should make the sacrifices required to address the problem of global warming.

unrelenting economic growth. The German environmental movement was distinctive in that its activists directly entered the political arena as the Green Party, which came to have a substantial role in German national politics. One of the Greens' main concerns was opposition to nuclear energy. Beyond addressing environmental pollution, Western activists focused much attention on wilderness issues, opposing logging, road building, and other development efforts in remaining unspoiled areas.

Quite quickly, during the 1970s and 1980s, environmentalism took root in the developing countries as well. There it often assumed a different character—it was more locally based and had fewer large national organizations than in the West; it involved poor people rather than affluent members of the middle class; it was less engaged in political lobbying and corporate strategies; it was more concerned with issues of food security, health, and basic survival than with the rights of nature or

Environmentalism in Action These South Korean environmental activists are wearing death masks and holding crosses representing various countries during an antinuclear protest in Seoul in 1996, exactly ten years after a large-scale nuclear accident at Chernobyl in the Soviet Union. The lead protester holds a placard reading "Don't forget Chernobyl!" (AP Images/Yun Hai-Huoung)

wilderness protection; and it was more closely connected to movements for social justice.[27] Thus, whereas Western environmentalists defended forests where few people lived, the Chikpo or "tree-hugging" movement in India sought to protect the livelihood of farmers, artisans, and herders living in areas subject to extensive defor- estation. A massive movement to prevent or limit the damming of India's Narmada River derived from the displacement of local people; similar anti-dam protests in the American Northwest were more concerned with protecting salmon runs.

Western environmentalists often called on individuals to change their values by turning away from materialism toward an appreciation of the intricate and fragile web of life that sustains us all. In the Philippines, by contrast, environmental activists confronting the operation of foreign mining companies have sought fundamental changes in the political and social structure of their country. Thus environmental protest has overlapped with other movements seeking to challenge established power structures and social hierarchies. Coalitions of numerous local groups— representing various religious, women's, human rights, indigenous peoples', peasant, and political organizations—frequently mobilized large-scale grassroots movements against the companies rather than seeking to negotiate with them. These movements have not been entirely nonviolent; occasionally they have included guerrilla warfare actions by "green armies." Such mass mobilization contributed to the decision of the Australian-based Western Mining Corporation in 2000 to abandon its plans for developing a huge copper mine in Mindanao.

By the late twentieth century, environmentalism had become a matter of global concern. Such an awareness motivated legislation aimed at pollution control in many countries; it pushed many businesses in a "green" direction; it fostered research on alternative and renewable sources of energy; it stimulated UN conferences on global warming; it persuaded millions of people to alter their way of life; and it generated a number of international agreements addressing matters such as whaling, ozone depletion, and global warming.

The globalization of environmentalism also disclosed sharp conflicts, particularly between the Global North and South. Both activists and governments in the developing countries have often felt that Northern initiatives to address atmospheric pollution and global warming would curtail their industrial development, leaving the North/South gap intact. "The threat to the atmospheric commons has been building over centuries," argued Indian environmentalist Vandana Shiva, "mainly because of industrial activity in the North. Yet…the North refuses to assume extra responsibility for cleaning up the atmosphere. No wonder the Third World cries foul when it is asked to share the costs." A Malaysian official put the dispute succinctly: "The developed countries don't want to give up their extravagant lifestyles, but plan to curtail our development."[28] The United States' refusal in the late 1990s to ratify the Kyoto protocol, aimed at reducing greenhouse gas emissions, seemed to confirm the unwillingness of the world's largest emitter to seriously limit those emissions and proved offensive to many of the 164 countries that had ratified it by 2006. Yet another North/South environmental issue arose over the export of hazardous wastes, generated in the rich countries, to disposal sites in the developing countries.

Beyond these and other conflicts, global environmentalism, more than any other widespread movement, came to symbolize "one-world" thinking, a focus on the common plight of humankind across the artificial boundaries of nation-states. It also marked a challenge to modernity itself, particularly its consuming commitment to endless growth. The ideas of sustainability and restraint, certainly not prominent in any list of modern values, entered global discourse and marked the beginnings of a new environmental ethic, though one based on concepts dating back to the Paleolithic era. This change in thinking was perhaps the most significant achievement of global environmentalism.

Final Reflections: Pondering the Uses of History

The end of a history book is an appropriate place to ask the fundamental question: just what is it good for, this field of study we call history? What, in short, are the uses of the past, and particularly of the global past?

At one level, philosophers, scholars, and thoughtful people everywhere have long used history to probe the significance of human experience. Does an examination of the past disclose any purpose, meaning, or pattern, or is it "just one damned thing after another"? Some sages, of course, have discerned divine purpose in the unfolding of the human story. To Saint Augustine, an early Christian thinker and writer, that purpose was the building of the "heavenly city," while events in this world were but steps in God's great plan. Chinese thinkers often viewed history as the source of moral lessons and related the behavior of rulers to the rise and fall of their dynasties. Europeans and others operating within the Enlightenment tradition have seen history in secular terms as a record of progress toward greater freedom or rationality in human affairs. Karl Marx viewed the past as a succession of economic changes and class struggles culminating in the creation of socialism, a secular utopia that would forever banish war, inequality, and social conflict.

Most contemporary historians are skeptical of such grand understandings of the human past, especially those that depend on some unseen hand directing the course of history to a defined end or those that reflect a particular set of values. But if "purpose" is hard to detect in the human story, some general "directions" over the long run are perhaps more evident.

One such trend lies in growing human numbers, which are linked to greater control over the natural environment as our ways of living moved from gathering and hunting, to agriculture, and most recently to industrial societies. Accompanying this broad direction in world history has been the growing complexity of human societies. Small hunting bands of a few dozen people gave way to agricultural villages of several thousands, to cities populated by tens or hundreds of thousands, to states and empires consisting of many millions. As the scale of human communities enlarged, so too did the pace of change in human affairs. In recent centuries, change has become both expected and valued in ways that would surely seem strange to most of the world's earlier inhabitants. A final possible direction in world history has been toward greater connection among the planet's diverse cultures and peoples. To early links among neighboring settlements or villages were later added networks of exchange and communication that operated among distant civilizations, across whole hemispheres, and after 1500 on a genuinely global level.

A word of caution, however, about finding direction in world history. None of this happened smoothly, evenly, or everywhere, and all of it was accompanied by numerous ups and downs, reversals, and variations. Furthermore, the notion of direction in history is quite different from that of progress. It is an observation rather than a judgment. One might consider growing populations, control over nature, increasing complexity, more rapid change, and global integration as great achievements and evidence of human "success." Alternatively, one might regard them as a burden or a curse, more of a disease than a triumph. We do well in studying the past to separate as much as possible our descriptions about what happened from our opinions about those events and processes.

In addition to discovering meaning or, even more modestly, direction in history, the uses of the past have long included efforts by political authorities to inculcate national, religious, civic, patriotic, or other values in their citizens. Furious debates in recent decades about history curricula in the schools of the United States, Japan, China, and elsewhere testify to the continuing impulse to use history in this way. In democratic societies, many people also express the hope that grounding in history will generate wiser public policies and more informed and effective participation by citizens. It is not always easy to find evidence for such outcomes of historical study, for the lessons of the past are many, varied, and conflicting, and the world, as always, hovers on the knife edge of possibility and disaster. Nonetheless, advocates for historical study continue to believe that probing the past enhances public life.

On a more personal level, many people have found in the study of history endless material for musing, for pondering those matters of the heart and spirit that all of us must confront as we make our way in the world. Consider, for example, the question of suffering. History is, among other things, a veritable catalog of the varieties of human suffering. It provides ample evidence, should we need it, that suffering is a common and bedrock human experience—and that none of us is exempt. But the study of history also highlights the indisputable fact that much of human suffering has come at our own hands in the shape of war, racism, patriarchy, exploitation, inequality, oppression, and neglect.

Is it possible that some exposure to the staggering sum of human suffering revealed in the historical record can soften our hearts, fostering compassion for our own suffering and that of others? In short, can the study of history generate kindness, both at the level of day-to-day personal interactions and at the wider level of acting to repair the brokenness of the world?

For those who choose to practice kindness or to seek justice in public life—overcoming global poverty, promoting equality between men and women, seeking understanding among religious traditions, encouraging environmental sustainability—history offers some encouragement. For one thing, it provides a record of those who have struggled long, hard, and on occasion with some success. Abolitionists contributed to the ending of slavery. Colonized peoples broke free of empire. Women secured the vote and challenged patriarchy. Socialists and communists challenged the inequities of capitalism, while popular protest brought repressive communist regimes to their knees in the Soviet Union and Eastern Europe. Brave people have spoken truth to power. In short, things changed, and sometimes people changed things.

There is yet another way in which history might assist our personal journeys through life. We are, most of us, inclined to be insular, to regard our own ways as the norm, to be fearful of difference. Nor is this tendency largely our own fault. We all have limited experience. Few of us have had much personal encounter with cultures beyond our own country, and none of us, of course, knows personally what life was like before our birth. But we do know that a rich and mature life involves opening up to a wider world. If we base our understanding of life only on what we personally experience, we are impoverished indeed.

In this task of opening up, history in general and world history in particular have much to offer. They provide a marvelous window into the unfamiliar. They confront us with the whole range of human achievement, tragedy, and sensibility. They give context and perspective to our own limited experience. They allow us some modest entry into the lives of people far removed from us in time and place. They offer us company for the journeys of our own lives. If we take it seriously, historical study can assist us in enlarging and enriching our sense of self. In helping us open up to the wider experience of "all under heaven," as the Chinese put it, history can assist us in becoming wiser and more mature people. What more might one ask from any field of study?

Second Thoughts

What's the Significance?

neo-liberalism	Prague Spring	Islamic renewal
reglobalization	Che Guevara	Osama bin Laden/al-Qaeda
transnational corporations	second-wave feminism	global warming
North/South gap	fundamentalism	environmentalism
antiglobalization	Hindutva	

To assess your mastery of the material in this chapter, see the **Online Study Guide** at bedfordstmartins.com/strayer.

Big Picture Questions

1. To what extent did the processes discussed in this chapter (economic globalization, feminism, fundamentalism, environmentalism) represent something new in the twentieth century? In what respects did they have roots in the more distant past?
2. In what ways did the global North/South divide find expression in the twentieth century?
3. What have been the benefits and drawbacks of globalization since 1945?
4. Does the twentieth century as a whole confirm or undermine Enlightenment predictions about the future of humankind?
5. "The twentieth century marks the end of the era of Western dominance in world history." What evidence might support this statement? What evidence might contradict it?
6. To what extent do you think the various liberation movements of the twentieth century — communism, nationalism, democracy, feminism, internationalism — have achieved their goals?
7. Based on material in Chapters 21, 22, and 24, how might you define the evolving roles of the United States in the history of the twentieth century?

Next Steps: For Further Study

For Web sites and documents related to this chapter, see **Make History** at bedfordstmartins.com/strayer.

Karen Armstrong, *The Battle for God* (2000). A comparison of Christian, Jewish, and Islamic fundamentalism in historical perspective.

Nayan Chanda, *Bound Together: How Traders, Preachers, Adventurers, and Warriors Shaped Globalization* (2007). An engaging, sometimes humorous, long-term view of the globalization process.

Jeffrey Frieden, *Global Capitalism: Its Fall and Rise in the Twentieth Century* (2006). A thorough, thoughtful, and balanced history of economic globalization.

Michael Hunt, *The World Transformed* (2004). A thoughtful global history of the second half of the twentieth century.

J. R. McNeill, *Something New under the Sun: An Environmental History of the Twentieth Century World* (2001). A much-acclaimed global account of the rapidly mounting human impact on the environment during the most recent century.

Bonnie Smith, ed., *Global Feminisms since 1945* (2000). A series of essays about feminist movements around the world.

"No Job for a Woman," http://www.iwm.org.uk/upload/package/30/women/index.htm. A Web site illustrating the impact of war on the lives of women in the twentieth century.

Notes

Chapter 13

1. Brian Fagan, *Ancient North America* (London: Thames and Hudson, 2005), 503.

2. Quoted in Charles C. Mann, *1491: New Revelations of the Americas before Columbus* (New York: Alfred A. Knopf, 2005), 334.

3. Louise Levanthes, *When China Ruled the Seas* (New York: Simon and Schuster, 1994), 175.

4. Niccolò Machiavelli, *The Prince* (New York: New American Library, 1952), 90, 94.

5. Frank Viviano, "China's Great Armada," *National Geographic*, July 2005, 34.

6. John J. Saunders, ed., *The Muslim World on the Eve of Europe's Expansion* (Englewood Cliffs, N.J.: Prentice Hall, 1966), 41–43.

7. Leo Africanus, *History and Description of Africa* (London: Hakluyt Society, 1896), 824–25.

8. Quoted in Patricia Risso, *Merchants and Faith* (Boulder, Colo.: Westview Press, 1995), 49.

9. Quoted in Stuart B. Schwartz, ed., *Victors and Vanquished* (Boston: Bedford/St. Martin's, 2000), 8.

10. Quoted in Michael E. Smith, *The Aztecs* (London: Blackwell, 2003), 108.

11. Smith, *The Aztecs*, 220.

12. Miguel León-Portilla, *Aztec Thought and Culture*, translated by Jack Emory Davis (Norman: University of Oklahoma Press, 1963), 7; Miguel León-Portilla, *Fifteen Poets of the Aztec World* (Norman: University of Oklahoma Press, 1992), 80–81.

13. Terence N. D'Altroy, *The Incas* (London: Blackwell, 2002), chaps. 11, 12.

14. Pedro de Cieza de León, *The Incas*, translated by Harriet de Onis (Norman: University of Oklahoma Press, 1959), 177–78.

15. For a summary of this practice among the Aztecs and Incas, see Karen Vieira Powers, *Women in the Crucible of Conquest* (Albuquerque: University of New Mexico Press, 2005), chap. 1.

16. Powers, *Women in the Crucible of Conquest*, 25.

17. Louise Burkhart, "Mexica Women on the Home Front," in *Indian Women of Early Mexico*, edited by Susan Schroeder et al. (Norman: University of Oklahoma Press, 1997), 25–54.

18. The "web" metaphor is derived from J. R. McNeill and William H. McNeill, *The Human Web* (New York: W. W. Norton, 2003).

19. Graph from David Christian, *Maps of Time* (Berkeley: University of California Press, 2004), 343.

Part Four

1. Victor Lieberman, "Transcending East–West Dichotomies," *Modern Asian Studies* 31 (1997): 463–546; John Richards, *The Unending Frontier* (Berkeley: University of California Press, 2003), 22–24.

Chapter 14

1. *Taipei Times*, October 11, 1999, http://uyghuramerican.org/articles/145/1/Fight-for-East-Turkestan/Fight-for-East-Turkestan.html.

2. Winona LaDuke, "We Are Still Here: The 500 Years Celebration," *Sojourners Magazine*, October 1991.

3. Quoted in Thomas E. Skidmore and Peter H. Smith, *Modern Latin America* (New York: Oxford University Press, 2001), 15.

4. George Raudzens, ed., *Technology, Disease, and Colonial Conquest* (Boston: Brill Academic, 2003), xiv.

5. Alfred W. Crosby, "The Columbian Voyages, the Columbian Exchange, and Their Historians," in *Islamic and European Expansion*, edited by Michael Adas (Philadelphia: Temple University Press, 1993), 160.

6. Quoted in Noble David Cook, *Born to Die: Disease and the New World Conquest* (Cambridge: Cambridge University Press, 1998), 202.

7. Quoted in Cook, *Born to Die*, 206.

8. Quoted in Charles C. Mann, *1491* (New York: Alfred A. Knopf, 2005), 56.

9. Felipe Fernandez-Armesto, "Empires in Their Global Context," in *The Atlantic in Global History*, edited by Jorge Canizares-Esguerra and Erik R. Seeman (Upper Saddle River, N.J.: Prentice-Hall, 2007), 105.

10. Quoted in Anthony Padgen, "Identity Formation in Spanish America," in *Colonial Identity in the Atlantic World, 1500–1800*, edited by Nicholas Canny and Anthony Padgen (Princeton, N.J.: Princeton University Press, 1987), 56.

11. Quoted in Marjorie Wall Bingham, *An Age of Empire, 1200–1750* (Oxford: Oxford University Press, 2005), 116.

12. Derived from Skidmore and Smith, *Modern Latin America*, 25.

13. Quoted in James Lockhart and Stuart B. Schwartz, *Early Latin America* (Cambridge: Cambridge University Press, 1983), 206.

14. From Kevin Reilly et al., eds., *Racism: A Global Reader* (Armonk, N.Y.: M. E. Sharpe, 2003), 136–37.

15. Felipe Fernandez-Armesto, *The Americas: A Hemispheric History* (New York: Modern Library, 2003), 58–59.

16. Willard Sutherland, *Taming the Wild Fields: Colonization and Empire on the Russian Steppe* (Ithaca, N.Y.: Cornell University Press, 2004), 223–24.

17. Quoted in Michael Khodarkovsky, *Russia's Steppe Frontier* (Bloomington: Indiana University Press, 2002), 216.

18. Khodarkovsky, *Russia's Steppe Frontier*, 222.

19. Quoted in Kappeler, *The Russian Empire*, 114.

20. Figures derived from Andreas Kappeler, *The Russian Empire* (New York: Longman, 2001), 115–17, 397–99.

21. Geoffrey Hosking, "The Freudian Frontier," *Times Literary Supplement*, March 10, 1995, 27.

22. Peter C. Perdue, *China Marches West* (Cambridge, Mass.: Harvard University Press, 2005); Nicola Di Cosmo, "Qing Colonial Administration in Inner Asia," *International History Review* 20, no. 2 (June 1998): 287–309.

23. Perdue, *China Marches West*, 10–11.

24. Quoted in Stephen F. Dale, "The Islamic World in the Age of European Expansion," in *The Cambridge Illustrated History of the Islamic World*, edited by Francis Robinson (Cambridge: Cambridge University Press, 1996), 80.

25. Quoted in Stanley Wolpert, *A New History of India* (New York: Oxford University Press, 1993), 160.

26. Jane I. Smith, "Islam and Christendom," in *The Oxford History of Islam*, edited by John Esposito (Oxford: Oxford University Press, 1999), 342.

27. Quoted in Alfred J. Andrea and James H. Overfield, *The Human Record* (New York: Houghton Mifflin Company, 2001), 2:91.

28. Jean Bodin, "The Rise and Fall of Commonwealths," chap. 7, http://www.constitution.org/bodin/bodin_4.htm.

29. Lord Wharncliffe, ed., *The Letters and Works of Lady Mary Wortley Montagu* (London: Henry G. Bohn, 1861), 1:298–300.

Chapter 15

1. Jacob Wheeler, "From Slave Post to Museum," *Christian Science Monitor*, December 31, 2002.

2. Quoted in Paul Lunde, "The Coming of the Portuguese," *Saudi Aramco World*, July–August 2005, 56.

3. Philip Curtin, *Cross Cultural Trade in World History* (Cambridge: Cambridge University Press, 1984), 144.

4. Quoted in Patricio N. Abinales and Donna J. Amoroso, *State and Society in the Philippines* (Lanham: Rowman and Littlefield, 2005), 50.

5. Anthony Reid, *Southeast Asia in the Age of Commerce, 1450–1680* (New Haven: Yale University Press, 1993), 2:274, 290.

6. Anthony Reid, *Charting the Shape of Early Modern Southeast Asia* (Chiang Mai: Silkworm Books, 1999), 227.

7. Andre Gunder Frank, *ReOrient: Global Economy in the Asian Age* (Berkeley: University of California Press, 1998), 131.

8. Quoted in Richard von Glahn, "Myth and Reality of China's Seventeenth Century Monetary Crisis," *Journal of Economic History* 56, no. 2 (June 1996): 132.

9. Kenneth Pomeranz and Steven Topik, *The World That Trade Created* (Armonk, N.Y.: M. E. Sharpe, 2006), 151–54.

10. Dennis O. Flynn and Arturo Giraldez, "Born with a 'Silver Spoon,'" *Journal of World History* 6, no. 2 (Fall 1995): 210.

11. Quoted in Mark Elvin, *The Retreat of the Elephant* (New Haven: Yale University Press, 2004), 37.

12. Quoted in Robert Marks, *The Origins of the Modern World* (Lanham: Rowman and Littlefield, 2002), 81.

13. See John Richards, *The Endless Frontier* (Berkeley: University of California Press, 2003), part 4. Much of this section is drawn from this source.

14. Elspeth M. Veale, *The English Fur Trade in the Later Middle Ages* (Oxford: Clarendon Press, 1966), 141.

15. Quoted in Richards, *The Endless Frontier*, 499.

16. Richards, *The Endless Frontier*, 504.

17. Quoted from "The Iroquois Confederacy," Portland State University, 2001, http://www.iroquoisdemocracy.pdx.edu/html/furtrader.htm.

18. David Brion Davis, *Challenging the Boundaries of Slavery* (Cambridge, Mass.: Harvard University Press, 2003), 13.

19. Quoted in Bernard Lewis, *Race and Slavery in the Middle East* (New York: Oxford University Press, 1990), 52–53.

20. Audrey Smedley, *Race in North America* (Boulder, Colo.: Westview Press, 1993).

21. Kevin Reilly et al., eds., *Racism: A Global Reader* (Armonk, N.Y.: M. E. Sharpe, 2003), 131.

22. Thomas Phillips, "A Journal of a Voyage Made in the Hannibal of London in 1694," in *Documents Illustrative of the History of the Slave Trade to America*, edited by Elizabeth Donnan (Washington, D.C.: Carnegie Institute, 1930), 399–410.

23. John Thornton, *Africa and Africans in the Making of the Atlantic World* (Cambridge: Cambridge University Press, 1998), 72.

24. Basil Davidson, trans., *The African Past* (London: Little Brown, 1964), 191–94.

25. Quoted in Anne Bailey, *African Voices in the Atlantic Slave Trade* (Boston: Beacon Press, 2005), 39.

26. Phillips, "A Journal of a Voyage," 399–410.

27. Erik Gilbert and Jonathan T. Reynolds, *Africa in World History* (Upper Saddle River, N.J.: Pearson, 2004), 160.

28. Adapted from Philip Curtin, *The Slave Trade: A Census* (Madison: University of Wisconsin Press, 1969).

29. Adapted from Lynn Hunt et al., *The Making of the West: Peoples and Cultures* (Boston: Bedford/St. Martin's, 2009), 521.

30. Paul Adams et al., *Experiencing World History* (New York: New York University Press, 2000), 334.

31. Bailey, *African Voices*, 153–54.

32. The present-day state of Benin was the location of the earlier kingdom of Dahomey. The ancient kingdom of Benin was located within present-day Nigeria.

Chapter 16

1. Michelle Goldberg, "The New Monkey Trial," January 10, 2005, http://www.salon.com/news/feature/2005/01/10/evolution/index.html.

2. Dr. Peter Hammond, "The Reformation," http://www.frontline.org.za/articles/thereformation_lectures.htm.

3. Glenn J. Ames, *Vasco da Gama: Renaissance Crusader* (New York: Pearson Education, 2005), 50.

4. Cecil Jane, ed. and trans., *Selected Documents Illustrating the Four Voyages of Columbus* (London: Hakluyt Society, 1930–1933), 2:2–18.

5. Kenneth Mills, *Idolatry and Its Enemies* (Princeton, N.J.: Princeton University Press, 1997), chap. 9.

6. Quoted in U.S. Library of Congress, *Country Studies: Peru*, http://countrystudies.us/peru/5.htm.

7. Quoted in Nicolas Griffiths, *The Cross and the Serpent* (Norman: University of Oklahoma Press, 1996), 263.

8. See James Lockhart, *The Nahuas after Conquest* (Stanford, Calif.: Stanford University Press, 1992), chap. 6.

9. Quoted in Joanna Waley-Cohen, *The Sextants of Beijing* (New York: W. W. Norton, 1999), 76–77.

10. Richard M. Eaton, "Islamic History as Global History," in *Islamic and European Expansion*, edited by Michael Adas (Philadelphia: Temple University Press, 1993), 25.

11. Robert Bly and Jane Hirshfield, trans., *Mirabai: Ecstatic Poems* (Boston: Beacon Press, 2004), ix–xi.

12. Quoted in Steven Shapin, *The Scientific Revolution* (Chicago: University of Chicago Press, 1996), 66.

13. This section draws heavily on Toby E. Huff, *The Rise of Early Modern Science* (Cambridge: Cambridge University Press, 2003), 48, 52, 76.

14. Huff, *The Rise of Early Modern Science*, 87, 288.

15. Jerome Cardano, *The Book of My Life*, translated by Jean Stoner (London: J. M. Dent, 1931), 189.

16. Quoted in Shapin, *The Scientific Revolution*, 28.

17. Quoted in Shapin, *The Scientific Revolution*, 61.

18. Quoted in Shapin, *The Scientific Revolution*, 33.

19. Quoted in Shapin, *The Scientific Revolution*, 68.

20. Stillman Drake, trans., *Discoveries and Opinions of Galileo* (Garden City, N.Y.: Doubleday, 1957).

21. H. S. Thayer, ed., *Newton's Philosophy of Nature: Selections from His Writings* (New York: Hafner Library of Classics, 1953), 42.

22. Immanuel Kant, "What Is Enlightenment?" translated by Peter Gay, in *Introduction to Contemporary Civilization in the West* (New York: Columbia University Press, 1954), 1071.

23. Voltaire, *A Treatise on Toleration* (1763), chap. 22.

24. Margaret C. Jacob, *The Enlightenment* (Boston: Bedford/St. Martin's, 2001), 103.

25. Marquis de Condorcet, *Historical View of the Progress of the Human Mind: The Tenth Stage* (1794).

26. Quoted in Jonathan Spence, *The Search for Modern China* (New York: Norton, 1999), 104.

27. Waley-Cohen, *The Sextants of Beijing*, 105–14.

28. Benjamin A. Elman, *On Their Own Terms: Science in China, 1550–1900* (Cambridge, Mass.: Harvard University Press, 2005).

29. Quoted in David R. Ringrose, *Expansion and Global Interaction, 1200–1700* (New York: Longman, 2001), 188.

30. Ekmeleddin Ihsanoglu, *Science, Technology, and Learning in the Ottoman Empire* (Burlington, Vt.: Ashgate, 2004).

Part Five

1. Quoted in Ross Dunn, *The New World History* (Boston: Bedford/St. Martin's, 2000), 17.

2. William H. McNeill, "*The Rise of the West* after 25 Years," *Journal of World History* 1, no. 1 (Spring 1990): 7.

Chapter 17

1. Quoted in Keith M. Baker, "A World Transformed," *Wilson Quarterly*, Summer 1989, 37.

2. Quoted in Thomas Benjamin et al., *The Atlantic World in the Age of Empire* (Boston: Houghton Mifflin, 2001), 205.

3. Jack P. Greene, "The American Revolution," *American Historical Review* 105, no. 1 (February 2000): 96–97.

4. Quoted in Greene, "The American Revolution," 102.

5. Quoted in Susan Dunn, *Sister Revolutions* (New York: Faber and Faber, 1999), 11, 12.

6. Quoted in Dunn, *Sister Revolutions*, 9.

7. Quoted in Lynn Hunt et al., *The Making of the West* (Boston: Bedford/St. Martin's, 2003), 625.

8. From James Leith, "Music for Mass Persuasion during the Terror," a collection of texts, tapes, and slides, copyright James A. Leith, Queen's University Kingston.

9. Franklin W. Knight, "The Haitian Revolution," *American Historical Review* 105, no. 1 (February 2000): 103.

10. Quoted in David P. Geggus, *Haitian Revolutionary Studies* (Bloomington: Indiana University Press, 2002), 27.

11. John C. Chasteen, *Born in Blood and Fire* (New York: Norton, 2006), 103.

12. Peter Winn, *Americas: The Changing Face of Latin America and the Caribbean* (Berkeley: University of California Press, 2006), 83.

13. Quoted in Thomas E. Skidmore and Peter H. Smith, *Modern Latin America* (New York: Oxford University Press, 2001), 33.

14. James Walvin, "The Public Campaign in England against Slavery," in *The Abolition of the Atlantic Slave Trade*, edited by David Eltis and James Walvin (Madison: University of Wisconsin Press, 1981), 76.

15. Michael Craton, "Slave Revolts and the End of Slavery," in *The Atlantic Slave Trade*, edited by David Northrup (Boston: Houghton Mifflin, 2002), 200.

16. Quoted in Northrup, *The Atlantic Slave Trade*, 175.

17. Eric Foner, *Nothing but Freedom* (Baton Rouge: Louisiana State University Press, 1983).

18. Quoted in Daniel Moran and Arthur Waldron, eds., *The People in Arms: Military Myth and National Mobilization since the French Revolution* (Cambridge: Cambridge University Press, 2003), 14.

19. Barbara Winslow, "Feminist Movements: Gender and Sexual Equality," in *A Companion to Gender History*, edited by Teresa A. Meade and Merry E. Weisner-Hanks (London: Blackwell, 2004), 186.

20. Olympe de Gouges, *The Declaration of the Rights of Woman*, 1791, http://www.pinn.net/~sunshine/book-sum/gouges.html.

21. Bonnie S. Anderson, *Joyous Greetings: The First International Women's Movement, 1830–1860* (Oxford: Oxford University Press, 2000).

22. Quoted in Claire G. Moses, *French Feminism in the Nineteenth Century* (Albany: SUNY Press, 1984), 135.

Chapter 18

1. "Mahatma Gandhi on Industrialization," http://www.tinytechindia.com/gandhi3.htm#1.

2. Joel Mokyr, *The Lever of Riches* (New York: Oxford University Press, 1990), 40–44.

3. Lynda Shaffer, "Southernization," *Journal of World History* 5, no. 1 (Spring 1994): 1–21.

4. Kenneth Pomeranz, *The Great Divergence* (Princeton, N.J.: Princeton University Press, 2000).

5. Pier Vries, "Are Coal and Colonies Really Crucial?" *Journal of World History* 12, no. 2 (Fall 2001): 411.

6. E. L. Jones, *The European Miracle* (Cambridge: Cambridge University Press, 1981), 119.

7. David Christian, *Maps of Time* (Berkeley: University of California Press, 2004), 390.

8. Quoted in Mokyr, *The Lever of Riches*, 188.

9. Quoted in Prasannan Parthansaranthi, "Rethinking Wages and Competitiveness in the Eighteenth Century," *Past and Present* 158 (February 1998): 79.

10. Maxine Berg, *Luxury and Pleasure in Eighteenth-Century Britain* (Oxford: Oxford University Press, 2005), 79–84.

11. Peter Stearns, *The Industrial Revolution in World History* (Boulder, Colo.: Westview Press, 1998), 36.

12. Jack Goldstone, "Efflorescences and Economic Growth in World History," *Journal of World History* 13, no. 2 (Fall 2002): 367–79.

13. Eric Hopkins, *Industrialization and Society* (London: Routledge, 2000), 2.

14. Mokyr, *The Lever of Riches*, 81.

15. Eric Hobsbawm, *Industry and Empire* (New York: New Press, 1999), 58. This section draws heavily on Hobsbawm's celebrated account of British industrialization.

16. Lynn Hunt et al., *The Making of the West: Peoples and Cultures* (Boston: Bedford/St. Martin's, 2009), 656.

17. Samuel Smiles, *Thrift* (London: John Murray, 1875), 30–40.

18. Hobsbawm, *Industry and Empire*, 65.

19. Peter Stearns and John H. Hinshaw, *Companion to the Industrial Revolution* (Santa Barbara: ABC-CLIO, 1996), 150.

20. http://www.workersliberty.org/node/view/3359?PHPSESSID=93d.

21. Hobsbawm, *Industry and Empire*, 171.

22. Derived from Paul Kennedy, *The Rise and Fall of the Great Powers* (New York: Random House, 1987), 149.

23. John Charles Chasteen, *Born in Blood and Fire* (New York: W. W. Norton, 2006), 181.

24. Peter Bakewell, *A History of Latin America* (Oxford: Blackwell, 1997), 425.

25. Michael Adas, *Machines as the Measure of Men* (Ithaca, N.Y.: Cornell University Press, 1990).

Chapter 19

1. *People's Daily*, April 6, 2001, http://english.peopledaily.com.cn/english/200104/06/eng20010406_66955.html.

2. Quoted in Heinz Gollwitzer, *Europe in the Age of Imperialism* (London: Thames and Hudson, 1969), 136.

3. Robert Knox, *Races of Man* (Philadelphia: Lea and Blanchard, 1850), v.

4. Quoted in Ralph Austen, ed., *Modern Imperialism* (Lexington, Mass.: D. C. Heath, 1969), 70–73.

5. Quoted in Julian Burger, "Echoes of History," *The New Internationalist*, August 1988, http://www.newint.org/issue186/echoes.htm.

6. Dun J. Li, ed., *China in Transition, 1517–1911* (New York: Van Nostrand Reinhold, 1969).

7. Quoted in Jonathan D. Spence, *The Search for Modern China* (New York: W. W. Norton, 1999), 169.

8. Hsin-Pao Chang, ed., *Commissioner Lin and the Opium War* (New York: Norton, 1970), 226–27.

9. Barbara Hodgson, *Opium: A Portrait of the Heavenly Demon* (San Francisco: Chronicle Books, 1999), 32.

10. Quoted in Magali Morsy, *North Africa: 1800–1900* (London: Longman, 1984), 79.

11. Marius B. Jansen, *The Making of Modern Japan* (Cambridge, Mass.: Harvard University Press, 2002), 33.

12. Quoted in Carol Gluck, "Themes in Japanese History," in *Asia in Western and World History*, edited by Ainslie T. Embree and Carol Gluck (Armonk, N.Y.: M. E. Sharpe, 1997), 754.

13. Quoted in S. Hanley and K. Yamamura, *Economic and Demographic Change in Pre-Industrial Japan* (Princeton, N.J.: Princeton University Press, 1977), 88–90.

14. Quoted in Harold Bolitho, "The Tempo Crisis," in *The Cambridge History of Japan,* vol. 5, *The Nineteenth Century*, edited by Maurice B. Jansen (Cambridge: Cambridge University Press, 1989), 230.

15. Kenneth Henshall, *A History of Japan* (New York: Palgrave, 2004), 67.

16. Quoted in James L. McClain, *Japan: A Modern History* (New York: W. W. Norton, 2002), 177.

17. Selcuk Esenbel, "Japan's Global Claim to Asia and the World of Islam," *American Historical Review,* October 2004, par. 1, 9, http://www.historycooperative.org/journals/ahr/109.4/esenbel.html.

Chapter 20

1. Quoted in Robert Strayer, *The Making of Mission Communities in East Africa* (London: Heinemann, 1978), 89.

2. Quoted in John Iliffe, *Africans: The History of a Continent* (Cambridge: Cambridge University Press, 1995), 191.

3. Quoted in Nicholas Tarling, "The Establishment of Colonial Regimes," in *The Cambridge History of Southeast Asia*, edited by Nicholas Tarling (Cambridge: Cambridge University Press, 1992), 2:76.

4. R. Meinertzhagen, *Kenya Diary* (London: Oliver and Boyd, 1957), 51–52.

5. Quoted in Neil Jamieson, *Understanding Vietnam* (Berkeley: University of California Press, 1993), 49–57.

6. Quoted in Donald R. Wright, *The World and a Very Small Place in Africa* (Armonk, N.Y.: M. E. Sharpe, 2004), 170.

7. Quoted in Scott B. Cook, *Colonial Encounters in the Age of High Imperialism* (New York: HarperCollins, 1996), 53.

8. D. R. SarDesai, *Southeast Asia: Past and Present* (Boulder, Colo.: Westview Press, 1997), 95–98.

9. Quoted in G. C. K. Gwassa and John Iliffe, *Records of the Maji Maji Rising*, part I (Nairobi: East African Publishing House, 1967), 4–5.

10. Iliffe, *Africans*, 216.

11. Quoted in Basil Davidson, *Modern Africa* (London: Longman, 1983), 79, 81.

12. This section draws heavily on Margaret Jean Hay and Sharon Stichter, eds., *African Women South of the Sahara* (London: Longman, 1984), especially chaps. 1–5.

13. Quoted in Robert A. Levine, "Sex Roles and Economic Change in Africa," in *Black Africa*, edited by John Middleton (London: Macmillan, 1970), 178.

14. Elizabeth Schmidt, *Peasants, Traders, and Wives: Shona Women in the History of Zimbabwe, 1870–1939* (Portsmouth, N.H.: Heinemann, 1992), chap. 4.

15. Derived from Adam McKeown, "Global Migration, 1846–1940," *Journal of World History* 15, no. 2 (June 2004): 156.

16. Josiah Kariuki, *Mau Mau Detainee* (London: Oxford University Press, 1963), 5.

17. Quoted in Harry Benda and John Larkin, *The World of Southeast Asia* (New York: Harper and Row, 1967), 182–85.

18. Rammohun Roy, *The English Works of Raja Rammohun Roy* (Allahabad: Panini Office, 1906), 471–74.

19. James Aggrey, "The Parable of the Eagle," in Edward W. Smith, *Aggrey of Africa* (London: SCM Press, 1929).

20. C. A. Bayly, *The Birth of the Modern World* (Oxford: Blackwell, 2004), 343.

21. William Theodore de Bary, ed., *Sources of Indian Tradition* (New York: Columbia University Press, 1958), 2:100.

22. Nirad Chaudhuri, *Autobiography of an Unknown Indian* (London: John Farquharson, 1968), 229.

23. Edward Blyden, *Christianity, Islam, and the Negro Race* (Edinburgh: Edinburgh University Press, 1967), 124.

24. John Iliffe, *A Modern History of Tanganyika* (Cambridge: Cambridge University Press, 1979), 324.

Part Six

1. J. R. McNeill, *Something New under the Sun* (New York: W. W. Norton, 2000), 3–4.

Chapter 21

1. "Scotland's Oldest Man Turns 107," *Scotsman*, June 25, 2003, http://www.aftermathww1.com/oldestscot.asp; MSNBC, November 21, 2005, http://www.msnbc.msn.com/id/10138446/.

2. Quoted in John Keegan, *The First World War* (New York: Vintage Books, 1998), 3.

3. Adapted from Lynn Hunt et al., *The Making of the West: Peoples and Cultures* (Boston: Bedford/St. Martin's, 2001), 1024.

4. Stanley Payne, *History of Fascism, 1914–1945* (Madison: University of Wisconsin Press, 1995), 208.

5. Richard Bessel, ed., *Fascist Italy and Nazi Germany: Comparisons and Contrasts* (Cambridge: Cambridge University Press, 1996), 8.

6. Quoted in Laurence Rees, *The Nazis: A Warning from History* (New York: New Press, 1997), 62.

7. James L. McClain, *Japan: A Modern History* (New York: W. W. Norton, 2002), 378.

8. Quoted in McClain, *Japan*, 414.

9. Bernd Martin, *Japan and Germany in the Modern World* (Providence: Berghahn Books, 1995), 155–81.

10. Quoted in Marius B. Jansen, *The Making of Modern Japan* (Cambridge, Mass.: Harvard University Press, 2000), 607.

11. Quoted in Jansen, *The Making of Modern Japan*, 639.

12. Quoted in John Keegan, *The Second World War* (New York: Viking Penguin, 1989), 186.

13. John Lewis Gaddis, *We Now Know: Rethinking Cold War History* (Oxford: Oxford University Press, 1997), 52.

14. Adam Gopnik, "The Big One: Historians Rethink the War to End All Wars," *The New Yorker*, August 23, 2004, 78.

Chapter 22

1. BBC, "On This Day," November 9, 1989, http://news.bbc.co.uk/onthisday/hi/witness/november/9/newsid_3241000/3241641.stm.

2. Quoted in Ronald Suny, *The Soviet Experiment* (Oxford: Oxford University Press, 1998), 357.

3. Yuan-tsung Chen, *The Dragon's Village* (New York: Penguin Books, 1980), 85.

4. Such figures are often highly controversial. See Maurice Meisner, *Mao's China and After* (New York: Free Press, 1999), 413–25; Roderick MacFarquhar, ed., *The Politics of China* (Cambridge: Cambridge University Press, 1997), 243–45.

5. Richard Rusk, *As I Saw It* (New York: Norton, 1990), 245.

6. Quoted in John L. Gaddis, *The Cold War: A New History* (New York: Penguin Press, 2005), 57.

7. Ronald Steel, *Pax Americana* (New York: Viking Press, 1970), 254.

8. Quoted in Donald W. White, *The American Century* (New Haven: Yale University Press, 1996), 164.

9. David Potter, *People of Plenty* (Chicago: University of Chicago Press, 1954), 139.

10. Quoted in John M. Thompson, *A Vision Unfulfilled* (Lexington, Mass.: D. C. Heath, 1996), 383.

11. Deng Xiaoping, "The Necessity of Upholding the Four Cardinal Principles in the Drive for the Four Modernizations," in *Major Documents of the People's Republic of China* (Beijing: Foreign Language Press, 1991), 54.

12. Mikhail Gorbachev, *Perestroika: New Thinking for Our Country and the World* (New York: Harper and Row, 1987), 64.

13. Quoted in Abraham Brumberg, *Chronicle of a Revolution* (New York: Pantheon Books, 1990), 225–26.

Chapter 23

1. "I Am Prepared to Die" (Nelson Mandela statement at the Rivonia trial, April 20, 1964), http://www.anc.org.za/ancdocs/history/rivonia.html.

2. Quoted in Jim Masselos, *Nationalism on the Indian Subcontinent* (Melbourne: Nelson, 1972), 122.

3. Mohandas Gandhi, *Hind Swaraj*, 1909, http://www.mkgandhi-sarvodaya.org/hindswaraj.htm.

4. Quoted in Stanley Wolpert, *A New History of India* (Oxford: Oxford University Press, 1993), 331.

5. This information is drawn from the World Bank, *World Development Report 2006* (Oxford: Oxford University Press, 2005), Tables 1, 2.

6. Quoted in Bernard Lewis, *The Emergence of Modern Turkey* (London: Oxford University Press, 1968), 268–69.

7. *The Sayings of Ayatollah Khomeini* (New York: Bantam Books, 1980), 3–29.

Chapter 24

1. BBC News, March 5, 2002, http://news.bbc.co.uk/2/hi/middle_east/1856558.stm.

2. Jeffrey Frieden, *Global Capitalism* (New York: W. W. Norton, 2006), 476.

3. Jan Aart Scholte, *Globalization: A Critical Introduction* (New York: Palgrave, 2005), 117.

4. Based on constant 2004 U.S. dollars. Earth Policy Institute, "Eco-Economy Indicators," http://www.earth-policy.org/Indicators/Econ/Econ_data.htm.

5. United Nations, *Human Development Report, 1997*, 2, http://hdr.undp.org/reports/global/1997/en.

6. Michael Hunt, *The World Transformed* (Boston: Bedford/St. Martin's, 2004), 442.

7. Quoted in Frieden, *Global Capitalism*, 408.

8. Quoted in Manfred B. Steger, *Globalization: A Very Short Introduction* (Oxford: Oxford University Press, 2003), 122.

9. Quoted in Frieden, *Global Capitalism*, 459.

10. Charles S. Maier, *Among Empires: American Ascendancy and Its Predecessors* (Cambridge, Mass.: Harvard University Press, 2006), chap. 5.

11. Quoted in Donald W. White, *The American Century: The Rise and Decline of the United States as a World Power* (New Haven: Yale University Press, 1996), 395.

12. Quoted in Sarah Shaver Hughes and Brady Hughes, *Women in World History* (Armonk, N.Y.: M. E. Sharpe, 1997), 2:268.

13. Susan Kent, "Worlds of Feminism," in *Women's History in Global Perspective*, edited by Bonnie G. Smith (Urbana: University of Illinois Press, 2004), 1:305–6.

14. Quoted in Wilhelmina Oduol and Wanjiku Mukabi Kabira, "The Mother of Warriors and Her Daughters: The Women's Movement in Kenya," in *Global Feminisms since 1945*, edited by Bonnie Smith (London: Routledge, 2000), 111.

15. Elisabeth Jay Friedman, "Gendering the Agenda," *Women's Studies International Forum* 26, no. 4 (2003): 313–31.

16. Quoted in Mary E. Hawkesworth, *Globalization and Feminist Activism* (New York: Rowman and Littfield, 2006), 124.

17. Phyllis Schlafly, *The Power of the Christian Woman* (Cincinnati: Standard, 1981), 117.

18. Karen Armstrong, *The Battle for God* (New York: Alfred A. Knopf, 2000), xi.

19. Quoted in Armstrong, *The Battle for God*, 273.

20. Quoted in John Esposito, *Unholy War* (Oxford: Oxford University Press, 2002), 57.

21. Quoted in Esposito, *Unholy War*, 63.

22. Text of Fatwah Urging Jihad against Americans, http://www.ict.org.il/articles/fatwah.htm.

23. Anwar Ibrahim, "The Ardent Moderates," *Time*, September 23, 1996, 24.

24. See J. R. McNeill, *Something New under the Sun: An Environmental History of the Twentieth Century World* (New York: Norton, 2001).

25. Adapted from Lynn Hunt et al., *The Making of the West: Peoples and Cultures* (Boston: Bedford/St. Martin's, 2009), 968.

26. Ramachandra Guha, *Environmentalism: A Global History* (New York: Longman, 2000), part 1.

27. Timothy Doyle, *Environmental Movements in Minority and Majority Worlds: A Global Perspective* (New Brunswick, N.J.: Rutgers University Press, 2005).

28. Quoted in Shiraz Sidhva, "Saving the Planet: Imperialism in a Green Garb," *The UNESCO Courier*, April 2001, 41–43.

Acknowledgments

Chapter 13

Miguel Leon-Portilla. "Like a painting, we will be erased." From *Fifteen Poets of the Aztec World* by Miguel Leon-Portilla, editor and translator. Copyright © 1992 by the University of Oklahoma Press, Norman. Reprinted by permission.

Chapter 15

Mark Elvin. "Rarer too their timber grew." Excerpt (4 lines) from *Retreat of the Elephants* by Mark Elvin. Copyright © 2004 by Mark Elvin. Used by permission of Yale University Press.

Chapter 16

Mirabai. "What I paid was my social body. . . ." From *Mirabai: Ecstatic Poems* by Robert Bly and Jane Hirshfeld. Copyright © by Robert Bly and Jane Hirshfield. Reprinted by Beacon Press, Boston.

Chapter 20

Neil Jamieson. "Fine wine but no good friends." From *Understanding Vietnam* by Neil Jamieson, translator. Copyright © 1993 by University of California Press. Reproduced with permission of University of California Press in the format Textbook via Copyright Clearance Center.

Maps

Map 15.4 is adapted from Craig Lockard, *Societies, Networks, and Transitions: A Global History* (Houghton, 2008). Map 18.2 is adapted from John Mack Faragher et al., *Out of Many: A History of the American People* (Prentice Hall, 1997). Map 18.3 is adapted from John Charles Chasteen, *Born in Blood and Iron: A Concise History of Latin America* (Norton, 2006). Map 19.1 is adapted from Jerry H. Bentley and Herbert F. Ziegler, *Traditions and Encounters,* Second Edition (McGraw-Hill, 2003). Map 24.1 is adapted from Felipe Fernández-Armesto, *The World* (Prentice Hall, 2007). Map 24.3 (bottom) is adapted from http://www.princeton.edu/~ina/infographics/starbucks.html (2003).

Index

Names of individuals in **boldface**

(f) figures, including charts and graphs

(i) illustrations, including photographs and artifacts

(m) maps

(t) tables

Abbasid caliphate, 379
Abd al-Hamid II (r. 1876–1909), 576
Abd al-Rahman al-Jabarti, 572
Abd al-Wahhab (1703–1792), 474, 474*(m)*
abolitionist movements, 510, 514, 514*(i)*
Aboriginal people, Australia, 365–366
Achebe, Chinua, 367
Addams, Jane, 521
Afghanistan
   communism in, 661
   Islamic renewal in, 745–746
   Soviet war in, 623*(t)*, 676, 745
   U.S. action in, 733
Afonso (king, Kongo), 400*(t)*, 453
Africa
   agriculture in, 366–367
   antidote to Eurocentrism and, 494
   cash crop farming in, 601
   colonial era and, 493, 497*(t)*, 592
   Columbian exchange in, 408
   communism in, 661
   conquest and resistance in, 593*(m)*
   decolonization in, 620, 623*(t)*
   democracy rejected in, 706–708
   diaspora from, 409, 449–450
   disparities in, 730
   economic growth in, 711, 712–713, 719
   feminism in, 737, 739
   fifteenth century, 364*(t)*, 389, 390*(m)*
   independence in, 692, 693
   landmarks of European movement in, 496–497*(t)*
   Marxism in, 681
   missionaries in, 493, 607, 609*(i)*, 609–610
   Paleolithic persistence in, 365
   pastoral societies in, 369
   political experiments in, 706–710, 709*(m)*
   Portuguese trade and, 375*(t)*, 436–437
   Prester John in, 435
   privatization in, 711
   scramble for, 592, 593*(m)*
   slave trade in, 367, 450, 452–453, 455–457
   in World War I, 629
   in World War II, 650, 652
African Americans, 736
African identity, 611–613
African National Congress, 691, 700*(t)*, 702, 703
Africanus, Leo, 381
Afrikaners, 700–704
Aggrey, James, 609
Agricultural Revolution, hunter/gatherers and, 366
agriculture
   in Africa, 604–605
   African slave trade and, 456
   in Australia, 365–366
   Aztec, 384, 410
   in Burma, 601
   in China, 371, 670–671
   colonization and, 416, 590, 604–605
   Columbian exchange in, 407–408
   communist collectivization of, 670–671, 683, 685
   environmental impact of, 748–749
   European, 378
   firestick farming, 366
   fur trade and, 445
   globalization of, 730
   in Great Britain, 531, 534, 535
   in Haiti, 509
   Inca, 387
   Industrial Revolution and, 528–529
   in Jamaica, 515
   in Japan, 578
   Native American women in, 368
   rice in China, 378
   Russian Empire, 419
   slavery and, 450–452
   tariffs and, 730
   webs of exchange in, 389
   women in, 711–712
   World War I stimulation of, 634
   See also irrigation; plantations; sugar production
Ahmad Sirhindi (1564–1624), 425
AIDS (acquired immune deficiency syndrome), 739
Akbar (r. 1556–1605), 424–425, 427
Akiko, Yosano, 642
algebra, Arab development of, 478
Algeria, 496*(t)*, 575, 696, 727, 742, 745
Algonquians, European trade with, 447
All-India Muslim League, 699
All Quiet on the Western Front (Remarque), 630
Amazon basin, 389, 550
America. *See* United States of America
American Federation of Labor, 544
Americanos, 512
American Revolution (1775–1783), 483, 496*(t)*, 499, 501–504
   See also United States of America
Americas
   European empires, 403–407, 405*(m)*
   northern *versus* southern continents, 416–417
   Paleolithic persistence in, 365
   pre-Columbian societies, 382–388, 383*(m)*
   separation of from Afro-Eurasia, 389, 390
   See also Mesoamerica; North America; South America
Amritsar massacre (India), 697–698
Anatolia, Turkey, 571
   Ottoman Empire in, 378, 427

al-Andalus. *See* Spain
Andes mountains
    Christian missions in, 468–470
    demographic collapse in, 407
    gender systems, 388
    Inca Empire, 382, 386–388
    social structures in, 410
Anglo-Japanese Treaty (1902), 584
Angola, 455
anticolonialism, 617, 618
Anti-Comintern Pact, 650(t)
antiglobalization movements, 730–731
anti-Semitism, 639, 640(i), 640–641
Aotearoa. *See* New Zealand
apartheid, 597, 700–701
    end of, 623(t), 700–704
    established, 700(t)
    Gandhi on, 698
    international opposition to, 703
    Mandela and, 691
appeasement policies, 648
Arab Empire
    end of, 692
    globalization by, 724
Arabia
    Islamic renewal in, 474, 474(m)
    Wahhabi movement in, 474, 496(t)
Arabs
    after World War I, 632
    cultural flowering of, 493
    Six-Day War (1967), 623(t)
    sugar production by, 413
    in World War I, 629
Argentina, 549, 550, 552
aristocracy
    in France, 505
    in Great Britain, 531–532, 534–535
    privilege of, 500
Aristotle, 478
    worldview of, 479–480
Armenia, 441, 632
art
    in Australia, 366
    Benin bronzes, 367, 367(i)
    in China, 475, 682
    in communism, 668
    Mughal Empire, 424–425
    Renaissance, 373
    slave trade in spread of African, 450
    Soviet Union, 684–685

Asante, West Africa, 515
Assyria, 692
astronomy
    Arab achievements in, 478, 479(i)
    in China, 471
Atahualpa, 406
Atatürk, Mustafa Kemal
    (1881–1938), 713, 716, 716(i)
Atlantic Revolutions, 500–501, 501(t)
Atlantic slave trade. *See* slave trade
Aurangzeb (1658–1707), 425, 473
Australia, 629
    colonization of, 592, 594
    Paleolithic persistence in, 365–366
Austria, 634, 637, 648
    railroads in, 535(f)
    royal family of, 574(i)
    in Triple Alliance, 627
    in World War II, 650, 650(t)
Austrian Empire, 426, 428(i), 429, 517, 693
Axis powers (Italy, Germany, Japan), 636, 649(m)
Aztec Empire, 364(t), 382–386, 384, 386
    Christianity and, 468
    conquest of, 400(t), 406, 410–412
    cultural flowering of, 493
    dissent in, 406
    gender system, 387–388
    Inca Empire compared with, 386
    population rebound among, 416
    religious syncretism based on, 487
    resentment against, 406

Bacon, Francis (1561–1626), 480(t)
Balkans, 427
bananas, 550
Bangladesh, 748
Bantustans, 701, 704(m)
Barbie and Ken dolls, 723, 727
Battle of Midway (1942), 650(t)
Battle of Stalingrad (1943), 650(t)
Beijing Conference (1995), 739
Belgian Congo, 696
Belgium, 531(m), 599
Bengal, 596, 607
Benin, 367, 367(i), 400(t), 452, 456
Berlin Wall, 659, 675, 685
Bharatiya Janata Party (BJP, India), 742
Bill of Rights, 504

Bini people, 367
bin Laden, Osama, 742, 745–746
birth control, 444, 712, 739
al-Biruni (973–1048), 479(i)
Black Consciousness movement, 700(t), 702–703
Black Death, 434
Black Shirts, 637–638
Blake, William, 749
blitzkrieg, 648
Blyden, Edward (1832–1912), 611–612
Bodin, Jean, 428–429
Boer War (1899–1902), 497(t), 700(t), 701
Bohemia, 531(m)
Bolivar, Simón (1783–1830), 496(t), 500, 501, 504, 512, 512(i)
Bolivia, 549, 550, 661
    silver mines in, 435, 442, 443(i), 443–444
Bolsheviks, 663(m), 663–664
    authoritarianism of, 664
    support for, 667
    Western opposition to, 668
    See also Russian Revolution
Bombay, India, 440
Bonsu, Osei, 515
Botswana, 605
Boxer Rebellion (1899–1901), 497(t), 569(m), 570
Bradford, Governor of Plymouth, 407
Brahmin caste, 597
brain drain, 727
Brazil
    abolishment of slavery in, 497(t), 514
    African religions in, 473
    diamonds in, 412
    economic development in, 554, 714–715(t)
    ethnic composition of, 414
    feminism in, 738(i)
    first railroads in, 497(t)
    gold rush in, 412
    Great Depression in, 634
    independence of, 501(t), 549
    industrialization in, 530
    Islam in, 473
    migration to, 552
    Portuguese colonies in, 412, 413

slavery in, 413, 415, 454(f), 455, 515, 549
war with Paraguay, 549
women's movement and, 523
Bretton Woods system, 725
Britain. *See* British Empire; Great Britain
British East India Company, 439, 440, 592, 596
British Empire, 493, 502–503, 587–589(i)
British Royal Society, 533
British West Indies, 514
British Women's Social and Political Union, 521
Broz, Josef (Tito), 665
Bruno, Giordano, 482
Buddhism
    in China, 471
    as cultural anchor, 389
    in East Asia, 462
    globalization of, 740
    in Neo-Confucianism, 474–475
    socially engaged, 747
Buganda, East Africa, 594, 608
Bulgaria, 572, 664–665, 685–686
Burma
    independence in, 692
    Japanese military operations in, 647
    Portugal resisted by, 437
    rice crops in, 601
Buthelezi, Gatsha, 703
Byzantine Empire (Byzantium)
    end of, 364(t)
    Ottoman Empire and, 379, 425, 427

Cabot, John, 375(t)
calendars, 505
caliphs, 379, 576
Cambodia, 661, 681, 682
Cameroon, 604
Canada, 497(t), 629
canal systems, 533
Candomble, 473
capitalism
    abolition of slavery and, 514
    in Africa, 707
    apparent triumph of, 687
    British colonies and, 415
    communist opposition to, 674

early modern rise of, 434
fundamentalism and, 741
globalization of, 725
Great Depression as unraveling of, 633–636
Hitler on, 640
Industrial Revolution and, 530
instabilities in, 633–634
Islam and, 743–744
in Japan, 578
Jews blamed for, 640(i)
versus socialism, 539
socialist revolution and, 661
carbon dioxide emissions, 715(t), 750(m)
The Cardinal Principles of Our National Polity, 644
Caribbean islands, 407, 412(i), 412–415, 454(f), 455, 507–510
Carnegie, Andrew, 543–544
Carson, Rachel, 749
cartaz (pass), 437
cash crops, 600–605
cassava, 408, 408(i), 456
caste system, in India, 399, 476–477
Caste War of Yucatán (1847–1904), 549
Castro, Fidel, 661, 676–677
Catherine the Great (r. 1762–1796), 419, 546
Catholicism. *See* Roman Catholic Church
cattle, Columbian exchange in, 407–408, 408(i)
caudillos, 549
Central America
    as developing country, 705, 705(m)
    economic development in, 730
    exports from, 550
    United Fruit Company in, 554
Ceylon, 372
Chavín civilization, 386
Chechnya, 575
checks and balances, 533
Chernobyl nuclear accident, 751(i)
Chiang Kai-Shek, 666
chiefdoms, 365
    in Africa, 612
    Native American, 366
Chikpo movement, 751
Chile, 497(t), 550, 634, 678, 738
Chimu civilization, 386

China, 370–372, 569(m)
    Boxer Rebellion in, 497(t), 569(m), 570
    Buddhism and, 389
    carbon dioxide emissions in, 750(m)
    Christianity and, 487, 740
    in the cold war, 675
    collective agriculture in, 670, 671, 683
    Columbian exchange in, 408
    communism in, 620, 632, 652, 660, 662, 665–667, 668, 682–684, 706
    Communist Party founded, 622(t)
    cultural flowering of, 493
    as developing country, 705, 705(m)
    early modern, 397, 399, 444–445
    economic growth in, 683, 687, 712, 714–715(t), 730
    education in, 479
    end of Empire in, 577
    European dominance and, 441, 494, 565
    expansion of, 369
    globalization and, 723, 724
    Great Leap Forward, 671, 673
    Great Proletarian Cultural Revolution, 673, 674–675, 681, 682, 735
    imperialism in, 375–378, 393, 404, 421, 422, 422(m), 422–424
    imperial system's collapse in, 665
    indentured servants from, 515
    in Indian Ocean trade, 406, 435
    industrialization in, 530, 671–672, 673, 711
    inequality in, 730
    isolationism in, 372
    Japan and, 584
    Japanese invasion of, 632, 666, 667
    kaozheng movement, 475, 485
    land reform in, 666, 711
    long-distance migration and, 606(t)
    Long March, 622(t), 665(i)
    manufacturing output and, 548(t)
    miners from, 604
    missionaries in, 398, 400(t), 468, 470–472, 531–532, 568
    nationalism and, 520
    Neo-Confucianism, 474–475
    nuclear capability of, 681

China (*continued*)
opium in, 566–567
versus Ottoman Empire, 577
Philippines and, 438
plantation workers from, 602
Portuguese trade bases in, 436
Rape of Nanjing, 650, 650(t)
regional specialization in, 444
scientific innovation in, 478, 479, 485, 529
silver trade with, 438(t), 442(m), 442–443, 444–445
Soviet opposition to, 681
Spanish American silver trade with, 433
special enterprise zones, 683
spheres of influence in, 558–559(i), 569(m)
Taiwan tensions with, 687
technological advancements in, 529
Tiananmen Square demonstration, 684
Tibet and, 747
Treaty of Friendship, 661
Uighurs in, 403
view of history in, 753
Voltaire on, 483
women's rights in, 523, 669–670, 735
in world economy, 458
in World War I, 629
in World War II, 559–560, 645, 646(m), 647, 650, 650(t)
Zheng He naval expeditions, 363, 365, 374–378
Chinese Communist Party (CCP), 665–667, 667, 681
Chinese Revolution (1911), 497(t), 577
Chinese Revolution (1949), 618, 622(t), 688
Chinggis Khan (1162–1227), 424
chlorofluorocarbons, 749
Christianity
African religions and, 472–473
in Americas, 493
in the Balkans, 427
conversion to, 596
cultural borrowing and, 486–487
European imperialism and, 563, 564
evolution and, 484
globalization of, 462–472, 740

imperialism and, 377, 406, 467–470, 694
in Indian Ocean Trade, 435
Islam and, 438
in Japan, 441
missionaries and, 609–610
Ottoman Empire and, 388–389, 390(m), 427–428
Protestant Reformation, 463–467
Renaissance and, 373–374
resistance to, 469
Russian Empire, 419, 420
saints in, 469–470
Scientific Revolution and, 482
Spanish America imperialism and, 412
syncretism in, 487
Taiping Uprising and, 565–566
Westernization and, 392
as world religion, 397, 461
Chulalongkorn (king, Siam), 608(i)
Churchill, Winston, 652
circumcision, female, 737
cities
of colonial world, 604
early modern, 398, 434
fifteenth-century, 369, 370
in Great Britain, 537–538
in Japan, 583
in Russia, 546
city-states. Europe, fifteenth-century, 372
civilizations, in Americas, 382–388
Civil Rights Movement, 623(t), 734, 736
civil service examination system, 371, 479
Civil War, U.S. (1861–1865), 497(t), 515, 562(i), 642
class distinctions
in agricultural village societies, 367
British colonial, 416
in China, 570
in France, 504–505
in India, 597
Industrial Revolution and, 534–541
in Japan, 578–579
Marx on, 484–485
modern age and, 392
in Ottoman Empire, 575

revolutions and, 523
role of enemies in, 674–675
in Russia, 545
socialism and, 539
in Southeast Asia, 604
in Spanish America, 410–411, 411(i)
Spanish American Revolutions and, 511
in U.S., 415, 503, 544
clergy (first estate), in France, 498–499(i), 504
climate changes, 749
greenhouse gases in, 619
Kyoto protocol on, 623(t)
UN conferences on, 752
See also environment
Club of Rome, 749–750
coal industry, 533, 543(m), 546
See also mining
coffee crops, 507, 509, 550, 600
cofradias, 469
cold war, 620, 675–681, 676(m)
arms race and, 677(i), 677–678
communist countries in, 680–681
communist threat in, 659–660
division of humanity in, 618
ending of, 623(t), 685–686
on the third world, 705
third world aid after, 710
United Nations and, 653
colonial rule
in Africa, 515
African nationalism and, 612
different version of, 596–598
of Europe, 561
by Europeans, 590
in Haiti, 508
Japan and, 584
in Latin America, 500, 510, 554
local leaders and, 595
racial boundaries and, 589
racism and, 597
colonial tribalism, 611–613
Columbian exchange, 407–409, 619
Columbus, Christopher
Christianity spread by, 467
influence of, 365
Native American views of, 403
voyage of, 362–363(i), 363, 374, 375, 375(t), 400(t), 434

comfort women, Korean, 559
Comintern, 661
commerce. *See* trade
Committee of Public Safety (France),
    505
communication
    colonization and, 595
    fifteenth-century webs of, 388–389,
        390*(m)*
    fundamentalism's use of, 741
    in globalization, 725
    globalization of, 457
communism, 619–620, 622*(t)*, 659–689
    abandonment of, 620, 623*(t)*, 659, 660
    accomplishments of, 754
    arms race and, 677*(i)*, 677–678
    Atlantic revolutions and, 500
    centralized planning in, 671
    in China, 577, 632
    collapse of, 681–687, 725
    failures of, 682
    fascism on, 636–637, 638
    globalization of, 724
    Great Depression and, 635
    in the Holocaust, 652
    Jews blamed for, 640*(i)*
    legacy of, 687–688
    Lenin in, 659
    of Marx, 539
    NATO and, 654–655
    protest movements in, 734–735
    revolutionary origins of, 620,
        662–667
    role of enemies in, 674–675
    in Russia, 542
    Russian Revolution in, 662–665
    significance of, 659–660
    societal change and, 620
    undermining of, 674–675
    World War II and, 652
    World War I in development of, 630
    See also cold war
Communist Manifesto (Marx), 496*(t)*, 539
Condorcet, Marquis de (1743–1794),
    483–484, 520
Confucianism
    versus Christianity, 468
    conservative modernism and, 570
    versus Islam, 577
    in Japan, 578, 582

Jesuits on, 470–471, 487
    Ming dynasty revival of, 373
    Neo-, 474–475
    science and, 478, 479
    in Vietnam, 595
    under Yongle, 371
Congo, 600*(i)*, 678, 714–715*(t)*
Congo Free State, 599–600
Congress Party (India), 699
conquistadores, 410–411, 411*(i)*
Constantinople, Ottoman seizure of,
    364*(t)*, 379, 400*(t)*, 427, 451
constitutions, 482–483
    of Japan, 581, 582*(t)*
    in Latin America, 549
    of Mexico, 553
    in Ottoman Empire, 576
    of United States of America, 496*(t)*,
        501*(t)*, 504
containerized shipping, 725
context, 754–755
Copernicus, Nicolaus (1473–1543),
    400*(t)*, 477, 479, 480–481, 480*(t)*,
    486
copper mining, 543*(m)*, 550
corn. *See* maize
Cortés, Hernán, 384, 406, 411
Cossacks, 419*(i)*
cotton production
    British/Chinese trade in, 567*(t)*
    forced growth of, 600
    in India, 445
    Industrial Revolution and, 528, 532
    slave labor and, 409, 414–415, 451, 532
Council of Trent (1545–1563), 465–466
Council on Mutual Economic
    Assistance, 661
Counter-Reformation, 465–466, 510
Creek Indians, 447
creoles, 510–512, 549
Crimean War (1854–1856), 546
Crusades, 379, 462–463
    Prester John and, 435
    sugar spread by, 451
Cuba
    abolition of slavery in, 497*(t)*
    communism in, 661, 676–677, 681,
        706
    economic reforms in, 687
    education in, 711

exports from, 550
    first railroads in, 497*(t)*
    labor migration in, 727
    missile crisis, 623*(t)*, 676–678
    nationalization in, 693
    Santeria in, 473
    slavery in, 510, 515, 549
    U.S. and, 687, 733
    women's rights in, 735
Cuban Revolution, 735, 735*(i)*
cultivation system, 600
cultural imperialism, 731, 732*(m)*,
    733–734
Cultural Revolution (China). *See* Great
    Proletarian Cultural Revolution
currency
    Bretton Woods system of, 725
    euro, 654
    globalization of, 726–727
    international, 457
    U.S., after World War II, 679
Cuzco, Peru, 387
Czechoslovakia
    communism and, 664–665,
        685–686
    division of, 687
    German annexation of, 648, 650*(t)*
    independence of, 630, 631*(m)*
    Prague Spring, 623*(t)*, 680*(i)*, 734

Dahomey, 400*(t)*, 456–457
daimyo (feudal lords), 441, 578–579, 581
Dalai Lama, 747
dams, protests against, 751
Daoism
    Jesuits in China and, 471
    in Neo-Confucianism, 474–475
Darwin, Charles (1809–1882), 484,
    485, 564
da Vinci, Leonardo, 374
Davison, Emily, 521
de Beauvoir, Simone, 735–736
de Bry, Theodore, 362–363*(i)*, 363
Decade for Women, 738–739
Declaration of Independence (U.S.),
    501, 501*(t)*, 504
Declaration of the Rights of Man and
    Citizen (France), 504
Declaration of the Rights of Women
    (de Gouges), 520

decolonization, 620, 754
    after World War II, 652, 656
    freedom struggles in, 696–704
    India, 696–700
    planning for, 695–696
    significance of, 691–692
    World War II and, 645, 646(m), 647
deforestation
    in China, 444
    global warming and, 749
    in Japan, 444
democracy
    in Africa, 706–708, 710
    in America, 504
    in China, 683–684
    collapse of communism and, 687
    versus colonial dictatorships, 598
    Enlightenment and, 513
    experiments in, 706, 735
    fascism on, 636–637
    fundamentalism and, 746
    future of, 719
    history education in, 754
    human rights and, 682
    imperialism and, 679, 694, 706, 734
    as liberation, 734
    Nazism on, 641
    Soviet Union, 685
demographics. *See* population
Deng Xiaoping, 623(t), 682–684
Descartes, Rene (1596–1650), 477,
    480(t), 481
The Descent of Man (Darwin), 484
Dessalines, Jean-Jacques, 509
detribalization, 598
developing countries, 619–620, 622(t)
    brain drains in, 727
    decolonization in, 691–696
    disparities among, 730
    economic development experiments
        in, 710–713
    environmentalism in, 750–751
    feminism in, 737–738
    political experiments in, 705(m),
        705–719
devshirme, 427
diamonds, 412, 604, 701
Díaz, Porfirio (1876–1911), 552, 553
dictatorships, 706
Diego, Juan, 461

diet, Spanish America, 412
Diop, C. A., 611
disease
    Black Death, 434
    European imperialism and, 406–407
    fur trade and, 447, 448
    germ theory of, 563
    globalization of, 398
    imperialism and indigenous people,
        406
    Russian Empire, 419
    Siberia, 448
    in sugar plantations, 414
    tropical, Europeans and, 452
    wage laborers and, 602
Disraeli, Benjamin, 538
divine rights of kings, 500
divorce
    in China, 669
    feminism on, 737
    in Ottoman Empire, 576
    Soviet Union, 669
    women's movement and, 521
A Doll's House (Ibsen), 522
domestication of plants and animals. *See*
    Agricultural Revolution
The Dream of the Red Chamber (Cao
    Xueqin), 475
Dubcek, Alexander, 734
DuBois, W. E. B., 612
Duma (Russia), 547
durbar (Mughal assembly), 402–403(i),
    587–589(i)

East Africa
    Portuguese bases in, 436–437
    slave trade in, 497(t), 515
Eastern Europe
    aid to Indonesia from, 678
    in the Cold War, 675, 676(m)
    communism in, 660, 664–665,
        681–682, 685–686, 686(m)
    miracle year in, 685–686
Eastern Orthodox Christianity, 389
    Constantinople as capital of, 463
    versus Roman Catholic Church, 462
    in Russia, 542, 545
eastern Roman Empire. *See* Byzantine
    Empire
East Germany, 664–665, 685–686, 687

East India companies, 400(t), 438(t),
    439–440, 457
economic development
    African slave trade and, 456
    in Africa since independence,
        707–708
    after World War II, 655–656
    capitalism and, 633
    in China, 666, 672(t), 683–684
    Chinese Great Leap Forward, 671
    communist failures in, 682
    environmental impact of, 748–752
    experiments in, 710–713, 735
    in fascist Italy, 638
    feminism and, 737
    globalization and, 621, 727–728,
        729(m)
    in Global South, 714–715(t)
    internationalism and, 653
    market dependence and, 711
    Soviet Union, 669(i)
    sustainable, 749–752
    third world, 705–706, 706
    twentieth-century technology
        and, 619
    urban bias in, 711–712
    women in, 739
economic growth
    abolition of slavery and, 514
    in American colonies, 503
    in China, 569
    Industrial Revolution and, 534
    in Japan, 578
    in Latin America, 550–552, 554
    Protestant Reformation and,
        463–464
    slums and, 543–544
    of U.S., 542
economy
    Adam Smith on, 482
    Aztec, 384
    colonialism and, 598–606
    Columbian exchange and, 408–409
    early modern development of,
        433–442
    forced labor and, 599–600
    globalization of, 723–734
    Inca, 387
    of Japan, 581
    neo-liberalism in, 725

of Ottoman Empire, 573
transnational corporations in, 727
Ecuador, 550
Edict of Nantes (1598), 465
Edo (Tokyo), 578
education
in Africa, 707
in China, 479, 668, 673
colonial rule and, 595, 606–609, 613
in communism, 668
in Cuba, 681, 711
curriculum debates in, 754
feminism and, 520–521
globalization and inequality in, 728
imperialism and, 710
in India, 608–609
in Iran, 718
in Japan, 578–579, 582, 582(t), 642,
644
Jesuits in, 470–471
in Ottoman Empire, 574–575, 576
Protestant Reformation and, 465
racism and, 596–597
Rousseau on, 484
in Russia, 546, 547
in South Africa, 597
in Soviet Union, 671
spread of Islam and, 473
in Turkey, 713
See also literacy
education, Islamic
in madrassas, 478–479
in Malacca, 382
science in, 486
in Timbuktu, 381, 382
Edward VII (king, England), 587–589(i)
Egypt
African identity and, 611
American influence resisted by, 733
economic development in, 714–715(t)
French invasion of, 500
in Indian Ocean trade, 435
invasion by France of, 572
Islam and, 742, 744, 745
Muslim Brotherhood, 744(i)
Soviet aid to, 678
Wahhabi movement in, 474
women's movement and, 523
Egypt for the Egyptians movement,
519–520

Eisenhower, Dwight (U.S. president,
1953–1961), 679
elites
in American colonies, 503
in Argentina, 552
in Buganda, 594
in China, 570
in colonial Africa, 607–608, 608(i)
colonization and, 595
in India, 597
in Latin America, 560
in Siam, 608(i)
social conservatism and, 510
in Southeast Asia, 604
in Spanish America, 511
in Vietnam, 595
See also aristocracy
El Salvador, 678
empires
early modern, 403–404
of Europe, 518(m)
informal, 568, 577, 590
of Japan, 578, 584
nineteenth century, 596–598
See also individual empires
England. See Great Britain
Enlightenment, 401(t)
abolition of slavery and, 514
in France, 505
Nazism on, 641
on religion, 740
revolutions and, 523
science and, 482–485
U.S. Constitution and, 504
World War I disillusionment with,
630
environment, 623(t), 749
antiglobalization on, 731
Columbian exchange and, 408
deforestation in China and, 444
fossil fuels and, 747–748
fur trade impact on, 433–434,
445–446
globalization and, 621, 726, 730,
747–752
population growth and, 619
equality, 500, 501
abolition of slavery and, 514
among Native Americans, 368
Atlantic revolutions and, 500

education and, 607
feminism and, 520–521
in Haiti, 508–509
as Iroquois League value, 368
in Latin America, 549
Nazism on, 641
Equal Rights Amendment, U.S., 739
Estates General, in France, 498–499(i),
504
Ethiopia
American influence resisted by, 733
avoidance of colonization by, 594
as developing country, 705, 705(m)
Italian invasion of, 638
ethnicity
in Africa, 612, 707
colonial Latin America, 414(t)
former Soviet Union and, 687
imperialism and, 692
Qing dynasty China, 422
Russian Empire, 419, 420, 421(t)
Spanish America, 411(i), 411–412
Eurocentrism, 429, 491–494
Europe
American empires of, 404–417,
405(m)
Christianity in, 462–463
end of imperialism by, 692–694,
694(m)
feminism in, 520
fifteenth-century, 364(t), 372–374,
373(m)
global relationships of, 390–391
imperialism by, 626(m), 626–627
industrialization and, 561–564
Industrial Revolution in, 529–532,
531(m)
industry and empire in, 561–564
legal system in, 478
long-distance migration and, 606(t)
manufacturing output and, 548(t)
Marshall Plan in, 654
modern age prominence of, 365,
392–393
nations and empires of, 518(i)
naval power of, 404, 406
Ottoman Empire and, 378, 425–429,
426(m)
railroads in, 534
recovery of after World War II, 653–656

Europe (*continued*)
rise of, 393
rivalries in, 627–629
Scientific Revolution in, 392, 398
slave trade to, 455
twentieth-century, 618
in world economy, 457–458
World War I in, 625–632
World War II in, 647–648, 652
European Coal and Steel Community, 654
European Economic Community, 622(t), 654
European Union
established, 623(t), 654
expansion of, 655(m)
formation of, 626
former communist states in, 687
evolution
Darwin on, 484
fundamentalism on, 741
imperialism and, 564
intelligent design and, 461
racial images and, 564(i)
Ewe people, 604
Ewuare (Benin king), 367
exchange networks. *See* trade
extinctions, 748

family
in China, 670
communism on, 669, 670
family values and, 633
Inca, 387, 388
in the Soviet Union, 670
Family Law Code (Morocco), 737
farming. *See* agriculture
fascism, 636–638
federalism, 504, 549
Federalist Papers, 504
The Feminine Mystique (Friedan), 736
feminism, 392
beginnings of, 520–523
communist, 669–670
fascism on, 636–637
globalization of, 621, 734–739
in Great Britain, 541
international, 738–739
in Japan, 642

nationalism and, 519
women's suffrage and, 522(i)
Ferdinand, Franz, Archduke, 627
Ferdinand VII (king, Spain), 511
Ferry, Jules, 564
feudalism
end of, in France, 505, 507
in England, breakdown of, 415
Japan, 441
Fiji, 389
Finland, 519, 521
firestick farming, 366
First Opium War (1838–1842), 496(t)
First World War. *See* World War I
Florentine Codex, 385(i)
food production
African slave trade in spread of, 450
Columbian exchange and, 619
environmentalism and, 750–751
Native American, 366
population growth and, 397
women and, 604
foot binding, in China, 566
Ford, Henry, 543
foreign direct investment, 683, 701, 712, 726, 726(m), 728(t)
Fourteen Points, 632
France
American empire of, 404, 405(m)
colonial Asia and, 591(m)
communism in, 661
democratic socialism in, 635
East India Company, 439
fascism in, 637
feminism in, 735–736
fur trade, 445
Huguenots in, 465
Hundred Years' War in, 372
Industrial Revolution in, 531(m), 541
invasion of Egypt by, 572
invasion of Vietnam by, 494
League of Nation mandates of, 631(m), 632
manufacturing output and, 548(t)
middle class in, 536(i)
nationalism and, 519
Native American alliances with, 447
Ottoman alliances with, 429
railroads in, 535(f)
religion in, 533, 740

in Russian Revolution, 664
slave trade, 455
Southeast Asian colonies of, 646(m), 647
student protests in, 623(t), 734
three estates of, 498–499(i), 504
in Triple Entente, 627
Franciscans, 467
Franco-Prussian War (1870–1871), 627
Freetown, Sierra Leone, 514
French Revolution (1789–1799), 496(t), 499, 501(t), 504–507
communist revolutions influenced by, 662
Enlightenment thought in, 483
Jefferson and, 500
mass conscription and, 516, 517(t)
social tensions and, 498–499(i)
sovereignty of people and, 516
Terror (1793–1794), 501(t)
violence and, 523–524
Freud, Sigmund (1856–1939), 485
Friedan, Betty, 736
Fukuzawa Yukichi, 581
Fulbe people, 369, 376(m)
fundamentalism
alternatives to, 746–747
Christian, 740–742
globalization of, 621, 740–742
Hindu, 742
Islamic, 742–746
fur trade
early modern, 433–434, 446(m)
global, 445–448
Russian Empire, 417, 419

Galileo Galilei (1564–1642), 477, 480(t), 481, 482
Gama, Vasco da, 378, 400(t), 467
voyage of, 374, 375, 375(t), 434, 438(t)
Gandhi, Mohandas (Mahatma) (1869–1948), 527, 696, 697(i), 698–699, 700, 702
Garvey, Marcus, 612
gathering and hunting peoples
complex or affluent, 366
North American, 366
persistence of, 365–366
Gatling gun, 562(i)

gender
  Aztec, 387–388
  communist movements and, 668,
    669–670
  early modern, 399
  economic development and,
    711–712
  fundamentalism and, 741
  Inca, 387–388
  parallelism, 388
  science on, 477
  See also men; patriarchy; women
genocide
  Armenian, 632
  Cambodia, 682
  Holocaust, 618, 622*(t)*, 641, 650*(t)*,
    651–652
  in Rwanda, 708
Germany
  arms race in, 629
  Berlin wall removed in, 659
  environmentalism in, 750
  fascism in, 637
  Great Depression in, 633–634, 635*(f)*,
    636
  Industrial Revolution and, 531*(m)*,
    541–542
  manufacturing output and, 548*(t)*
  Nazism in, 625–626, 638–641
  peasant revolts, 464
  railroads in, 535*(f)*
  recovery of after World War II, 653
  reunification of, 687
  socialism and, 539
  Thirty Years' War, 465
  Treaty of Versailles on, 631–632
  in Triple Alliance, 627
  unification of, 496*(t)*, 517, 517*(t)*,
    562, 627
  war socialism in, 630
  World War I reparations by, 634
  in World War II, 647–648, 649*(m)*
germ theory of disease, 563
Ghana (modern state)
  cacao farming in, 604
  democracy in, 708, 709*(m)*
  Great Depression in, 634
  independence in, 705
  military coups in, 706
  nationalist movement in, 695–696

Ghana (West African kingdom), slave
    trade in, 433, 456
Gikuyu people, 603
glasnost, 684–685
globalization, 723–756
  Africa in, 620
  Asia in, 620
  biological, 409
  of Christianity, 462–472
  definition of, 724
  early modern, 397
  economic, 457–458
  environmental impact of, 747–752
  ethics of, 747
  Europe and, 390–391, 408–409, 491,
    493, 528, 561, 564
  of fundamentalism, 620, 740–742
  Great Depression and, 634–635
  history of, 724
  imperialism in, 404
  indicators of, 728*(t)*
  of industrialization, 541, 555
  inequality in, 727–728
  Islam and, 746
  of liberation, 734–739
  markers of, 622–623*(t)*
  modern age, 390–391
  North America and, 491
  protests against, 623*(t)*
  reglobalization and, 725–727
  resistance to, 728, 730–731
  twentieth-century, 619, 620
global justice movement, 730–731
global warming, 749, 752
goats, 407–408
Gokalp, Ziya, 576
gold
  in Africa, 435, 453, 604
  Brazil, 412
  South Africa, 701
  Spanish American, 410
  in U.S., 543*(m)*
  See also mining
Gold Coast, 601, 634
Gorbachev, Mikhail, 623*(t)*, 682,
    684–686
de Gouges, Olympe, 520
government
  in British American colonies, 416
  in China, 371, 423

commerce supported by, 457
constitutional, 482–483
early modern, 398, 399
economic development and, 710
the Enlightenment on, 482–483
freedom and, 501
Inca, 386–387, 388
Industrial Revolution and, 530
of Japan, 580
legitimacy of, 710
limited, as Iroquois League value, 368
neo-liberalism and, 725
New Deal agencies in, 636
postindependence experiments in,
    705–719
Grameen Bank, 712*(i)*
Great Britain
  abolition of slavery and, 514
  American empire of, 404, 405*(m)*,
    415–417, 420–421
  arms race in, 629
  cities in, 434
  colonial Asia and, 591*(m)*
  control over American colonies and,
    503
  democratic socialism in, 635
  fascism in, 637
  fur trade, 445
  Great Depression in, 635*(f)*
  Hundred Years' War in, 372
  imperialism, India and, 425
  India Sikhs and, 477
  India under, 438*(t)*, 696–700
  Industrial Revolution in, 528,
    532–533
  investments in Argentina by, 550
  Irish home rule and, 517
  League of Nation mandates of,
    631*(m)*, 632
  manufacturing output and, 548*(t)*
  Native American alliances with, 447
  neo-liberalism in, 725
  parliamentary government in, 415,
    416
  pollution and, 526–527*(i)*
  railroads in, 535*(f)*
  religion in, 740
  in Russian Revolution, 664
  slave trade, 455
  South Africa and, 700–701

Great Britain (*continued*)
  Southeast Asian colonies of, 646(m), 647
  in Triple Entente, 627
  in World War II, 648
Great Depression, 622(t), 633–636,
    634(i), 635(f)
  in globalization, 724
  impact of, 724
  in Japan, 643, 644
  reglobalization after, 725–727
  rise of Nazism after, 639
  socialist movements and, 544
  World War I and, 625
Great Law of Peace, 368
Great Leap Forward (1958–1960), 671,
    673, 682
Great Proletarian Cultural Revolution
    (China), 673, 674–675, 681, 682, 735
Great Trek (South Africa), 700(t)
Greece
  communism in, 661
  cultural traditions and, 493
  independence of, 517, 517(t), 572
  Renaissance based on, 373
  Scientific Revolution influenced by,
    479
Greenpeace, 623(t)
Guam, 389
guano, 550
Guatemala, 550, 678, 714–715(t)
guerrilla warfare, 666, 735, 735(i)
Guevara, Che, 735, 735(i)
guilds, 531
guillotine, 505, 506(i)
gulag, 674, 682
gunpowder, 398, 406
  Ottoman use of, 380(i)
Guomindang (China), 665–666, 667,
    667(m)
Gupta dynasty (320–600 C.E.), 696
Guru Granth, 477
Gypsies, 652

haciendas, 549, 553
Haiti, 414, 473, 483, 515, 727
Haitian Revolution (1791–1803), 494,
    496(t), 499, 501(t), 507–510, 509(i),
    524
hajj, 389
Hamas, 744(i), 745

Haruko (empress, Japan), 523
Harvey, William (1578–1657), 480(t)
Hawaii, 515
  See also Pearl Harbor attack
health care
  colonial rule and, 606
  in Cuba, 681, 711
  environmentalism and, 750–751
  globalization and inequality in, 728
Hellenistic world. *See* Greece
Henry IV (France), 465
Henry the Navigator, 375(t)
Hezbollah, 745
Hidalgo-Morelos rebellion (Mexico;
    1810–1813), 496(t), 501(t), 511–512
Hinduism, 381, 610–611, 698–699
  bhakti, 476
  British colonial rule and, 494
  Christianity and, 468
  fundamentalism in, 742
  in India, 424–425, 462, 608
  Indian independence and, 697
  in Indian Ocean trade, 435
  Islam and, 388–389, 390(m), 473
  sacred cattle and, 596
  Sikhism and, 476–477
  in the West, 610(i)
Hindutva, 742
Hiroshima bombing, 622(t), 647, 650,
    650(t), 651(i)
Hispaniola, 362–363(i), 363
Hitler, Adolf (1889–1945), 618, 622(t),
    632, 638(i), 638–641, 648, 649
Ho Chi Minh, 504, 660, 696
Holland. *See* Netherlands
Holocaust, 618, 622(t), 641, 650(t),
    651–652, 657
Holy Roman Empire, 465
home rule, in Ireland, 517
homosexuality
  feminism on, 736
  in the Holocaust, 652
Hong Kong, 568, 712
Hong Rengan, 566
Hong Xiuquan (1814–1864), 565–566
Hormuz, 436
horses
  Columbian exchange in, 407
  European imperialism and, 406
  in Nigeria, 389

Huguenots, 465
Huitzilopochtli (deity, Aztec), 385
human rights
  communism and, 682, 688
  environmentalism and, 750–751
  feminism and, 738
  globalization and, 731
  women's rights as, 738–739
human sacrifice
  Aztec, 384–385
  Inca, 387
Hundred Years' War (1337–1453), 372
Hungary
  collapse of communism in, 685–686
  communist takeover of, 664–665
  fascism in, 637
  independence movement and, 517
  railroads in, 535(f)
  Soviet invasion of, 680
hunter/gatherers. *See* gathering and
    hunting peoples
Hurons, 447
Hussein, Saddam, 733

Ibn Khaldun (1332–1406), 452
Ibn Saud, Muhammad, 474
Ibrahim, Anwar, 746–747
Ibsen, Henrik, 522
Igbo peoples, 367, 605, 613
imperialism
  Asia and, 560
  and China, 566–569, 577
  in China, 666–667
  Chinese rejection of, 371–372,
    375–378
  Christianity and, 467–470
  colonization and, 594
  competition in, 627–628
  credibility of, 693–694
  diseases carried in, 406–407
  early modern, 397
  East India Companies trading post,
    439–440
  economic development and, 710
  Egyptian revolt against, 517(t)
  elites in, 695
  end of, 618, 626, 656, 691–694
  Eurocentrism and, 429
  European, 377, 393, 403–407, 560,
    562, 590

globalization and, 458, 724
infrastructure development in, 697, 710
Islamic renewal on, 746
of Japan, 578, 585, 642, 645–647
legacy of, 403–404, 692
military intervention and, 554
modern, 403
and Philippines, 437–439
Portuguese trading post, 436–437, 438(t)
Russian, 417–421
scientific knowledge from, 409
Treaty of Versailles on, 631–632
U.S. and, 693, 731–734
World War I and, 629, 632
See also decolonization
Inca Empire, 364(t), 382, 386–388
Christianity and, 468
conquest of, 406, 410–412
cultural flowering of, 493
gender system, 387–388
integration in, 389
population rebound among, 416
wealth of, 379
indentured workers, 451, 515, 602
independence
decolonization and, 692–696
economic development and, 710–713
experiments in, 705–719
India and, 527
in Latin America, 511(m), 513, 516, 549
from Russian Empire, 584
of Spanish American colonies, 510–511, 513
of U.S. colonies, 501(t), 517(t)
See also individual countries
India, 364(t), 399, 678
American influence resisted by, 733
British conquest of, 438(t), 496(t), 592, 602
British East India Company in, 440
carbon dioxide emissions in, 750(m)
Chikpo movement, 751
Christianity in, 610–611
cultural identity in, 696–697
da Gama voyage to, 434
democracy in, 706, 707
economic development in, 711, 712, 714–715(t), 730

environmentalism in, 751
fundamentalism in, 742
Hinduism in, 560
Hindu/Muslim divisions in, 698, 699–700
indentured servants from, 515
independence in, 606, 632, 692, 695, 696–700, 701
Indian Ocean trade, 406
industrialization in, 530
Islamic expansion in, 473
long-distance migration and, 606(t)
manufacturing output and, 548(t)
microloan programs, 712(i)
Mughal Empire, 364(t), 381–382, 424(m), 424–425
Muslims in, 560
nationalism in, 520, 695–696, 707
opium in, 567
Pakistan divided from, 699–700
pepper trade in, 437(i)
plantation workers from, 602
Portuguese voyages to, 374, 375, 436
privatization in, 711
racism in, 596–597
reform societies in, 608–609
religion in, 476–477, 487
scientific advancements in, 529
spice trade, 437, 437(i)
technological advancements in, 529
textile industry, 445, 532
Timur invasion of, 364(t), 369
trade in Asia, 441–442
in World War I, 629, 632
in World War II, 650
See also South Asia
Indian National Congress (INC), 497(t), 517(t), 520, 697, 698, 699
Indian Ocean
Chinese power in, 371–372, 375–378
East India Companies and, 439–440
European dominance of, 378, 435, 436(m), 492
in globalization, 724
Islamic commerce in, 381–382
monsoons, 406
Portuguese commerce in, 435–437
spice trade and, 433
Indian Rebellion (1857–1858), 493, 497(t), 596

Indigenous Women's Network, 403
indigo, plantation economy in, 414–415
individualism
in Africa, 707
Buddhism and, 475
communist China on, 673
fascism on, 636–637
materialism and, 633
Protestant Reformation and, 467
Indochina, 497(t), 647
Indonesia, 530
colonial rule and, 592
communism in, 661, 678
Dutch control of, 439, 440, 592
economic development in, 714–715(t)
independence in, 692
Japanese military operations in, 647
nationalist movement in, 695–696
indulgences (Roman Catholic), 463
industrialization, 391, 528
abolition of slavery and, 514
carbon dioxide emissions in, 750(m)
Chinese, 671–672, 673, 683, 711
city-based, 711–712
communism and, 618, 661, 662, 668, 671–673
environmental impact of, 749
in Europe, 561, 563
fundamentalism and, 741
increases in, 619
of India, 527, 697(i), 698
international, 457
in Japan, 577–578, 582–583, 642, 644
military-industrial complex and, 629, 679
overproduction by, 634
societies and, 526–527(i), 653
South Africa, 701
Soviet Union, 672–673
third world, 705–706
in U.S., 541–545, 542
without socialism, 542–545
World War I in, 629, 634
Industrial Revolution, 392
Asian influence on, 493
colonial conquests and, 590
in Europe, 527–528, 531(m)
explanation of, 528–529
globalization and, 458, 724
in Great Britain, 496(t), 534–541

Industrial Revolution (*continued*)
  imperialism and, 409, 429, 626
  in Japan, 444
  Latin America and, 548–554
  manufacturing output and, 548(t)
  origins of, 365
  in population growth, 619
  in Russia, 545–548
  science in, 477
  in U.S., 541–545
infant mortality, 715(t), 728
inflation
  colonial silver trade and, 443–444
  in France, 505
  in Germany, 639
influenza epidemics, after World War II,
  697
informal empires, 568, 577, 590
information revolution, 479, 682
inheritance practices, 611, 739
Inkatha Freedom Party (South Africa),
  703
intelligent design, 461
International Criminal Court, 733
International Monetary Fund, 653, 725
International Women's Year, 738
Internet, 619, 728, 728(t)
Inti (deity, Inca), 386
inventions, 528, 532, 533
  See also patents
Iran
  economic development in, 705,
    705(m), 714–715(t), 717–719
  Islamic Revolution, 623(t)
  Islam in, 717–719, 742, 745
  Sara and Dara dolls, 723
  U.S. intervention in, 678
Iraq
  independence in, 632, 692
  Islam in, 745
  as League of Nations mandate,
    631(m)
Iraq War, 623(t), 656, 657, 733, 734
Ireland, 452, 517
Iron Curtain, 675
iron industry
  Industrial Revolution and, 533
  in U.S., 543(m)
ironworking technology, European
  imperialism and, 406

Iroquois League of Five Nations, 364(t),
  368, 448
irrigation, in China, 570
Islam
  in Africa, 560
  Christianity opposed by, 438,
    462–463, 468
  Crusades and, 379, 462–463
  cultural encounters with, 389
  defensive modernization and, 571
  early modern, 398, 399
  economic development and, 713,
    716–719
  European opposition to, 375
  expansion of, 364(t), 378–382, 462,
    473–474
  feminism and, 739
  fundamentalism in, 742
  future of, 719
  Gandhi on, 698–699
  globalization of, 724, 740
  Hindu interaction with, 388–389,
    390(m)
  independent centers of civilization,
    577
  in India, 476–477
  in Iran, 717–719
  Japan and, 584
  Malacca in spread of, 382
  in Ottoman Empire, 575
  renewal movements, 473–474, 623(t)
  Sara and Dara dolls, 723
  scientific innovation and, 478–479, 529
  second flowering of, 381–382
  Shia, 380
  slavery in, 450
  Sunni, 380
  Sunni/Shia hostility in, 426
  syncretism in, 487
  technological advancements in, 529
  terrorism and, 733
  trade and, 389
  in Turkey, 426–427, 713, 716–717
  unification of, 378, 379
  Wahhabi, 474, 474 (m), 486
  women and, 717, 718
  See also Muslims; Ottoman Empire;
    Safavid Empire; Songhay Empire
Islamic Jihad (Egypt), 745
Islamic law. *See sharia*

Islamic Salvation Front (Algeria), 745
Israel, 623(t), 692, 742–743
Istanbul, 427
Italy
  communism in, 661
  fascism in, 637–638, 639, 641
  immigrant farm workers from, 553
  Industrial Revolution in, 531(m)
  racism in, 641
  railroads in, 535(f)
  Renaissance in, 373
  in Triple Alliance, 627, 628(m)
  unification of, 496(t), 517, 517(t), 562
  in World War II, 648, 649(m)
Ito Hirobumi, 582(t)
Ivan the Great (1462–1505), 364(t)
Ivory Coast, 604

Jahan, Shah, 402–403(i), 403
Jamaica, 515
Jamestown, Virginia, 400(t)
Janissaries, 380(i), 573, 575
Japan
  air pollution in, 749
  assassinations in, 643
  authoritarianism in, 641–645
  Buddhism and, 389
  and China, 584, 622(t), 632, 665–667
  Christianity and, 398, 401(t), 438(t),
    468(i), 487
  civil war in, 364(t)
  closed to Western trade, 485–486
  colonial Asia and, 591(m)
  colonization by, 584–585, 594
  constitution in, 581, 582(t), 644
  economic development in, 714–715(t)
  European impact on, 441
  Great Depression in, 636
  Hiroshima/Nagasaki bombing,
    622(t), 647, 650(t), 651(i)
  industrialization in, 529, 530
  manufacturing output and, 548(t)
  modernization of, 580–584
  nationalism and, 520
  opening of, 580(i)
  Perry arrives in, 497(t)
  Philippines and, 438
  population growth, 444
  Portugal resisted by, 437
  rise of, 577–585, 585(m)

Russia and, 547, 582(t), 584
in Russian Revolution, 664
scientific innovation in, 485–486
silver mines, 442, 443, 444
urbanization in, 398
women's movement and, 523
World War I and, 632, 642
World War II and, 559–560, 645,
    646(m), 647, 650–651, 653, 655–656
See also Pearl Harbor attack; samurai
    warriors
Java, 382, 600, 602
Jefferson, Thomas, 500, 504
Jehangir, 424
Jerusalem, 426
Jesuits. See Society of Jesus
Jesus of Nazareth, 483
Jews. See Judaism/Jewish people
jihad, 369, 743–744, 745
Jinnah, Muhammad Ali, 699
jizya (Islamic tax), 424, 425
John Paul II (pope), 747
Jordan, 632, 692, 745
Judaism/Jewish people
    Holocaust, 618, 650(t), 651–652
    in Indian Ocean Trade, 435
    Nazis on, 639, 640(i), 640–641
    Ottoman Empire, 427
    World War I and, 639

Kamil, Mustafa, 584
Kangxi (Chinese emperor), 472
Kant, Immanuel (1724–1804), 482
kaozheng, 475, 485
Kennedy, John F., 677
Kenya
    democracy in, 708, 709(m)
    independence in, 696, 702(i)
    land ownership in, 603–604
    Luo people in, 605
    wage workers in, 604
    women's group movement in, 737
Kenyatta, Jomo, 702(i)
Kepler, Johannes (1571–1630), 480(t),
    481, 486
Keynes, John Maynard, 635
Khomeini, Ayatollah Ruholla,
    717–719, 718(i)
Khrushchev, Nikita, 677, 680, 681
Kierkegaard, Soren, 719

kings and kingdoms, parliaments as
    checks on, 415
kinship
    African slave trade and, 453
    agricultural village, 366–367
Knox, Robert, 563
Kongo, Kingdom of, 364(t), 453, 456
Korea
    Buddhism in, 389
    in the cold war, 675
    communism in, 660
    Japanese annexation of, 582(t),
        585(m), 594
Korean War (1950–1953), 655, 675
Kranz, Erna, 640
Kristallnacht (1938), 641
Kyoto, Japan, 578
Kyoto protocol, 623(t), 733, 752

labor
    Americas, demographic collapse and,
        407
    globalization and, 726, 728, 730
    in Great Britain, 537–538
    imperialism and indigenous people
        in, 410, 412
    Inca, 387
    migration for, 727
    social protest and, 538–541
    Spanish colonial, 439, 443
    for sugar production, 413(i),
        413–414
    women in, 736
labor laws, 730, 731
labor movements
    in fascist Italy, 638
    in Germany, 542
    Islamic, 745
    in Japan, 582(t), 584, 642, 644
    Nazi Germany on, 639
    New Deal, 636
    in Russia, 547
    Russian Revolution and, 662–663
    socialism and, 544
    South Africa, 703
    Soviet Union, 685–686
    in World War I, 630, 630(f)
labor unions. See unions
Labour Party (Great Britain), 539–540,
    541

land ownership
    in Africa, 602, 613
    in American colonies, 503
    in China, 568, 570
    in colonial America, 502
    in Great Britain, 534–535
    in Haiti, 515
    imperialism and, 410
    in Latin America, 552–553
    liberty and, 501
    modern wealth creation and,
        391–392
    in Russia, 545
    Spanish colonial, 439
    See also property ownership
land reform
    Afghanistan, 676
    in China, 666, 670–671, 711
    in Hungary, 665
    in Iran, 717
    in Poland, 665
    Russian Revolution, 663
    in the Soviet Union, 670, 671
languages
    colonial "tribalism" and, 611–613
    English as global, 679
    European, 560
    imperialism and, 692
    publishing industry and, 517
    Russian, nationalism and, 518–519
    Turkish, 576, 713, 716
Laos, 661, 687
Lateran Accords (1969), 638
Latin America, 551(m)
    economic growth in, 712
    independence in, 511(m), 549
    Industrial Revolution and, 548–554
    privatization in, 711
    social conservatism in, 510
    Spanish American Revolutions in,
        510–513
    wars of independence, 496(t)
Latin American revolutions, 499–500
Law of Family Rights (Turkey), 576
Law of the Sea Convention (1982), 623(t)
League of Nations, 631(m), 632, 645
Lebanon, 745
legal systems
    Islamic *sharia*, 745
    scientific innovation and, 478–479

Leibniz, Gottfried Wilhelm
(1646–1716), 531
Lenin (Vladimir Ulyanov), 547–548,
658–659(i), 659, 663–664, 674
Leopold II (king, Belgium), 599
levée en masse (mass conscription), 516
liberalism, 392, 519, 536, 636–637, 741
liberation theology, 747
Liberia, 594, 612
libraries, 478
life expectancies
Cuba, 711
globalization and, 728, 729(m)
twenty-first century, 715(t)
Limits to Growth (Club of Rome),
749–750
Lin Zexu, 568
literacy
in China, 668
colonial rule and, 607–609
globalization and, 728
imperialism and, 710
Islam and, 473
in Japan, 578–579
Protestantism on, 416
Protestant Reformation and, 465
Soviet Union, 671
women's movement and, 521
See also education
literature
Mughal Empire, 424–425
Neo-Confucianism in China and, 475
Renaissance, 373
Locke, John (1632–1704), 482–483,
500
Long March (1934–1935), 622(t), 665(i),
667(m)
Louisiana Purchase (1803), 496(t), 510
Louis XVI (king, France), 501(t), 504
Louverture, Toussaint, 509
Luce, Henry, 654
Luo people, 605
Luther, Martin, 463, 463(i), 465, 475

Macao, 436
Machiavelli, Niccolò (1469–1527), 374
machine guns, 563, 591
Machu Picchu, 387(i)
Macumba, 473
Madison, James, 504

madrassas (Islamic schools), 478–479
Magellan, Ferdinand, 375(t), 438
maize (corn), 408
African slave trade and, 456
population growth and, 397
Maji Maji rebellion in German East
Africa (1904–1905), 497(t)
Malacca, 364(t), 382, 436
Malaya, 515, 647, 661
Malaysia, 554, 604
male suffrage, 506, 513
Mali (modern state), democracy in, 708,
709(m)
Manchu dynasty. *See* Qing dynasty
Manchukuo, 645
Manchuria, 645, 646(m), 650, 650(t)
Mandela, Nelson, 690–691(i), 691,
696, 700(t), 702, 703
manufacturing
colonialism and, 599
early modern, 398–399
in Great Britain, 531–532
in Japan, 582(t)
in Latin America, 554
in U.S., 543(m)
Mao Zedong, 668, 670, 673(i), 681, 682
in communist revolution, 665–667
Great Leap Forward, 671, 673
Great Proletarian Cultural
Revolution, 673, 674–675, 682
Long March, 665(i)
mapmaking, 470–471, 471(i)
Mardana, 476(i)
Marie Antoinette, 505
maritime voyages, 370(m)
European, 374–375, 404, 406
of Zheng He, 363, 364, 364(f), 371(i)
market-based economies, Industrial
Revolution and, 530–531
marriage
in China, 471–472, 669
feminism on, 736, 737
labor shortages and, 601
Portugal, with Asians, 437
Qing dynasty China, 422
Russian Empire, 419
Soviet Union, 669
in Spanish America, 411(i), 411–412
Marshall, John, 503
Marshall Plan, 654, 664

Marx, Karl (1818–1883), 484–485, 494,
539, 548, 614, 660
communism based on, 618
Communist Manifesto of, 496(t)
influence of in China, 665
on religion, 740
view of history of, 753
Marxism, 661
Chinese, 666
on communist revolutions, 662
Leninist version of, 663–664
on nationalism, 680
role of enemies in, 674–675
women's movement and, 522
Mary, mother of Jesus, 464(t)
MasterCard, 727
mathematics
Chinese, 485, 487
Islamic, 478
matrilineal systems, Africa, 367
Mattel Corporation, 727
Mauritania, 455
Mauryan dynasty, 696
Mawdudi, Mawlana, 743
Maxim guns, 591
Maya civilization, Caste War of Yucatán
and, 549
McCarthyism, 661
McDonald's, 679, 732(m)
Mecca
Turkic control of, 426
Wahhabi movement in, 474
medicine
anatomy studies in, 481, 483(i)
in China, 487
Islamic development of, 478
in population growth, 619
medicine men, 610
Medina, Arabia, 426
Mediterranean basin
Ottoman power in, 427
slavery and, 450
sugar production in, 413
Meiji restoration, 580, 582(t), 585(m)
Mein Kampf (My Struggle) (Hitler), 640
men
colonization and, 590
division of labor in colonial Africa
and, 604
See also male suffrage; patriarchy

mercantilism, 409–410
merchants
  Aztec, 384
  colonialism and, 599
  in Great Britain, 531–532
  in Haiti, 507
  Industrial Revolution and, 530
  in Japan, 578, 579
  in Ottoman Empire, 573
Mesoamerica
  Aztec Empire, 382–386
  Christian missions in, 468–470
  demographic collapse in, 407
  gender systems of, 388
  Inca Empire, 382
  social structures in, 410
mestizo, 411*(i)*, 411–412
Mexican-American War (1845–1848),
  496*(t)*
Mexican Revolution (1910–1920), 553,
  553*(i)*, 693
Mexica people. *See* Aztec Empire
Mexico
  air pollution in, 749
  Chiapas rebellion, 730
  Christian missions in, 469
  cofradías, 469
  demographic collapse in, 407
  diet in, 412
  economic development in, 714–715*(t)*
  European diseases in, 407
  exports from, 550
  first school for girls in, 497*(t)*
  globalization and, 730
  Hidalgo-Morelos rebellion in, 496*(t)*,
    501*(t)*, 511–512
  independence in, 511
  industrialization in, 530
  labor migration in, 727
  landowners in, 552
  mestizos in, 411*(i)*, 411–412
  oil nationalization in, 693
  religious syncretism in, 469–470,
    487
  silver mines in, 408–409, 435
  U.S. and, 549, 550
  Virgin of Guadalupe, 460–461*(i)*
  women's movement and, 523
  See also Maya civilization;
    Mesoamerica; North America

Michelangelo, 374
microloan programs, 712*(i)*
middle class, 536–537, 541, 544, 546, 552
Middle East, 364*(t)*
  economic development in,
    712–715*(t)*, 730
  Ottoman Empire and, 425, 426*(m)*
  population growth in, 573
Middle Passage, 449, 451*(i)*, 455
  See also slave trade
migrant laborers, colonization and, 590
migration
  in age of empire, 606*(t)*
  to Argentina, 552, 553
  British America, 415–417
  and China, 423, 439
  Europe and, 561
  globalization and, 727
  Inca, 386–387
  Japanese, to the Philippines, 439
  of labor, 604–605, 727
  of Muslims, 740
  nations and, 516
  in Russian Empire, 419
  twentieth-century, 724
  of wage laborers, 602–603
  women in, to North America, 414
military-industrial complex, 679, 680
military organization
  in Africa, 708
  Aztec, 388
  in China, 671
  European imperialism and, 563
  Inca, 388
  industrialization and, 629
  in Japan, 644
  in Ottoman Empire, 573, 574
  in Russia, 420, 546
  U.S., 654–655, 678–679, 732*(m)*, 733
military technology, 423, 441, 570
Ming dynasty (1368–1644), 364*(t)*,
  370–372
  exploration during, 370*(m)*, 371–372
  Jesuits in, 470–472
  Neo-Confucianism in, 474–475
  Ottoman Empire compared with,
    379
mining
  of coal, 533, 543*(m)*, 546
  of copper, 543*(m)*, 550

  environmentalism and, 751
  of gold, 410, 412, 435, 453, 543*(m)*,
    604, 701
  in Great Britain, 531–532
  in Japan, 582*(t)*
  of silver, 408–410, 433, 435, 438*(t)*,
    442–445, 443*(i)*
  of tin in Bolivia, 550
  of tin in Malaysia, 604
  in U.S., 543*(m)*
  wage laborers and, 604
Mirabai (1498–1547), 476
missionaries
  in Africa, 493, 607, 609–610
  in China, 470–472, 471*(i)*, 568
  colonization and, 595
  European imperialism and, 564
  imperialism and, 467–468
  in Japan, martyred, 468*(i)*
  in Kenya, 589
  Philippines, 438–439
Mississippi River valley, 389
mita (Inca labor service), 387
mixed-race people, in Latin America,
  549
Moctezuma, 411
modern era, 390–391, 397–399
modernity
  in China, 570–571
  European, 560
  Islamic world and, 571
  science as, 462
modernization
  in Africa, 707
  in China, 569
  colonial rule and, 606
  colonization and, 597–598
  in communism, 618
  communist movements and, 662, 668
  Islamic renewal and, 742–746
  in Islamic world, 571
  in Japan, 580–584, 642
  in Ottoman Empire, 573
Mohawk people, 368
monarchs and monarchies
  the Enlightenment on, 482–483
  French Revolution and, 505
  Industrial Revolution and, 530
  parliamentary systems in Britain, 415,
    416

monarchs and monarchies (*continued*)
  in Russia, 545
  taxation under, 434
  See also kings
money. *See* currency
Mongol Empire
  in China, 370–371, 422–423
  end of, 364*(t)*, 692
  globalization by, 724
  influence of, 368–369
  Russian Empire and, 417, 418*(m)*
  under Timur, 369
Mongol peoples, 492
monsoons, 406
Morelos, José, 511
Morocco, 737
Moscow, 372, 417
Moses, 483
Mozambique, 600, 696
Mughal Empire, 364*(t)*, 379*(m)*, 381–382,
  400*(t)*, 402–403*(i)*, 424*(m)*,
  424–425, 592, 596
  British East India Company and, 440
  European impact on, 441
  Hindu/Muslim interaction in, 404
  Islam in, 473
  Portugal resisted by, 437
  unification by, 381–382, 696
  webs of exchange in, 388–389
Muhammad (prophet) (570–632 C.E.),
  571
  Treatise of Three Imposters on, 483
Muhammad Ali (r. 1805–1948),
  496*(t)*
mulattoes, 414, 415
music
  Africa and, 450
  U.S., influence of, 679
Muslim League, 699
Muslims
  in India, 494, 611
  Indian Ocean trade controlled by, 435
  Japan and, 584
  offensive pigs and, 596
  in Ottoman Empire, 574–575
  rejection of materialism by,
    575–576
  revolts of (1855–1873), 569*(m)*
  See also Islam; Shia Muslims; Sunni
    Muslims

Mussolini, Benito (1883–1945),
  637–638, 638*(i)*, 640, 641
Mwene Mutapa, 364*(t)*

Nagasaki, Japan, 485–486, 622*(t)*, 647,
  650, 650*(t)*, 651*(i)*
Nanak, Guru (1469–1539), 476 *(i)*,
  476–477
Nanjing Massacre, 559
Napoleon Bonaparte (r. 1799–1814),
  496*(t)*, 501*(t)*, 507, 508*(m)*, 509–510,
  627
  conquests of, 496*(t)*, 511, 516, 572
National American Woman Suffrage
  Association, 521
nationalism, 392
  in Africa, 494, 612
  after World War II, 652
  in Asia, 494
  Atlantic revolutions and, 500
  in China, 570–571, 666–667, 684
  colonial rule and, 606
  communism on, 680, 681
  decolonization and, 693–694, 694,
    694*(m)*, 695–696
  in Europe, 562
  fascism and, 636–638
  growth of in nineteenth century,
    516–520, 517*(t)*
  imperialism and, 692–693
  in India, 707
  Islamic world and, 571
  Japanese, 643–644
  as liberation, 734
  Marxism and, 680
  in Mexico, 553
  Nazi, 638–641
  in Ottoman Empire, 573, 576
  in South Africa, 703
  in Soviet Union, 673, 686
  World War I and, 627–630
National Party (South Africa), 702
National Rejuvenation Study Society,
  570
Native Americans, 368, 410, 443, 451,
  487
  alcohol and, 447–448
  Christian conversion of, 468–470
  in colonial Latin America, 414
  on Columbus, 403

  demographic collapse of, 406–407,
    416, 429, 447
  European diseases and, 492–493
  fur trade and, 445–448
  as hunter/gatherers, 366
  in Latin America, 510–512
  mourning wars, 447
  post-Columbian decimation of, 365
  transformed by Columbian
    exchange, 408
native Australians. *See* Aboriginal people, Australia
naval technologies
  European, 406
  Portuguese, Indian Ocean trade and,
    435–437
Nazca civilization, 386
Nazism, 638–641, 674, 675
  communist resistance to, 665
  genocide by, 632
  Holocaust, 651–652
  rise of in Germany, 625–626
  World War II and, 647–648, 649
Nehru, Jawaharlal, 696, 699, 706, 742
Neo-Confucianism, 474–475
neo-liberalism, 725, 730–731
Netherlands
  American empire of, 404, 405*(m)*
  cities as commercial centers in, 434
  colonial Asia and, 591*(m)*
  East India Company, 439–440
  fascism in, 637
  forced labor and, 599–600
  fur trade, 445
  merchants in, 530
  religion in, 740
  slave trade, 455
  Southeast Asian colonies of, 646*(m)*,
    647
  trade with Japan, 485–486
Netherlands East Indies (Indonesia),
  599–600
New Deal (1933–1942), 635–636
New Guinea, 366, 609*(i)*
Newton, Isaac (1642–1727), 401*(t)*,
  477, 480*(t)*, 481, 482, 486
New Zealand, 521, 592, 594, 609–610,
  629
Nezahualcoyotl (1402–1472), 385–386
Nguyen Khuyen (1835–1909), 595

Nguyen Thai Hoc, 608
Nian Rebellion (1853–1868), 569(m)
Nicholas II, Tsar of Russia, 662
Nigeria, 389, 592, 597, 605, 613, 708,
   714–715(t)
Nightingale, Florence, 521
Nike, 727
Ninety-five Theses (Luther), 463, 463(i)
nitrates, from Chile, 550
Nkrumah, Kwame, 606, 696, 705
noble savages, 563
nomadic peoples, 365
   eliminated as historical actors, 424
   influence of, 368–369
   Russian Empire, 417
   See also pastoral societies
nonviolence philosophy, 698–699, 702
North Africa
   Ottoman Empire and, 425, 426(m)
   in World War II, 648
North America
   agriculture in, 366
   European diseases carried to, 407
   feminism in, 520
   fur trade in, 433–434, 445–447,
      446(m)
   gathering and hunting peoples in,
      366
   global dominance of, 491
   plantation economy in, 414–415
   settler colonies in, 415–417
   slaves shipped to, 454(f)
   slave trade to, 455
   in world economy, 457–458
   See also Canada; Mesoamerica;
      Mexico; United States of America
North American Free Trade Agreement
   (NAFTA), 623(t)
North Atlantic Treaty Organization
   (NATO), 654–655, 661, 675,
   676(m), 687, 733
North Korea, 687
nuclear power, 529, 719, 750
nuclear weapons
   arms race and, 651(i), 660, 677(i),
      677–678, 719
   in China, 681
   in cold war conflicts, 676(m)
   Hiroshima/Nagasaki bombing,
      622(t), 647, 650, 650(t), 651(i)

   in North Korea, 687
   in World War II, 649
Nupe people, 605
Nyakyusa people, 612

Ogodei, 393
oil industry, 546, 712, 719, 747–748
Oman, 437
Oneida people, 368
Onondaga people, 368
OPEC, 623(t)
Opium Wars, 497(t), 566–568
The Origin of Species (Darwin), 484
Orthodox Christianity. See Eastern
      Orthodox Christianity
Ottoman Empire, 378–380, 425–429,
   426(m)
   Armenian genocide by, 632
   Christian interaction with, 373(m),
      388–389, 390(m), 404
   collapse of, 693
   compared with China, 577
   conquest of Constantinople, 463
   constitution established (1875), 497(t)
   contraction of, 572(m)
   Crusades against, 379
   decline of, 632
   expansion of, 364(t)
   fur trade, 448
   Greek independence from, 517, 517(t)
   Indian nationalism and, 697
   influence of, 378–379
   Janissaries, 380(i)
   nationalism and, 520
   reform in, 497(t), 573–575
   Safavid Empire hostility with, 389
   siege of Vienna by, 379
   slave trade, 451
   trade in, 389
   urban riots in, 573
   Vienna siege by, 364, 393
   and the West, 486, 571–577, 574(i)
   in World War I, 629
Owen, Robert (1771–1858), 539
Oyo, 456, 457
ozone layer, 749, 752

Pacific islands, 364(t)
   colonization of, 592
   missionaries in, 609–610

Pahlavi, Muhammad Reza
   (r. 1941–1979), 717
Pakistan, 548(t), 692, 699–700, 742
Palau, 389
Paleolithic era/peoples, 365–366
Palestine
   Hamas, 744(i)
   Islamic renewal in, 745
   as League of Nations mandate,
      631(m)
   Zionist movement and, 517, 517(t)
Palmares, Brazil, 401(t)
Pan Africanist Congress, 703
Panama Canal, 497(t), 554
pantheism, 483
parliaments, 581, 638–639, 643
Pascal, Blaise (1623–1662), 481
pastoral societies, 365
   Americas, 383(m)
   eliminated as historical actors, 424
   influence of, 368–369
   and Russian Empire, 417
patents, 529, 533
   See also inventions
patriarchy
   challenges to, 520
   communism on, 735
   decline of, 738
   women as heads of households and,
      605
   women's liberation and, 736
Peace of Westphalia (1648), 465
Peace Preservation Law (1925, Japan), 642
Pearl Harbor attack (1941), 647, 650(t)
peasant rebellions
   in China, 560, 565–566, 573
   in Japan, 579, 582(t), 583
peasants
   in China, 493
   colonization and, 590, 596, 598–600
   in France, 505
   in Japan, 578–579
   in Latin America, 553
   modern age diminishment of, 392
   in Russia, 515
peninsulares, 411
People's Liberation Army (China), 666
perestroika, 684
Perry, Matthew, 497(t), 577, 578, 580,
   580(i), 582(t)

Persia
  Portugal resisted by, 437
  Safavid Empire, 364(t), 380, 400(t)
  Timur in, 369
Peru
  communism in, 661
  conflict with Bolivia, 549
  exports from, 550
  indentured servants in, 515
  indigenous people in, 412
  silver mines in, 408–409
  Taki Onqoy, 469, 487
  Tupac Amaru revolt in, 412, 501(t),
    512
Peter the Great (r. 1689–1725), 401(t),
  546
Philip II (king, Spain), 437
Philippine islands
  communism in, 661
  dictatorships in, 706
  economic development in, 714–715(t)
  environmentalism in, 751–752
  Japanese military operations in, 647
  missionaries in, 467–468
  religious syncretism in, 487
  in silver trade, 442
  Spanish control of, 400(t), 437–439,
    441
  U.S. takeover of, 594, 678
Pinochet, Augusto, 738
pirates, 436
plague, 370, 372, 434
plantations, 400(t), 401(t)
  in Cuba, 510
  European-owned, 602
  in Haiti, 507–509
  in Latin America, 549
  slave trade and, 409, 449(m), 450, 514
  sugar production and, 412(i), 412–415
pochteca (Aztec merchants), 384
poetry
  Aztec, 385–386
  bhakti, 476
  Vietnamese, 595
Poland
  collapse of communism in, 685–686
  communist takeover of, 664–665
  Holocaust in, 651–652
  independence and, 517, 630, 631(m)
  invasions of, 500, 648, 650(t), 680

nationalism and, 519, 519(i)
  Russian Revolution in, 663
political parties
  in Great Britain, 539–540, 539–541,
    541
  in India, 699, 742
  in Italy, 638
  in Japan, 581
  in Russia, 547
  in South Africa, 702, 703
  in U.S., 503, 544–545
political systems
  African slave trade and, 456
  Aztec, 388
  in Europe, 562
  Inca, 387, 388
  Machiavelli on, 374
  in Ottoman Empire, 575, 576
  Protestant Reformation and,
    463–464
  in Russia, 547
  Spanish America, 410–411, 411(i)
  West Africa, fifteenth-century, 367
pollution, 526–527(i), 749, 752
  See also environment
polygamy, 576, 737
popes, authority of, 463–464, 464(t)
popular sovereignty, 500, 503, 510
population
  in Africa, 455–456, 609–610
  Aztec, 384
  birth control and, 712
  Bolivia, Potosí, 443
  of China, 370, 561, 565
  Columbian exchange and, 408
  density, fifteenth-century, 369, 370
  early modern growth of, 397–398
  environmental impact of, 619, 747,
    753
  in Europe, 434
  fifteenth-century, 369, 370
  of French West Africa, 595
  Global South, 705
  of Haiti, 507
  Inca records on, 386
  Islamic, 743(m)
  in Latin America, 552
  of London, 537
  modern age growth of, 391, 391(f)
  Philippines, 439

pre-Columbian Western Hemisphere,
    407
  of Russian Empire, 420, 421(t)
  Siberia, 419
  third world, 706
  twentieth-century growth in,
    618–619
  world, 623(t)
population growth
  in globalization, 725
  in Great Britain, 531
  in Middle East, 573
  twenty-first century, 714(t)
  worldwide, 748(f)
Portugal
  American empire of, 404, 405(m)
  Christian missions by, 467
  commercial empire of, 435–437
  East India Companies and, 439
  enforced cotton cultivation and,
    600
  exploration by, 364(t), 374–375, 375(t),
    376(m), 378, 400(t)
  independence of Brazil from,
    501(t)
  Islamic trade opposed by, 435
  search for sea route to the East, 434,
    435
  in slave trade, 451, 452, 453, 454(f),
    455
  in spice trade, 435–437, 437(i)
potato crops, 397, 408
Potosí, Bolivia, 443(i), 443–444
pottery, Asian, 493
poverty
  in Africa, 713
  in American colonies, 503
  in China, 565, 683
  feminism on, 736, 737
  globalization and, 728
  in Great Britain, 538, 538(i), 541
  in Haiti, 510
  imperialism and, 694
  in India, 606
  in Latin America, 554
  modern age, 392
  third world, 706
Prague Spring, 623(t), 680(i), 734
Prester John, 435
The Prince (Machiavelli), 374

printing
  the Enlightenment and, 482
  nations and, 517
  Ottoman, 401*(t)*
  Protestant Reformation and, 465
  sacred texts and, 493
privatization, 711, 725
Progressives, in U.S., 545
proletariat, 539
propaganda
  Soviet Union, 680
  World War I, 630, 630*(f)*
  World War II, 650
property ownership
  in China, 669, 670–671
  communism on, 660, 662
  in Iran, 719
  in Japan, 644
  opium wars and, 568
  See also land ownership
prostitution
  child, in Brazil, 738*(i)*
Protestant Reformation, 389, 400*(t)*,
  463–467, 464*(t)*, 465–467, 466*(m)*
Ptolemy, 479–480
Puerto Rico, 554
Puritans, 416, 467

al-Qaeda, 733, 745–746
Qianlong (emperor, China), 564–565
Qing dynasty (Manchu dynasty
  1644–1912), 401*(t)*, 475, 568
  collapse of, 570–571
  imperialism in, 404, 421, 422*(m)*,
  422–424
  Jesuits in, 470–472
  Neo-Confucianism in, 474–475
  peasant rebellion and, 565–566
Quakers, 416, 465, 514, 514*(i)*
Quechua language, 387
quinine, discovery of, 562
quipus (Inca counting devices), 386
Qutb, Sayyid, 743, 744

racial segregation. *See* segregation laws
racism, 492
  in British America, 416
  in colonial Brazil, 415
  in colonial Latin America, 411–412,
  414

evolution and, 564
feminism and, 736
Gandhi on, 698
in Germany, 519
in Haiti, 507–510
imperialism and, 596–598, 607, 692,
  694
in India, 596
Japan and, 644, 645
in Nazism, 639
Russian Empire, 419–420
scientific, 477, 641
slavery and, 449–450, 450–452,
  451–452, 515
South Africa, 700–704
railroads
  in Brazil, 497*(t)*
  in Chile, 497*(t)*
  in China, 568
  in Cuba, 497*(t)*
  in Europe, 534
  Industrial Revolution and, 534*(i)*
  in Japan, 582*(t)*, 583, 583*(i)*
  labor strikes and, 544
  in Latin America, 550
  pilgrimages in India and, 493
  in Russia, 546
  in U.S., 502*(m)*, 542
Ramayana, 424–425
Rape of Nanjing (1937–1938), 559, 650,
  650*(t)*
Raphael, 374
rationalism, 500
  modern, 392
  Nazism on, 641
Red Guards (China), 674
Reformation. *See* Protestant
  Reformation
Reform Bill (1832), 536
reform societies, in India, 608–609
religions
  in Australia, 366
  awakenings and revivals, 484
  Aztec, 384–385, 388
  colonial rule and, 412, 609–611, 692
  the Enlightenment on, 483
  European imperialism and, 563
  evolution and, 484
  feminism and, 739
  freedom of, 416, 507

fundamentalism, 740–742
future of, 719
globalization and, 740–746
Inca, 386, 388
in Japan, 582
and modernity, 392
Ottoman Empire, 427, 576
pantheism, 483
versus science, 461, 462, 477, 478–479
slavery and, 450, 514
Soviet Union, 684
suppression of native, 468–469
syncretism, 412, 468–470, 472–474,
  486–487
Taiping Uprising and, 565–566
webs of exchange and, 388–389,
  390*(m)*
See also individual religions
religious toleration, 500
  in Great Britain, 533
  Huguenots in France, 465
  in Mughal Empire, 424–425
  in Ottoman Empire, 427
  in Russian Empire, 419
religious wars. *See* Crusades; jihad
Remarque, Erich, 630
remittances, 727
Renaissance, 364*(t)*, 373–374, 400*(t)*
republicanism, 500, 504, 510, 513
revolutions. *See individual revolutions*
Rhodes, Cecil, 562
Ricci, Matteo, 400*(t)*, 470
rice crops
  in Burma, 601
  in China, 378
  Columbian exchange in, 407
  in Japan, 578
  plantation economy and, 414–415
roads. *See* Silk Roads; trade
Robertson, Pat, 741
Robespierre, Maximilien, 505, 506*(i)*
rock-and-roll, 679
Rockefeller, John D., 543
Roman Catholic Church (Catholicism)
  Copernicus and, 480–481
  Counter-Reformation and, 465–466,
  510
  versus Eastern Orthodoxy, 389, 462
  European autonomy of, 478
  in fascist Italy, 638

Roman Catholic Church
(Catholicism) *(continued)*
in France, 506
indulgences in, 463
on Jesuit policy of accommodation,
472
Lateran Accords, 638
Mexico and, 460*(i)*, 460–461*(i)*, 553
opposition of to science, 481–482
papal authority in, 463–464, 464*(t)*
political life in Latin America and,
549
Protestant Reformation and,
463–467, 464*(t)*
in Spanish imperialism, 438–439
syncretism and, 469–470, 487
Roman Empire/Rome
collapse of, 692
fascist Italy as new, 638
Ottomans as successors to, 379
Romania, 572, 637, 664–665, 685–686
Romantic movement, 484
Roosevelt, Franklin, 635–636, 652
Roosevelt, Theodore, 545
Rousseau, Jean-Jacques (1712–1778),
484, 504–505
Roy, Ram Mohan (1772–1833), 608
Royal Dutch Shell, 727
rubber crops, 550, 554, 599
rum, global connections in production
of, 457
Russia
communism in, 620
early modern, 397
economic development in, 714–715*(t)*
expansion of, 369, 594
fifteenth-century, 372
French invasion of, 500
Industrial Revolution in, 529,
545–548
long-distance migration and, 606*(t)*
manufacturing output and, 548*(t)*
Mongol conquest of, 364*(t)*
nationalism and, 518–519
Polish insurrections against, 517*(t)*
railroads in, 535*(f)*
Revolution in, 497*(t)*, 662–665
serfs in, 514, 515
Siberian expansion by, 400*(t)*
slave trade, 450

Timur in, 369
in Triple Entente, 627
war with Japan, 547, 582*(t)*, 584
women's movement and, 523
World War I in, 630
Russian Empire, 404, 417–421, 418*(m)*,
626*(m)*
Asia under, 423–424
Chinese imperialism and, 423
Christianity in, 419, 420, 467
collapse of, 403, 693
fur trade, 448, 448*(i)*
globalization by, 724
independence from, 584
Russian Orthodox Church, 467
Russian Revolution (1905), 547, 547*(m)*
Russian Revolution (1917), 547, 622*(t)*,
662–665, 663*(m)*
as beginning of era, 617
cold war and, 675
as inspiration, 661
justice in, 688
Lenin in, 659
societal change in, 618
World War I in development of, 630
Russo-Japanese War (1904–1905),
497*(t)*, 547, 582*(t)*, 584, 645
Rwanda, 708

Sadat, Anwar, 744, 745
Safavid Empire, 364*(t)*, 379*(m)*, 380,
381–382, 389, 400*(t)*, 426
Safi al-Din (1252–1334), 380
Sahara Desert
trade routes across, 380–381
Saint Augustine (354–430 C.E.), 753
Saint Domingue. *See* Haiti
Samarkand, 369
Samoa, 389
samurai warriors, 441, 578–581, 582*(t)*,
644
San Martín, José, 512
Santeria, 473
Sara and Dara dolls, 723
sati, 425, 476
satyagraha, 698
Saudi Arabia, 486, 530, 714–715*(t)*
Scandinavia, 635
Schaeffer, Francis (1912–1984), 741
scheduled caste. *See* caste system

Schlafly, Phyllis, 739
science
birth of modern, 477–486
China, 475, 485
Enlightenment challenged by,
484–485
fundamentalism and, 741
Islamic, 745
Japan, 485–486
modern emphasis on, 392
and religion, 461, 462, 477, 516, 740
in U.S., 543
Western, in Japan, 581
scientific racism, 563, 596–598
Scientific Revolution, 392, 477–486
in Great Britain, 533
imperialism and, 409, 429, 626
influence of, 477
Islam and, 478–479, 493
and population growth, 619
religious opposition to, 461, 462
transformation by, 398
scramble for Africa, 592, 593*(m)*
The Second Sex (Beauvoir), 735–736
Second World War. *See* World War II
secular humanism, fundamentalism on,
741
secularism, in Turkey, 713, 716–717
segregation laws, 515, 604
Self-Strengthening Movement, 570
Selim III, 574, 575
Seneca people, 368
Senegal, 423*(i)*, 433, 708, 709*(m)*
Senghor, Léopold, 607
separation of church and state, 504
September 11, 2001, attacks, 617, 623*(t)*,
742, 746
Serbia, 517, 572, 627
serfs
in France, 505
in Russia, 496*(t)*, 514, 515, 542, 545
settler colonies, 592
sexual behavior
fundamentalism on, 741
women's movement and, 521, 736,
737
sex workers, 727
Shaka, 700*(t)*
Sharawi, Huda, 523
sharecropping, in Southern U.S., 515

sharia (Islamic law), 743–745
  alternatives to, 746–747
  in Iran, 718
  scientific innovation and, 478–479
  in Turkey, 713
sheep, 407–408
Shia Muslims, 380, 426, 717–719, 743*(m)*
Shinto, 582
Shiva, Vandana, 752
shoguns, 400*(t)*, 441, 578–579
Shona people, 605
Siam (Thailand), 594
Siberia, 417–421, 467, 487
  fur trade in, 433–434, 448
  Paleolithic persistence in, 365–366
Sikhism, 476 *(i)*, 476–477, 487
Silent Spring (Carson), 749
Silk Roads
  China and, 423–424
  globalization by, 724
  in webs of exchange, 389
silk trade
  after World War I, 643
  British/Chinese, 567*(t)*
  China, silver trade and, 444
silver
  Bolivia, 435
  fur trade and, 448
  global commerce in, 442*(m)*, 442–445
  Industrial Revolution and, 532
  Mexico, 435, 550
  opium trade and, 567
  slave trade and, 453
  Spanish American, 410, 433, 435,
    438*(t)*
  in U.S., 543*(m)*
  See also mining
Singapore, 712
Sino-Japanese War (1894–1985), 582*(t)*,
  584
Six-Day War (1967), 623*(t)*, 742
Skagit people, 366
slave revolts, 473, 509–510
slavery
  abolition of, 500, 513–516, 754
  abolition of, in Brazil, 497*(t)*
  abolition of, in Cuba, 497*(t)*
  abolition of, in France, 505
  abolition of, in Latin America, 549
  Aztec, 384–385

Banda Islands, 440
  cotton and, 532
  ending of, 524
  globalization and, 458
  in Haiti, 507, 509–510
  Haitian Revolution and, 493, 509
  as illegitimate, 618
  Islam and, 473
  life expectancy in, 415
  as metaphor for oppression, 450
  in North America, 415, 503, 542
  religious syncretism and, 472–473
  runaway slave communities, 401*(t)*
  Russian, 417
slave trade, 449–457
  Africa and, 398, 409, 515
  beginning of, 375*(t)*, 400*(t)*
  Columbus in development of, 365
  East African, 497*(t)*
  economic links in, 397
  Eurocentrism and, 429
  European imperialism and, 407, 563
  as global commerce, 432–433*(i)*, 433
  impact of on African societies, 367
  legacy of, 433
  mortality rate in, 449, 455
  numbers transported in, 449, 453,
    454*(f)*, 455
  peak of, 401*(t)*
  plantations and, 409, 449*(m)*, 450
  population impact of, 398
  practice of, 452–455
  prevalence of, 450
  racial mixing through, 449–450
  racism and, 450–452
  silver in, 443
  societal impact of, 449
  sugar production and, 413*(i)*, 413–415
smallpox, 407
Smiles, Samuel, 536, 581
Smith, Adam (1723–1790), 482, 503
social Darwinism, 564
Social-Democratic Labor Party
  (Russia), 547
social hierarchies, colonization and, 598
socialism, 392, 660
  accomplishments of, 754
  Atlantic revolutions and, 500
  in China, 494, 668–675
  and communism, 659–660

  democratic, 635
  in Great Britain, 541
  of Marx, 484–485, 539
  nationalism and, 519
  on social inequality, 633
  in the Soviet Union, 547–548,
    668–675
  in U.S., 544–545
  and war, 630
  See also communism
Socialist Party of America, 544
Social Security, 636
social structure
  in Africa, 708
  agricultural village, 366–368
  colonial American, 409–410
  communist revolutions and changes
    in, 618, 620, 662, 668
  fifteenth-century, 365–369
  imperialism and, 692
  independence movements and, 708
  military-industrial complex and, 679
  and modernity, 391–392
  Protestant Reformation and, 463–464
  Russian Empire, 418
  slave trade, source of slaves and, 455
  in sugar colonies, 412–415, 414*(t)*
  women's movement and, 521
Society of Jesus (Jesuits), 466, 485, 487
  in China, 467, 470–472, 471 *(i)*, 485,
    531–532
Society of Righteous and Harmonious
  Fists, 570
Songhay Empire, 364*(t)*, 379*(m)*,
  380–381, 400*(t)*
  Islamization of, 381–382
  trade with, 367
Sonni Ali (r. 1465–1492), 381
Sony, 727
South Africa
  after apartheid, 704*(m)*
  Boer War in, 497*(t)*
  democracy in, 706
  Dutch settlement in, 401*(t)*
  end of apartheid in, 623*(t)*, 691
  Gandhi in, 698
  history of, 700*(t)*
  indentured servants in, 515
  independence in, 700–704
  industrialization in, 530

South Africa (*continued*)
land ownership in, 602–603
Mandela and, 691
nationalist movement in, 695–696
racism in, 597
rise of Zulu kingdom in, 496(t)
in World War I, 629
South America
agricultural village societies in, 366–367
as developing country, 705, 705(m)
Inca Empire, 386–388
missionaries in, 467–470
slaves shipped to, 454(f)
South Asia
British East India Company and, 592
cultural flowering of Indians in, 493
fifteenth century, 364(t)
labor migration from, 727
manufacturing output and, 548(t)
See also India
Southeast Asia
Buddhism as cultural link in, 389
colonization of, 592
elites in, 604
Great Depression in, 634
highland minority groups in Vietnam and, 494
plantations in, 602
in World War I, 629
South Korea, 530, 711, 712, 730, 738, 751(i)
South Pacific, colonization of, 592
soviets, 547
Soviet Union. *See* Union of Soviet Socialist Republics
Soweto, South Africa, protests, 702–703
Spain
American empire of, 404, 405(m), 416, 420–421, 467, 468–470
Aztec conquest by, 406, 410–412
Christian missions from, 467
fascism in, 637
Inca conquest by, 406, 410–412
Philippines under, 437–439
reconquest of, 364(t)
silver mines, 408–409, 433, 442–445, 443(i)
Spanish-American Revolutions (1810–1825), 501(t), 510–513
Spanish-American War (1898–1902), 438, 497(t), 594
Special Enterprise Zones, 683

Spice Islands, 439–440, 441
spice trade
African slave trade and, 453
East India Companies in, 439–440
European entry into, 433, 434
India, 437(i)
Portuguese, 435–437, 437(i)
silver in, 443
Stalin, Joseph, 622(t), 652, 664–665, 668–674, 678, 680, 682, 684
Stanton, Elizabeth Cady, 521
steam engine, 528, 533
steamship technology, 550, 562
strikes
class conflict and, 541
in Japan, 584
laboring classes and, 539
in Latin America, 552
in Russia, 546–547
sub-Saharan Africa, 452, 473
Suez Canal, 497(t)
suffrage. *See* male suffrage; voting rights; women's suffrage
Sufism
bhakti compared with, 476
in Islamic renewal, 744
missionaries to Southeast Asia, 382
Mughal Empire, 425
Safavid Empire, 380
in Turkey, 713
Wahhabi movement and, 474
sugar production, 507, 509, 510, 514
Columbian exchange in, 407
from Cuba, 550
as first modern industry, 451
peasant farmers and, 600
slavery and, 409, 451, 532
social structure and, 412–415, 414(t)
suicide bombers, 744(i)
Sukarno, 696
Suleiman, 400(t), 428
Sumatra (Indonesia), 382, 575
Sunni Muslims, 380, 426, 743(m)
survival of the fittest, 543–544, 564
sustainability, 751–752
Swinton, William O., 492
Syria, 631(m), 632

Taino peoples, 362–363(i), 363, 509
Taiping Uprising (1850–1864), 497(t), 565–566, 569(m), 570, 573, 580

Taiwan, 584, 594, 687, 712
Taj Mahal, 400(t)
Taki Onqoy (dancing sickness), 469, 487
Taliban, 746
Tamerlane. *See* **Timur**
Tanzania, 497(t), 714–715(t)
Tanzimat reforms, 496(t), 574, 575
tariffs, 503, 510, 533, 535, 554, 568, 730
See also taxation
taxation
British control over American colonies and, 503
in China, 442–445, 565
European, 372, 434
in France, 504
in Japan, 581, 583
Ottoman Empire, 427, 573
Spanish colonial, 439, 510
in U.S., 542
without representation, 503
technology
African slave trade and, 456
in economic growth, 619
European, 555
fundamentalism's use of, 741
in globalization, 725
in Great Britain, 533
Industrial Revolution and, 528–529
Islam and, 745
as modern, 391
steamships as, 550
of West, Japan and, 581
telegraph, European expansion and, 562
telescope, 480(t), 481
Temple of Reason (Cathedral of Notre Dame), 506
Temujin. *See* **Chinggis Khan**
Tennyson, Alfred Lord, 537
Tenochtitlán, 384
Teotihuacán, Mexico, 384
terrorism
fundamentalist, 741
global war against, 733
Islamic, 742, 744(i), 745–746
September 11, as era marker, 617
textile industry
African slave trade and, 453
Asian, 493
China and, 444–445

from Europe, 561
Great Britain and, 415, 534, 599
Inca, 387
India and, 445, 532
Industrial Revolution and, 528
in Japan, 583
in New England, 542
in Russia, 546
slave trade and, 452–453
Thailand, 530, 705, 705(m)
Things Fall Apart (Achebe), 367
Third World, 622(t), 678, 735
Thirty Years' War (1618–1648), 400(t), 465
Tiananmen Square demonstration, 499, 684
Tibet, 389, 423, 747
Timbuktu, 381
Timur, 364(t), 369, 370(m)
Tlacaelel (1398–1480), 385
Tlatelolco, Aztec market, 384
tobacco, 414–415, 451
de Tocqueville, Alexis, 542
Tokugawa shogunate, 400(t), 441, 444, 578–579
Toltec civilization, 384
Tonga, 389
torture, 599–600, 733, 734, 738
totalitarianism, in communism, 668
total war, 630, 650
Toure, Samori, 497(t)
tourism, 727
Toyota, 726
trade
    Australia, fifteenth-century, 366
    Aztec, 384
    Bretton Woods system of, 725
    cash crops and, 601
    Chinese, 371–372, 422
    colonial rule and, 606
    European, 375, 377, 406, 530–531
    fifteenth-century, 389
    globalization and, 725–726
    global silver, 442(m), 442–445
    Great Depression's impact on, 633
    Inca, 387
    Islamic, 381–382
    in Japan, 581
    Latin America and, 550
    in opium, 567, 568(i)
    pros and cons of, 712

religion and, 389, 390(m)
Songhay Empire, 380–381
webs of, fifteenth-century, 389
in West Africa, 605
trading post empires, 436–437, 438(t), 439–440
Transjordan, as League of Nations mandate, 631(m)
transnational corporations (TNCs), 727, 728(t)
Treaty of Nanjing (1842), 568
Treaty of Nerchinsk (1689), 423
Treaty of Tordesillas, 400(t)
Treaty of Versailles (1919), 622(t), 631–632, 637, 639, 642, 647–648
tribalism
    in Africa, 598, 612–613
    colonialism and, 611–613
    in India, 597
    See also kinship
tribunals, in Ottoman Empire, 574–575
tribute system
    Aztec, 384, 386
    China, Ming dynasty, 371–372
    Chinese, imperialism and, 422
    Inca, 387
    Russian Empire, 419, 448
    Spanish colonial, 439
Triple Alliance (1428, Aztec), 384
Triple Alliance (Germany, Austria, Italy), 627, 628(m)
Triple Entente (Russia, France, Britain), 627, 628(m)
Tu Duc, 594
Tulalip people, 366
Tupac Amaru revolt (Peru), 412, 501(t), 512
Turkey, 576, 577
    creation of, 713
    as developing country, 705, 705(m)
    economic development in, 711, 713, 714–715(t), 716–719
    independence of, 631(m), 632
    Islamic renewal in, 745
    Westernization of, 713, 716, 716(i)
Turks
    papal ban on weapons sales to, 429
    prominence of in Islam, 426–427
    See also Ottoman Empire
Tursum, Muhammet, 403
Twinings of London, 726

Uganda, 706
Ukraine, 517, 517(t), 519, 663
ulama (Islamic scholars), 424, 575–576
Ulyanov, Vladimir. *See* **Lenin**
UN Convention to Eliminate Discrimination against Women, 739
unequal treaties, 568, 580
Union of Soviet Socialist Republics (USSR)
    Afghanistan war, 623(t), 676
    on anticolonialism, 618, 694–695
    in arms race, 677(i), 677–678
    Chernobyl, 751(i)
    Chinese opposition to, 681
    cold war and, 675–681
    collapse of, 403, 421, 617, 623(t), 681–682, 684–687, 686(m), 693
    collective agriculture in, 670, 671
    creation of, 664–665
    in Cuban missile crisis, 676–677
    economic development in, 682
    feminism in, 669, 670
    Great Depression and, 635
    industrialization in, 672–673
    Japan threatened by, 647
    military-industrial complex in, 680, 681
    NATO and, 654–655
    post-World War II credibility of, 652
    Purges in, 674
    recovery of after World War II, 653
    religion in, 740
    rock-and-roll music in, 679
    as Russian Empire, 693
    in spread of communism, 660, 661
    Treaty of Friendship with China, 661
    U.S. and, 660, 733
    women in, 735
    in World War II, 648, 649, 649(m), 651
unions
    among laboring classes, 538–539
    in Great Britain, 533
    in Japan, 584
    legalization of, 539
    in U.S., 544–545
United Fruit Company, 554
United Kingdom. *See* Great Britain
United Nations (U.N.)
    anticolonialism of, 695
    creation of, 653

United Nations (U.N.) (*continued*)
Decade for Women, 738–739
global warming conferences, 752
International Women's Year, 738
United States of America (U.S.A.),
502(*m*)
abolition of slavery in, 515
anticolonialism of, 618, 694–695
anti-Japanese immigration policies
in, 645
in arms race, 677(*i*), 677–678
balance of trade, 733
cold war in, 675–681
communism in, 661, 688
criticisms of, 733–734
cultural influence of, 679
economic development in, 714–715(*t*)
energy use by, 748
and globalization, 724–725, 731–734
Great Depression in, 633–634, 634(*i*),
635(*f*)
imperialism by, 693
imperial presidency in, 679, 734
Industrial Revolution in, 529,
541–545, 543(*m*)
intrusion into Japan by, 579–580
Kyoto protocol and, 752
labor shift in, 730
Latin America and, 551(*m*), 693
manufacturing output of, 548(*t*)
military buildup in, 681
nationalism and, 519
neo-liberalism in, 725
New Deal, 635–636
and Russian Revolution, 664
slavery in, 450
Soviet rivalry with, 660
as superpower, 632, 653–655,
678–679, 733
triangular diplomacy in, 681, 723
in Western civilization, 653–654
westward expansion of, 594
in World War I, 629, 632, 634
in World War II, 647, 648, 651
See also American Revolution; Civil
War, U.S.; North America
urbanization
in China under Deng, 683
Dutch, 439
early modern, 398

in Great Britain, 537–538
industrialization and, 711–712
in Japan, 578, 642
in Latin America, 552
modern age, 391–392
Protestant Reformation and, 464
Renaissance, 374
Soviet Union, 671
Uruguay, 549, 552
U.S. Steel Corporation, 542
utopianism
of Robery Owen, 539
of Soviet feminism, 669

Vatican, as sovereign state, 638
Venice, 435, 530
Vesalius, Andreas (1514–1564), 480(*t*),
483(*i*)
Vienna, Ottoman siege of, 364(*t*), 379,
393, 400(*t*), 401(*t*), 427, 428(*i*), 463
Vietnam
communism in, 660–661, 706
communist reforms in, 687
French invasion of, 494
nationalist movement in, 695–696
wage laborers in, 602
Vietnam War (1965–1973), 623(*t*), 656,
657, 675, 681, 733, 734
Vijayanagara kingdom, 381
Villa, Pancho, 553
Viracocha (deity, Inca), 386
Virgin of Guadalupe, 460–461(*i*)
Vivekandanda, Swami, 610, 610(*i*), 612
Vodou, 473
Voltaire (1694–1778), 483, 500
voting rights
in American colonies, 503
Atlantic revolutions and, 500
in France, 506
in Great Britain, 536
Japan, 642
in Mexico, 553
in New World, 513
in Southern U.S., 515
for women in France, 521
See also male suffrage; women's suffrage

Wahhabi movement of Islamic renewal,
474, 496(*t*)
Waldseemüller, Martin, 377(*m*)

WalMart, 726
Wang Dayue, 444
Wang Yangmin (1472–1529), 475
warfare
in American colonies, 503
arms race and, 677(*i*), 677–678
Aztec, 385
blitzkrieg, 648
Chinese, 422, 666
cold war, 675–677
European imperialism and, 564
in European state building, 372
fascism on, 638
and fur trade in North America, 447
industrialized, 629, 630
male prestige in, 368
naval, Indian Ocean trade and, 436
Nazism on, 648
Ottoman, Janissaries in, 380(*i*)
preemptive, 733
religious, Thirty Years' War, 465
Russian Empire, 418–419
technology in, 649
total, 630, 650
trench, 630
See also weapons
Warsaw Pact, 661, 675, 676(*m*)
Washington, Booker T., 612
weapons
colonization and, 590–591
European expansion and, 406, 563
hydrogen bombs, 677(*i*)
industrialization and, 629, 630
Native Americans and, 447
Ottoman, 380(*i*)
papal ban on sales to Turks, 429
Russian Empire, 418
during U.S. Civil War, 562(*i*)
in World War I, 629
in World War II, 649
See also warfare
weaving
colonization and, 596
in India, 599
Weimar Republic, 639
West Africa, 494
cash crop farming in, 601
forced labor in, 599
independence in, 695
Islam in, 473

labor migration in, 727
migration to, 594
nationalism and, 520
political development in, 367
Slave Coast, 453
slave trade in, 451, 515
Songhay Empire, 364(t), 380–381
wars of Islamic renewal, 401(t)
Western Europe
global dominance of, 491
Industrial Revolution in, 528,
    541–542
See also Europe
Western Hemisphere, biological
    diversity in, 409
Westernization
economic, 457
modern age and, 392–393
Russia, 401(t)
West Indies, labor migration in, 727
whaling, 752
wheat, 407
wilderness, preservation of, 749
Wilhelm, Kaiser, 627
Wilson, Woodrow, 545, 630, 632
witchcraft, 472
women
in agricultural village societies, 367,
    368
Aztec, 385(i)
in bhakti Hinduism, 476
in China, 566
in colonial Africa, 604(i), 604–605
colonization and, 590
in economic development, 711–712
effects of World War I on, 633
equality of, 500
in fascist Italy, 638
Inca, 387
in India, 699
Islamic renewal and, 744
in Japan, 582(t)
laboring class and, 538
Mexican Revolution and, 553(i)
middle class and, 536–537
missionaries and, 609–610
in Ottoman Empire, 429, 576
Philippines, religious participation by,
    439

Protestantism on, 464–465
Sikhism on, 476–477
as victims of patriarchy, 613
voting rights in Great Britain and, 536
wage discrepancies and, 602
in World War I, 630, 630(f)
in World War II, 650–651
See also feminism
Women's Bible, 521
Women's Federation (China), 669–670
women's movements, 669–670
women's rights
fundamentalism on, 746
as human rights, 738–739
in Japan, 642
in Turkey, 716, 717
United Nations and, 738–739
See also feminism
Women's Rights Convention (Seneca
    Falls, NY), 496(t), 521
women's suffrage, 521, 522(i), 630,
    630(f), 633, 716, 754
Wordsworth, William, 749
working class
colonialism and, 598–606
in Great Britain, 537–538, 541
in Japan, 583–584
in Russia, 547
socialist ideas among, 539
in U.S., 543–544
World Bank, 653, 711, 725
World Conferences on Women, 739
World Peace Summit (2000), 747
World Social Forum, 623(t), 731
World Trade Center attacks, 623(t), 742,
    746
World Trade Organization, 623(t), 731
World War I (WWI), 622(t), 624–625(i),
    625–632
Africans and, 612
as beginning of era, 617
causes of, 618
economic contraction after, 724
and globalization, 724
and imperialism, 629
India in, 697–698
Japan in, 642
legacies of, 629–632
lessons from, 656–657

nationalism and, 517
number of deaths in, 629
outbreak of, 497(t)
paintings of, 624(i), 625
Russian Revolution and, 547–548,
    662–664, 663(m)
World War II (WWII), 622(t), 645–653
in Asia, 645, 646(m), 647
causes of, 618
European recovery from, 653–656
globalization after, 724–725
Great Depression ended by, 636
imperialism and, 693
Japanese aggression during, 559
lessons from, 656–657
Nanjing Massacre during, 559
number of deaths in, 648–650
Soviet Union in, 665
U.S. and, 647, 679
Wounded Knee massacre (1890), 497(t)

Xinjiang, 423

Yalta Conference (1945), 650(t)
Yap, 364(t), 389
yasak (tribute), 419
Yathrib. *See* Medina, Arabia
yellow peril, 563
Yongle, Emperor of China
    (r. 1402–1422), 371, 372
Yoruba people, 367
Young Ottomans, 575–576
Young Turks, 497(t), 576
Yugoslavia, 630, 631(m), 665, 680, 687, 727

zaibatsu, 644
Zaire, 708
Zambia, 708, 709(m)
Zapata, Emiliano, 553
Zheng He, 365, 375, 376(m), 422
    expedition of, 363, 364(t), 371–372
Zhenotdel (Women's Department,
    USSR), 669
Zhou Enlai, 523
Zimbabwe, 364(t), 696
Zionism, 517, 517(t)
Zoroastrianism, Mughal Empire, 424
Zulu state, 496(t), 700(t), 703
Zunghars, 422–423